Adobe

ADOBE® COLDFUSION® 8
Getting Started

web application construction kit
VOLUME 1

Ben Forta and Raymond Camden
with Charlie Arehart

Adobe ColdFusion 8 Web Application Construction Kit, Volume 1: Getting Started
Ben Forta and Raymond Camden
with Charlie Arehart

This Adobe Press book is published by Peachpit.

Peachpit Press
1249 Eighth Street
Berkeley, CA 94710
510/524-2178
510/524-2221 (fax)

Find us on the Web at: www.peachpit.com
To report errors, please send a note to errata@peachpit.com

Peachpit is a division of Pearson Education

Editor: Judy Ziajka
Technical Reviewer: Marc A. Garrett
Production Editor: Lupe Edgar
Compositor: Maureen Forys, Happenstance Typo-O-Rama
Proofreader: Liz Welch
Illustration: Jeff Wilson, Happenstance Typo-O-Rama
Indexer: Ron Strauss
Cover design: Charlene Charles-Will

ISBN 13: 978-0-321-51548-3

ISBN 10: 0-321-51548-X

9 8 7 6 5 4 3

Printed and bound in the United States of America

Dedications

Ben Forta

The book is dedicated to my first acquisitions editor, Angela Kozlowski, who helped me create the first edition of this book and more than a dozen other titles in the decade that followed. Without her, I'd still be struggling to get that first book out of the door. Angela, thank you for helping me to become a published author!

Raymond Camden

To my wife, Jeanne. You are my best supporter, my best friend, and the absolute best thing in my life. Thank you.

Charlie Arehart

I'd like to dedicate this book to my wife of seven years and the love of my life, Kim. I couldn't do all I do without your patience, support, and encouragement. Thank you, my love. God truly blessed me when he brought you into my life.

Acknowledgments

Ben Forta

Thanks to my co-authors, Ray Camden and Charlie Arehart, for their outstanding contributions. Although this book is affectionately known to thousands as "the Ben Forta book," it is, in truth, as much theirs as it is mine. An extra thank you to Ray Camden for once again bravely accepting the role of lead co-author. Thanks to Nancy Ruenzel and the crew at Peachpit for allowing me the creative freedom to build these books as I see fit. Thanks to Wendy Sharp for stepping in as acquisitions editor on this revision and to Judy Ziajka for so ably shepherding this book through the publication process. Thanks to Marc Garrett for his incredibly thorough technical editing. Thanks to the thousands of you who write to me with comments, suggestions, and criticism (thankfully not too much of the latter)— I do read each and every message (and even attempt to reply to them all, eventually), and all are appreciated. And last, but by no means least, a loving thank you to my wife Marcy and our children for putting up with (and allowing) my often hectic work schedule. Their love and support make all that I do possible.

Raymond Camden

I want to thank my wife and kids for understanding while I worked night after night. I want to thank Ben for once again asking me to help with this 600-page monster of a book (and that's just the first book). Thank you to Adobe for answering my unending stream of questions and also putting up with my suggestions. (They were all good ideas—really!)

Charlie Arehart

First, I want to thank Ben for having me as a contributor to this series. With so many excellent authors among the current and past contributors, I really feel privileged. I also want to thank him for all his contributions to the ColdFusion community. Again, as with my fellow authors, I follow in the footsteps of giants. In that regard, I want to acknowledge the awesome ColdFusion community. I've so enjoyed being a part of it, as both beneficiary and contributor, since 1997. This book's for you.

Biographies

Ben Forta

Ben Forta is senior technical evangelist for Adobe System Incorporated and has more than two decades of experience in the computer software industry in product development, support, training, and marketing. Ben is the author of the best-selling ColdFusion book of all time, *Macromedia ColdFusion MX 7 Web Application Construction Kit*, as well as books on SQL, Java Server Pages, Windows development, Regular Expressions, and more. More than half a million Ben Forta books have been printed in more than a dozen languages worldwide. Ben helped create the official Adobe ColdFusion training material, as well as the certification tests and study guides for those tests. He writes regular columns on ColdFusion and Internet development and spends a considerable amount of time lecturing and speaking on application development worldwide. Ben welcomes your e-mail at ben@forta.com and invites you to visit his Web site at http://forta.com/ and his blog at http://forta.com/blog.

Raymond Camden

Raymond Camden is the owner of Camden Media, Inc., a Web development and training company. A long-time ColdFusion user, Ray has worked on numerous ColdFusion books, including *Macromedia ColdFusion MX 7 Web Application Construction Kit*, and has contributed to the *Fusion Authority Quarterly Update* and the *ColdFusion Developers Journal*. He has also made presentations at numerous conferences and contributes to online Webzines. He has founded many community Web sites, including CFLib.org, ColdFusionPortal.org, and ColdFusionCookbook.org, and is the author of open source applications, including the popular BlogCFC (www.blogcfc.com) blogging application. Ray can be reached at his blog (http://www.coldfusionjedi.com) or via email at ray@camdenfamily.com. He is the happily married, proud father of three kids and is somewhat of a Star Wars nut.

Charlie Arehart

A veteran ColdFusion developer since 1997, Charlie Arehart is a longtime contributor to the community and a recognized Adobe community expert. He's a certified advanced ColdFusion developer and instructor for ColdFusion 4, 5, 6, and 7 and served as technical editor of the *ColdFusion Developers Journal* until 2003. Now an independent contractor (http://carehart.org) living in Alpharetta, Georgia, Charlie provides high-level troubleshooting and tuning assistance and training and mentoring for ColdFusion teams. He also helps run the Online ColdFusion Meetup (http://coldfusionmeetup.com, an online CF user group) and is frequently invited to speak to developer conferences and user groups worldwide.

CONTENTS AT A GLANCE

CONTENTS

Introduction

Who Should Use This Book

This book is written for anyone who wants to create cutting-edge Web-based applications.

If you are a Webmaster or Web page designer and want to create dynamic, data-driven Web pages, this book is for you. If you are an experienced database administrator who wants to take advantage of the Web to publish or collect data, this book is for you, too. If you are starting out creating your Web presence, but know you want to serve more than just static information, this book will help get you there. If you have used ColdFusion before and want to learn what's new in ColdFusion 8, this book is also for you. Even if you are an experienced ColdFusion user, this book provides you with invaluable tips and tricks and also serves as the definitive ColdFusion developer's reference.

This book teaches you how to create real-world applications that solve real-world problems. Along the way, you acquire all the skills you need to design, implement, test, and roll out world-class applications.

How to Use This Book

This is the eighth edition of *ColdFusion Web Application Construction Kit*, and what started off as a single volume a decade ago has had to grow to three volumes to adequately cover ColdFusion 8. The books are organized as follows:

- **Volume 1—***Adobe ColdFusion 8 Web Application Construction Kit, Volume 1: Getting Started (ISBN 0-321-51548-X)* contains Chapters 1–23 and is targeted at beginning ColdFusion developers.

- **Volume 2—***Adobe ColdFusion 8 Web Application Construction Kit, Volume 2: Application Development (ISBN 0-321-51546-3)* contains Chapters 24–40 and covers the ColdFusion features and language elements that are used by most ColdFusion developers most of the time.

- **Volume 3**—*Adobe ColdFusion 8 Web Application Construction Kit, Volume 3: Advanced Application Development (ISBN 0-321-51547-1)* contains Chapters 41–81 and covers the more advanced ColdFusion functionality, including extensibility features, as well as security and management features that will be of interest primarily to those responsible for larger and more critical applications.

These books are designed to serve two different, but complementary, purposes.

First, as the books used by most ColdFusion developers, they are a complete tutorial covering everything you need to know to harness ColdFusion's power. As such, the books are divided into parts, or sections, and each section introduces new topics building on what has been discussed in prior sections. Ideally, you will work through these sections in order, starting with ColdFusion basics and then moving on to advanced topics. This is especially true for the first two books.

Second, the books are invaluable desktop references. The appendixes and accompanying Web site contain reference chapters that will be of use to you while developing ColdFusion applications. Those reference chapters are cross-referenced to the appropriate tutorial sections, so that step-by-step information is always readily available to you.

The following describes the contents of *Adobe ColdFusion 8 Web Application Construction Kit, Volume 1: Getting Started*.

Part I: Getting Started

Part I of this book introduces ColdFusion and explains what exactly it is that ColdFusion enables you to accomplish. Internet fundamentals are also introduced; a thorough understanding of these is a prerequisite to ColdFusion application development. This part also covers databases, SQL, Adobe Dreamweaver, Eclipse and the ColdFusion Eclipse plug-ins, and everything else you need to know to get up and running quickly.

Chapter 1, "Introducing ColdFusion," teaches you how ColdFusion works and explains the various components that comprise it.

Chapter 2, "Choosing a Development Environment," introduces Dreamweaver and Eclipse as ColdFusion development environments.

Chapter 3, "Accessing the ColdFusion Administrator," introduces the ColdFusion Administrator program. This Web-based program, written in ColdFusion itself, manages and maintains every aspect of your ColdFusion Application Server.

To whet your appetite, Chapter 4, "Previewing ColdFusion," walks you through the creation of two real working applications using Dreamweaver code generation, and manual coding, too.

Chapter 5, "Building the Databases," provides a complete overview of databases and related terms. Databases are an integral part of almost every ColdFusion application, so database concepts and technologies must be well understood. Databases are mechanisms for storing and retrieving information, and almost every Web-based application you build will sit on top of a database of some kind. Key database concepts, such as tables, rows, columns, datatypes, keys, and indexes, are taught, as are the basics of the relational database model. You also learn the differences between client server–based and shared file–based databases, as well as the pros and cons of each.

In Chapter 6, "Introducing SQL," you learn the basics of the SQL language. SQL is a standard language for interacting with database applications, and all ColdFusion database manipulation is performed using SQL statements. The link between ColdFusion and your database itself is via database drivers, so this chapter introduces this technology and walks you through the process of creating data sources. This chapter also teaches you how to use the SQL SELECT statement.

Chapter 7, "SQL Data Manipulation," introduces three other important SQL statements: INSERT, UPDATE, and DELETE.

Part II: Using ColdFusion

With the introductions taken care of, Part II quickly moves on to real development. Starting with language basics, and progressing to database-driven applications and more, the chapters here will make you productive using ColdFusion faster than you thought possible.

Chapter 8, "The Basics of CFML," introduces ColdFusion templates and explains how these are created and used. Variables are explained (including complex variable types, such as arrays and structures), as are CFML functions and the <cfset> and <cfoutput> tags.

Chapter 9, "Programming with CFML," teaches all the major CFML program flow language elements. From if statements (using <cfif>) to loops (using <cfloop>) to switch statements (using <cfswitch> and <cfcase>) to template reuse (using <cfinclude>), almost every tag used regularly by ColdFusion developers is explained here, and all with real, usable examples.

Chapter 10, "Creating Data-Driven Pages," is where you create your first data-driven ColdFusion application, albeit a very simple one. You also learn how to use <cfquery> to create queries that extract live data from your databases and how to display query results using <cfoutput>. Various formatting techniques, including using tables and lists, are taught as well. One important method of displaying data on the Web is data drill-down, and this approach to data interaction is also taught.

As applications grow in size and complexity, so does the need for structure and organizations. Chapter 11, "The Basics of Structured Development," introduces ColdFusion Components, and explains how these should be used to build n-tier applications. Dreamweaver wizards and shortcuts for working with ColdFusion Components are explained as well.

In Chapter 12, "ColdFusion Forms," you learn how to collect user-supplied data via HTML forms. This data can be used to build dynamic SQL statements that provide you with infinite flexibility in creating dynamic database queries. This chapter also teaches you how to create search screens that enable visitors to search on as many different fields as you allow.

Continuing with the topic of collecting data from users, Chapter 13, "Form Data Validation," explains the various techniques and options available for data validation. ColdFusion can generate both client-side and server-side validation code automatically, and these features are explored in detail. You will learn how to use all of the various validation features offered by ColdFusion, as well as how to provide your own validation rules.

Chapter 14, "Using Forms to Add or Change Data," teaches you how to use forms to add, update, and delete data in database tables. The ColdFusion tags <cfinsert> and <cfupdate> are introduced, and you learn how <cfquery> can be used to insert, update, and delete data.

Basic HTML forms can suffice for basic data entry, but Web developers quickly find them to be restrictive and cumbersome to work with. Chapter 15, "Beyond HTML Forms: ColdFusion-Powered Ajax," introduces the ColdFusion form control extensions and the powerful Ajax-based controls.

In Chapter 16, "Graphing, Printing, and Reporting," you learn how to generate business charts, printable Web pages, and data-driven reports using the new ColdFusion Report Builder.

Chapter 17, "Debugging and Troubleshooting," teaches you the types of things that can go wrong in ColdFusion application development and what you can do to rectify them. You learn how to use ColdFusion's debugging and logging features and how to trace your own code; most importantly, you learn tips and techniques that can help you avoid problems in the first place.

Part III: Building ColdFusion Applications

Part II concentrated on ColdFusion coding. In Part III, all the ideas and concepts are brought together in the creation of complete applications.

Experienced developers know that it takes careful planning to write good code. Chapter 18, "Planning an Application," teaches important design and planning techniques you can use in your own development.

In Chapter 19, "Introducing the Web Application Framework," you learn how to take advantage of the ColdFusion Web application framework to facilitate the use of persistent variables, sophisticated parameter and variable manipulation, and customized error message handling. You also learn how to use the application template to establish applicationwide settings and options and how to use the APPLICATION scope.

Chapter 20, "Working with Sessions," teaches you all you need to know about CLIENT and SESSION variables, as well as HTTP cookies. These special data types play an important part in creating a complete application that can track a client's state.

Chapter 21, "Interacting with Email" (online), introduces ColdFusion's email capabilities. ColdFusion enables you to create SMTP-based email messages using its <cfmail> tag. You learn how to send email messages containing user-submitted form fields, how to email the results of a database query, and how to do mass mailings to addresses derived from database tables. Additionally, you learn how to retrieve mail from POP mailboxes using the <CFPOP> tag.

Chapter 22, "Online Commerce" (online), teaches you how to conduct real-time e-commerce, including credit card authorization. You build an entire working shopping cart application—one you can use as a stepping stone when writing your own shopping applications.

Chapter 23, "Securing Your Applications" (online), introduces important security concepts and explains which you should worry about and why. You learn how to create login screens, access control, and more.

Part IV: Appendixes

Appendix A, "Installing ColdFusion and Development Environments," presents system, hardware, and operating system prerequisites and explains how to install ColdFusion. Installation of the sample applications used in this book is also explained.

Appendix B, "Sample Application Data Files," lists the format of the database tables used in the sample applications throughout this book.

The Web Site

The accompanying Web site contains everything you need to start writing ColdFusion applications, including:

- Links to obtain ColdFusion 8

- Links to obtain Adobe Dreamweaver

- An explanation of how to obtain Eclipse and the ColdFusion Eclipse plug-ins

- Source code and databases for all the examples in this book

- Electronic versions of some chapters

- An errata sheet, should one be required

- An online discussion form

The book Web page is at `http://www.forta.com/books/032151548X`.

And with that, turn the page and start reading. In no time, you'll be creating powerful applications powered by ColdFusion 8.

PART I

Getting Started

Introducing ColdFusion

The Basics

If you're embarking on learning ColdFusion, then you undoubtedly have an interest in Web-based applications. ColdFusion is built on top of the Internet (and the World Wide Web), so a good understanding of the Internet and related technologies is a must before getting started.

There is no need to introduce you to the Internet and the Web. The fact that you're reading this book is evidence enough that these are important to you. The Web is everywhere, and Web site addresses appear on everything from toothpaste commercials to movie trailers to cereal boxes to car showrooms. In August 1981, 213 host computers were connected to the Internet. By the turn of the millennium that number had grown to about 100 million! And most of them are accessing the Web.

What has made the World Wide Web so popular? Most people give two primary reasons:

- **Ease of use.** Publishing and browsing for information on the Web are relatively easy.

- **Quantity of content.** With millions of Web pages from which to choose and thousands more being created each day, there are sites and pages to cater to almost every surfer's tastes.

Of course, not all Web sites and pages are public facing. Indeed, many organizations have far more internal Web content than they do public-facing content. But regardless of the audience and visibility, well-designed (and thus frequently used) Web sites try to take advantage of all sorts of features and technologies, including:

- Dynamic, data-driven Web pages

- Database connectivity

- Intelligent, user-customized pages

- Sophisticated data collection and processing

- Powerful report generation

- Email interaction

- Rich and engaging user interfaces

- Access to any existing back-ends and systems

ColdFusion enables you to do all this—and more.

Understanding ColdFusion

Millions of Web sites exist that attract millions of visitors daily. Many Web sites are being used as electronic replacements for newspapers, magazines, brochures, and bulletin boards. The Web offers ways to enhance these publications using audio, images, animation, multimedia, and even virtual reality.

These sites add value to the Net because information is knowledge, and knowledge is power. All this information is literally at your fingertips. But because of the underlying technology that makes the Web tick, sites can be much more than electronic versions of paper publications. Users can interact with you and your company, collect and process mission-critical information in real time (allowing you to provide new levels of user support), and much more.

The Web isn't merely the electronic equivalent of a newspaper or magazine—it's a communication medium limited only by the innovation and creativity of Web site designers.

The Dynamic Page Advantage

Dynamic pages—pages that contain dynamic content—are what bring the Web to life. Linking your Web site to live data is a tremendous advantage, but the benefits of database interaction go beyond extending your site's capabilities.

To see why dynamic Web pages are becoming the norm, compare them to static pages:

- **Static Web pages.** Static Web pages are made up of text, images, and HTML formatting tags. These pages are manually created and maintained so that when information changes, so must the page. This usually involves loading the page into an editor, making the changes, reformatting text if needed, and then saving the file. And not everyone in the organization can make these changes. The webmaster or Web design team is responsible for maintaining the site and implementing all changes and enhancements. This often means that by the time information finally makes it onto the Web site, it's out of date.

- **Dynamic Web pages.** Dynamic Web pages contain very little text. Instead, they pull needed information from other applications. Dynamic Web pages communicate with databases to extract employee directory information, spreadsheets to display accounting figures, client-server database management systems to interact with order processing applications, and more. A database already exists. Why re-create it for Web page publication?

Creating dynamic pages lets you create powerful applications that can include features such as these:

- Querying existing database applications for data
- Creating dynamic queries, facilitating more flexible data retrieval
- Executing stored procedures (in databases that support them)
- Executing conditional code on the fly to customize responses for specific situations
- Enhancing the standard HTML form capabilities with data validation functions
- Dynamically populating form elements
- Customizing the display of dates, times, and currency values with formatting functions
- Using wizards to ease the creation of data entry and data drill-down applications
- Creating printable content
- Generating email automatically (in response to form submissions, for example)
- Data-driven reports in Adobe FlashPaper and PDF formats
- Shopping carts and e-commerce sites
- Data syndication and affiliate programs

Understanding Web Applications

Web sites are powered by Web servers, and Web servers do just that: they serve. Web browsers make requests, and Web servers fulfill those requests—they serve up the requested information to the browser. These are usually HTML files, as well as the other file types discussed previously.

And that's really all Web servers do. In the grand scheme of things, Web servers are actually pretty simple applications—they sit and wait for requests that they attempt to fulfill as soon as they arrive. Web servers don't let you interact with a database; they don't let you personalize Web pages; they don't let you process the results of a user's form submission. They do none of that; all they do is serve pages.

So how do you extend your Web server to do all the things listed above? That's where Web application servers come into play. A *Web application server* is a piece of software that extends the Web server, enabling it to do things it can't do by itself—kind of like teaching an old dog new tricks.

Here's how it all works. When a Web server receives a request from a Web browser, it looks at that request to determine whether it is a simple Web page or a page that needs processing by a Web application server. It does this by looking at the MIME type (or file extension). If the MIME type indicates that the file is a simple Web page (for example, it has an .htm extension), the Web server fulfills the request and sends the file to the requesting browser as is. But if the MIME type indicates that the requested file is a page that needs processing by a Web application server (for example, it has a .cfm extension), the Web server passes it to the appropriate Web application server and returns the results it gets back rather than the actual page itself.

In other words, Web application servers are *page preprocessors*. They process the requested page before it's sent back to the client (the browser), and in doing so they open the door to developers to do all sorts of interesting things on the server, such as:

- Creating guest books

- Conducting surveys

- Changing your pages on the fly based on date, time, first visit, and whatever else you can think of

- Personalizing pages for your visitors

- In fact, all the features listed previously

What Is ColdFusion?

Initially, developing highly interactive and data-rich sites was a difficult process. Writing custom Web-based applications was a job for experienced programmers only. A good working knowledge of Unix was a prerequisite, and experience with traditional development or scripting languages was a must.

But all that has changed. Adobe ColdFusion enables you to create sites every bit as powerful and capable, without a long and painful learning curve. In fact, rather than being painful, the process is actually fun!

So, what exactly is ColdFusion? Simply put, ColdFusion is an application server—one of the very best out there, as well as the very first. (ColdFusion actually created the application server category back in 1995).

ColdFusion doesn't require coding using traditional programming languages, although traditional programming constructs and techniques are fully supported. Instead, you create applications by extending your standard HTML files with high-level formatting functions, conditional operators, and database commands. These commands are instructions to the ColdFusion processor and form the blocks on which to build industrial-strength applications.

Creating Web applications this way has significant advantages over conventional application development:

- ColdFusion applications can be developed rapidly because no coding is required, other than use of simple HTML style tags.

- ColdFusion applications are easy to test and roll out.

- The ColdFusion language contains all the processing and formatting functions you'll need (and the capability to create your own functions if you run into a dead end).

- ColdFusion applications are easy to maintain because no compilation or linking step is required. (Files actually are compiled, but that happens transparently, as I'll explain shortly.) The files you create are the files used by ColdFusion.

- ColdFusion provides all the tools you need to troubleshoot and debug applications, including a powerful development environment and debugger.

- ColdFusion comes with all the hooks necessary to link to almost any database application and any other external system.

- ColdFusion is fast, thanks to its scalable, multithreaded, service-based architecture.

- ColdFusion is built on industry-standard Java architecture, and supports all major standards and initiatives.

ColdFusion and Your Intranet, Extranet, and Portal

Everything explained here applies not just to Internet Web sites. Indeed, the benefits of ColdFusion apply to intranets, extranets, and portals, too.

Most companies have masses of information stored in various systems. Users often don't know what information is available or even how to access it.

ColdFusion bridges the gap between existing and legacy applications and your employees. It gives employees the tools to work more efficiently.

ColdFusion Explained

You're now ready to take a look at ColdFusion so you can understand what it is and how it works its magic.

And if you're wondering why you went through all this discussion about the Internet and Web servers, here's where it will all fit together.

The ColdFusion Application Server

ColdFusion is an application server—a piece of software that (usually) resides on the same computer as your Web server, enabling the Web server to do things it wouldn't normally know how to do.

ColdFusion is actually made up of several pieces. The ColdFusion Application Server is the program that actually parses (reads and compiles) and processes any supplied instructions.

Instructions are passed to ColdFusion using *templates*. A template looks much like any HTML file, with one big difference. Unlike HTML files, ColdFusion templates can contain special tags that instruct ColdFusion to perform specific operations. Here is a sample ColdFusion template that you'll use later in this book.

```
<!--- Get movies sorted by release date --->
<cfquery datasource="ows" name="movies">
 SELECT MovieTitle, DateInTheaters
 FROM Films
 ORDER BY DateInTheaters
</cfquery>

<!--- Create HTML page --->
<HTML>
<HEAD>
<TITLE>Movies by Release Date</TITLE>
</HEAD>

<BODY>

<H1>Movies by Release Date</H1>

<!--- Display movies in list format --->
<UL>
<cfoutput query="movies">
 <LI><STRONG>#Trim(MovieTitle)#</STRONG> - #DateFormat(DateInTheaters)#</LI>
</cfoutput>
</UL>

</BODY>

</HTML>
```

Earlier in this chapter, I said that Web servers typically return the contents of a Web page without paying any attention to the file contents.

That's exactly what ColdFusion *doesn't* do. When ColdFusion receives a request, it parses through the template looking for special ColdFusion tags (they all begin with CF) or ColdFusion variables and functions (always surrounded by number [#] signs). HTML or plain text is left alone and is output to the Web server untouched. Any ColdFusion instructions are processed, and any existing results are sent to the Web server. The Web server can then send the entire output back to the requester's browser. As explained earlier, the request file type tells the Web server that a request is to be handled by an application server. All ColdFusion files have an extension of .cfm or .cfml, like this:

```
http://www.forta.com/books/index.cfm
```

When ColdFusion is installed, it configures your Web server so it knows that any file with an extension of .cfm (or .cfml) is a ColdFusion file. Then, whenever a ColdFusion file is requested, the Web server knows to pass the file to ColdFusion for processing rather than return it.

It's worth noting that ColdFusion doesn't actually need a Web server because it has one built in. So as not to conflict with any other installed Web servers (like Apache and Microsoft IIS) the internal Web server runs on port 8500 or 8300 (depending on the type of installation performed) instead of the default port 80. During ColdFusion installation you'll be asked whether you want to run Cold-Fusion in stand-alone mode (bound to the integrated Web server) or using an existing Web server. If you opt to use the internal Web server you'll need to specify the port number in all URLs.

NOTE

The examples in this book use the internal Web server, so they include the port number. If you're using an external Web server, just drop the port number from the URLs.

CAUTION

Adobe doesn't recommend that the internal Web server (stand-alone mode) be used on production boxes. ColdFusion's integrated HTTP server is intended for use on development boxes only.

The ColdFusion Markup Language

I said earlier that ColdFusion is an application server; that's true, but that's not all it is. In fact, ColdFusion is two distinct technologies:

- The ColdFusion Application Server
- The CFML language

Although the ColdFusion Application Server itself is important, ColdFusion's power comes from its capable and flexible language. ColdFusion Markup Language (CFML) is modeled after HTML, which makes it very easy to learn.

CFML extends HTML by adding tags with the following capabilities:

- Read data from, and update data to, databases and tables
- Create dynamic data-driven pages
- Perform conditional processing
- Populate forms with live data
- Process form submissions
- Generate and retrieve email messages
- Interact with local files
- Perform HTTP and FTP operations
- Perform credit-card verification and authorization
- Read and write client-side cookies

And that's not even the complete list.

The majority of this book discusses ColdFusion pages (often called templates) and the use of CFML.

Linking to External Applications

One of ColdFusion's most powerful features is its capability to connect to data created and maintained in other applications. You can use ColdFusion to retrieve or update data in many applications, including the following:

- Corporate databases
- Client/server database systems (such as Microsoft SQL Server and Oracle)
- Spreadsheets
- XML data
- Contact-management software
- ASCII-delimited files
- Javabeans, JSP tag libraries, and EJBs
- .NET classes and assemblies
- Web Services

Extending ColdFusion

As installed, ColdFusion will probably do most of what you need, interacting with most of the applications and technologies you'll be using. But in the event that you need something more, ColdFusion provides all the hooks and support necessary to communicate with just about any application or service in existence. Integration is made possible via:

- C and C++
- Java
- .NET
- COM
- CORBA
- XML
- Web Services

These technologies and their uses are beyond the scope of this book and are covered in detail in the sequels, *ColdFusion Web Application Construction Kit, Volume 2: Application Development* and *ColdFusion Web Application Construction Kit, Volume 3: Advanced Application Development*.

Inside ColdFusion 8

ColdFusion 8 is the most remarkable ColdFusion to date, and is built on top of ColdFusion MX, the first completely redesigned and rebuilt ColdFusion since the product was first created back in

1995. Understanding the inner workings of ColdFusion isn't a prerequisite to using the product, but knowing what ColdFusion is doing under the hood will help you make better use of this remarkable product.

I said earlier that ColdFusion is a page preprocessor—it processes pages and returns the results as opposed to the page itself. To do this ColdFusion has to read each file, check and validate the contents, and then perform the desired operations. But there is actually much more to it than that. In fact, within ColdFusion is a complete J2EE (Java 2 Enterprise Edition) server that provides the processing power ColdFusion needs.

NOTE

Don't worry, you don't need know any Java at all to use ColdFusion.

First, a clarification. When people talk about Java they generally mean two very different things:

- The Java language is just that, a programming language. It is powerful and not at all easy to learn or use.

- The Java platform, a complete set of building blocks and technologies to build rich and powerful applications.

Of the two, the former is of no interest (well, maybe little interest) to ColdFusion developers. After all, why write complex code in Java to do what CFML can do in a single tag? But Java the platform? Now that's compelling. The Java platform provides the wherewithal to:

- Access all sorts of databases

- Interact with legacy systems

- Support mobile devices

- Use directory services

- Create multilingual and internationalized applications

- Leverage transactions, queuing, and messaging

- Create robust and highly scalable applications

In the past you'd have had to write Java code in order to leverage the Java platform, but not any more. ColdFusion runs on top of the Java platform, providing the power of underlying Java made accessible via the simplicity of CFML.

NOTE

By default, the Java engine running ColdFusion is Adobe's own award-winning J2EE server, JRun. ColdFusion can also be run on top of third-party J2EE servers like IBM WebSphere, BEA WebLogic, and JBoss. See Appendix A, "Installing ColdFusion and Development Environments," for more information.

But don't let the CFML (and CFM files) fool you—when you create a ColdFusion application you are actually creating a Java application. In fact, when ColdFusion processes your CFM pages it actually creates Java source code and compiles it into Java bytecode for you, all in the background.

This behavior was first introduced in ColdFusion MX. Using ColdFusion you can truly have the best of both worlds—the power of Java, and the simplicity of ColdFusion, and all without having to make any sacrifices at all.

Powered by ColdFusion

You were probably planning to use ColdFusion to solve a particular problem or fill a specific need. Although this book helps you do just that, I hope that your mind is now racing and beginning to envision just what else ColdFusion can do for your Web site.

In its relatively short life, ColdFusion has proven itself to be a solid, reliable, and scalable development platform. ColdFusion is the tenth major release of this product, and with each release it becomes an even better and more useful tool. It is easy to learn, fun to use, and powerful enough to create real-world, Web-based applications. With a minimal investment of your time, your applications can be powered by ColdFusion.

Choosing a Development Environment

ColdFusion applications are made up of files—lots and lots of files. These files are plain text files containing CFML, HTML, SQL, JavaScript, CSS, and more. Because they are plain text files, ColdFusion developers are free to use any editor they like to write and edit their applications.

But of all of the applications and editors out there, two are primarily used by ColdFusion developers: Adobe Dreamweaver and Eclipse. This chapter introduces you to them both.

CAUTION

Although you can indeed use any editor, you must use editors that save files as plain text. This means that you should not use word processors (like Microsoft Word) to edit source code.

TIP

You can use both editors! Indeed, most ColdFusion developers use more than one editor, switching back and forth as needed based on what they are doing, and which features they need at any given time.

Using Adobe Dreamweaver

Dreamweaver is the industry standard for Web page creation and editing and is used by millions of developers and designers the world over. Many of these users are writing ColdFusion code, and for good reason.

NOTE

Dreamweaver is a big and powerful program, and this brief introduction barely scratches the surface of what the product can do. To really learn Dreamweaver, read one of the many books dedicated entirely to the product. You may want to start with *Dreamweaver CS3 for Windows and Macintosh: Visual QuickStart Guide* (ISBN-10: 0-321-50302-3; ISBN-13: 978-0-321-50302-2) from Peachpit Press.

Why Use Dreamweaver for ColdFusion Development

Dreamweaver is a general-purpose Web page designer and editor, and it appeals primarily to those working extensively with Web technologies. Much of Dreamweaver focuses on the design and layout aspects of Web application development, and so Dreamweaver tends to appeal more to Web page designers and new developers than it does to highly experienced coders.

Here are some of the benefits of Dreamweaver:

- A highly customizable workspace
- Multiple viewing options: a code view, a design view, and a hybrid mixed view
- Extensive menus, toolbars, and shortcuts
- Code awareness and source code coloring
- Drag-and-drop editing
- Tag editors to simplify tag attribute use
- Built-in behaviors for fast code generation
- The capability to work with local and remote files
- Support for lots of server-side languages, including CFML

For a ColdFusion developer, the reasons to use Dreamweaver include all of the above, plus included ColdFusion-specific functionality:

- Language support for all of CFML
- Support for ColdFusion RDS (allowing access to remote files and data sources)
- Sophisticated ColdFusion Component support
- Integrated ColdFusion debugging
- And much more

NOTE

This first volume of *ColdFusion 8 Web Application Construction Kit* uses Dreamweaver almost exclusively. Volumes 2 and 3, however, make far more use of Eclipse.

A Brief Introduction to Dreamweaver

NOTE

If you have not yet installed Dreamweaver, refer to Appendix A, "Installing ColdFusion and Development Environments."

When you launch Dreamweaver, you will see a screen similar to the one shown in Figure 2.1. (The exact screen layout you see may differ, depending on the operating system you're using and the installation options you select.)

Figure 2.1

The Dreamweaver
start screen contains
links that you can
use to create new files
and open recently
used files.

Notice these important details about the Dreamweaver screen:

- The Files panel (shown on the left in the figure, although it can be moved elsewhere) is used to browse and open sites and files. You should generally always have this panel open.

- Above the Files panel are other useful panels, including the Application panel, which ColdFusion developers can use to access ColdFusion data sources and more.

- The main screen area displays startup options when Dreamweaver is first started. This area is also the editor area when you are creating or editing a file.

- Above the main screen area are toolbars and buttons used for working with language elements and features.

TIP

You can open and close panels by clicking the triangle to the left of the panel name.

Dreamweaver ColdFusion Support

Dreamweaver CS3 (the current version of Dreamweaver) comes with built-in ColdFusion support. However, Dreamweaver CS3 was released several months before ColdFusion 8 was completed, and so the most up-to-date ColdFusion support could not be included in Dreamweaver when it shipped.

Fortunately, Dreamweaver allows updates and extensions to be installed at any time, and ColdFusion comes with an update file that you definitely should install.

Dreamweaver extensions are shipped as MXP files (a special extension format used by Dreamweaver, Adobe Flash, and more). To install the ColdFusion extensions, do the following:

1. Locate the MXP file and run it. (If you don't have the MXP file, refer to Appendix A, "Installing ColdFusion and Development Environments," for information on how to obtain it.) You will see a screen prompting you to accept the license.

2. Accept the license.

   The extension will be installed. When installation is complete you'll see a summary screen listing all installed extensions, including the ColdFusion 8 Dreamweaver extensions.

Now you're ready to use Dreamweaver to write ColdFusion applications.

Getting Started

Application developers often have to work on lots of different projects, and each project is usually made up of lots of files and assets. To help manage the files and settings for each project, Dreamweaver encourages you to create a *site* for each.

Throughout this book, we'll be creating all sorts of files, and so before we go any further, we need to create a site for our applications.

NOTE

Dreamweaver allows you to work on files directly, without creating a site first. But without a site, some functionality (such as the capability to directly launch ColdFusion pages) will be unavailable. Therefore, you must create a site to be able to follow the steps in upcoming chapters.

Here are the steps to create our site (which we'll name ows, for *Orange Whip Studios*):

1. Locate the Dreamweaver Site menu and choose New Site.

   The Site Definition screen appears (Figure 2.2). This screen has two modes: Basic and Advanced. We'll use Basic for now.

2. In the field that asks you to name your site, enter ows. In the HTTP address field, type the address for the site. If you are using a default installation (with the integrated HTTP server), this will be http://localhost:8500/ows. Then click Next.

3. You will be asked if you want to use a server technology. Select Yes and then choose ColdFusion from the drop-down list (Figure 2.3). Then click Next.

4. The next screen asks where you want to edit and test files. We'll be doing the development and testing locally, so select the first option, Edit and Test Locally.

Figure 2.2

Use the Site
Definition screen to
define sites in
Dreamweaver.

Figure 2.3

If your site will be used
to develop ColdFusion
applications, be sure
to choose ColdFusion
as the site server
technology.

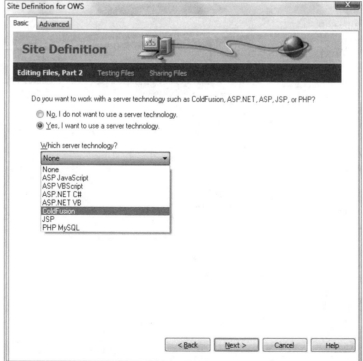

5. Specify the location to store the files by entering the path to a folder under the ColdFusion Web root (the default path will be `C:\ColdFusion8\wwwroot\OWS\` on a Windows machine and `Applications\ColdFusion8\wwwroot\OWS\` on the Mac). Then click Next.

6. Specify the URL to the root of your application. If you are using a default installation (with the integrated HTTP server), this path will be `http://localhost:8500/ows`. Then click the Test URL button and make sure you get a success dialog (like the one shown in Figure 2.4). Then click Next.

Figure 2.4

Verify that your site has the correct URL before proceeding, or you will not be able to browse or test any of the code you write.

7. The next screen asks if you want to use a remote server. You use a remote server only when you are going to deploy your applications to production servers, so select No. Then click Next.

8. You should see a summary page (like the one shown in Figure 2.5). Verify that the information is correct and then click Done.

Figure 2.5

The Site Definition Summary page is a good place to check your site settings before you create the site.

You now have a site set up for use with our project. The new site will automatically be opened in the Files panel. If ever the site is not opened, you can open it by selecting ows from the drop-down list at the top of the panel.

NOTE
> You can change site settings after a site is created by choosing the Site > Manage Sites menu option. You can also switch the site editing screen to Advanced mode to see more configuration options.

Working with Files

Now that you've successfully defined the ows site, we'll quickly practice working with files in Dreamweaver. In Chapter 4, "Previewing ColdFusion," you will learn more about working with Dreamweaver. For now, let's get you set up and practicing a few basic techniques.

Creating a Work Directory and File

To simplify organization of the code created in this book, each chapter's code will go in its own directory.

To create a directory for this chapter, do the following:

1. Right-click (Windows) or Control-click (Mac) the ows folder at the top of the Files panel and choose New Folder.

2. Name the folder 2 (for Chapter 2) and press Enter (Windows) or Return (Mac).

Now you'll create a file. The file will go in the new 2 directory and will be named index.cfm.

1. Right-click (Windows) or Control-click (Mac) the 2 directory on the Site tab in the Files panel and choose New File.

2. Name the file index.cfm and press Enter (Windows) or Return (Mac).

3. Double-click the new file to open it in the editor.

TIP
> You can also create files by choosing New from the File menu or by pressing Ctrl-N (Windows) or Command-N (Mac).

Let's name the file right away (with an HTML name, the one that appears in the browser title bar).

1. Above the editor window is a toolbar, and one of the options is a field for the HTML title. By default, the file is named Untitled Document; change it to Orange Whip Studios by typing that text in the field.

2. Press Enter (Windows) or Return (Mac) to update the title; the HTML below will reflect the change (Figure 2.6).

Figure 2.6

ColdFusion developers will find that they spend most of their time in Dreamweaver's code view.

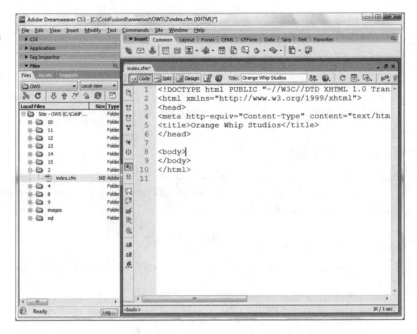

Saving, Closing, and Opening Files

Before you go any further, you need to know how to save, close, and open files.

To save a file, do one of the following:

- Press Ctrl-S (Windows) or Command-S (Mac).

- Choose Save from the File menu.

- Right-click (Windows) or Control-click (Mac) the file name tab (beneath the editor) and choose Save.

TIP

If a file has changed since the last save operation and therefore needs to be saved again, an asterisk will appear after the file's name on the tab.

To close a file, do one of the following:

- Press Ctrl-W (Windows) or Command-W (Mac).

- Choose Close from the File menu.

- Right-click (Windows) or Control-click (Mac) the file name tab and choose Close.

TIP

Windows users can press Ctrl-F4 to close an open file.

To open a file, do one of the following:

- Press Ctrl-O (Windows) or Command-O (Mac).
- Choose Open from the File menu.
- Double-click the file in the site list.

TIP

The Standard toolbar, which can be enabled from the View > Toolbars menu, contains buttons for creating, opening, closing, and saving files.

Testing the Page

Now that you have created a page, you should make sure it's accessible from a Web browser. Open your browser and enter the URL for the page. If you are using the integrated HTTP server, this will be the URL:

```
http://localhost:8500/ows/2/index.cfm
```

The file displayed will be empty (you've put nothing in it), but as long as you don't receive a browser error and the browser title bar reflects the specified title, you'll know that it's working properly. You can now create ColdFusion pages in Dreamweaver and access them via ColdFusion using your browser.

TIP

You can launch a browser directly from within Dreamweaver by pressing F12 or by choosing a browser from the File > Preview in Browser menu.

And with that, you're ready to being ColdFusion development using Dreamweaver.

Using Eclipse

Eclipse is an open-source, Java-based application development environment, and it is used by millions of developers working in all sorts of programming languages. Eclipse has long been supported by the ColdFusion community as well as by the ColdFusion team at Adobe.

Why Use Eclipse for ColdFusion Development

Eclipse is a code editor, and it is designed for experienced coders. Eclipse lacks the design tools that many users love in Dreamweaver, but by concentrating on just what hard-core coders need, it does a better job of addressing this group's unique requirements.

These are the main benefits of using Eclipse:

- Cost—Eclipse is open source and is free to download
- Single editor environment for development in numerous languages: Java, Flex, SQL, Regular Expressions, and more

- Code awareness and source code coloring

- Powerful version control integration

- Lots of third-party add-ons

For a ColdFusion developer, reasons to use Eclipse include all of the preceding plus these:

- Sophisticated ColdFusion application-creation wizards

- Powerful ColdFusion interactive debugger

- Real-time log file viewing

- And much more

Another important reason to use Eclipse is that it is the platform on which Adobe Flex Builder is built, and because many ColdFusion developers also write Flex applications, Eclipse can provide a single environment to work on both.

A Brief Introduction to Eclipse

When you launch Eclipse (with the ColdFusion plug-ins installed, as will be described shortly), you will see a screen similar to the one in Figure 2.7. (The exact screen layout may differ depending on the operating system you're using and the plug-ins that you have installed.)

Figure 2.7

The Eclipse environment allocates the most screen real estate to the editor itself.

Notice these important details about the Eclipse screen:

- The Navigator panel (shown on the left in the figure, though it can be moved elsewhere) is used to browse and open projects and files.

- At the bottom of the screen are important panels that show the results of searches, error messages, and more.

- Above the main screen area are toolbars and buttons used for working with language elements and features.

TIP

Panels can be moved around and repositioned as desired.

Eclipse ColdFusion Support

Eclipse does not ship with built-in ColdFusion support. To develop ColdFusion applications in Eclipse, you must manually install the ColdFusion Eclipse plug-ins.

For full ColdFusion support in Eclipse, you will need to install two plug-ins:

- ColdFusion 8 comes with plug-ins that provide wizards, helps, the debugger, and more. These are distributed as an Eclipse archive .zip file, and can be downloaded from Adobe (as explained in Appendix A).

- The ColdFusion Eclipse plug-in does not provide core CFML language awareness. For that, you will need to install the free community-created CFEclipse plug-in, which is available from http://www.cfeclipse.org/.

Both plug-ins can be installed using the Eclipse software installer screens located at Help > Software Updates > Find & Install.

NOTE

Eclipse plug-in installation is a bit more complex than Dreamweaver extension installation, and so detailed steps are not provided here. Refer to the documentation for instructions.

With these plug-ins installed, you're ready to use Eclipse to write ColdFusion applications.

Getting Started

Much as Dreamweaver lets developers set up sites, Eclipse allows developers to create *projects* for the applications they are working on.

Here are the steps to create our project (which we'll name ows, as before):

1. Locate the Eclipse File menu and choose File > New > Project.

2. Expand the CFEclipse branch and select CFML Project (Figure 2.8). Then click Next.

Figure 2.8

The list of available Eclipse project types varies based on the Eclipse extensions installed.

3. Specify OWS as the project name, and specify the application path as the location (as before, on a Windows computer with the default configuration, the path should be C:\ColdFusion8\wwwroot\OWS\). Then click Next.

4. The next screen may ask you if your project references any other projects. If so, leave the selections blank and click Finish.

You now have a project set up for use with our applications. The new project will automatically be opened in the Navigator panel. If ever the project is not opened, you can open it by right-clicking it in the Navigator panel and choosing Open Project.

Using Perspectives

As already noted, Eclipse can be used for many types of languages and development, and each language has different editor needs. To address all of the different requirements of different languages, Eclipse supports a feature called *perspectives*.

A perspective is a simple a group of configuration settings that you can activate as needed. As a rule, when writing ColdFusion code, you'll want to use the CFEclipse perspective. The exception to this rule is when you are debugging ColdFusion code, in which case you'll want to use the Debug perspective.

You can change the current perspective by using the Window > Open Perspective menu option. In addition, recently used perspectives are usually displayed at the top right of the screen for easy selection.

Working with Files

Now that you've successfully defined the ows site, you should quickly practice working with files in Dreamweaver. In Chapter 4, you will learn more about working with Dreamweaver. For now, let's get you set up and practicing a few basic techniques.

Creating Files

To create new files in Eclipse, simply select the folder to contain the new file, right-click (Windows) or Control-click (Mac), and choose New > CFML Page.

Saving, Closing, and Opening Files

Before you go any further, you need to know how to save, close, and open files.

To save a file, do one of the following:

- Press Ctrl-S (Windows) or Command-S (Mac).
- Choose Save from the File menu.
- Click the Save button on the toolbar (it is a picture of a diskette).

To close a file, do one of the following:

- Press Ctrl-W (Windows) or Command-W (Mac).
- Choose Close from the File menu.

TIP

Windows users can press Ctrl-F4 to close an open file.

To open a file, do one of the following:

- Choose Open from the File menu.
- Double-click the file in the Navigator panel.

And with that, you're ready to begin ColdFusion development using Eclipse.

CHAPTER 3

Accessing the ColdFusion Administrator

The ColdFusion server is a piece of software—an application. As explained in Chapter 1, "Introducing ColdFusion," the software usually runs on a computer running Web server software. Production servers (servers that run finished and deployed applications) usually are connected to the Internet with a high-speed always-on connection. Development machines (used during the application development phase) often are stand-alone computers or workstations on a network and usually run locally installed Web server software and ColdFusion.

The ColdFusion Application Server software—I'll just call it ColdFusion for readability's sake—has all sorts of configuration and management options. Some must be configured before features will work (for example, connections to databases). Others are configured only if necessary (for example, the extensibility options). Still others are purely management and monitoring related (for example, log file analysis).

All these configuration options are managed via a special program, the ColdFusion Administrator. The Administrator is a Web-based application; you access it using any Web browser, from any computer with an Internet connection. This is important because:

- Local access to the computer running ColdFusion is often impossible (especially if hosting with an ISP or in an IT department).

- ColdFusion servers can be managed easily, without needing to install special client software.

- ColdFusion can be managed from any Web browser, even those running on platforms not directly supported by ColdFusion, and even on browsers not running on PCs.

Of course, such a powerful Web application needs to be secure—otherwise, anyone would be able to reconfigure your ColdFusion server! At install time, you were prompted for a password with which to secure the ColdFusion Administrator. Without that password, you won't be able to access the program.

NOTE

In addition to the Web-based ColdFusion Administrator, developers and administrators can create their own Administration screens, consoles, and applications using a special Administrative API. This feature is beyond the scope of this book and is covered in *ColdFusion Web Application Construction Kit, Volume 3: Advanced Application Development*.

TIP

Many ColdFusion developers abbreviate ColdFusion Administrator to CF Admin. So if you hear people talking about "CF Admin," you'll know what they're referring to.

Logging Into (and Out of) the ColdFusion Administrator

When ColdFusion is installed (on Windows), a program group named Adobe, ColdFusion 8 is created. Within that group is an option named Administrator that, when selected, launches the Cold-Fusion Administrator.

NOTE

Depending on installation options selected, the menu item might be named Administrator or ColdFusion 8 Administrator.

It's important to note that this menu option is just a shortcut; you can also access the ColdFusion Administrator by specifying the appropriate URL directly. This is especially important if Cold-Fusion isn't installed locally, or if you simply want to bookmark the Administrator directly.

TIP

If you're serious about ColdFusion development, you should install a server locally. Although you can learn ColdFusion and write code against a remote server, not having access to the server will complicate both your learning and your ongoing development.

The URL for the local ColdFusion Administrator is `http://localhost/CFIDE/administrator/index.cfm`.

As explained in Chapter 1, ColdFusion has an integrated (stand-alone) Web server that may be used for development. That server is usually on port `8500` or `8300` (instead of the default Web port of `80`), so any URLs referring to the integrated Web server must specify that port. As such, the URL for the local ColdFusion Administrator (when using the integrated Web server) is `http://localhost:8500/CFIDE/administrator/index.cfm` or `http://localhost:8300/CFIDE/administrator/index.cfm`.

NOTE

If, for some reason `localhost` doesn't work, the IP address 127.0.0.1 can be used instead: `http://127.0.0.1/CFIDE/administrator/index.cfm`.

TIP

To access the ColdFusion Administrator on a remote server, use the same URL but replace `localhost` with the DNS name (or IP address) of that remote host.

Using the Program Group option or any of the URLs listed previously, start your ColdFusion Administrator. You should see a login screen like the one in Figure 3.1.

Figure 3.1

To prevent
unauthorized
use, access to
the ColdFusion
Administrator is
password protected.

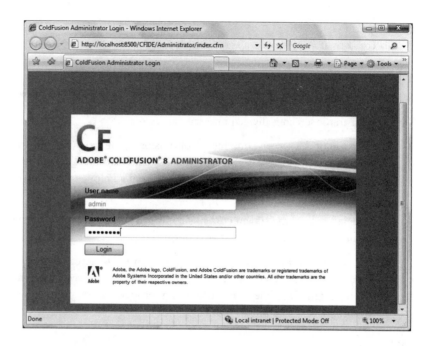

Enter your password, then click the Login button. Assuming your password is correct (you'll know
if it isn't), you'll see the Administrator Welcome Page, as shown in Figure 3.2.

Figure 3.2

The Administrator
Welcome Page.

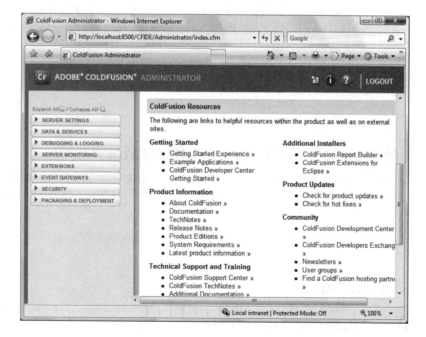

NOTE

The ColdFusion Administrator password is initially set during ColdFusion installation.

NOTE

The exact contents of the Administrator Welcome page will vary, depending on the installation type and edition being used.

The Administrator screen is divided into several regions:

- The top of the screen contains a ColdFusion home icon (use this to get back to the home page if you get lost), a resources icon, a system information icon (used to obtain system configuration information), a Logout link, and a help icon (this provides additional context-sensitive help as necessary).

- The left side of the screen contains menus that may be expanded to display the administrative and configuration options.

- To the right of the menus is the main Administrator screen, which varies based on the menu options selected. When at the home page, this screen contains links to documentation, online support, training, product registration, community sites, the Security Zone, and much more.

NOTE

Use the System Information link at the top of the ColdFusion Administrator screen to install or change your ColdFusion license and serial number (perhaps to upgrade from Standard to Enterprise).

Try logging out of the Administrator (use the Logout button) and then log in again. You should get in the habit of always logging out of the Administrator when you are finished using it.

TIP

If you are logged into the Administrator, your login will time out after a period of inactivity (forcing you to log in again), but don't rely on this. If you leave your desk, or you work in an environment where others can access your computer, always explicitly log out of the ColdFusion Administrator when you're finished or when you leave.

Using the ColdFusion Administrator

Let's take a brief look at the Administrator, and then configure the few options needed so that you can begin development. If you have logged out of the ColdFusion Administrator (or if you have yet to log in), log in now.

→ This chapter provides an overview of the ColdFusion Administrator. Chapter 28, "ColdFusion Server Configuration," in Vol. 2, *Application Development,* covers every Administrator option in detail.

Creating a Data Source

One of the most important uses of the ColdFusion Administrator is to create and define *data sources*, which are connections that ColdFusion uses to interact with a databases. Data sources are defined using the Data Sources menu option (it's in the section labeled Data & Services).

We'll be discussing data sources in detail in Chapter 6, "Introducing SQL," so we'll postpone creating the data source needed for our example applications until we get to that chapter.

Defining a Mail Server

In Chapter 21, "Interacting with Email," online, you will learn how to generate email messages with ColdFusion. ColdFusion doesn't include a mail server; therefore, to generate email the name of a mail server (an SMTP server) must be provided.

NOTE

> If you don't have access to a mail server or don't know the mail server name, don't worry. You won't be using this feature for a while, and omitting this setting now won't keep you from following along in the next lessons.

To set up your SMTP mail server, do the following:

1. In the ColdFusion Administrator, select the Mail menu option (it's in the section labeled Server Settings); you'll see a screen like the one in Figure 3.3.

Figure 3.3

The Mail Server Settings screen is used to define the default SMTP mail server and other mail-related options.

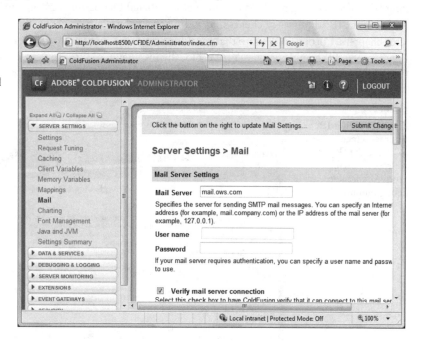

2. The first field, titled Mail Server, prompts for the mail server host (either the DNS name or IP address). Provide this information as requested.

3. Before you submit the form, you always should ensure that the specified mail server is valid and accessible. To do this, check the Verify Mail Server Connection checkbox lower down the page.

4. Click the Submit Changes button (there is one at both the top and the bottom of the screen). Assuming the mail server was accessible, you'll see a success message at the top of the screen. You'll see an error message if the specified server could not be accessed.

You have now configured your mail server and can use ColdFusion to generate SMTP email.

Enabling Debugging

The debugging screens are another important set of screens that you should be familiar with, starting with the Debugging Output Settings screen. To access this screen, select Debugging Output Settings (it's in the section labeled Debugging & Logging).

I don't want you to turn on any of these options now, but I do want you to know where these options are and how to get to them, so that you'll be ready to use them in Chapter 10, "Creating Data-Driven Pages."

Now go to the Debugging IP Address screen shown in Figure 3.4. To get to it, select the Debugging IP Addresses option; it's also in the section labeled Debugging & Logging. This screen is used to define the IP addresses of clients that will receive debug output (this will make more sense in later chapters, I promise). Ensure that the addresses 127.0.0.1 and 0:0:0:0:0:0:0:1 are listed; if they're not, add them. If you don't have a locally installed ColdFusion (and are accessing a remote ColdFusion server), add your own IP address, too: type it and click the Add button.

Figure 3.4

The Debugging IP Address screen is used to define the IP address that will receive generated debug output.

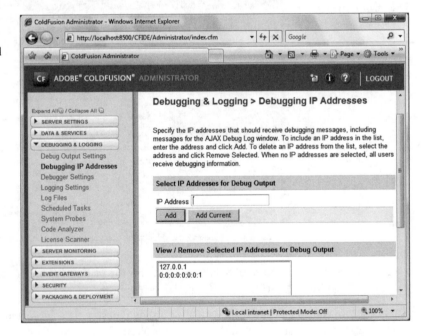

TIP

You can click the Add Current button to add your own IP address. If you are accessing the ColdFusion Administrator using `localhost`, then IP address `127.0.0.1` or `0:0:0:0:0:0:0:1` will be added; otherwise your actual IP address will be added.

Debugging and the generated debug output are an important part of application development, as you'll see later in the book.

➜ Chapter 17, "Debugging and Troubleshooting," covers the debugging options in detail.

Viewing Settings

The final screen I'd like to show you is the Settings Summary screen. As its name implies, this reports all ColdFusion settings, including all defined data sources. To access this screen, select the Settings Summary menu option; it's in the Server Setting section. ColdFusion Administrator will read all settings and then generate a complete report. Settings are also linked, allowing quick access to the appropriate screens if changes are to be made.

TIP

It's a good idea to keep a copy of this screen so that you'll have all the settings readily available if you ever have to restore them.

For now, you are finished with the ColdFusion Administrator. So log out and proceed to the next chapter.

TIP

To log out of the ColdFusion Administrator, click the Logout button at the top right.

NOTE

Feel free to browse through the other administrator screens, but resist the urge to make changes to any settings until you have studied Chapter 28.

CHAPTER 4

Previewing ColdFusion

Preparing to Learn ColdFusion

You're just about ready to go. But before you do, you need to know a little about the sample applications you'll be using.

Orange Whip Studio is a low-budget movie studio waiting for its first big break. To help it get there, you need to create a series of Web applications. These include:

- A public Web site that will allow viewers to learn about the movies

- Intranet screens for movie management (budgets, actors, directors, and more)

- A public e-commerce site allowing fans to purchase movie goodies and memorabilia

Your job throughout this book is to build these and other applications.

TIP

Most of the applications created in this book share common resources (images and data, for example) but are actually stand-alone, meaning they don't require components or code created elsewhere. Although this isn't typical of real-world application development, in this book it is deliberate and by design.

Here are a few things you must know about how to manage code and resources:

- You'll create and store the Orange Whip Studio applications in a folder named ows beneath the Web root.

- ows contains a folder named images, which—this should come as no surprise—contains images used in many of the applications.

- The database used by our application resides in a special folder under the ColdFusion root.

- Web applications are usually organized into a directory structure that maps to application features or sections. However, you won't do that here. To simplify the learning process, you'll create a folder beneath ows for each chapter in the book: 4 for Chapter 4, 5 for Chapter 5, and so on. The files you create in each chapter should go in the appropriate folders.

Assuming you are running ColdFusion locally (this is advised), and assuming you installed the files in the default locations, the URL to access the ows folder will be `http://localhost:8500/ows/` if you're using the integrated HTTP server, or `http://localhost/ows/` if you're using an external HTTP server. You would then access folders beneath ows, such as the folder for this chapter, as `http://localhost:8500/ows/4/` or `http://localhost/ows/4/` (again, depending on whether you're using ColdFusion's integrated HTTP server).

NOTE

Once again, `8500` is the default port used by ColdFusion's integrated Web server. The default port used by the integrated Web server in a JRun/ColdFusion installation is `8300`. If you are using an external Web server (IIS or Apache, for example) then the default port of `80` will likely be used (and can also be entirely omitted from URLs).

TIP

If you have problems resolving host `localhost`, try using IP address `127.0.0.1` instead. `127.0.0.1` is a special IP address that always refers to your own host, and `localhost` is the host name that should always resolve to `127.0.0.1`.

Adobe Dreamweaver is a development environment for creating Web sites and applications. As a ColdFusion developer, you'll be using Dreamweaver extensively, which is why I introduced you to this product previously (see Chapter 2, "Choosing a Development Environment"). For now, to give you a sneak peek at what ColdFusion is all about, you'll use Dreamweaver to build two applications:

- A data browser that displays database contents and contains links for moving from one page of the listing to another
- An age calculator that asks for your date of birth and calculates your age

You'll set up both of these applications using Dreamweaver, but you'll create each very differently. The former will use Dreamweaver features that require no coding at all, and you'll code the latter manually.

And now you're *really* ready to go.

Using Dreamweaver Code Generation

The data used by the Orange Whip Studios applications hasn't been set up yet, so for this first application we'll use one of the example databases that is installed with ColdFusion, and we'll display a list of available art items from an art database.

If you haven't already done so, open Dreamweaver. Your screen should look something like the one shown in Figure 4.1, although you may have different panels open. You can expand and collapse panels as needed by clicking the little arrow to the left of the panel name; when the arrow points downward, the panel is expanded; when the arrow points right, the panel is collapsed.

Figure 4.1

Dreamweaver features a large editor window and many surrounding panels.

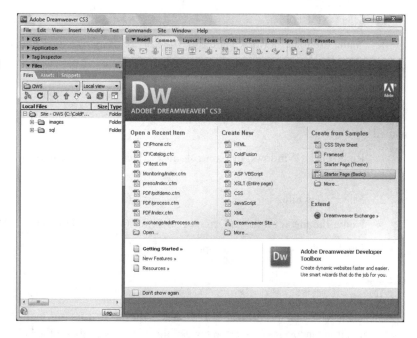

The most important panel for developers is the Files panel, which provides access to all your code, so make sure you have Files expanded and ready for use.

Preparing to Create an Application

Before you can start using Dreamweaver to write ColdFusion code, the following steps must have been performed:

- Create the application root directory.

- Define a site in Dreamweaver.

- Verify that the application directory is set up properly and ready to use.

➜ If you did not complete these steps back in Chapter 2, please refer to that chapter before continuing.

Make sure that the ows site (created in Chapter 2) is open.

Creating a Work Directory and File

As explained previously, to simplify organizing the code created in this book, each chapter's code goes in its own directory.

To create a directory for this chapter, do the following:

1. Right-click (Windows) or Control-click (Mac) the site name in the Site tab in the Files panel.

2. Select New Folder.

3. Name the folder 4 (for Chapter 4); then press (Windows) or Return (Mac).

TIP

Remember these steps, as you'll need to repeat them for most of the chapters in this book.

Now you'll create a file to display the art list. The file will go in the new 4 directory, and will be named art.cfm.

1. Right-click (Windows) or Control-click (Mac) the 4 directory in the Site tab in the Files panel.

2. Select New File.

3. Name the file art.cfm, and then press Enter (Windows) or Return (Mac).

4. Double-click the new file to open it in the editor.

TIP

You can also create files by selecting New from the File menu, or by pressing Ctrl-N (Windows) or Command-N (Mac).

Let's name the file right away (with an HTML name, the one that appears in the Browser title bar). Above the editor window is a toolbar, and one of the options is a field for the HTML title. By default it will be Untitled Document, so change it to Art List by typing that text in the field. Press Enter (Windows) or Return (Mac) to update the title; the HTML below will reflect the change as seen in Figure 4.2.

Figure 4.2

The editor window contains your code and reflects any changes made using toolbars or menu options.

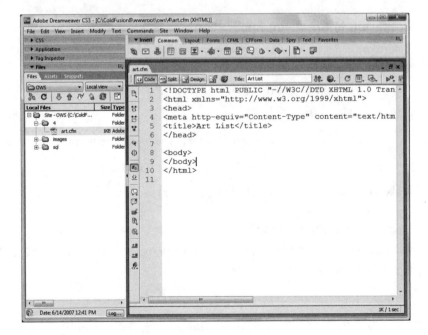

Testing the Page

Now that you have created a page, you should make sure it is accessible via a Web browser. First, save the file (because you just made changes to it). Open your browser and enter the URL to the page. If you are using the integrated HTTP server, the URL will be:

```
http://localhost:8500/ows/4/art.cfm
```

or

```
http://localhost:8300/ows/4/art.cfm
```

If you are using a local external Web server, the URL will probably be:

```
http://localhost/ows/4/art.cfm
```

The file displayed will be empty (you've put nothing in it), but as long as you don't receive a browser error, and the browser title bar reflects the specified title, you'll know it's working properly. You can now create ColdFusion pages in Dreamweaver and access them via ColdFusion using your browser.

TIP

Windows users can launch a browser directly from within Dreamweaver by pressing F12.

Creating an Application in Dreamweaver

Most of this book teaches ColdFusion coding, so you won't be using Dreamweaver's code-generation (*codegen* for short) features very much. However, to create the art list application quickly (without writing any code at all), you'll let Dreamweaver do the work.

The application is rather simple; it displays a list of available art items along with the description and price for each. As this list could include lots of items, the application displays just ten at a time, so you'll need navigation options to move from page to page, as well as to the start and end of the list.

As you won't be coding manually right now, you'll switch Dreamweaver from Code view to Code and Design view (you could use Design view, but it's kind of fun to see Dreamweaver writing the code for you). To do so, click the Show Code and Design Views button on the toolbar above the editor window (it's the second button from the left, the one with the word Split on it).

TIP

If you're having a hard time finding the buttons to switch views, just select the desired view from the View menu.

Dreamweaver will display a split screen, as seen in Figure 4.3, with the code at the top and a design window beneath it. As you add design elements and features at the bottom, Dreamweaver will update the code above.

Figure 4.3

Dreamweaver features a Code view, a Design view, or a Code and Design view in split-screen mode.

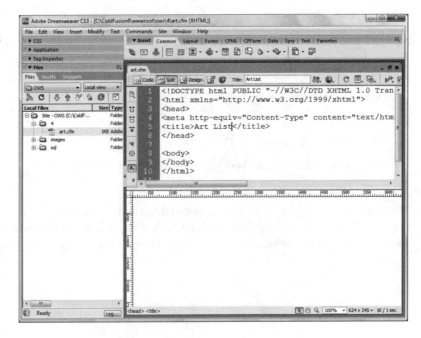

Creating a Recordset

We'll be displaying the art list retrieved from a database, and so the first thing you need to do is to tell Dreamweaver how to get that data. In Dreamweaver this is done by creating a recordset.

➡ Chapter 6, "Introducing SQL," and Chapter 7, "SQL Data Manipulation," cover databases, recordsets, SQL, and more in detail.

You'll now create a recordset that retrieves all items sorted alphabetically by title:

1. In the Application panel, select the Bindings tab. This tab displays any defined bindings (there are none yet), and allows you to define bindings of your own. Click the plus (+) button and select Recordset (query) to display the Recordset window seen in Figure 4.4.

2. Name the recordset art, then select cfartgallery from the list of available data sources. This will populate a list of available tables as seen in Figure 4.5.

3. Select the ART table (it may be displayed as APP.ART). Additional options allow you to specify the columns to retrieve and filter information; leave those as is for now.

4. In the Sort field, select ARTNAME to sort the returned data by title.

5. The selections you just made built a SQL query (I'll explain that in Chapters 6 and 7). To test that the query is working properly, click the Test button to execute it. You should see a display like the one shown in Figure 4.6. If it looks correct, click OK to return to the Recordset window.

Figure 4.4

To define recordsets, you must provide database and selection information.

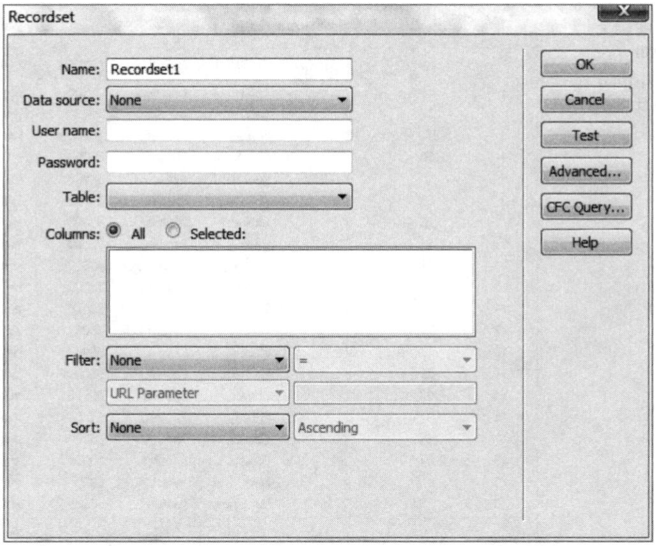

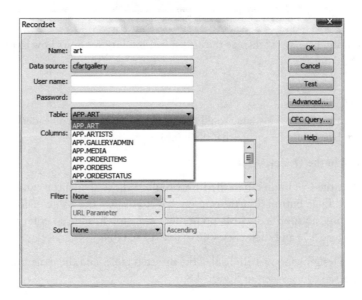

Figure 4.5

Recordsets are built interactively, and the options and selections available will vary based on prior selections.

TIP

For access to the generated SQL and additional options, click the Advanced button in the Recordset window.

6. Click OK to save the recordset. You'll notice that Dreamweaver has inserted the database query into the code at the top of the editor.

Figure 4.6

The Test button executes SQL queries and displays returned results.

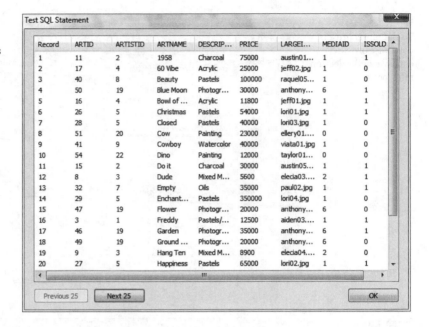

Record	ARTID	ARTISTID	ARTNAME	DESCRIP...	PRICE	LARGEI...	MEDIAID	ISSOLD
1	11	2	1958	Charcoal	75000	austin01...	1	1
2	17	4	60 Vibe	Acrylic	25000	jeff02.jpg	1	0
3	40	8	Beauty	Pastels	100000	raquel05...	1	0
4	50	19	Blue Moon	Photogr...	30000	anthony...	6	1
5	16	4	Bowl of ...	Acrylic	11800	jeff01.jpg	1	1
6	26	5	Christmas	Pastels	54000	lori01.jpg	1	1
7	28	5	Closed	Pastels	40000	lori03.jpg	1	0
8	51	20	Cow	Painting	23000	ellery01....	0	0
9	41	9	Cowboy	Watercolor	40000	viata01.jpg	1	0
10	54	22	Dino	Painting	12000	taylor01...	0	0
11	15	2	Do it	Charcoal	30000	austin05...	1	1
12	8	3	Dude	Mixed M...	5600	elecia03...	2	1
13	32	7	Empty	Oils	35000	paul02.jpg	1	1
14	29	5	Enchant...	Pastels	350000	lori04.jpg	1	0
15	47	19	Flower	Photogr...	20000	anthony...	6	0
16	3	1	Freddy	Pastels/...	12500	aiden03....	1	1
17	46	19	Garden	Photogr...	35000	anthony...	6	1
18	49	19	Ground ...	Photogr...	20000	anthony...	6	0
19	9	3	Hang Ten	Mixed M...	8900	elecia04....	2	0
20	27	5	Happiness	Pastels	65000	lori02.jpg	1	1

Previous 25   Next 25   OK

This ColdFusion page won't display the art list yet, but it now knows how to obtain that information from the database.

Displaying Dynamic Data

Next, you want to display the data. You'll use an HTML table with a header above each column, and you'll let Dreamweaver create that table for you:

1. Click in the Design window.

2. Select the Common tab in the Insert toolbar above the editor window, and click the Insert Table button (fourth from the left) to display the Table dialog. You want 2 rows, 3 columns, no specified width, no border, and a top header, so enter those settings (as seen in Figure 4.7) and then click OK to insert the table.

3. The Design window will display the inserted table, and the generated HTML code will appear above, as seen in Figure 4.8.

NOTE

If you select any code in the Code window, that highlights the corresponding design element in the Design window. Similarly, selecting any design element in the Design window highlights its code in the Code window.

Figure 4.7

The Insert Table dialog prompts for table information, and then generates the complete HTML table.

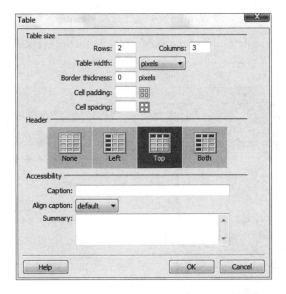

Figure 4.8

Dreamweaver automatically syncs highlighted code in the Code window with design elements in the Design window.

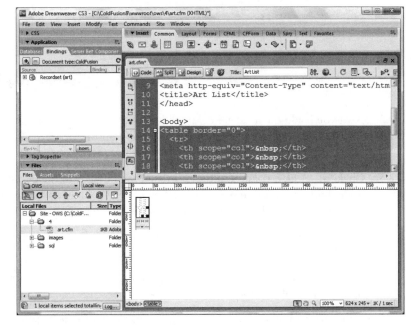

Next you'll add the titles and database columns to the HTML table:

1. Type Title in the top-left table cell, Description in the top-center table cell, and Price in the top-right table cell. These will be the headers, as seen in Figure 4.9.

Figure 4.9

Edits may be made in either the Code window or the Design window.

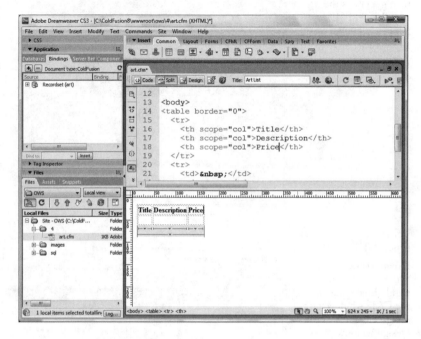

2. Next you'll add the database columns (the ones you retrieved in the recordset earlier). The Bindings tab in the Application panel contains the art recordset. Click the + sign to the left of the recordset to expand it and display its columns.

3. Click the ARTNAME column in the recordset, then drag it to the design window, dropping it in the bottom-left cell in your HTML table. The column name will appear in curly braces (so that you know it's dynamic content, not text).

4. Click the DESCRIPTION column in the recordset, and drag it to bottom-center cell in your HTML table.

5. Repeat the last step, this time dragging column PRICE to the bottom-right cell. Your page should now look like the one in Figure 4.10.

Save your changes, and reload the page in your browser (refer to the "Testing the Page" section earlier in this chapter if you need help). You should see output similar to that in Figure 4.11—a single item listed beneath the specified headers.

Figure 4.10

In Design view, dynamic data is highlighted and surrounded by curly braces.

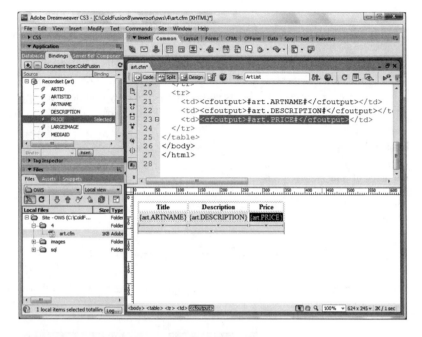

Figure 4.11

When building dynamic content, keep checking the results in a browser as you work.

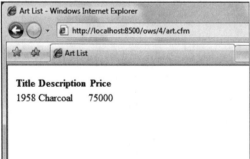

Displaying Multiple Rows

So far, so good—but the page displayed just the first item, and as Figure 4.6 earlier in this chapter shows, the database actually contains lots more. So why did only the first item display? Because you didn't tell Dreamweaver to show any more.

Your next task is to define a Repeat Region, a block of code or design that will repeat once per row retrieved. Here are the steps:

1. Select the Server Behaviors tab in the Application panel. You'll see the recordset listed along with the three dynamic elements, the database columns you dragged into the page.

2. Before you can create a Repeat Region, you need to specify exactly what it is you want to repeat. Select the entire second row of the HTML table, as that is what you'd like to repeat for each art item.

TIP

If you place the pointer just to the left of the table row, it will turn into a left-facing arrow, allowing you to click-select the entire row.

3. Now that you've selected the second row, click the + button in the Server Behaviors tab and select Repeat Region to display the Repeat Region dialog seen in Figure 4.12. The correct recordset will be listed (as that is the only one defined right now), and the default value of "show 10 records at a time" will work, so click OK to create the Repeat Region.

Figure 4.12

A Repeat Region is a block of code or design that is repeated once per database record.

Save your changes and refresh the browser to test your new code. You'll now see the first ten rows as seen in Figure 4.13.

Figure 4.13

Refresh your browser anytime you want to test changes you've made to the code.

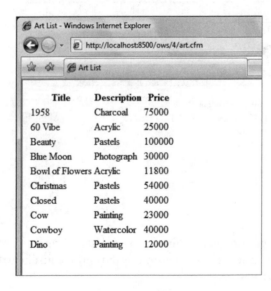

Implementing Page Navigation

This new version is much better, but now you need a way to get to the next page or any other page. Dreamweaver can generate the code for this too, using Recordset Paging behaviors. Here are the steps:

1. First of all, you need the text that the user will click, so insert a line above the table (just press Enter in Windows or Return on the Mac) and type the following:

   `[<< First] [< Previous] [Next >] [Last >>]`

2. When the user clicks << First, the list should jump to the first page of art items. So highlight that text without the square brackets.

3. Click the + button in the Server Behaviors tab (in the Application panel), and select Recordset Paging, then Move to First Page. Verify your selections in the dialog (seen in Figure 4.14), then click OK to create the behavior.

Figure 4.14

When creating Recordset Paging, you verify each behavior before applying it.

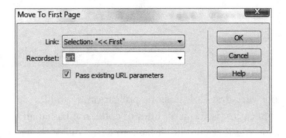

4. Highlight < Previous to create the previous page link (this one will take the user to the previous page), click the + button in the Server Behaviors tab, and select Recordset Paging, then Move to Previous Page. When the dialog appears, click OK to apply the behavior.

5. Now create the next page link (this one will go to the next page). Highlight Next > and apply the Move to Next Page behavior to it.

6. Finally, create the last page link (it will go to the last page). Highlight Last >> and apply the Move to Last Page behavior to it.

Now save the page and test it once again in your browser. As seen in Figure 4.15, the page displays the first ten items, and navigation links allow you to move between pages and jump to the first or last page.

Figure 4.15

Always test all options and links in your application.

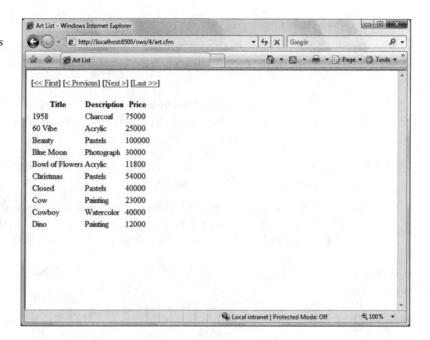

And there you have it—your very first ColdFusion application. If you look at the code window, you'll see that the entire application is about 40 lines of code, not bad at all for this much functionality (and even better considering that you didn't have to write any of the code yourself).

Trying It Yourself

Codegen is OK for some tasks (and is wonderful for rapid prototyping), but more often than not it won't be enough. This is why most of this book discusses coding. To give you a taste of what's to come, try this small (and very simple) application. I won't go into the details of the code itself; for now, concentrate on creating and executing CFM files so they work. If you can get all these to function, you'll have a much easier time working through the book.

The bday application is really simple; it prompts you for your name and date of birth and calculates your age, using simple date arithmetic. The application is made up of two files:

- bday1.cfm (shown in Listing 4.1) is the form that prompts for the name and date of birth.

- bday2.cfm (shown in Listing 4.2) processes the form and displays the results.

Using Dreamweaver, create these two new files, saving them both in the 4 directory. Then enter the code that follows in each file exactly as it appears here—your files should contain this code and nothing else.

Listing 4.1 bday1.cfm

```
<html>
<body>
<form action="bday2.cfm" method="post">
Name: <input type="text" name="name">
<br>
Date of birth: <input type="text" name="dob">
<br>
<input type="submit" value="calculate">
</form>
</body>
</html>
```

The code in bday1.cfm is simple HTML—there's no ColdFusion code at all. In fact, you could have named the file with an .html extension and it would have worked properly.

bday1.cfm contains an HTML form with two form fields: name for the user name and dob for the date of birth.

Listing 4.2 bday2.cfm

```
<html>
<body>
<cfoutput>
Hello #FORM.name#,
you are #DateDiff("YYYY", FORM.dob, Now())#.
</cfoutput>
</body>
</html>
```

The code in bday2.cfm is a mixture of HTML and CFML. The name form field displays the Hello message, and the dob field calculates the age.

To try the application, open a browser and go to the following URL:

```
http://localhost:8500/ows/4/bday1.cfm
```

NOTE

If you aren't using the integrated HTTP server, adjust the URL accordingly.

A form, as shown in Figure 4.16, will prompt you for your name and date of birth. Fill in the two fields, and then click the form submission button to display your age (see Figure 4.17).

Was that a little anticlimactic after the Dreamweaver–generated application? Perhaps. But you've now learned all you need to know about creating, saving, and executing ColdFusion applications.

Figure 4.16

ColdFusion forms are created using standard HTML tags.

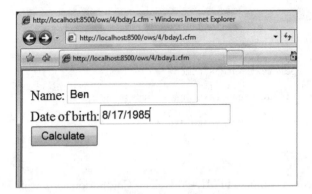

Figure 4.17

ColdFusion generates output displayed in a browser.

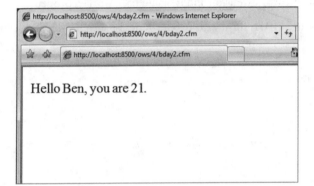

Browsing the Examples and Tutorials

ColdFusion comes with extensive examples, tutorials, and help. These are installed along with ColdFusion (assuming that they were actually selected during the installation). The Getting Started applications are available via links in the ColdFusion Administrator welcome screen.

Two of the options on this page deserve special mention:

- Select Explore Real-World Example Applications to browse two applications that demonstrate lots of ColdFusion functionality, along with the code used to build them.

- Select Code Snippets by Feature and Task to display a Code Snippet Explorer that provides you with instant access to ColdFusion code used to perform various tasks, as well as narrated and interactive tutorials.

Conclusion

I hope that this chapter has given you a taste for what is to come. But before we continue learning ColdFusion, we need to take a little detour into the world of databases and SQL.

CHAPTER 5

Building the Databases

Database Fundamentals

You have just been assigned a project: you must create and maintain a list of all the movies produced by your employer, Orange Whip Studios.

What do you use to maintain this list? Your first thought might be to use a word processor. You could create the list, one movie per line, and manually enter each movie's name so the list is alphabetical and usable. Your word processor provides you with sophisticated document-editing capabilities, so adding, removing, or updating movies is no more complicated than editing any other document.

Initially, you might think you have found the perfect solution—that is, until someone asks you to sort the list by release date and then alphabetically for each date. Now you must re-create the entire list, again sorting the movies manually and inserting them in the correct sequence. You end up with two lists to maintain. You must add new movies to both lists and possibly remove movies from both lists as well. You also discover that correcting mistakes or even just making changes to your list has become more complicated because you must make every change twice. Still, the list is manageable. You have only the two word-processed documents to be concerned with, and you can even open them both at the same time and make edits simultaneously.

The word processor isn't the perfect solution, but it's still a manageable solution—that is, until someone else asks for the list sorted by director. As you fire up your word processor yet again, you review the entire list-management process in your mind. New movies must now be added to all three lists. Likewise, any deletions must be made to the three lists. If a movie tag line changes, you must change all three lists.

And then, just as you think you have the entire process worked out, your face pales and you freeze. What if someone else wants the list sorted by rating? And then, what if yet another department needs the list sorted in some other way? You panic, break out in a sweat, and tell yourself, "There must be a better way!"

This example is a bit extreme, but the truth is that a better way really does exist. You need to use a database.

Databases: A Definition

Let's start with a definition. A *database* is simply a structured collection of similar data. The important words here are *structured* and *similar*, and the movie list is a perfect example of both.

Imagine the movie list as a two-dimensional grid or table, similar to that shown in Figure 5.1. Each horizontal row in the table contains information about a single movie. The rows are broken up by vertical columns. Each column contains a single part of the movie record. The `MovieTitle` column contains movie titles, and so on.

Figure 5.1

Databases display data in an imaginary two-dimensional grid.

Movies

Movie Title	Rating	Budget
Being Unbearably Light	5	300000
Charlie's Devils	1	750000
Closet Encounters of the Odd Kind	5	350000
Four Bar-Mitzvahs and a Circumcision	1	175000

The movie list contains similar data for all movies. Every movie record, or row, contains the same type of information. Each has a title, tag line, budget amount, and so on. The data is also structured in that the data can be broken into logical columns, or fields, that contain a single part of the movie record.

Here's the rule of thumb: any list of information that can be broken into similar records of structured fields should probably be maintained in a database. Product prices, phone directories, invoices, invoice line items, vacation schedules, and lists of actors and directors are all database candidates.

Where Are Databases Used?

You probably use databases all the time, often without knowing it. If you use a software-based accounting program, you are using a database. All accounts payable, accounts receivable, vendor, and customer information is stored in databases. Scheduling programs use databases to store appointments and to-do lists. Even email programs use databases for directory lists and folders.

These databases are designed to be hidden from you, the end user. You never add accounts receivable invoice records into a database yourself. Rather, you enter information into your accounting program, and it adds records to the database.

Clarification of Database-Related Terms

Now that you understand what a database is, I must clarify some important database terms for you. In the SQL world (you will learn about SQL in depth in Chapter 6, "Introducing SQL"), this collection of data is called a *table*. The individual records in a table are called *rows*, and the fields that make up the rows are called *columns*. A collection of tables is called a *database*.

Picture a filing cabinet. The cabinet houses drawers, each of which contains groups of data. The cabinet is a way to keep related but dissimilar information in one place. Each cabinet drawer contains a set of records. One drawer might contain employee records, and another drawer might contain sales records. The individual records within each drawer are different, but they all contain the same type of data, in fields.

The filing cabinet shown in Figure 5.2 is the database—a collection of drawers or tables containing related but dissimilar information. Each drawer contains one or more records, or rows, made up of different fields, or columns.

Figure 5.2

Databases store information in tables, columns, and rows, the way records are filed in a filing cabinet.

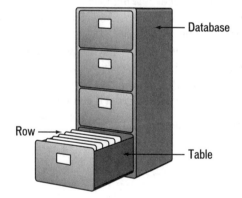

Data Types

Each row in a database table is made up of one or more columns. Each column contains a single piece of data, part of the complete record stored in the row. When a table is created, each of its columns needs to be defined. Defining columns involves specifying the column's name, size, and data type. The data type specifies what data can be stored in a column.

Data types specify the characteristics of a column and instruct the database as to what kind of data can be entered into it. Some data types allow the entry of free-form alphanumeric data. Others restrict data entry to specific data, such as numbers, dates, or true or false flags. A list of common data types is shown in Table 5.1.

Table 5.1 Common Database Data Types and How They Are Used

DATA TYPE	RESTRICTIONS	TYPICAL USE
Character	Upper and lowercase text, numbers, symbols	Names, addresses, descriptions
Numeric	Positive and negative numbers, decimal points	Quantities, numbers
Date	Dates, times	Dates, times
Money	Positive and negative numbers, decimal points	Prices, billing amounts, invoice line items
Boolean	Yes and No or True and False	On/off flags, switches
Binary	Non-text data	Pictures, sound, and video data

There are several reasons for using data types, instead of just entering all data into simple text fields. One of the main reasons is to control or restrict the data a user can enter into that field. A field that has to contain a person's age, for example, could be specified as a numeric field. This way, the user can't enter letters into it—only the digits 0–9. This restriction helps keep invalid data out of your database.

Various data types are also used to control how data is sorted. Data entered in a text field is sorted one character at a time, as if it were left justified. The digit 0 comes before 1, which comes before 9, which comes before a, and so on. Because each character is evaluated individually, a text field containing the number 10 is listed after 1 but before 2 because 10 is greater than 1 but less than 2, just as a 0 is greater than a but less than b. If the value being stored in this column is a person's age, correctly sorting the table by that column would be impossible. Data entered into a numeric field, however, is evaluated by looking at the complete value rather than a character at a time; 10 is considered greater than 2. Figure 5.3 shows how data is sorted if numbers are entered into a text field.

Figure 5.3

Unless you use the correct data type, data may not be sorted the way you want.

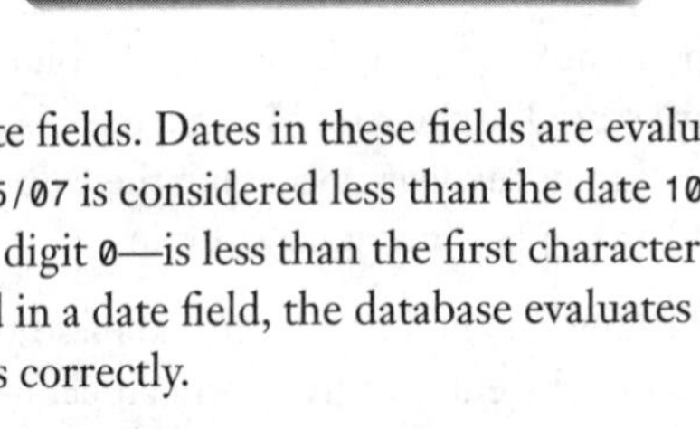

```
1000
2
248
39
7
```

The same is true for date fields. Dates in these fields are evaluated one character at a time, from left to right. The date 02/05/07 is considered less than the date 10/12/99 because the first character of the date 02/05/07—the digit 0—is less than the first character of the date 10/12/99—the digit 1. If the same data is entered in a date field, the database evaluates the date as a complete entity and therefore sorts the dates correctly.

The final reason for using various data types is the storage space that plain-text fields take up. A text field big enough to accommodate up to 10 characters takes up 10 bytes of storage. Even if only 2 characters are entered into the field, 10 bytes are still stored. The extra space is reserved for possible future updates to that field. Some types of data can be stored more efficiently when not treated as text. For example, a 4-byte numeric field can store numeric values from 0 to over 4,000,000,000! Storing 4,000,000,000 in a text field requires 10 bytes of storage. Similarly, a 4-byte date/time field can store the date and time with accuracy to the minute. Storing that same information in a text field would take a minimum of 14 bytes or as many as 20 bytes, depending on how the data is formatted.

TIP

In addition to what has been said about picking the appropriate data types, it's also important to note that picking the wrong type can have a significant impact on performance.

NOTE

Different database applications use different terms to describe the same data type. For example, Microsoft Access uses the term text to describe a data type that allows the entry of all alphanumeric data. Microsoft SQL Server calls this same data type char and uses text to describe variable-length text fields. After you determine the type of data you want a column to contain, refer to your database application's manuals to ensure that you use the correct term when making data type selections.

When you're designing a database, you should give careful consideration to data types. You usually can't easily change the type of a field after the table is created. If you do have to change the type, you might have to create a new table and write routines to convert the data from one table to the new one.

Planning the size of fields is equally important. With most databases, you can't change the size of a field after the table is created. Getting the size right the first time and allowing some room for growth can save you much aggravation later.

CAUTION

When you're determining the size of data fields, always try to anticipate future growth. If you're defining a field for phone numbers, for example, realize that not all phone numbers follow the three-digit area code plus seven-digit phone number convention used in the United States and Canada. Paris, France, for example, has eight-digit phone numbers, and area codes in small towns in England can contain four or five digits.

Using a Database

Back to the example. At this point, you have determined that a film database will make your job easier and might even help preserve your sanity. You create a table with columns for movie title, tag line, release date, and the rest of the required data. You enter your movie list into the table, one row at a time, and are careful to put the correct data in each column.

Next, you instruct the database application to sort the list by movie title. The list is sorted in a second or less, and you print it out. Impressed, you try additional sorts—by rating and by budgeted amount.

You now have two or more lists, but you had to enter the information only once; because you were careful to break the records into multiple columns, you can sort or search the list in any way necessary. You just need to reprint the lists whenever your records are added, edited, or deleted. And the new or changed data is automatically sorted for you.

A Database Primer

You have just seen a practical use for a database. The movie list is a simple database that involves a single table and a small set of columns. Most well-designed database applications require many tables and ways to link them. You'll revisit the movie list when we discuss relational databases.

Your first table was a hit. You have been able to accommodate any list request, sorted any way anyone could need. But just as you are beginning to wonder what you're going to do with all your new-found spare time, your boss informs you that he'll need reports sorted by the director name.

"No problem," you say. You open your database application and modify your table. You add two new columns, one for the director's first name and one for the last name. Now, every movie record can contain the name of the director, and you even create a report of all movies including director information. Once again, you and your database have saved the day, and all is well—or so you think.

Just when things are looking good, you get a memo asking you to include movie expenses in your database so as to be able to run reports containing this information.

You think for a few moments and come up with two solutions to this new problem. The first solution is simply to add lots more columns to the table, three for each expenses item (date, description, and amount).

But you realize this isn't a long-term solution at all. How many expenses should you allow space for? Every movie can, and likely will, have a different set of expenses, and you have no way of knowing how many you should accommodate for. Inevitably, whatever number you pick won't be enough at some point. In addition, adding all these extra columns, which won't be used by most records, is a tremendous waste of disk space. Furthermore, data manipulation becomes extremely complicated if data is stored in more than one column. If you need to search for specific expenses, you'd have to search multiple columns. This situation greatly increases the chance of incorrect results. It also makes sorting data impossible because databases sort data one column at a time, and you have data that must be sorted together spread over multiple columns.

NOTE

An important rule in database design is that if columns are seldom used by most rows, they probably don't belong in the table.

Your second solution is to create additional rows in the table, one for each expense for each movie. With this solution, you can add as many expenses as necessary without creating extra columns.

This solution, though, isn't workable. Although it does indeed solve the problem of handling more than a predetermined number of expenses, doing so introduces a far greater problem. Adding additional rows requires repeating the basic movie information—things such as title and tag line—over and over, for each new row.

Not only does reentering this information waste storage space, it also greatly increases the likelihood of your being faced with conflicting data. If a movie title changes, for example, you must be sure to change every row that contains that movie's data. Failing to update all rows would result in queries and searches returning conflicting results. If you do a search for a movie and find two rows, each of which has different ratings, how would you know which is correct?

This problem probably isn't too serious if the conflicting data is the spelling of a name, but imagine that the data is customer-billing information. If you reenter a customer's address with each order and then the customer moves, you could end up shipping orders to an incorrect address.

You should avoid maintaining multiple live copies of the same data whenever possible.

NOTE

Another important rule in database design is that data should never be repeated unnecessarily. As you multiply the number of copies you have of the same data, the chance of data-entry errors also multiplies.

TIP

One point worth mentioning here is that the "never duplicate data" rule does not apply to backups of your data. Backing up data is incredibly important, and you can never have too many backup plans. The rule of never duplicating data applies only to live data—data to be used in a production environment on an ongoing basis.

And while you are thinking about it, you realize that even your earlier solution for including director names is dangerous. After all, what if a movie has two directors? You've allocated room for only one name.

Understanding Relational Databases

The solution to your problem is to break the movie list into multiple tables. Let's start with the movie expenses.

The first table, the movie list, remains just that—a movie list. To link movies to other records, you add one new column to the list, a column containing a unique identifier for each movie. It might be an assigned movie number or a sequential value that is incremented as each new movie is added to the list. The important thing is that no two movies have the same ID.

TIP

It's generally a good idea never to reuse record-unique identifiers. If the movie with ID number 105 is deleted, for example, that number should never be reassigned to a new movie. This policy guarantees that there is no chance of the new movie record getting linked to data that belonged to the old movie.

Next, you create a new table with several columns: movie ID, expense date, expense description, and expense amount. As long as a movie has no associated expenses, the second table—the expenses table—remains empty. When an expense is incurred, a row is added to the expenses table. The row contains the movie that uniquely identifies this specific movie and the expense information.

The point here is that no movie information is stored in the expenses table except for that movie ID, which is the same movie ID assigned in the movie list table. How do you know which movie the record is referring to when expenses are reported? The movie information is retrieved from the movie list table. When displaying rows from the expenses table, the database relates the row back to the movie list table and grabs the movie information from there. This relationship is shown later in this chapter, in Figure 5.4.

This database design is called a *relational database*. With it you can store data in various tables and then define *links*, or *relationships*, to find associated data stored in other tables in the database. In this example, a movie with two expenses would have two rows in the expenses table. Both of these rows contain the same movie ID, and therefore both refer to the same movie record in the movie table.

NOTE

The process of breaking up data into multiple tables to ensure that data is never duplicated is called normalization.

Primary and Foreign Keys

Primary key is the database term for the column(s) that contains values that uniquely identify each row. A primary key is usually a single column, but doesn't have to be.

There are only two requirements for primary keys:

- **Every row must have a value in the primary key.** Empty fields, sometimes called null fields, are not allowed.

- **Primary key values can never be duplicated.** If two movies were to have the same ID, all relationships would fail. In fact, most database applications prevent you from entering duplicate values in primary key fields.

When you are asked for a list of all expenses sorted by movie, you can instruct the database to build the relationship and retrieve the required data. The movie table is scanned in alphabetical order, and as each movie is retrieved, the database application checks the expenses table for any rows that have a movie ID matching the current primary key. You can even instruct the database to ignore the movies that have no associated expenses and retrieve only those that have related rows in the expenses table.

TIP

Many database applications support a feature that can be used to auto-generate primary key values. Microsoft Access refers to this as an Auto Number field, SQL Server uses the term Identity, and other databases use other terms for essentially the same thing. Using this feature, a correct and safe primary key is automatically generated every time a new row is added to the table.

NOTE

Not all data types can be used as primary keys. You can't use columns with data types for storing binary data, such as sounds, images, variable-length records, or OLE links, as primary keys.

The movie ID column in the expenses table isn't a primary key. The values in that column are not unique if any movie has more than one expense listed. All records of a specific movie's expenses contain the same movie ID. The movie ID is a primary key in a different table—the movie table. This is a *foreign key*. A foreign key is a non-unique key whose values are contained within a primary key in another table.

To see how the foreign key is used, assume that you have been asked to run a report to see which movies incurred expenses on a specific date. To do so, you instruct the database application to scan the expenses table for all rows with expenses listed on that date. The database application uses the value in the expenses table's movie ID foreign key field to find the name of the movie; it does so by using the movie table's primary key. This relationship is shown in Figure 5.4.

Figure 5.4

The foreign key values in one table are always primary key values in another table, which allows tables to be *related* to each other.

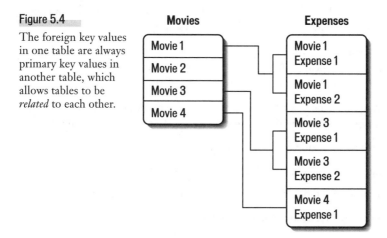

The relational database model helps overcome scalability problems. A database that can handle an ever-increasing amount of data without having to be redesigned is said to *scale well*. You should always take scalability into consideration when designing databases.

Now you've made a significant change to your original database, but what you've created is a manageable and scalable solution. Your boss is happy once again, and your database management skills have saved the day.

Different Kinds of Relationships

The type of relationship discussed up to this point is called a *one-to-many* relationship. This kind of relationship allows an association between a single row in one table and multiple rows in another table. In the example, a single row in the movie list table can be associated with many rows in the expenses table. The one-to-many relationship is the most common type of relationship in a relational database.

Two other types of relational database relationships exist: one-to-one and many-to-many.

The *one-to-one relationship* allows a single row in one table to be associated with no more than one row in another table. This type of relationship is used infrequently. In practice, if you run into a situation in which a one-to-one relationship is called for, you should probably revisit the design. Most tables that are linked with one-to-one relationships can simply be combined into one large table.

The *many-to-many relationship* is also used infrequently. The many-to-many relationship allows one or more rows in one table to be associated with one or more rows in another table. This type of relationship is usually the result of bad design. Most many-to-many relationships can be more efficiently managed with multiple one-to-many relationships.

Multi-Table Relationships

Now that you understand relational databases, let's look at the directors problem again. You will recall that the initial solution was to add the directors directly into the movie table, but that was not a viable solution because it would not allow for multiple directors in a single movie.

Actually, an even bigger problem exists with the suggested solution. As I said earlier, relational database design dictates that data never be repeated. If the director's name was listed with the movie, any director who directed more than one movie would be listed more than once.

Unlike expenses—which are always associated with a single movie—directors can be associated with multiple movies, and movies can be associated with multiple directors. Two tables won't help here.

The solution to this type of relationship problem is to use three database tables:

- Movies are listed in their own table, and each movie has a unique ID.

- Directors are listed in their own table, and each director has a unique ID.

- A new third table is added, which relates the two previous tables.

For example, if movie number 105 was directed by director ID number 3, a single row would be added to the third table. It would contain two foreign keys, the primary keys of each of the movie and director tables. To find out who directed movie number 105, all you'd have to do is look at that third table for movie number 105 and you'd find that director 3 was the director. Then, you'd look at the directors table to find out who director 3 is.

That might sound overly complex for a simple mapping, but bear with me—this is all about to make a lot of sense.

If movie number 105 had a second director (perhaps director ID 5), all you would need to do is add a second row to that third table. This new row would also contain 105 in the movie ID column, but it would contain a different director ID in the director column. Now you can associate two, three, or more directors with each movie. You associate each director with a movie by simply adding one more record to that third table.

And if you wanted to find all movies directed by a specific director, you could do that too. First, you'd find the ID of the director in the directors table. Then, you'd search that third table for all movie IDs associated with the director. Finally, you'd scan the movies table for the names of those movies.

This type of multi-table relationship is often necessary in larger applications, and you'll be using it later in this chapter. Figure 5.5 summarizes the relationships used.

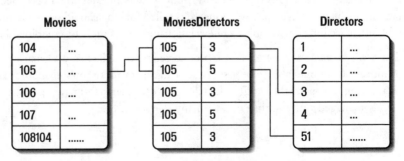

Figure 5.5

To relate multiple rows to multiple rows, you should use a three-way relational table design.

Movies			MoviesDirectors			Directors	
104	...		105	3		1	...
105	...		105	5		2	...
106	...		105	3		3	...
107	...		105	5		4	...
108104	......		105	3		51	......

To summarize, two tables are used if the rows in one table might be related to multiple rows in a second table and when rows in the second table are only related to single rows in the first table. If rows in both tables might be related to multiple rows, however, three tables must be used.

Indexes

Database applications make extensive use of a table's primary key whenever relationships are used. It's therefore vital that accessing a specific row by primary key value be fast. When data is added to a table, you have no guarantee that the rows are stored in any specific order. A row with a higher primary key value could be stored before a row with a lower value. Don't make any assumptions about the actual physical location of any rows within your table.

Now take another look at the relationship between the movie list table and the expenses table. You have the database scan the expenses table to learn which movies have incurred expenses on specific dates; only rows containing that date are selected. This operation, however, returns only the movie IDs—the foreign key values. To determine to which movies these rows are referring, you have the database check the movie list table. Specific rows are selected—the rows that have this movie ID as their primary-key values.

To find a specific row by primary-key value, you could have the database application sequentially read through the entire table. If the first row stored is the one needed, the sequential read is terminated. If not, the next row is read, and then the next, until the desired primary key value is retrieved.

This process might work for small sets of data. Sequentially scanning hundreds, or even thousands of rows is a relatively fast operation, particularly for a fast computer with plenty of available system memory. As the number of rows increases, however, so does the time it takes to find a specific row.

The problem of finding specific data quickly in an unsorted list isn't limited to databases. Suppose you're reading a book on mammals and are looking for information on cats. You could start on the first page of the book and read everything, looking for the word *cat*. This approach might work if you have just a few pages to search through, but as the number of pages grows, so does the difficulty of locating specific words and the likelihood that you will make mistakes and miss references.

To solve this problem, books have indexes. An index allows rapid access to specific words or topics spread throughout the book. Although the words or topics referred to in the index are not in any sorted order, the index itself is. *Cat* is guaranteed to appear in the index somewhere after *bison*, but before *cow*. To find all references to *cat*, you would first search the index. Searching the index is a quick process because the list is sorted. You don't have to read as far as *dog* if the word you're looking for is *cat*. When you find *cat* in the index list, you also find the page numbers where cats are discussed.

Databases use indexes in much the same way. Database indexes serve the same purpose as book indexes—allowing rapid access to unsorted data. Just as book indexes list words or topics alphabetically to facilitate the rapid location of data, so do database table indexes list the values indexed in a sorted order. Just as book indexes list page numbers for each index listing, database table indexes list the physical location of the matching rows, as shown in Figure 5.6. After the database application knows the physical location of a specific row, it can retrieve that row without having to scan every row in the table.

Figure 5.6

Database indexes are lists of rows and where they appear in a table.

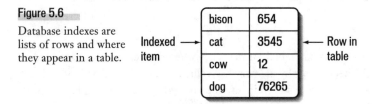

There are two important differences between an index at the back of a book and an index to a database table. First, an index to a database table is *dynamic*. This means that every time a row is added to a table, the index is automatically modified to reflect this change. Likewise, if a row is updated or deleted, the index is updated to reflect this change. As a result, the index is always up to date and always useful. Second, unlike a book index, the table index is never explicitly browsed by the end user. Instead, when the database application is instructed to retrieve data, it uses the index to determine how to complete the request quickly and efficiently.

The database application maintains the index and is the only one to use it. You, the end user, never actually see the index in your database, and in fact, most modern database applications hide the actual physical storage location of the index altogether.

When you create a primary key for a table, it's automatically indexed. The database assumes the primary key will be used constantly for lookups and relationships and therefore does you the favor of creating that first index automatically.

When you run a report against the expenses table to find particular entries, the following process occurs. First, the database application scans the expenses table to find any rows that match the desired date. This process returns the IDs of any matching expenses. Next, the database application retrieves the matching movie for each expense row it has retrieved. It searches the primary key index to find the matching movie record in the movie list table. The index contains all movie IDs in order and, for each ID, lists the physical location of the required row. After the database application finds the correct index value, it obtains a row location from the index and then jumps directly to that location in the table. Although this process might look involved on paper, it actually happens very quickly and in less time than any sequential search would take.

Using Indexes

Now revisit your movies database. Movie production is up, and the number of movies in your movies table has grown, too. Lately, you've noticed that database operations are taking longer than they used to. The alphabetical movie list report takes considerably longer to run, and performance drops further as more movies are added to the table. The database design was supposed to be a scalable solution, so why is the additional data bringing the system to its knees?

The solution here is the introduction of additional indexes. The database application automatically creates an index for the primary key. Any additional indexes have to be explicitly defined. To improve sorting and searching by rating, you just need an index on the rating column. With this index, the database application can instantly find the rows it's looking for without having to sequentially read through the entire table.

The maximum number of indexes a table can have varies from one database application to another. Some databases have no limit at all and allow every column to be indexed. That way, all searches or sorts can benefit from the faster response time.

CAUTION

Some database applications limit the number of indexes any table can have. Before you create dozens of indexes, check to see whether you should be aware of any limitations.

Before you run off and create indexes for every column in your table, you have to realize the trade-off. As we saw earlier, a database table index is dynamic, unlike an index at the end of a book. As data changes, so do the indexes—and updating indexes takes time. The more indexes a table has, the longer write operations take. Furthermore, each index takes up additional storage space, so unnecessary indexes waste valuable disk space.

So when should you create an index? The answer is entirely up to you. Adding indexes to a table makes read operations faster and write operations slower. You have to decide the number of indexes to create and which columns to index for each application. Applications that are used primarily for data entry have less need for indexes. Applications that are used heavily for searching and reporting can definitely benefit from additional indexes.

In our example, you should probably index the movie list table by rating because you often will be sorting and searching by movie rating. Likewise, the release date column might be a candidate for indexing. But you will seldom need to sort by movie summary, so there's no reason to index the summary column. You still can search or sort by summary if the need arises, but the search will take longer than a rating search. Whether you add indexes is up to you and your determination of how the application will be used.

TIP

With many database applications, you can create and drop indexes as needed. You might decide that you want to create additional temporary indexes before running a batch of infrequently used reports. They enable you to run your reports more quickly. You can drop the new indexes after you finish running the reports, which restores the table to its previous state. The only downside to doing so is that write operations are slower while the additional indexes are present. This slowdown might or might not be a problem; again, the decision is entirely up to you.

Indexing on More than One Column

Often, you might find yourself sorting data on more than one column; an example is indexing on last name plus first name. Your directors table might have more than one director with the same last name. To correctly display the names, you need to sort on last name plus first name. This way, Jack Smith always appears before Jane Smith, who always appears before John Smith.

Indexing on two columns—such as last name plus first name—isn't the same as creating two separate indexes (one for last name and one for first name). You have not created an index for the first name column itself. The index is of use only when you're searching or sorting the last name column, or both the last name and first name.

As with all indexes, indexing more than one column often can be beneficial, but this benefit comes with a cost. Indexes that span multiple columns take longer to maintain and take up more disk space. Here, too, you should be careful to create only indexes that are necessary and justifiable.

Understanding the Various Types of Database Applications

All the information described to this point applies equally to all databases. The basic fundamentals of databases, tables, keys, and indexes are supported by all database applications. At some point, however, databases start to differ—in price, performance, features, security, scalability, and more.

One decision you should make very early in the process is whether to use a *shared file–based* database, such as Microsoft Access, or a *client/server* database application, such as Microsoft SQL Server and Oracle. Each has advantages and disadvantages, and the key to determining which will work best for you is understanding the difference between shared file–based applications and client/server systems.

Shared File-Based Databases

Databases such as Microsoft Access and FileMaker are shared file–based databases. They store their data in data files that are shared by multiple users. These data files usually are stored on network drives so they are easily accessible to all users who need them, as shown in Figure 5.7.

Figure 5.7

The data files in a shared file–based database are accessed by all users directly.

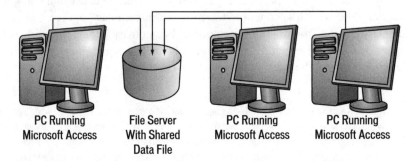

PC Running Microsoft Access   File Server With Shared Data File   PC Running Microsoft Access   PC Running Microsoft Access

When you access data from a Microsoft Access table, for example, that data file is opened on your computer. Any data you read is also read by Microsoft Access running on your computer. Likewise, any data changes are made locally by the copy of Microsoft Access running on your computer.

Considering this point is important when you're evaluating shared file–based database applications. The fact that every running copy of Microsoft Access has the data files open locally has serious implications:

- **Shared data files are susceptible to data corruption.** Each user accessing the tables has the data files open locally. If the user fails to terminate the application correctly or the computer hangs, those files don't close gracefully. Abruptly closing data files like this can corrupt the file or cause garbage data to be written to it.

- **Shared data files create a great deal of unnecessary network traffic.** If you perform a search for specific expenses, the search takes place on your own computer. The database application running on your computer has to determine which rows it wants and which it does not. The application has to know of all the records—including those it will discard for this particular query—for this determination to occur. Those discarded records have to travel to your computer over a network connection. Because the data is discarded anyway, unnecessary network traffic is created.

- **Shared data files are insecure.** Because users have to open the actual data files they intend to work with, they must have full access to those files. This also means that users can either intentionally or accidentally delete the entire data file with all its tables.

This isn't to say that you should never use shared file–based databases. The following are some reasons to use this type of database:

- **Shared file–based databases are inexpensive.** Unless you choose an open-source database such as MySQL, the software itself costs far less than client/server database software. And unlike client/server software, shared file–based databases don't require dedicated hardware for database servers.

- **Shared file–based databases are easier** to learn and use than with client/server-based databases.

Client/Server-Based Databases

Databases such as Microsoft SQL Server, Oracle, and MySQL are client/server-based databases. Client/server applications are split into two distinct parts. The *server* portion is a piece of software that is responsible for all data access and manipulation. This software runs on a computer called the *database server*. In the case of Microsoft SQL Server, it's a computer running Windows and the SQL Server software.

Only the server software interacts with the data files. All requests for data, data additions and deletions, and data updates are funneled through the server software. These requests or changes come from computers running client software. The *client* is the piece of software the user interacts with. If you request a list of movies sorted by rating, for example, the client software submits that request over the network to the server software. The server software processes the request; it filters, discards, and sorts data as necessary, and sends the results back to your client software. This process is illustrated in Figure 5.8.

All this action occurs transparently to you, the user. The fact that data is stored elsewhere or that a database server is even performing all this processing for you is hidden. You never need to access the data files directly. In fact, most networks are set up so that users have no access to the data, or even the drives on which it's stored.

Figure 5.8

Client/server
databases enable
clients to perform
database operations
that are processed by
the server software.

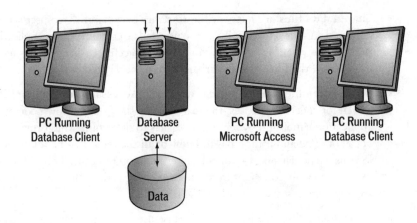

Client/server–based database servers overcome the limitations of shared file-based database applications in the following ways:

- **Client/server-based data files are less susceptible to data corruption caused by incorrect application termination.** If a user fails to exit a program gracefully, or if their computer locks up, the data files do not get damaged. That is because the files are never actually open on that user's computer.

- **Client/server-based database servers use less network bandwidth.** Because all data filtering occurs on the server side, all unnecessary data is discarded before the results are sent back to the client software. Only the necessary data is transmitted over the network.

- **End users in a client/server database environment need never have access to the actual physical data files.** This lack of access helps ensure that the files are not deleted or tampered with.

- **Client/server databases offer greater performance.** This is true of the actual database server itself. In addition, client/server databases often have features not available in shared file–based databases that can provide even greater performance.

As you can see, client/server databases are more secure and more robust than shared-file databases—but all that extra power and security comes with a price:

- **Running client/server databases is expensive.** The software itself is far more expensive than shared-file database applications. In addition, you need a database server to run a client/server database. It must be a high-powered computer that is often dedicated for just this purpose.

- **Client/server databases are more difficult to set up, configure, and administer.** Many companies hire full-time database administrators to do this job.

Which Database Product to Use

Now that you have learned the various types of database systems you can use, how do you determine which is right for your application?

Unfortunately, this question has no simple answer. You really need to review your application needs, the investment you are willing to make in the system, and which systems you already have in place.

To get started, try to answer as many of the following questions as possible:

- Do you have an existing database system in place? If yes, is it current technology that is still supported by the vendor? Do you need to link to data in this system, or are you embarking on a new project that can stand on its own feet?

- Do you have any database expertise or experience? If yes, with which database systems are you familiar?

- Do you have database programmers or administrators in-house? If yes, with which systems are they familiar?

- How many users do you anticipate will use the system concurrently?

- How many records do you anticipate your tables will contain?

- How important is database uptime? What is the cost associated with your database being down for any amount of time?

- Do you have existing hardware that can be used for a database server?

These questions are not easy to answer, but the effort is well worth your time. The more planning you do up front, the better chance you have of making the right decision. Getting the job done right the first time will save you time, money, and aggravation later.

Of course, there is no way you can anticipate all future needs. At some point you might, in fact, need to switch databases. If you ever have to migrate from one database to another, contact the database vendor to determine which migration tools are available. As long as you select known and established solutions from reputable vendors, you should be safe.

TIP

As a rule, shared file-based databases should never be used on production servers. Most developers opt to use client/server databases for production applications because of the added security and scalability. But shared-file databases are often used on development and testing machines because they are cheaper and easier to use. This is a good compromise, and one that is highly recommended if it isn't possible to run client/server databases on all machines—client/server on production machines, shared-file on development machines (if necessary).

ColdFusion comes with a built-in DBMS called Apache Derby (a free, open source, Java application). Derby can be used in two ways: as a file-based database that uses local files (this is called Apache Derby Embedded) and as a client/server database that accesses a Derby server. The database for all examples in this book uses Apache Derby Embedded.

Understanding the OWS Database Tables

Now that you've reviewed the important database fundamentals, let's walk through the tables used in the Orange Whip Studios application (the database you'll be using throughout this book).

NOTE
> Tables and table creation scripts for additional databases can be found on the book Web site at http://www.forta.com/ books/032151548X.

The database is made up of 12 tables, all of which are related.

NOTE
> What follows isn't a complete definition of the tables; it's a summary intended to provide a quick reference that will be of use to you when building the applications. You might want to bookmark this page for future reference.

→ See Appendix B, "Sample Application Data Files," for a more thorough description of the tables used.

The Films Table

The Films table (Table 5.2) contains the movies list. The primary key for this table is the FilmID column.

This table contains a single foreign key:

- The RatingID column is related to the primary key of the FilmsRatings table.

Table 5.2 The Films Table

COLUMN	DATA TYPE	DESCRIPTION AND SIZE
FilmID	Numeric	Unique ID for each movie; can be populated manually when rows are inserted or automatically (if defined as an Auto Number field)
MovieTitle	Text	Movie title
PitchText	Text	Movie pitch text; the tag line
AmountBudgeted	Numeric, currency	Amount budgeted for movie (may not be equal to the actual cost plus expenses)
RatingID	Numeric	ID of associated rating in the FilmsRatings table
Summary	Memo or long text	Full movie summary stored in a variable-length text field (to enable longer summaries)
ImageName	Text	File name of associated image (if there is one)
DateInTheaters	Date	Expected movie release date

The Expenses Table

The Expenses table (Table 5.3) contains the expenses associated with any movies listed in the Films table.

Table 5.3   The Expenses Table

COLUMN	DATA TYPE	DESCRIPTION AND SIZE
ExpenseID	Numeric	Unique ID for each expense; can be populated manually when rows are inserted or automatically (if defined as an Auto Number field)
FilmID	Numeric	ID of associated movie
ExpenseAmount	Numeric, or currency	Expense amount
Description	Text	Expense description
ExpenseDate	Date	Expense date

The primary key for this table is the ExpenseID column.

This table contains a single foreign key:

- The FilmID column is related to the primary key of the Films table.

The Directors Table

The Directors table (Table 5.4) contains the list of directors. This table is related to the Films table via the FilmsDirectors table.

Table 5.4   The Directors Table

COLUMN	DATA TYPE	DESCRIPTION AND SIZE
DirectorID	Numeric	Unique ID for each director; can be populated manually when rows are inserted or automatically (if defined as an Auto Number field)
FirstName	Text	Director's first name
LastName	Text	Director's last name

The primary key for this table is the DirectorID column.

This table contains no foreign keys.

The FilmsDirectors Table

The FilmsDirectors table (Table 5.5) is used to relate the Films and Directors tables (so as to associate directors with their movies).

Table 5.5   The `FilmsDirectors` Table

COLUMN	DATA TYPE	DESCRIPTION AND SIZE
FDRecID	Numeric	Unique ID for each row; can be populated manually when rows are inserted or automatically (if defined as an Auto Number field)
FilmID	Numeric	ID of associated movie
DirectorID	Numeric	ID of associated director
Salary	Numeric, or currency	Director's salary

The primary key for this table is the `FDRecID` column.

This table contains two foreign keys:

- The `FilmID` column is related to the primary key of the `Films` table.
- The `DirectorID` column is related to the primary key of the `Directors` table.

The `Actors` Table

The `Actors` table (Table 5.6) contains the list of actors. This table is related to the `Films` table via the `FilmsActors` table.

Table 5.6   The `Actors` Table

COLUMN	DATA TYPE	DESCRIPTION AND SIZE
ActorID	Numeric	Unique ID for each actor; can be populated manually when rows are inserted or automatically (if defined as an Auto Number field)
NameFirst	Text	Actor's first name
NameLast	Text	Actor's last name
Age	Numeric	Actor's age
NameFirstReal	Text	Actor's real first name
NameLastReal	Text	Actor's real last name
AgeReal	Numeric	Actor's real age (this one actually increases each year)
IsEgomaniac	Bit or Yes/No	Flag specifying whether actor is an egomaniac
IsTotalBabe	Bit or Yes/No	Flag specifying whether actor is a total babe
Gender	Text	Actor's gender (M or F)

The primary key for this table is the `ActorID` column.

This table contains no foreign keys.

The `FilmsActors` Table

The `FilmsActors` table (Table 5.7) is used to relate the `Films` and `Actors` tables (so as to associate actors with their movies).

Table 5.7 The `FilmsActors` Table

COLUMN	DATA TYPE	DESCRIPTION AND SIZE
FARecID	Numeric	Unique ID for each row; can be populated manually when rows are inserted or automatically (if defined as an Auto Number field)
FilmID	Numeric	ID of associated movie
ActorID	Numeric	ID of associated actor
IsStarringRole	Bit or Yes/No	Flag specifying whether this is a starring role
Salary	Numeric or currency	Actor's salary

The primary key for this table is the `FARecID` column.

This table contains two foreign keys:

- The `FilmID` column is related to the primary key of the `Films` table.
- The `ActorID` column is related to the primary key of the `Actors` table.

The `FilmsRatings` Table

The `FilmsRatings` table (Table 5.8) contains a list of film ratings used in the `Films` table (which is related to this table).

Table 5.8 The `FilmsRatings` Table

COLUMN	DATA TYPE	DESCRIPTION AND SIZE
RatingID	Numeric	Unique ID for each rating; can be populated manually when rows are inserted or automatically (if defined as an Auto Number field)
Rating	Text	Rating description

The primary key for this table is the `RatingID` column.

This table contains no foreign keys.

The `UserRoles` Table

The `UserRoles` table (Table 5.9) defines user security roles used by secures applications. This table isn't related to any of the other tables.

Table 5.9 The UserRoles Table

COLUMN	DATA TYPE	DESCRIPTION AND SIZE
UserRoleID	Numeric	Unique ID of user roles; can be populated manually when rows are inserted or automatically (if defined as an Auto Number field)
UserRoleName	Text	User role name (title)
UserRoleFunction	Text	User role description

The primary key for this table is the UserRoleID column.

This table contains no foreign keys.

The Contacts Table

The Contacts table (Table 5.10) contains a list of all contacts (including customers).

Table 5.10 The Contacts Table

COLUMN	DATA TYPE	DESCRIPTION AND SIZE
ContactID	Numeric	Unique ID for each contact; can be populated manually when rows are inserted or automatically (if defined as an Auto Number field)
FirstName	Text	Contact first name
LastName	Text	Contact last name
Address	Text	Contact address
City	Text	Contact city
State	Text	Contact state (or province)
Zip	Text	Contact ZIP code (or postal code)
Country	Text	Contact country
Email	Text	Contact email address
Phone	Text	Contact phone number
UserLogin	Text	Contact login name
UserPassword	Text	Contact login password
MailingList	Bit or Yes/No	Flag specifying whether this contact is on the mailing list
UserRoleID	Numeric	ID of associated security level

The primary key for this table is the ContactID column.

This table contains a single foreign key:

- The UserRoleID column is related to the primary key of the UserRoles table.

The Merchandise Table

The Merchandise table (Table 5.11) contains a list of merchandise for sale. Merchandise is associated with movies, so this table is related to the Films table.

Table 5.11   The Merchandise Table

COLUMN	DATA TYPE	DESCRIPTION AND SIZE
MerchID	Numeric	Unique ID for each item of merchandise; can be populated manually when rows are inserted or automatically (if defined as an Auto Number field)
FilmID	Numeric	ID of associated movie
MerchName	Text	Item name
MerchDescription	Text	Item description
MerchPrice	Numeric or currency	Item price
ImageNameSmall	Text	File name of small image of item (if present)
ImageNameLarge	Text	File name of large image of item (if present)

The primary key for this table is the MerchID column.

This table contains a single foreign key:

- The FilmID column is related to the primary key of the Films table.

The MerchandiseOrders Table

The MerchandiseOrders table (Table 5.12) contains the orders for movie merchandise. Orders are associated with contacts (the buyer), so this table is related to the Contacts table.

Table 5.12   The MerchandiseOrders Table

COLUMN	DATA TYPE	DESCRIPTION AND SIZE
OrderID	Numeric	Unique ID of order (order number); can be populated manually when rows are inserted or automatically (if defined as an Auto Number field)
ContactID	Numeric	ID of associated contact
OrderDate	Date	Order date
ShipAddress	Text	Order ship to address
ShipCity	Text	Order ship to city
ShipState	Text	Order ship to state (or province)
ShipZip	Text	Order ship to ZIP code (or postal code)
ShipCountry	Text	Order ship to country
ShipDate	Date	Order ship date (when shipped)

The primary key for this table is the OrderID column.

This table contains a single foreign key:

- The ContactID column is related to the primary key of the Contacts table.

The MerchandiseOrdersItems Table

The MerchandiseOrdersItems table (Table 5.13) contains the individual items within an order. Order items are associated with an order and the merchandise being ordered, so this table is related to both the MerchandiseOrders and Merchandise tables.

Table 5.13 The MerchandiseOrdersItems Table

COLUMN	DATA TYPE	DESCRIPTION AND SIZE
OrderItemID	Numeric	Unique ID of order items; can be populated manually when rows are inserted or automatically (if defined as an Auto Number field)
OrderID	Numeric	ID of associated order
ItemID	Numeric	ID of item ordered
OrderQty	Numeric	Item quantity
ItemPrice	Numeric or currency	Per-item price

The primary key for this table is the OrderItemID column.

This table contains two foreign keys:

- The OrderID column is related to the primary key of the MerchandiseOrders table.
- The ItemID column is related to the primary key of the Merchandise table.

CHAPTER **6**

Introducing SQL

SQL—pronounced "sequel" or "S-Q-L"—is an acronym for Structured Query Language, a language you use to access and manipulate data in a relational database. It was designed to be easy to learn and extremely powerful, and its mass acceptance by many database vendors proves that it has succeeded in both.

In 1970, Dr. E. F. Codd, the man called the father of the relational database, described a universal language for data access. In 1974, engineers at IBM's San Jose Research Center created the Structured English Query Language, or SEQUEL, built on Codd's ideas. This language was incorporated into System R, IBM's pioneering relational database system.

Toward the end of the 1980s, two of the most important standards bodies, the American National Standards Institute (ANSI) and the International Standards Organization (ISO), published SQL standards, opening the door to mass acceptance. With these standards in place, SQL was poised to become the de facto standard used by every major database vendor.

Although SQL has evolved a great deal since its early SEQUEL days, the basic language concepts and its founding premises remain the same. The beauty of SQL is its simplicity. But don't let that simplicity deceive you. SQL is a powerful language, and it encourages you to be creative in your problem solving. You can almost always find more than one way to perform a complex query or to extract desired data. Each solution has pros and cons, and no solution is explicitly right or wrong.

Lest you panic at the thought of learning a new language, let me reassure you: SQL is easy to learn. In fact, you need to learn only four statements to be able to perform almost all the data manipulation you will need on a regular basis. Table 6.1 lists these statements.

Table 6.1 SQL-Based Data Manipulation Statements

STATEMENT	DESCRIPTION
SELECT	Queries a table for specific data.
INSERT	Adds new data to a table.
UPDATE	Updates existing data in a table.
DELETE	Removes data from a table.

Each of these statements takes one or more keywords as parameters. By combining various statements and keywords, you can manipulate your data in as many ways as you can imagine.

ColdFusion provides you with all the tools you need to add Web-based interaction to your databases. ColdFusion itself has no built-in database, however. Instead, it communicates with whatever database you select, passing updates and requests and returning query results.

TIP

This chapter (and the next) is by no means a complete SQL tutorial, so a good book on SQL is a must for ColdFusion developers. If you want a crash course on all the major SQL language elements, you might want to pick a copy of my *Sams Teach Yourself SQL in 10 Minutes* (ISBN: 0-672-32567-5).

Understanding Data Sources

As explained in Chapter 5, "Building the Databases," a database is a collection of tables that store related data. Databases are generally used in one of two ways:

- Directly within a DBMS application such as Microsoft Access or SQL Server's Enterprise Manager. These applications tend to be very database specific (they are usually designed by the database vendor for use with specific databases).

- Via third-party applications, commercial or custom, that know how to interact with existing external databases.

ColdFusion is in the second group. It isn't a database product, but it let you write applications that interact with databases.

How do third-party applications interact with databases, which are usually created by other vendors? That's where data sources come in to the picture. But first, we need to look at the *database driver*. Almost every database out there has available database drivers—special bits of software that provide access to the database. Each database product requires its own driver (the Oracle driver, for example, won't work for SQL Server), although a single driver can support multiple databases (the same SQL Server driver can access many different SQL Server installations).

There are two primary standards for databases drivers:

- ODBC has been around for a long time, and is one of the most widely used database driver standards. ODBC is primarily used on Windows, although other platforms are supported, too.

- JDBC is Java's database driver implementation, and is supported on all platforms and environments running Java.

NOTE

ColdFusion 5 and earlier used ODBC database drivers. ColdFusion MX and later, which are Java based, primarily use JDBC instead.

Regardless of the database driver or standard used, the purpose of the driver is the same—to hide databases differences and provide simplified access to databases. For example, the internal workings of Microsoft Access and Oracle are very different, but when accessed via a database driver they look the same (or at least more alike). This allows the same application to interact with all sorts of databases, without needing to be customized or modified for each one. Database drivers are very database specific, so access to databases need not be database specific at all.

Of course, different database drivers need different information. For example, the Microsoft Access and Apache Derby Embedded drivers simply need to know the name and location of the data files to be used, whereas the Oracle and SQL Server database drivers require server information and an account login and password.

This driver-specific information could be provided each time it's needed, or a data source could be created. A data source is simply a driver plus any related information stored for future use. Client applications, like ColdFusion, use data sources to interact with databases.

Creating a Data Source

Data sources must be created on the computer actually running ColdFusion. If you are developing using a local ColdFusion installation, the data sources will be local, too; but if you are developing against a remote server, the data sources will need to be defined on that remote server.

ColdFusion data sources are usually created using the ColdFusion Administrator (introduced in Chapter 3, "Accessing the ColdFusion Administrator"). Here are the steps to follow to create the ows data source:

NOTE

If you haven't yet installed the sample file and databases, see the end of Appendix A, "Installing ColdFusion and Development Environments."

1. Log into the ColdFusion Administrator as described in Chapter 3.

2. Select the Data Sources menu option (it's in the section labeled Data & Services). You'll see a screen like the one in Figure 6.1, though with your own available data sources.

Figure 6.1

The Data Sources screen lists all available data sources.

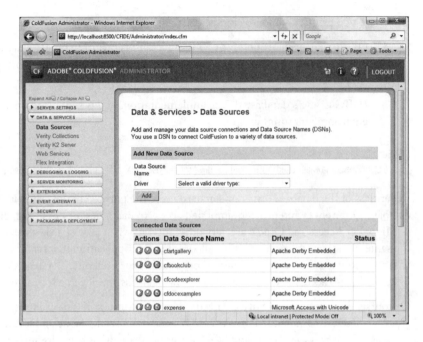

3. All defined data sources are listed in this screen, and they can be added and edited here as well. At the top of the screen, enter ows as the name for the new data source and set the driver type to Apache Derby Embedded (as shown in Figure 6.2); then click the Add button.

Figure 6.2

Data sources can be defined (and edited) from within the Data Sources screen.

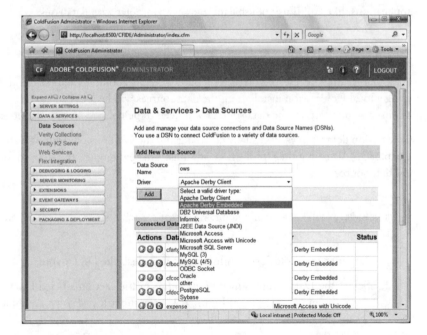

4. The Data Sources definition screen, shown in Figure 6.3, prompts for any information necessary to define the data source. The only field necessary for an Apache Derby Embedded data source is the name of the database folder, so provide the full path to the ows data folder in this field (usually `c:\coldfusion8\db\ows` on Windows systems and `/Applications/ColdFusion8/db/ows` on Mac OS X). You also can click the Browse Server button to display a tree control created using a Java applet that can be used to browse the server's hard drive to locate the file interactively.

Figure 6.3

The Data Sources screen varies based on the driver selected.

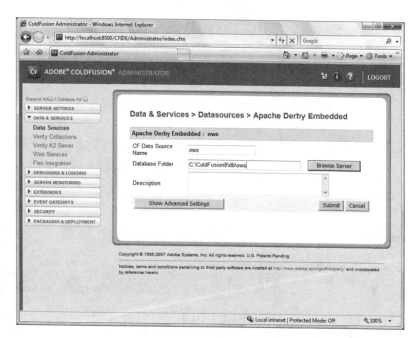

5. When you have filled in any required fields, click the Submit button to create the new data source. The list of data sources will be redisplayed, and the new ows data source will be listed with a status of OK. The screen will report that the data source was successfully updated (Figure 6.4). If an error status message is returned (Figure 6.5), click ows to make any necessary corrections.

NOTE

The options required in a data source definitions vary based on the driver used. As such, the screen used to create and edit data sources varies based on the driver used.

Figure 6.4

Newly created data sources are automatically verified, and the verification status is displayed.

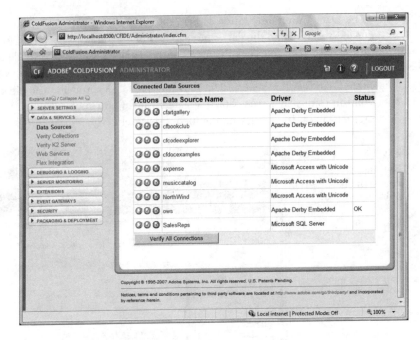

Figure 6.5

If the data source can't be used, the status will indicate a failure.

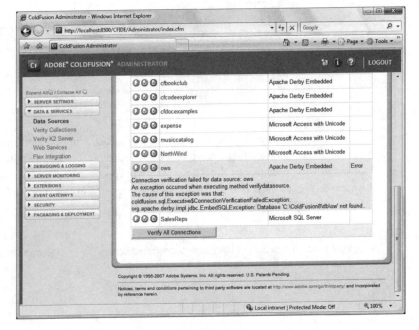

Preparing to Write SQL Queries

Now that you have a data source, all you need is a client application with which to access the data. Ultimately, the client you will use is ColdFusion via CFML code; after all, that is why you're reading this book. But to start learning SQL, we'll use something simpler, a SQL Query Tool (written in ColdFusion). The tool is accessed via a file named `index.cfm` in a directory named `sql` under the `ows` directory, and so the path to it (if using the integrated Web server) will be:

```
http://localhost:8500/ows/sql/index.cfm
```

NOTE

If you are using the integrated server in a multi-server installation, use port 8300 instead of 8500.

The SQL Query Tool, shown in Figure 6.6, allows you to enter SQL statements in the box provided; they are executed when the Execute button is clicked. Results are displayed in the bottom half of the screen.

Figure 6.6

The SQL Query Tool allows SQL statements to be entered manually and then executed.

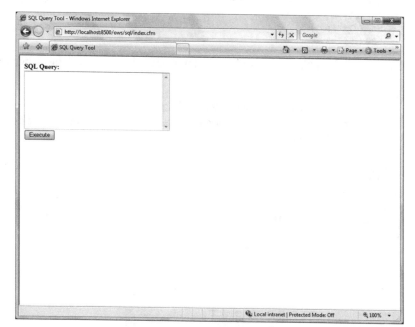

CAUTION

The SQL Query Tool is provided here as a convenience to you. It's not for use on development computers and should never be installed on live (production) servers.

NOTE

The SQL Query Tool allows SQL statements to be executed against databases. This type of tool is dangerous, as it could be used to delete or change data (accidentally or maliciously). To help prevent this, SQL Query Tool has several built-in security measures: by default it only allows `SELECT` statements; it has a hard-coded data source; and it only allows SQL statements to be executed locally (local IP address only). To use SQL Query Tool remotely, you must explicitly allow your own IP address access to the tool by modifying the `Application.cfc` file specifying the address in the `ip_restrict` variable.

Creating Queries

With all the preliminaries taken care of, you can roll up your sleeves and start writing SQL. The SQL statement you will use most is the SELECT statement. As its name implies, you use SELECT to select data from a table.

Most SELECT statements require at least the following two parameters:

- What data you want to select, known as the select list. If you specify more than one item, you must separate each with a comma.

- The table (or tables) from which to select the data, specified with the FROM keyword.

The first SQL SELECT you will create is a query for a list of movies in the Films table. Type the code in Listing 6.1 in the SQL Query box and then execute the statement by clicking the Execute button.

Listing 6.1 Simple SELECT Statement

```
SELECT
MovieTitle
FROM Films
```

That's it! You've written your first SQL statement. The results will be shown as seen in Figure 6.7.

TIP

You can enter SQL statements on one long line or break them up over multiple lines. All white-space characters (spaces, tabs, newline characters) are ignored when the command is processed. Breaking a statement into multiple lines and indent parameters makes it easier to read and debug.

Figure 6.7

The SQL Query Tool displays query results in the bottom half of the screen along with the SQL used and the number of rows returned.

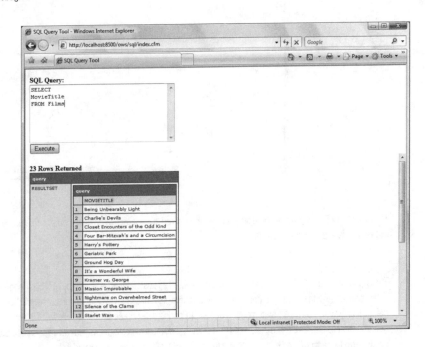

Here's another example. Type the code in Listing 6.2, then click the Execute button to display two columns as seen in Figure 6.8.

Listing 6.2   Multi-column `SELECT` Statement

```
SELECT
MovieTitle, PitchText
FROM Films
```

Figure 6.8

The SQL Query Tool displays the results of all specified columns.

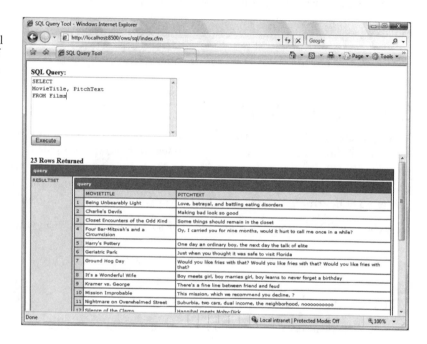

Before you go any further, take a closer look at the SQL code in Listing 6.2. The first parameter you pass to the `SELECT` statement is a list of the two columns you want to see. A column is specified by its name (for example, `MovieTitle`) or as `table.column` (such as `Films.MovieTitle`, where `Films` is the table name and `MovieTitle` is the column name).

Because you want to specify two columns, you must separate them with commas. No comma appears after the last column name, so if you have only one column in your select list, you don't need a comma.

Right after the select list, you specify the table on which you want to perform the query. You always precede the table name with the keyword `FROM`. The table is specified by name, in this case `Films`.

NOTE

SQL statements aren't case sensitive, so you can specify the `SELECT` statement as `SELECT`, `select`, `Select`, or however you want. Common practice, however, is to enter all SQL keywords in uppercase and parameters in lowercase or mixed case. This way, you can read the SQL code and spot typos more easily.

Now modify the `SELECT` statement so it looks like the code in Listing 6.3, then execute it.

Listing 6.3 SELECT All Columns

```
SELECT
*
FROM Films
```

This time, instead of specifying explicit columns to select, you use an asterisk (*). The asterisk is a special select list option that represents all columns. The data pane now shows all the columns in the table in the order in which they are returned by the database table itself.

CAUTION

Don't use an asterisk in the select list unless you really need every column. Each column you select requires its own processing, and retrieving unnecessary columns can dramatically affect retrieval times as your tables get larger.

Sorting Query Results

When you use the SELECT statement, the results are returned to you in the order in which they appear in the table. This is usually the order in which the rows were added to the table. Since that probably isn't the order you want, here is how to sort the query results. To sort rows, you need to add the ORDER BY clause. ORDER BY always comes after the table name; if you try to use it before, you generate a SQL error.

Now click the SQL button, enter the SQL code shown in Listing 6.4, and then click OK.

Listing 6.4 SELECT with Sorted Output

```
SELECT MovieTitle, PitchText, Summary
FROM Films
ORDER BY MovieTitle
```

Your output is then sorted by the MovieTitle column, as shown in Figure 6.9.

What if you need to sort by more than one column? No problem. You can pass multiple columns to the ORDER BY clause. Once again, if you have multiple columns listed, you must separate them with commas. The SQL code in Listing 6.5 demonstrates how to sort on more than one column by sorting by RatingID, and then by MovieTitle within each RatingID.

Listing 6.5 SELECT with Output Sorted on More than One Column

```
SELECT RatingID, MovieTitle, Summary
FROM Films
ORDER BY RatingID, MovieTitle
```

You also can use ORDER BY to sort data in descending order (Z–A). To sort a column in descending order, just use the DESC (short for descending) parameter. Listing 6.6 retrieves all the movies and sorts them by title in reverse order.

Listing 6.6 SELECT with Output Sorted in Reverse Order

```
SELECT MovieTitle, PitchText, Summary
FROM Films
ORDER BY MovieTitle DESC
```

Figure 6.9

You use the ORDER BY clause to sort SELECT output.

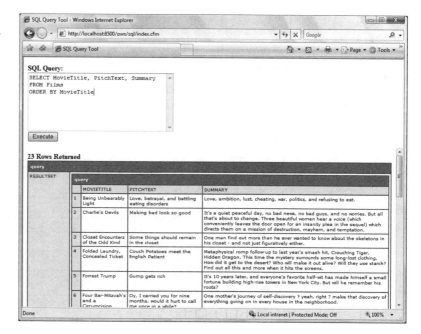

Filtering Data

So far, your queries have retrieved all the rows in the table. You also can use the SELECT statement to retrieve only data that matches specific search criteria. To do so, you must use the WHERE clause and provide a restricting condition. If a WHERE clause is present, when the SQL SELECT statement is processed, every row is evaluated against the condition. Only rows that pass the restriction are selected.

If you use a WHERE clause, it must appear after the table name. If you use both the ORDER BY and WHERE clauses, the WHERE clause must appear after the table name but before the ORDER BY clause.

Filtering on a Single Column

To demonstrate filtering, modify the SELECT statement to retrieve only movies with a RatingID of 1. Listing 6.7 contains the SELECT statement, and the resulting output appears in Figure 6.10.

Listing 6.7 SELECT with WHERE Clause

```
SELECT MovieTitle, PitchText, Summary
FROM Films
WHERE RatingID=1
ORDER BY MovieTitle DESC
```

Figure 6.10

Using the WHERE clause, you can restrict the scope of a SELECT search.

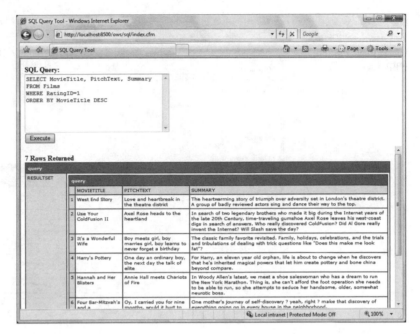

Filtering on Multiple Columns

The WHERE clause also can take multiple conditions. To search for Ben Forta, for example, you can specify a search condition in which the first name is Ben and the last name is Forta, as shown in Listing 6.8. As Figure 6.11 shows, only Ben Forta is retrieved.

Listing 6.8 SELECT with Multiple WHERE Clauses

```
SELECT FirstName, LastName, Email
FROM Contacts
WHERE FirstName='Ben' AND LastName='Forta'
```

CAUTION

Text passed to a SQL query must be enclosed within quotation marks. If you omit the quotation marks, the SQL parser thinks that the text you specified is the name of a column, and you receive an error because that column doesn't exist. Pure SQL allows strings to be enclosed within single quotation marks ('like this') or within double quotation marks ("like this"). But when passing text in a SQL statement to an ODBC or JDBC driver, you must use single quotation marks. If you use double ones, the parser treats the first double quotation mark as a statement terminator, and ignores all text after it.

The AND and OR Operators

Multiple WHERE clauses can be evaluated as AND conditions or OR conditions. The example in Listing 6.8 is an AND condition. Only rows in which both the last name is Forta *and* the first name is Ben will be retrieved. If you change the clause to the following, contacts with a first name of Ben will be retrieved (regardless of last name) and contacts with a last name of Forta will be retrieved (regardless of first name):

```
WHERE FirstName='Ben' OR LastName='Forta'
```

Figure 6.11

You can narrow your search with multiple WHERE clauses.

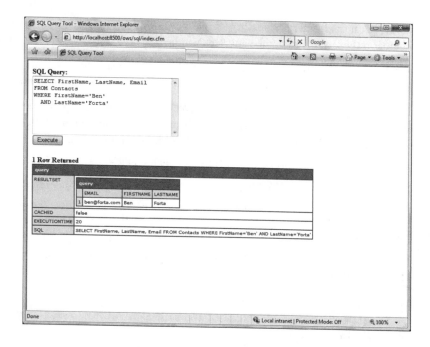

You can combine the AND and OR operators to create any search condition you need. Listing 6.9 shows a WHERE clause that can be used to retrieve only Ben Forta and Rick Richards.

Listing 6.9   Combining WHERE Clauses with AND and OR Operators

```
SELECT NameFirst, NameLast, Email
FROM Contacts
WHERE FirstName='Ben' AND LastName='Forta'
 OR FirstName='Rick' AND LastName='Richards'
```

Evaluation Precedence

When a WHERE clause is processed, the operators are evaluated in the following order of precedence:

- Parentheses have the highest precedence.

- The AND operator has the next level of precedence.

- The OR operator has the lowest level of precedence.

What does this mean? Well, look at the WHERE clause in Listing 6.9. The clause reads WHERE First-Name='Ben' AND LastName='Forta' OR FirstName='Rick' AND LastName='Richards'. AND is evaluated before OR so this statement looks for Ben Forta and Rick Richards, which is what we wanted.

But what would be returned by a WHERE clause of WHERE FirstName='Rick' OR FirstName='Ben' AND LastName= 'Forta'? Does that statement mean *anyone whose first name is either Rick or Ben, and whose last name is Forta*, or does it mean *anyone whose first name is Rick, and also Ben Forta*? The difference is subtle, but if the former is true, then only contacts with a last name of Forta will be retrieved, whereas if the latter is true, then any Rick will be retrieved, regardless of last name.

So which is it? Because AND is evaluated first, the clause means *anyone whose first name is Rick, and also Ben Forta*. This might be exactly what you want—and then again, it might not.

To prevent the ambiguity created by mixing AND and OR statements, parentheses are used to group related statements. Parentheses have a higher order of evaluation than both AND and OR, so they can be used to explicitly match related clauses. Consider the following WHERE clauses:

```
WHERE (FirstName='Rick' OR FirstName='Ben') AND (LastName='Forta')
```

This clause means *anyone whose first name is either Rick or Ben, and whose last name is Forta.*

```
WHERE (FirstName='Rick') OR (FirstName='Ben' AND LastName='Forta')
```

This clause means *anyone whose first name is Rick, and also Ben Forta.*

As you can see, the exact same set of WHERE clauses can mean very different things depending on where parentheses are used.

TIP

Always using parentheses whenever you have more than one WHERE clause is good practice. They make the SQL statement easier to read and easier to debug.

WHERE **Conditions**

In the examples so far, you have used only the = (equal to) operator. You filtered rows based on their being equal to a specific value. Many other operators and conditions can be used with the WHERE clause; they're listed in Table 6.2.

Feel free to experiment with different SELECT statements, using any of the WHERE clauses listed here. The SQL Query tool is safe. By default, it won't update or modify data (by default), so there's no harm in using it to play around with statements and clauses.

Table 6.2 WHERE Clause Search Conditions

CONDITION	DESCRIPTION
=	Equal to. Tests for equality.
<>	Not equal to. Tests for inequality.
<	Less than. Tests that the value on the left is less than the value on the right.
<=	Less than or equal to. Tests that the value on the left is less than or equal to the value on the right.
>	Greater than. Tests that the value on the left is greater than the value on the right.
>=	Greater than or equal to. Tests that the value on the left is greater than or equal to the value on the right.

Table 6.2 (CONTINUED)

CONDITION	DESCRIPTION
EXISTS	Tests for the existence of rows returned by a subquery.
BETWEEN	Tests that a value is in the range between two values; the range is inclusive.
IN	Tests to see whether a value is contained within a list of values.
IS NULL	Tests to see whether a column contains a NULL value.
IS NOT NULL	Tests to see whether a column contains a non-NULL value.
LIKE	Tests to see whether a value matches a specified pattern.
NOT	Negates any test.

Testing for Equality: =

You use the = operator to test for value equality. The following example retrieves only contacts whose last name is Smith:

```
WHERE LastName = 'Smith'
```

Testing for Inequality: <>

You use the <> operator to test for value inequality. The following example retrieves only contacts whose first name is not Kim:

```
WHERE FirstName <> 'Kim'
```

Testing for Less Than: <

By using the < operator, you can test that the value on the left is less than the value on the right. The following example retrieves only contacts whose last name is less than C, meaning that their last name begins with an A or a B:

```
WHERE LastName < 'C'
```

Testing for Less Than or Equal To: <=

By using the <= operator, you can test that the value on the left is less than or equal to the value on the right. The following example retrieves actors aged 21 or less:

```
WHERE Age <= 21
```

Testing for Greater Than: >

You use the > operator to test that the value on the left is greater than the value on the right. The following example retrieves only movies with a rating of 3 or higher (greater than 2):

```
WHERE RatingID > 2
```

Testing for Greater Than or Equal To: >=

You use the >= operator to test that the value on the right is greater than or equal to the value on the left. The following example retrieves only contacts whose first name begins with the letter J or higher:

```
WHERE FirstName >= 'J'
```

BETWEEN

Using the BETWEEN condition, you can test whether a value falls into the range between two other values. The following example retrieves only actors aged 20 to 30. Because the test is inclusive, ages 20 and 30 are also retrieved:

```
WHERE Age BETWEEN 20 AND 30
```

The BETWEEN condition is actually nothing more than a convenient way of combining the >= and <= conditions. You also could specify the preceding example as follows:

```
WHERE Age >= 20 AND Age <= 30
```

Using the BETWEEN condition makes the statement easier to read.

EXISTS

Using the EXISTS condition, you can check whether a subquery returns any rows.

➡ Subqueries are explained in Chapter 41, "More About SQL and Queries," online.

IN

You can use the IN condition to test whether a value is part of a specific set. The set of values must be surrounded by parentheses and separated by commas. The following example retrieves contacts whose last name is Black, Jones, or Smith:

```
WHERE LastName IN ('Black', 'Jones', 'Smith')
```

The preceding example is actually the same as the following:

```
WHERE LastName = 'Black' OR LastName = 'Jones' OR LastName = 'Smith'
```

Using the IN condition has two advantages. First, it makes the statement easier to read. Second, and more importantly, you can use the IN condition to test whether a value is within the results of another SELECT statement (providing a complete SELECT statement in between (and) so as to match whatever that statement returned).

IS NULL and IS NOT NULL

A NULL value is the value of a column that is empty. The IS NULL condition tests for rows that have a NULL value; that is, the rows have no value at all in the specified column. IS NOT NULL tests for rows that have a value in a specified column.

The following example retrieves all contacts whose Email column is empty:

```
WHERE Email IS NULL
```

To retrieve only the contacts who have an email address, use the following example:

```
WHERE Email IS NOT NULL
```

LIKE

Using the LIKE condition, you can test for string pattern matches using wildcards. Two wildcard types are supported. The % character means that anything from that position on is considered a match. You also can use [ ] to create a wildcard for a specific character.

The following example retrieves actors whose last name begins with the letter S. To match the pattern, a last name must have an S as the first character.

```
WHERE LastName LIKE 'S%'
```

To retrieve actors with an S anywhere in their last names, you can use the following:

```
WHERE LastName LIKE '%S%'
```

You also can retrieve just actors whose last name ends with S, as follows:

```
WHERE LastName LIKE '%S'
```

The LIKE condition can be negated with the NOT operator. The following example retrieves only actors whose last name doesn't begin with S:

```
WHERE LastName NOT LIKE 'S%'
```

Using the LIKE condition, you also can specify a wildcard on a single character. If you want to find all actors named Smith but aren't sure whether the one you want spells his or her name Smyth, you can use the following:

```
WHERE LastName LIKE 'Sm[iy]th'
```

This example retrieves only names that start with Sm, then have an i or a y, and then a final th. As long as the first two characters are Sm and the last two are th, and as long as the middle character is i or y, the name is considered a match.

TIP

Using the powerful LIKE condition, you can retrieve data in many ways. But everything has its price, and the price here is performance. Generally, LIKE conditions take far longer to process than other search conditions, especially if you use wildcards at the beginning of the pattern. As a rule, use LIKE and wildcards only when absolutely necessary.

For even more powerful searching, LIKE may be combined with other clauses using AND and OR. And you may even include multiple LIKE clauses in a single WHERE clause.

CHAPTER 7

SQL Data
Manipulation

Chapter 6, "Introducing SQL," introduced data drivers, data sources, SQL, and data retrieval (using the SELECT statement). You'll probably find that you spend far more time retrieving data than you do inserting, updating, or deleting it (which is why we concentrated on SELECT first).

NOTE

As in the previous chapter, the SQL Query Tool in the ows / sql directory will be used to execute the SQL statements. For security's sake (to prevent accidental data changes) the SQL Query Tool by default allows execution of SELECT statements, but no other SQL statements.

To change this behavior, edit the Application.cfc file in the ows/sql directory. You will see a series of variables that are set, one of which is THIS.select_only. This flag is set to yes (the default setting) instructing the utility to execute only SELECT statements. Change this value to no before proceeding (and save the updated Application.cfc file) with the examples in this chapter (or an error will be thrown).

When you're done, set the flag back to yes, just to be safe.

Adding Data

You will need to insert data into tables at some point, so let's look at data inserting using the INSERT statement.

NOTE

In this chapter, you will add, update, and delete rows from tables in the ows data source. The reason you delete any added rows is to ensure that any example code and screen shots later in the book actually look like the way they're supposed to. Feel free to add more rows if you'd like, but if you don't clean up when you're finished, your screens will look different from the ones shown in the figures. This isn't a problem, just something to bear in mind.

Using the `INSERT` Statement

You use the `INSERT` statement to add data to a table. `INSERT` is usually made up of three parts:

- The table into which you want to insert data, specified with the `INTO` keyword.

- The column(s) into which you want to insert values. If you specify more than one item, each must be separated by a comma.

- The values to insert, which are specified with the `VALUES` keyword.

The `Directors` table contains the list of movie directors working with or for Orange Whip Studios. Directors can't be assigned projects (associated with movies) if they aren't listed in this table, so any new directors must be added immediately.

→ See Appendix B, "Sample Application Data Files," for an explanation of each of the data files and their contents.

Now you're ready to add the new director. The following code contains the SQL `INSERT` statement:

```
INSERT INTO Directors(FirstName, LastName)
VALUES('Benjamin', 'FORTA')
```

Enter this statement into the SQL Query field as seen in Figure 7.1. Feel free to replace my name with your own. When you're finished, click the Execute button to insert the new row. Assuming no problems occur, you should see a confirmation screen like the one in Figure 7.2.

Figure 7.1

Type the statement into the SQL Query field, then click Execute.

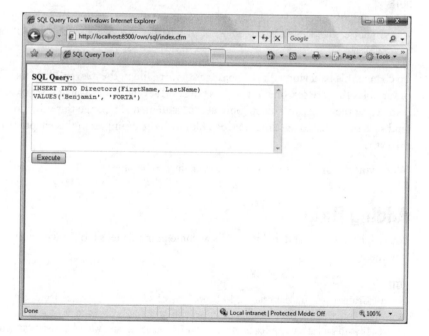

Figure 7.2

As INSERT statements don't return data, no results will be returned.

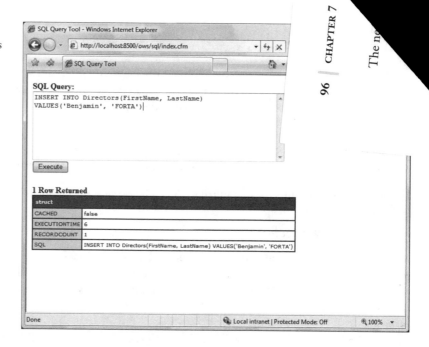

Understanding INSERT

Now that you've successfully inserted a row using the SQL INSERT statement, take a minute to look at the statement's syntax.

The first line of your statement reads:

```
INSERT INTO Directors(FirstName, LastName)
```

The text immediately following the INTO keyword is the name of the table into which the new row is being inserted—in this case, the Directors table.

Next, the columns being added are specified. The columns are listed within parentheses, and since multiple columns are specified, they are separated by a comma. A row in the Directors table requires both a FirstName and a LastName, so the INSERT statement specifies both columns.

NOTE

When you insert a row into a table, you can provide values for as few or as many columns as you like. The only restriction is that any columns defined as NOT NULL columns—meaning they can't be left empty—must have values specified. If you don't set a value for a NOT NULL column, the database driver returns an error message and the row is not inserted.

xt line reads:

```
VALUES('Benjamin', 'FORTA')
```

A value must be specified for every column listed whenever you insert a row. Values are passed to the VALUES keyword; all values are contained within parentheses, just like their column names. Two columns are specified, so two values are passed to the VALUES keyword.

NOTE

When inserting rows into a table, columns can be specified in any order. But be sure that the order of the values in the VALUES keyword exactly matches the order of the columns after the table name, or you'll insert the wrong data into the columns.

To verify that the new director was added to the table, retrieve the complete list of directors using the following SQL statement:

```
SELECT * FROM Directors
```

As explained in Chapter 6, SELECT * means select all columns. As you can see in Figure 7.3, the new row was added to the table. Make a note of the DirectorID value, which you'll need later to update or delete this row (and the ID generated for you may not be the same as the 14 generated for me).

Figure 7.3

You can use SELECT statements to verify that INSERT operations were successful.

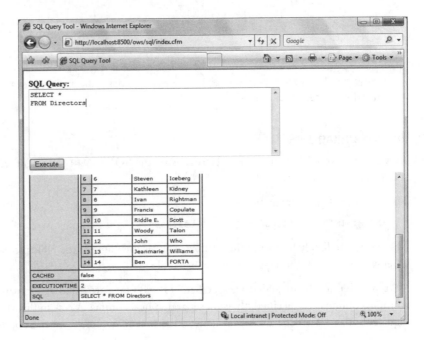

NOTE

In the previous INSERT statement, no value was provided for the DirectorID column. So where did that value come from? The Directors table was set up to automatically assign primary key values every time a new row is inserted. This is a feature supported by many databases—Access calls these AutoNumber columns, SQL Server and Derby use the term *Identity*, and other databases have their own names. As a result, you don't have to worry about creating unique values because the database does that for you.

TIP

> `INSERT` can usually insert only one row at a time, and so multiple insertions require multiple `INSERT` statements. However, some DBMSs, including Derby, allow multiple `VALUE` clauses to be passed to `INSERT`. If you look at the scripts used to populate the example tables, you will see how this syntax is used.

Modifying Data

You use the SQL `UPDATE` statement to update one or more columns. This usually involves specifying the following:

- The table containing the data you want to update.

- The column or columns you want to update, preceded by the `SET` keyword. If you specify more than one item, each must be separated by a comma.

- An optional `WHERE` clause to specify which rows to update. If no `WHERE` clause is provided, all rows are updated.

Try updating a row. Enter the following SQL statement (ensuring that the ID number used in the `WHERE` clause is the `DirectorID` you noted earlier).

```
UPDATE Directors
SET FirstName='Ben'
WHERE DirectorID = 14
```

Click Execute to perform the update. Again, no results will be displayed, as `UPDATE` doesn't return data (although the SQL, execution time, and other information will indeed be displayed).

If you now select the contents of the `Directors` table, you see that the new director's first name has been changed.

Understanding UPDATE

Now, take a closer look at the SQL statement you just used. The first line issued the `UPDATE` statement and specified the name of the table to update. As with the `INSERT` and `DELETE` statements, the table name is required.

You next specified the column you wanted to change and its new value:

```
SET FirstName='Ben'
```

This is an instruction to update the `FirstName` column with the text `Ben`. The `SET` keyword is required for an `UPDATE` operation, because updating rows without specifying what to update makes little sense.

The `SET` keyword can be used only once in an `UPDATE` statement. If you are updating multiple rows—for example, to change `Benjamin` to `Ben` and to set the `LastName` to `Forta` in one operation—the `SET` keyword would look like this:

```
SET FirstName='Ben', LastName='Forta'
```

When updating multiple columns, each column must be separated by a comma. The complete (revised) UPDATE statement would then look like this:

```
UPDATE Directors
SET FirstName='Ben', LastName='Forta'
WHERE DirectorID = 14
```

The last line of the code listing specifies a WHERE clause. The WHERE clause is optional in an UPDATE statement. Without it, all rows will be updated. The following code uses the primary key column to ensure that only a single row gets updated:

```
WHERE DirectorID = 14
```

To verify that the updates worked, try retrieving all the data from the Directors table. The results should be similar to those seen in Figure 7.4 (showing the updated final row).

Figure 7.4

When experimenting with updates, it's a good idea to retrieve the table contents to check that the update worked properly.

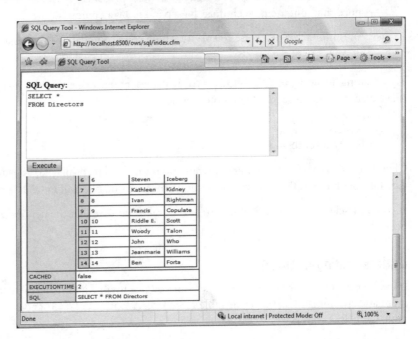

Making Global Updates

Occasionally, you will want to update all rows in a table. To do this, you use UPDATE, too—you just omit the WHERE clause, or specify a WHERE clause that matches multiple rows.

When updating multiple rows using a WHERE clause, always be sure to test that WHERE clause with a simple SELECT statement before executing the UPDATE. If the SELECT returns the correct data (i.e., the data you want updated), you'll know that it is safe to use with UPDATE. If you don't, you might update the wrong data!

Before executing INSERT, UPDATE, or DELETE operations that contain complex statements or WHERE conditions, you should test the statement or condition by using it in a SELECT statement. If SELECT returns incorrect statement results or an incorrect subset of data filtered by the WHERE clause, you'll know that the statement or condition is incorrect. Unlike INSERT, UPDATE, and DELETE, the SELECT statement never changes any data. So if an error exists in the statement or condition, you'll find out about it before any damage is done.

Deleting Data

Deleting data from a table is even easier than adding or updating data—perhaps too easy.

You use the SQL DELETE statement to delete data. The statement takes only two parameters—one required and one optional:

- The name of the table from which to delete the data must be specified immediately following the words DELETE FROM.

- An optional WHERE clause can be used to restrict the scope of the deletion process.

The DELETE statement is dangerously easy to use. Look at the following line of code (but don't execute it):

```
DELETE FROM Directors
```

This statement removes all directors from the Directors table, and does it without any warnings or confirmation.

Some databases, in particular client/server databases (such as Microsoft SQL Server and Oracle), offer safeguards against accidental or malicious deletions. There generally are two approaches to preventing mass deletion. One is to create a trigger (a piece of code that runs on the server when specific operations occur) that verifies every DELETE statement and blocks any DELETE without a WHERE clause. A second is to restrict the use of DELETE without a WHERE clause based on login name. Only certain users, usually those with administrative rights, are granted permission to execute DELETE without a WHERE clause. Any other user attempting a mass DELETE will receive an error message, and the operation will abort. Not all database systems support these techniques. Consult the database administrator's manuals to ascertain which safeguards are available to you.

The DELETE statement is most often used with a WHERE clause. For example, the following SQL statement deletes a single director (the one you just added) from the Directors table:

```
DELETE FROM Directors
WHERE DirectorID=14
```

To verify that the row was deleted, retrieve all the Directors one last time.

As with all WHERE clauses, the DELETE statement's WHERE clause can be a SELECT statement that retrieves the list of rows to delete. If you do use a SELECT statement for a WHERE clause, be careful to test the SELECT statement first to ensure that it retrieves all the values you want, and only those values.

TIP

Feel free to INSERT, UPDATE, and DELETE rows as necessary, but when you're finished either clean up the changes or just copy overwrite the data file with the original (to restore it to its original state).

NOTE

Primary key values are never reused. If you INSERT rows after you have performed delete operations, the new rows will be assigned brand-new IDs, and the old (deleted) IDs will not be reused. This behavior is a required part of how relational databases work, and was explained in Chapter 5, "Building the Databases."

PART II

Using ColdFusion

CHAPTER **8**

The Basics of CFML

Working with Templates

Back in Chapter 4, "Previewing ColdFusion," I walked you through creating several simple applications. ColdFusion applications are made up of one or more files, each with a `.cfm` extension. These files often are referred to as *templates*; you'll see the terms templates, files, and even pages used somewhat interchangeably. Just so you know, they all refer to the same thing. I'll explain why the term templates is used in a few moments.

NOTE

As explained in Chapter 3, "Accessing the ColdFusion Administrator," the URL used with ColdFusion will vary based on whether or not an external Web server is being used. For the sake of simplicity, all URLs used in this and future chapters assume that ColdFusion is being used in conjunction with the integrated Web server ("stand-alone" mode). As such, you'll see the port address :8500 specified in all URLs (both in the content and the figures). If you are not using the integrated Web server simply omit the :8500 from any URLs.

Creating Templates

As already explained, ColdFusion templates are plain text files. As such, they can be created using many different programs. Good choices for ColdFusion developers, as already seen, are Adobe Dreamweaver and Eclipse. Most of the lessons and examples in this book use Dreamweaver, but you are free to use whatever editor you prefer.

To create a new ColdFusion file—or template; as I said, the terms are used interchangeably—simply start Dreamweaver. The editor will be ready for you to start typing code, and what you save is the ColdFusion file, as long as you save it with a `.cfm` extension, that is.

NOTE

There are two other file extensions used with ColdFusion, `.cfc` and `.cfr`. We'll look at those files in future chapters.

The following code is the contents of a simple ColdFusion file named `hello1.cfm`. Actually, at this point no ColdFusion code exists in the listing—it is all straight HTML and text, but we'll change that soon. Launch Dreamweaver (if it is not already open), and type the code as shown next (see Listing 8.1).

Listing 8.1 `hello1.cfm`

```
<html>
<head>
 <title>Hello 1</title>
</head>

<body>

Hello, and welcome to ColdFusion!

</body>
</html>
```

TIP

Tag case is not important, so `<BODY>` or `<body>` or `<Body>` can be used–it's your choice.

Saving Templates

Before ColdFusion can process pages, they must be saved onto the ColdFusion server. If you are developing against a local server, with ColdFusion running on your own computer, you can save the files locally. If you are developing against a remote server, you must save your code on that server.

Where you save your code is extremely important. The URL used to access the page is based on where files are saved, and how directories and paths are configured on the server.

As explained back in Chapter 2, "Choosing a Development Environment," all the files you create throughout this book will go in directories beneath the ows directory under the Web root. To save the code you just typed, create a new directory named 8 under ows and then save the code as `hello1.cfm`. To save the file, do one of the following:

- Select Save from the File menu.

- Right-click (Windows) or Control-click (Mac) on the file tab, and select Save.

- Press Ctrl-S (Windows) or Command-S (Mac).

TIP

Forgotten how to create directories in Dreamweaver? Here's a reminder: In the Files window select the directory in which the new directory is to be created, right-click (Windows) or Control-click (Mac) in the file pane below, and select New Folder.

Executing Templates

Now, let's test the code. There are several ways to do this. The simplest is to right-click (Windows) or Control-click (Mac) on the file in the Files window and select Preview in Browser (selecting your browser off the list).

You may also execute the page directly yourself. Simply open your Web browser and go to this URL:

```
http://localhost:8500/ows/8/hello1.cfm
```

TIP

Not using the integrated Web server? See the note at the start of this chapter.

You should see a page like the one in Figure 8.1. I admit that this is somewhat anticlimactic, but wait; it'll get better soon enough.

Figure 8.1

ColdFusion-generated output usually is viewed in any Web browser.

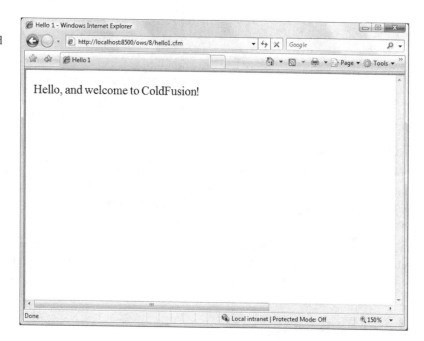

There's another way to browse the code you write. Assuming it is a page that can be executed directly (meaning it is not one that needs to be processed after another page—for example, a page that expects to be processed after a form is submitted), you can browse it directly in Dreamweaver by switching to Design view and activating Live Data view as seen in Figure 8.2.

NOTE

For Live Data view to work, your site must be configured so that Dreamweaver knows how to pass the page to ColdFusion for processing. Sites and how to define them are explained in Chapter 2; refer to that chapter if necessary.

Figure 8.2

If you configure your site correctly, you'll be able to browse much of your ColdFusion code within Dreamweaver itself.

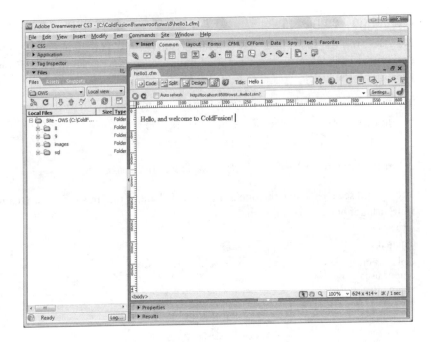

Templates Explained

I promised to explain why ColdFusion files are often referred to as templates. Chapter 1, "Introducing ColdFusion," explains that ColdFusion pages are processed differently from Web pages. When requested, Web pages are sent to the client (the browser) as is, whereas ColdFusion files are processed and the generated results are returned to the client instead.

In other words, ColdFusion files are never sent to the client, but what they create is. And depending on what a ColdFusion file contains, it likely will generate multiple different outputs all from that same single .cfm file—thus the term *template*.

Using Functions

This is where it starts to get interesting. CFML (the ColdFusion Markup Language) is made up of two primary language elements:

- **Tags.** These perform operations, such as accessing a database, evaluating a condition, and flagging text for processing.

- **Functions.** These return (and possibly process) data and do things such as getting the current date and time, converting text to uppercase, and rounding a number to its nearest integer.

Writing ColdFusion code requires the use of both tags and functions. The best way to understand this is to see it in action. Here is a revised hello page. Type Listing 8.2 in a new page, and save it as `hello2.cfm` in the `ows/8` directory.

Listing 8.2   `hello2.cfm`

```
<html>
<head>
 <title>Hello 2</title>
</head>

<body>

Hello, and welcome to ColdFusion!
<br>
<cfoutput>
It is now #Now()#
</cfoutput>

</body>
</html>
```

After you have saved the page, try it by browsing it either in a Web browser or right within Dreamweaver. (If using a Web browser the URL will be `http://localhost:8500/ows/8/hello2.cfm`.) The output should look similar to Figure 8.3 (except that your date and time will probably be different).

Before we go any further, let's take a look at Listing 8.2. You will recall that when ColdFusion processes a `.cfm` file, it looks for CFML code to be processed and returns any other code to the client as is. So, the first line of code is

```
<html>
```

Figure 8.3

ColdFusion code can contain functions, including one that returns the current date and time.

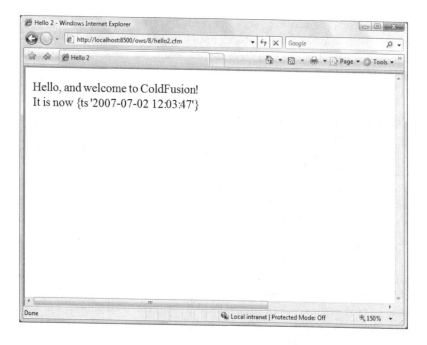

That is not CFML code—it's plain HTML. Therefore, ColdFusion ignores it and sends it on its way (to the client browser). The next few lines are also HTML code:

```
<title>Hello 2</title>
</head>

<body>

Hello, and welcome to ColdFusion!
<br>
```

No ColdFusion language elements exist there, so ColdFusion ignores the code and sends it to the client as is.

But the next three lines of code are not HTML:

```
<cfoutput>
It is now #Now()#
</cfoutput>
```

`<cfoutput>` is a ColdFusion tag (all ColdFusion tags begin with `CF`). `<cfoutput>` is used to mark a block of code to be processed by ColdFusion. All text between the `<cfoutput>` and `</cfoutput>` tags is parsed, character by character, and any special instructions within that block are processed.

In the example, the following line was between the `<cfoutput>` and `</cfoutput>` tags:

```
It is now #Now()#
```

The text `It is now` is not an instruction, so it is sent to the client as is. But the text `#Now()#` *is* a ColdFusion instruction— instructions within strings of text are delimited by number signs (the `#` character). `#Now()#` is an instruction telling ColdFusion to execute a function named `Now()`—a function that returns the current date and time. Thus the output in Figure 8.3 is generated.

The entire block of text from `<cfoutput>` until `</cfoutput>` is referred to as a "`<cfoutput>` block." Not all the text in a `<cfoutput>` block need be CFML functions. In the previous example, literal text was used, too, and that text was sent to the client untouched. As such, you also could have entered the code like this:

```
It is now <cfoutput>#Now()#</cfoutput>
```

Only the `#Now()#` expression needs ColdFusion processing, so only it really needs to be within the `<cfoutput>` block. But what if you had not placed the expression within a `<cfoutput>` block? Try it; remove the `<cfoutput>` tags, save the page, and execute it. You'll see output similar to that in Figure 8.4—obviously not what you want. Because any content not within a `<cfoutput>` block is sent to the client as is, using `Now()` outside a `<cfoutput>` block causes the text `Now()` to be sent to the client instead of the data returned by `Now()`. Why? Because if it is outside a `<cfoutput>` block (and not within any other CFML tag), ColdFusion will never process it.

Omitting the number signs has a similar effect. Put the `<cfoutput>` tags back where they belong, but change `#Now()#` to `Now()` (removing the number signs from before and after it). Then save the page, and execute it. The output will look similar to Figure 8.5. Why? Because all `<cfoutput>` does is flag a block of text as needing processing by ColdFusion. However, ColdFusion does not process *all* text between the tags—instead, it looks for expressions delimited by number signs, and any text *not* within number signs is assumed to be literal text that is to be sent to the client as is.

Figure 8.4

If expressions are sent to the browser, it usually means you have omitted the `<cfoutput>` tags.

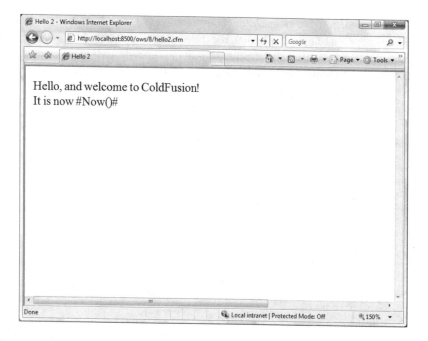

Figure 8.5

Number signs (#) are needed around all expressions; otherwise, the expression is sent to the client instead of being processed.

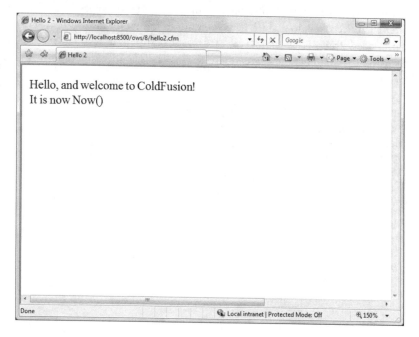

NOTE

`<cfoutput>` has another important use when working with database-driven content. More information about that can be found in Chapter 10, "Creating Data-Driven Pages."

Now() is a function, one of many functions supported in CFML. Now() is used to retrieve information from the system (the date and time), but the format of that date is not entirely readable. Another function, DateFormat(), can help here. DateFormat() is one of ColdFusion's output formatting functions, and its job is to format dates so they are readable in all types of formats. Here is a revision of the code you just used (see Listing 8.3); save it as hello3.cfm and browse the file to see output similar to what is shown in Figure 8.6.

Listing 8.3 hello3.cfm

```
<html>
<head>
 <title>Hello 3</title>
</head>

<body>

Hello, and welcome to ColdFusion!
<br>
<cfoutput>
It is now #DateFormat(Now())#
</cfoutput>

</body>
</html>
```

DateFormat() is an example of a function that accepts (and requires) that data must be passed to it—after all, it needs to know which date you want to format for display. DateFormat() can accept dates as hard-coded strings (as in #DateFormat("8/17/2004")#), as well as dates returned by other expressions, such as the Now() function. #DateFormat(Now())# tells ColdFusion to format the date returned by the Now() function.

Figure 8.6

ColdFusion features a selection of output formatting functions that can be used to better control generated output.

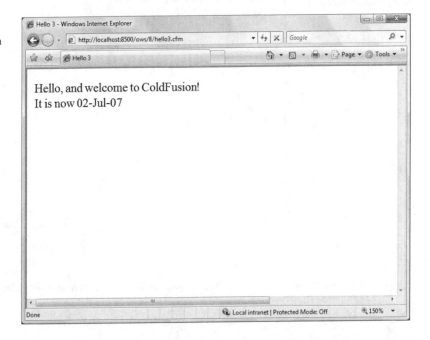

Passing a function as a parameter to another function is referred to as "nesting." In this chapter's example, the `Now()` function is said to be nested in the `DateFormat()` function.

`DateFormat()` takes a second optional attribute, too: a format mask used to describe the output format. Try replacing the `#DateFormat(Now())#` in your code with any of the following, and try each to see what they do:

- `#DateFormat(Now(), "MMMM-DD-YYYY")#`

- `#DateFormat(Now(), "MM/DD/YY")#`

- `#DateFormat(Now(), "DDD, MMMM DD, YYYY")#`

Parameters passed to a function are always separated by commas. Commas are not used if a single parameter is passed, but when two or more parameters exist, every parameter must be separated by a comma.

You've now seen a function that takes no parameters, a function that takes a required parameter, and a function that takes both required and optional parameters. All ColdFusion functions, and you'll be using many of them, work the same way—some take parameters, and some don't. But all functions, regardless of parameters, return a value.

It is important to remember that # is not part of the function. The functions you used here were `DateFormat()` and `Now()`. The number signs were used to delimit (mark) the expressions, but they are not part of the expression itself.

I know I've already said this, but it's worth repeating: CFML code is processed on the server, not on the client. The CFML code you write is *never* sent to the Web browser. What is sent to the browser? Most browsers feature a View Source option that displays code as received. If you view the source of for page `hello3.cfm` you'll see something like this:

```
<html>
<head>
 <title>Hello 3</title>
</head>

<body>

Hello, and welcome to ColdFusion!
<br>

It is now 02-Jul-07


</body>
</html>
```

As you can see, there is no CFML code here at all. The `<cfoutput>` tags, the functions, the number signs—all have been stripped out by the ColdFusion Server, and what was sent to the client is the output that they generated.

TIP

Viewing the generated source is an invaluable debugging trick. If you ever find that output is not being generated as expected, viewing the source can help you understand exactly what was generated and why.

Using Variables

Now that you've had the chance to use some basic functions, it's time to introduce variables. Variables are an important part of just about every programming language, and CFML is no exception. A *variable* is a container that stores information in memory on the server. Variables are named, and the contents of the container are accessed via that name. Let's look at a simple example. Type the code in Listing 8.4 into a new file (feel free to use your own name instead of mine), save it as hello4.cfm, and browse it. You should see a display similar to the one shown in Figure 8.7.

Listing 8.4 hello4.cfm

```
<html>
<head>
 <title>Hello 4</title>
</head>

<body>

<cfset FirstName="Ben">

<cfoutput>
Hello #FirstName#, and welcome to ColdFusion!
</cfoutput>

</body>
</html>
```

Figure 8.7

Variables are replaced by their contents when content is generated.

This code is similar to the previous code listings. It starts with plain HTML, which is sent to the client as is. Then a new tag is used, `<cfset>`:

```
<cfset FirstName="Ben">
```

`<cfset>` is used to set variables. Here, a variable named `FirstName` is created, and a value of `Ben` is stored in it. After it's created, that variable will exist until the page has finished processing and can be used, as seen in the next line of code:

```
Hello #FirstName#, and welcome to ColdFusion!
```

This line of code was placed in a `<cfoutput>` block so ColdFusion will know to replace `#FirstName#` with the contents of `FirstName`. The generated output is then:

```
Hello Ben, and welcome to ColdFusion!
```

Variables can be used as many times as necessary, as long as they exist. Try moving the `<cfset>` statement after the `<cfoutput>` block, or delete it altogether. Executing the page now will generate an error, similar to the one seen in Figure 8.8. This error message is telling you that you referred to (tried to access) a variable that doesn't exist. The error message includes the name of the variable that caused the problem, as well as the line and column in your code, to help you find and fix the problem easily. More often than not, this kind of error is caused by typos.

Figure 8.8

ColdFusion produces an error if a referenced variable doesn't exist.

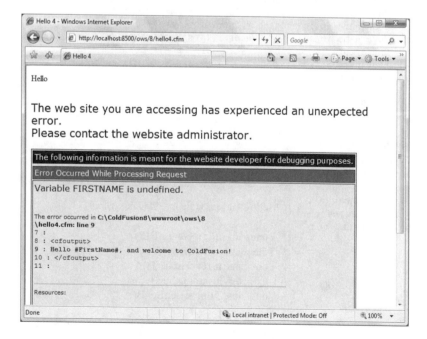

NOTE

If the error message doesn't contain line numbers (or displays less detail than seen in Figure 8.8), you'll need to access the ColdFusion Administrator (as explained in Chapter 3), go to the Debugging Output Settings page, and turn on Enable Robust Exception Information.

NOTE

Regular variables exist only in the page that creates them. If you define a variable named `FirstName` in one page, you can't use it in another page unless you explicitly pass it to that page (see Chapter 10). An exception to this rule does exist. In Chapter 20, "Working with Sessions," you learn how to create and use variables that persist across requests. (Each page access is known as a request.)

Here is a new version of the code, this time using the variable `FirstName` six times. Save Listing 8.5 as `hello5.cfm`, and then try this listing for yourself (feel free to replace my name with your own). The output is shown in Figure 8.9.

Listing 8.5 `hello5.cfm`

```
<html>
    <head>
     <title>Hello 5</title>
    </head>

    <body>

    <cfset firstName="ben">
    <cfoutput>
    Hello #firstName#, and welcome to ColdFusion!<p>
    Your name in uppercase: #UCase(firstName)#<br>
    Your name in lowercase: #LCase(firstName)#<br>
    Your name in reverse: #Reverse(firstName)#<br>
    Characters in your name: #Len(firstName)#<br>
    Your name 3 times: #RepeatString(firstName, 3)#<br>
    </cfoutput>

    </body>
    </html>
```

Figure 8.9

There is no limit to the number of functions that can be used in one page, which enables you to render content as you see fit.

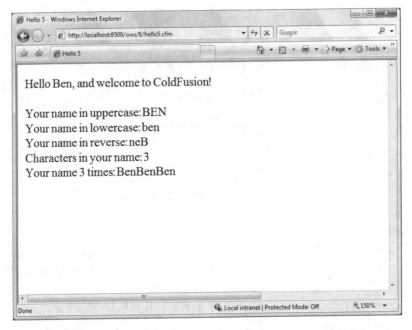

Hello 5 - Windows Internet Explorer

http://localhost:8500/ows/8/hello5.cfm

Hello Ben, and welcome to ColdFusion!

Your name in uppercase: BEN
Your name in lowercase: ben
Your name in reverse: neB
Characters in your name: 3
Your name 3 times: BenBenBen

Let's take a look at the previous code. A `<cfset>` is used to create a variable named `FirstName`. That variable is used once by itself (the Hello message), and then five times with functions. `UCase()` converts a string to uppercase, `LCase()` converts a string to lowercase, `Reverse()` reverses the string, `Len()` returns the length of a string (the number of characters in it), and `RepeatString()` repeats a string a specified number of times.

But functions such as `UCase()` don't truly convert strings; instead, they return converted strings. The difference is subtle but important. Look at the following line of code:

```
Your name in uppercase: #UCase(firstName)#
```

`UCase()` returns `FirstName` converted to uppercase, but the contents of `FirstName` itself are intact and are not converted to anything at all. `FirstName` was not modified; a copy was made and modified instead, and that copy was returned. To save the uppercase `FirstName` to a variable, you must do something like this:

```
<CFSET UpperFirstName=UCase(FirstName)>
```

Here a new variable, `UpperFirstName`, is created. `UpperFirstName` is assigned the value that is returned by `UCase(FirstName)`, the uppercase `FirstName`. And this new variable can be used like any other variable, and as often as necessary. Listing 8.6 is a modified version of Listing 8.5. Try it for yourself—the output will be exactly the same as in Figure 8.9.

Listing 8.6   `hello6.cfm`

```
<html>
<head>
 <title>Hello 6</title>
</head>

<body>

<cfset firstName="ben">
<cfset upperFirstname=UCase(firstName)>
<cfset lowerFirstname=LCase(firstName)>
<cfset reverseFirstname=Reverse(firstName)>
<cfset lenFirstName=Len(firstName)>
<cfset repeatFirstName=RepeatString(firstName, 3)>

<cfoutput>
Hello #FirstName#, and welcome to ColdFusion!<p>
Your name in uppercase: #upperFirstName#<br>
Your name in lowercase: #lowerFirstName#<br>
Your name in reverse: #reverseFirstName#<br>
Characters in your name: #lenFirstName#<br>
Your name 3 times: #repeatFirstName#<br>
</cfoutput>

</body>
</html>
```

This code deserves a closer look. Six `<cfset>` tags now exist, and six variables are created. The first creates the `firstName` variable, just like in the previous examples. The next creates a new variable named `upperFirstName`, which contains the uppercase version of `firstName`. And then lowerFirstName, reverseFirstName, lenFirstName, and repeatFirstName are each created with additional <cfset> statements.

The <cfoutput> block here contains no functions at all. Rather, it just displays the contents of the variables that were just created. In this particular listing there is actually little value in doing this, aside from the fact that the code is a bit more organized this way. The real benefit in saving function output to variables is realized when a function is used many times in a single page. Then, instead of using the same function over and over, you can use it once, save the output to a variable, and just use that variable instead.

One important point to note here is that variables can be overwritten. Look at the following code snippet:

```
<cfset firstName="Ben">
<cfset firstName="Ray">
```

Here, firstName is set to Ben and then set again to Ray. Variables can be overwritten as often as necessary, and whatever the current value is when accessed (displayed, or passed to other functions), that's the value that will be used.

Knowing that, what do you think the following line of code does?

```
<cfset firstName=UCase(FirstName)>
```

This is an example of variable overwriting, but here the variable being overwritten is the variable itself. I mentioned earlier that functions such as UCase() don't convert text; they return a converted copy. So how could you really convert text? By using code such as the line just shown. <cfset firstName=UCase(firstName)> sets firstName to the uppercase version of firstName, effectively overwriting itself with the converted value.

Variable Naming

This would be a good place to discuss variable naming. When you create a variable you get to name it, and the choice of names is up to you. However, you need to know a few rules about variable naming:

- Variable names can contain alphanumeric characters but can't begin with a number (so result12 is okay, but 4thresult is not).

- Variable names can't contain spaces. If you need to separate words, use underscores (for example, monthly_sales_figures instead of monthly sales figures).

- Aside from the underscore, non-alphanumeric characters can't be used in variable names (so Sales!, SSN#, and first-name are all invalid).

- Variable names are case insensitive (FirstName is the same as FIRSTNAME, which is the same as firstname, which is the same as firstName).

Other than that, you can be as creative as necessary with your names. Pick any variable name you want; just be careful not to overwrite existing variables by mistake.

TIP

Avoid the use of abbreviated variable names, such as `fn` or `c`. Although these are valid names, what they stand for is not apparent just by looking at them. Yes, `fn` is fewer keystrokes than `FirstName`, but the first time you (or someone else) must stare at the code trying to figure out what a variable is for, you'll regret saving that little bit of time. As a rule, make variable names descriptive.

Using Prefixes

ColdFusion supports many variable types, and you'll become very familiar with them as you work through this book. For example, local variables (the type you just created) are a variable type. Submitted form fields are a variable type, as are many others.

ColdFusion variables can be referenced in two ways:

- The variable name itself.

- The variable name with the type as a prefix.

For example, the variable `firstName` that you used a little earlier is a local variable (type VARIABLES). That variable can be referred to as `firstName` (as you did previously) and as `VARIABLES.firstName`. Both are valid, and both will work (you can try editing file `hello6.cfm` to use the VARIABLES prefix to try this).

So, should you use prefixes? Well, there are pros and cons. Here are the pros:

- Using prefixes improves performance. ColdFusion will have less work to do finding the variable you are referring to if you explicitly provide the full name (including the prefix).

- If multiple variables exist with the same name but are of different types, the only way to be 100 percent sure that you'll get the variable you want is to use the prefix.

As for the cons, there is just one:

- If you omit the prefix, multiple variable types will be accessible (perhaps form fields and URL parameters, which are discussed in the following chapters). If you provide the type prefix, you restrict access to the specified type, and although this does prevent ambiguity (as just explained), it does make your code a little less reusable.

The choice is yours, and there is no real right or wrong. You can use prefixes if you see fit, and not use them if not. If you don't specify the prefix, ColdFusion will find the variable for you. And if multiple variables of the same name do exist (with differing types) then a predefined order of precedence is used. (Don't worry if these types are not familiar yet, they will become familiar soon enough, and you can refer to this list when necessary.) Here is the order:

- Function local (user-defined functions and CFC methods)

- Thread local (within a `<CFTHREAD>` statement)

- Query results

- Function ARGUMENTS

- Local variables (VARIABLES)

- CGI variables

- FILE variables

- URL parameters

- FORM fields

- COOKIE values

- CLIENT variables

In other words, if you refer to #firstName# (without specifying a prefix) and that variable exists both as a local variable (VARIABLES.firstName) and as a FORM field (FORM.firstName), VARIABLES.first-Name will be used automatically.

NOTE

An exception to this does exist. Some ColdFusion variable types must always be accessed with an explicit prefix; these are covered in later chapters.

Working with Expressions

I've used the term *expressions* a few times in this chapter. What is an expression? The official Cold-Fusion documentation explains that expressions are "language constructs that allow you to create sophisticated applications." A better way to understand it is that expressions are strings of text made up of one or more of the following:

- Literal text (strings), numbers, dates, times, and other values

- Variables

- Operators (+ for addition, & for concatenation, and so on)

- Functions

So, UCase(FirstName) is an expression, as are "Hello, my name is Ben", 12+4, and DateFormat(Now()). And even though many people find it hard to articulate exactly what an expression is, realize that expressions are an important part of the ColdFusion language.

Building Expressions

Expressions are entered where necessary. Expressions can be passed to a <cfset> statement as part of an assignment, used when displaying text, and passed to almost every single CFML tag (except for the few that take no attributes).

Simple expressions can be used, such as those discussed previously (variables, functions, and combinations thereof). But more complex expressions can be used, too, and expressions can include arithmetic, string, and decision operators. You'll use these in the next few chapters.

When using expressions, number signs are used to delimit ColdFusion functions and variables within a block of text. So, how would you display the # itself? Look at the following code snippet:

```
<cfoutput>
#1: #FirstName#
</cfoutput>
```

You can try this yourself if you so feel inclined; you'll see that ColdFusion generates an error when it processes the code (see Figure 8.10).

Figure 8.10

Number signs in text must be escaped; otherwise, ColdFusion produces an error.

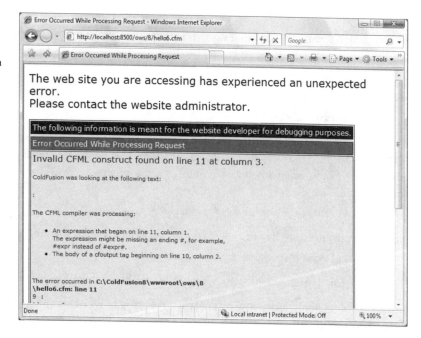

What causes this error? When ColdFusion encounters the # at the start of the line, it assumes you are delimiting a variable or a function and tries to find the matching # (which of course does not exist, as this is not a variable reference at all). The solution is to *escape* the number sign (flag it as being a real number sign), as follows:

```
<cfoutput>
##1: #FirstName#
</cfoutput>
```

When ColdFusion encounters ##, it knows that # is not delimiting a variable or function. Instead, it correctly displays a single #.

When to Use #, and When Not To

Before we go any further, let's clarify exactly when number signs are needed and when they're not.

Simply put, number signs are needed to flag functions and variables within a string of text.

In this first example, the number signs are obviously needed:

```
Hello #VARIABLES.FirstName#
```

But what about when a variable is used within a tag, like this?

```
<cfset UpperFirstName=UCase(FirstName)>
```

Here number signs are not necessary because ColdFusion assumes that anything passed to a tag is a function or variable unless explicitly defined as a string. So the following is incorrect:

```
<cfset #UpperFirstName#=#UCase(FirstName)#>
```

This code will actually work (ColdFusion is very forgiving), but it is still incorrect and should not be used.

This next example declares a variable and assigns a value that is a string, so no number signs are needed here:

```
<cfset FirstName="Ben">
```

But if the string contains variables, number signs would be necessary. Look at this next example: `FullName` is assigned a string, but the string contains two variables (`FirstName` and `LastName`) and those variables must be enclosed within number signs (otherwise ColdFusion will assign the text, not the variable values):

```
<cfset FullName="#FirstName# #LastName#">
```

Incidentally, the previous line of code is functionally equivalent to the following:

```
<CFSET FullName=FirstName & " " & LastName>
```

Here number signs are not necessary because the variables are not being referred to within a string.

Again, the rule is: Only use number signs when referring to variables and functions within a block of text. It's as simple as that.

Using ColdFusion Data Types

The variables you have used thus far are simple variables, are defined, and contain a value. ColdFusion supports three advanced data types that I'll briefly introduce now: lists, arrays, and structures.

> **NOTE**
>
> This is just an introduction to lists, arrays, and structures. All three are used repeatedly throughout the rest of this book, so don't worry if you do not fully understand them by the time you are done reading this chapter. Right now, the intent is to ensure that you know these exist and what they are. You'll have lots of opportunities to use them soon enough.

Lists

Lists are used to group together related information. Lists are actually strings (plain text)—what makes them lists is that a delimiter is used to separate items within the string. For example, the following is a comma-delimited list of five U.S. states:

```
California,Florida,Michigan,Massachusetts,New York
```

The next example is also a list. Even though it might not look like a list, a sentence is a list delimited by spaces:

```
This is a ColdFusion list
```

Lists are created just like any other variables. For example, this next line of code uses the `<cfset>` tag to create a variable named `fruit` that contains a list of six fruits:

```
<cfset fruit="apple,banana,cherry,grape,mango,orange">
```

The code in Listing 8.7 demonstrates the use of lists. Type the code and save it as `list.cfm` in the 8 directory; then execute it. You should see an output similar to the one shown in Figure 8.11.

Figure 8.11

Lists are useful for grouping related data into simple sets.

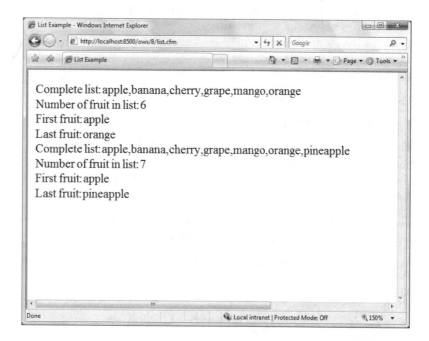

Listing 8.7 `list.cfm`

```
<html>
<head>
 <title>List Example</title>
</head>

<body>

<cfset fruit="apple,banana,cherry,grape,mango,orange">
<cfoutput>
Complete list: #fruit#<BR>
Number of fruit in list: #ListLen(fruit)#<BR>
First fruit: #ListFirst(fruit)#<BR>
Last fruit: #ListLast(fruit)#<BR>
<cfset fruit=ListAppend(fruit, "pineapple")>
Complete list: #fruit#<BR>
```

Listing 8.7 (CONTINUED)

```
Number of fruit in list: #ListLen(fruit)#<BR>
First fruit: #ListFirst(fruit)#<BR>
Last fruit: #ListLast(fruit)#<BR>
</cfoutput>

</body>
</html>
```

Let's walk through the code in Listing 8.7. A <cfset> is used to create a list. As a list is simply a string, a simple variable assignment can be used.

Next comes the <cfoutput> block, starting with displaying #fruit# (the complete list). The next line of code uses the ListLen() function to return the number of items in the list (there are six of them). Individual list members can be retrieved using ListFirst() (used here to get the first list element), ListLast() (used here to get the last list element), and ListGetAt() (used to retrieve any list element, but not used in this example).

Then another <cfset> tag is used, as follows:

```
<cfset fruit=ListAppend(fruit, "pineapple")>
```

This code uses the ListAppend() function to add an element to the list. You will recall that functions return copies of modified variables, not modified variables themselves. So the <cfset> tag assigns the value returned by ListAppend() to fruit, effectively overwriting the list with the new revised list.

Then the number of items, as well as the first and last items, is displayed again. This time 7 items are in the list, and the last item has changed to pineapple.

As you can see, lists are very easy to use and provide a simple mechanism for grouping related data.

NOTE

I mentioned earlier that a sentence is a list delimited by spaces. The default list delimiter is indeed a comma. Actually, though, any character can be used as a list delimiter, and every list function takes an optional delimiter attribute if necessary.

Arrays

Arrays, like lists, store multiple values in a single variable. But unlike lists, arrays can contain far more complex data (including lists and even other arrays).

Unlike lists, arrays support multiple dimensions. A single-dimensional array is actually quite similar to a list: It's a linear collection. A two-dimensional array is more like a grid (imagine a spreadsheet), and data is stored in rows and columns. ColdFusion also supports three-dimensional arrays, which can be envisioned as cubes of data.

If this all sounds somewhat complex, well, it is. Arrays are not as easy to use as lists, but they are far more powerful (and far quicker). Here is a simple block of code that creates an array and displays part of it; the output is shown in Figure 8.12. To try it out, type the code in Listing 8.8 and save it as array1.cfm.

Listing 8.8   `array1.cfm`

```
<html>
<head>
 <title>Array Example 1</title>
</head>

<body>

<cfset names=ArrayNew(2)>
<cfset names[1][1]="Ben">
<cfset names[1][2]="Forta">
<cfset names[2][1]="Ray">
<cfset names[2][2]="Camden">
<cfset names[3][1]="Leon">
<cfset names[3][2]="Chalnick">

<cfoutput>
The first name in the array is #names[1][1]# #names[1][2]#
</cfoutput>

</body>
</html>
```

Figure 8.12

Arrays treat data as if they were in a one-, two-, or three-dimensional grid.

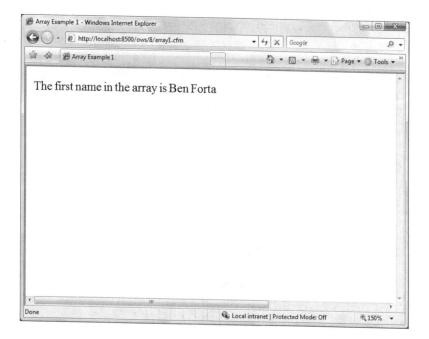

Arrays are created using the `ArrayNew()` function. `ArrayNew()` requires that the desired dimension be passed as a parameter, so the following code creates a two-dimensional array named `names`:

```
<cfset names=ArrayNew(2)>
```

Array elements are set using `<cfset>`, just like any other variables. But unlike other variables, when array elements are set the element number must be specified using an index (a relative position starting at 1). So, in a one-dimensional array, `names[1]` would refer to the first element and `names[6]` would refer to the sixth. In two-dimensional arrays, both dimensions must be specified, as seen in these next four lines (taken from the previous code listing):

```
<cfset names[1][1]="Ben">
<cfset names[1][2]="Forta">
<cfset names[2][1]="Ray">
<cfset names[2][2]="Camden">
```

`names[1][1]` refers to the first element in the first dimension—think of it as the first column of the first row in a grid. `names[1][2]` refers to the second column in that first row, and so on.

When accessed, even for display, the indexes must be used. Therefore, the following line of code

```
The first name in the array #names[1][1]# #names[1][2]#
```

generates this output:

```
The first name in the array Ben Forta
```

For a better view into an array, you can use a tag named `<cfdump>`. Listing 8.9 contains the code for array2.cfm (the same as `array1.cfm`, but with different output code). The output is shown in Figure 8.13.

Figure 8.13

`<cfdump>` is a great way to inspect array contents.

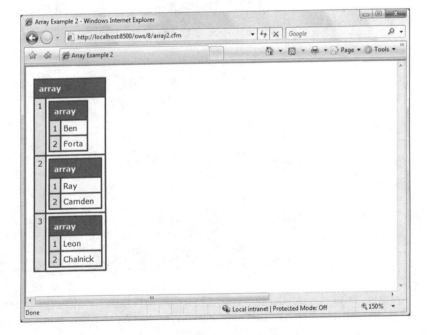

Listing 8.9   array2.cfm

```
<html>
<head>
 <title>Array Example 2</title>
</head>

<body>

<cfset names=ArrayNew(2)>
<cfset names[1][1]="Ben">
<cfset names[1][2]="Forta">
<cfset names[2][1]="Ray">
<cfset names[2][2]="Camden">
<cfset names[3][1]="Leon">
<cfset names[3][2]="Chalnick">

<cfdump var="#names#">
</body>
</html>
```

We'll take a look at `<cfdump>` again in a moment. But for now, as you can see, although they're not as easy to use as lists, arrays are a very flexible and powerful language feature.

As you have seen, arrays are first created using `ArrayNew()`, and then elements are added as needed. Thus far, elements were added to specific array locations (`[2][1]`, for example). Array elements can also be appended using `ArrayAppend()`, as seen here:

```
<cfset names=ArrayNew(1)>
<cfset ArrayAppend(names, "Ben")>
<cfset ArrayAppend(names, "Ray")>
<cfset ArrayAppend(names, "Leon")>
```

This example creates a single-dimensional array and then appends three elements to it.

When working with single-dimensional arrays, ColdFusion provides a shortcut syntax that can create and populate an array in a single step. The following snippet is functionally identical to the previous example:

```
<cfset names=["Ben","Ray","Leon"]>
```

As you can see, single-dimensional arrays can be created and populated without the use of any array functions at all.

TIP

ColdFusion can process arrays far more quickly than it can lists. For very short sets of data, you'll probably not see much of a difference between arrays and lists, but as the amount of data in sets grows, the performance benefit of arrays of lists will become more apparent.

Structures

Structures are the most powerful and flexible data type within ColdFusion, so powerful in fact that many internal variables are actually structures.

Simply put, structures provide a way to store data within data. Unlike arrays, structures have no special dimensions and are not like grids. Rather, they can be thought of as top-level folders that can store data, or other folders, which in turn can store data, or other folders, and so on. Structures can contain lists, arrays, and even other structures.

To give you a sneak peek at what structures look like, here is some code. Give it a try yourself; save the file as `structure.cfm` (see Listing 8.10), and you should see output as shown in Figure 8.14.

Listing 8.10 `structure.cfm`

```
<html>
<head>
 <title>Structure Example</title>
</head>

<body>

<cfset contact=StructNew()>
<cfset contact.FirstName="Ben">
<cfset contact.LastName="Forta">
<cfset contact.EMail="ben@forta.com">

<cfoutput>
e-mail:
<a href="mailto:#contact.EMail#">#contact.FirstName# #contact.LastName#</a>
</cfoutput>

</body>
</html>
```

Figure 8.14

Structures are one of the most important data types in ColdFusion and are used internally extensively.

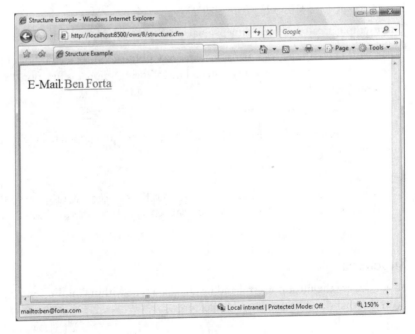

Structures are created using `StructNew()`, which—unlike `ArrayNew()`—takes no parameters. After a structure is created, variables can be set inside it. The following three lines of code all set variables with the `contact structure`:

```
<cfset contact.FirstName="Ben">
<cfset contact.LastName="Forta">
<cfset contact.EMail="ben@forta.com">
```

To access structure members, simply refer to them by name. `#contact.FirstName#` accesses the `FirstName` member of the `contact` structure. Therefore, the code

```
<a href="mailto:#contact.EMail#">#contact.FirstName# #contact.LastName#</a>
```

generates this output:

```
<a href="mailto:ben@forta.com">Ben Forta</a>
```

And that's just scratching the surface. Structures are incredibly powerful, and you'll use them extensively as you work through this book.

Like arrays, structures can be implicitly created and populated without the need to use `StructNew()`. The following snippet replaces the four `<cfset>` statements in the previous example:

```
<cfset contact={FirstName="Ben",
                LastName="Forta",
                EMail="ben@forta.com"}>
```

For simplicity's sake, I have described only the absolute basic form of structure use. ColdFusion features an entire set of structure manipulation functions that can be used to better take advantage of structures—you use some of them in the next chapter, "Programming with CFML."

"Dumping" Expressions

I showed you a tag named `<cfdump>` in Listing 8.9. This tag is never used in live applications, but it's an invaluable testing and debugging tool. `<cfdump>` lets you display any expression in a cleanly formatted table. You saw an example of dumping an array previously; now let's try another example. Type the following code into a new document (see Listing 8.11), save it as `cfdump1.cfm`, and then execute it in your browser. The output is shown in Figure 8.15.

Listing 8.11 `cfdump1.cfm`

```
<html>
<head>
 <title>&lt;cfdump&gt; Example 1</title>
</head>

<body>

<cfset contact=StructNew()>
<cfset contact.FirstName="Ben">
<cfset contact.LastName="Forta">
<cfset contact.EMail="ben@forta.com">

<cfdump var="#contact#">

</body>
</html>
```

Figure 8.15

<cfdump> is an invaluable diagnostics and debugging tool capable of displaying all sorts of data in a clean and easy-to-read format.

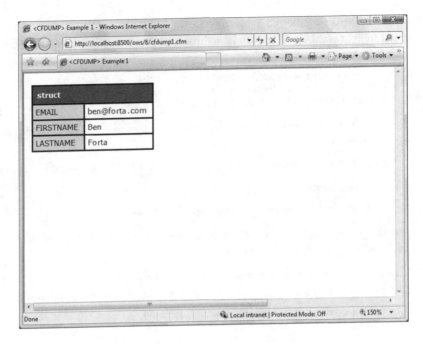

In this listing we've removed the <cfoutput> block. Instead, a <cfdump> tag is being used to dump (display) the contents of the contact structure. As you can see in Figure 8.15, <cfdump> creates a nicely formatted table containing the data contained within the structure. Our structure was pretty simple (three members, and no nested data types) but as the variables and data types you work with grow in complexity you'll find <cfdump> to be an invaluable utility tag.

Here is one final <cfdump> example, this time dumping the contents of two special variable scopes. SERVER is a structure (that contains two other structures) containing ColdFusion and operating system information. CGI is a structure that contains all sorts of data provided by the Web browser, Web server, and ColdFusion. Type the following code into a new document (see Listing 8.12), save it as cfdump2.cfm, and then execute it in your browser. The output is shown in Figure 8.16.

Listing 8.12 cfdump2.cfm

```
<html>
<head>
 <title>&lt;cfdump&gt; Example 2</title>
</head>

<body>

<h1>SERVER</h1>
<cfdump var="#SERVER#">
<h1>CGI</h1>
<cfdump var="#CGI#">

</body>
</html>
```

Figure 8.16

`<cfdump>` can display all ColdFusion data types, including nested data types.

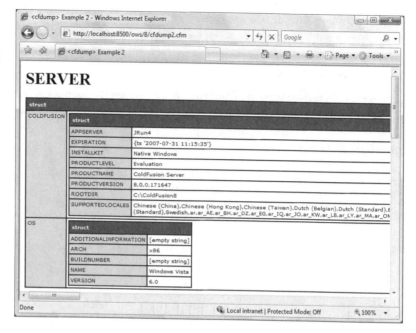

`<cfdump>` actually does more than just paint an HTML table. Try clicking on any of the boxes with colored backgrounds; you'll be able to collapse and expand them as needed. When working with very large complex expressions this feature is incredibly useful, and to make it work ColdFusion automatically generates DHTML code (with supporting JavaScript) all automatically. To appreciate just how much work this little tag does, View Source in your Web browser.

Commenting Your Code

The last introductory topic I want to mention is commenting your code. Many books leave this to the very end, but I believe it is so important that I am introducing the concept right here—before you start real coding.

The code you have worked with thus far has been short, simple, and pretty self-explanatory. But as you start building bigger and more complex applications, your code will become more involved and more complex, and comments become vital. Here is why you should comment your code:

- If you make code as self-descriptive as possible, when you revisit it at a later date you'll remember what you did, and why.

- This is even truer if others have to work on your code. The more detailed and accurate comments are, the easier (and safer) it will be to make changes or corrections when necessary.

- Commented code is much easier to debug than uncommented code.

- Commented code tends to be better organized.

And that's just the start of it.

Listing 8.13 is a revised version of hello6.cfm; all that has changed is the inclusion of comments. And as you can see from Figure 8.17, this has no impact on generated output whatsoever.

Listing 8.13 hello7.cfm

```
<!---
Name:       hello7.cfm
Author:     Ben Forta (ben@forta.com)
Description: Demonstrate use of comments
Created:    07/01/2007
--->
<html>
<head>
 <title>Hello 7</title>
</head>

<body>

<!--- Save name --->
<cfset firstName="ben">

<!--- Save converted versions of name --->
<cfset upperFirstname=UCase(firstName)>
<cfset lowerFirstname=LCase(firstName)>
<cfset reverseFirstname=Reverse(firstName)>
<!--- Save name length --->
<cfset lenFirstName=Len(firstName)>
<!--- Save repeated name --->
<cfset repeatFirstName=RepeatString(firstName, 3)>

<!--- Display output --->
<cfoutput>
Hello #FirstName#, and welcome to ColdFusion!<p>
Your name in uppercase: #upperFirstName#<br>
Your name in lowercase: #lowerFirstName#<br>
Your name in reverse: #reverseFirstName#<br>
Characters in your name: #lenFirstName#<br>
Your name 3 times: #repeatFirstName#<br>
</cfoutput>

</body>
</html>
```

Comments are typed between <!--- and ---> tags. Comments should never be nested and should never be mismatched (such as having a starting tag without an end tag, or vice versa).

Figure 8.17

ColdFusion comments in your code are never sent to the client browser.

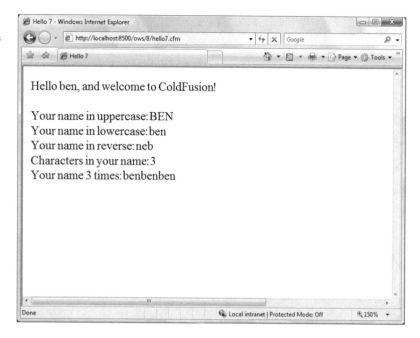

ColdFusion uses <!--- and ---> to delimit comments. HTML uses <!-- and --> (two hyphens instead of three). Within Cold-Fusion code, always use ColdFusion comments and not HTML comments. The latter will be sent to the client (they won't be displayed, but they will still be sent), whereas the former won't.

Be sure not to mix comment styles, using two hyphens on one end of the comment and three on the other. Doing so could cause your code to not be executed as expected.

Commenting code is a useful debugging technique. When you are testing code and need to eliminate specific lines, you can comment them out temporarily by wrapping them within <!--- and ---> tags.

Programming with CFML

Working with Conditional Processing

Chapter 8, "The Basics of CFML," introduced two ColdFusion tags (`<cfoutput>` and `<cfset>`), functions, and variables. This chapter takes CFML one big step further, adding conditional and programmatic processing, the stuff that starts to add real power to your code.

The code you wrote in the last chapter was linear—ColdFusion started at the top of the page and processed every line in order. And although that works for simple applications, more often than not you'll need to write code that does various things based on conditions, such as:

- Displaying different messages based on the time of day or day of the week

- Personalizing content based on user login

- Informing users of the status of searches or other operations

- Displaying (or hiding) options based on security level

All these require intelligence within your code to facilitate decision making. Conditional processing is the mechanism by which this is done, and ColdFusion supports two forms of conditional processing:

- If statements, created using `<cfif>` and related tags

- Switch statements, created using `<cfswitch>` and `<cfcase>`

Let's start by taking a look at these in detail.

If Statements

If statements are a fundamental part of most development languages. Though the syntax varies from one language to the next, the basic concepts and options are the same. If statements are used to create conditions that are evaluated, enabling you to perform actions based on the result.

The conditions passed to if statements always evaluate to TRUE or FALSE, and any condition that can be expressed as a TRUE / FALSE (or YES / NO) question is valid. Here are some examples of valid conditions:

- Is today Monday?

- Does variable FirstName exist?

- Were any rows retrieved from a database?

- Does variable one equal variable two?

- Is a specific word in a sentence?

More complex conditions (multiple conditions) are allowed, too:

- Is today Sunday or Saturday?

- Was a credit card number provided, and if yes, has it been validated?

- Does the currently logged-in user have a first name of Ben and a last name of Forta, or a first name of Ray and a last name of Camden?

The common denominator here is that all these conditions can be answered with TRUE or FALSE, so they are all valid conditions.

NOTE

In ColdFusion, the words TRUE and FALSE can be used when evaluating conditions. In addition, YES can be used in lieu of TRUE, and NO can be used in lieu of FALSE. It is also worth noting that all numbers are either TRUE or FALSE: 0 is FALSE, and any other number (positive or negative) is TRUE.

Basic If Statements

ColdFusion if statements are created using the <cfif> tag. <cfif> takes no attributes; instead, it takes a condition. For example, the following <cfif> statement checks to see whether a variable named FirstName contains the value Ben:

```
<cfif FirstName IS "Ben">
```

The keyword IS is an operator used to test for equality. Other operators are supported, too, as listed in Table 9.1.

As seen in Table 9.1, most CFML operators have shortcut equivalents that you can use. The IS operator used in the previous code example is actually a shortcut for EQUAL, and that condition is:

```
<cfif FirstName EQUAL "Ben">
```

To test whether FirstName is not Ben, you could use the following code:

```
<cfif FirstName IS NOT "Ben">
```

or

```
<cfif FirstName NEQ "Ben">
```

or

```
<cfif FirstName NOT EQUAL "Ben">
```

or even

```
<cfif NOT FirstName IS "Ben">
```

In this last snippet, the NOT operator is used to negate a condition.

Table 9.1 CFML Evaluation Operators

OPERATOR	SHORTCUT	DESCRIPTION
EQUAL	IS, EQ	Tests for equality
NOT EQUAL	IS NOT, NEQ	Tests for nonequality
GREATER THAN	GT	Tests for greater than
GREATER THAN OR EQUAL TO	GTE	Tests for greater than or equal to
LESS THAN	LT	Tests for less than
LESS THAN OR EQUAL TO	LTE	Tests for less than or equal to
CONTAINS		Tests whether a value is contained within a second value
DOES NOT CONTAIN		Tests whether a value is not contained within a second value

Ready to try <cfif> yourself? What follows is a simple application that checks to see whether today is the weekend (Listing 9.1). Save the file as if1.cfm, and execute it from within Dreamweaver or your Web browser (if the latter then the URL to use will be http://localhost:8500/ows/9/if1.cfm if the integrated Web server is being used). The output is shown in Figure 9.1 (if today is Sunday).

Listing 9.1 if1.cfm

```
<!---
Name:         if1.cfm
Author:       Ben Forta (ben@forta.com)
Description:  Demonstrate use of <cfif>
Created:      07/01/2007
--->

<html>
<head>
 <title>If 1</title>
</head>

<body>

<!--- Is it the weekend? --->
<cfif DayOfWeek(Now()) IS 1>
 <!--- Yes it is, great! --->
 It is the weekend, yeah!
</cfif>

</body>
</html>
```

Figure 9.1

<cfif> statements can be used to display output conditionally.

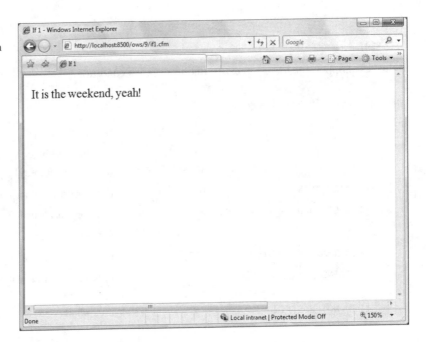

TIP
Don't forget to create the **9** directory under **ows**; all the code created in this chapter should go in that directory.

The code in Listing 9.1 should be self-explanatory. A comment header describes the code, and the standard HTML <head> and <body> tags are used to create the page. Then comes the <cfif> statement:

```
<cfif DayOfWeek(Now()) IS 1>
```

As you already have seen, Now() is a function that returns the current system date and time. DayOfWeek() is a function that returns the day of the week for a specified date (a variable, a literal, or another function). DayOfWeek(Now()) returns the current day of the week: 1 for Sunday, 2 for Monday, 3 for Tuesday, and so on. The condition DayOfWeek(Now()) IS 1 then simply checks to see whether it is Sunday. If it is Sunday, the condition evaluates to TRUE; if not, it evaluates to FALSE.

If the condition is TRUE, the text between the <cfif> and </cfif> tags is displayed. It's as simple as that.

Multiple-Condition If Statements

A couple of problems exist with the code in Listing 9.1, the most important of which is that weekends include both Sundays and Saturdays. Therefore, the code to check whether it is the weekend needs to check for both days.

Here is a revised version of the code (see Listing 9.2); save this file as if2.cfm, and then execute it.

TIP

So as not to have to retype all the code as you make changes, use Dreamweaver's File > Save As menu option to save the file with the new name, and then edit the newly saved file.

Listing 9.2 if2.cfm

```
<!---
Name:         if2.cfm
Author:       Ben Forta (ben@forta.com)
Description: Demonstrate use of multiple conditions
Created:      07/01/2007
--->

<html>
<head>
 <title>If 2</title>
</head>

<body>

<!--- Is it the weekend? --->
<cfif (DayOfWeek(Now()) IS 1) OR (DayOfWeek(Now()) IS 7)>
 <!--- Yes it is, great! --->
 It is the weekend, yeah!
</cfif>

</body>
</html>
```

The code is the same as Listing 9.1, except for the <cfif> statement itself:

```
<cfif (DayOfWeek(Now()) IS 1) OR (DayOfWeek(Now()) IS 7)>
```

This statement contains two conditions, one that checks whether the day of the week is 1 (Sunday), and one that checks whether it is 7 (Saturday). If it is Sunday or Saturday, the message is displayed correctly. Problem solved.

To tell ColdFusion to test for either condition, the OR operator is used. By using OR if either of the specified conditions is TRUE, the condition returns TRUE. FALSE is returned only if *neither* condition is TRUE. This is in contrast to the AND operator, which requires that *both* conditions be TRUE and returns FALSE if only one or no conditions are TRUE. Look at the following code snippet:

```
<cfif (FirstName IS "Ben") AND (LastName IS "Forta")>
```

For this condition to be TRUE, the FirstName must be Ben and the LastName must be Forta. Ben with any other LastName or Forta with any other FirstName fails the test.

AND and OR are logical operators (sometimes called *Boolean* operators). These two are the most frequently used logical operators, but others are supported, too, as listed in Table 9.2.

Table 9.2 CFML Logical Operators

OPERATOR	DESCRIPTION
AND	Returns TRUE only if both conditions are TRUE
OR	Returns TRUE if at least one condition is TRUE
XOR	Returns TRUE if either condition is TRUE, but not if both or neither are TRUE
EQV	Tests for equivalence and returns TRUE if both conditions are the same (either both TRUE or both FALSE, but not if one is TRUE and one is FALSE)
IMP	Tests for implication; returns FALSE only when the first condition is TRUE and the second is FALSE
NOT	Negates any other logical operator

TIP

You probably noticed that when multiple conditions (either **AND** or **OR**) were used, each condition was enclosed within parentheses. This is not required but is generally good practice. Not only does it make the code cleaner and easier to read, but it also prevents bugs from being introduced by expressions being evaluated in ways other than you expected. For example, if both **AND** and **OR** are used in a condition, **AND** is always evaluated before **OR**, which might or might not be what you want. Parentheses are evaluated before **AND**, so by using parentheses you can explicitly manage the order of evaluation.

If and Else

The code in Listing 9.2 is logically correct: If it is Sunday or Saturday, then it is indeed the weekend, and the weekend message is displayed. But what if it is not Sunday or Saturday? Right now, nothing is displayed at all; so let's fix that.

Listing 9.3 contains the revised code, capable of displaying a non-weekend message if necessary (see Figure 9.2). Save this code as if3.cfm, and then execute it.

Listing 9.3 if3.cfm

```
<!---
Name:        if3.cfm
Author:      Ben Forta (ben@forta.com)
Description: Demonstrate use of <cfif> and <cfelse>
Created:     07/01/2007
--->

<html>
<head>
 <title>If 3</title>
</head>

<body>

<!--- Is it the weekend? --->
<cfif (DayOfWeek(Now()) IS 1) OR (DayOfWeek(Now()) IS 7)>
 <!--- Yes it is, great! --->
 It is the weekend, yeah!
```

Listing 9.3 (CONTINUED)

```
<cfelse>
<!--- No it is not :-( --->
No, it's not the weekend yet, sorry!
</cfif>

</body>
</html>
```

Figure 9.2

`<cfelse>` enables the creation of code to be executed when a `<cfif>` test fails.

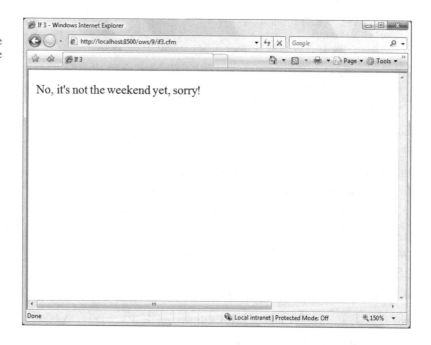

The only real difference between Listings 9.2 and 9.3 is the introduction of a new tag—`<cfelse>`. `<cfif>` is used to define code to be executed when a condition is TRUE, and `<cfelse>` defines code to be executed when a condition is FALSE. `<cfelse>` takes no attributes and can be used only between `<cfif>` and `</cfif>` tags. The new code will now display It is the weekend, yeah! if it is Sunday or Saturday and No, it's not the weekend yet, sorry! if not. Much better.

But before you move on, Listing 9.4 contains one more refinement—a cleaner `<cfif>` statement. Save Listing 9.4 as if4.cfm, and then execute it (it should do exactly what Listing 9.3 did).

Listing 9.4 if4.cfm

```
<!---
Name:        if4.cfm
Author:      Ben Forta (ben@forta.com)
Description: Demonstrate saving <cfif> results
Created:     07/01/2007
--->

<html>
<head>
```

Listing 9.4 (CONTINUED)

```
  <title>If 4</title>
  </head>

  <body>

  <!--- Is it the weekend? --->
  <cfset weekend=(DayOfWeek(Now()) IS 1) OR (DayOfWeek(Now()) IS 7)>

  <!--- Let the user know --->
  <cfif weekend>
   <!--- Yes it is, great! --->
   It is the weekend, yeah!
  <cfelse>
   <!--- No it is not :-( --->
   No, it's not the weekend yet, sorry!
  </cfif>

  </body>
  </html>
```

The more complex conditions become, the harder they are to read, so many developers prefer to save the results of executed conditions to variables for later use. Look at this line of code (from Listing 9.4):

```
  <cfset weekend=(DayOfWeek(Now()) IS 1) OR (DayOfWeek(Now()) IS 7)>
```

Here, <cfset> is used to create a variable named weekend. The value stored in this variable is whatever the condition returns. So, if it is a weekend (Sunday or Saturday), weekend will be TRUE, and if it is not a weekend then weekend will be FALSE.

➜ See Chapter 8 for detailed coverage of the <cfset> tag.

The <cfset> statement could be broken down further if required, like this:

```
  <!--- Get day of week --->
  <cfset dow=DayOfWeek(Now())>
  <!--- Is it the weekend? --->
  <cfset weekend=(dow IS 1) OR (dow IS 7)>
```

The end result is the same, but this code is more readable.

After weekend is set, it can be used in the <cfif> statement:

```
  <cfif weekend>
```

If weekend is TRUE, the first block of text is displayed; otherwise, the <cfelse> text is displayed.

But what is weekend being compared to? In every condition thus far, you have used an operator (such as IS) to test a condition. Here, however, no operator is used. So what is weekend being tested against?

Actually, weekend is indeed being tested; it is being compared to TRUE. Within a <cfif> the comparison is optional, and if it's omitted, a comparison to TRUE is assumed. So, <cfif weekend> is functionally the same as

```
  <cfif weekend IS TRUE>
```

The weekend variable contains either TRUE or FALSE. If it's TRUE, the condition is effectively

```
<cfif TRUE IS TRUE>
```

which obviously evaluates to TRUE. But if weekend is FALSE, the condition is

```
<cfif FALSE IS TRUE>
```

which obviously is FALSE.

I said that weekend contained either TRUE or FALSE, but you should feel free to test that for yourself. If you add the following line to your code, you'll be able to display the contents of weekend:

```
<cfoutput>#weekend#</cfoutput>
```

As you can see, you have a lot of flexibility when it comes to writing `<cfif>` statements.

Multiple If Statements

There's one more feature of `<cfif>` that you need to look at—support for multiple independent conditions (as opposed to one condition made up of multiple conditions).

The best way to explain this is with an example. In the previous listings, you displayed a message on weekends. But what if you wanted to display different messages on Sunday and Saturday? You could create multiple `<cfif> </cfif>` blocks, but there is a better way.

Listing 9.5 contains yet another version of the code; this time the file name should be if5.cfm.

Listing 9.5 `if5.cfm`

```
<!---
Name:          if5.cfm
Author:        Ben Forta (ben@forta.com)
Description:   Demonstrate <cfelseif> use
Created:       07/01/2007
--->

<html>
<head>
 <title>If 5</title>
</head>

<body>

<!--- Get day of week --->
<cfset dow=DayOfWeek(Now())>

<!--- Let the user know --->
<cfif dow IS 1>
 <!--- It's Sunday --->
 It is the weekend! But make the most of it, tomorrow it's back to work.
<cfelseif dow IS 7>
 <!--- It's Saturday --->
 It is the weekend! And even better, tomorrow is the weekend too!
<cfelse>
 <!--- No it is not :-( --->
```

Listing 9.5 (CONTINUED)

```
    No, it's not the weekend yet, sorry!
</cfif>

</body>
</html>
```

Let's take a look at the previous code. A `<cfset>` is used to create a variable named dow, which contains the day of the week (the value returned by `DayOfWeek(Now())`, a number from 1 to 7).

The `<cfif>` statement checks to see whether dow is 1, and if TRUE, displays the Sunday message (see Figure 9.3). Then a `<cfelseif>` is used to provide an alternative `<cfif>` statement:

```
    <cfelseif dow IS 7>
```

Figure 9.3

If dow is 1, the Sunday message is displayed.

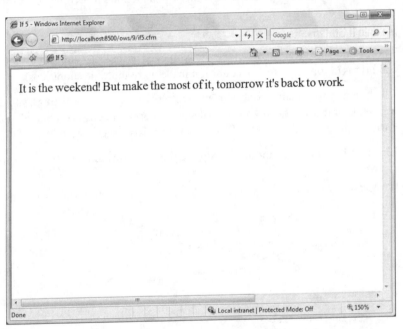

The `<cfelseif>` checks to see whether dow is 7, and if TRUE, displays the Saturday message (see Figure 9.4). Finally, `<cfelse>` is used to display text if neither the `<cfif>` nor the `<cfelseif>` is TRUE. `<cfelseif>` is essentially a combined `<cfelse>` and `<cfif>`; hence its name.

Saving conditions' results to variables, as you did here with the dow variable and previously with weekend, instead of repeating code makes your code more readable. But it also has another benefit. If you use the exact same expressions (getting the day of the week, say) in multiple places, you run the risk that one day you'll update the code and not make all the changes in all the required locations. If just a single expression must be changed, that potential problem is avoided.

No limit exists to the number of `<cfelseif>` statements you use within a `<cfif>` tag, but you can never use more than one `<cfif>` or `<cfelse>`.

Figure 9.4

If dow is 7, the
Saturday message is
displayed.

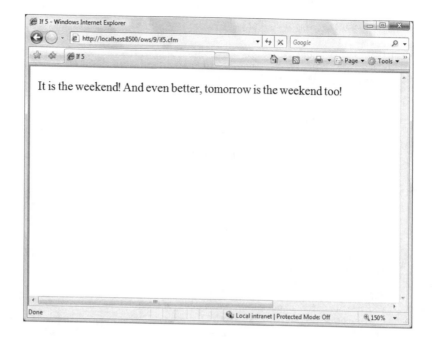

It is the weekend! And even better, tomorrow is the weekend too!

NOTE

Use of `<cfelseif>` and `<cfelse>` is optional. However, if `<cfelse>` is used, it must always be the last tag before the `</cfif>`.

Putting It All Together

`<cfif>` is one of the most frequently used tags in CFML. So before we move on to the next subject, let's walk through one more example—a slightly more complex one.

Guess the Number is a simple game: *I'm thinking of a number between 1 and 10; guess what number I am thinking of.* ColdFusion selects a random number, you guess a number, and ColdFusion will tell you whether you guessed the correct one.

Listing 9.6 contains the code for guess1.cfm. Save it in the 9 directory, but don't execute it from within Dreamweaver. Instead, use this URL to execute it:

```
http://localhost:8500/ows/9/guess1.cfm?guess=n
```

Replace n with a number from 1 to 10. For example, if you guess 5, use this URL:

```
http://localhost:8500/ows/9/guess1.cfm?guess=5
```

You must pass the guess URL parameter, or an error will be thrown. When you pass that parameter you'll see an output similar to the ones shown in Figures 9.5 and 9.6. (Actually, if you reload the page often enough, you'll see both figures.)

Listing 9.6 guess1.cfm

```
<!---
Name:        guess1.cfm
Author:      Ben Forta (ben@forta.com)
Description: if statement demonstration
Created:     07/01/2007
--->

<html>
<head>
 <title>guess the number - 1</title>
</head>

<body>

<!--- Pick a random number --->
<cfset RandomNumber=RandRange(1, 10)>

<!--- Check if matched --->
<cfif RandomNumber IS URL.guess>
 <!--- It matched --->
 <cfoutput>
 You got it, I picked #RandomNumber#! Good job!
 </cfoutput>
<cfelse>
 <!--- No match --->
 <cfoutput>
 Sorry, I picked #RandomNumber#! Try again!
 </cfoutput>
</cfif>

</body>
</html>
```

Figure 9.5

URL.guess matched the number ColdFusion picked.

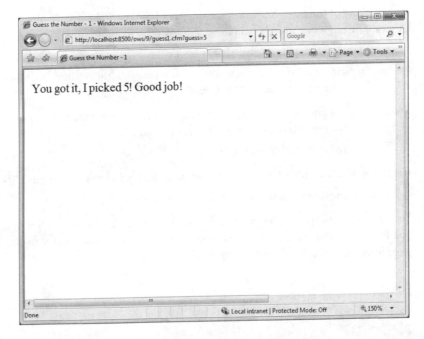

Figure 9.6

URL.guess did not match the number ColdFusion picked.

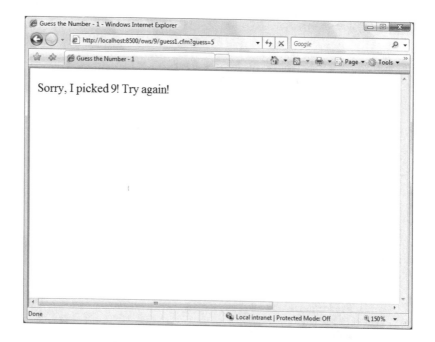

The first thing the code does is pick a random number. To do this, the RandRange() function is used. RandRange() takes two parameters (the range) and returns a random number within that range. The following line of code thus returns a random number from 1 to 10 (inclusive) and saves it in a variable named RandomNumber:

```
<cfset RandomNumber=RandRange(1, 10)>
```

Next, the randomly generated number is compared to the guessed number (which was passed as a URL parameter) using the following <cfif> statement:

```
<cfif RandomNumber IS URL.guess>
```

URL.guess is the variable containing the guess value provided in the URL. If the two match, the first message is displayed; if they don't, the second message is displayed.

➜ URL variables and their use are covered in detail in Chapter 10, "Creating Data-Driven Pages." For now, it's sufficient to know that variables passed as parameters to a URL are accessible via the URL scope.

But what if no guess parameter was specified? You will recall from Chapter 8 that referring to a variable that doesn't exist generates an error. Therefore, you should modify the code to check that URL.guess exists before using it. Listing 9.7 contains the modified version of the code; save this file as guess2.cfm.

NOTE

This is why I said not to try guess1.cfm from within Dreamweaver. If you had, the code would have been executed without allowing you to pass the necessary URL parameter, and an error would have been generated.

Listing 9.7 guess2.cfm

```
<!---
Name:         guess2.cfm
Author:       Ben Forta (ben@forta.com)
Description:  if statement demonstration
Created:      07/01/2007
--->

<html>
<head>
 <title>Guess the Number - 2</title>
</head>

<body>

<!--- Pick a random number --->
<cfset RandomNumber=RandRange(1, 10)>

<!--- Check if number was passed --->
<cfif IsDefined("URL.guess")>

 <!--- Yes it was, did it match? --->
 <cfif RandomNumber IS URL.guess>
 <!--- It matched --->
 <cfoutput>
 You got it, I picked #RandomNumber#! Good job!
 </cfoutput>
 <cfelse>
 <!--- No match --->
 <cfoutput>
 Sorry, I picked #RandomNumber#! Try again!
 </cfoutput>
 </cfif>

<cfelse>

 <!--- No guess specified, give instructions --->
 You did not guess a number.<BR>
 To guess a number, reload this page adding
 <B>?guess=n</B> (where n is the guess, for
 example, ?guess=5). Number should be between
 1 and 10.

</cfif>

</body>
</html>
```

Listing 9.7 introduces a new concept in `<cfif>` statements—nested `<cfif>` tags (one set of `<cfif>` tags within another). Let's take a look at the code. The first `<cfif>` statement is

```
<cfif IsDefined("URL.guess")>
```

IsDefined() is a CFML function that checks whether a variable exists. IsDefined("URL.guess") returns TRUE if guess was passed on the URL and FALSE if not. Using this function, you can process the guess only if it actually exists. So the entire code block (complete with `<cfif>` and `<cfelse>`

tags) is within the TRUE block of the outer `<cfif>`, and the original `<cfif>` block is now nested—it's a `<cfif>` within a `<cfif>`.

This also enables you to add another `<cfelse>` block, on the outer `<cfif>`. Remember, the outer `<cfif>` checks whether URL.guess exists, so `<cfelse>` can be used to display a message if it doesn't. Therefore, not only will the code no longer generate an error if guess was not specified, it will also provide help and instruct the user appropriately (see Figure 9.7).

Figure 9.7

By checking for the existence of expected variables, your applications can provide assistance and instructions if necessary.

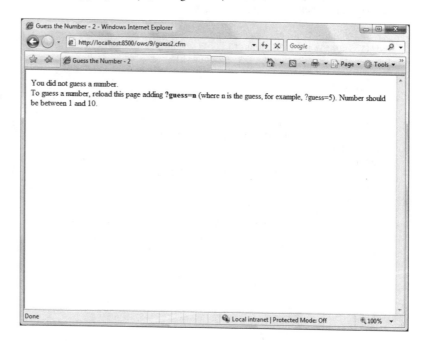

NOTE

The code in Listing 9.7 clearly demonstrates the value of indenting your code. The code within each `<cfif>` block is indented, and the deeper the nesting, the further the indentation. This type of formatting is extremely popular among professional developers because it makes finding matching (or mismatched) code blocks much easier.

As a rule, nesting should be avoided unless absolutely necessary. And nesting really isn't necessary in this game. Listing 9.8 takes the game code one step further, this time using `<cfelseif>` and multiple clause conditions to create tighter (and better performing) code. Save Listing 9.8 as guess3.cfm.

Listing 9.8 guess3.cfm

```
<!---
Name:        guess3.cfm
Author:      Ben Forta (ben@forta.com)
Description: if statement demonstration
Created:     07/01/2007
--->

<html>
```

Listing 9.8 (CONTINUED)

```
<head>
 <title>Guess the Number - 3</title>
</head>

<body>

<!--- Pick a random number --->
<cfset RandomNumber=RandRange(1, 10)>

<!--- Check if number was passed --->
<cfif IsDefined("URL.guess")
      AND (RandomNumber IS URL.guess)>
 <!--- It matched --->
 <cfoutput>
 You got it, I picked #RandomNumber#! Good job!
 </cfoutput>
<cfelseif IsDefined("URL.guess")
          AND (RandomNumber IS NOT URL.guess)>
 <!--- Did not match --->
 <cfoutput>
 Sorry, I picked #RandomNumber#! Try again!
 </cfoutput>
<cfelse>
 <!--- No guess specified, give instructions --->
 You did not guess a number.<BR>
 To guess a number, reload this page adding
 <B>?guess=n</B> (where n is the guess, for
 example, ?guess=5). Number should be between
 1 and 10.
</cfif>

</body>
</html>
```

Again, the code starts with the random number generation. Then this `<cfif>` statement is used:

```
<cfif IsDefined("URL.guess")
      AND (RandomNumber IS URL.guess)>
```

As explained earlier, AND requires that both conditions be TRUE. Therefore, the first message is displayed only if URL.guess exists and if the numbers match. The second condition is in a `<cfelseif>` statement:

```
<cfelseif IsDefined("URL.guess")
          AND (RandomNumber IS NOT URL.guess)>
```

Here too, IsDefined() is used to check that URL.guess exists. The second condition is TRUE only when the numbers don't match, in which case the second message is displayed.

NOTE

Notice that the `<cfif>` and `<cfelseif>` statements in Listing 9.8 are split over two lines. ColdFusion ignores white space (including line breaks), so code can be spread over as many lines as needed, and shorter lines of code (as used here) can be easier to read.

The `<cfelse>` here is evaluated only if `<cfif>` and `<cfelseif>` are both not evaluated, in which case it would be clear that `URL.guess` was not defined.

The same result occurs, but this time without nesting.

CAUTION

As a rule, don't nest unless you really have to. Although nesting is legal within your code, nested code tends to be easier to make mistakes in, harder to debug, and slower to execute.

Take a look at this line of code again:

```
<cfif IsDefined("URL.guess")
        AND (RandomNumber IS URL.guess)>
```

You might be wondering why an error would not be generated if `URL.guess` did not exist. After all, if the `IsDefined()` returns `FALSE`, shouldn't the next condition cause an error because `URL.guess` is being referred to?

The answer is no, because ColdFusion supports *short-circuit evaluation*. This means that conditions that don't affect a result are never evaluated. In an `AND` condition, if the first condition returns `FALSE`, then the result will always be `FALSE`, regardless of whether the second condition returns `TRUE` or `FALSE`. Similarly, in an `OR` condition, if the first condition is `TRUE`, the result will always be `TRUE`, regardless of whether the second condition is `TRUE` or `FALSE`. With short-circuit evaluation, conditions that don't affect the final result aren't executed, to save processing time. So in the previous example, if `IsDefined("URL.guess")` returns `FALSE`, `RandomNumber IS URL.guess` is never even evaluated.

Let's finish this game application with one last revision. Listing 9.9 should be saved as file `guess4.cfm`.

Listing 9.9 `guess4.cfm`

```
<!---
Name:        guess4.cfm
Author:      Ben Forta (ben@forta.com)
Description: if statement demonstration
Created:     07/01/2007
--->

<html>
<head>
 <title>Guess the Number - 4</title>
</head>

<body>

<!--- Set range --->
<cfset GuessLow=1>
<cfset GuessHigh=10>

<!--- Pick a random number --->
<cfset RandomNumber=RandRange(GuessLow, GuessHigh)>
```

Listing 9.8 (CONTINUED)

```
<!--- Was a guess specified? --->
<cfset HaveGuess=IsDefined("URL.guess")>

<!--- If specified, did it match? --->
<cfset Match=(HaveGuess)
        AND (RandomNumber IS URL.guess)>

<!--- Feedback --->
<cfoutput>
<cfif Match>
 <!--- It matched --->
 You got it, I picked #RandomNumber#! Good job!
<cfelseif HaveGuess>
 <!--- Did not match --->
 Sorry, I picked #RandomNumber#! Try again!
<cfelse>
 <!--- No guess specified, give instructions --->
 You did not guess a number.<BR>
 To guess a number, reload this page adding
 <B>?guess=n</B> (where n is the guess, for
 example, ?guess=5). Number should be between
 #GuessLow# and #GuessHigh#.
</cfif>
</cfoutput>

</body>
</html>
```

Quite a few changes were made in Listing 9.9. First, the range high and low values are now variables, defined as follows:

```
<!--- Set range --->
<cfset GuessLow=1>
<cfset GuessHigh=10>
```

By saving these to variables, changing the range (perhaps to allow numbers 1–20) will be easier. These variables are passed to the RandRange() function and are used in the final output (when instructions are given if no guess was specified) so that the allowed range is included in the instructions.

Next, the simple assignment `<cfset HaveGuess=IsDefined("URL.guess")>` sets variable HaveGuess to either TRUE (if guess was specified) or FALSE. The next assignment sets a variable named Match to TRUE if the numbers match (and guess was specified) or to FALSE. In other words, two simple `<cfset>` statements contain all the necessary intelligence and decision making, and because the results are saved to variables, using this information is very easy indeed.

This makes the display code much cleaner. `<cfif Match>` displays the first message if the correct guess was provided. `<cfelseif HaveGuess>` is executed only if the `<cfif>` failed, which must mean the guess was wrong. In addition, the `<cfelse>` displays the instructions (with the correct range included automatically).

It doesn't get much cleaner than that.

NOTE

Listing 9.9 demonstrates a coding practice whereby logic (or intelligence) and presentation are separated. This is a practice that should be adopted whenever possible, as the resulting code will be both cleaner and more reusable.

Switch Statements

All the conditional processing used thus far has involved `<cfif>` statements. But as I stated at the beginning of this chapter, ColdFusion also supports another form of conditional processing: *switch statements*.

The best way to understand switch statements is to see them used. Listing 9.10 should be saved as file `switch.cfm`.

When you have executed Listing 9.10, you'll notice that it does exactly what Listing 9.5 (file `if5.cfm`) does. The code here is very different, however.

Listing 9.10 `switch.cfm`

```
<!---
Name:         switch.cfm
Author:       Ben Forta (ben@forta.com)
Description:  Demonstrate use of <cfswitch> and <cfcase>
Created:      07/01/2007
--->

<html>
<head>
<title>Switch</title>
</head>

<body>

<!--- Get day of week --->
<cfset dow=DayOfWeek(Now())>

<!--- Let the user know --->
<cfswitch expression="#dow#">

 <!--- Is it Sunday? --->
 <cfcase value="1">
 It is the weekend! But make the most of it, tomorrow it's back to work.
 </cfcase>

 <!--- Is it Saturday? --->
 <cfcase value="7">
 It is the weekend! And even better, tomorrow is the weekend too!
 </cfcase>

 <!--- If code reaches here it's not the weekend --->
 <cfdefaultcase>
 No, it's not the weekend yet, sorry!
 </cfdefaultcase>
</cfswitch>

</body>
</html>
```

First the day of the week is saved to variable dow (as it was earlier), but that variable is then passed to a <cfswitch> statement:

```
<cfswitch expression="#dow#">
```

<cfswitch> takes an expression to evaluate; here, the value in dow is used. The expression is a string, so number signs are needed around dow. Otherwise, the text dow will be evaluated instead of the value of that variable.

<cfswitch> statements include <cfcase> statements, which each match a specific value that expression could return. The first <cfcase> is executed if expression is 1 (Sunday) because 1 is specified as the value in <cfcase value="1">. Similarly, the second <cfcase> is executed if expression is 7 (Saturday). Whichever <cfcase> matches the expression is the one that is processed, and in this example, the text between the <cfcase> and </cfcase> tags is displayed.

If no <cfcase> matches the expression, the optional <cfdefaultcase> block is executed. <cfdefaultcase> is similar to <cfelse> in a <cfif> statement.

As I said, the end result is exactly the same as in the example using <cfif>. So, why would you use <cfswitch> over <cfif>? For two reasons:

- <cfswitch> usually executes more quickly than <cfif>.

- <cfswitch> code tends to be neater and more manageable.

You can't always use <cfswitch>, however. Unlike <cfif>, <cfswitch> can be used only if all conditions are checking against the same expression. In other words, when the conditions are all the same, and only the values being compared against differ. If you need to check a set of entirely different conditions, <cfswitch> would not be an option, which is why you couldn't use it in the game example.

TIP

Although the example here uses <cfswitch> to display text, that is not all this tag can do. In fact, just about any code you can imagine can be placed between <cfcase> and </cfcase>. <cfcase> tags are evaluated in order, so it makes sense to place the values that you expect to match more often before those that will match much less often. Doing so can improve application performance slightly because ColdFusion won't have to evaluate values unnecessarily. This is also true of sets of <cfif> and <cfelseif> statements: Conditions that are expected to match more frequently should be moved higher up the list.

Using Looping

Loops are another fundamental language element supported by most development platforms. Loops do just that—they loop. Loops provide a mechanism with which to repeat tasks, and ColdFusion supports several types of loops, all via the <cfloop> tag:

- Index loops, used to repeat a set number of times

- Conditional loops, used to repeat until a specified condition becomes FALSE

- Query loops, used to iterate through database query results

- List loops, used to iterate through a specified list

- Collection loops, used to loop through structures

- File loops, used to loop through the lines in a file

You won't use all these loop types here, but to acquaint you with <cfloop>, let's look at a few examples.

The Index Loop

One of the most frequently used loops is the index loop, used to loop a set number of times (from a specified value to another specified value). To learn about this loop, you'll generate a simple list (see Figure 9.8). Type the code in Listing 9.11, and save it in 9 as loop1.cfm.

Listing 9.11 loop1.cfm

```
<!---
Name:        loop1.cfm
Author:      Ben Forta (ben@forta.com)
Description: Demonstrate use of <cfloop from to>
Created:     07/01/2007
--->

<html>
<head>
 <title>Loop 1</title>
</head>

<body>

<!--- Start list --->
<ul>

<!--- loop from 1 to 10 --->
<cfloop from="1" to="10" index="i">
 <!--- Write item --->
 <cfoutput><li>Item #i#</li></cfoutput>
</cfloop>

<!--- end list --->
</ul>

</body>
</html>
```

Figure 9.8

Loops can build lists and other display elements automatically.

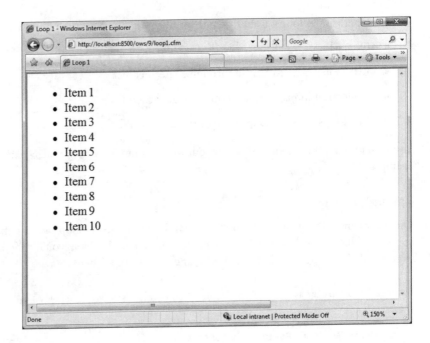

`<cfloop>` is used to create a block of code to be executed over and over. The code in Listing 9.11 creates a simple loop that displays a list of numbers in an HTML unordered list from 1 to 10. The HTML unordered list is started before the `<cfloop>` (you wouldn't want to start it in the loop, because you'd be starting a new list on each iteration) and ends after the `</cfloop>`. The loop itself is created using the following code:

```
<cfloop from="1" to="10" index="i">
```

In an index loop the `from` and `to` values must be specified and the code between `<cfloop>` and `</cfloop>` is repeated that many times. Here, `from="1"` and `to="10"`, so the loop repeats 10 times. Within the loop itself, a variable named in the index attribute contains the current increment, so `i` will be 1 the first time around, 2 the second time, and so on.

Within the loop, the value of `i` is displayed in a list item using the following code:

```
<cfoutput><li>Item #i#</li></cfoutput>
```

The first time around, when `i` is 1, the generated output will be

```
<li>Item 1</li>
```

and on the second loop it will be

```
<li>Item 2</li>
```

and so on.

TIP

Want to loop backwards? You can. Use the `step` attribute to specify how to count from the `from` value to the `to` value. `step="-1"` makes the count go backward, one number at a time.

The List Loop

List loops are designed to make working with ColdFusion lists simple and error-free. Whether it is lists created by form submissions, manual lists, lists derived from database queries (regardless of the origin), any list (with any delimiter) can be iterated over using `<cfloop>`.

➜ For an introduction to lists, see Chapter 8.

The following example uses a list created in Chapter 8 and loops through the list displaying one element at a time (see Figure 9.9). Save Listing 9.12 as `loop2.cfm`.

Listing 9.12 `loop2.cfm`

```
<!---
Name:        loop2.cfm
Author:      Ben Forta (ben@forta.com)
Description: Demonstrate use of <cfloop list>
Created:     07/01/2007
--->

<html>
<head>
 <title>Loop 2</title>
</head>

<body>

<!--- Create list --->
<cfset fruit="apple,banana,cherry,grape,mango,orange,pineapple">

<!--- Start list --->
<ul>

<!--- Loop through list --->
<cfloop list="#fruit#" index="i">
 <!--- Write item --->
 <cfoutput><li>#i#</li></cfoutput>
</cfloop>

<!--- end list --->
</ul>

</body>
</html>
```

Figure 9.9

Any lists, with any delimiter, can be iterated using `<cfloop>`.

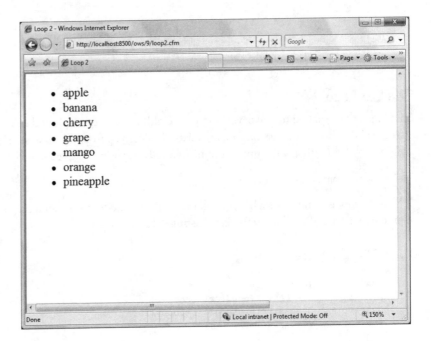

`<cfset>` is used to create the list—a comma-delimited list of fruit. `<cfloop>` takes the list to be processed in the `list` attribute, and because `list` accepts a string, number signs must be used around the variable name `fruit`.

`<cfloop>` repeats the loop once for every element in the list. In addition, within the loop, it makes the current element available in the variable specified in the `index` attribute—in this example, `i`. So, `i` is `apple` on the first iteration, `banana` on the second iteration, and so on.

NOTE

Lists also can be looped over using index loops. `from="1" to="#ListLen(fruit)#"` sets the `to` and `from` properly. Within the loop, `ListGetAt()` can be used to obtain the element.

Nested Loops

Like the `<cfif>` and `<cfswitch>` statements, loops can be nested. Nesting loops lets you create extremely powerful code, as long as you are very careful in constructing the loops. Listing 9.13 contains a practical example of nested loops, using three loops to display a table of Web browser–safe colors (seen in Figure 9.10). Save the code as `loop3.cfm`.

Listing 9.13 `loop3.cfm`

```
<!---
Name:         loop3.cfm
Author:       Ben Forta (ben@forta.com)
Description:  Demonstrate use of nested loops
Created:      07/01/2007
--->

<html>
```

```
<head>
 <title>Loop 3</title>
</head>

<body>

<!--- Hex value list --->
<cfset hex="00,33,66,99,CC,FF">

<!--- Create table --->
<table>

<!--- Start RR loop --->
<cfloop index="red" list="#hex#">
 <!--- Start GG loop --->
 <cfloop index="green" list="#hex#">
  <tr>
  <!--- Start BB loop --->
  <cfloop index="blue" list="#hex#">
   <!--- Build RGB value --->
   <cfset rgb=red&green&blue>
   <!--- And display it --->
   <cfoutput>
   <td bgcolor="###rgb#" width="100" align="center">#rgb#</td>
   </cfoutput>
  </cfloop>
  </tr>
 </cfloop>
</cfloop>

</table>

</body>
</html>
```

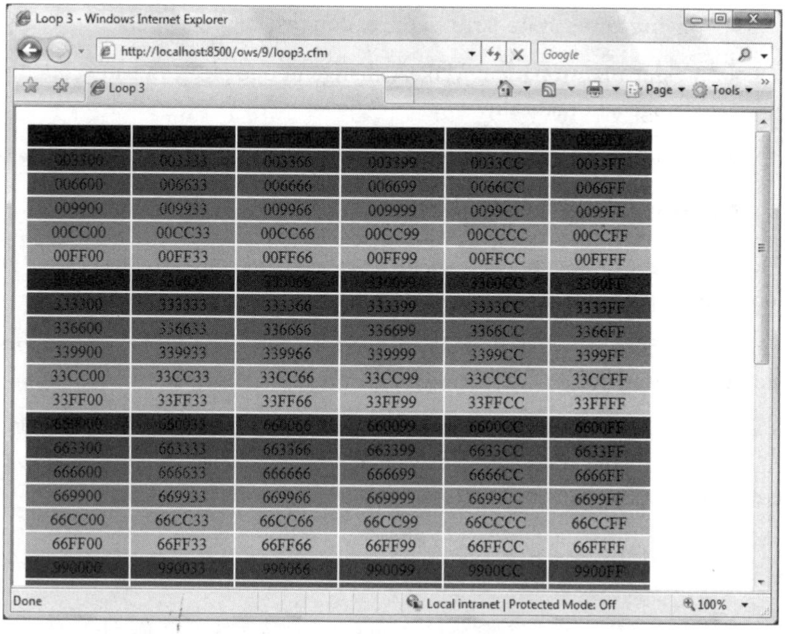

Figure 9.10

Displaying the Web browser–safe color palette requires the use of three nested loops.

Listing 9.13 warrants explanation. Colors in Web pages are expressed as RGB values (as in red, green, blue). The idea is that by adjusting the amount of red, green, and blue within a color, every possible color can be created. RGB values are specified using hexadecimal notation. Don't panic if you have forgotten base-n arithmetic—it's quite simple, actually. The amount of color is specified as a number, from `0` (none) to `255` (all). But instead of `0–255`, the hexadecimal equivalents (`00–FF`) are used. So, pure red is all red and no green or blue, or `FF0000`; yellow is all red and green and no blue, or `FFFF00`.

Still confused? Execute the code and you'll see a complete list of colors and the RGB value for each.

To list all the colors, the code must loop through all possible combinations—list all shades of red, and within each shade of red list each shade of green, and within each shade of green list each shade of blue. In the innermost loop, a variable named `rgb` is created as follows:

```
<cfset rgb=red&green&blue>
```

On the very first iteration red, green, and blue are all `00`, so `rgb` is `000000`. On the next iteration red and green are still `00`, but blue is `33`, so `rgb` is `000033`. By the time all the loops have been processed, a total of 216 colors have been generated (6 to the power of 3 for you mathematicians out there, because each color has six possible shades as defined in variable `hex`).

The exact mechanics of RGB value generation aren't important here. The key point is that loops can be nested quite easily and within each loop the counters and variables created at an outer loop are visible and usable.

Reusing Code

All developers write—or should write—code with reuse in mind. There are many reasons why this is a good idea:

- **Saving time.** If it's written once, don't write it again.
- **Easier maintenance.** Make a change in one place and any code that uses it gets that change automatically.
- **Easier debugging.** Fewer copies exist out there that will need to be fixed.
- **Group development.** Developers can share code more easily.

Most of the code reuse in this book involves ColdFusion code, but to demonstrate basic reuse, let's look at a simple example.

Orange Whip Studios is building a Web site, slowly. Figure 9.11 shows a Home page (still being worked on), and Figure 9.12 shows a Contact page (also being worked on).

The pages have a lot in common—both have the same header, the same logo, and the same copyright notice. If you were writing plain HTML, you'd have no choice but to copy all the code that creates those page components into every page you were creating.

Figure 9.11

The Home page contains basic logos and branding.

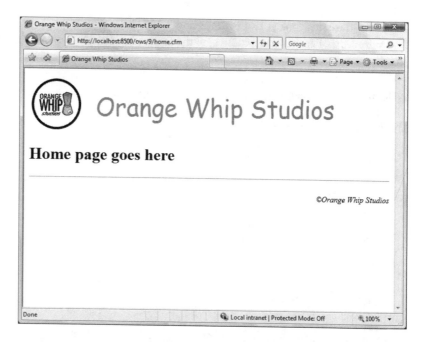

Figure 9.12

The Contact page contains the same elements as the Home page.

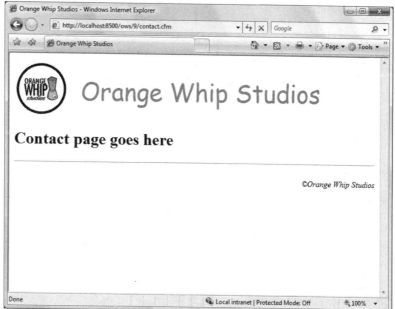

But you're using ColdFusion, and ColdFusion makes code reuse incredibly simple. The CFML `<cfinclude>` tag is used to include one page in another. `<cfinclude>` specifies the name of a file to include. At runtime, when ColdFusion encounters a `<cfinclude>` tag, it reads the contents of the specified file and processes it as if it were part of the same file.

To demonstrate this, look at Listings 9.14 and 9.15. The former is `ows_header.cfm`, and the latter is `ows_footer.cfm`. Between the two files, all the formatting for the Orange Whip Studios pages is present.

Listing 9.14 `ows_header.cfm`

```
<!---
Name:          ows_header.cfm
Author:        Ben Forta (ben@forta.com)
Description: <cfinclude> header
Created:       07/01/2007
--->

<html>
<head>
 <title>Orange Whip Studios</title>
</head>

<body>

<!--- header --->
<table width="100%">
<tr>
<td>
 <img src="../images/logo_c.gif"
      width="101"
      height="101"
      alt=""
      border="0">
</td>
<td>
 <font face="Comic Sans MS" size="7" color="#ff8000">Orange Whip Studios</font>
</td>
</tr>
</table>
<p>
```

Listing 9.15 `ows_footer.cfm`

```
<!---
Name:          ows_footer.cfm
Author:        Ben Forta (ben@forta.com)
Description: <cfinclude> footer
Created:       07/01/2007
--->

<p>
<hr>
<p align="right">
<i>&copy;Orange Whip Studios</i>
</p>

</body>
</html>
```

Now that the page header and footer have been created, `<cfinclude>` can be used to include them in the pages. Listing 9.16 is `home.cfm`, and Listing 9.17 is `contact.cfm`.

Listing 9.16   `home.cfm`

```
<!---
Name:        home.cfm
Author:      Ben Forta (ben@forta.com)
Description: Demonstrate use of <cfinclude>
Created:     07/01/2007
--->

<!--- Include page header --->
<cfinclude template="ows_header.cfm">

<h1>Home page goes here</h1>

<!--- Include page footer --->
<cfinclude template="ows_footer.cfm">
```

Listing 9.17   `contact.cfm`

```
<!---
Name:        contact.cfm
Author:      Ben Forta (ben@forta.com)
Description: Demonstrate use of <cfinclude>
Created:     07/01/2007s
--->

<!--- Include page header --->
<cfinclude template="ows_header.cfm">

<h1>Contact page goes here</h1>

<!--- Include page footer --->
<cfinclude template="ows_footer.cfm">
```

As you can see, very little code exists in Listings 9.16 and 9.17. Each listing contains two `<cfinclude>` statements: The first includes file `ows_header.cfm` (Listing 9.14), and the second includes file `ows_footer.cfm` (Listing 9.15). ColdFusion includes those two files and generates the output seen previously in Figures 9.11 and 9.12. The content that is unique to each page can be placed between the two `<cfinclude>` tags.

To see the real value of this approach, modify `ows_header.cfm` (change colors, text, or anything else) and then reload `home.cfm` and `contact.cfm` to see your changes automatically applied to both.

➜ We'll revisit this subject in detail in Chapter 11, "The Basics of Structured Development."

Revisiting Variables

Another important tag is `<cfparam>`. You won't use this tag here, but in preparation for the next chapters, I'll explain what this tag is and how it is used.

Earlier in this chapter, you used a function named IsDefined(), which is used to check whether a variable exists. You used IsDefined() to simply check for a variable's existence, but what if you wanted to create a variable with a default value if it did not exist? You could do something similar to this:

```
<cfif NOT IsDefined("FirstName")>
 <cfset FirstName="Ben">
</cfif>
```

Why would you want to do this? Well, as a rule, you should not include data validation code in the middle of your core code. This is bad practice for several reasons, the most important of which are that it helps create unreliable code, makes debugging difficult, and makes code reuse very difficult. So, best practices dictate that all variable validation occur before your core code. If required variables are missing, throw an error, redirect the user to another page, or do something else. If optional variables are missing, define them and assign default values. Either way, by the time you get to your core code, you should have no need for variable checking of any kind. It should all have been done already.

And thus the type of code I just showed you.

<cfparam> has several uses, but the most common use is simply a way to shortcut the previous code. Look at the following:

```
<cfparam name="FirstName" default="Ben">
```

When ColdFusion processes this line, it checks to see whether a variable named FirstName exists. If it does, the tag is ignored and processing continues. If, however, the variable doesn't exist, it will be created right then and there and assigned the value specified in default. So by using <cfparam>, you can ensure that after that tag has been processed, one way or another the variable referred to exists. And that makes writing clean code that much easier.

TIP

<CFPARAM> can be used to check for (and create) variables in specific scopes, including URL and FORM. This can greatly simplify the processing of passed values, as you will see in the coming chapters.

CHAPTER 10

Creating Data-Driven Pages

Accessing Databases

In the past few chapters, you created and executed ColdFusion templates. You worked with different variable types, conditional processing, code reuse, and more.

But this chapter is where it starts to get really interesting. Now it's time to learn how to connect to databases to create complete dynamic and data-driven pages.

NOTE

The examples in this chapter, and indeed all the chapters that follow, use the data in the **ows** data sources and database. These must be present before continuing. And I'll remind you just this once, all the files created in this chapter need to go in a directory named **10** under the application root (the **ows** directory under the Web root).

For your first application, you will create a page that lists all movies in the Films table.

Static Web Pages

Before you create your first data-driven ColdFusion template, let's look at how *not* to create this page.

Listing 10.1 contains the HTML code for the movie list Web page. The HTML code is relatively simple; it contains header information and then a list of movies, one per line, separated by line breaks (the HTML <br> tag).

Listing 10.1 `movies.htm`—HTML Code for Movie List

```
<html>
<head>
 <title>Orange Whip Studios - Movie List</title>
</head>

<body>
```

Listing 10.1 (CONTINUED)

```
<h1>Movie List</h1>

Being Unbearably Light<br>
Charlie's Devils<br>
Closet Encounters of the Odd Kind<br>
Folded Laundry, Concealed Ticket<br>
Forrest Trump<br>
Four Bar-Mitzvahs and a Circumcision<br>
Geriatric Park<br>
Gladly Ate Her<br>
Ground Hog Day<br>
Hannah and Her Blisters<br>
Harry's Pottery<br>
It's a Wonderful Wife<br>
Kramer vs. George<br>
Mission Improbable<br>
Nightmare on Overwhelmed Street<br>
Raiders of the Lost Aardvark<br>
Silence of the Clams<br>
Starlet Wars<br>
Strangers on a Stain<br>
The Funeral Planner<br>
The Sixth Nonsense<br>
Use Your ColdFusion II<br>
West End Story<br>

</body>
</html>
```

Figure 10.1 shows the output this code listing generates.

Figure 10.1

You can create the movie list page as a static HTML file.

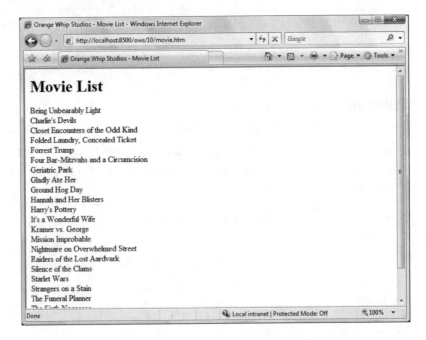

Dynamic Web Pages

Why is a static HTML file not the way to create the Web page? What would you have to do when a new movie is created, or when a movie is dropped? What would you do if a movie title or tag line changed?

You could directly modify the HTML code to reflect these changes, but you already have all this information in a database. Why would you want to have to enter it all again? You'd run the risk of making mistakes—information being misspelled, entries out of order, and possibly missing movies altogether. As the number of movies in the list grows, so will the potential for errors. In addition, visitors will be looking at inaccurate information during the period between updating the table and updating the Web page.

A much easier and more reliable solution is to have the Web page display the contents of your `Films` table. This way, any table changes are immediately available to all viewers. The Web page would be dynamically built based on the contents of the `Films` table.

To create your first data-driven ColdFusion template, enter the code as it appears in Listing 10.2 and save it in the `10` directory as `movies1.cfm`. (Don't worry if the ColdFusion code doesn't make much sense yet; I will explain it in detail in just a moment.)

Listing 10.2   `movies1.cfm`—The Basic Movie List

```
<!---
Name:        movies1.cfm
Author:      Ben Forta (ben@forta.com)
Description: First data-driven Web page
Created:     07/01/07
--->

<!--- Get movie list from database --->
<cfquery name="movies" datasource="ows">
SELECT MovieTitle
FROM Films
ORDER BY MovieTitle
</cfquery>

<!--- Create HTML page --->
<html>
<head>
 <title>Orange Whip Studios - Movie List</title>
</head>

<body>

<h1>Movie List</h1>

<!--- Display movie list --->
<cfoutput query="movies">
#MovieTitle#<br>
</cfoutput>

</body>
</html>
```

Now, execute this page in your browser as

```
http://localhost:8500/ows/10/movies1.cfm
```

TIP

As a reminder, the port number (**8500** in the above URL) is only needed if you are using the integrated HTTP server. If you are using ColdFusion with an external HTTP server then don't specify the port.

The results are shown in Figure 10.2.

Figure 10.2

Ideally, the movie list page should be generated dynamically, based on live data.

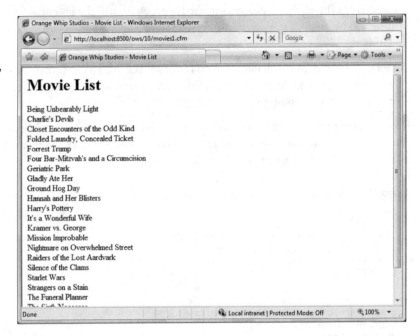

You could also browse the page right from within Dreamweaver as seen in Figure 10.3. To do this, switch to Design View (click the Show Design View button, or select Design from the View menu) and turn on Live Data View (click the Live Data View button, select Live Data from the View menu, or press Ctrl-Shift-R [Windows] or Command-Shift-R [Mac]).

Understanding Data-Driven Templates

Now compare Figure 10.1 to Figure 10.2. Can you see the difference between them? Look carefully.

Give up? The truth is that there is no difference at all (well, other than the file extension in the URL, that is). The screen shots are identical, and if you looked at the HTML source that generated Figure 10.2, you'd see that aside from a lot of extra white space, the dynamically generated code is exactly the same as the static code you entered in Listing 10.1 and nothing like the (much shorter) dynamic code you entered in Listing 10.2.

Figure 10.3

ColdFusion pages may
be browsed directly
within Dreamweaver
by switching to
Design View with Live
Data View enabled.

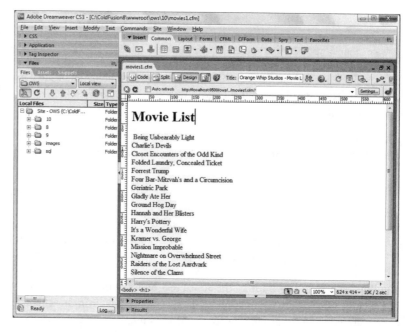

How did the code in Listing 10.2 become the HTML source code that generated Figure 10.1? Let's
review the code listing carefully.

The `<cfquery>` Tag

Listing 10.2 starts off with a comment block (as should all the code you write). Then comes a Cold-
Fusion tag called `<cfquery>`, which submits a SQL statement to a specified data source. The SQL
statement is usually a SQL SELECT statement, but it could also be an INSERT, an UPDATE, a DELETE, a
stored procedure call, or any other SQL statement.

➝ See Chapter 6, "Introducing SQL," for an overview of data sources, SQL, and SQL statements.

The `<cfquery>` tag has several attributes, or parameters, that are passed to it when used. The
`<cfquery>` in Listing 10.2 uses only two attributes:

- name—This attribute is used to name the query and any returned data.

- datasource—This attribute contains the name of the data source to be used.

The query name you specified is movies. This name will be used later when you process the results
generated by the query.

CAUTION

Don't use reserved words (words that have special meaning to ColdFusion) as your query name. For example, don't name a query
URL, as URL is a reserved prefix.

> Query names passed to `<cfquery>` need not be unique to each query within your page. If you do reuse query names, subsequent `<cfquery>` calls will overwrite the results retrieved by the earlier query.

You specified ows for the `datasource` attribute, which is the name of the data source created earlier. `datasource` is required; without it ColdFusion would not know which database to execute the SQL statement against.

The SQL statement to be executed is specified between the `<cfquery>` and `</cfquery>` tags. The following SQL statement was used, which retrieves all movie titles sorted alphabetically:

```
SELECT MovieTitle
FROM Films
ORDER BY MovieTitle
```

TIP
> The SQL statement in Listing 10.2 is broken up over many lines to make the code more readable. Although it's perfectly legal to write a long SQL statement that is wider than the width of your editor, these generally should be broken up over as many lines as needed.

ColdFusion pays no attention to the actual text between the `<cfquery>` and `</cfquery>` tags (unless you include CFML tags or functions, which we'll get to later in this chapter). Whatever is between those tags gets sent to the data source for processing.

When ColdFusion encounters a `<cfquery>` tag, it creates a query request and submits it to the specified data source. The results, if any, are stored in a temporary buffer and are identified by the name specified in the name attribute. All this happens before ColdFusion processes the next line in the template.

NOTE
> You'll recall that ColdFusion tags (including the `<cfquery>` tag) are never sent to the Web server for transmission to the browser. Unlike HTML tags, which are browser instructions, CFML tags are ColdFusion instructions.

NOTE
> ColdFusion doesn't validate the SQL code you specify. If syntax errors exist in the SQL code, ColdFusion won't let you know because that's not its job. The data source will return error messages if appropriate, and ColdFusion will display those to you. But it's the data source (and the database or database driver) that returns those error messages, not ColdFusion.

It's important to note that, at this point, no data has been displayed. `<cfquery>` retrieves data from a database table, but it doesn't display that data. Actually, it does nothing at all with the data—that's your job. All it does is execute a specified SQL statement when the `</cfquery>` tag is reached. `<cfquery>` has no impact on generated content at all, and retrieved data is never sent to the client (unless you send it).

The next lines in the template are standard HTML tags, headers, title, and headings. Because these aren't ColdFusion tags, they are sent to the Web server and then on to the client browser.

Using `<cfoutput>` to Display `<cfquery>` Data

Next, the query results are displayed, one row per line. To loop through the query results, the `<cfoutput>` tag is used.

`<cfoutput>` is the same ColdFusion output tag you used earlier (in Chapter 8, "The Basics of CFML"). This time, however, you use it to create a code block that is used to output the results of a `<cfquery>`. For ColdFusion to know which query results to output, the query name is passed to `<cfoutput>` in the query attribute. The name provided is the same that was assigned to the `<cfquery>` tag's name attribute. In this case, the name is movies.

CAUTION

The query name passed to `<cfquery>` must be a valid (existing) query; otherwise, ColdFusion will generate an error.

The code between `<cfoutput query="movies">` and `</cfoutput>` is the output code block. Cold-Fusion uses this code once for every row retrieved. Because 23 rows are currently in the Films table, the `<cfoutput>` code is looped through 23 times. And any HTML or CFML tags within that block are repeated as well—once for each row.

NOTE

So what is the minimum number of times a `<cfoutput>` code block will be processed? It depends on whether you are using the query attribute. Without a query, the code block is processed once. With a query block, it's processed once if a single row exists in the query, and not at all if the query returned no results.

TIP

You'll notice that I put the SQL query at the very top of the page instead of right where it was needed (in the middle of the output). This is the recommended way to write your code–queries should be organized at the top of the page, all together. This will help you write cleaner code and will also simplify any testing and debugging if (or rather, when) the need arises.

Using Table Columns

As explained in Chapter 8, ColdFusion uses # to delimit expressions and variables. ColdFusion expressions also can be columns retrieved by a `<cfquery>`. Whatever column name is specified is used; ColdFusion replaces the column name with the column's actual value. When ColdFusion processed the output block, it replaced #MovieTitle# with the contents of the MovieTitle column that was retrieved in the movies query. Each time the output code block is used, that row's MovieTitle value is inserted into the HTML code.

ColdFusion-generated content can be treated as any other content in an HTML document; any of the HTML formatting tags can be applied to them. In this example, the query results must be separated by a line break (the `<br>` tag).

Look at the following line of code:

```
#MovieTitle#<br>
```

That first row retrieved is movie *Being Unbearably Light*, so when processing the first row the above code will generate the following:

```
Being Unbearably Light<br>
```

Figure 10.2 shows the browser display this template creates. It's exactly the same result as Figure 10.1, but without any actual data in the code. The output of Listing 10.2 is dynamically generated—each time the page is refreshed, the database query is executed and the output is generated.

NOTE

Want to prove this for yourself? Open the database and make a change to any of the movie titles and then refresh the Web page—you'll see that the output will reflect the changes as soon as they are made.

If you are thinking that constantly rereading the database tables seems unnecessary and likely to affect performance, you're right. Chapter 31, "Improving Performance," in *ColdFusion 8 Web Application Construction Kit, Volume 2: Application Development*, teaches tips and techniques to optimize the performance of data-driven sites.

The Dynamic Advantage

To see the real power of data-driven pages, take a look at Listing 10.3. This is the same code as in Listing 10.2, but a column has been added to the SQL statement (retrieving PitchText as well now) and the output has been modified so that it displays both the MovieTitle and PitchText columns. Save this file as movies2.cfm (you can edit movies1.cfm and use the Save As option (in the File menu) to save it as movies2.cfm, if you find that easier). Now, execute this page in your browser as follows:

```
http://localhost:8500/ows/10/movies2.cfm
```

TIP

Again, drop the port if not using the internal HTTP server.

Figure 10.4 shows the output generated by the revised code.

Figure 10.4

Data-driven pages are easy to modify because only the template needs changing, not every single row.

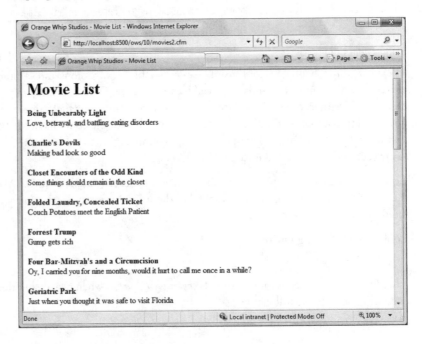

Listing 10.3 `movies2.cfm`—The Extended Movie List

```
<!---
Name:        movies2.cfm
Author:      Ben Forta (ben@forta.com)
Description: Retrieving multiple database columns
Created:     07/01/07
--->

<!--- Get movie list from database --->
<cfquery name="movies" datasource="ows">
SELECT MovieTitle, PitchText
FROM Films
ORDER BY MovieTitle
</cfquery>

<!--- Create HTML page --->
<html>
<head>
 <title>Orange Whip Studios - Movie List</title>
</head>

<body>

<h1>Movie List</h1>

<!--- Display movie list --->
<cfoutput query="movies">
<strong>#MovieTitle#</strong><br>
#PitchText#<p>
</cfoutput>

</body>
</html>
```

As you can see, two table columns are now used, each delimited by number signs. The `MovieTitle` is displayed in bold (using `<strong>` and `</strong>` tags) and is followed by a line break; on the next line `PitchText` is displayed followed by a paragraph break. So, for the first row displayed, the previous code becomes

```
<strong>#MovieTitle#</strong><br>
#PitchText#<p>
```

Compare that to what you'd have had to change in `movies.htm` to update a static page to look like Figure 10.4, and you'll start to appreciate the dynamic page advantage.

Excited? You should be. Welcome to ColdFusion and the wonderful world of dynamic data-driven Web pages!

Displaying Database Query Results

Listings 10.2 and 10.3 displayed data in simple line-by-line outputs. But that's not all you can do with ColdFusion—in fact, there is no type of output that *can't* be generated with it. ColdFusion has absolutely nothing to do with formatting and generating output; as long as you can write what you want (in HTML, JavaScript, Flash, DHTML, or any other client technology), ColdFusion generates the output dynamically.

To better understand this, let's look at some alternative output options.

Displaying Data Using Lists

HTML features support for two list types—ordered lists (in which each list item is automatically numbered) and unordered lists (in which list items are preceded by bullets). Creating HTML lists is very simple:

1. Start the list with `<ul>` (for an unordered list) or `<ol>` (for an ordered list).

2. End the list with a matching end tag (`</ul>` or `</ol>`).

3. Between the list's start and end tags, specify the list members (called *list items*) between `<li>` and `</li>` tags.

For example, the following is a simple bulleted (unordered) list containing three names:

```
<ul>
 <li>Ben Forta</li>
 <li>Nate Weiss</li>
 <li>Ray Camden</li>
</UL>
```

The numbered (ordered) equivalent of this list would be:

```
<ol>
 <li>Ben Forta</li>
 <li>Nate Weiss</li>
 <li>Ray Camden</li>
</ol>
```

So, how would you display the movie list in an unordered list? Listing 10.4 contains the code, which you should save as `movies3.cfm`. Execute the code in your browser (or in Dreamweaver, if you prefer); the output should look like Figure 10.5.

Figure 10.5

HTML unordered lists provide a simple way to display data-driven output.

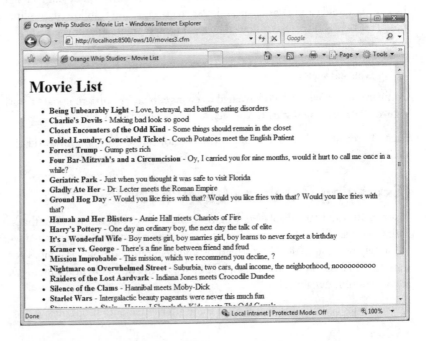

Listing 10.4 `movies3.cfm`—The Movie List in an Unordered List

```
<!---
Name:        movies3.cfm
Author:      Ben Forta (ben@forta.com)
Description: Data-driven HTML list
Created:     07/01/07
--->

<!--- Get movie list from database --->
<cfquery name="movies" datasource="ows">
SELECT MovieTitle, PitchText
FROM Films
ORDER BY MovieTitle
</cfquery>

<!--- Create HTML page --->
<html>
<head>
 <title>Orange Whip Studios - Movie List</title>
</head>

<body>

<h1>Movie List</h1>

<!--- Display movie list --->
<ul>
 <cfoutput query="movies">
  <li><strong>#MovieTitle#</strong> - #PitchText#</li>
 </cfoutput>
</ul>

</body>
</html>
```

Let's review Listing 10.4 together. It should look familiar because it's essentially the same code as Listing 10.3 (`movies2.cfm`), only the actual data output has changed. The new output code is:

```
<ul>
 <cfoutput query="movies">
  <li><strong>#MovieTitle#</strong> - #PitchText#</li>
 </cfoutput>
</ul>
```

As you can see, the list is started before the `<cfoutput>` tag, and it's ended after the `</cfoutput>` tag. This is important—everything within the output block is repeated once for every row retrieved. Therefore, if the list was started inside the output block, 23 lists would be generated, with each containing a single movie, instead of a single list containing 23 movies. Only the data to be repeated should be placed inside the output block.

The output code itself is simple. For the first row, the code

```
<li><strong>#MovieTitle#</strong> - #PitchText#</li>
```

becomes

```
<li><strong>Being Unbearably Light</strong>
 - Love, betrayal, and battling eating disorders</li>
```

which is a valid list item with the movie title in bold (using `<strong>` and `</strong>`) is followed by the tag line.

NOTE

As you can see, changing output formatting affects (or should affect) only an isolated portion of your code. As such, many developers first test whether their code works using simple output (line breaks or lists) before they write complex user interfaces. This can make development much easier (debugging core code and the user interface at the same time is no fun).

CAUTION

Be careful when placing code within an output block. Only code that is to be repeated for each row should be placed between `<cfoutput>` and `</cfoutput>`. Any other code should go outside the tags.

Displaying Data Using Tables

Probably the layout feature most frequently used (and most useful) is tables. HTML tables enable you to create grids that can contain text, graphics, and more. Tables are used to facilitate a more controlled page layout, including placing content side by side, in columns, and wrapped around images.

Creating tables involves three sets of tags:

- `<table>` and `</table>`—Used to create the table

- `<tr>` and `</tr>`—Used to create rows in the table

- `<td>` and `</td>`—Used to insert cells within a table row (`<th>` and `</th>` also can be used for header cells—essentially data cells formatted a little differently, usually centered and in bold)

So, a simple table with a header row, two columns, and three rows of data (as seen in Figure 10.6) might look like this:

```
<table>
 <tr>
  <th>First Name</th>
  <th>Last Name</th>
 </tr>
 <tr>
  <td>Ben</td>
  <td>Forta</td>
 </tr>
 <tr>
  <td>Nate</td>
  <td>Weiss</td>
 </tr>
 <tr>
  <td>Ray</td>
  <td>Camden</td>
 </tr>
</table>
```

TIP

The Dreamweaver Tables toolbar contains buttons and shortcuts to simplify table creation and manipulation.

Figure 10.6

HTML tables are constructed using tags to create the table, rows, and individual cells.

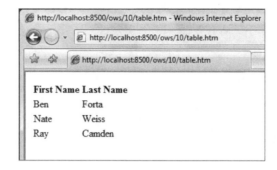

With that brief intro to HTML tables, let's modify the movie listing to display the list in an HTML table. Listing 10.5 contains a modified version of the code (again, you can use Save As to create a copy of the previous version for editing). Save the file as movies4.cfm, and then execute it to display an output similar to that shown in Figure 10.7.

Listing 10.5   movies4.cfm—The Movie List in an HTML Table

```
<!---
Name:        movies4.cfm
Author:      Ben Forta (ben@forta.com)
Description: Data-driven HTML table
Created:     07/01/07
--->

<!--- Get movie list from database --->
<cfquery name="movies" datasource="ows">
SELECT MovieTitle, PitchText
FROM Films
ORDER BY MovieTitle
</cfquery>

<!--- Create HTML page --->
<html>
<head>
 <title>Orange Whip Studios - Movie List</title>
</head>

<body>

<h1>Movie List</h1>

<!--- Display movie list --->
<table border="1">
 <cfoutput query="movies">
  <tr>
   <td>#MovieTitle#</td>
   <td>#PitchText#</td>
  </tr>
 </cfoutput>
</table>

</body>
</html>
```

Figure 10.7

Tables provide a convenient mechanism for displaying data in a grid-like format.

Once again, the code in Listing 10.5 is similar to the previous examples, and once again, it's only the output block that has changed.

The table is created using the code `<table border="1">`—a table with a border. The `<table>` and `</table>` tags are placed *outside* the output block (you want a single table, not a table for each row).

The table needs a new table row for each row in the query. So, the `<tr>` and `</tr>` tags are within the output loop, and within them are two cells (containing `MovieTitle` and `PitchText`).

As you can see in Figure 10.7, this code creates a single table with as many rows as there are query rows (23 in this example).

TIP

Viewing the source code generated by ColdFusion is useful when debugging template problems. When you view the source, you are looking at the complete output as it was sent to your browser. If you ever need to ascertain why a Web page doesn't look the way you intended it to look, a good place to start is comparing your template with the source code it generated.

You'll probably find yourself using tables extensively. To ensure that dynamic HTML table creation is properly understood, another example is in order.

This time the table will contain two rows for each query row. The first will contain two cells—one for the title and tag line and one for the release date. The second row will contain the movie summary (and because the summary can be lengthy, its cell spans both columns). The output generated can be seen in Figure 10.8.

Listing 10.6 contains the revised code; this time save the file as `movies5.cfm` and execute it in your browser.

Listing 10.6 `movies5.cfm`—The Movie List in an HTML Table

```
<!---
Name:        movies5.cfm
Author:      Ben Forta (ben@forta.com)
Description: Data-driven HTML table
Created:     07/01/07
--->

<!--- Get movie list from database --->
<cfquery name="movies" datasource="ows">
SELECT MovieTitle, PitchText,
       Summary, DateInTheaters
FROM Films
ORDER BY MovieTitle
</cfquery>

<!--- Create HTML page --->
<html>
<head>
 <title>Orange Whip Studios - Movie List</title>
</head>

<body>

<!--- Start table --->
<table>
 <tr>
  <th colspan="2">
   <font size="+2">Movie List</font>
  </th>
 </tr>
 <!--- loop through movies --->
 <cfoutput query="movies">
  <tr bgcolor="##cccccc">
   <td>
    <strong>#MovieTitle#</strong>
    <br>
    #PitchText#
   </td>
   <td>
    #DateFormat(DateInTheaters)#
   </td>
  </tr>
  <tr>
   <td colspan="2">
    <font size="-2">#Summary#</font>
   </td>
  </tr>
 </cfoutput>
 <!--- End of movie loop --->
</table>

</body>
</html>
```

A few changes have been made in Listing 10.6. First, the `<cfquery>` SELECT statement has been modified to retrieve two additional columns—Summary contains the movie summary, and DateInTheaters contains the movie's public release date.

In addition, the following HTML code has been added *before* the `<cfoutput>` tag:

```
<tr>
  <th colspan="2">
    <font size="+2">Movie List</font>
  </th>
</tr>
```

This creates a header cell (header contents usually are centered and displayed in bold) containing the text Movie List as a table title. Because the table is two columns wide, the title must span both columns, so the optional attribute colspan="2" is specified.

The output block itself creates two rows (two sets of `<tr>` and `</tr>` tags) per movie. The first contains two cells—one with the MovieTitle and PitchText (with a line break between them) and the other with the release date formatted for display using the DateFormat() function. The second row contains a single cell spanning both columns and displaying Summary.

➡ The DateFormat() function was introduced in Chapter 8.

Figure 10.8

For greater control, HTML tables can contain cells that span two or more columns (and rows).

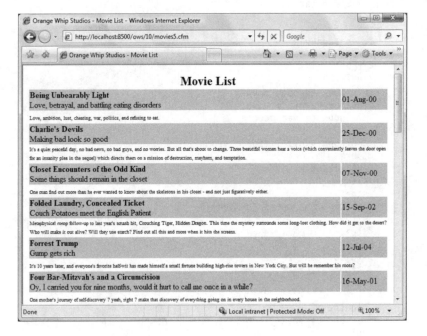

As seen in Figure 10.8, the table row containing the title and tag line has a colored background. To set the background color of a table row (or a specific table cell, or even the entire table for that matter) the bgcolor attribute is used, and the color is specified using known named (like red and green) or RGB values in hexadecimal notation as follows:

```
<tr bgcolor="#cccccc">
```

Hexadecimal values are preceded by a #, the same character used to delimit ColdFusion expressions. If the above code were used in our <cfoutput> block, ColdFusion would have generated an error message complaining about a missing closing # (it would think that cccccc was an expression needing a closing #). As such, our table code escapes the # as follows:

```
<tr bgcolor="##cccccc">
```

➜ Escaping # was covered in Chapter 8.

TIP

Pay close attention to which code you place within and without the <cfoutput> block. Misplacing a <tr> or </td> tag could result in a badly formatted HTML table, and some browsers might opt to not even display that table.

As you can see, as long as you know the basic HTML syntax and know what needs to be repeated for each database row and what doesn't, creating dynamic data-driven output is quick and painless.

TIP

ColdFusion features a tag named <cftable> that can be used to automate the entire process of creating data-driven HTML tables. Although this tag works, I recommend against using it. HTML tables aren't difficult to learn and create, and doing so is well worth the effort because you'll find that you have far more control over the exact format and output.

CAUTION

I know I've said it several times already, but because this is one of the most common beginners' mistakes (and a very aggravating one to debug at that), I'll say it one last time: When creating dynamic output, pay special attention to what needs to be repeated and what does not. Anything that needs to be displayed once per row (either before or after the row) must go in the output block; anything else must not.

Using Result Variables

So far, you have displayed data retrieved using database queries. But sometimes you'll need access to data about queries (and not just data within queries). For example, if you wanted to display the number of movies retrieved, where would you get that count from?

To simplify this type of operation, ColdFusion can return special variables with every query using the optional RESULT structure. Table 10.1 lists these variables, and as you can see, RecordCount can provide the number of rows retrieved.

Table 10.1 Query RESULT Variables

VARIABLE	DESCRIPTION
Cached	Flag indicating whether or not returned query is a cached copy
ColumnList	Names of columns in query results (comma-delimited list)
ExecutionTime	Query execution time (in milliseconds)
RecordCount	Number of rows in a query
SQL	The SQL statement as submitted for processing

To demonstrate using these special variables, create the file movies6.cfm, as shown in Listing 10.7. This code, which is based on movies5.cfm, generates the output seen in Figure 10.9. Save the code, and execute it in your browser.

Listing 10.7 movies6.cfm—Using Query Variables

```
<!---
Name:        movies6.cfm
Author:      Ben Forta (ben@forta.com)
Description: Using query variables
Created:     07/01/07
--->

<!--- Get movie list from database --->
<cfquery name="movies" datasource="ows" result="result">
SELECT MovieTitle, PitchText,
       Summary, DateInTheaters
FROM Films
ORDER BY MovieTitle
</cfquery>

<!--- Create HTML page --->
<html>
<head>
 <title>Orange Whip Studios - Movie List</title>
</head>

<body>

<!--- Start table --->
<table>
 <tr>
  <th colspan="2">
   <font size="+2">
   <cfoutput>
   Movie List (#result.RecordCount# movies)
   </cfoutput>
   </font>
  </th>
 </tr>
 <!--- loop through movies --->
 <cfoutput query="movies">
  <tr bgcolor="##cccccc">
```

Listing 10.7   (CONTINUED)

```
   <td>
    <strong>#CurrentRow#: #MovieTitle#</strong>
    <br>
    #PitchText#
   </td>
   <td>
    #DateFormat(DateInTheaters)#
   </td>
  </tr>
  <tr>
   <td colspan="2">
    <font size="-2">#Summary#</font>
   </td>
  </tr>
 </cfoutput>
 <!--- End of movie loop --->
 </table>

</body>
</html>
```

Figure 10.9

RecordCount can be accessed to obtain the number of rows in a query.

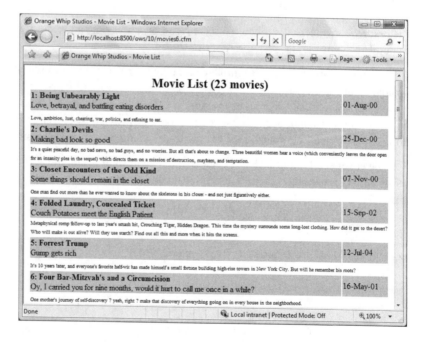

So what changed here? Only three modifications were made to this code. First, the `<cfquery>` RESULT attribute was specified so that, when processed, the structure named `result` would be created containing the query execution results. In addition, the title (above the output block) now reads as follows:

```
Movie List (#result.RecordCount# movies)
```

`#result.RecordCount#` returns the number of rows retrieved—in this case, 23. Like any other expression, the text `result.RecordCount` must be enclosed within number signs and must be between `<cfoutput>` and `</cfoutput>` tags. But unlike many other expressions, here the prefix `result` is required. Why? Because this code isn't referring to a column in a named query. Rather, `RecordCount` is a member of a structure named `result`, and so the fully qualified variable name must be specified.

TIP

Here the query name prefix is required because the query was not specified in the `<cfoutput>` loop. Within an output loop, the query name isn't required, but it can be used to prevent ambiguity (for example, if there were variables with the same names as table columns).

Here you use `RecordCount` purely for display purposes. But as you will see later in this chapter, it can be used in other ways, too (for example, checking to see whether a query returned any data at all).

The other line of code that changed is the movie title display, which now has `#CurrentRow#`: in front of it. `CurrentRow` is another special variable, but this time it's in `<cfoutput>` instead of `<cfquery>`. Within an output loop, `CurrentRow` keeps a tally of the iterations—it contains 1 when the first row is processed, 2 when the second row is processed, and so on. In this example, it's used to number the movies (as seen in Figure 10.9).

`CurrentRow` can also be used it to implement fancy formatting, for example, alternating the background color for every other row (a *green paper* effect) as seen in Figure 10.10. Listing 10.8 is `movies7.cfm`, a modified version of `movies4.cfm` (I used that older version as it's simpler and looks better for this example). Background color, as previously seen, is set using the `bgcolor` attribute, but unlike in the previous example, here the colors are being set dynamically and programmatically.

The big change in Listing 10.8 is the `<cfif>` statement right inside the `<cfoutput>` loop. As you will recall, `<cfif>` is used to evaluate if statements (conditions), and here the following `<cfif>` statement is used:

```
<cfif CurrentRow MOD 2 IS 1>
```

➡ `<cfif>` was introduced back in Chapter 9, "Programming with CFML."

Listing 10.8 `movies7.cfm`—Implementing Alternating Colors

```
<!---
Name:         movies7.cfm
Author:       Ben Forta (ben@forta.com)
Description:  Implementing alternating colors
Created:      07/01/07
--->

<!--- Get movie list from database --->
<cfquery name="movies" datasource="ows">
SELECT MovieTitle, PitchText
FROM Films
ORDER BY MovieTitle
</cfquery>
```

Listing 10.8 (CONTINUED)

```html
<!--- Create HTML page --->
<html>
<head>
 <title>Orange Whip Studios - Movie List</title>
</head>

<body>

<h1>Movie List</h1>

<!--- Display movie list --->
<table>
 <cfoutput query="movies">
  <!--- What color should this row be? --->
   <cfif CurrentRow MOD 2 IS 1>
    <cfset bgcolor="MediumSeaGreen">
   <cfelse>
    <cfset bgcolor="White">
   </cfif>
   <tr bgcolor="#bgcolor#">
   <td>#MovieTitle#</td>
   <td>#PitchText#</td>
  </tr>
 </cfoutput>
</table>

</body>
</html>
```

Figure 10.10

RecordCount can be
used to alternate
output colors.

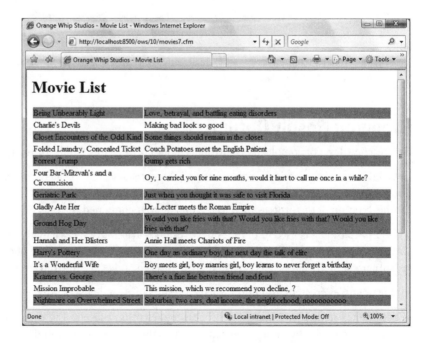

`CurrentRow` contains the current loop counter as previously explained. `MOD` is an arithmetic operator that returns the reminder of an equation, and so testing for `MOD 2` is a way to check for odd or even numbers (divide a number by 2, if the remainder is 1 the number is odd otherwise the number is even). So checking `MOD 2 IS 1` is effectively checking that *the number is odd*.

Within the `<cfif>` statement one of two `<cfset>` tags will be called; if the `CurrentRow` is odd then the first is called (setting a variable named `bgcolor` to `MediumSeaGreen`), and if even then the second is called (setting `bgcolor` to `white`). Once the `</cfif>` is reached a variable named `bgcolor` will exist and will contain a color (`MediumSeaGreen` or `white`, depending on whether `CurrentRow` is odd or even). As the `<cfif>` code is within the `<cfoutput>` block it's processed once for every row, and so `bgcolor` is reset on each row.

➡ See Chapter 8 for an introduction to the `<cfset>` tag.

Then `bgcolor` is then passed to the `<tr>` tag's `bgcolor` attribute so that on odd rows the `<TR>` tag becomes:

```
<tr bgcolor="">
```

and on even rows it becomes:

```
<tr bgcolor="White">
```

The result is shown in Figure 10.10.

TIP

You'll notice that I named the variable in Listing 10.8 `bgcolor`, the same as the HTML attribute with which it was used. This isn't required (you may name variables as you wish) but doing so makes the code clearer as the variable's use is then blatantly obvious.

NOTE

The value in `CurrentRow` isn't the row's unique ID (primary key). In fact, the number has nothing to do with the table data at all. It's merely a loop counter and should never be relied on as anything else.

Grouping Result Output

Before a new level of complexity is introduced, let's review how ColdFusion processes queries.

In ColdFusion, data queries are created using the `<cfquery>` tag. `<cfquery>` performs a SQL operation and retrieves results if any exist. Results are stored temporarily by ColdFusion and remain only for the duration of the processing of the template that contained the query.

The `<cfoutput>` tag is used to output query results. `<cfoutput>` takes a query name as an attribute and then loops through all the rows that were retrieved by the query. The code block between `<cfoutput>` and `</cfoutput>` is repeated once for each and every row retrieved.

All the examples created until now displayed results in a single list or single table.

What would you do if you wanted to process the results in subsets? For example, suppose you wanted to list movies by rating. You could change the SQL statement in the `<cfquery>` to retrieve the rating ID and set the sort order to be `RatingID` and then by `MovieTitle`.

This would retrieve the data in the correct order, but how would you display it? If you used <cfoutput> as you have until now, every row created by the <cfoutput> block would have to be the same. If one had the rating displayed, all would have to because every row that is processed is processed with the same block of code.

Look at Figure 10.11. As you can see, the screen contains nested lists. The top-level list contains the rating IDs, and within each rating ID is a second list containing all the movies with that rating. How would you create an output like this?

Listing 10.9 contains the code for a new page; save this as `ratings1.cfm` and execute it in your browser.

Listing 10.9 `ratings1.cfm`—Grouping Query Output

```
<!---
Name:        ratings1.cfm
Author:      Ben Forta (ben@forta.com)
Description: Query output grouping
Created:     07/01/07
--->

<!--- Get movie list from database --->
<cfquery name="movies" datasource="ows">
SELECT MovieTitle, RatingID
FROM Films
ORDER BY RatingID, MovieTitle
</cfquery>

<!--- Create HTML page --->
<html>
<head>
 <title>Orange Whip Studios - Movie List</title>
</head>

<body>

<h1>Movie List</h1>

<!--- Display movie list --->
<ul>
 <!--- Loop through ratings --->
 <cfoutput query="movies" group="RatingID">
  <li>#RatingID#</li>
  <ul>
   <!--- For each rating, list movies --->
   <cfoutput>
    <li>#MovieTitle#</li>
   </cfoutput>
  </ul>
 </cfoutput>
</ul>

</body>
</html>
```

Figure 10.11

Grouping provides a means with which to display data grouped into logical sets.

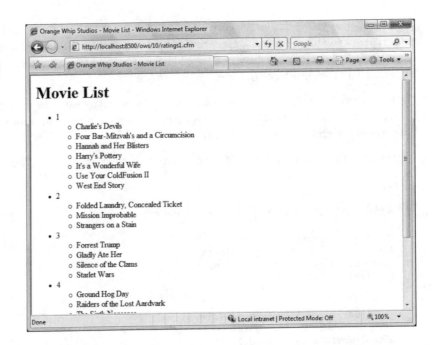

Listing 10.9 starts with the comment block, followed by a `<cfquery>` that retrieves all the movies (title and rating only) sorted by `RatingID` and `MovieTitle` (by `RatingID` and within each `RatingID` by `MovieTitle`).

The display section of the code starts by creating an unordered list—this is the outer list, which contains the ratings.

Then, `<cfoutput>` is used again to create an output block, but this time the `group` attribute has been added. `group="RatingID"` tells the output block to loop through the outer loop only when `RatingID` changes. In other words, the outer loop is processed once per group value. So, in this example, it's processed once per `RatingID` value—regardless of the number of movies with that `RatingID`.

Then the `RatingID` is displayed, and a second unordered list is started—this is for the inner list within each `RatingID`.

Next, comes a second `<cfoutput>` block that displays the `MovieTitle`. No `query` is specified here; ColdFusion doesn't need one. Why? Because `group` is being used, ColdFusion knows which query is being used and loops through the inner `<cfoutput>` only as long as `RatingID` doesn't change.

As soon as `RatingID` changes, the inner `<cfoutput>` loop stops and the inner list is terminated with a `</ul>`.

This repeats until all rows have been processed, at which time the outer `<cfoutput>` terminates and the final `</ul>` is generated.

So, how many times is each `<cfoutput>` processed? The movie list contains 23 rows with a total of 6 ratings. So the outer loop is processed 6 times, and the inner loop is processed 23 times. This outer list contains 6 items (each `RatingID` value), and each item contains a sub-list containing the movies with that `RatingID`.

NOTE

For grouping to work, groups must be created in the exact same order as the sort order (the **ORDER BY** clause) in the SQL statement itself.

Listing 10.10 contains a modified version of Listing 10.9, this time displaying the results in an HTML table (as seen in Figure 10.12). Save Listing 10.10 as `ratings2.cfm`, and then execute it in your browser.

Listing 10.10 `ratings2.cfm`—Grouping Query Output

```
<!---
Name:        ratings2.cfm
Author:      Ben Forta (ben@forta.com)
Description: Query output grouping
Created:     07/01/07
--->

<!--- Get movie list from database --->
<cfquery name="movies" datasource="ows">
SELECT MovieTitle, RatingID
FROM Films
ORDER BY RatingID, MovieTitle
</cfquery>
<!--- Create HTML page --->
<html>
<head>
 <title>Orange Whip Studios - Movie List</title>
</head>

<body>

<h1>Movie List</h1>

<!--- Display movie list --->
<table>
 <!--- Loop through ratings --->
 <cfoutput query="movies" group="RatingID">
  <tr valign="top">
   <td bgcolor="##000000">
    <font color="##FFFFFF">Rating #RatingID#</font>
   </td>
   <td>
    <!--- For each rating, list movies --->
    <cfoutput>
    #MovieTitle#<br>
    </cfoutput>
   </td>
  </tr>
 </cfoutput>
</table>

</body>
</html>
```

Figure 10.12

Grouped data can be used in lists, tables, and any other form of data presentation.

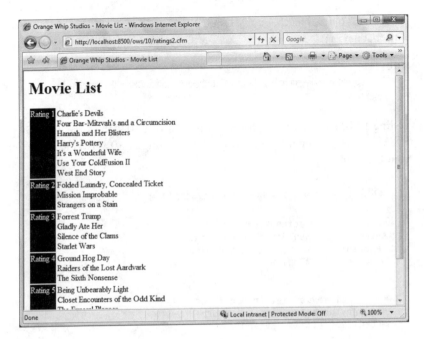

The only thing that has changed in Listing 10.10 is the output code. Again, the `<cfoutput>` tags are nested—the outer loops through `RatingID` and the inner loops through the movies.

The HTML table is created before any looping occurs (you want only one table). Then, for each `RatingID` a new table row is created containing two cells. The left cell contains the `RatingID`, and the right cell contains the movies.

To do this, the inner `<cfoutput>` loop is used in that right cell (between the `<TD>` and `</td>` tags) so that, for each `RatingID` listed on the left, all the appropriate movies are listed on the right.

TIP

A single level of grouping is used here, but there is no limit to the number of levels in which data can be grouped. To group multiple levels (groups within groups), you simply need an additional `<cfoutput>` per group (and of course, the SQL statement must sort the data appropriately).

Using Data Drill-Down

Now that you've learned almost everything you need to know about the `<cfoutput>` tag, let's put it all together in a complete application.

Data drill-down is a popular form of user interface within Web applications because it enables the progressive and gradual selection of desired data. Data drill-down applications usually are made up of three levels of interface:

- A search screen

- A results screen (displaying the results of any searches)

- A details screen (displaying the details for any row selected in the results screen)

You won't create the search screen here (forms are introduced in the next chapter), but you will create the latter two screens. Your application will display a list of movies (similar to the screens created earlier in this chapter) and will allow visitors to click any movie to see detailed information about it.

Introducing Dynamic SQL

You've used lots of `<cfquery>` tags thus far, and each of them has contained hard-coded SQL—SQL that you typed and that stays the same (the results may differ if the data in the database changes, but the SQL itself always stays the same). But SQL passed to ColdFusion need not be static and hard-coded; the real power of `<cfquery>` is seen when SQL is constructed dynamically.

To demonstrate what we mean, Listing 10.11 contains the code for a new file named `dynamicsql.cfm`. Save the code and execute it to see a screen like the one shown in Figure 10.13.

Listing 10.11 `dynamicsql.cfm`—Dynamic SQL Demonstration

```
<!---
Name:        dynamicsql.cfm
Author:      Ben Forta (ben@forta.com)
Description: Dynamic SQL demonstration
Created:     07/01/07
--->

<!--- Create FilmID variable --->
<cfset FilmID=1>

<!--- Get a movie from database --->
<cfquery name="movie"
         datasource="ows"
         result="results">
SELECT FilmID, MovieTitle, PitchText
FROM Films
WHERE FilmID=#FilmID#
</cfquery>

<h1>Dump Returned Query (NAME)</h1>
<cfdump var="#movie#">
<h1>Dump Returned Result (RESULT)</h1>
<cfdump var="#results#">
```

Figure 10.13

The `<cfquery>`
result structure
contains the final
(post–dynamic
processing) SQL and
additional
information.

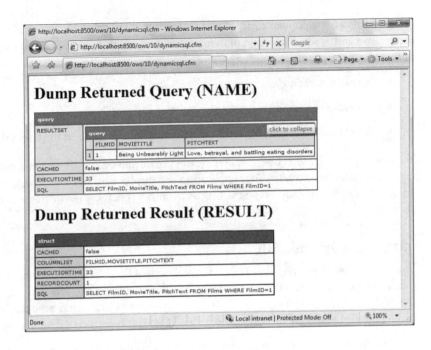

Listing 10.11 starts by creating a variable as follows:

```
<cfset FilmID=1>
```

Next comes a `<cfquery>` tag containing the following SQL:

```
SELECT FilmID, MovieTitle, PitchText
FROM Films
WHERE FilmID=#FilmID#
```

The WHERE clause specifies the row to be retrieved, and would usually be an actual value. For example, to retrieve the movie with a FilmID of 1 you would use this SQL:

```
SELECT FilmID, MovieTitle, PitchText
FROM Films
WHERE FilmID=1
```

→ See Chapter 6, "Introducing SQL," for a detailed explanation of the SELECT statement and its WHERE clause.

And this is exactly what the code in Listing 10.11 does. #FilmID# is a ColdFusion expression, and so ColdFusion will process it, returning the value of FilmID which is 1 (as set in the `<cfset>` earlier).

In other words, the SQL used here is dynamic in that the actual SQL statement itself can change (in this example based on the value of FilmID). If you wanted to retrieve a different movie you could simply update FilmID so that it contained a different value.

The last block of code contains two `<cfdump>` tags:

```
<h1>Display Data</h1>
<cfdump var="#movie#">
<h1>Display cfquery Results</h1>
<cfdump var="#results#">
```

The former simply dumps the returned query (the data contained in the `movie` variable). The latter dumps the `results` structure, exposing a field named `SQL` that contains the SQL used, and additional information (including the same query variables listed in Table 10.1 earlier in this chapter).

As seen previously, the use of `result` is always optional, but if needed it can expose useful information about tag execution.

NOTE

The result structure may contain additional members, depending on the `<cfquery>` attributes used.

Implementing Data Drill-Down Interfaces

Now that you've seen how dynamic SQL is used, let's return to data drill-down pages. The first screen you need to create is the details page—the one that will be displayed when a movie is selected. Figure 10.14 shows the details for one movie.

Listing 10.12 contains the code for the file `details1.cfm`. Save the code, and then execute it in your browser with this URL:

```
http://localhost:8500/ows/10/details1.cfm?FilmID=2
```

You should see a screen like the one in Figure 10.14.

Listing 10.12   `details1.cfm`—Data Drill-Down Details

```
<!---
Name:        details1.cfm
Author:      Ben Forta (ben@forta.com)
Description: Data drill-down details
Created:     07/01/07
--->

<!--- Get a movie from database --->
<cfquery name="movie" datasource="ows">
SELECT FilmID, MovieTitle,
       PitchText, Summary,
       DateInTheaters, AmountBudgeted
FROM Films
WHERE FilmID=#URL.FilmID#
</cfquery>

<!--- Create HTML page --->
<html>
<head>
 <title>Orange Whip Studios - Movie Details</title>
</head>

<body>

<!--- Display movie details --->
<cfoutput query="movie">

<table>
 <tr>
```

Listing 10.12 (CONTINUED)

```
   <td colspan="2">
    <img src="../images/f#filmid#.gif"
         alt="#movietitle#"
         align="middle">
    <strong>#MovieTitle#</strong>
   </td>
  </tr>
  <tr valign="top">
   <th align="right">Tag line:</th>
   <td>#PitchText#</td>
  </tr>
  <tr valign="top">
   <th align="right">Summary:</th>
   <td>#Summary#</td>
  </tr>
  <tr valign="top">
   <th align="right">Released:</th>
   <td>#DateFormat(DateInTheaters)#</td>
  </tr>
  <tr valign="top">
   <th align="right">Budget:</th>
   <td>#DollarFormat(AmountBudgeted)#</td>
  </tr>
 </table>

</cfoutput>

</body>
</html>
```

Figure 10.14

In data drill-down applications, the details page displays all of the details for a specific record.

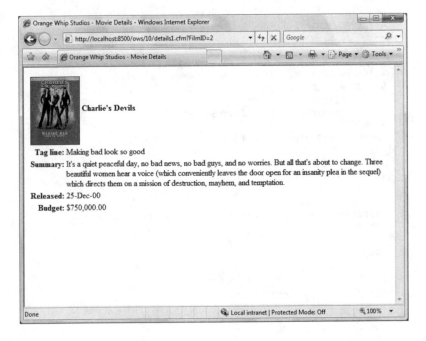

There are several important things to point out in Listing 10.12. Let's start with the SQL statement:

```
SELECT FilmID, MovieTitle,
       PitchText, Summary,
       DateInTheaters, AmountBudgeted
FROM Films
WHERE FilmID=#URL.FilmID#
```

The WHERE clause here is used to select a specific movie by its primary key (FilmID). But instead of comparing it to a real number, a ColdFusion variable is used—#URL.FilmID#. This is dynamic SQL, similar to the example in Listing 10.11 above. When ColdFusion encounters #URL.FilmID#, it replaces that expression with whatever the value of the URL parameter FilmID is. So, if the URL parameter FilmID had a value of 2, the generated SQL would look like this:

```
SELECT FilmID, MovieTitle,
       PitchText, Summary,
       DateInTheaters, AmountBudgeted
FROM Films
WHERE FilmID=2
```

This is why I had you append ?FilmID=2 to the URL when you executed this page. Without a FilmID parameter, this code would have failed, but we'll get to that in a moment.

The beauty of this technique is that it allows the same details page to be used for an unlimited number of database records—each FilmID specified generates a different page. If FilmID were 10, the SQL statement would have a WHERE clause of FilmID=10, and so on.

➜ URL variables were briefly introduced in Chapter 9.

The rest of the code in Listing 10.12 is self-explanatory. The details are displayed in an HTML table with the title spanning two columns. Dates are formatted using the DateFormat() function, and monetary amounts are formatted using the DollarFormat() function (which, as its name suggests, formats numbers as dollar amounts).

NOTE

Support for other currencies also are available via the locale functions.

One interesting line of code, though, is the <img> tag (used to display the movie poster image):

```
<img src="../images/f#filmid#.gif"
     alt="#movietitle#"
     align="middle">
```

Binary data, like images, can be stored in databases just like any other data, but accessing these images requires special processing that is beyond the scope of this chapter. And so in this application images are stored in a directory and named using the primary key values. Therefore, in this example, the image for FilmID 2 is f2.gif, and that image is stored in the images directory under the application root. By using #FilmID# in the file name, images can be referred to dynamically. In this example, for FilmID 2 the <img> tag becomes

```
<img src="../images/f2.gif"
     alt="Charlie's Devils"
     align="middle">
```

Try executing Listing 10.12 again, but this time don't pass the `FilmID` parameter. What happens when you execute the code? You probably received an error message similar to the one in Figure 10.15 telling you that you were referring to a variable that doesn't exist. You can't use `URL.FilmID` in your SQL statement if no `URL` parameter named `FilmID` exists.

Figure 10.15

Do not refer to a variable that does not exist; if you do, an error message will be generated.

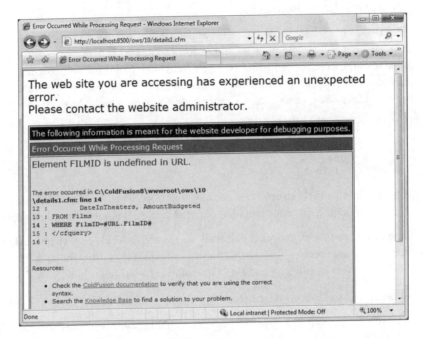

The solution (which you looked at briefly in Chapter 9) is to check that the variable exists before using it. Listing 10.13 contains an updated version of the code; save it as `details2.cfm` and execute it. What happens now if no `FilmID` is specified?

Listing 10.13 `details2.cfm`—Data Drill-Down Details

```
<!---
Name:        details2.cfm
Author:      Ben Forta (ben@forta.com)
Description: Data drill-down details
             with basic validation
Created:     07/01/07
--->

<!--- Make sure FilmID was passed --->
<cfif not IsDefined("URL.filmid")>
 <!--- it wasn't, send to movie list --->
 <cflocation url="movies6.cfm">
</cfif>

<!--- Get a movie from database --->
<cfquery name="movie" datasource="ows">
SELECT FilmID, MovieTitle,
```

Listing 10.13 (CONTINUED)

```
            PitchText, Summary,
            DateInTheaters, AmountBudgeted
FROM Films
WHERE FilmID=#URL.FilmID#
</cfquery>

<!--- Create HTML page --->
<html>
<head>
<title>Orange Whip Studios - Movie Details</title>
</head>

<body>

<!--- Display movie details --->
<cfoutput query="movie">

<table>
 <tr>
  <td colspan="2">
   <img src="../images/f#filmid#.gif"
        alt="#movietitle#"
        align="middle">
   <strong>#MovieTitle#</strong>
  </td>
 </tr>
 <tr valign="top">
  <th align="right">Tag line:</th>
  <td>#PitchText#</td>
 </tr>
 <tr valign="top">
  <th align="right">Summary:</th>
  <td>#Summary#</td>
 </tr>
 <tr valign="top">
  <th align="right">Released:</th>
  <td>#DateFormat(DateInTheaters)#</td>
 </tr>
 <tr valign="top">
  <th align="right">Budget:</th>
  <td>#DollarFormat(AmountBudgeted)#</td>
 </tr>
</table>

</cfoutput>

</body>
</html>
```

The only thing that has changed in Listing 10.13 is the inclusion of the following code *before* the
<CFQUERY> tag:

```
<!--- Make sure FilmID was passed --->
<cfif not IsDefined("URL.filmid")>
 <!--- it wasn't, send to movie list --->
 <cflocation url="movies6.cfm">
</cfif>
```

If FilmID was not passed, users should never have gotten to this page. You could simply display an error message, but instead, why not send them where they need to go? <cflocation> is a Cold-Fusion tag that redirects users to other pages (or even other sites). So, the <cfif> statement checks to see whether URL.FilmID exists (using the IsDefined() function). If it does not, the user is sent to the movies6.cfm page automatically. Now the SQL code won't execute without a FilmID because if no FilmID exists, the <cfquery> tag is never even reached.

➔ The IsDefined() function was introduced in Chapter 9.

So far so good, but you're not there yet. Two other possible trouble spots still exist. Try executing the following URL:

```
http://localhost:8500/ows/10/details2.cfm?FilmID=1
```

1 is a valid FilmID, so the movie details are displayed. But FilmID 1 doesn't have a movie image, which means the <img> tag is pointing to a nonexistent image, causing a browser error (as seen in Figure 10.16).

Figure 10.16

When referring to images dynamically, take care to ensure that the image actually exists.

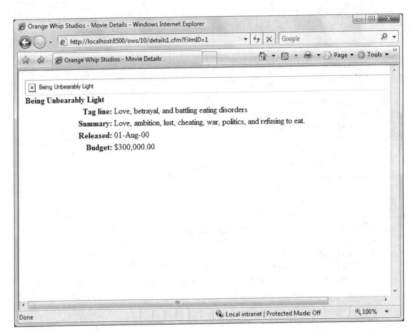

In addition, try this URL:

```
http://localhost:8500/ows/10/details2.cfm?FilmID=1000
```

No movie with a FilmID of 1000 exists, so no movie is displayed, but no error message is displayed either.

Neither of these problems is critical, but they should be addressed anyway. Listing 10.14 contains a final version of the details page; save this file as details3.cfm.

Listing 10.14 details3.cfm—Data Drill-Down Details

```
<!---
Name:        details3.cfm
Author:      Ben Forta (ben@forta.com)
Description: Data drill-down details
             with complete validation
Created:     07/01/07
--->

<!--- Movie list page --->
<cfset list_page="movies8.cfm">

<!--- Make sure FilmID was passed --->
<cfif not IsDefined("URL.filmid")>
 <!--- it wasn't, send to movie list --->
 <cflocation url="#list_page#">
</cfif>

<!--- Get a movie from database --->
<cfquery name="movie" datasource="ows" result="result">
SELECT FilmID, MovieTitle,
       PitchText, Summary,
       DateInTheaters, AmountBudgeted
FROM Films
WHERE FilmID=#URL.FilmID#
</cfquery>

<!--- Make sure have a movie --->
<cfif result.RecordCount IS 0>
 <!--- It wasn't, send to movie list --->
 <cflocation url="#list_page#">
</cfif>

<!--- Build image paths --->
<cfset image_src="../images/f#movie.FilmID#.gif">
<cfset image_path=ExpandPath(image_src)>

<!--- Create HTML page --->
<html>
<head>
 <title>Orange Whip Studios - Movie Details</title>
</head>

<body>

<!--- Display movie details --->
<cfoutput query="movie">

<table>
 <tr>
  <td colspan="2">
   <!--- Check of image file exists --->
   <cfif FileExists(image_path)>
    <!--- If it does, display it --->
    <img src="#image_src#"
       alt="#movietitle#"
```

Listing 10.14 (CONTINUED)

```
            align="middle">
     </cfif>
     <strong>#MovieTitle#</strong>
     </td>
   </tr>
   <tr valign="top">
     <th align="right">Tag line:</th>
     <td>#PitchText#</td>
   </tr>
   <tr valign="top">
     <th align="right">Summary:</th>
     <td>#Summary#</td>
   </tr>
   <tr valign="top">
     <th align="right">Released:</th>
     <td>#DateFormat(DateInTheaters)#</td>
   </tr>
   <tr valign="top">
     <th align="right">Budget:</th>
     <td>#DollarFormat(AmountBudgeted)#</td>
   </tr>
   </table>

   <p>

   <!--- Link back to movie list --->
   [<a href="#list_page#">Movie list</a>]

   </cfoutput>

   </body>
   </html>
```

A lot has changed here, so let's walk through the code together.

The first line of code is a `<cfset>` statement that sets a variable named `list_page` to `movies8.cfm`. You'll see why this was done in a moment.

Next comes the check for the URL parameter `FilmID`. If it's not present, `<cflocation>` is used to redirect the user to the page referred to in variable `list_page` (the movie list, same as before).

Then comes the query itself—same as before; no changes there.

After the query comes a new `<cfif>` statement that checks to see whether `result.RecordCount IS 0`. You will recall that `RecordCount` lets you know how many rows were retrieved by a query, so if `RecordCount IS 0`, you know that no rows were retrieved. The only way this could happen is if an invalid `FilmID` were specified, in which case `<cflocation>` would be used to send the user back to the movie list page—one problem solved. (Earlier I said that I'd show you an alternative use for `RecordCount`; well, I just did.)

Next comes a set of two `<cfset>` statements:

```
<!--- Build image paths --->
<cfset image_src="../images/f#movie.FilmID#.gif">
<cfset image_path=ExpandPath(image_src)>
```

The goal here is to check that the movie image exists before the `<img>` tag is used to insert it. Cold-Fusion provides a function named `FileExists()` that can be used to check for the existence of files, but there is a catch.

Images always have at least two paths by which they are referred—the actual path on disk and the URL (usually a relative URL). So, in this example, the image for `FilmID 2` would have a path on disk that might look similar to `c:\coldfusion8\wwwroot\ows\images\f2.gif` and a URL that might look similar to `../images/f2.gif`. Usually, you care about only the URL—the actual physical location of a file isn't important within the browser. But to check for a file's existence, you do need the actual path (that is what you must pass to `FileExists()`). And the code you used to build the path (using `#FilmID#` in the SRC) was a relative path. Enter the two `<cfset>` statements. The first simply creates a variable named `image_src` that contains the dynamically generated relative file name (in the case of `FilmID 2`, it would be `../images/f2.gif`), the same technique used in the `<img>` tag in the previous versions of this code. The second uses a ColdFusion function named `ExpandPath()` that converts relative paths to complete physical paths (here saving that path to `image_path`).

At this point, no determination has been made as to whether to display the image. All you have done is created two variables, each containing a path—one physical, suitable for using with `FileExists()`, and one relative, suitable for use in an `<img>` tag.

Next comes the details display, which is the same as it was before, except now the `<img>` tag is enclosed within a `<cfif>` statement that checks whether `FileExists(image_path)`. If the image exists, `FileExists()` returns TRUE and the `<img>` tag is inserted using `image_src` as the SRC. If `FileExists()` returns FALSE (meaning the movie had no image), the `<img>` tag isn't generated—problem number two solved.

NOTE

Of course, the two variables `image_path` and `image_src` aren't actually necessary, and the code would have worked if the processing was all done inline. But the approach used here is cleaner, more intuitive, and easier to read, and it will help you write better code.

At the very bottom of the page is a new link that enables users to get back to the movie list page. This link also uses the `list_page` variable. And by now, I hope the reason that a variable for the movie link URL is used is blatantly obvious. The code now has three locations that refer to the movie list file. Had they all been hard-coded, making changes would involve more work and would be more error-prone (the likelihood of you missing one occurrence grows with the number of occurrences). By using a variable, all that needs to change is the variable assignment at the top of the page—the rest all works as is.

The last thing to do is to update the movie-listing page so it contains links to the new `details3.cfm` page. Listing 10.15 contains the revised movie listing code (based on `movies6.cfm`). Save it as `movies8.cfm`, and then execute it to see a page similar to the one shown in Figure 10.17.

Listing 10.15 `movies8.cfm`—Data Drill-Down Results Page

```
<!---
Name:        movies8.cfm
Author:      Ben Forta (ben@forta.com)
Description: Data drill-down
```

Listing 10.15 (CONTINUED)

```
Created:      07/01/07
--->

<!--- Get movie list from database --->
<cfquery name="movies" datasource="ows" result="result">
SELECT FilmID, MovieTitle, PitchText,
        Summary, DateInTheaters
FROM Films
ORDER BY MovieTitle
</cfquery>

<!--- Create HTML page --->
<html>
<head>
 <title>Orange Whip Studios - Movie List</title>
</head>
<body>

<!--- Start table --->
<table>
 <tr>
  <th colspan="2">
   <font size="+2">
   <cfoutput>
   Movie List (#result.RecordCount# movies)
   </cfoutput>
   </font>
  </th>
 </tr>
 <!--- loop through movies --->
 <cfoutput query="movies">
  <tr bgcolor="##cccccc">
   <td>
    <strong>
    #CurrentRow#:
    <a href="details3.cfm?FilmID=#URLEncodedFormat(Trim(FilmID))#">#MovieTitle#</a>
    </strong>
    <br>
    #PitchText#
   </td>
   <td>
    #DateFormat(DateInTheaters)#
   </td>
  </tr>
  <tr>
   <td colspan="2">
    <font size="-2">#Summary#</font>
   </td>
  </tr>
 </cfoutput>
 <!--- End of movie loop --->
</table>

</body>
</html>
```

Figure 10.17

Dynamically generated URLs make creating data drill-down interfaces easy.

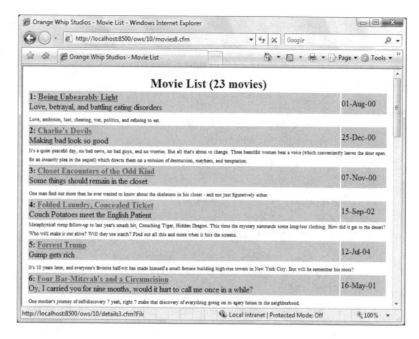

Just two changes have been made in Listing 10.15. The SELECT statement in the `<cfquery>` now also retrieves the FilmID column—you need that to pass to the details page. (You will recall that the details page needs the FilmID passed as a URL parameter.)

The display of MovieTitle has been changed to read

```
<a href="details3.cfm?FilmID=#URLEncodedFormat(Trim(FilmID))#">
#MovieTitle#</a>
```

The HTML `<a href>` tag is used to create links to other pages. The text between the `<a>` and `</a>` tags is clickable, and when it's clicked, the user is taken to the URL specified in the href attribute. So, the tag `<a href="details3.cfm">Click here</a>` displays the text Click here, which, if clicked, takes the user to page details3.cfm.

But you need FilmID to be passed to the details page, so for FilmID 1 the href needed would read

```
<a href="details3.cfm?FilmID=1">Being Unbearably Light</a>
```

And for FilmID 2 it would have to be

```
<a href="details3.cfm?FilmID=2">Charlie's Devils</a>
```

These links are created using the FilmID column so that the URL parameter FilmID is correctly populated with the appropriate value for each movie. As ColdFusion loops through the movies, it creates a link for each one of them. The links all point to the same page—details3.cfm. The only thing that differs is the value passed to the FilmID parameter, and this value is then used in details3.cfm to display the correct movie. So, for the movie with FilmID of 1, the URL correctly becomes

```
<a href="details3.cfm?FilmID=1">Being Unbearably Light</a>
```

Try it out; you should be able to click any movie to see the details and then click the link at the bottom of the details page to get back.

Pretty impressive for just two files containing fewer than 150 lines of ColdFusion code (including all HTML and comments).

NOTE

You probably noticed that when constructing URLs for an HREF, two functions were used, `Trim()` and `URLEncodedFormat()`, instead of just referring to the column directly.

`Trim()` was used to get rid of any extra spaces (if any existed). URLs have size limitations, and care should be taken to not waste URL space.

The `URLEncodedFormat()` function is even more important. As you already know, `?` is used to separate the URL from any parameters passed to it, `=` is used to assign parameter values, and `&` is used to separate parameters. Of course, this means that these characters can't be used within URL parameter values; many others can't be used, either (spaces, periods, and so on).

So how are these values passed? They're passed using a special format in which characters are replaced by a set of numbers that represent them. On the receiving end, the numbers can be converted back to the original characters (and ColdFusion does this for you automatically).

The `URLEncodedFormat()` function takes a string and returns a version of it that is URL safe.

When you populate a URL from a variable (any variable, including a database column), you run the risk that the values used might contain these illegal characters—characters that need to be converted. Therefore, you always should use `URLEncodedFormat()` (as was done in the previous example) so that if any invalid characters exist, they will be converted automatically and transparently. (Even in this chapter's example, in which you know `FilmID` contains only numbers that are safe, it still pays to encode the values in case someone changes something someday.)

Displaying Data Using Frames

Another form of data drill-down involves the use of HTML *frames*. Frames enable you to split your browser window in two or more windows and control what gets displayed within each. ColdFusion templates are very well suited for use within frames.

NOTE

Frames have proven to be rather unpopular, and most large public-facing and high-profile applications avoid their use. But frames are indeed useful, and understanding how they can be used in dynamic data-driven drill-down applications remains important. As such, they are briefly covered here.

Creating frames involves creating multiple templates (or HTML pages). Each window in a frame typically displays a different template; you need two templates if you have two windows. In addition, one more page is always used to lay out and create the frames.

When the frames are created, each window is titled with a unique name. In a non-framed window, the new page is opened in the same window every time you select a hyperlink, replacing whatever contents were there previously. In a framed window, you can use the window name to control the destination for any output.

Figure 10.18

Frames-based interfaces are effective for data drill-down applications.

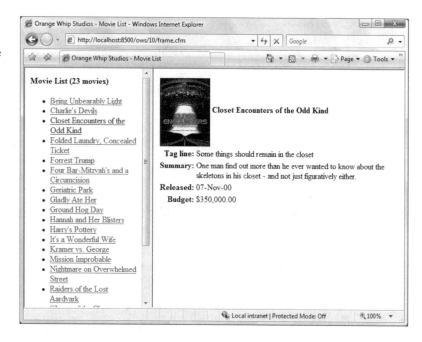

Figure 10.18 shows a frames-based version of the movie listing application. As you can see, movies are listed on the left, and when a movie is selected its details are displayed on the right.

Now that you know how frames work, the first thing you need to do is create the template to define and create the frames. The code for template `frame.cfm` is shown in Listing 10.16.

This template first defines the frames. `<frameset cols="250,*">` creates two columns (or windows) —one 250 pixels wide and the other as wide as the remaining space allows.

TIP

Sizes also can be specified as percentages, so `<frameset cols="50%,50%">` would create two windows, each 50 percent of the width of the browser.

Listing 10.16 `frame.cfm`—ColdFusion-Powered Frames

```
<!---
Name:        frame.cfm
Author:      Ben Forta (ben@forta.com)
Description: Frames for frames-based data drill-down
Created:     07/01/07
--->

<html>
<head>
 <title>Orange Whip Studios - Movie List</title>
</head>

<!--- frames --->
```

Listing 10.16 (CONTINUED)

```
<frameset cols="250,*">
 <frame name="left" src="frame_movies.cfm">
 <frame name="right" src="frame_blank.cfm">
</frameset>

</html>
```

The two columns are then defined: `<frame name="left" src="frame_movies.cfm">` creates the left frame; the name attribute names the window; and the src attribute specifies the name of the template to initially display within the window when the frame is first displayed. Listing 10.17 contains the code for the file frame_movies.cfm.

Listing 10.17 frame_movies.cfm—Movie List for Left Frame

```
<!---
Name:        frame_movies.cfm
Author:      Ben Forta (ben@forta.com)
Description: Left frame for data drill-down
Created:     07/01/07
--->

<!--- Get movie list from database --->
<cfquery name="movies" datasource="ows" result="result">
SELECT FilmID, MovieTitle
FROM Films
ORDER BY MovieTitle
</cfquery>

<body>

<!--- title and movie count --->
<cfoutput>
<strong>
Movie List (#result.RecordCount# movies)
</strong>
</cfoutput>

<!--- Movie list --->
<ul>
 <cfoutput query="movies">
 <li><a href="frame_details.cfm?filmid=#URLEncodedFormat(Trim(FilmID))#"
        target="right">#MovieTitle#</a>
 </cfoutput>
</ul>

</body>
```

No movie is selected when the frame is first displayed, and therefore no information exists to display in the details window (the right frame). You obviously can't display movie information in that frame before the user selects the movie to view, so instead you display an empty page. `SRC="frame_blank.cfm"` loads a blank page in the frame named right, the source for which is shown in Listing 10.18.

Listing 10.18 `frame_blank.cfm`—Initial Blank Right Frame

```
<!---
Name:        frame_blank.cfm
Author:      Ben Forta (ben@forta.com)
Description: Blank initial frame content
Created:     07/01/07
--->

<body>
</body>
```

Listing 10.17 (`frame_movies.cfm`) contains code similar to the code used in previous listings in this chapter. The only difference is the link itself. The `<a>` tag now contains a new attribute: `target="right"`. `target` specifies the name of the target window in which to open the URL. Because you named the right window `right` (you named the left window `left`), when a link is clicked in the left window, the appropriate URL is opened in the right window.

TIP

Frames can be named with any names you want, but be careful not to reuse frame names unless you want to reuse the same frame. To open links in a new window (effectively creating a frame as needed), use the target of **_new**.

The link itself is a file named `frame_details.cfm` (a modified version of the details files created earlier). Listing 10.19 contains the source for this file.

Listing 10.19 `frame_details.cfm`—Movie Details for Right Frame

```
<!---
Name:        frame_details.cfm
Author:      Ben Forta (ben@forta.com)
Description: Detail for frames-based data drill-down
Created:     07/01/07
--->

<!--- Make sure FilmID was passed --->
<cfif not IsDefined("URL.filmid")>
 <!--- This should never happen --->
 <cflocation url="frame_blank.cfm">
</cfif>

<!--- Get a movie from database --->
<cfquery name="movie" datasource="ows" result="result">
SELECT FilmID, MovieTitle,
       PitchText, Summary,
       DateInTheaters, AmountBudgeted
FROM Films
WHERE FilmID=#URL.FilmID#
</cfquery>

<!--- Make sure have a movie --->
<cfif result.RecordCount IS 0>
 <!--- This should never happen --->
  <cflocation url="frame_blank.cfm">
</cfif>
```

Listing 10.19 (CONTINUED)

```
<!--- Build image paths --->
<cfset image_src="../images/f#movie.FilmID#.gif">
<cfset image_path=ExpandPath(image_src)>

<!--- Create HTML page --->
<body>

<!--- Display movie details --->
<cfoutput query="movie">

<table>
 <tr>
  <td colspan="2">
   <!--- Check of image file exists --->
   <cfif FileExists(image_path)>
    <!--- If it does, display it --->
    <img src="../images/f#filmid#.gif"
       alt="#movietitle#"
       align="middle">
   </cfif>
   <strong>#MovieTitle#</strong>
  </td>
 </tr>
 <tr valign="top">
  <th align="right">Tag line:</th>
  <td>#PitchText#</td>
 </tr>
 <tr valign="top">
  <th align="right">Summary:</th>
  <td>#Summary#</td>
 </tr>
 <tr valign="top">
  <th align="right">Released:</th>
  <td>#DateFormat(DateInTheaters)#</td>
 </tr>
 <tr valign="top">
  <th align="right">Budget:</th>
  <td>#DollarFormat(AmountBudgeted)#</td>
 </tr>
</table>

</cfoutput>

</body>
```

Just like the code for frame_blank.cfm, the code for frame_details.cfm is missing `<html>...</html>`, and `<head><title>...</title></head>`.

Listing 10.18 should be self-explanatory by this point. The only real change here is that if no FilmID is passed, or if FilmID is invalid (neither condition should ever actually occur, but it pays to be safe), file blank.cfm is loaded. You could change this to display an appropriate error message if you want.

After you have created all four files (`frame.cfm`, `frame_blank.cfm`, `frame_movies.cfm`, and `frame_details.cfm`), execute the application in your browser by going to the following URL:

```
http://localhost:8500/ows/10/frame.cfm
```

You should see a screen like the one previously in Figure 10.18. Try clicking any link on the left; the appropriate movie will be displayed on the right.

And there you have it—two simple tags, `<cfquery>` and `<cfoutput>`, generating any output you can imagine.

Debugging Dynamic Database Queries

Before we finish this chapter, there is something you should be aware of. Look at the following code:

```
<!--- Get a movie from database --->
<cfquery name="movie" datasource="ows">
SELECT FilmID, MovieTitle,
       PitchText, Summary,
       DateInTheaters, AmountBudgeted
FROM Films
WHERE FilmID=#URL.FilmID#
</cfquery>
```

As you now know, this code builds a dynamic SQL statement—the expression `#URL.FilmID#` is replaced by the contents of that variable to construct a complete SQL SELECT statement at runtime.

This particular example is a simple one; a single expression is used in a simple WHERE clause. But as the complexity of the expressions (or the number of them) increases, so does the chance that you'll introduce problems in your SQL. And to find these problems, you'll need to know exactly what SQL was generated by ColdFusion—taking into account all dynamic processing.

I already showed you one way to obtain the dynamically generated SQL (using the optional `<cfquery>` result attribute). But here is another option.

In Chapter 3, "Accessing the ColdFusion Administrator," I mentioned the debugging screens (and told you that we'd use them in this chapter). The debugging screens can be used to append debug output to the bottom of generated pages, as seen in Figure 10.19.

As you can see, the appended output contains database query information (including the SQL, number of rows retrieved, and execution time), page execution time, passed parameters, CGI variables, and much more.

To try this for yourself, see Chapter 3 for instructions on turning on debug output. Once enabled, execute any page in your browser and the debug output will be appended automatically.

Figure 10.19

Dynamic SQL information is displayed along with the standard ColdFusion debugging output.

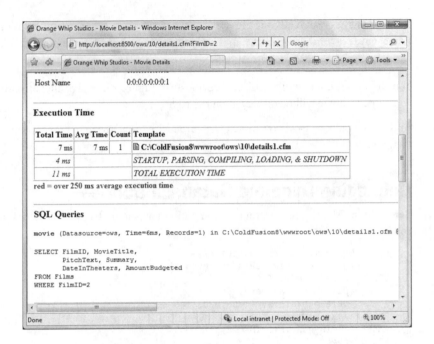

If you are browsing files within Dreamweaver the debug output will be displayed in the results window beneath the editor.

Most ColdFusion developers find that the tags you have learned thus far, `<cfquery>`, `<cfoutput>`, `<cfset>`, `<cfif>`, and `<cflocation>`, account for almost all the CFML code they ever write. As such, it's highly recommended that you try every example in this chapter before proceeding.

CHAPTER 11

The Basics of Structured Development

You have now seen just how easy dynamic page development is using ColdFusion. Combining SQL queries (even dynamically created queries) and output code is the key to building just about any Web-based applications.

We still have much to cover, but before going any further I'd like to take a little detour to revisit dynamic page generation and consider structured development.

Understanding Structured Development

The best way to understand structured development—what it does and the problems it solves—is to look at an example. Listing 11.1 should be familiar; it's the first data-driven example we looked at in Chapter 10, "Creating Data-Driven Pages."

Listing 11.1   `movies1.cfm`—The Basic Movie List

```
<!---
Name:        movies1.cfm
Author:      Ben Forta (ben@forta.com)
Description: First data-driven Web page
Created:     07/01/07
--->

<!--- Get movie list from database --->
<cfquery name="movies" datasource="ows">
SELECT MovieTitle
FROM Films
ORDER BY MovieTitle
</cfquery>

<!--- Create HTML page --->
<html>
<head>
```

Listing 11.1 (CONTINUED)

```
  <title>Orange Whip Studios - Movie List</title>
  </head>

  <body>

  <h1>Movie List</h1>

  <!--- Display movie list --->
  <cfoutput query="movies">
  #MovieTitle#<br>
  </cfoutput>

  </body>
  </html>
```

As explained in Chapter 10, this code first retrieves data from a database, then loops through the returned results, outputting one movie at a time. `#MovieTitle#` in the `<cfoutput>` loop refers to the `MovieTitle` column in the `Films` database table, the column retrieved in the `<cfquery>` tag.

Simple, right? Maybe not. As innocent as Listing 11.1 looks, the makings of a developer's nightmare lurk in its depths. Let me explain.

Consider what would happen if the database table changed. Maybe you had to rename a column; or maybe you were rethinking your table layout and needed to split a table into multiple tables; or maybe your field name was `Movie Title` (with a space, which will work in some databases, but is a really bad practice) and you needed to change it to a legal name; or...

You get the idea. If the table field name changed, any and all SQL that referred to that field would have to change too. As we saw in Chapter 10, when you build applications you end up with references to database tables in lot of different files very quickly. If a table changes, each file that referred to that table would need to change. Failure to do so would generate errors because the SQL would be invalid.

"No problem," you think. "A quick find-and-replace will locate all those queries." And you may be right; locating every `<cfquery>` in your application isn't that difficult. Dreamweaver—and just about any editor out there—will allow searching across multiple files and folders.

But that won't be enough. Why? Because if `MovieTitle` were changed you'd need to update your SQL and any CFML code that refers to that column. That `#MovieTitle#` in the `<cfoutput>` block would need updating too.

"Okay," you think, "I can do a search for `#MovieTitle#` as well, and do another find-and-replace." But that won't work, because you'd also need to find code like this:

```
  <cfoutput>#UCase(MovieTitle)#</cfoutput>
```

and this

```
  <cfset display="Title: " & MovieTitle>
```

and more.

Single-Tier Applications

The problem with the code in Listing 11.1 (and indeed, all of the code written in the last chapter) is that the presentation code is closely tied to the data access code. Developers refer to this type of application as being *single tiered*. Basically there is one layer or tier to the application, and it contains everything from database code to application logic.

→ The processing of the guessing game in Chapter 9, "Programming with CFML," is an example of application logic.

For simple applications, this may not be a problem. But as applications grow in complexity and size, so does the likelihood of something breaking later when you least expect it. Too many applications have been broken by simple changes in one part of an application that had unforeseen implications elsewhere.

And the problem isn't just the risk of something breaking. Take a look at the SQL code used in the various <cfquery> tags in the listing in Chapter 10. You'll notice that they are all similar and many are exactly the same, copied from file to file. That isn't efficient use of code. If you were to tweak a query—perhaps to improve performance—you'd need to do so for lots of queries. If you were to make security-related changes to your queries you'd need to do those all over the place too, and more.

→ The security issues to be aware of when using <cfquery> and dynamically constructed SQL will be explained in Chapter 41, "More About SQL and Queries," online.

So we have two different but related problems: presentation and content are too closely coupled; and code is repeated multiple times in multiple files.

Fortunately, there is a single solution to both problems.

Multi-Tier Applications

As we said, a single-tiered application is just that, with everything thrown into a single tier. A *multi-tiered* application (or an *n-tier* application) is an application that is broken into different layers, each responsible for just part of the complete application.

This may sound complex, bit it needn't be. Consider the code in Listing 11.1 (and all of the data-driven code in Chapter 10). That code could be broken up as follows:

- Data is stored in the database.

- All database access queries are stored in a special file. This file does no data presentation (it doesn't generate HTML, for example) and all database access is via this file.

- All presentation (the HTML and <cfoutput> blocks) goes in another file. This file doesn't contain any database interaction; rather, it relies on the previous file for that.

Breaking applications into tiers forces developers to think about data and application logic differently than presentation, and this is a good thing. Consider the following:

- If you made changes to a back-end database, only code in the data access layer would need to change; presentation code would not.

- As the same data access code can be used by multiple presentation files, any changes made once will be applied to all uses of that code.

- You're free to change the presentation at will, be it colors, tables, adding alternative client technologies (like Macromedia Flash), or more. These changes are presentation-tier changes, so the database access code will remain as is.

I know this sounds a little abstract, but bear with me. It will all make sense in a moment. The key is a special type of file called a ColdFusion Component.

Introducing ColdFusion Components

Like the ColdFusion templates you have already seen, ColdFusion Components are ColdFusion files that you create and use. Both are plain text files and both contain CFML code, but that's where the similarities end.

- ColdFusion templates have no fixed format, and can contain all sorts of tags in any order. ColdFusion Components have a very strict and rigid format.

- ColdFusion templates are processed starting at the top of the file and working downward. ColdFusion Components have one or more starting and ending points, essentially different blocks of functionality within a single file.

- ColdFusion templates have a `.cfm` extension. ColdFusion Components have a `.cfc` extension.

- ColdFusion templates are designed to be invoked by a user (in a browser). ColdFusion Components are generally invoked by other code (and not by end users directly).

NOTE

If you have experience with object-oriented development and are familiar with the concept of objects, much of this will be familiar. ColdFusion Components are a form of object, essentially providing the basics of object functionality without the pain associated with so many object-oriented languages. If you have no idea what an object is, don't let that scare you. In true form, ColdFusion makes this all as simple as CFML.

You will be using ColdFusion Components (CFCs for short) extensively throughout the rest of this book. In this chapter we will revisit examples from the previous chapter, this time using CFCs.

As already explained, CFCs are plain text files, so they can be created using any editor, including Dreamweaver. However, Dreamweaver comes with sophisticated built-in support for creating and using CFCs, and we'll use these features shortly.

NOTE

Developers use the term *refactor* to describe the process of taking applications and restructuring them to make them more reusable and more efficient.

Creating Your First CFC

To create ColdFusion Components, you need to learn some important new CFML tags. We'll start by creating a CFC manually. Later in the chapter you will get to use Dreamweaver's CFC wizard.

NOTE

As before, examples in this chapter use the data in the ows data sources and database. These must be present before continuing.

All the files created in this chapter need to go in a directory named 11 under the application root (the ows directory under the Web root).

The first thing you need to create a ColdFusion Component is a new file, so create a file named intro.cfc in the 11 folder. Delete any automatically generated content, and make sure that the file is empty.

The `<cfcomponent>` Tag

ColdFusion Components are defined using a tag named `<cfcomponent>`. (Intuitive, eh?) All of the code that makes up the CFC must be placed in between `<cfcomponent>` and `</cfcomponent>` tags (Listing 11.2). Nothing may be placed before the opening `<cfcomponent>` or after the closing `</cfcomponent>`.

Listing 11.2   `intro.cfc`—Introduction CFC Step 1

```
<!--- This is the introductory CFC --->
<cfcomponent>

</cfcomponent>
```

Once you have typed in this code, save your new file as intro.cfc. You have just created a ColdFusion Component. It does absolutely nothing at this point, but it's a ColdFusion Component nonetheless.

TIP

I just stated that nothing can be before the opening `<cfcomponent>` or after the closing `</cfcomponent>`, but as you can see in Listing 11.2 that isn't entirely accurate. No code may be outside of those tags, but comments are indeed allowed (and should be used).

The `<cffunction>` Tag

ColdFusion Components usually contain one or more *functions* (often called *methods*; the two terms are effectively interchangeable). A function is simply a block of code that performs an operation, and usually returns results. Each function is defined using a tag named `<cffunction>` and terminated with the matching closing tag `</cffunction>`.

`<cffunction>` takes a series of attributes, but only two are really important:

- name is the name of the function (it must be unique within the CFC; the same method name may be used in two different CFCs but not twice in the same CFC).

- returntype is the type of the results that will be returned (string, date, array, query, etc.).

Listing 11.3 is `intro.cfc` again, but this time we've introduced three functions.

Listing 11.3 `intro.cfc`—Introduction CFC Step 2

```
<!--- This is the introductory CFC --->
<cfcomponent>

<!--- Get today's date --->
<cffunction name="today" returntype="date">

</cffunction>

<!--- Get tomorrow's date --->
<cffunction name="tomorrow" returntype="date">

</cffunction>

<!--- Get yesterday's date --->
<cffunction name="yesterday" returntype="date">

</cffunction>

</cfcomponent>
```

As you can see, each function is defined with a pair of `<cffunction>` tags. The functions in Listing 11.3 have no content yet. If there were content—and there will be shortly—it would go in between those tags. Each function is uniquely named, and each function has its return data type specified. In this example all three functions return a `date`, today's date, tomorrow's date, and yesterday's date, respectively.

TIP

The `returntype` attribute may be omitted, but you should get into the habit of always defining the return type. This provides greater error checking and will ensure safer function use.

The `<cfreturn>` Tag

When a ColdFusion Component is used, the name of the function to be executed is specified. Any code in that function is processed, and a result is returned back to the calling code. To return data, a `<cfreturn>` tag is used. Listing 11.4 is a modified version of the previous listing, this time with `<cfreturn>` tags included in the body.

Listing 11.4 `intro.cfc`—Introduction CFC Step 3

```
<!--- This is the introductory CFC --->
<cfcomponent>

<!--- Get today's date --->
<cffunction name="today" returntype="date">
    <cfreturn Now()>
</cffunction>

<!--- Get tomorrow's date --->
<cffunction name="tomorrow" returntype="date">
```

```
    <cfreturn DateAdd("d", 1, Now())>
  </cffunction>

  <!--- Get yesterday's date --->
  <cffunction name="yesterday" returntype="date">
    <cfreturn DateAdd("d", -1, Now())>
  </cffunction>

</cfcomponent>
```

Usually CFC functions contain lots of processing and then a result is returned by `<cfreturn>`. But that need not be the case, as seen here. These three functions have single-line bodies, expressions being calculated right within `<cfreturn>` tags. The `today` function returns `Now()`, `tomorrow` uses `DateAdd()` to add 1 day to `Now()`. `yesterday` adds `-1` day to `Now()`, essentially subtracting a day from today's date.

→ The `Now()` function was introduced in Chapter 8, "The Basics of CFML."

Of course, performing calculations in the returned expression is optional, and this code:

```
  <!--- Get tomorrow's date --->
  <cffunction name="tomorrow" returntype="date">
    <cfreturn DateAdd("d", 1, Now())>
  </cffunction>
```

could have been written as:

```
  <!--- Get tomorrow's date --->
  <cffunction name="tomorrow" returntype="date">
    <cfset result=DateAdd("d", 1, Now())>
    <cfreturn result>
  </cffunction>
```

This latter form is what most CFC functions tend to look like.

TIP

Every CFC function should have one–and only one–`<cfreturn>` tag. Avoid the bad practice of having multiple `<cfreturn>` tags in a single function.

TIP

Technically, functions need not return a result, but best practices dictate that every CFC function return something, even if it is a simple true/false flag.

The `<cfargument>` Tag

The functions defined thus far are simple ones, in that they accept no data and return a result. But many of the functions that you'll create will need to accept data. For example, if you were creating a CFC function that returned movie details, you'd need to pass the desired movie ID to the function.

In CFC lingo, passed data are called *arguments* and the tag that is used to define arguments is the `<cfargument>` tag. If used, `<cfargument>` must be the very first code within a `<cffunction>`, and multiple `<cfargument>` tags may be used if needed.

The following code snippet demonstrates the use of `<cfargument>`:

```
<cfargument name="radius" type="numeric" required="yes">
```

This code (which would go into a `<cffunction>`) defines an argument named `radius` that is required and must be a `numeric` value. `type` and `required` are both optional, and if not specified then any type will be accepted, as would no value at all.

To demonstrate the use of arguments, here is a complete function:

```
<!--- Perform geometric calculations --->
<cffunction name="geometry" returntype="struct">
    <!--- Need a radius --->
    <cfargument name="radius" type="numeric" required="yes">
    <!--- Define result variable --->
    <cfset var result=StructNew()>
    <!--- Save radius --->
    <cfset result.radius=radius>
    <!--- First circle --->
    <cfset result.circle=StructNew()>
    <!--- Calculate circle circumference --->
    <cfset result.circle.circumference=2*Pi()*radius>
    <!--- Calculate circle area --->
    <cfset result.circle.area=Pi()*(radius^2)>
    <!--- Now sphere --->
    <cfset result.sphere=StructNew()>
    <!--- Calculate sphere volume --->
    <cfset result.sphere.volume=(4/3)*Pi()*(radius^3)>
    <!--- Calculate sphere surface area --->
    <cfset result.sphere.surface=4*result.circle.area>
    <!--- Return it --->
    <cfreturn result>
</cffunction>
```

The `geometry` function performs a series of geometric calculations. Provide it with a `radius` value and it will return a structure containing two structures. The first is named `circle` and contains the calculated circumference and area of a circle of the specified `radius`. The second is named `sphere` and contains the calculated surface area and volume of a sphere of the specified `radius`.

If all that sounds like something from a long-forgotten math class, don't worry. The point isn't the geometry itself, but the fact that these calculations can be buried within a CFC function. (That, and the fact that I really do love math.)

As before, the function is named using the `<cffunction>` `name` attribute, and this time `returntype="struct"` (a structure). The `<cfargument>` tag accepts a required `numeric` value as the radius.

The code then uses the following code to define a structure named `result` that will contain the values to be returned:

```
<!--- Define result variable --->
<cfset var result=StructNew()>
```

→ Structures and the `StructNew()` function were introduced in Chapter 8.

The rest of the code defines two nested structures, and then uses <cfset> tags to perform the actual calculations (saving the results of the calculations into the result structure). The last line of code returns the structure with a <cfreturn> tag.

NOTE

You may have noticed that the <cfset> used to create the result structure included the word var. We'll explain this in later chapters. For now, suffice to say that all local variables within CFC functions should be defined using var as seen here.

Listing 11.5 contains the final complete intro.cfc.

Listing 11.5 intro.cfc—Introduction CFC Step 4

```
<!--- This is the introductory CFC --->
<cfcomponent>

<!--- Get today's date --->
<cffunction name="today" returntype="date">
   <cfreturn Now()>
</cffunction>

<!--- Get tomorrow's date --->
<cffunction name="tomorrow" returntype="date">
   <cfreturn DateAdd("d", 1, Now())>
</cffunction>

<!--- Get yesterday's date --->
<cffunction name="yesterday" returntype="date">
   <cfreturn DateAdd("d", -1, Now())>
</cffunction>

<!--- Perform geometric calculations --->
<cffunction name="geometry" returntype="struct">
   <!--- Need a radius --->
   <cfargument name="radius" type="numeric" required="yes">
   <!--- Define result variable --->
   <cfset var result=StructNew()>
   <!--- Save radius --->
   <cfset result.radius=radius>
   <!--- First circle --->
   <cfset result.circle=StructNew()>
   <!--- Calculate circle circumference --->
   <cfset result.circle.circumference=2*Pi()*radius>
   <!--- Calculate circle area --->
   <cfset result.circle.area=Pi()*(radius^2)>
   <!--- Now sphere --->
   <cfset result.sphere=StructNew()>
   <!--- Calculate sphere volume --->
   <cfset result.sphere.volume=(4/3)*Pi()*(radius^3)>
   <!--- Calculate sphere surface area --->
   <cfset result.sphere.surface=4*result.circle.area>
   <!--- Return it --->
   <cfreturn result>
</cffunction>

</cfcomponent>
```

You now have a complete ColdFusion Component containing four methods. Great—but how do you actually use your new creation?

Using ColdFusion Components

ColdFusion Components are used by other ColdFusion code, although rather than used, CFCs are said to be *invoked*. A special tag is used to invoke ColdFusion Components, and not surprisingly the tag is named `<cfinvoke>`. To invoke a ColdFusion Component you'll need to specify several things:

- The name of the CFC to be used.

- The name of the method to be invoked (CFCs may contain multiple methods).

- The name of a variable that should contain any returned data.

- In addition, if the CFC method being invoked accepts arguments, those arguments are to be provided.

Listing 11.6 is a simple file named `testcfc.cfm`. As its name suggests, it tests the CFC file you just created.

Listing 11.6   testcfc.cfm—CFC Tester Step 1

```
<!---
Name:        testcfc.cfm
Author:      Ben Forta (ben@forta.com)
Description: Quick CFC test
Created:     07/01/07
--->

<!--- Title --->
<h1>Testing intro.cfc</h1>

<!--- Get today's date --->
<cfinvoke component="intro"
          method="today"
          returnvariable="todayRet">

<!--- Output --->
<cfoutput>
Today is #DateFormat(todayRet)#<br>
</cfoutput>
```

Let's take a quick look at this code. The `<cfinvoke>` needs to know the name of the component to be used, and `component="intro"` tells ColdFusion to find a file named `intro.cfc` in the current folder. As already seen, CFCs can contain multiple functions, so ColdFusion needs to know which method in the CFC to invoke. `method="today"` tells ColdFusion to find the function named `today` and invoke it. `today` returns a value (today's date), and so `returnvariable="todayRet"` tells Cold-Fusion to save whatever `today` returns in a variable named `todayRet`.

NOTE

If the variable name specified in `returnvariable` doesn't exist, it will be created. If it does exist it will be overwritten.

When ColdFusion processes the `<cfinvoke>` tag it locates and opens the `intro.cfc` file, finds the `today` function, executes it, and saves the result in a variable named `todayRet`. The code then displays that value using a simple `<cfoutput>` block.

If you were to run `testcfc.cfm` you would see a result like the one in Figure 11.1.

Figure 11.1

CFC processing is hidden from ColdFusion-generated output.

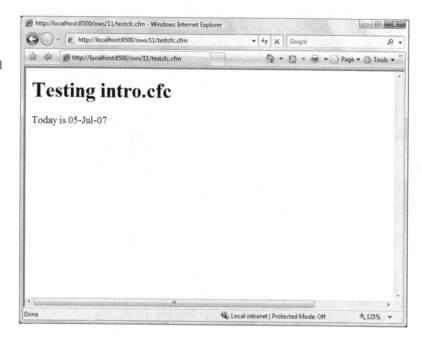

NOTE

Be sure to run the `.cfm` file and not the `.cfc` file or the results won't be what you expect.

Pretty simple, right? Well, it gets even simpler when using Dreamweaver.

Using Dreamweaver CFC Support

Dreamweaver features sophisticated support for ColdFusion Components. This includes:

- Drag-and-drop CFC method invocation
- Wizard-based CFC creation
- Support for CFC based recordsets

We'll now look at each of these.

Simplified CFC Method Invocation

You have seen how to use `<cfinvoke>` to invoke a ColdFusion Component method. You'll now learn how to invoke a CFC method without writing any code at all. Here are the steps:

1. Open the Dreamweaver Application panel, and select the Components tab. In the drop-down control at the top of that tab, make sure that CF Components is selected (and not Web Services) as seen in Figure 11.2.

Figure 11.2

The Components tab in the Application panel displays available ColdFusion Components.

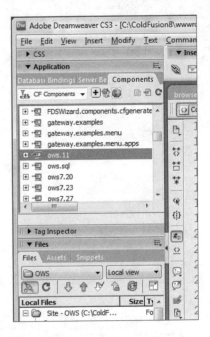

2. This tab displays a list of all known ColdFusion Components, ordered by the folder they are in. By default, every CFC known to ColdFusion is shown, but you can use two toggle buttons to select between all CFCs (click the little button with a picture of a globe) or just CFCs in the current site (click the little button with a picture of a house).

3. You should see a folder named ows.11 listed; ows.11 is folder 11 within folder ows (dot notation is used in folder path names).

4. Once you have located the folder, click the plus (+) button to its left to display the ColdFusion Components within it (there'll be just one named intro, the file created previously).

5. Click the plus (+) next to intro to display the methods it contains.

6. As seen in Figure 11.3, Dreamweaver lists all CFC methods, along with their return type, and any arguments (if a plus (+) is shown).

Figure 11.3

Components may be
expanded to display
methods (and
arguments if
applicable).

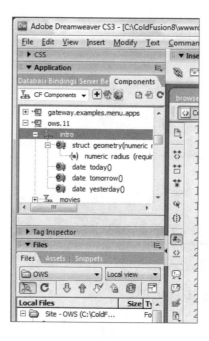

7. Make sure that file `testcfc.cfm` is open and visible in Dreamweaver, then select the
   `tomorrow()` method in the Components tab and drag it into the editor (after the existing
   `<cfinvoke>` and before the `<cfoutput>` block).

8. Dreamweaver will generate a complete `<cfinvoke>` tag for you, specifying the correct
   `component` and `method`, and defining a `returnvariable` of `tomorrowRet`.

9. Add the following code into the `<cfoutput>` block (after the existing line of code):

```
Tomorrow is #DateFormat(tomorrowRet)#<br>
```

`testcfc.cfm` should now look like Listing 11.7.

Listing 11.7   `testcfc.cfm`—CFC Tester Step 2

```
<!---
Name:       testcfc.cfm
Author:     Ben Forta (ben@forta.com)
Description: Quick CFC test
Created:    07/01/07
--->

<!--- Title --->
<h1>Testing intro.cfc</h1>

<!--- Get today's date --->
<cfinvoke component="intro"
          method="today"
          returnvariable="todayRet">
<!--- Get tomorrow's date --->
```

Listing 11.7 (CONTINUED)

```
<cfinvoke
 component="ows.11.intro"
 method="tomorrow"
 returnvariable="tomorrowRet">
</cfinvoke>

<!--- Output --->
<cfoutput>
Today is #DateFormat(todayRet)#<br>
Tomorrow is #DateFormat(tomorrowRet)#<br>
</cfoutput>
```

Run `testcfc.cfm`. You should see a page like the one in Figure 11.4.

Figure 11.4

Be sure to test ColdFusion Component invocations by executing test code.

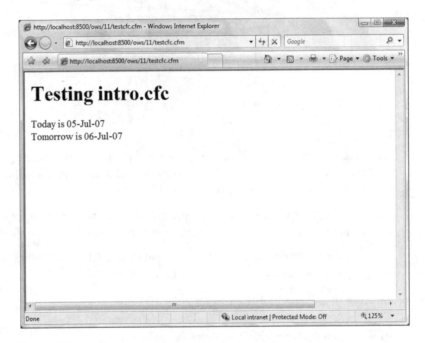

You'll notice that Dreamweaver generated a closing `</cfinvoke>` tag. This was not needed in our simple invocation, but it does no harm being there either.

NOTE

The CFC path generated by Dreamweaver is the full path (starting from the Web root). This is only required when accessing a component in another directory, but does no harm here. You can change `component="ows.11.intro"` to `component="intro"` if you like.

The ColdFusion Component method you just used is a simple one. It accepts no arguments and returns a simple value. Let's try this again, but now using a more complicated method, the `geometry` method. Here are the steps:

1. Locate the `ows.11.geometry` method in the Application panel's Components tab.

2. Drag the `geometry` method from the Application panel into the editor (you can place it the very end of the page).

3. Dreamweaver generates a `<cfinvoke>` that looks like this:

```
<cfinvoke
 component="ows.11.intro"
 method="geometry"
 returnvariable="geometryRet">
   <cfinvokeargument name="radius" value="enter_value_here"/>
</cfinvoke>
```

4. `<cfinvokeargument>` is used within `<cfinvoke>` tags to pass arguments to invoked methods. As the `geometry` method requires that an argument (the `radius`) be passed to it, Dreamweaver generates a `<cfinvokeargument>` tag. The argument `name` is automatically set by Dreamweaver (`name="radius"`), but you need to specify the `value`. So replace the words `enter_value_here` with a number of your choice (any positive number, for example, `10`).

5. The geometry method returns a structure, and the simplest way to see the results is to use `<cfdump>`, so add the following after the `</cfinvoke>` tag:

```
<!--- Display it --->
<cfdump var="#geometryRet#">
```

The final test code should look like Listing 11.8. Run the page. You should see output that looks like that in Figure 11.5.

Figure 11.5

Use `<cfdump>` to quickly display complex data types.

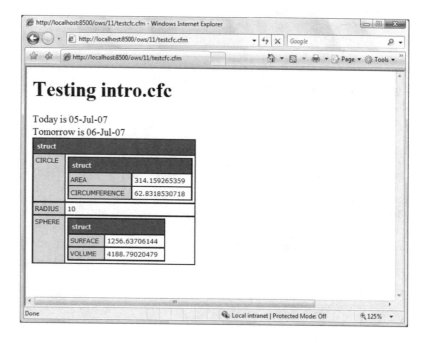

Listing 11.8　`testcfc.cfm`—CFC Tester Step 3

```
<!---
Name:        testcfc.cfm
Author:      Ben Forta (ben@forta.com)
Description: Quick CFC test
Created:     07/01/07
--->

<!--- Title --->
<h1>Testing intro.cfc</h1>

<!--- Get today's date --->
<cfinvoke component="intro"
          method="today"
          returnvariable="todayRet">
<!--- Get tomorrow's date --->
<cfinvoke
 component="ows.11.intro"
 method="tomorrow"
 returnvariable="tomorrowRet">
</cfinvoke>

<!--- Output --->
<cfoutput>
Today is #DateFormat(todayRet)#<br>
Tomorrow is #DateFormat(tomorrowRet)#<br>
</cfoutput>
<!--- Geometry test --->
<cfinvoke
 component="ows.11.intro"
 method="geometry"
 returnvariable="geometryRet">
   <cfinvokeargument name="radius" value="10"/>
</cfinvoke>
<!--- Display it --->
<cfdump var="#geometryRet#">
```

Before we go any further, let's take another look at the invocation of the `geometry` method. This is the code generated by Dreamweaver:

```
<cfinvoke
 component="ows.11.intro"
 method="geometry"
 returnvariable="geometryRet">
   <cfinvokeargument name="radius" value="10"/>
</cfinvoke>
```

`<cfinvoke>` takes the name of the component, the method, and the name of the `returnvariable`, as it did previously. The `radius` that must be passed to `geometry` is passed using a `<cfinvokeargument>` tag that takes a `name` (the argument name) and a `value` (the value for that argument). If multiple arguments were needed then multiple `<cfinvokeargument>` tags could be used.

NOTE

You can now see why Dreamweaver inserted a closing `</cfinvoke>` tag, as this is needed when nested `<cfinvokeargument>` tags are used.

There is another way to pass arguments to a CFC method, without using `<cfinvokeargument>`. Take a look at this code snippet:

```
<cfinvoke
  component="ows.11.intro"
  method="geometry"
  radius="10"
  returnvariable="geometryRet">
```

This code is functionally identical to the previous snippet, but it doesn't use `<cfinvokeargument>`. Instead, it simply passes the argument as a `name=value` pair, in this case `radius="10"`. Although Dreamweaver generates the former when using drag-and-drop method selection; you are feel free to use either syntax.

TIP

Many developers find the name=value syntax better suited for simple methods without lots of arguments, and the `<cfinvokeargument>` better suited for more complex methods with lots of arguments (and possibly optional arguments).

As you have seen, Dreamweaver makes using existing ColdFusion Components very easy. Over time you will likely accumulate quite a collection of ColdFusion Components, and being able to simply select and invoke them is very handy.

Wizard-Based CFC Creation

You have now created a ColdFusion Component manually, and invoked that component both manually and using Dreamweaver-generated code. Now I'd like to show you how Dreamweaver can actually help you write ColdFusion Components too.

NOTE

In case you're wondering why I first made you do it manually and am only now showing you the shortcut, it's because ColdFusion Components are incredibly important, and a good understanding of exactly how they work (and the syntax used) is critical. Now that you know what CFCs are and how they are used, I can show you the shortcuts.

In Chapter 10 we created an application that listed all Orange Whip Studios movies, and allowed them to be clicked on to display more details. The final versions of those files (`movies8.cfm` and `details3.cfm` in the `10` folder) each contain `<cfquery>` tags, and refer to query columns in `<cfoutput>` blocks.

We'll now revisit that application, this time moving the database interaction out of the two `.cfm` files and into a new file named `movies.cfc`. But instead of creating `movies.cfc` from scratch, we'll use Dreamweaver's Create Component wizard. Here are the steps to follow:

1. Locate the Dreamweaver Application panel, and make sure the Components tab is selected (and the drop-down control shows CF Components).

2. Click the plus (+) button at the top of the tab to display the Create Component wizard.

3. The wizard contains multiple sections (screens) that are selected using the Sections list to the left. The first section is Components, and this is used to name the component (the `.cfc` file) and to specify its location (the folder it is to be placed in). In the Name field type `movies` (without the `.cfc` extension), and in the Component Directory field specify the full path to the `ows/11` folder (as seen in Figure 11.6).

Figure 11.6

The Create Component wizard first prompts for CFC name and location.

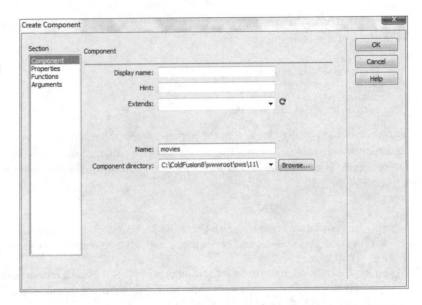

4. Now you need to define the methods needed. This is done in the Functions section, so select Functions from the Section list on the left to display that screen (seen in Figure 11.7).

Figure 11.7

The Create Component wizard's Functions screen is used to list CFC methods.

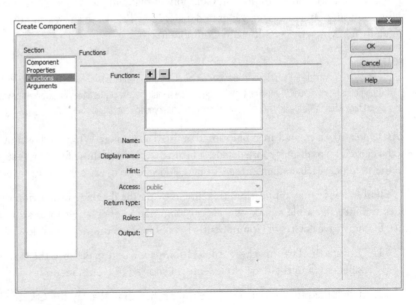

5. `movies.cfc` will need two methods, one to list all movies and one to return movie details. Click the plus (+) button twice to add two functions (as seen in Figure 11.8). You may now click on each function to specify its name and other attributes.

Figure 11.8

The Create Component wizard assigns default method names, which should be changed.

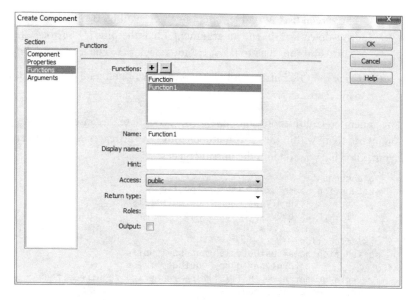

6. Click on the first function. Change the Name to List, and select query as the Return Type. You can ignore the other attributes for now.

7. Click on the second function. Change the Name to GetDetails, and select query as the Return Type.

8. The List method needs no arguments (it simply returns all movies), but GetDetails requires that a movie id be passed as an argument. Arguments are defined in the Arguments section, so click on Arguments in the Section list to display that screen (seen in Figure 11.9).

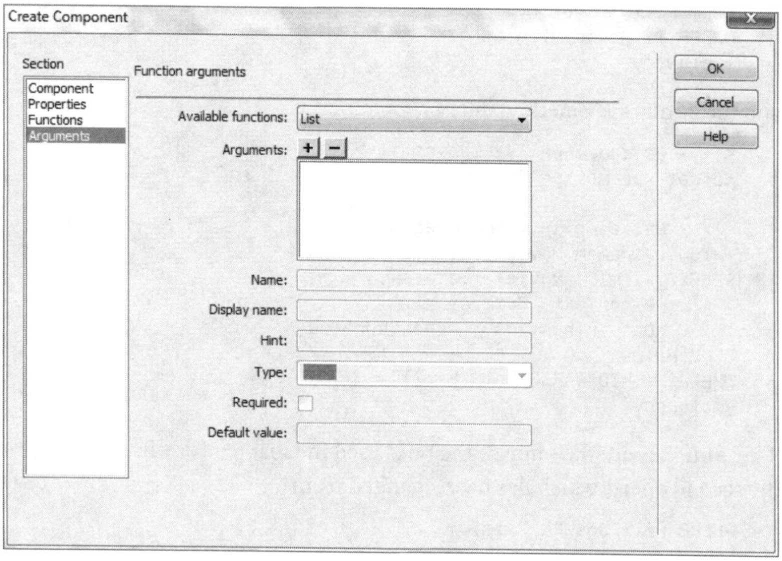

Figure 11.9

Method arguments are defined in the Create Component wizard's Arguments screen.

9. The screen lists Available functions (there will be two listed); select `GetDetails` from the drop-down list. To add an argument, click the plus (+) button. Change the Name to `FilmID` and the Type to `Numeric`, and check the `Required` check box.

10. Click the OK button, and Dreamweaver will generate a ColdFusion Component shell named `movies.cfc` in the `11` folder.

The generated ColdFusion Components isn't complete, because Dreamweaver can't know what you intend to do within the CFC methods. But Dreamweaver was able to create the following basic layout, allowing you to fill in the missing pieces:

```
<cfcomponent>
<cffunction name="List" access="public"
            returnType="query" output="false">
   <!--- List body --->
   <cfreturn >
  </cffunction>
<cffunction name="GetDetails" access="public"
            returnType="query" output="false">
   <cfargument name="FilmID" type="numeric" required="true">
   <!--- GetDetails body --->
   <cfreturn >
  </cffunction>
</cfcomponent>
```

Notice that Dreamweaver inserted comments where you need to place your method body code. You now need to insert a query into each of the methods. The `List` method query should be:

```
<!--- Define local variables --->
<cfset var movies="">

<!--- Get movie list from database --->
<cfquery name="movies" datasource="ows">
SELECT FilmID, MovieTitle, PitchText,
       Summary, DateInTheaters
FROM Films
ORDER BY MovieTitle
</cfquery>
```

and the `GetDetails` method query should be:

```
<!--- Define local variables --->
<cfset var movie="">

<!--- Get a movie from database --->
<cfquery name="movie" datasource="ows">
SELECT FilmID, MovieTitle,
       PitchText, Summary,
       DateInTheaters, AmountBudgeted
FROM Films
WHERE FilmID=#ARGUMENTS.FilmID#
</cfquery>
```

These queries are the same as the ones used in Chapter 10, with the exception of the `WHERE` clause in the second query, which has been changed from

```
WHERE FilmID=#URL.FilmID#
```

to

```
WHERE FilmID=#ARGUMENTS.FilmID#
```

as the `FilmID` is now a CFC method argument instead of a URL parameter.

TIP

Feel free to copy and paste the `<cfquery>` tags from `movies8.cfm` and `details3.cfm` in the `10` folder.

Now that each method contains its query, edit the `<cfreturn>` tag in each so that the query is returned. Listing 11.9 contains what your final edited `movies.cfc` should look like.

Listing 11.9 `movies.cfc`—Movie Data-Abstraction Component

```
<cfcomponent>

<cffunction name="List" access="public"
            returnType="query" output="false">

    <!--- Define local variables --->
    <cfset var movies="">

    <!--- Get movie list from database --->
    <cfquery name="movies" datasource="ows">
    SELECT FilmID, MovieTitle, PitchText,
           Summary, DateInTheaters
    FROM Films
    ORDER BY MovieTitle
    </cfquery>

    <cfreturn movies>
</cffunction>

<cffunction name="GetDetails" access="public"
            returnType="query" output="false">
    <cfargument name="FilmID" type="numeric" required="true">

    <!--- Define local variables --->
    <cfset var movies="">

    <!--- Get a movie from database --->
    <cfquery name="movie" datasource="ows">
    SELECT FilmID, MovieTitle,
           PitchText, Summary,
           DateInTheaters, AmountBudgeted
    FROM Films
    WHERE FilmID=#ARGUMENTS.FilmID#
    </cfquery>

    <cfreturn movie>
</cffunction>

</cfcomponent>
```

The code in Listing 11.9 should be quite familiar by now. It contains two methods, `List` and `GetDetails`. `List` executes a query to obtain all movies and returns that `movies` query. `GetDetails` accepts `FilmID` as an argument, then uses `<cfquery>` to retrieve that movie, then returns that `movie` query. Both methods populate local variables, the query results generated by `FilmID`, so those variables are first defined using `<cfset>` and the `FilmID` keyword (as mentioned previously).

TIP

Check the ColdFusion Components listed in the Dreamweaver Application panel's Components tab. It should show your new `movies.cfc` ready for use. If it does not, click the Refresh button (the one with the circular blue arrow) to update the list.

Now that you have `movies.cfc` complete, you need the `.cfm` pages that will invoke the CFC methods. Listing 11.10 contains `movies.cfm` (which is based on `10/movies8.cfm`) and Listing 11.11 contains `details.cfm` (which is based on `10/details3.cfm`).

TIP

To save time and typing, feel free to start by copying from the two aforementioned files in the `10` folder.

Listing 11.10 `movies.cfm`—CFC-Driven Movie List

```
<!---
Name:        movies.cfm
Author:      Ben Forta (ben@forta.com)
Description: CFC driven data drill-down
Created:     07/01/07
--->

<!--- Get movie list --->
<cfinvoke
 component="movies"
 method="List"
 returnvariable="movies">

<!--- Create HTML page --->
<html>
<head>
 <title>Orange Whip Studios - Movie List</title>
</head>

<body>

<!--- Start table --->
<table>
 <tr>
  <th colspan="2">
   <font size="+2">
   <cfoutput>
   Movie List (#Movies.RecordCount# movies)
   </cfoutput>
   </font>
  </th>
 </tr>
 <!--- loop through movies --->
 <cfoutput query="movies">
  <tr bgcolor="##cccccc">
   <td>
    <strong
```

Listing 11.10 (CONTINUED)

```
      #CurrentRow#:<a href="details.cfm?FilmID=
        #URLEncodedFormat(Trim(FilmID))#">#MovieTitle#</a>
    </strong>
    <br>
    #PitchText#
   </td>
   <td>
    #DateFormat(DateInTheaters)#
   </td>
  </tr>
  <tr>
   <td colspan="2">
    <font size="-2">#Summary#</font>
   </td>
  </tr>
 </cfoutput>
 <!--- End of movie loop --->
</table>

</body>
</html>
```

Listing 11.11 details.cfm—CFC-Driven Movie Details

```
<!---
Name:        details.cfm
Author:      Ben Forta (ben@forta.com)
Description: CFC driven data drill-down details
             with complete validation
Created:     07/01/07
--->

<!--- Movie list page --->
<cfset list_page="movies.cfm">

<!--- Make sure FilmID was passed --->
<cfif not IsDefined("URL.filmid")>
 <!--- it wasn't, send to movie list --->
 <cflocation url="#list_page#">
</cfif>

<!--- Get movie details --->
<cfinvoke
 component="movies"
 method="GetDetails"
 returnvariable="movie"
 FilmID="#URL.filmid#">

<!--- Make sure have a movie --->
<cfif movie.RecordCount IS 0>
 <!--- It wasn't, send to movie list --->
 <cflocation url="#list_page#">
</cfif>

<!--- Build image paths --->
```

Listing 11.11 (CONTINUED)

```cfml
<cfset image_src="../images/f#movie.FilmID#.gif">
<cfset image_path=ExpandPath(image_src)>

<!--- Create HTML page --->
<html>
<head>
 <title>Orange Whip Studios - Movie Details</title>
</head>

<body>

<!--- Display movie details --->
<cfoutput query="movie">

<table>
 <tr>
  <td colspan="2">
   <!--- Check of image file exists --->
   <cfif FileExists(image_path)>
    <!--- If it does, display it --->
    <img src="../images/f#filmid#.gif"
       alt="#movietitle#"
       align="middle">
   </cfif>
   <b>#MovieTitle#</b>
  </td>
 </tr>
 <tr valign="top">
  <th align="right">Tag line:</th>
  <td>#PitchText#</td>
 </tr>
 <tr valign="top">
  <th align="right">Summary:</th>
  <td>#Summary#</td>
 </tr>
 <tr valign="top">
  <th align="right">Released:</th>
  <td>#DateFormat(DateInTheaters)#</td>
 </tr>
 <tr valign="top">
  <th align="right">Budget:</th>
  <td>#DollarFormat(AmountBudgeted)#</td>
 </tr>
</table>

<p>

<!--- Link back to movie list --->
[<a href="#list_page#">Movie list</a>]

</cfoutput>

</body>
</html>
```

I'm not going to walk through all of Listings 11.10 and 11.11, as most of that code was explained in detail in Chapter 10. However, notice that in both listings the <cfquery> tags have been removed and replaced with <cfinvoke> tags. The <cfinvoke> in Listing 11.10 passes no arguments and receives a query as a result (which I named movies to match the original name so as to not have to change any other code). The <cfinvoke> in Listing 11.11 passes URL.FilmID as an argument to GetDetails (previously it had been used in a <cfquery> directly).

Run movies.cfm. The code should execute exactly as it did in Chapter 10, but this time you are running a multi-tiered application, one that will be much easier to manage and maintain in the future.

Now that we are done, let's consider the solution. Have we actually solved any problems? Haven't we merely moved the problem from one file to another? To go back to our original concern—the fact that data access code and presentation code were too closely tied—isn't that still the case? If a table column name changed, wouldn't presentation code still break?

Actually, we've made life much better. True, all we did was move the SQL from one file to another, but in doing so we reduced the number of times SQL statements occur, and also divorced the presentation code from the data access code. If a table column name did change, all you'd need to do is modify the method that accesses the data. The methods could still return the column names you expected previously (perhaps using SQL aliases, or by building queries manually), so while you'd need to update the relevant CFC methods, you should not need to update anything else at all. This is definitely a major improvement.

Using CFCs as Recordsets

Dreamweaver features all sorts of sophisticated page layout and code generation options, some of which were introduced in Chapter 2, "Choosing a Development Environment." Many of these features work with *recordsets* (Dreamweaver-speak for queries; the data returned by a <cfquery> tag is used by Dreamweaver as a recordset).

Dreamweaver can also use ColdFusion Component methods as a way to obtain recordsets. To demonstrate this, we'll create a movie-browsing application without writing any code at all (and leveraging the movies.cfc that you already created).

Here are the steps to follow:

1. Create a new file (in the 11 folder) named browse.cfm. Delete any auto-generated content from the file; make sure it is empty.

2. Open this new file (the Dreamweaver Application panel can't be used unless a file is open).

3. Locate the Dreamweaver Application panel and select the Bindings tab. No bindings will be listed.

4. Click the plus (+) button to display the available bindings types (as seen in Figure 11.10) and select Recordset (Query) to display the Recordset dialog.

Figure 11.10

Click plus to display available bindings types.

5. The Recordset dialog can be used to define a SQL statement, but we don't want to do that. Rather, we want to use ColdFusion Components, so click the CFC Query button to switch from the Recordset dialog to the CFC Query dialog (seen in Figure 11.11).

Figure 11.11

The CFC Query dialog is used to create CFC-driven bindings.

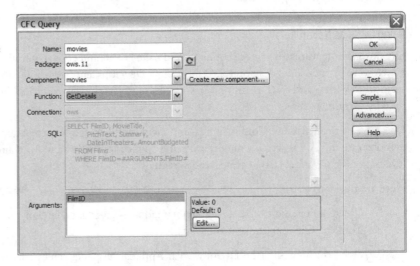

6. If you didn't have an existing ColdFusion Component to use, you could click the Create New Component button to quickly create a ready-to-use .cfc (complete with a <cfquery> tag written for you). However, we do have an existing .cfc, so there's no need to use that button now.

7. Change the Name to `movies` (this will be the name of the method `returnvariable`). The Package should be `ows.11` (the folder). Select the `Movies` component from the drop-down list, and select `List` from the Function drop-down list.

8. Click OK and Dreamweaver will insert a `<cfinvoke>` tag for you.

9. Notice that the CFC query is now listed in Application panel's Bindings tab, and you can even expand the query to display the individual column names (as seen in Figure 11.12). These can be dragged into the editor if needed.

Figure 11.12

Once defined, CFC Queries are listed in the Bindings tab, and may be expanded if needed.

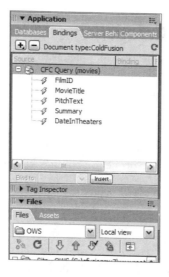

10. Now to add the data display. From the Dreamweaver Insert menu select Application Objects > Dynamic Data > Dynamic Table to display the Dynamic Table dialog (seen in Figure 11.13).

Figure 11.13

Recordset-driven tables can be defined in the Dynamic Table dialog.

11. Dreamweaver knows that the only available query is `movies` (returned by the `<cfinvoke>`), so that is already selected. The defaults are all right, so click OK to insert the data-driven HTML table.

12. The code could actually be run as is; it would display the first ten movies in a table. But let's add one more feature, record paging, so as to be able to move back and forth through the movie list. Place the cursor between the `<cfinvoke>` and the start of the HTML `<table>`.

13. From the Dreamweaver Insert menu select Application Objects > Recordset Paging > Recordset Navigation Bar to insert navigation code and links.

And that's it. Save the file and run `browse.cfm`. ColdFusion will display the movies and page browsing links using the `movies.cfc` created previously.

More On Using ColdFusion Components

You've now had firsthand experience with ColdFusion Components, and you'll be using them extensively as you work through this book. ColdFusion Components make it easy to tier applications, and this results in:

- Cleaner code

- More reusable code

- More maintainable code (code that is less prone to breakage when changes are made)

But before closing this chapter, there are a few additional points about ColdFusion Components worth mentioning.

Where to Save CFCs

The ColdFusion Components created in this chapter (and indeed, throughout this book) are stored within the work folder. This is ideal when learning ColdFusion, but in practice this isn't what you'd want to do.

Most developers create a specific `cfc` folder (or several of them) and store all common ColdFusion Components in them. This will make it easier to locate and maintain them. As you have seen, Dreamweaver automatically accommodates for path considerations when generating `<cfinvoke>` tags.

Unit Testing

One important benefit of ColdFusion Components not mentioned thus far is testing. As you build applications you'll want to test your work regularly. And the larger and more complex an application becomes, the harder testing becomes. This is even more problematic when code gets in the way. For example, if you were testing the SQL in a `<cfquery>` you wouldn't want HTML layout issues to unnecessarily complicate the testing.

Breaking code into tiers greatly simplifies testing. Once you've written your ColdFusion Component you can (and should) create a simple test page, one that doesn't have complex display code and simply invokes methods and dumps their output—much like we did in the `geometry` example earlier in this chapter. Experienced developers typically have simple test front-ends for each ColdFusion Component they create. This practice is highly recommended.

Documenting ColdFusion Components

As your ColdFusion Component collection grows, so will the uses you find for them. So will the number of developers who will want to take advantage of them, assuming you're working with other developers. As such, it is really important to document your ColdFusion Components, explaining what they do, what each method does, and what you expect passed to any arguments.

Documenting ColdFusion Components is so important that self-documenting features are built right into the tags used to create them. Each of the CFC tags used in this chapter, <cfcomponent>, <cffunction>, and <cfargument>, take an optional attribute named hint. As you can see in Listing 11.12, the hint attribute has been used to add little snippets of documentation to our movies.cfc file.

Listing 11.12 movies.cfc—Providing CFC Hints

```
<!--- Movie component --->
<cfcomponent hint="Movie database abstraction">

 <!--- List method --->
 <cffunction name="List" access="public"
             returnType="query" output="false"
             hint="List all movies">

  <!--- Define local variables --->
  <cfset var movies="">

  <!--- Get movie list from database --->
  <cfquery name="movies" datasource="ows">
  SELECT FilmID, MovieTitle, PitchText,
         Summary, DateInTheaters
  FROM Films
  ORDER BY MovieTitle
  </cfquery>
  <cfreturn movies>
 </cffunction>

 <!--- GetDetails method --->
 <cffunction name="GetDetails" access="public"
             returnType="query" output="false"
             hint="Get movie details for a specific movie">
 <cfargument name="FilmID" type="numeric"
             required="true" hint="Film ID">

  <!--- Define local variables --->
  <cfset var movie="">

  <!--- Get a movie from database --->
  <cfquery name="movie" datasource="ows">
  SELECT FilmID, MovieTitle,
         PitchText, Summary,
         DateInTheaters, AmountBudgeted
  FROM Films
  WHERE FilmID=#ARGUMENTS.FilmID#
  </cfquery>
  <cfreturn movie>
 </cffunction>

</cfcomponent>
```

So what do these hints do? They have absolutely no impact on the actual processing of the Cold-Fusion Components. Rather, they are used by ColdFusion to generate documentation on the fly, as seen in Figure 11.14.

Figure 11.14

ColdFusion auto-generates ColdFusion Component documentation using the information gleaned from the tags used to create it.

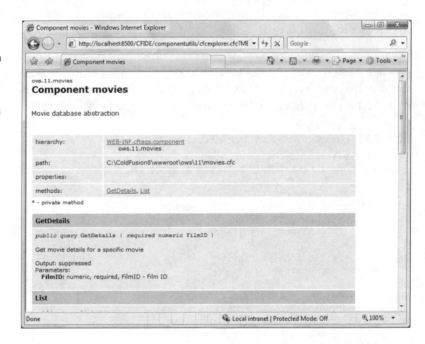

Earlier in this chapter I told you not to run the .cfc directly, and said that if you did, the result might not be what you'd expect. Well, the result is actually documentation, like the example shown in Figure 11.14. To access this documentation you can:

- Specify the URL to the .cfc in your browser.

- Browse the .cfc in Dreamweaver.

- From within the Dreamweaver Application panel's Components tab, right-click on any Component and select Get Description.

NOTE

When you browse CFC documentation you may be asked for your ColdFusion Administrator's password.

You can type hints manually, if you like. In addition, the Create Component wizard used earlier in this chapter allows hint text to be provided while building the CFC. However you decide to do it, providing hint text is highly recommended.

12

ColdFusion Forms

Using Forms

In Chapter 10, "Creating Data-Driven Pages," you learned how to create ColdFusion templates that dynamically display data retrieved from databases. The `Films` table has just 23 rows, so the data fit easily in a Web browser window and required only minimal scrolling.

What do you do if you have hundreds or thousands of rows? Displaying all that data in one long list is impractical. Scrolling through lists of movies to find the one you want just doesn't work well. The solution is to enable users to search for what they want by specifying what they are looking for. You can allow them to enter a title, an actor's name, or part of the tag line. You can then display only the movies that meet the search criteria.

To accomplish this, you need to do two things. First, you must create your search form using the HTML `<form>` tags. Second, you must create a template that builds SQL `SELECT` statements dynamically based on the data collected and submitted by the form.

➜ See Chapter 6, "Introducing SQL," for an explanation of the `SELECT` statement.

Creating Forms

Before you can create a search form, you need to learn how ColdFusion interacts with HTML forms. Listing 12.1 contains the code for a sample form that prompts for a first and last name. Create this template, then save it in a new folder named 12 (under the application root) as `form1.cfm`.

TIP

As a reminder, the files created in this chapter are in directory 12, so use that in your URLs too.

Listing 12.1 `form1.cfm`—HTML Forms

```
<!---
Name:         forms.cfm
Author:       Ben Forta (ben@forta.com)
Description:  Introduction to forms
Created:      07/01/07
--->

<html>
<head>
 <title>Learning ColdFusion Forms 1</title>
</head>

<body>

<!--- Movie search form --->
<form action="form1_action.cfm" method="POST">

Please enter the movie name and then click
<strong>Process</strong>.
<p>
Movie:
<input type="text" name="MovieTitle">
<br>
<input type="submit" value="Process">

</form>

</body>
</html>
```

Execute this code to display the form, as shown in Figure 12.1.

Figure 12.1

You can use HTML forms to collect data to be submitted to ColdFusion.

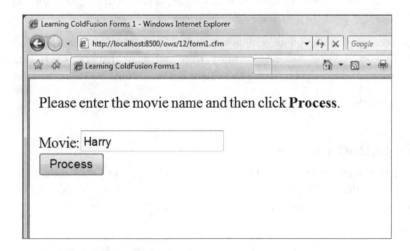

This form is simple, with a single-data entry field and a submit button, but it helps clearly demonstrate how forms are used to submit data to ColdFusion.

Using HTML Form Tags

You create HTML forms by using the `<form>` tag. `<form>` usually takes two parameters passed as tag attributes. The `action` attribute specifies the name of the script or program that the Web server should execute in response to the form's submission. To submit a form to ColdFusion, you specify the name of the ColdFusion template that will process the form. The following example specifies that the template `form1_action.cfm` should process the submitted form:

```
action="form1_action.cfm"
```

The `method` attribute specifies how data is sent back to the Web server. As a rule, all ColdFusion forms should be submitted as type `post`.

CAUTION

The default submission type is not `post`; it is usually `get`. If you omit the `method="post"` attribute from your form tag, you run the risk of losing form data, particularly in long forms or forms with `textarea` controls.

Your form has only a single data entry field: `<input type="text" name="MovieTitle">`. This is a simple text field. The `name` attribute in the `<input>` tag specifies the name of the field, and Cold-Fusion uses this name to refer to the field when it is processed.

Each field in a form is usually given a unique name. If two fields have the same name, both sets of values are returned to be processed and are separated by a comma. You usually want to be able to validate and manipulate each field individually, so each field should have its own name. The notable exceptions are the check box and radio button input types, which we'll describe shortly.

The last item in the form is an `<input>` of type `submit`. The submit `<input>` type creates a button that, when clicked, submits the form contents to the Web server for processing. Almost every form has a submit button (or a graphic image that acts like a submit button). The `value` attribute specifies the text to display within the button, so `<input type="submit" value="Process">` creates a submit button with the text `Process` in it.

TIP

When you're using an `input` type of submit, you should always specify button text by using the `value` attribute. If you don't, the default text `Submit Query` (or something similar) is displayed, which is likely to confuse your users.

Form Submission Error Messages

If you enter a movie title into the field and submit the form right now, you will receive a Cold-Fusion error message like the one in Figure 12.2. This error says that file `form1_action.cfm` can't be found.

This error message is perfectly valid, of course. You submitted a form to be passed to ColdFusion and processed it with a template, but you haven't created that template yet. So your next task is to create a template to process the form submission.

Figure 12.2

ColdFusion returns an error message when it can't process your request.

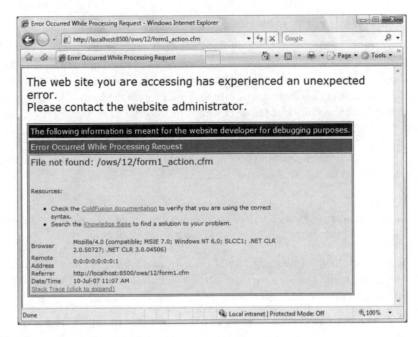

Processing Form Submissions

To demonstrate how to process returned forms, you must create a simple template that echoes the movie title you entered. The template is shown in Listing 12.2.

Listing 12.2 `form1_action.cfm`—Processing Form Fields

```
<!---
Name:        form1_action.cfm
Author:      Ben Forta (ben@forta.com)
Description: Introduction to forms
Created:     07/01/07
--->

<html>
<head>
 <title>Learning ColdFusion Forms 1</title>
</head>

<body>

<!--- Display search text --->
<cfoutput>
<strong>Movie title:</strong> #FORM.MovieTitle#
</cfoutput>

</body>
</html>
```

Processing Text Submissions

By now the `<cfoutput>` tag should be familiar to you; you use it to mark a block of code that Cold-Fusion should parse and process. The line `<strong>Movie title:</strong> #FORM.MovieTitle#` is processed by ColdFusion. `#FORM.MovieTitle#` is replaced with the value you entered in the `MovieTitle` form field.

NOTE

Use of the prefix **FORM** is optional. Using it prevents ambiguity and improves performance, but it also makes the code less reusable.

➜ See Chapter 8, "The Basics of CFML," for a detailed discussion of the ColdFusion `<cfoutput>` tag.

Create a template called `form1_action.cfm` that contains the code in Listing 12.2 and save it. Then resubmit your movie's name by clicking the form's submit button again. This time you should see a browser display similar to the one shown in Figure 12.3. Whatever name you enter in the Movie field in the form is displayed.

Figure 12.3

Submitted form fields can be displayed simply by referring to the field name.

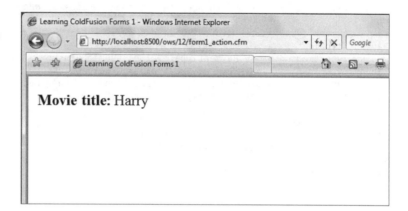

As you can see, `FORM` fields are used in ColdFusion like any other variable type.

Processing Check Boxes and Radio Buttons

Other input types you will frequently use are check boxes and radio buttons:

- **Check boxes** are used to select options that have one of two states: on or off, yes or no, and true or false. To ask a visitor whether they want to be added to a mailing list, for example, you would create a check box field. If the user selects the box, their name is added to the mailing list; if the user doesn't select the box, their name is not added.

- **Radio buttons** are used to select one of at least two mutually exclusive options. You can implement a field prompting for payment type with options such as Cash, Check, Credit card, or P.O.

The code example in Listing 12.3 creates a form that uses both option buttons and check box fields.

Listing 12.3 `form2.cfm`—Using Check Boxes and Radio Buttons

```
<!---
Name:        form2.cfm
Author:      Ben Forta (ben@forta.com)
Description: Introduction to forms
Created:     07/01/07
--->

<html>

<head>
 <title>Learning ColdFusion Forms 2</title>
</head>

<body>

<!--- Payment and mailing list form --->
<form action="form2_action.cfm" method="POST">

Please fill in this form and then click <strong>Process</strong>.
<p>
<!--- Payment type radio buttons --->
Payment type:<br>
<input type="radio" name="PaymentType" value="Cash">Cash<br>
<input type="radio" name="PaymentType" value="Check">Check<br>
<input type="radio" name="PaymentType" value="Credit card">Credit card<br>
<input type="radio" name="PaymentType" value="P.O.">P.O.
<p>
<!--- Mailing list checkbox --->
Would you like to be added to our mailing list?
<input type="checkbox" name="MailingList" value="Yes">
<p>
<input type="submit" value="Process">

</form>

</body>

</html>
```

Figure 12.4 shows how this form appears in your browser.

Before you create `form2_action.cfm` to process this form, you should note a couple of important points. First, look at the four lines of code that make up the Payment Type radio button selection:

```
<input type="radio" name="PaymentType" value="Cash">Cash<br>
<input type="radio" name="PaymentType" value="Check">Check<br>
<input type="radio" name="PaymentType" value="Credit card">Credit card<br>
<input type="radio" name="PaymentType" value="P.O.">P.O.
```

Each one contains the exact same name attribute—name="PaymentType". The four <input> fields have the same name so your browser knows they are part of the same set. If each radio button had a separate name, the browser wouldn't know that these buttons are mutually exclusive and thus would allow the selection of more than one button.

Figure 12.4

You can use input types of option buttons and check boxes to facilitate the selection of options.

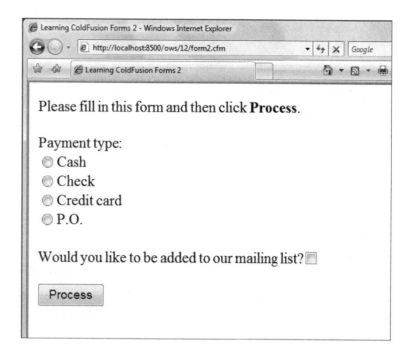

Another important point: Unlike <input> type text, radio buttons don't prompt the user for any textual input. Therefore, you must use the value attribute for the browser to associate a particular value with each radio button. The code value="Cash" instructs the browser to return the value Cash in the PaymentType field if that radio button is selected.

Now that you understand radio button and check box fields, you're ready to create a template to process them. Create a template called form2_action.cfm using the template code in Listing 12.4.

Listing 12.4 form2_action.cfm—Processing Option Buttons and Check Boxes

```
<!---
Name:        form2_action.cfm
Author:      Ben Forta (ben@forta.com)
Description: Introduction to forms
Created:     07/01/07
--->

<html>

<head>
 <title>Learning ColdFusion Forms 2</title>
</head>

<body>

<!--- Display feedback to user --->
<cfoutput>
```

Listing 12.4 (CONTINUED)

```
<!--- Payment type --->
Hello,<br>
You selected <strong>#FORM.PaymentType#</strong> as your payment type.<br>

<!--- Mailing list --->
<cfif MailingList IS "Yes">
 You will be added to our mailing list.
<cfelse>
 You will not be added to our mailing list.
</cfif>

</cfoutput>

</body>

</html>
```

The form processing code in Listing 12.4 displays the payment type the user selects. The field `PaymentType` is fully qualified with the `FORM` field type to prevent name collisions.

When the check box is selected, the value specified in the `value` attribute is returned; in this case, the value is `Yes`. If the `value` attribute is omitted, the default value of `on` is returned.

→ See Chapter 9, "Programming with CFML," for details on using the `<CFIF>` tag.

Now, execute `form2.cfm` in your browser, select a payment option, and select the mailing list check box. Click the Process button. Your browser display should look like Figure 12.5.

Figure 12.5

You can use ColdFusion templates to process user-selected options.

That worked exactly as intended, so now get ready to complicate things a little. Reload template `form2.cfm` and submit it without selecting a payment type or by leaving the `MailingList` check box unselected. ColdFusion generates an error message, as shown in Figure 12.6. As you can see, the field you don't select generates an `element is undefined` error.

Figure 12.6

Option buttons or
check boxes that are
submitted with no
value generate a
ColdFusion error.

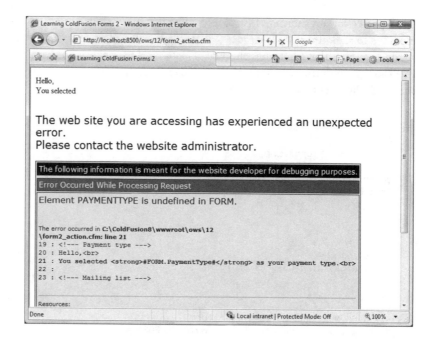

Check the code in Listing 12.3 to verify that the form fields do in fact exist. Why does ColdFusion report that the form field doesn't exist? That is one of the quirks of HTML forms. If you select a check box, the `on` value is submitted; but, *nothing* is submitted if you don't select the check box—not even an empty field. The same is true of radio buttons: If you make no selection, the field isn't submitted at all. (This behavior is the exact opposite of the text `<input>` type, which returns empty fields as opposed to no field.)

How do you work around this limitation? You could modify your form processing script to check which fields exist by using the `#IsDefined()#` function and, if the field exists, process it.

But the simpler solution is to prevent the browser from omitting fields that aren't selected. You can modify the radio button field so that one radio button is pre-selected. This way, users will have to make a selection or use the pre-selected option. To pre-select a radio button, just add the attribute `checked` to it.

Check boxes are trickier because by their nature they must be able to be turned off. Check boxes are used for on/off states, and, when the check box is off, there is no value to submit. The solution here is to set a default value in the `action` template. As you have already learned, this can be done easily using the `<cfparam>` tag. Look at this code:

```
<cfparam NAME="FORM.MailingList" default="No">
```

When ColdFusion encounters this line, it checks to see whether a variable named `FORM.MailingList` exists. If it does, processing continues. If it doesn't exist, ColdFusion creates the variable and sets the value to whatever is specified in the `default` attribute. The key here is that either way—whether the variable exists or not—the variable does exist after the `<cfparam>` tag is processed. It is therefore safe to refer to that variable further down the template code.

The updated form is shown in Listing 12.5. The first option button in the PaymentType field is modified to read `<input type="radio" name="PaymentType" value="Cash" checked>`. The checked attribute ensures that a button is checked. The MailingList check box has a value of Yes when it is checked, and the `<cfparam>` in the action page ensures that if MailingList is not checked, the value automatically is set to No.

Listing 12.5   form3.cfm—Pre-selecting Form Field Values

```
<!---
Name:        form3.cfm
Author:      Ben Forta (ben@forta.com)
Description: Introduction to forms
Created:     07/01/07
--->

<html>

<head>
 <title>Learning ColdFusion Forms 3</title>
</head>

<body>
<!--- Payment and mailing list form --->
<form action="form3_action.cfm" method="POST">

Please fill in this form and then click <strong>Process</strong>.
<p>
<!--- Payment type radio buttons --->
Payment type:<br>
<input type="radio" name="PaymentType" value="Cash" CHECKED>Cash<br>
<input type="radio" name="PaymentType" value="Check">Check<br>
<input type="radio" name="PaymentType" value="Credit card">Credit card<br>
<input type="radio" name="PaymentType" value="P.O.">P.O.
<p>
<!--- Mailing list checkbox --->
Would you like to be added to our mailing list?
<input type="checkbox" name="MailingList" value="Yes">
<p>
<input type="submit" value="Process">

</form>

</body>

</html>
```

Create and save this template as form3.cfm. Then create a new file named form3_action.cfm containing the code in form2_action.cfm, and add the following code to the top of the page (right below the comments):

```
<!--- Initialize variables --->
<cfparam name="MailingList" default="No">
```

Try using it and experiment with the two fields. You'll find that this form is reliable and robust, and it doesn't generate ColdFusion error messages, no matter which options are selected (or not).

Processing List Boxes

Another field type you will frequently use is the *list box*. Using list boxes is an efficient way to enable users to select one or more options. If a list box is created to accept only a single selection, you can be guaranteed that a value is always returned. If you don't set one of the options to be pre-selected, the first one in the list is selected. An option always has to be selected.

List boxes that allow multiple selections also allow no selections at all. If you use a multiple-selection list box, you once again have to find a way to ensure that ColdFusion doesn't generate `variable is undefined` errors.

Listing 12.6 contains the same data-entry form you just created, but it replaces the option buttons with a list box. Save this template as `form4.cfm`, and then test it with your browser.

Listing 12.6 `form4.cfm`—Using a `<select>` List Box for Options

```
<!---
Name:        form4.cfm
Author:      Ben Forta (ben@forta.com)
Description: Introduction to forms
Created:     07/01/07
--->

<html>

<head>
 <title>Learning ColdFusion Forms 4</title>
</head>

<body>

<!--- Payment and mailing list form --->
<form action="form3_action.cfm" method="POST">

Please fill in this form and then click <strong>Process</strong>.
<p>
<!--- Payment type select list --->
Payment type:<br>
<select name="PaymentType">
 <option value="Cash">Cash</option>
 <option value="Check">Check</option>
 <option value="Credit card">Credit card</option>
 <option value="P.O.">P.O.</option>
</select>
<p>
<!--- Mailing list checkbox --->
Would you like to be added to our mailing list?
<input type="checkbox" name="MailingList" value="Yes">
<p>
<input type="submit" value="Process">

</form>

</body>

</html>
```

For this particular form, the browser display shown in Figure 12.7 is probably a better user interface. The choice of whether to use radio buttons or list boxes is yours, and no hard and fast rules exist as to when to use one versus the other. The following guidelines, however, might help you determine which to use:

- If you need to allow the selection of multiple items or of no items at all, use a list box.

- List boxes take up less screen space. With a list box, 100 options take up no more precious real estate than a single option.

- Radio buttons present all the options to the users without requiring mouse clicks. (Statistically, users more often select options that are readily visible.)

Figure 12.7

You can use HTML list boxes to select one or more options.

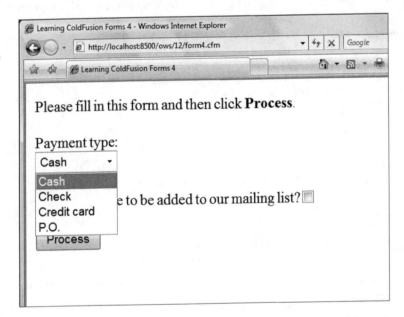

Processing Text Areas

Text area fields are boxes in which the users can enter free-form text. When you create a text area field, you specify the number of rows and columns of screen space it should occupy. This area, however, doesn't restrict the amount of text users can enter. The field scrolls both horizontally and vertically to enable the users to enter more text.

Listing 12.7 creates an HTML form with a text area field for user comments. The field's width is specified as a number of characters that can be typed on a single line; the height is the number of lines that are displayed without scrolling.

TIP

The `<textarea>` `cols` attribute is specified as a number of characters that can fit on a single line. This setting is dependent on the font in which the text is displayed, and the font is browser specific. Be sure you test any `<textarea>` fields in more than one browser because a field that fits nicely in one might not fit at all in another.

Listing 12.7 form5.cfm—Using a <textarea> Field

```
<!---
Name:        form5.cfm
Author:      Ben Forta (ben@forta.com)
Description: Introduction to forms
Created:     07/01/07
--->

<html>

<head>
 <title>Learning ColdFusion Forms 5</title>
</head>

<body>

<!--- Comments form --->
<form action="form5_action.cfm" method="POST">
Please enter your comments in the box provided, and then click
<strong>Send</strong>.
<p>
<textarea name="Comments" rows="6" cols="40"></textarea>
<p>
<input type="submit" value="Send">

</form>

</body>

</html>
```

Listing 12.8 contains ColdFusion code that displays the contents of a <textarea> field.

Listing 12.8 form5_action.cfm—Processing <textarea> Fields

```
<!---
Name:        form5_action.cfm
Author:      Ben Forta (ben@forta.com)
Description: Introduction to forms
Created:     07/01/07
--->

<html>

<head>
 <title>Learning ColdFusion Forms 5</title>
</head>

<body>

<!--- Display feedback to user --->
<cfoutput>

Thank you for your comments. You entered:
<p>
<strong>#FORM.comments#</strong>
```

Listing 12.8   (CONTINUED)

```
</cfoutput>

</body>

</html>
```

Figure 12.8 shows the `<textarea>` field you created, and Figure 12.9 shows how ColdFusion displays the field.

Figure 12.8

The HTML `<textarea>` field is a means by which you can accept free-form text input from users.

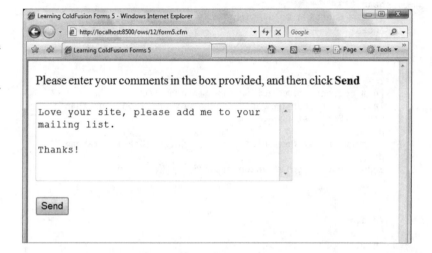

Figure 12.9

Without ColdFusion output functions, `<textarea>` fields are not displayed with line breaks preserved.

Try entering line breaks (by pressing the Enter [Windows] or Return [Mac]) in the text field and then submit it. What happens to the line breaks? Line break characters are considered white-space characters (just like spaces) by your browser, and all white space is ignored by browsers.

```
WHITE SPACE IS IGNORED
```

is displayed no differently than

```
WHITE SPACE          IS          IGNORED
```

The only way to display line breaks is to replace the line break with an HTML paragraph tag: <p>. You therefore have to parse through the entire field text and insert <p> tags wherever necessary. Fortunately, ColdFusion makes this task a simple one. The ColdFusion #ParagraphFormat()# function automatically replaces every double line break with a <p> tag. (Single line breaks aren't replaced because ColdFusion has no way of knowing whether the next line is a new paragraph or part of the current one.)

NOTE

The ColdFusion `Replace()` and `ReplaceList()` functions can be used instead of `ParagraphFormat()` to have greater control over the paragraph formatting.

The code in Listing 12.9 contains the same comments form as the one in Listing 12.7, with two differences. First, default field text is provided. Unlike other <input> types, <textarea> default text is specified between <textarea> and </textarea> tags—not in a value attribute. Second, you use the wrap attribute to wrap text entered into the field automatically. wrap="virtual" instructs the browser to wrap to the next line automatically, just as most word processors and editors do.

Listing 12.9 `form6.cfm`—The HTML `<textarea>` Field

```
<!---
Name:        form6.cfm
Author:      Ben Forta (ben@forta.com)
Description: Introduction to forms
Created:     07/01/07
--->

<html>

<head>
 <title>Learning ColdFusion Forms 6</title>
</head>

<body>

<!--- Comments form --->
<form action="form6_action.cfm" method="POST">

Please enter your comments in the box provided, and then click
<strong>Send</strong>.
<p>
<textarea name="Comments" rows="6" cols="40" wrap="virtual">
Enter your comments here ...
</textarea>
<p>
<input type="submit" value="Send">

</form>

</body>

</html>
```

Listing 12.10 shows the template to display the user-supplied comments. The Comments field code is changed to #ParagraphFormat(FORM.Comments)#, ensuring that multiple line breaks are maintained and displayed correctly, as shown in Figure 12.10.

Figure 12.10

You should use
the ColdFusion
ParagraphFormat()
function to display
<textarea> fields
with their line breaks
preserved.

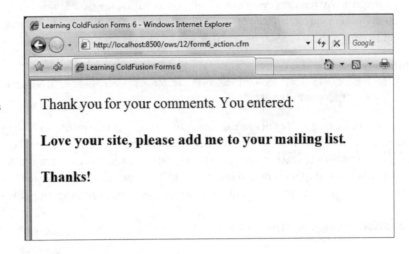

Listing 12.10 form6_action.cfm—Using ParagraphFormat

```
<!---
Name:        form6_action.cfm
Author:      Ben Forta (ben@forta.com)
Description: Introduction to forms
Created:     07/01/07
--->

<html>

<head>
 <title>Learning ColdFusion Forms 6</title>
</head>

<body>

<!--- Display feedback to user --->
<cfoutput>

Thank you for your comments. You entered:
<p>
<strong>#ParagraphFormat(FORM.comments)#</strong>

</cfoutput>

</body>

</html>
```

Processing Buttons

The HTML forms specification supports only two types of buttons. Almost all forms, including all the forms you create in this chapter, have a *submit* button. Submit, as its name implies, instructs the browser to submit the form fields to a Web server.

TIP

Most newer browsers actually require no submit button at all, and force a submit if the Enter (Windows) or Return (Mac) key is pressed.

The second supported button type is reset. *Reset* clears all form entries and restores default values if any existed. Any text entered into <input type="text"> or <textarea> fields is cleared, as are any check box, list box, and option button selections. Many forms have reset buttons, but you never need more than one.

On the other hand, you might want more than one submit button. For example, if you're using a form to modify a record, you could have two submit buttons: one for Update and one for Delete. (Of course, you also could use two forms to accomplish this task.) If you create multiple submit buttons, you must name the button with the name attribute and be sure to assign a different value attribute for each. The code in Listing 12.11 contains a reset button and two submit buttons.

Listing 12.11 form7.cfm—Template with a Reset

```
<!---
Name:        form7.cfm
Author:      Ben Forta (ben@forta.com)
Description: Introduction to forms
Created:     07/01/07
--->

<html>

<head>
 <title>Learning ColdFusion Forms 7</title>
</head>

<body>

<!--- Update/delete form --->
<form action="form7_action.cfm" method="POST">

<p>

Movie:
<input type="text" name="MovieTitle">

<p>
<!--- Submit buttons --->
<input type="submit" name="Operation" value="Update">
<input type="submit" name="Operation" value="Delete">
<!--- Reset button --->
<input type="reset" value="Clear">

</form>

</body>

</html>
```

The result of this code is shown in Figure 12.11.

Figure 12.11

When you're using multiple submit buttons, you must assign a different value to each button.

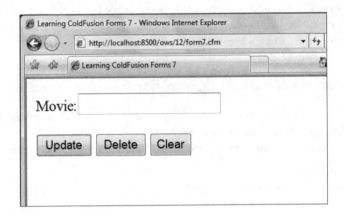

When you name submit buttons, you treat them as any other form field. Listing 12.12 demonstrates how to determine which submit button was clicked. The code `<cfif FORM.Operation IS "Update">` checks whether the Update button was clicked, and `<cfelseif FORM.Operation IS "Delete">` checks whether Delete was clicked, but only if Update was not clicked.

Listing 12.12 `form7_action.cfm`—Multiple Submit Button Processing

```
<!---
Name:        form7_action.cfm
Author:      Ben Forta (ben@forta.com)
Description: Introduction to forms
Created:     07/01/07
--->

<html>
<head>
 <title>Learning ColdFusion Forms 7</title>
</head>

<body>

<!--- User feedback --->
<cfoutput>

<cfif FORM.Operation IS "Update">
 <!--- Update button clicked --->
 You opted to <strong>update</strong> #MovieTitle#
<cfelseif FORM.Operation IS "Delete">
 <!--- Delete button clicked --->
 You opted to <strong>delete</strong> #MovieTitle#
</cfif>

</cfoutput>

</body>

</html>
```

Creating Dynamic SQL Statements

This section uses `<cfquery>` tags for data access, and the example here should use ColdFusion Components as was described in the last chapter. However, to keep the examples simpler I will violate the rules I just taught you. I guess I'm saying that every rule has exceptions.

Now that you're familiar with forms and how ColdFusion processes them, you can return to creating a movie search screen. The first screen enables visitors to search for a movie by title. Because this requires text input, you will need an `<input>` field of type text. The field name can be anything you want, but using the same name as the table column to which you're comparing the value is generally a good idea.

When you're creating search screens, you can give your form fields any descriptive name you want. When first starting to build Cold-Fusion applications, however, you may want to make sure that the field names match the table column names, to make matching HTML form fields and SQL easier.

The code in Listing 12.13 contains a simple HTML form not unlike the test forms you created earlier in this chapter. The form contains a single text field called `MovieTitle` and a submit button.

Listing 12.13   `search1.cfm`—Code Listing for Movie Search Screen

```
<!---
Name:        search1.cfm
Author:      Ben Forta (ben@forta.com)
Description: Creating search screens
Created:     07/01/07
--->

<html>

<head>
 <title>Orange Whip Studios - Movies</title>
</head>

<body>

<!--- Page header --->
<cfinclude template="header.cfm">

<!--- Search form --->
<form action="results1.cfm" method="POST">

<table align="center" border="1">
 <tr>
  <td>
  Movie:
  </td>
  <td>
  <input type="text" name="MovieTitle">
  </td>
 </tr>
```

Listing 12.13 (CONTINUED)

```
<tr>
 <td colspan="2" align="center">
 <input type="submit" value="Search">
 </td>
</tr>
</table>

</form>

</body>

</html>
```

Save this form as `search1.cfm`, then execute it to display a screen like the one in Figure 12.12.

Figure 12.12

The movie search screen enables users to search by movie title.

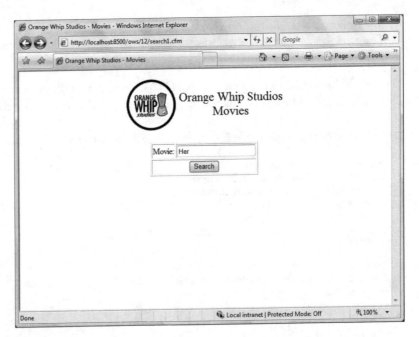

Listing 12.13 starts off with a comment block, followed by the standard HTML headers and `<body>` tag. Then a `<cfinclude>` tag is used to include a common header, file `header.cfm` (which puts the logo and title at the top of the page).

→ See Chapter 9 for information on using the `<cfinclude>` tag.

The form itself is placed inside an HTML table. This is a very popular technique that can be used to better control form field placement. The form contains a single field, `MovieTitle`, and a submit button.

The `<form>` `action` attribute specifies which ColdFusion template should be used to process this search. The code `action="results1.cfm"` instructs ColdFusion to use the template `results1.cfm`, which is shown in Listing 12.14. Create this template and save it as `results1.cfm`.

Listing 12.14 results1.cfm—Passed Form Field in a SQL WHERE Clause

```
<!---
Name:        results1.cfm
Author:      Ben Forta (ben@forta.com)
Description: Creating search screens
Created:     07/01/07
--->

<!--- Get movie list from database --->
<cfquery name="movies" datasource="ows">
SELECT MovieTitle, PitchText,
       Summary, DateInTheaters
FROM Films
WHERE MovieTitle LIKE '%#FORM.MovieTitle#%'
ORDER BY MovieTitle
</cfquery>

<!--- Create HTML page --->
<html>
<head>
 <title>Orange Whip Studios - Movies</title>
</head>

<body>

<!--- Page header --->
<cfinclude template="header.cfm">

<!--- Display movie list --->
<table>
 <tr>
  <th colspan="2">
   <cfoutput>
   <font size="+3">Movie List (#Movies.RecordCount# movies)</font>
   </cfoutput>
  </th>
 </tr>
 <cfoutput query="movies">
  <tr>
   <td>
   <font size="+2"><strong>#CurrentRow#: #MovieTitle#</strong></font><br>
   <font size="+1"><em>#PitchText#</em></font>
   </td>
   <td>Released: #DateFormat(DateInTheaters)#</td>
  </tr>
  <tr>
   <td colspan="2">#Summary#</td>
  </tr>
 </cfoutput>
</table>

</body>
</html>
```

The code in Listing 12.14 is based on the movie lists created in the last chapter, so most of the code should be very familiar. The only big change here is in the <cfquery> tag.

The WHERE clause in Listing 12.14 contains a ColdFusion field rather than a static value. You will recall that when ColdFusion parses templates, it replaces field names with the values contained within the field. So, look at the following WHERE clause:

```
WHERE MovieTitle LIKE '%#FORM.MovieTitle#%'
```

#FORM.MovieTitle# is replaced with whatever was entered in the MovieTitle form field. If the word Her was entered then the WHERE clause becomes

```
WHERE MovieTitle LIKE '%Her%'
```

which will find all movies with the text her anywhere in the MovieTitle. If you search for all movies containing C, the code WHERE MovieTitle LIKE '%#FORM.MovieTitle#%' would become WHERE MovieTitle LIKE '%C%', and so on. You can do this with any clauses, not just the LIKE operator.

> **NOTE**
>
> If no search text is specified at all, the clause becomes WHERE MovieTitle LIKE '%%'—a wildcard search that finds all records.

➜ See Chapter 10 for an introduction to the <CFQUERY> tag.

➜ See Chapter 6 for an explanation of the LIKE operator.

You use a LIKE clause to enable users to enter partial text. The clause WHERE MovieTitle = 'Her' finds only movies with a title of her; movies with her in the name along with other text are not retrieved. Using a wildcard, as in WHERE MovieTitle LIKE '%Her%', enables users to also search on partial names.

Try experimenting with different search strings. The sample output should look like the output shown in Figure 12.13. Depending on the search criteria you specify, you'll see different search results, of course.

Figure 12.13

By building WHERE clauses dynamically, you can create different search conditions on the fly.

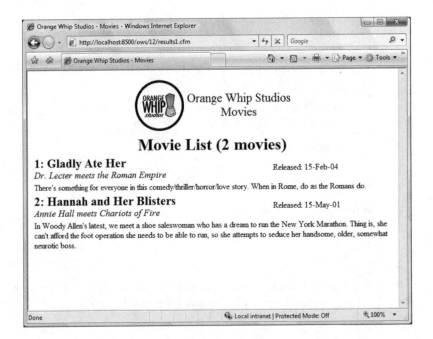

To complete the application, try copying the movie detail page (created in Chapter 10) and modify `results1.cfm` so that it enables the drill-down of the displayed search results. You'll then have a complete drill-down application.

Building Truly Dynamic Statements

No sooner do you roll out your movie search screen at Orange Whip Studios, but you immediately find yourself inundated with requests. "Searching by title is great, but what about searching by tag line or rating?" your users ask. Now that you have introduced the ability to search for data, your users want to be able to search on several fields.

Adding fields to your search screen is simple enough. Add two fields: one for tag line and one for rating. The code for the updated search screen is shown in Listing 12.15.

Listing 12.15 `search2.cfm`—Movie Search Screen

```
<!---
Name:        search2.cfm
Author:      Ben Forta (ben@forta.com)
Description: Creating search screens
Created:     07/01/07
--->

<html>

<head>
 <title>Orange Whip Studios - Movies</title>
</head>

<body>

<!--- Page header --->
<cfinclude template="header.cfm">

<!--- Search form --->
<form action="results2.cfm" method="POST">

<table align="center" border="1">
 <tr>
  <td>
  Movie:
  </td>
  <td>
  <input type="text" name="MovieTitle">
  </td>
 </tr>
 <tr>
  <td>
  Tag line:
  </td>
  <td>
  <input type="text" name="PitchText">
  </td>
```

Listing 12.15 (CONTINUED)

```
</tr>
<tr>
 <td>
 Rating:
 </td>
 <td>
 <input type="text" name="RatingID"> (1-6)
 </td>
</tr>
<tr>
 <td colspan="2" align="center">
 <input type="submit" value="Search">
 </td>
</tr>
</table>

</form>

</body>

</html>
```

This form lets users specify text in one of three fields, as shown in Figure 12.14.

Figure 12.14

The movie search screen now allows searching by three fields.

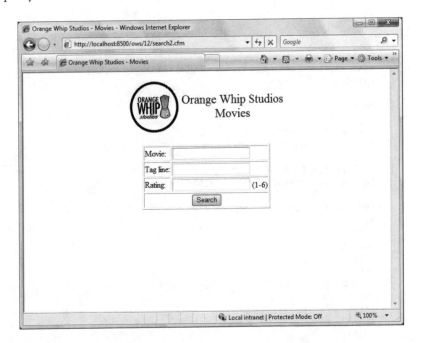

You must create a search template before you can actually perform a search. The complete search code is shown in Listing 12.16; save this file as `results2.cfm`.

Listing 12.16 results2.cfm—Building SQL Statements Dynamically

```
<!---
Name:        results2.cfm
Author:      Ben Forta (ben@forta.com)
Description: Creating search screens
Created:     07/01/07
--->

<!--- Get movie list from database --->
<cfquery name="movies" datasource="ows">
SELECT MovieTitle, PitchText, Summary, DateInTheaters
FROM Films
<!--- Search by movie title --->
<cfif FORM.MovieTitle IS NOT "">
 WHERE MovieTitle LIKE '%#FORM.MovieTitle#%'
</cfif>
<!--- Search by tag line --->
<cfif FORM.PitchText IS NOT "">
 WHERE PitchText LIKE '%#FORM.PitchText#%'
</cfif>
<!--- Search by rating --->
<cfif FORM.RatingID IS NOT "">
 WHERE RatingID = #FORM.RatingID#
</cfif>
ORDER BY MovieTitle
</cfquery>

<!--- Create HTML page --->
<html>
<head>
 <title>Orange Whip Studios - Movies</title>
</head>

<body>

<!--- Page header --->
<cfinclude template="header.cfm">

<!--- Display movie list --->
<table>
<tr>
 <cfoutput>
 <th colspan="2">
 <font size="+3">Movie List (#Movies.RecordCount# movies)</font>
 </TH>
 </cfoutput>
</tr>
<cfoutput query="movies">
<tr>
 <td>
 <font size="+2"><strong>#CurrentRow#: #MovieTitle#</strong></font><br>
 <font size="+1"><em>#PitchText#</em></font>
 </td>
 <td>Released: #DateFormat(DateInTheaters)#</td>
</tr>
<tr>
```

Listing 12.16 (CONTINUED)

```
  <td colspan="2">#Summary#</td>
</tr>
</cfoutput>
</table>

</body>
</html>
```

Understanding Dynamic SQL

Before you actually perform a search, take a closer look at the template in Listing 12.16. The `<cfquery>` tag is similar to the one you used in the previous search template, but in this one the SQL SELECT statement in the SQL attribute is incomplete. It doesn't specify a WHERE clause with which to perform a search, nor does it specify a search order. No WHERE clause is specified because the search screen has to support not one, but four search types, as follows:

- If none of the three search fields is specified, no WHERE clause should be used, so that all movies can be retrieved.

- If a movie title is specified, the WHERE clause must filter data to find only movies containing the specified title text. For example, if the is specified as the search text, the WHERE clause has to be WHERE MovieTitle LIKE '%the%'.

- If tag-line text is specified, the WHERE clause needs to filter data to find only movies containing the specified text. For example, if bad is specified as the search text, the WHERE clause must be WHERE PitchText LIKE '%bad%'.

- If you're searching by rating and specify 2 as the search text, a WHERE clause of WHERE RatingID = 2 is necessary.

How can a single search template handle all these search conditions? The answer is dynamic SQL.

When you're creating dynamic SQL statements, you break the statement into separate common SQL and specific SQL. The common SQL is the part of the SQL statement you always want. The sample SQL statement has two common parts:

```
SELECT MovieTitle, PitchText, Summary, DateInTheaters
FROM Films
```

and

```
ORDER BY MovieTitle
```

The common text is all the SQL statement you need if no search criteria is provided. If, however, search text is specified, the number of possible WHERE clauses is endless.

Take another look at Listing 12.16 to understand the process of creating dynamic SQL statements. The code `<cfif FORM.MovieTitle IS NOT "">` checks to see that the MovieTitle form field isn't empty. This condition fails if no text is entered into the MovieTitle field in the search form, in which case any code until the </CFIF> is ignored.

→ See Chapter 9 for details on using <CFIF>.

If a value does appear in the MovieTitle field, the code WHERE MovieTitle LIKE '#FORM.Movie Title#%' is processed and appended to the SQL statement. #FORM.MovieTitle# is a field and is replaced with whatever text is entered in the MovieTitle field. If the is specified as the text for which to search, this statement translates to WHERE MovieTitle LIKE '%the%'. This text is appended to the previous SQL statement, which now becomes the following:

```
SELECT MovieTitle, PitchText, Summary, DateInTheaters
FROM Films
WHERE MovieTitle LIKE '%the%'
```

All you need now is the ORDER BY clause. Even though ORDER BY is fixed and doesn't change with different searches, it must be built dynamically because the ORDER BY clause must come after the WHERE clause, if one exists. After ColdFusion processes the code ORDER BY MovieTitle, the finished SQL statement reads as follows:

```
SELECT MovieTitle, PitchText, Summary, DateInTheaters
FROM Films
WHERE MovieTitle LIKE '%the%'
ORDER BY MovieTitle
```

NOTE

You may not use double quotation marks in a SQL statement. When ColdFusion encounters a double quotation mark, it thinks it has reached the end of the SQL statement. It then generates an error message because extra text appears where ColdFusion thinks there should be none. To include text strings with the SQL statement, use only single quotation marks.

Similarly, if a RatingID is specified (for example, the value 2) as the search text, the complete SQL statement reads as follows:

```
SELECT MovieTitle, PitchText, Summary, DateInTheaters
FROM Films
WHERE RatingID = 2
ORDER BY MovieTitle
```

The code <cfif FORM.MovieTitle IS NOT ""> evaluates to FALSE because FORM.MovieTitle is actually empty; ColdFusion therefore checks the next condition, which is also FALSE, and so on. Because RatingID was specified, the third <CFIF> condition is TRUE and the previous SELECT statement is generated.

NOTE

You may have noticed that there are single quotation marks around FORM.MovieTitle and FORM.PitchText but not FORM.RatingID. Why? Because MovieTitle and PitchText have text datatypes in the database table, whereas RatingID is numeric. SQL is not typeless, and it will require that you specify quotes where needed to create strings if that is what is expected.

So, one template is capable of generating four different sets of SQL SELECT statements, of which the values can be dynamic. Try performing various searches, but for now, use only one form field at a time.

Concatenating SQL Clauses

Now try entering text in two search fields, or all three of them. What happens? You probably generated an error like the one in Figure 12.15.

Figure 12.15

Dynamic SQL must be generated carefully to avoid building invalid SQL.

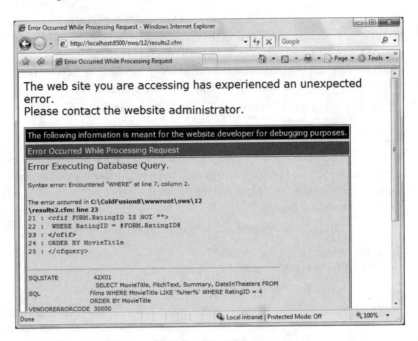

Why did this happen? Well, suppose the was specified as the MovieTitle and 2 as the RatingID. Walk through the <cfif> statements to work out what the generated SQL would look like. The first condition will be TRUE, the second will be FALSE, and the third will be TRUE. The SELECT statement would therefore look like this:

```
SELECT MovieTitle, PitchText, Summary, DateInTheaters
FROM Films
WHERE MovieTitle LIKE '%the%'
WHERE RatingID = 2
ORDER BY MovieTitle
```

Obviously, this is not a valid SELECT statement—only one WHERE clause is allowed. The correct syntax for this statement is

```
SELECT MovieTitle, PitchText, Summary, DateInTheaters
FROM Films
WHERE MovieTitle LIKE '%the%'
  AND RatingID = 2
ORDER BY MovieTitle
```

So how would you generate this code? You couldn't hard-code any condition with a WHERE or an AND, because you wouldn't know whether it was the first clause. The MovieTitle clause, if used, will always be the first, but it might not always be used.

One obvious solution (which I suggest you avoid at all costs) is to use embedded `<cfif>` statements to intelligently include WHERE or AND as necessary. However, this type of code is very complex and error prone.

A better solution would be to never need WHERE at all—only use AND. How can you do this? Look at the following SQL statement:

```
SELECT MovieTitle, PitchText, Summary, DateInTheaters
FROM Films
WHERE 0=0
 AND MovieTitle LIKE '%the%'
 AND RatingID = 2
ORDER BY MovieTitle
```

WHERE 0=0 is a dummy clause. Obviously 0 is equal to 0, so WHERE 0=0 retrieves every row in the table. For each row the database checks to see whether 0 is 0, which of course it always is. This is a legal WHERE clause, but it does nothing because it is always TRUE.

So why use it? Simple. Now that there is a WHERE clause, you can safely use AND for every dynamic condition. If no other condition exists, then only the WHERE 0=0 will be evaluated. But if additional conditions do exist, no matter how many, they can all be appended using AND.

NOTE

There is nothing magical about WHERE 0=0. You can use any condition that will always be TRUE: WHERE 'A'='A', WHERE primary key = primary key (using the table's primary key), and just about anything else you want.

Listing 12.17 contains a revised search page (this time using a drop-down list box for the rating); save it as search3.cfm. Figure 12.16 shows the new and improved search screen.

Figure 12.16

Drop-down list boxes are well suited for selections of one of a set of finite options.

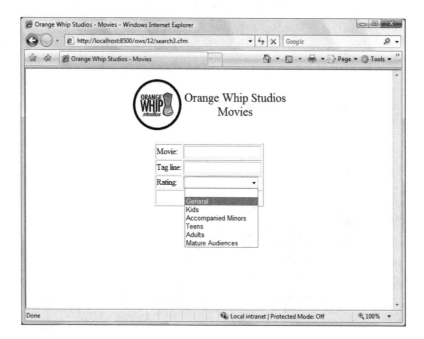

Listing 12.18 contains the revised results page; save it as `results3.cfm`.

Listing 12.17   `search3.cfm`—Revised Movie Search Screen

```
<!---
Name:        search3.cfm
Author:      Ben Forta (ben@forta.com)
Description: Creating search screens
Created:     07/01/07
--->

<html>

<head>
 <title>Orange Whip Studios - Movies</title>
</head>

<body>

<!--- Page header --->
<cfinclude template="header.cfm">

<!--- Search form --->
<form action="results3.cfm" method="POST">

<table align="center" border="1">
 <tr>
  <td>
  Movie:
  </td>
  <td>
  <input type="text" name="MovieTitle">
  </td>
 </tr>
 <tr>
  <td>
  Tag line:
  </td>
  <td>
  <input type="text" name="PitchText">
  </td>
 </tr>
 <tr>
  <td>
  Rating:
  </td>
  <td>
   <select name="RatingID">
    <option value=""></option>
    <option value="1">General</option>
    <option value="2">Kids</option>
    <option value="3">Accompanied Minors</option>
    <option value="4">Teens</option>
    <option value="5">Adults</option>
    <option value="6">Mature Audiences</option>
   </select>
  </td>
```

Listing 12.17 (CONTINUED)

```
 </tr>
 <tr>
  <td colspan="2" align="center">
  <input type="submit" value="Search">
  </td>
 </tr>
</table>

</form>

</body>

</html>
```

The only change in Listing 12.17 is the drop-down list box for the RatingID. Manually entering 1 to 6 isn't intuitive, and is highly error prone. For finite lists such as this drop-down list, boxes are a better option. This doesn't change the form field processing, though. Either way, RatingID is sent to the action page, shown in Listing 12.18.

Listing 12.18 results3.cfm—Concatenating SQL Clauses

```
<!---
Name:        results3.cfm
Author:      Ben Forta (ben@forta.com)
Description: Creating search screens
Created:     07/01/07
--->

<!--- Get movie list from database --->
<cfquery name="movies" datasource="ows">
SELECT MovieTitle, PitchText, Summary, DateInTheaters
FROM Films
WHERE 0=0
<!--- Search by movie title --->
<cfif FORM.MovieTitle IS NOT "">
 AND MovieTitle LIKE '%#FORM.MovieTitle#%'
</cfif>
<!--- Search by tag line --->
<cfif FORM.PitchText IS NOT "">
 AND PitchText LIKE '%#FORM.PitchText#%'
</cfif>
<!--- Search by rating --->
<cfif FORM.RatingID IS NOT "">
 AND RatingID = #FORM.RatingID#
</cfif>
ORDER BY MovieTitle
</cfquery>

<!--- Create HTML page --->
<html>
<head>
 <title>Orange Whip Studios - Movies</title>
</head>

<body>
```

Listing 12.18 (CONTINUED)

```
<!--- Page header --->
<cfinclude template="header.cfm">

<!--- Display movie list --->
<table>
 <tr>
  <th colspan="2">
   <cfoutput>
   <font size="+3">Movie List (#Movies.RecordCount# movies)</font>
   </cfoutput>
  </th>
 </tr>
 <cfoutput query="movies">
  <tr>
   <td>
    <font size="+2"><strong>#CurrentRow#: #MovieTitle#</strong></font><br>
    <font size="+1"><em>#PitchText#</em></font>
   </td>
   <td>Released: #DateFormat(DateInTheaters)#</td>
  </tr>
  <tr>
   <td colspan="2">#Summary#</td>
  </tr>
 </cfoutput>
</table>

</body>
</html>
```

The `<cfquery>` in Listing 12.18 now contains a dummy clause and then three optional AND clauses, each within a `<cfif>` statement. So what will this do?

- If no form fields are filled in, only the dummy WHERE clause will be used.

- If any single form field is filled in, the WHERE clause will contain the dummy and a single real clause appended using AND.

- If any two form fields are filled in, the WHERE clause will have three clauses, one dummy and two real.

- If all three clauses are filled in, the WHERE clause will contain four clauses, one dummy and three real.

In other words, a single template can now generate eight different combinations of WHERE clauses, and each can have an unlimited number of values. All that in less than 20 lines of code—it doesn't get much more powerful than that.

After you create the template, use your browser to perform various combinations of searches. You'll find that this new search template is both powerful and flexible. Indeed, this technique for creating truly dynamic SQL SELECT statements will likely be the basis for some sophisticated database interaction in real-world applications.

TIP

Debugging dynamic SQL statement creation can be tricky, and troubleshooting requires that you know exactly what SQL your ColdFusion code created. To do this, use the techniques described in Chapter 10 (debug output and obtaining a `result` from `<cfquery>`).

Creating Dynamic Search Screens

There is one final improvement to be made to your application. The list of ratings used in the search form has been hard-coded (refer to Listing 12.17). Remember that you're creating data-driven applications. Everything in your application should be data-driven. You don't want to have to manually enter data, not even in list boxes. Rather, you want the list box to be driven by the data in the `FilmsRatings` table. This way, you can acquire changes automatically when ratings are added or when a rating name changes.

Listing 12.19 is identical to Listing 12.17, with the exception of the addition of a new `<cfquery>` and a `<cfoutput>` block to process its contents.

Listing 12.19   `search4.cfm`—Data-Driven Forms

```
<!---
Name:        search4.cfm
Author:      Ben Forta (ben@forta.com)
Description: Creating search screens
Created:     07/01/07
--->

<!--- Get ratings --->
<cfquery datasource="ows" name="ratings">
SELECT RatingID, Rating
FROM FilmsRatings
ORDER BY RatingID
</cfquery>

<html>

<head>
 <title>Orange Whip Studios - Movies</title>
</head>

<body>

<!--- Page header --->
<cfinclude template="header.cfm">

<!--- Search form --->
<form action="results3.cfm" method="POST">

<table align="center" border="1">
 <tr>
  <td>
  Movie:
  </td>
```

Listing 12.19 (CONTINUED)

```
<td>
<input type="text" name="MovieTitle">
</td>
</tr>
<tr>
<td>
Tag line:
</td>
<td>
<input type="text" name="PitchText">
</td>
</tr>
<tr>
<td>
Rating:
</td>
<td>
<select name="RatingID">
 <option value=""></option>
 <cfoutput query="ratings">
  <option value="#RatingID#">#Rating#</option>
 </cfoutput>
</select>
</td>
</tr>
<tr>
<td colspan="2" align="center">
<input type="submit" value="Search">
</td>
</tr>
</table>

</form>

</body>

</html>
```

The code in Listing 12.19 demonstrates a data-driven form. The <cfquery> at the top of the template should be familiar to you by now. It creates a result set called ratings, which contains the ID and name of each rating in the database.

The drop-down list box also has been changed. The <select> tag creates the list box, and it is terminated with the </select> tag, as before. The individual entries in the list box are specified with the <option> tag, but here that tag is within a <cfoutput> block. This block is executed once for each row retrieved by the <cfquery>, creating an <OPTION> entry for each one.

As it loops through the ratings resultset, the <cfquery> block creates the individual options, using the RatingID field as the value and Rating as the description. So when ColdFusion processes RatingID 1 (General), the code generated is:

```
<option value="1">General</option>
```

The end result is exactly the same as the screen shown previously in Figure 12.16, but this time it is populated by a database query (instead of being hard-coded).

Also notice that a blank `<option>` line is included in the list box. Remember that list boxes always must have a selection, so if you want to allow your users to not select any option, you need to give them a *no option* option (the blank option).

And there you have it: dynamic data-driven forms used to perform dynamic data-driven searches using dynamic data-driven SQL.

Form Data Validation

Understanding Form Validation

HTML forms are used to collect data from users by using several field types. Forms are used for data entry, as front-end search engines, for filling out orders, for signing guest books, for providing user names and passwords to secure applications, and much more. Although forms have become one of the most important features in HTML, these forms provide almost no data validation tools.

This becomes a real problem when developing Web-based applications. As a developer, you need to be able to control what data users can enter into what fields. Without that, your programs will constantly be breaking due to mismatched or unanticipated data. And thus far, you have used forms only as search front ends—when forms are used to insert or update database tables (as you'll see in Chapter 14, "Using Forms to Add or Change Data"), this becomes even more critical.

Thankfully, ColdFusion provides a complete and robust set of tools with which to implement form data validation, both client-side and server-side.

Since its inception, HTML has always provided Web page developers with a variety of ways to format and display data. With each revision to the HTML specification, additional data display mechanisms have been made available. As a result, HTML is a powerful data-publishing tool.

Although its data presentation options continue to improve, HTML's data collection capabilities leave much to be desired. In fact, they have barely changed at all since the language's very early days.

HTML data collection is performed using forms. HTML forms support the following field types:

- Free-form text fields
- Select box (or drop-down list boxes)
- Radio buttons
- Check boxes
- Multi-line text boxes
- Password (hidden input) boxes

➜ See Chapter 12, "ColdFusion Forms," for more information about HTML forms and using them with ColdFusion.

So what's wrong with this list? Actually, nothing. These field types are all the standard fields you would expect to be available to you in any development language. What is wrong, however, is that these fields have extremely limited capabilities. There are two primary limitations:

- Inability to mark fields as required
- Inability to define data types or filters, for example, to only accepting digits, a ZIP code, an e-mail address, or a phone number

What this means is that there is no simple way to tell HTML to disallow form submission if certain fields are left empty. Similarly, HTML can't be instructed to accept only certain values or types of data in specific fields.

HTML itself has exactly one validation option, the `maxlength` attribute, which can be used to specify the maximum number of characters that can be entered in a text field. That's it—no other validation options are available.

To work around these limitations, HTML developers have typically adopted two forms of validation options:

- Server-side validation
- Client-side validation

Comparing Server-Side and Client-Side Validation

Server-side validation involves checking for required fields or invalid values after a form has been submitted. The script on the server first validates the form and then continues processing only if all validation requirements are met. Typically, an error message is sent back to the user's browser if validation fails; the user then goes back to the page, makes the corrections, and resubmits the form. Of course, the form submission must be validated again upon resubmission, and the process must be repeated if the validation fails again.

Client-side scripting lets the developer embed instructions to the browser within the HTML code. Because HTML itself provides no mechanism for doing this, developers have resorted to using scripting languages, such as JavaScript, which is supported by just about every browser. These interpreted languages support basic data manipulation and user feedback and are thus well suited for form validation. To validate a form, the page author would create a function to be executed as soon as a Submit button is clicked. This function would perform any necessary validation right inside of the browser, and allow the submission to proceed only if the validation check was successful. The advantage of this approach is that the user doesn't have to submit a form to find out an error occurred in it. Notification of any errors occurs prior to form submission.

Pros and Cons of Each Option

Neither of these options is perfect, and they are thus often used together, complementing each other. Table 13.1 lists the pros and cons of each option.

Table 13.1 The Pros and Cons of Client and Server Form Validation

VALIDATION TYPE	PROS	CONS
Server-side	Very safe, will always work, regardless of the browser used and any browser settings	Not very user-friendly, user must submit form before validation occurs; any errors require resubmission
Client-side	More user-friendly, users prefer knowing what is wrong before form submission	Less safe, not supported by some older browsers; can be disabled, scripting languages have a lengthy learning curve

From a user's perspective, client-side validation is preferable. Obviously, users want to know what's wrong with the data they entered *before* they submit the form for processing. From a developer's perspective, however, server-side validation is simpler to code, guaranteed to always work regardless of the browser used, and less likely to fall victim to browser incompatibilities.

TIP

Form field validation should never be considered optional, and you should get in the habit of always using some type of validation in each and every form you create. Failure to do so will inevitably cause errors and broken applications later.

Using Server-Side Validation

As mentioned earlier, server-side validation involves adding code to your application that performs form field validation after the form is submitted. In ColdFusion this usually is achieved with a series of `<cfif>` statements that check each field's value and data types. If any validation steps fail, processing can be terminated with the `<cfabort>` function, or the user can be redirected to another page (maybe the form itself) using `<cflocation>`.

Using Manual Server-Side Validation

The code shown in Listing 13.1 is a simple login prompt used to gain access to an intranet site. The file (which you should save as `login1.cfm` in a new directory named `13`) prompts for a user ID and password. HTML's only validation rule, `maxlength`, is used in both form fields to restrict the number of characters that can be entered. The form itself is shown in Figure 13.1.

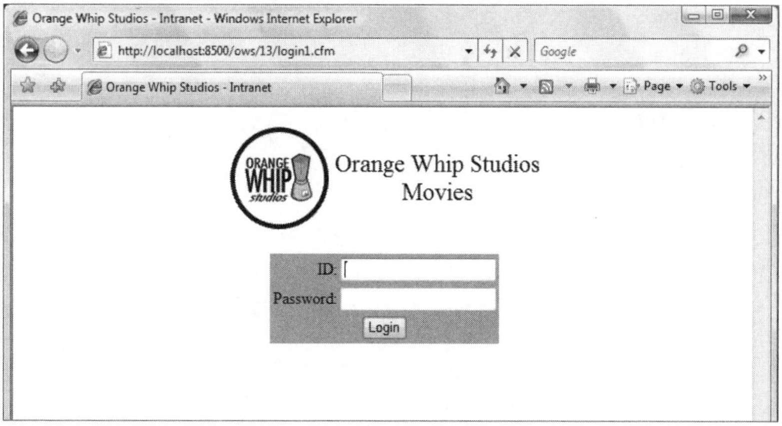

Figure 13.1

HTML forms support basic field types, such as text and password boxes.

Listing 13.1 `login1.cfm`—Simple Login Screen

```
<!---
Name:        login1.cfm
Author:      Ben Forta (ben@forta.com)
Description: Basic server-side validation
Created:     07/01/07
--->

<html>

<head>
  <title>Orange Whip Studios - Intranet</title>
</head>

<body>

<!--- Page header --->
<cfinclude template="header.cfm">

<!--- Login form --->
<form action="process1.cfm" method="post">

<table align="center" bgcolor="orange">
  <tr>
    <td align="right">
      ID:
    </td>
    <td>
      <input type="text"
             name="LoginID"
             maxlength="5">
    </td>
  </tr>
  <tr>
    <td align="right">
      Password:
    </td>
    <td>
      <input type="password"
             name="LoginPassword"
             maxlength="20">
    </td>
  </tr>
  <tr>
    <td colspan="2" align="center">
      <input type="submit" value="Login">
    </td>
 </tr>
</table>

</form>

</body>

</html>
```

This particular form gets submitted to a template named process1.cfm (specified in the action attribute). That template is responsible for validating the user input and processing the login only if all the validation rules passed. The validation rules necessary here are:

- Login ID is required.

- Login ID must be numeric.

- Login password is required.

To perform this validation, three `<cfif>` statements are used, as shown in Listing 13.2.

Listing 13.2 process1.cfm—Basic Server-Side Login Validation Code

```
<!---
Name:         process1.cfm
Author:       Ben Forta (ben@forta.com)
Description:  Basic server-side validation
Created:      07/01/07
--->

<html>

<head>
  <title>Orange Whip Studios - Intranet</title>
</head>

<body>

<!--- Page header --->
<cfinclude template="header.cfm">

<!--- Make sure LoginID is not empty --->
<cfif Len(Trim(LoginID)) IS 0>
 <h1>ERROR! ID can't be left blank!</h1>
 <cfabort>
</cfif>

<!--- Make sure LoginID is a number --->
<cfif IsNumeric(LoginID) IS "No">
 <h1>ERROR! Invalid ID specified!</h1>
 <cfabort>
</cfif>

<!--- Make sure LoginPassword is not empty --->
<cfif Len(Trim(LoginPassword)) IS 0>
 <h1>ERROR! Password can't be left blank!</h1>
 <cfabort>
</cfif>

<p align="center">
<h1>Intranet</h1>
</p>

Intranet would go here.

</body>

</html>
```

The first `<cfif>` checks the length of `LoginID` after trimming it with the `Trim()` function. The `Trim()` function is necessary to trap space characters that are technically valid characters in a text field but are not valid here. If the `Len()` function returns `0`, an error message is displayed, and the `<cfabort>` statement halts further processing.

TIP

Checking the length of the trimmed string (to determine whether it's empty) is functionally the same as doing a comparison against an empty string, like this:

```
<cfif Trim(LoginID) IS "">
```

The reason I used `Len()` to get the string length (instead of comparing it to `" "`) is that numeric comparisons are generally processed more quickly than string comparisons. For even greater performance, I could have eliminated the comparison value and used the following:

```
<cfif not Len(Trim(LoginID))>
```

The second `<cfif>` statement checks the data type. The `IsNumeric()` function returns `TRUE` if the passed value was numeric (contained only digits, for example) or `FALSE` if not. Once again, if the `<cfif>` check fails, an error is displayed and `<cfabort>` halts further processing, as shown in Figure 13.2. The third `<cfif>` checks that a password was specified (and that that the field was not left blank).

Figure 13.2

`<cfif>` statements can be used to perform validation checks and then display error messages if the checks fail.

This form of validation is the most powerful and flexible of all the validation options available to you. There's no limit to the number of `<cfif>` statements you can use, and there's no limit to the number of functions or tags you can use within them. You can even perform database operations (perhaps to check that a password matches) and use the results in comparisons.

TIP

`<cfif>` statements can be combined using **AND** and **OR** operators if necessary. For example, the first two `<cfif>` statements shown in Listing 13.2 could be combined to read

```
<cfif (Len(Trim(LoginID)) IS 0) OR (NOT IsNumeric(LoginID))>
```

Of course, there is a downside to all of this. Managing and maintaining all of those `<cfif>` statements can get tedious and complex, especially since most of your forms will likely contain more than just two controls, as ours did here.

Using `<cfparam>` Server-Side Validation

One solution to the proliferation of `<cfif>` statements in Listing 13.2 is to use the `<cfparam>` tag (first introduced in Chapter 9, "Programming with CFML"). The `<cfparam>` tag has two distinct functions:

- Providing default values for variables
- Performing field value validation

The difference is whether or not a `default` is provided. Look at this example:

```
<cfparam name="LoginID">
```

No default value is provided, and so `LoginID` is required, and if not present an error will be thrown.

By contrast, this next example has a `default` value:

```
<cfparam name="color" default="red">
```

In this example `color` isn't required, and if not present, the default value of `red` will be used.

`<cfparam>` also supports one additional attribute, a `type`, as seen in this example:

```
<cfparam name="LoginID" type="integer">
```

In this example `LoginID` is required (because no `default` is specified). In addition, it must be an `integer` (a number), and if it's something other than an `integer` an error will be thrown. Cold-Fusion supports a complete range of validation types, as listed in Table 13.2.

Table 13.2 Supported Validation Types

TYPE	DESCRIPTION
any	Allows any value
array	A ColdFusion array
binary	A binary value
boolean	true (yes, true, or any non-zero number) or false (no, false, or 0)
creditcard	A 13- or 16-digit credit card number that matches the MOD10 algorithm
date	A date and time value (same as time)
email	A well-formatted e-mail address
eurodate	A date value in dd/mm/yy format
float	A numeric value (same as numeric)
guid	A UUID in the form xxxxxxxx-xxxx-xxxx-xxxx-xxxxxxxxxxxx
integer	An integer value
numeric	A numeric value (same as float)
query	A ColdFusion query
range	A range of numbers (range must be specified)

Table 13.2 (CONTINUED)

TYPE	DESCRIPTION
regex	A regular expression pattern (same as `regular_expression`)
regular_expression	A regular expression pattern (same as `regex`)
social_security_number	A US format social security number (same as `ssn`)
ssn	A US format Social Security number (same as `social_security_number`)
string	A string of one or more characters
struct	A ColdFusion structure
telephone	A US format phone number
time	A date and time value (same as `date`)
url	A `file`, `ftp`, `http`, `https`, `mailto`, or `news` URL
usdate	A date value in `mm/dd/yy` format
uuid	A ColdFusion UUID in the form xxxxxxxx-xxxx-xxxx-xxxxxxxxxxxxxxx
variablename	A string that meets ColdFusion variable naming rules
xml	An XML object or string
zipcode	A US 5- or 5+4-digit ZIP code

Listing 13.3 is an updated version of Listing 13.2, this time replacing the `<cfif>` statements with `<cfparam>` tags.

Listing 13.3 process2.cfm—`<cfparam>` Server-Side Validation

```
<!---
Name:        process2.cfm
Author:      Ben Forta (ben@forta.com)
Description: <cfparam> server-side validation
Created:     07/01/07
--->

<!--- Form field validation --->
<cfparam name="FORM.LoginID" type="integer">
<cfparam name="FORM.LoginPassword">

<html>

<head>
  <title>Orange Whip Studios - Intranet</title>
</head>

<body>

<!--- Page header --->
<cfinclude template="header.cfm">
```

Listing 13.3 (CONTINUED)

```
<p align="center">
<h1>Intranet</h1>
</p>

Intranet would go here.

</body>

</html>
```

The code in Listing 13.3 is much cleaner and simpler than the code in Listing 13.2., yet it accomplishes the same thing. To test this code, modify `login1.cfm` and change the `<form>` tag so that `action="process2.cfm"`. Try submitting the form with errors and you'll see a screen like the one shown in Figure 13.3.

Figure 13.3

When using embedded form field validation, ColdFusion automatically displays an error message listing which checks failed.

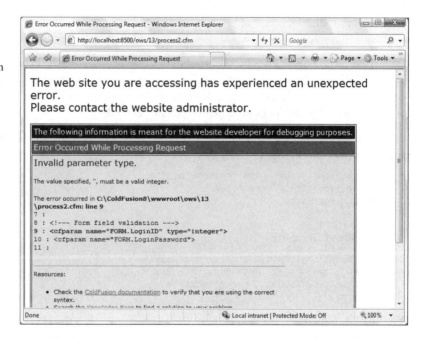

As you can see, there's a trade-off here. `<cfparam>` makes validation much simpler, but you lose control over formatting and presentation. `<cfif>` statements are a lot more work, but you retain total control over ColdFusion processing.

NOTE

The screen shown in Figure 13.3 is the default ColdFusion error screen. This screen can be changed using the `<cferror>` tag, which will be introduced in Chapter 19, "Introducing the Web Application Framework."

There is, however, a downside with both forms of server-side validation. If you were to add or rename a field, for example, you'd have to remember to update the destination page (the page to which the fields get submitted, as specified in the `<form>` action attribute), as well as the form itself. As your forms grow in complexity, so does the likelihood of your forms and their validation rules getting out of sync.

Using Automatic Server-Side Validation

Server-side validation is the safest and most secure form of form field validation, but it can also become a maintenance nightmare. ColdFusion to the rescue!

ColdFusion enables developers to embed basic form validation instructions within an HTML form. These instructions are embedded as hidden form fields. They get sent to the user's browser along with the rest of the form fields, but they aren't displayed to the user. When the user submits the form back to the Web server, however, those hidden fields are submitted too—and ColdFusion can then use them to perform automatic field validation.

These hidden form fields serve as validation rules, and ColdFusion can generate them for you automatically. It does this via some new tags, `<cfform>` and `<cfinput>`. But first, an explanation.

As you have already seen, `<form>`, `<input>`, and related tags are used by browsers to display HTML forms. ColdFusion doesn't process `<form>` or `<input>` tags when it sees them in your code (as it did in Listing 13.1). It simply passes them down to the browser. ColdFusion only processes CFML tags (or expressions without blocks to be processed), not HTML tags.

`<cfform>` is ColdFusion's version of `<form>`, and `<cfinput>` is ColdFusion's version of `<input>`. The tags can be used interchangeably, and this code:

```
<form action="process.cfm" method="post">
 <input type="text" name="search">
 <input type="submit">
</form>
```

is functionally identical to:

```
<cfform action="process.cfm" method="post">
 <cfinput type="text" name="search">
 <cfinput type="submit" name="submit">
</cfform>
```

When ColdFusion processes the `<cfform>` tag it simply generates the HTML `<form>` tag, and when it processes `<cfinput>` it generates `<input>`. So why bother doing this? Because these tags essentially intercept the form generation, allowing ColdFusion to insert other code as needed, such as validation code. For example, look at the following code snippet:

```
<cfinput type="password"
         name="LoginPassword"
         maxlength="20"
         required="yes"
         message="Password is required!"
         validateAt="onServer">
```

This tag accepts a password, just like the `<input>` seen in Listing 13.1. But unlike the tag in that listing, here a `<cfinput>` tag is used. And once `<input>` has been replaced with `<cfinput>`, additional attributes (that are instructions to ColdFusion) may be introduced. `required="yes"` tells Cold-Fusion that the `password` field is required, `message` contains the error message to be displayed if validation fails, and `validateAt="onServer"` instructs ColdFusion to validate the page on the server after form submission. When ColdFusion processes this tag it generates an `<input>` tag (because Web browsers would have no idea what `<cfinput>` was anyway), along with other code that it writes for you, hidden form fields that contain validation rules that ColdFusion can process upon form submission.

CAUTION

`<cfinput>` must be used within `<cfform>` tags; you can't use `<cfinput>` with `<form>`. Doing so will throw an error.

Listing 13.4 contains an updated login screen, this time containing `<cfform>` and `<cfinput>` tags providing validation rules.

Listing 13.4 `login2.cfm`—Embedded Server-Side Validation Rules

```
<!---
Name:        login2.cfm
Author:      Ben Forta (ben@forta.com)
Description: Form field validation demo
Created:     07/01/07
--->

<html>

<head>
  <title>Orange Whip Studios - Intranet</title>
</head>

<body>

<!--- Page header --->
<cfinclude template="header.cfm">

<!--- Login form --->
<cfform action="process2.cfm">

<table align="center" bgcolor="orange">
  <tr>
    <td align="right">
      ID:
    </td>
    <td>
      <cfinput type="text"
               name="LoginID"
               maxlength="5"
               required="yes"
               message="A valid numeric ID is required!"
               validate="integer"
               validateAt="onServer">
    </td>
  </tr>
  <tr>
    <td align="right">
```

Listing 13.4 (CONTINUED)

```
          Password:
        </td>
        <td>
          <cfinput type="password"
                   name="LoginPassword"
                   maxlength="20"
                   required="yes"
                   message="Password is required!"
                   validateAt="onServer">
        </td>
      </tr>
      <tr>
        <td colspan="2" align="center">
          <cfinput type="submit"
                   name="submit"
                   value="Login">
        </td>
      </tr>
    </table>

  </cfform>

  </body>

  </html>
```

NOTE

When using `<cfinput>` every form field must have a name, even `type="button"`.

If you were to run this code, it would look exactly as it did before (Figure 13.1). That's because ColdFusion generated the same HTML form code as we did before. So where is the difference? Do a View Source, and you'll see that the form generated by ColdFusion looks like this:

```
<html>

<head><script type="text/javascript" src="/CFIDE/scripts/cfform.js"></script>
<script type="text/javascript" src="/CFIDE/scripts/masks.js"></script>

  <title>Orange Whip Studios - Intranet</title>

<script type="text/javascript">
    if (window.ColdFusion) ColdFusion.required['LoginID']=true;
</script>

<script type="text/javascript">
    if (window.ColdFusion) ColdFusion.required['LoginPassword']=true;
</script>
<script type="text/javascript">
<!--
    _CF_checkCFForm_1 = function(_CF_this)
    {
        //reset on submit
        _CF_error_exists = false;
        _CF_error_messages = new Array();
```

```
            _CF_error_fields = new Object();
            _CF_FirstErrorField = null;


        //display error messages and return success
        if( _CF_error_exists )
        {
            if( _CF_error_messages.length > 0 )
            {
                // show alert() message
                _CF_onErrorAlert(_CF_error_messages);
                // set focus to first form error, if the field supports js focus().
                if( _CF_this[_CF_FirstErrorField].type == "text" )
                { _CF_this[_CF_FirstErrorField].focus(); }

            }
            return false;
        }else {
            return true;
        }
    }
//-->
</script>
</head>

<body>




<table align="center">
 <tr>
  <td><img src="../images/logo_c.gif" alt="Orange Whip Studios"></td>
  <td align="center"><font size="+2">Orange Whip Studios<br>Movies</font></td>
 </tr>
</table>


<form name="CFForm_1" id="CFForm_1" action="process2.cfm" method="post"
onsubmit="return _CF_checkCFForm_1(this)">

<table align="center" bgcolor="orange">
  <tr>
    <td align="right">
      ID:
    </td>
    <td>
      <input name="LoginID" id="LoginID"  type="text" maxlength="5"  />
    </td>
  </tr>
  <tr>
    <td align="right">
      Password:
    </td>
    <td>
      <input name="LoginPassword" id="LoginPassword"  type="password" maxlength="20"
/>
```

```
       </td>
     </tr>
     <tr>
       <td colspan="2" align="center">
         <input name="submit" id="submit"  type="submit" value="Login" />
       </td>
  </tr>
</table>

<input type='hidden' name='LoginID_CFFORMINTEGER' value='A valid numeric ID is
required!'>
<input type='hidden' name='LoginID_CFFORMREQUIRED' value='A valid numeric ID is
required!'>
<input type='hidden' name='LoginPassword_CFFORMREQUIRED' value='Password is
required!'>
</form>


</body>

</html>
```

There is no `<cfform>` in this code, no `<cfinput>`, and no closing `</cfform>`. ColdFusion generated the standard HTML form tags, and also made some other changes:

- Listing 13.4 had no method specified, but `<cfform>` knew to automatically set `method="post"`.

- `<cfform>`, `<cfinput>`, and `</cfform>` were replaced with `<form>`, `<input>`, and `</form>` respectively.

- Three hidden fields were added to the form; these contain the validation rules that ColdFusion will use when processing the form submission.

- Other changes were made too, but those relate to client-side validation, which we'll get to shortly.

Run `login2.cfm` and submit the form with missing or invalid values. You'll see an error screen like the one shown in Figure 13.4.

Figure 13.4

Validation errors caught by embedded server-side validation throw a more friendly error message screen.

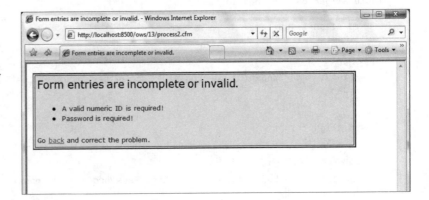

NOTE

The screen shown in Figure 13.4 is the default validation error screen. This screen too can be changed using the `<cferror>` tag.

As you can see, the ColdFusion validation rules are simple and effective. And because the validation rules are embedded into the form itself, your forms and their rules are less likely to get out of sync.

NOTE

The validation rules seen here were generated by ColdFusion automatically. If needed, you can embed the hidden validation rules yourself, although you'll seldom have to. In previous versions of ColdFusion this was necessary, as no automatic generation existed.

Of course, when validation errors occur the user will still have to go back to the form to make any corrections. The benefits of embedded validation rules are really only for developers. Embedded validation does nothing to improve the user experience—for that you need client-side validation.

Using Client-Side Validation

The biggest drawback in using server-side validation is that the validation occurs after form submission. This means that if any validation rules fail, the user must go back to the form, make the corrections, and resubmit it to the server. To make matters worse, some browsers lose the data in the form fields when the Back button is clicked, forcing the user to reenter all the data.

Obviously, this hardly creates a user-friendly interface. Too many good Web sites have lost visitors because their forms were aggravating to work with.

Fortunately, an alternative is available: client-side validation.

Understanding Client-Side Validation

To perform client-side validation, you add a series of browser instructions to your Web page. The browser interprets these instructions and executes them right on the user's computer (i.e., on the client side) before the form ever gets submitted to the server.

These instructions are written in scripting languages, such as JavaScript (supported by almost all browsers) or VBScript (based on Visual Basic and supported by Microsoft Internet Explorer only). These are interpreted languages that enable you to control browser behavior.

NOTE

Don't confuse JavaScript with Java. Java is a true compiled object-oriented application development language, one that can be used to write entire programs. JavaScript (including JScript, which is a variant of JavaScript) is an interpreted language designed to control Web browsers. Unlike Java, JavaScript can't access anything on your computer other than your Web browser.

To validate a form, you write a script that will trap the form submission and allow it to proceed only if a series of validation checks have passed. If any checks fail, you would display an error message and prevent the form from being submitted.

Of course, to do this, you'd have to learn JavaScript.

Client-Side Validation Via `<cfform>`

You've already seen how ColdFusion can dramatically simplify server-side validation by automatically generating code for you. Well, it can do the same for client-side validation, generating the JavaScript needed to validate form fields. And the best part is that you already know the tags you need to make this work: they are `<cfform>` and `<cfinput>`.

Listing 13.5 contains `login3.cfm`, a slightly modified version of `login2.cfm`. Make that very slightly modified. Can you even see the change?

Listing 13.5 `login3.cfm`—Client-Side Validation Rules

```
<!---
Name:        login3.cfm
Author:      Ben Forta (ben@forta.com)
Description: Form field validation demo
Created:     07/01/07
--->

<html>

<head>
  <title>Orange Whip Studios - Intranet</title>
</head>

<body>

<!--- Page header --->
<cfinclude template="header.cfm">

<!--- Login form --->
<cfform action="process2.cfm">

<table align="center" bgcolor="orange">
  <tr>
    <td align="right">
      ID:
    </td>
    <td>
      <cfinput type="text"
               name="LoginID"
               maxlength="5"
               required="yes"
               message="A valid numeric ID is required!"
               validate="integer"
               validateAt="onSubmit">
    </td>
  </tr>
  <tr>
    <td align="right">
      Password:
    </td>
    <td>
```

Listing 13.5 (CONTINUED)

```
        <cfinput type="password"
                 name="LoginPassword"
                 maxlength="20"
                 required="yes"
                 message="Password is required!"
                 validateAt="onSubmit">
      </td>
    </tr>
    <tr>
      <td colspan="2" align="center">
        <cfinput type="submit"
                 name="submit"
                 value="Login">
      </td>
    </tr>
  </table>

</cfform>

</body>

</html>
```

Listings 13.4 and 13.5 are almost identical. The only change is the `validateAt` attribute in the two `<cfinput>` tags, which has been changed from

```
validateAt="onServer"
```

to

```
validateAt="onSubmit"
```

`onServer` tells ColdFusion to generate validation code that will be processed on the server (as seen previously). `onSubmit` tells ColdFusion to generate code that will be processed by the browser when the form is about to be submitted. `validateAt="onSubmit"` generates JavaScript code, which it embeds into your form (in the much the same way as it embedded hidden form fields for server-side validation).

Run `login3.cfm`; the form should look exactly as it did before. But now if you generate an error you'll see a pop-up window right in your browser, as seen in Figure 13.5.

Using client-side validation, the form was never submitted, because it failed the validation test. `onSubmit` validation essentially traps the form submission, and only allows it to continue if it passes all validation tests. This is obviously a far friendlier user experience; if users see a pop-up message like the one in Figure 13.5 they will be able to make corrections and resubmit the form.

NOTE

The pop-up error box is a standard browser dialog that varies from browser to browser, and there is no way to change what it looks like. The only thing you can change are the actual error messages themselves.

e validation
ssages are
d in a browser
box.

It is worth noting that a lot is going on under the hood to make all this work, and ColdFusion has successfully shielded you from it. But do a View Source and you'll see that the generated code has gotten quite lengthy and complex:

```html
<html>

<head><script type="text/javascript" src="/CFIDE/scripts/cfform.js"></script>
<script type="text/javascript" src="/CFIDE/scripts/masks.js"></script>

  <title>Orange Whip Studios - Intranet</title>

<script type="text/javascript">
    if (window.ColdFusion) ColdFusion.required['LoginID']=true;
</script>

<script type="text/javascript">
    if (window.ColdFusion) ColdFusion.required['LoginPassword']=true;
</script>
<script type="text/javascript">
<!--
    _CF_checkCFForm_1 = function(_CF_this)
    {
        //reset on submit
        _CF_error_exists = false;
        _CF_error_messages = new Array();
        _CF_error_fields = new Object();
        _CF_FirstErrorField = null;

        //form element LoginID required check
        if( _CF_hasValue(_CF_this['LoginID'], "TEXT", false ) )
```

```
            {
                //form element LoginID 'INTEGER' validation checks
                if (!_CF_checkinteger(_CF_this['LoginID'].value, true))
                {
                    _CF_onError(_CF_this, "LoginID", _CF_this['LoginID'].value, "A valid
numeric ID is required!");
                    _CF_error_exists = true;
                }

        }else {
                _CF_onError(_CF_this, "LoginID", _CF_this['LoginID'].value, "A valid
numeric ID is required!");
                _CF_error_exists = true;
        }

        //form element LoginPassword required check
        if( !_CF_hasValue(_CF_this['LoginPassword'], "PASSWORD", false ) )
        {
                _CF_onError(_CF_this, "LoginPassword", _CF_this['LoginPassword'].value,
"Password is required!");
                _CF_error_exists = true;
        }


        //display error messages and return success
        if( _CF_error_exists )
        {
            if( _CF_error_messages.length > 0 )
            {
                // show alert() message
                _CF_onErrorAlert(_CF_error_messages);
                // set focus to first form error, if the field supports js focus().
                if( _CF_this[_CF_FirstErrorField].type == "text" )
                { _CF_this[_CF_FirstErrorField].focus(); }

            }
            return false;
        }else {
            return true;
        }
    }
//-->
</script>
</head>

<body>



<table align="center">
 <tr>
  <td><img src="../images/logo_c.gif" alt="Orange Whip Studios"></td>
  <td align="center"><font size="+2">Orange Whip Studios<br>Movies</font></td>
 </tr>
</table>
```

```
<form name="CFForm_1" id="CFForm_1" action="process2.cfm" method="post"
onsubmit="return _CF_checkCFForm_1(this)">

<table align="center" bgcolor="orange">
  <tr>
    <td align="right">
      ID:
    </td>
    <td>
      <input name="LoginID" id="LoginID"  type="text" maxlength="5"  />
    </td>
  </tr>
  <tr>
    <td align="right">
      Password:
    </td>
    <td>
      <input name="LoginPassword" id="LoginPassword"  type="password" maxlength="20"
/>
    </td>
  </tr>
  <tr>
    <td colspan="2" align="center">
      <input name="submit" id="submit"  type="submit" value="Login" />
    </td>
  </tr>
</table>

</form>


</body>

</html>
```

That's a lot of code, and most of it is the JavaScript needed to validate form fields.

So what can client-side validation check for? The exact same checks that server-side validation does. Use `required="yes"` to make a form field required, and use `validate=` specifying any of the types listed in Table 13.2 previously. The same validation options are supported by both server-side and client-side validation, all you have to do is decide which you want and specify `validateAt="onServer"` or `validateAt="onSubmit"`.

NOTE

There is actually a third option supported by `validateAt`. To force client-side validation as soon as the user leaves the form field (either by clicking on another field or by tabbing between fields) specify `validateAt="onBlur"`. But use this option sparingly, as this type of validation can annoy your users.

TIP

If `validateAt` is not specified, the default of `validateAt="onSubmit"` will be used.

One of the validation types warrants special mention. `validate="range"` checks that a number is within a specified range, which means that you must provide the range of allowed values. This is done using the `range` attribute, as follows:

```
<cfinput type="text"
         name="age"
         validate="range"
         range="1,100">
```

This code snippet will allow numbers from 1 to 100. You may also specify just a minimum (and no maximum) by only providing one number in the `range`, as follows:

```
<cfinput type="text"
         name="age"
         validate="range"
         range="18">
```

This code will only allow 18 or higher. To specify a maximum but no minimum, just provide the second number, like this:

```
<cfinput type="text"
         name="age"
         validate="range"
         range=",17">
```

This code will only allow 17 or lower.

NOTE

The actual JavaScript validation code is in a file named `cfform.js` in the `cfide/scripts` directory beneath the Web root. This file is included dynamically using a `<script>` tag whenever any validation is used.

Extending `<cfinput>` Validation Options

You can't add your own validation types to `<cfinput>`, but you can extend the validation by providing *regular expressions*. A regular expression is a search pattern used to match strings. Full coverage of regular expressions is beyond the scope of this book, but here is an example to help explain the concept.

NOTE

Interested in learning more about regular xxpressions? You may want to get a copy of *Sams Teach Yourself Regular Expressions in 10 Minutes* (Sams, ISBN 0672325667).

Colors used in Web pages are often specified as RGB values (colors specified in amounts of red, green, and blue). RGB values are six characters long—three sets of two hexadecimal values (00 to FF). To obtain a set of RGB values in a form you could use three `<cfinput>` tags like this:

```
Red:
<cfinput type="text"
         name="color_r"
         validate="regex"
         pattern="[A-Fa-f0-9]{ 2,} "
         message="RGB value must be 00-FF"
         size="2"
```

```
            maxlength="2">
<br>
Green:
<cfinput type="text"
         name="color_g"
         validate="regex"
         pattern="[A-Fa-f0-9]{ 2,} "
         message="RGB value must be 00-FF"
         size="2"
         maxlength="2">
<br>
Blue:
<cfinput type="text"
         name="color_b"
         validate="regex"
         pattern="[A-Fa-f0-9]{ 2,} "
         message="RGB value must be 00-FF"
         size="2"
         maxlength="2">
<br>
```

validate="regex" specifies that regular expressions are to be used for validation. The regular expression itself is passed to the pattern attribute. [A-Fa-f0-9] matches a single character of A through F (upper- or lowercase) or 0 through 9. The { 2,} instructs the browser to only accept a minimum of 2 instances of the previous expression. That coupled with maxlength="2" provides the exact validation rule needed to accept RGB values.

As you can see, with minimal work you can write regular expressions to validate all sorts of things.

Specifying an Input Mask

We're not quite done yet. Client-side validation provides users with a far better experience than does server-side validation. But let's take this one step further.

All the validation thus far checks for errors after a user inputs data into a form field. Which begs the question, why let users type incorrect data into form fields in the first place? If a form field requires specific data (like LoginID in the forms above, which required a numeric ID), let's prevent the user from typing anything else.

As simple as that suggestion sounds, controlling user input at that level is rather complex, and requires some very sophisticated scripting. Fortunately, you don't have to write that validation code either. The <cfinput> tag supports an additional attribute named mask that accepts an input filter mask. A filter is a string made up of characters that identify what is allowed for each character entered. For example, 9 is used to allow only digits (0 through 9). So the following mask would only allow two digits and nothing else:

```
mask="99"
```

Table 13.3 lists the mask characters supported by <cfinput mask=>.

Table 13.3 Supported Mask Characters

CHARACTER	ALLOWS
A	A through Z (upper- or lowercase)
9	Any digit
X	A through Z (upper- or lowercase) and any digit
?	Any character
	Any other character inserts that actual character into the input text

So, for a US ZIP code you could use the following mask:

```
mask="99999-9999"
```

And this mask could work for Canadian postal codes:

```
mask="A9A 9A9"
```

And to mask a US Social Security number you could use:

```
mask="999-99-9999"
```

Of course, masking and validation may be combined, as seen in Listing 13.6, an update to our login page.

Listing 13.6 `login4.cfm`—Login Screen with Client-Side Validation Rules and Masking

```
<!---
Name:        login4.cfm
Author:      Ben Forta (ben@forta.com)
Description: Form field validation demo
Created:     07/01/07
--->

<html>

<head>
  <title>Orange Whip Studios - Intranet</title>
</head>

<body>

<!--- Page header --->
<cfinclude template="header.cfm">

<!--- Login form --->
<cfform action="process2.cfm">

<table align="center" bgcolor="orange">
  <tr>
    <td align="right">
      ID:
    </td>
    <td>
      <cfinput type="text"
```

Listing 13.6   (CONTINUED)

```
                name="LoginID"
                maxlength="5"
                required="yes"
                mask="99999"
                message="A valid numeric ID is required!"
                validate="integer"
                validateAt="onSubmit">
    </td>
  </tr>
  <tr>
    <td align="right">
      Password:
    </td>
    <td>
      <cfinput type="password"
               name="LoginPassword"
               maxlength="20"
               required="yes"
               message="Password is required!"
               validateAt="onSubmit">
    </td>
  </tr>
  <tr>
    <td colspan="2" align="center">
      <cfinput type="submit"
               name="submit"
               value="Login">
    </td>
  </tr>
</table>

</cfform>

</body>

</html>
```

Run this new login form. It will look just like the previous login screens, but see what happens when you try to type an alphabetical character into the LoginID field. And all it took was one more <cfinput> attribute.

Validation on the Server and Client

You've seen <cfinput> used to validate on the server and on the client. So far we used one or the other, but it need not be an either/or proposition. In fact, <cfinput> supports the use of multiple validation types at once. All you need to do is specify the types delimited by commas.

So, to validate the UserID field using masks, client-side validation, and server-side validation, you could do the following:

```
<cfinput type="text"
         name="LoginID"
         maxlength="5"
         required="yes"
```

```
mask="99999"
message="A valid numeric ID is required!"
validate="integer"
validateAt="onSubmit,onServer">
```

Preventing Multiple Form Submissions

I want to share one last `<cfinput>` goodie with you. All Web application developers face the problem of dealing with multiple form submissions. For example, a user fills in a form, clicks the Submit button, and then gets impatient and submits it again and again and again.

If your form was a front end to database searches, this would result in multiple searches being performed. And while this won't negatively impact your data, it will definitely slow the application. This becomes an even bigger issue when forms are used to insert data into database tables (as will be seen in the next chapter). Multiple form submissions then are a real problem, as users could inadvertently insert multiple rows to your table.

Once again, `<cfinput>` comes to the rescue with a special `validate` option that only applies to form buttons. `validate="SubmitOnce"` generates JavaScript code that prevents multiple form submissions. For example, to not allow our login form to be submitted multiple times, the button could be changed to:

```
<cfinput type="submit"
         name="submit"
         value="Login"
         validate="SubmitOnce">
```

Clean and simple, thanks to `<cfinput>`.

Putting It All Together

Before you run off and plug `<cfform>` and `<cfinput>` into all your templates, there are some other details that you should know:

- **Not all browsers support JavaScript.** Most newer ones do, but there still are older ones out there. Browsers that don't support JavaScript will generally ignore it, enabling your forms to be submitted without being validated if only client-side validation is used.

- **You should combine the use of JavaScript validation with server-side validation.** These will never fail validation if the browser does support JavaScript, and if the browser doesn't, at least you have some form of validation.

- **Don't rely solely on automatically generated server-side validation (via embedded hidden fields).** Clever hackers could quite easily remove those hidden fields and submit your form without server-side validation.

- **The JavaScript code can be quite lengthy.** This will slightly increase the size of your Web page and thus the time it takes to download it from your Web server.

- **Mix and match validation types.** Use `<cfinput>` to generate multiple validation types; the more validation you do the safer your applications will be.

- **Manual server-side validation is your last defense.** Regardless of the validation options used, it's safest to always use manual server-side tests (either using `<cfparam>` or `<cfif>` statements). If you are using `<cfinput>`, users will never get caught by those tests, so you may not need to even worry about prettying up the error messages. But for that mischievous user who just wants to find a way in, manual server-side validation is your last defense.

CHAPTER 14

Using Forms to Add or Change Data

Adding Data with ColdFusion

Now that you learned all about forms and form data validation in the previous two chapters, it's time to combine the two so as to be able to add and update database table data.

➜ See Chapter 12, "ColdFusion Forms," to learn about HTML forms and how to use them within your ColdFusion applications.

➜ See Chapter 13, "Form Data Validation," for coverage of form field validation techniques and options.

When you created the movie search forms in Chapter 12, you had to create two templates for each search. One creates the user search screen that contains the search form, and the other performs the actual search using the ColdFusion `<cfquery>` tag. ColdFusion developers usually refer to these as the `<form>` and `action` pages, because one contains the form and the other is the file specified as the `<form>` action.

Breaking an operation into more than one template is typical of ColdFusion, as well as all Web-based data interaction. As explained in Chapter 1, "Introducing ColdFusion," a browser's connection to a Web server is made and broken as necessary. An HTTP connection is made to a Web server whenever a Web page is retrieved. That connection is broken as soon as that page is retrieved. Any subsequent pages are retrieved with a new connection that is used just to retrieve that page.

There is no real way to keep a connection alive for the duration of a complete process—when searching for data, for example. Therefore, the process must be broken up into steps, and, as shown in Chapter 12, each step typically is a separate template.

Adding data via your Web browser is no different. You generally need at least two templates to perform the insertion. One displays the form you use to collect the data; the other processes the data and inserts the record.

Adding data to a table involves the following steps:

1. Display a form to collect the data. The names of any input fields should match the names of the columns in the destination table.

2. Submit the form to ColdFusion for processing. ColdFusion adds the row via the data source using a SQL statement.

Creating an Add Record Form

Forms used to add data are no different from the forms you created to search for data. As seen in Listing 14.1, the form is created using form tags, with a form control for each row table column to be inserted. Save this file as insert1.cfm (in the 14 directory under ows). You'll be able to execute the page to display the form, but don't submit it yet (you have yet to create the action page).

Listing 14.1 insert1.cfm—New Movie Form

```
<!---
Name:        insert1.cfm
Author:      Ben Forta (ben@forta.com)
Description: Table row insertion demo
Created:     07/01/07
--->

<!--- Get ratings --->
<cfquery datasource="ows" name="ratings">
SELECT RatingID, Rating
FROM FilmsRatings
ORDER BY RatingID
</cfquery>

<!--- Page header --->
<cfinclude template="header.cfm">

<!--- New movie form --->
<form action="insert2.cfm" method="post">

<table align="center" bgcolor="orange">
 <tr>
  <th colspan="2">
   <font size="+1">Add a Movie</font>
  </th>
 </tr>
 <tr>
  <td>
   Movie:
  </td>
  <td>
   <input type="Text"
          name="MovieTitle"
          size="50"
          maxlength="100">
  </td>
 </tr>
```

Listing 14.1 (CONTINUED)

```
<tr>
 <td>
  Tag line:
 </td>
 <td>
  <input type="Text"
         name="PitchText"
         size="50"
         maxlength="100">
 </td>
</tr
<tr>
 <td>
  Rating:
 </td>
 <td>
  <!--- Ratings list --->
  <select name="RatingID">
   <cfoutput query="ratings">
    <option value="#RatingID#">#Rating#</option>
   </cfoutput>
  </select>
 </td>
</tr>
<tr>
 <td>
  Summary:
 </td>
 <td>
  <textarea name="summary"
            cols="40"
            rows="5"
            wrap="virtual"></textarea>
 </td>
</tr>
<tr>
 <td>
  Budget:
 </td>
 <td>
  <input type="Text"
         name="AmountBudgeted"
         size="10"
         maxlength="10">
 </td>
</tr>
<tr>
 <td>
  Release Date:
 </td>
 <td>
  <input type="Text"
         name="DateInTheaters"
         size="10"
         maxlength="10">
```

Listing 14.1   (CONTINUED)

```
      </td>
     </tr>
     <tr>
      <td>
       Image File:
      </td>
      <td>
       <input type="Text"
              name="ImageName"
              size="20"
              maxlength="50">
      </td>
     </tr>
     <tr>
      <td colspan="2" align="center">
       <input type="submit" value="Insert">
      </td>
     </tr>
    </table>

   </form>

   <!--- Page footer --->
   <cfinclude template="footer.cfm">
```

NOTE

Listing 14.1 contains a form not unlike the forms created in Chapters 12 and 13. This form uses form techniques and validation options described in both of those chapters; refer to them if necessary.

The file `insert1.cfm`—and indeed all the files in this chapter—includes common header and footer files (`header.cfm` and `footer.cfm`, respectively). These files contain the HTML page layout code, including any logos. They are included in each file (using `<cfinclude>` tags) to facilitate code reuse (and to keep code listings shorter and more manageable). Listings 14.2 and 14.3 contain the code for these two files.

➝ `<cfinclude>` and code reuse are introduced in Chapter 9, "Programming with CFML."

Listing 14.2   `header.cfm`—Movie Form Page Header

```
   <!---
   Name:        header.cfm
   Author:      Ben Forta (ben@forta.com)
   Description: Page header
   Created:     07/01/07
   --->

   <html>

   <head>
    <title>Orange Whip Studios - Intranet</title>
   </head>

   <body>
```

Listing 14.2 (CONTINUED)

```
<table align="center">
 <tr>
  <td>
   <img src="../images/logo_c.gif" alt="Orange Whip Studios">
  </td>
  <td align="center">
   <font size="+2">Orange Whip Studios<br>Movie Maintenance</font>
  </td>
 </tr>
</table>
```

Listing 14.3 `footer.cfm`—Movie Form Page Footer

```
<!---
Name:        footer.cfm
Author:      Ben Forta (ben@forta.com)
Description: Page footer
Created:     07/01/07
--->

</body>

</html>
```

The `<form>` `action` attribute specifies the name of the template to be used to process the insertion; in this case it's `insert2.cfm`.

Each `<input>` (or `<cfinput>`, if used) field has a field name specified in the `name` attribute. These names correspond to the names of the appropriate columns in the `Films` table.

TIP

Dreamweaver users can take advantage of the built-in drag-and-drop features when using table and column names within your code. Simply open the Database tab in the Application panel, expand the data source, and then expand the tables item to display the list of tables within the data source. You can then drag the table name into your source code. Similarly, expanding the table name displays a list of the fields within that table, and those can also be dragged into your source code.

You also specified the `size` and `maxlength` attributes in each of the text fields. `size` is used to specify the size of the text box within the browser window. Without the `size` attribute, the browser uses its default size, which varies from one browser to the next.

The `size` attribute does not restrict the number of characters that can be entered into the field. `size="50"` creates a text field that occupies the space of 50 characters, but the text scrolls within the field if you enter more than 50 characters. To restrict the number of characters that can be entered, you must use the `maxlength` attribute. `maxlength="100"` instructs the browser to allow no more than 100 characters in the field.

The `size` attribute primarily is used for aesthetics and the control of screen appearance. `maxlength` is used to ensure that only data that can be handled is entered into a field. Without `maxlength`, users could enter more data than would fit in a field, and that data would be truncated upon database insertion (or might even generate database errors).

NOTE

You should always use both the `size` and `maxlength` attributes for maximum control over form appearance and data entry. Without them, the browser will use its defaults–and there are no rules governing what these defaults should be.

The `RatingID` field is a drop-down list box populated with a `<cfquery>`.

The Add a Movie form is shown in Figure 14.1.

Figure 14.1

HTML forms can be used as a front end for data insertion.

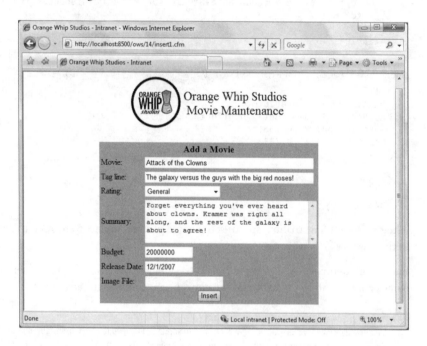

Processing Additions

The next thing you need is a template to process the actual data insertion—the ACTION page mentioned earlier. In this page use the SQL INSERT statement to add the new row to the `Films` table.

➜ See Chapter 7, "SQL Data Manipulation," for an explanation of the INSERT statement.

As shown in Listing 14.4, the `<cfquery>` tag can be used to pass any SQL statement—not just SELECT statements. The SQL statement here is INSERT, which adds a row to the `Films` table and sets the values in seven columns to the form values passed by the browser.

Listing 14.4   `insert2.cfm`—Adding Data with the SQL INSERT Statement

```
<!---
Name:        insert2.cfm
Author:      Ben Forta (ben@forta.com)
Description: Table row insertion demo
Created:     07/01/07
--->
```

Listing 14.4 (CONTINUED)

```
<!--- Insert movie --->
<cfquery datasource="ows">
INSERT INTO Films(MovieTitle,
                  PitchText,
                  AmountBudgeted,
                  RatingID,
                  Summary,
                  ImageName,
                  DateInTheaters)
VALUES('#Trim(FORM.MovieTitle)#',
       '#Trim(FORM.PitchText)#',
       #FORM.AmountBudgeted#,
       #FORM.RatingID#,
       '#Trim(FORM.Summary)#',
       '#Trim(FORM.ImageName)#',
       #CreateODBCDate(FORM.DateInTheaters)#)
</cfquery>

<!--- Page header --->
<cfinclude template="header.cfm">

<!--- Feedback --->
<cfoutput>
<h1>New movie '#FORM.MovieTitle#' added</h1>
</cfoutput>

<!--- Page footer --->
<cfinclude template="footer.cfm">
```

Listing 14.4 is pretty self-explanatory. The <cfquery> tag performs the actual INSERT operation. The list of columns into which values are to be assigned is specified, as is the matching VALUES list (these two lists must match exactly, both the columns and their order).

Each of the values used is from a FORM field, but some differences do exist in how the fields are used:

- All string fields have their values enclosed within single quotation marks.

- The two numeric fields (AmountBudgeted and RatingID) have no single quotation marks around them.

- The date field (DateInTheaters) is formatted as a date using the CreateODBCDate() function.

It's important to remember that SQL is not typeless, so it's your job to use quotation marks where necessary to explicitly type variables.

TIP

ColdFusion is very good at handling dates, and can correctly process dates in all sorts of formats. But occasionally a date may be specified in a format that ColdFusion can't parse properly. In that case, it will be your responsibility to format the date so ColdFusion understands it. You can do this using the DateFormat() function or the ODBC date function CreateODBCDate() (or the CreateODBCTime() and CreateODBCDateTime() functions). Even though ColdFusion uses JDBC database drivers, the ODBC format generated by the ODBC functions is understood by ColdFusion and will be processed correctly. Listing 14.4 demonstrates the use of the CreateODBCDate() function.

NOTE

> Notice that the `<cfquery>` in Listing 14.4 has no `name` attribute. `name` is an optional attribute and is necessary only if you need to manipulate the data returned by `<cfquery>`. Because the operation here is an `INSERT`, no data is returned; the `name` attribute is therefore unnecessary.

Save Listing 14.4 as `insert2.cfm`, and then try submitting a new movie using the form in `insert1.cfm`. You should see a screen similar to the one shown in Figure 14.2.

Figure 14.2

Data can be added via ColdFusion using the SQL INSERT statement.

NOTE

> You can verify that the movie was added by browsing the table using any of the search templates you created in Chapter 12.

Introducing `<cfinsert>`

The example in Listing 14.4 demonstrates how to add data to a table using the standard SQL `INSERT` command. This works very well if you have to provide data for only a few columns, and if those columns are always provided. If the number of columns can vary, using SQL `INSERT` gets rather complicated.

For example, assume you have two or more data-entry forms for similar data. One might collect a minimal number of fields, whereas another collects a more complete record. How would you create a SQL `INSERT` statement to handle both sets of data?

You could create two separate templates, with a different SQL `INSERT` statement in each, but that's a poor solution. You should always try to avoid having more than one template perform a given operation. That way, you don't run the risk of future changes and revisions being applied incorrectly. If a table name or column name changes, for example, you won't have to worry about forgetting one of the templates that references the changed column.

TIP

> As a rule, never create more than one template to perform a specific operation. This helps prevent introducing errors into your templates when updates or revisions are made. You're almost always better off creating one template with conditional code than creating two separate templates.

Another solution is to use dynamic SQL. You could write a basic INSERT statement and then gradually construct a complete statement by using a series of <cfif> statements.

This is a workable solution, but not a very efficient one. The conditional SQL INSERT code is far more complex than conditional SQL SELECT. The INSERT statement requires that both the list of columns and the values be dynamic. In addition, the INSERT syntax requires that you separate all column names and values by commas. This means that every column name and value must be followed by a comma except the last one in the list. Your conditional SQL has to accommodate these syntactical requirements when the statement is constructed.

A better solution is to use <cfinsert>, which is a special ColdFusion tag that hides the complexity of building dynamic SQL INSERT statements. <cfinsert> takes the following parameters as attributes:

- datasource—The name of the data source that contains the table to which the data is to be inserted.

- tablename—The name of the destination table.

- formfields—An optional comma-separated list of fields to be inserted. If this attribute isn't provided, all the fields in the submitted form are used.

Look at the following ColdFusion tag:

```
<cfinsert datasource="ows" tablename="FILMS">
```

This code does exactly the same thing as the <cfquery> tag in Listing 14.4. When ColdFusion processes a <cfinsert> tag, it builds a dynamic SQL INSERT statement under the hood. If a formfields attribute is provided, the specified field names are used. No formfields attribute was specified in this example, so ColdFusion automatically uses the form fields that were submitted, building the list of columns and the values dynamically. <cfinsert> even automatically handles the inclusion of single quotation marks where necessary.

CAUTION

When you use Apache Derby, table names passed to <cfinsert> must be uppercase.

While we are it, the form created in insert1.cfm did not perform any data validation, which could cause database errors to be thrown (try inserting text in a numeric field and see what happens).

Listing 14.5 contains a revised form (a modified version of insert1.cfm); save this file as insert3.cfm. Listing 14.6 contains a revised action page (a modified version of insert2.cfm); save this file as insert4.cfm.

Listing 14.5   insert3.cfm—Using <cfform> for Field Validation

```
<!---
Name:        insert3.cfm
Author:      Ben Forta (ben@forta.com)
Description: Table row insertion demo
Created:     07/01/07
--->
```

Listing 14.5 (CONTINUED)

```
<!--- Get ratings --->
<cfquery datasource="ows" name="ratings">
SELECT RatingID, Rating
FROM FilmsRatings
ORDER BY RatingID
</cfquery>

<!--- Page header --->
<cfinclude template="header.cfm">

<!--- New movie form --->
<cfform action="insert4.cfm">

<table align="center" bgcolor="orange">
 <tr>
  <th colspan="2">
   <font size="+1">Add a Movie</font>
  </th>
 </tr>
 <tr>
  <td>
   Movie:
  </td>
  <td>
   <cfinput type="Text"
            name="MovieTitle"
            message="MOVIE TITLE is required!"
            required="Yes"
            validateAt="onSubmit,onServer"
            size="50"
            maxlength="100">
  </td>
 </tr>
 <tr>
  <td>
   Tag line:
  </td>
  <td>
   <cfinput type="Text"
            name="PitchText"
            message="TAG LINE is required!"
            required="Yes"
            validateAt="onSubmit,onServer"
            size="50"
            maxlength="100">
  </td>
 </tr>
 <tr>
  <td>
   Rating:
  </td>
  <td>
   <!--- Ratings list --->
   <select name="RatingID">
    <cfoutput query="ratings">
```

Listing 14.5 (CONTINUED)

```
          <option value="#RatingID#">#Rating#</option>
        </cfoutput>
      </select>
    </td>
  </tr>
  <tr>
    <td>
      Summary:
    </td>
    <td>
      <textarea name="summary"
                cols="40"
                rows="5"
                wrap="virtual"></textarea>
    </td>
  </tr>
  <tr>
    <td>
      Budget:
    </td>
    <td>
      <cfinput type="Text"
               name="AmountBudgeted"
               message="BUDGET must be a valid numeric amount!"
               required="NO"
               validate="integer"
               validateAt="onSubmit,onServer"
               size="10"
               maxlength="10">
    </td>
  </tr>
  <tr>
    <td>
      Release Date:
    </td>
    <td>
      <cfinput type="Text"
               name="DateInTheaters"
               message="RELEASE DATE must be a valid date!"
               required="NO"
               validate="date"
               validateAt="onSubmit,onServer"
               size="10"
               maxlength="10">
    </td>
  </tr>
  <tr>
    <td>
      Image File:
    </td>
    <td>
      <cfinput type="Text"
               name="ImageName"
               required="NO"
               size="20"
```

Listing 14.5 (CONTINUED)

```
                maxlength="50">
  </td>
 </tr>
 <tr>
  <td colspan="2" align="center">
   <input type="submit" value="Insert">
  </td>
   </tr>
</table>

</cfform>

<!--- Page footer --->
<cfinclude template="footer.cfm">
```

Listing 14.6 is the same form used previously, except that `<input>` has been replaced with `<cfinput>` so as to validate submitted data, and form field validation has been included, using the techniques described in Chapter 13.

Listing 14.6   `insert4.cfm`—Adding Data with the `<cfinsert>` Tag

```
<!---
Name:        insert4.cfm
Author:      Ben Forta (ben@forta.com)
Description: Table row insertion demo
Created:     07/01/07
--->

<!--- Insert movie --->
<cfinsert datasource="ows" tablename="FILMS">

<!--- Page header --->
<cfinclude template="header.cfm">

<!--- Feedback --->
<cfoutput>
<h1>New movie '#FORM.MovieTitle#' added</h1>
</cfoutput>

<!--- Page footer --->
<cfinclude template="footer.cfm">
```

Try adding a movie with these new templates. You'll see that the database inserting code in Listing 14.6 does exactly the same thing as the code in Listing 14.4, but with a much simpler syntax and interface.

Controlling `<cfinsert>` Form Fields

`<cfinsert>` instructs ColdFusion to build SQL INSERT statements dynamically. ColdFusion automatically uses all submitted form fields when building this statement.

Sometimes you might want ColdFusion to not include certain fields. For example, you might have hidden fields in your form that aren't table columns, such as the hidden field shown in Listing 14.7.

That field might be there as part of a security system you have implemented; it isn't a column in the table. If you try to pass this field to <cfinsert>, ColdFusion passes the hidden Login field as a column to the database. Obviously, this generates an database error, as seen in Figure 14.3, because no Login column exists in the Films table.

Figure 14.3

An error message is generated if ColdFusion tries to insert fields that aren't table columns.

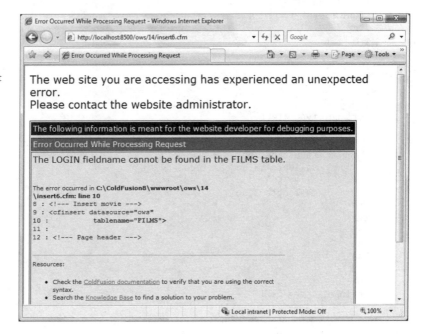

Listing 14.7 insert5.cfm—Movie Addition Form with Hidden Login Field

```
<!---
Name:         insert5.cfm
Author:       Ben Forta (ben@forta.com)
Description:  Table row insertion demo
Created:      07/01/07
--->

<!--- Get ratings --->
<cfquery datasource="ows" name="ratings">
SELECT RatingID, Rating
FROM FilmsRatings
ORDER BY RatingID
</cfquery>

<!--- Page header --->
<cfinclude template="header.cfm">

<!--- New movie form --->
<cfform action="insert6.cfm">

<!--- Login field --->
<cfinput type="hidden"
         name="Login"
```

Listing 14.7 (CONTINUED)

```
                value="Ben">

    <table align="center" bgcolor="orange">
     <tr>
      <th colspan="2">
       <font size="+1">Add a Movie</font>
      </th>
     </tr>
     <tr>
      <td>
       Movie:
      </td>
      <td>
       <cfinput type="Text"
                name="MovieTitle"
                message="MOVIE TITLE is required!"
                required="Yes"
                validateAt="onSubmit,onServer"
                size="50"
                maxlength="100">
      </td>
     </tr>
     <tr>
      <td>
       Tag line:
      </td>
      <td>
       <cfinput type="Text"
                name="PitchText"
                message="TAG LINE is required!"
                required="Yes"
                validateAt="onSubmit,onServer"
                size="50"
                maxlength="100">
      </td>
     </tr>
     <tr>
      <td>
       Rating:
      </td>
      <td>
       <!--- Ratings list --->
       <select name="RatingID">
        <cfoutput query="ratings">
         <option value="#RatingID#">#Rating#</option>
        </cfoutput>
       </select>
      </td>
     </tr>
     <tr>
      <td>
       Summary:
      </td>
      <td>
       <textarea name="summary"
                 cols="40"
                 rows="5"
```

Listing 14.7 (CONTINUED)

```
                            wrap="virtual"></textarea>
      </td>
     </tr>
     <tr>
      <td>
       Budget:
      </td>
      <td>
       <cfinput type="Text"
                name="AmountBudgeted"
                message="BUDGET must be a valid numeric amount!"
                required="NO"
                validate="integer"
                validateAt="onSubmit,onServer"
                size="10"
                maxlength="10">
      </td>
     </tr>
     <tr>
      <td>
       Release Date:
      </td>
      <td>
       <cfinput type="Text"
                name="DateInTheaters"
                message="RELEASE DATE must be a valid date!"
                required="NO"
                validate="date"
                validateAt="onSubmit,onServer"
                size="10"
                maxlength="10">
      </td>
     </tr>
     <tr>
      <td>
       Image File:
      </td>
      <td>
       <cfinput type="Text"
                name="ImageName"
                required="NO"
                size="20"
                maxlength="50">
      </td>
     </tr>
     <tr>
      <td colspan="2" align="center">
       <input type="submit" value="Insert">
      </td>
     </tr>
    </table>

   </cfform>

   <!--- Page footer --->
   <cfinclude template="footer.cfm">
```

To solve this problem, you must use the `formfields` attribute. `formfields` instructs ColdFusion to process only form fields that are in the list. Any other fields are ignored.

It's important to note that `formfields` isn't used to specify which fields ColdFusion should process. Rather, it specifies which fields should *not* be processed. The difference is subtle. Not all fields listed in the `formfields` value need be present. They are processed *if* they are present; if they aren't present, they aren't processed (so no error will be generated). Any fields not listed in the `formfields` list are ignored.

Listing 14.8 contains an updated data insertion template. The `<cfinsert>` tag now has a `formfields` attribute, so now ColdFusion knows to ignore the hidden `Login` field.

Listing 14.8 `insert6.cfm`—Using the `<cfinsert>` `formfields` Attribute

```
<!---
Name:        insert6.cfm
Author:      Ben Forta (ben@forta.com)
Description: Table row insertion demo
Created:     07/01/07
--->

<!--- Insert movie --->
<cfinsert datasource="ows"
          tablename="FILMS"
          formfields="MovieTitle,
                      PitchText,
                      AmountBudgeted,
                      RatingID,
                      Summary,
                      ImageName,
                      DateInTheaters">

<!--- Page header --->
<cfinclude template="header.cfm">

<!--- Feedback --->
<cfoutput>
<h1>New movie '#FORM.MovieTitle#' added</h1>
</cfoutput>

<!--- Page footer --->
<cfinclude template="footer.cfm">
```

Collecting Data for More Than One INSERT

Here's another situation where `<cfinsert>` `formfields` can be used: when a form collects data that needs to be added to more than one table. You can create a template that has two or more `<cfinsert>` statements by using `formfields`.

As long as each `<cfinsert>` statement has a `formfields` attribute that specifies which fields are to be used with each INSERT, ColdFusion correctly executes each `<cfinsert>` with its appropriate fields.

`<cfinsert>` **vs. SQL** `INSERT`

Adding data to tables using the ColdFusion `<cfinsert>` tag is simpler and helps prevent the creation of multiple similar templates.

So why would you ever *not* use `<cfinsert>`? Is there ever a reason to use SQL `INSERT` instead of `<cfinsert>`?

The truth is that both are needed. `<cfinsert>` can be used only for simple data insertion to a single table. If you want to insert the results of a `SELECT` statement, you can't use `<cfinsert>`. And you can't use `<cfinsert>` if you want to insert values other than `FORM` fields—variables or URL parameters, for example.

These guidelines will help you decide when to use which method:

- For simple operations (single table and no complex processing), use `<cfinsert>` to add data.

- If you find that you need to add specific form fields—and not all that were submitted—use the `<cfinsert>` tag with the `formfields` attribute.

- If `<cfinsert>` can't be used because you need a complex `INSERT` statement or are using fields that aren't form fields, use SQL `INSERT`.

TIP

I have seen many documents and articles attempt to dissuade the use of `<cfinsert>` (and `<cfupdate>` discussed below), primarily because of the limitations already mentioned. In my opinion there is nothing wrong with using these tags at all, recognizing their limitations of course. In fact, I'd even argue that their use is preferable as they are dynamic (if the form changes they may not need changing) and are type aware (they handle type conversions automatically). So don't let the naysayers get you down. CFML is all about making your development life easier, so if these tags make coding easier, use them.

Updating Data with ColdFusion

Updating data with ColdFusion is similar to inserting data. You generally need two templates to update a row—a data-entry form template and a data update one. The big difference between a form used for data addition and one used for data modification is that the latter needs to be populated with existing values. See the screen in Figure 14.4.

Building a Data Update Form

Populating an HTML form is a simple process. First, you must retrieve the row to be updated from the table. You do this with a standard `<cfquery>`; the retrieved values are then passed as attributes to the HTML form.

Figure 14.4

When you use forms to update data, the form fields usually need to be populated with existing values.

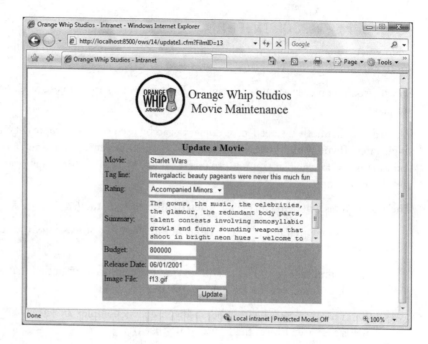

Listing 14.9 contains the code for update1.cfm, a template that updates a movie. Save it as update1.cfm, and then execute it. Be sure to append the FilmID—for example, ?FilmID=13—as a URL parameter. Your screen should look like Figure 14.4.

Listing 14.9 update1.cfm—Movie Update Form

```
<!---
Name:        update1.cfm
Author:      Ben Forta (ben@forta.com)
Description: Table row update demo
Created:     07/01/07
--->

<!--- Check that FilmID was provided --->
<cfif NOT IsDefined("URL.FilmID")>
 <h1>You did not specify the FilmID</h1>
 <cfabort>
</cfif>

<!--- Get the film record --->
<cfquery datasource="ows" name="film">
SELECT FilmID, MovieTitle, PitchText,
    AmountBudgeted, RatingID,
    Summary, ImageName, DateInTheaters
FROM Films
WHERE FilmID=#URL.FilmID#
</cfquery>

<!--- Get ratings --->
<cfquery datasource="ows" name="ratings">
```

Listing 14.9 (CONTINUED)

```
SELECT RatingID, Rating
FROM FilmsRatings
ORDER BY RatingID
</cfquery>

<!--- Page header --->
<cfinclude template="header.cfm">

<!--- Update movie form --->
<cfform action="update2.cfm">

<!--- Embed primary key as a hidden field --->
<cfoutput>
<input type="hidden" name="FilmID" value="#Film.FilmID#">
</cfoutput>

<table align="center" bgcolor="orange">
 <tr>
  <th colspan="2">
   <font size="+1">Update a Movie</font>
  </th>
 </tr>
 <tr>
  <td>
   Movie:
  </td>
  <td>
   <cfinput type="Text"
            name="MovieTitle"
            value="#Trim(film.MovieTitle)#"
            message="MOVIE TITLE is required!"
            required="Yes"
            validateAt="onSubmit,onServer"
            size="50"
            maxlength="100">
  </td>
 </tr>
 <tr>
  <td>
   Tag line:
  </td>
  <td>
   <cfinput type="Text"
            name="PitchText"
            value="#Trim(film.PitchText)#"
            message="TAG LINE is required!"
            required="Yes"
            validateAt="onSubmit,onServer"
            size="50"
            maxlength="100">
  </td>
 </tr>
 <tr>
  <td>
   Rating:
```

Listing 14.9 (CONTINUED)

```
    </td>
    <td>
     <!--- Ratings list --->
     <select name="RatingID">
      <cfoutput query="ratings">
       <option value="#RatingID#"
               <cfif ratings.RatingID IS film.RatingID>
               selected
               </cfif>>#Rating#
      </option>
      </cfoutput>
     </select>
    </td>
   </tr>
   <tr>
    <td>
     Summary:
    </td>
    <td>
     <cfoutput>
     <textarea name="summary"
               cols="40"
               rows="5"
               wrap="virtual">#Trim(Film.Summary)#</textarea>
     </cfoutput>
    </td>
   </tr>
   <tr>
    <td>
     Budget:
    </td>
    <td>
     <cfinput type="Text"
              name="AmountBudgeted"
              value="#Int(film.AmountBudgeted)#"
              message="BUDGET must be a valid numeric amount!"
              required="NO"
              validate="integer"
              validateAt="onSubmit,onServer"
              size="10"
              maxlength="10">
    </td>
   </tr>
   <tr>
    <td>
     Release Date:
    </td>
    <td>
     <cfinput type="Text"
              name="DateInTheaters"
              value="#DateFormat(film.DateInTheaters, "MM/DD/YYYY")#"
              message="RELEASE DATE must be a valid date!"
              required="NO"
              validate="date"
              validateAt="onSubmit,onServer"
```

Listing 14.9 (CONTINUED)

```
              size="10"
              maxlength="10">
   </td>
  </tr>
  <tr>
   <td>
    Image File:
   </td>
   <td>
    <cfinput type="Text"
              name="ImageName"
              value="#Trim(film.ImageName)#"
              required="NO"
              size="20"
              maxlength="50">
   </td>
  </tr>
  <tr>
   <td colspan="2" align="center">
    <input type="submit" value="Update">
   </td>
   </tr>
 </table>

 </cfform>

 <!--- Page footer --->
 <cfinclude template="footer.cfm">
```

There is a lot to look at in Listing 14.9. And don't submit the form yet; you have yet to create the action page.

To populate a form with data to be updated, you must first retrieve that row from the table. Therefore, you must specify a FilmID to use this template. Without it, ColdFusion wouldn't know which row to retrieve. To ensure that the FilmID is passed, the first thing you do is check for the existence of the FilmID parameter. The following code returns TRUE only if FilmID was not passed, in which case an error message is sent back to the user and template processing is halted with the <cfabort> tag:

```
<CFIF NOT IsDefined("URL.FilmID")>
```

Without the <cfabort> tag, ColdFusion continues processing the template. An error message is generated when the <cfquery> statement is processed because the WHERE clause WHERE FilmID = #URL.FilmID# references a nonexistent field.

The first <cfquery> tag retrieves the row to be edited, and the passed URL is used in the WHERE clause to retrieve the appropriate row. The second <cfquery> retrieves the list of ratings for the <select> control. To populate the data-entry fields, the current field value is passed to the <input> (or <cfinput>) value attribute. Whatever is passed to value is displayed in the field, so value="#Film.MovieTitle#" displays the MovieTitle table column.

NOTE

The query name is necessary here as a prefix because it isn't being used within a `<cfoutput>` associated with a query. `<cfinput>` is a ColdFusion tag, so you can pass variables and columns to it without needing to use `<cfoutput>`. If you were using `<input>` instead of `<cfinput>`, the `<input>` tags would need to be within a `<cfoutput>` block. This is actually another benefit of using `<cfinput>` instead of `<input>`–`<cfinput>` makes populating form fields with dynamic data much easier.

To ensure that no blank spaces exist after the retrieved value, the fields are trimmed with the Cold-Fusion `Trim()` function before they are displayed. Why would you do this? Some databases, such as Microsoft SQL Server, pad some text fields with spaces so they take up the full column width in the table. The `MovieTitle` field is a 255-character-wide column, so a movie title could have a lot of spaces after it. The extra space can be very annoying when you try to edit the field. To append text to a field, you'd first have to backspace or delete all those extra characters.

NOTE

When populating forms with table column values, you should always trim the field first. Unlike standard browser output, spaces in form fields aren't ignored. Removing them allows easier editing. The ColdFusion `Trim()` function removes spaces at the beginning and end of the value. If you want to trim only trailing spaces, you could use the `RTrim()` function instead.

Dates and numbers are also formatted specially. By default, dates are displayed in a rather unusable format (and a format that won't be accepted upon form submission). Therefore, `DateFormat()` is used to format the date in a usable format.

The `AmountBudgeted` column allows numbers with decimal points; to display the number within the trailing decimal point and zeros, the `Int()` function can be used to round the number to an integer. You also could have used `NumberFormat()` for more precise number formatting.

One hidden field exists in the FORM. The following code creates a hidden field called `FilmID`, which contains the ID of the movie being updated:

```
<input type="hidden" name="FilmID" value="#Film.FilmID#">
```

This hidden field must be present. Without it, ColdFusion has no idea which row you were updating when the form was actually submitted. Also, because it is an `<input>` field (not `<cfinput>`), it must be enclosed within `<cfoutput>` tags.

Remember that HTTP sessions are created and broken as necessary, and every session stands on its own two feet. ColdFusion might retrieve a specific row of data for you in one session, but it doesn't know that in the next session. Therefore, when you update a row, you must specify the primary key so ColdFusion knows which row to update. Hidden fields are one way of doing this because they are sent to the browser as part of the form, but are never displayed and thus can't be edited. However, they are still form fields, and they are submitted along with all other form fields intact upon form submission.

Processing Updates

As with adding data, there are two ways to update rows in a table. The code in Listing 14.10 demonstrates a row update using the SQL UPDATE statement.

➡ See Chapter 6, "Introducing SQL," for an explanation of the UPDATE statement.

Listing 14.10   `update2.cfm`—Updating a Table with SQL UPDATE

```
<!---
Name:        update2.cfm
Author:      Ben Forta (ben@forta.com)
Description: Table row update demo
Created:     07/01/07
--->

<!--- Update movie --->
<cfquery datasource="ows">
UPDATE Films
SET MovieTitle='#Trim(FORM.MovieTitle)#',
    PitchText='#Trim(FORM.PitchText)#',
    AmountBudgeted=#FORM.AmountBudgeted#,
    RatingID=#FORM.RatingID#,
    Summary='#Trim(FORM.Summary)#',
    ImageName='#Trim(FORM.ImageName)#',
    DateInTheaters=#CreateODBCDate(FORM.DateInTheaters)#
WHERE FilmID=#FORM.FilmID#
</cfquery>

<!--- Page header --->
<cfinclude template="header.cfm">

<!--- Feedback --->
<cfoutput>
<h1>Movie '#FORM.MovieTitle#' updated</h1>
</cfoutput>

<!--- Page footer --->
<cfinclude template="footer.cfm">
```

This SQL statement updates the seven specified rows for the movie whose ID is the passed `FORM.FilmID`.

To test this update template, try executing template `update1.cfm` with different `FilmID` values (passed as URL parameters), and then submit your changes.

Introducing `<cfupdate>`

As you saw earlier in regards to inserting data, hard-coded SQL statements are neither flexible nor easy to maintain. ColdFusion provides a simpler way to update rows in database tables.

CAUTION

If you are using Windows 98 or ME and are using Microsoft Access, you won't be able to use the `<cfupdate>` tag due to limitations with the Access database drivers on these platforms. You can still insert data using `<cfquery>` and `update`, and `<cfupdate>` will function correctly if you are using Access on Windows 2000, XP, or Vista.

The `<cfupdate>` tag is similar to the `<cfinsert>` tag discussed earlier in this chapter. `<cfupdate>` requires just two attributes—the data source and the name of the table to update—and supports an optional `formfields` too.

- `datasource`—The name of the data source that contains the table to which the data is to be updated.

- `tablename`—The name of the destination table.

- `formfields`—An optional comma-separated list of fields to be updated. If this attribute isn't provided, all the fields in the submitted form are used.

When using `<cfupdate>`, ColdFusion automatically locates the row you want to update by looking at the table to ascertain its primary key. All you have to do is ensure that the primary key value is passed, as you did in Listing 14.9 using a hidden field.

The code in Listing 14.11 performs the same update as that in Listing 14.10, but it uses the `<cfupdate>` tag rather than the SQL UPDATE tag. Obviously, this code is more readable, reusable, and accommodating of form-field changes you might make in the future.

Listing 14.11 update3.cfm—Updating Data with the `<cfupdate>` Tag

```
<!---
Name:         update3.cfm
Author:       Ben Forta (ben@forta.com)
Description: Table row update demo
Created:      07/01/07
--->

<!--- Update movie --->
<cfupdate datasource="ows" tablename="FILMS">

<!--- Page header --->
<cfinclude template="header.cfm">

<!--- Feedback --->
<cfoutput>
<h1>Movie '#FORM.MovieTitle#' updated</h1>
</cfoutput>

<!--- Page footer --->
<cfinclude template="footer.cfm">
```

To use this code, you must change the `<form>` action attribute in update1.cfm so that it points to update3.cfm. Make this change, and try updating several movies.

`<cfupdate>` vs. SQL UPDATE

As with adding data, the choice to use `<cfupdate>` or SQL UPDATE is yours. The following guidelines as to when to use each option are similar as well:

- Whenever appropriate, use `<cfupdate>` to update data.

- If you find you need to update specific form fields—not all that were submitted—use the `<cfupdate>` tag with the `formfields` attribute.

- If `<cfupdate>` can't be used because you need a complex UPDATE statement or you are using fields that aren't form fields, use SQL UPDATE.

- If you ever need to update multiple (or all) rows in a table, you must use SQL UPDATE.

Deleting Data with ColdFusion

ColdFusion is very efficient at adding and updating data, but not at deleting it. DELETE is always a dangerous operation, and the ColdFusion developers didn't want to make it too easy to delete data by mistake.

To delete data in a ColdFusion template, you must use the SQL DELETE statement, as shown in Listing 14.12. The code first checks to ensure that a FilmID was passed; if the URL.FilmID field isn't present, the statement terminates. If a FilmID is passed, a <cfquery> is used to pass a SQL DELETE statement to the data source.

→ See Chapter 6 for an explanation of the DELETE statement.

Listing 14.12 delete1.cfm—Deleting Table Data with SQL DELETE

```
<!---
Name:        delete1.cfm
Author:      Ben Forta (ben@forta.com)
Description: Table row delete demo
Created:     07/01/07
--->

<!--- Check that FilmID was provided --->
<cfif NOT IsDefined("FilmID")>
 <h1>You did not specify the FilmID</h1>
<cfabort>
</cfif>

<!--- Delete a movie --->
<cfquery datasource="ows">
DELETE FROM Films
WHERE FilmID=#FilmID#
</cfquery>

<!--- Page header --->
<cfinclude template="header.cfm">

<!--- Feedback --->
<h1>Movie deleted</h1>

<!--- Page footer --->
<cfinclude template="footer.cfm">
```

No <cfdelete> tag exists in ColdFusion. The only way to delete rows is to use a SQL DELETE.

NOTE

You will not be able to delete rows in the Films table that have related rows in other tables.

Reusing Forms

You can now add to as well as update and delete from your Films table. But what if you need to change the form? What if you needed to add a field, or change validation, or update colors? Any changes that need to be made to the Add form also must be made to the Update form.

With all the effort you have gone to in the past few chapters to prevent any duplication of effort, this seems counterproductive.

Indeed it is.

The big difference between an Add and an Update form is whether the fields are prefilled to show current values. Using ColdFusion conditional expressions, you can create a single form that can be used for both adding and updating data.

To do this, all you need is a way to conditionally include the value attribute in <input>. After all, look at the following two <input> statements:

```
<input type="text" name="MovieTitle">
<input type="text" name="MovieTitle" value="#MovieTitle#">
```

The first <input> is used for new data; there is no prefilled value. The second is for editing, and thus the field is populated with an initial value.

Therefore, it wouldn't be hard to create <input> fields with <cfif> statements embedded in them, conditionally including the value. Look at the following code:

```
<input type="text" name="MovieTitle"
<cfif IsDefined("URL.FilmID")>
value="#MovieTitle#"
</CFIF>
>
```

This <input> field includes the value attribute only if the FilmID was passed (meaning that this is an edit operation as opposed to an add operation). Using this technique, a single form field can be used for both adds and edits.

This is perfectly valid code, and this technique is quite popular. The only problem with it is that the code can get very difficult to read. All those embedded <cfif> statements, one for every row, make the code quite complex. There is a better solution.

value can be an empty string, the attribute value="" is perfectly legal and valid. So why not *always* use value, but conditionally populate it? The best way to demonstrate this is to try it, so Listing 14.13 contains the code for edit1.cfm—a new dual-purpose form.

Listing 14.13 edit1.cfm—Combination Insert and Update Form

```
<!---
Name:        edit1.cfm
Author:      Ben Forta (ben@forta.com)
Description: Dual purpose form demo
Created:     07/01/07
--->

<!--- Check that FilmID was provided --->
<!--- If yes, edit, else add --->
<cfset EditMode=IsDefined("URL.FilmID")>

<!--- If edit mode then get row to edit --->
<cfif EditMode>
```

Listing 14.13 (CONTINUED)

```
<!--- Get the film record --->
<cfquery datasource="ows" name="film">
SELECT FilmID, MovieTitle, PitchText,
        AmountBudgeted, RatingID,
        Summary, ImageName, DateInTheaters
FROM Films
WHERE FilmID=#URL.FilmID#
</cfquery>

<!--- Save to variables --->
<cfset MovieTitle=Trim(film.MovieTitle)>
<cfset PitchText=Trim(film.PitchText)>
<cfset AmountBudgeted=Int(film.AmountBudgeted)>
<cfset RatingID=film.RatingID>
<cfset Summary=Trim(film.Summary)>
<cfset ImageName=Trim(film.ImageName)>
<cfset DateInTheaters=DateFormat(film.DateInTheaters, "MM/DD/YYYY")>

<!--- Form text --->
<cfset FormTitle="Update a Movie">
<cfset ButtonText="Update">

<cfelse>

<!--- Save to variables --->
<cfset MovieTitle="">
<cfset PitchText="">
<cfset AmountBudgeted="">
<cfset RatingID="">
<cfset Summary="">
<cfset ImageName="">
<cfset DateInTheaters="">

<!--- Form text --->
<cfset FormTitle="Add a Movie">
<cfset ButtonText="Insert">

</cfif>

<!--- Get ratings --->
<cfquery datasource="ows" name="ratings">
SELECT RatingID, Rating
FROM FilmsRatings
ORDER BY RatingID
</cfquery>

<!--- Page header --->
<cfinclude template="header.cfm">

<!--- Add/update movie form --->
<cfform action="edit2.cfm">

<cfif EditMode>
<!--- Embed primary key as a hidden field --->
<cfinput type="hidden" name="FilmID"
        value="#Film.FilmID#">
```

Listing 14.13 (CONTINUED)

```
    </cfif>

    <table align="center" bgcolor="orange">
     <tr>
      <th colspan="2">
       <cfoutput>
       <font size="+1">#FormTitle#</font>
       </cfoutput>
      </th>
     </tr>
     <tr>
      <td>
       Movie:
      </td>
      <td>
       <cfinput type="Text"
                name="MovieTitle"
                value="#MovieTitle#"
                message="MOVIE TITLE is required!"
                required="Yes"
                validateAt="onSubmit,onServer"
                size="50"
                maxlength="100">
      </td>
     </tr>
    <tr>
      <td>
       Tag line:
      </td>
      <td>
       <cfinput type="Text"
                name="PitchText"
                value="#PitchText#"
                message="TAG LINE is required!"
                required="Yes"
                validateAt="onSubmit,onServer"
                size="50"
                maxlength="100">
      </td>
     </tr>
     <tr>
      <td>
       Rating:
      </td>
      <td>
       <!--- Ratings list --->
       <select name="RatingID">
        <cfoutput query="ratings">
         <option value="#RatingID#"
          <cfif ratings.RatingID IS VARIABLES.RatingID>
           selected
          </cfif>>
          #Rating#</option>
        </cfoutput>
       </select>
      </td>
```

Listing 14.13 (CONTINUED)

```
  </tr>
  <tr>
   <td>
    Summary:
   </td>
   <td>
    <cfoutput>
    <textarea name="summary"
              cols="40"
              rows="5"
              wrap="virtual">#Summary#</textarea>
    </cfoutput>
   </td>
  </tr>
  <tr>
   <td>
    Budget:
   </td>
   <td>
    <cfinput type="Text"
             name="AmountBudgeted"
             value="#AmountBudgeted#"
             message="BUDGET must be a valid numeric amount!"
             required="NO"
             validate="integer"
             validateAt="onSubmit,onServer"
             size="10"
             maxlength="10">
   </td>
  </tr>
  <tr>
   <td>
    Release Date:
   </td>
   <td>
    <cfinput type="Text"
             name="DateInTheaters"
             value="#DateInTheaters#"
             message="RELEASE DATE must be a valid date!"
             required="NO"
             validate="date"
             validateAt="onSubmit,onServer"
             size="10"
             maxlength="10">
   </td>
  </tr>
  <tr>
   <td>
    Image File:
   </td>
   <td>
    <cfinput type="Text"
             name="ImageName"
             value="#ImageName#"
             required="NO"
             size="20"
```

Listing 14.13 (CONTINUED)

```
                    maxlength="50">
     </td>
    </tr>
    <tr>
     <td colspan="2" align="center">
      <cfoutput>
      <input type="submit" value="#ButtonText#">
      </cfoutput>
     </td>
     </tr>
   </table>

   </cfform>

   <!--- Page footer --->
   <cfinclude template="footer.cfm">
```

The code first determines whether the form will be used for an Add or an Update. How can it know this? The difference between how the two are called is in the URL—whether FilmID is passed. The code `<cfset EditMode=IsDefined("URL.FilmID")>` created a variable named EditMode, which will be TRUE if URL.FilmID exists and FALSE if not. This variable can now be used as necessary throughout the page.

Next comes a `<cfif>` statement. If editing (EditMode is TRUE) then a `<cfquery>` is used to retrieve the current values. The fields retrieved by that `<cfquery>` are saved in local variables using multiple `<cfset>` tags. No `<cfquery>` is used if it is an insert operation, but `<cfset>` is used to create empty variables.

By the time the `</cfif>` has been reached, a set of variables has been created. They'll either contain values (from the Films table) or be empty. Either way, they're usable as value attributes in `<input>` and `<cfinput>` tags.

Look at the `<cfinput>` fields themselves. You'll notice that no conditional code exists within them, as it did before. Instead, every `<input>` tag has a value attribute, regardless of whether this is an insert or an update. The value in the value attribute is a ColdFusion variable—a variable that is set at the top of the template, not a database field.

The rest of the code in the template uses these variables, without needing any conditional processing. Even the page title and submit button text can be initialized in variables this way, so `<cfif>` tags aren't necessary for them, either.

The primary key, embedded as a hidden field, is necessary only if a movie is being edited, so the code to embed that field is enclosed within a `<cfif>` statement:

```
<cfif EditMode>
 <!--- Embed primary key as a hidden field --->
 <cfinput type="hidden" name="FilmID"
          value="#Film.FilmID#">
</cfif>
```

Even the form header at the top of the page and the text of the submit button are populated using variables. This way, the `<form>` is completely reusable:

```
<INPUT TYPE="submit" VALUE="#ButtonText#">
```

This form is submitted to the same `action` page regardless of whether data is being added or updated. Therefore, the `action` page also must support both additions and updates. Listing 14.14 contains the new `action` template, `edit2.cfm`.

Listing 14.14   `edit2.cfm`—Combination Insert and Update Page

```
<!---
Name:        edit2.cfm
Author:      Ben Forta (ben@forta.com)
Description: Dual purpose form demo
Created:     07/01/07
--->

<!--- Insert or update? --->
<cfset EditMode=IsDefined("FORM.FilmID")>

<cfif EditMode>
 <!--- Update movie --->
 <cfupdate datasource="ows" tablename="FILMS">
 <cfset action="updated">
<cfelse>
 <!--- Add movie --->
<cfinsert datasource="ows" tablename="FILMS">
 <cfset action="added">
</cfif>

<!--- Page header --->
<cfinclude template="header.cfm">

<!--- Feedback --->
<cfoutput>
<h1>Movie #FORM.MovieTitle# #action#</h1>
</cfoutput>

<!--- Page footer --->
<cfinclude template="footer.cfm">
```

This code also first determines the `EditMode`, this time by checking for a `FORM` field named `FilmID` (the hidden form field). If `EditMode` is `TRUE`, a `<cfupdate>` is used to update the row; otherwise, a `<cfinsert>` is used to insert it. The same `<cfif>` statement also is used to set a variable that is used later in the page when providing user feedback.

It's clean, simple, and reusable.

Creating a Complete Application

Now that you've created add, modify, and delete templates, let's put them all together and create a finished application—and this time, one that is constructed properly, using a CFC for database access.

The following templates are a combination of all you have learned in this and previous chapters.

Listing 14.15 is the ColdFusion Component that provides all database access (to get, add, update, and delete movies).

→ ColdFusion Components were introduced in Chapter 11, "The Basics of Structured Development."

Listing 14.15   `movies.cfc`—Movie Database Access

```
<!---
Name:        movies.cfc
Author:      Ben Forta (ben@forta.com)
Description: Movie database access component
Created:     07/01/07
--->

<cfcomponent hint="OWS movie database access">

 <!--- Set the datsources --->
 <cfset ds="ows">


 <!--- Get movie list --->
 <cffunction name="list"
             returntype="query"
             hint="List all movies">

  <cfquery datasource="#ds#"
           name="movies">
  SELECT FilmID, MovieTitle
  FROM Films
  ORDER BY MovieTitle
  </cfquery>
  <cfreturn movies>

 </cffunction>


 <!--- Get details for a movie --->
 <cffunction name="get"
             returntype="query"
             hint="Get movie details">
  <cfargument name="FilmID"
              type="numeric"
              required="yes"
              hint="Movie ID">

  <cfquery datasource="#ds#"
           name="movie">
  SELECT FilmID, MovieTitle,
         PitchText, AmountBudgeted,
         RatingID, Summary,
         ImageName, DateInTheaters
  FROM Films
  WHERE FilmID=#ARGUMENTS.FilmID#
  </cfquery>
```

Listing 14.15 (CONTINUED)

```
  <cfreturn movie>

</cffunction>


<!--- Add a movie --->
<cffunction name="add"
            returntype="boolean"
            hint="Add a movie">

  <!--- Method arguments --->
  <cfargument name="MovieTitle"
            type="string"
            required="yes"
            hint="Movie title">
  <cfargument name="PitchText"
            type="string"
            required="yes"
            hint="Movie tag line">
  <cfargument name="AmountBudgeted"
            type="numeric"
            required="yes"
            hint="Projected movie budget">
  <cfargument name="RatingID"
            type="numeric"
            required="yes"
            hint="Movie rating ID">
  <cfargument name="Summary"
            type="string"
            required="yes"
            hint="Movie summary">
  <cfargument name="DateInTheaters"
            type="date"
            required="yes"
            hint="Movie release date">
  <cfargument name="ImageName"
            type="string"
            required="no"
            default=""
            hint="Movie image file name">

  <!--- Insert movie --->
  <cfquery datasource="#ds#">
  INSERT INTO Films(MovieTitle,
                    PitchText,
                    AmountBudgeted,
                    RatingID,
                    Summary,
                    ImageName,
                    DateInTheaters)
  VALUES('#Trim(ARGUMENTS.MovieTitle)#',
         '#Trim(ARGUMENTS.PitchText)#',
         #ARGUMENTS.AmountBudgeted#,
         #ARGUMENTS.RatingID#,
         '#Trim(ARGUMENTS.Summary)#',
```

Listing 14.15   (CONTINUED)

```
            '#Trim(ARGUMENTS.ImageName)#',
            #CreateODBCDate(ARGUMENTS.DateInTheaters)#)
  </cfquery>
  <cfreturn true>

</cffunction>


<!--- Update a movie --->
<cffunction name="update"
            returntype="boolean"
            hint="Update a movie">
 <!--- Method arguments --->
 <cfargument name="FilmID"
            type="numeric"
            required="yes"
            hint="Movie ID">
 <cfargument name="MovieTitle"
            type="string"
            required="yes"
            hint="Movie title">
 <cfargument name="PitchText"
            type="string"
            required="yes"
            hint="Movie tag line">
 <cfargument name="AmountBudgeted"
            type="numeric"
            required="yes"
            hint="Projected movie budget">
 <cfargument name="RatingID"
            type="numeric"
            required="yes"
            hint="Movie rating ID">
 <cfargument name="Summary"
            type="string"
            required="yes"
            hint="Movie summary">
 <cfargument name="DateInTheaters"
            type="date"
            required="yes"
            hint="Movie release date">
 <cfargument name="ImageName"
            type="string"
            required="no"
            default=""
            hint="Movie image file name">

 <!--- Update movie --->
 <cfquery datasource="#ds#">
 UPDATE Films
 SET MovieTitle='#Trim(ARGUMENTS.MovieTitle)#',
     PitchText='#Trim(ARGUMENTS.PitchText)#',
     AmountBudgeted=#ARGUMENTS.AmountBudgeted#,
     RatingID=#ARGUMENTS.RatingID#,
     Summary='#Trim(ARGUMENTS.Summary)#',
```

Listing 14.15 (CONTINUED)

```
        ImageName='#Trim(ARGUMENTS.ImageName)#',
        DateInTheaters=#CreateODBCDate(ARGUMENTS.DateInTheaters)#
  WHERE FilmID=#ARGUMENTS.FilmID#
  </cfquery>
  <cfreturn true>

</cffunction>


<!--- Delete a movie --->
<cffunction name="delete"
            returntype="boolean"
            hint="Delete a movie">
  <cfargument name="FilmID"
              type="numeric"
              required="yes"
              hint="Movie ID">

  <cfquery datasource="#ds#">
  DELETE FROM Films
  WHERE FilmID=#ARGUMENTS.FilmID#
  </cfquery>
  <cfreturn true>

</cffunction>


<!--- Get movie ratings --->
<cffunction name="getRatings"
            returntype="query"
            hint="Get movie ratings list">

  <!--- Get ratings --->
  <cfquery datasource="#ds#"
           name="ratings">
  SELECT RatingID, Rating
  FROM FilmsRatings
  ORDER BY RatingID
  </cfquery>
  <cfreturn ratings>

</cffunction>


</cfcomponent>
```

movies.cfc contains six methods, list lists all movies, get gets a specific movie, getRatings returns a list of all possible ratings, and add, update, and delete add, update, and delete movies respectively.

NOTE

Notice that the value passed to all **datasource** attributes in Listing 14.15 is a variable (which is set at the top of the page) so as to not hard-code the value multiple times.

Listing 14.16 is the main movie maintenance page. It displays the movies returned from the Cold-Fusion Component and provides links to edit and delete them (using the data drill-down techniques discussed in previous chapters); it also has a link to add a new movie. The administration page is shown in Figure 14.5.

Figure 14.5

The movie administration page is used to add, edit, and delete movies.

Listing 14.16 `movies.cfm`—Movie List Maintenance Page

```
<!---
Name:         movies.cfm
Author:       Ben Forta (ben@forta.com)
Description:  Movie maintenance application
Created:      07/01/07
--->

<!--- Get all movies --->
<cfinvoke component="movies"
          method="list"
          returnvariable="movies">

<!--- Page header --->
<cfinclude template="header.cfm">

<table align="center" bgcolor="orange">

  <!--- Loop through movies --->
<cfoutput query="movies">
  <tr>
    <!--- Movie name --->
    <td><strong>#MovieTitle#</strong></td>
```

Listing 14.16 (CONTINUED)

```
   <!--- Edit link --->
   <td>
    [<a href="movie_edit.cfm?FilmID=#FilmID#">Edit</a>]
   </td>
   <!--- Delete link --->
   <td>
    [<a href="movie_delete.cfm?FilmID=#FilmID#">Delete</a>]
   </td>
  </tr>
 </cfoutput>

 <tr>
  <td></td>
  <!--- Add movie link --->
  <td colspan="2" align="center">
   [<a href="movie_edit.cfm">Add</a>]
  </td>
 </tr>

</table>

<!--- Page footer --->
<cfinclude template="footer.cfm">
```

Listing 14.15 uses a <cfinvoke> to obtain the movie list, then provides two links for each movie: an edit link (that links to movie_edit.cfm passing the FilmID) and a delete link (movie_delete.cfm, also passing the FilmID). The add link at the bottom of the page also points to movie_edit.cfm but doesn't pass a FilmID (so the form will be used as an add form).

→ Dynamic links and data drill-down were covered in Chapter 12.

Listing 14.17 is essentially the same reusable add and update form you created earlier, but with another useful shortcut.

Listing 14.17 movie_edit.cfm—Movie Add and Update Form

```
<!---
Name:        movie_edit.cfm
Author:      Ben Forta (ben@forta.com)
Description: Dual purpose movie edit form
Created:     07/01/07
--->

<!--- Check that FilmID was provided --->
<!--- If yes, edit, else add --->
<cfset EditMode=IsDefined("URL.FilmID")>

<!--- If edit mode then get row to edit --->
<cfif EditMode>

 <!--- Get the film record --->
 <cfinvoke component="movies"
           method="get"
           filmid="#URL.FilmID#"
```

Listing 14.17 (CONTINUED)

```
                    returnvariable="film">

    <!--- Save to variables --->
    <cfset MovieTitle=Trim(film.MovieTitle)>
    <cfset PitchText=Trim(film.PitchText)>
    <cfset AmountBudgeted=Int(film.AmountBudgeted)>
    <cfset RatingID=film.RatingID>
    <cfset Summary=Trim(film.Summary)>
    <cfset ImageName=Trim(film.ImageName)>
    <cfset DateInTheaters=DateFormat(film.DateInTheaters, "MM/DD/YYYY")>

    <!--- Form text --->
    <cfset FormTitle="Update a Movie">
    <cfset ButtonText="Update">

<cfelse>

    <!--- Save to variables --->
    <cfset MovieTitle="">
    <cfset PitchText="">
    <cfset AmountBudgeted="">
    <cfset RatingID="">
    <cfset Summary="">
    <cfset ImageName="">
    <cfset DateInTheaters="">

<!--- Form text --->
 <cfset FormTitle="Add a Movie">
 <cfset ButtonText="Insert">

</cfif>

<!--- Get ratings --->
 <cfinvoke component="movies"
           method="getRatings"
           returnvariable="ratings">

<!--- Page header --->
<cfinclude template="header.cfm">

<!--- Add/update movie form --->
<cfform action="movie_process.cfm">

<cfif EditMode>
 <!--- Embed primary key as a hidden field --->
 <cfoutput>
 <input type="hidden" name="FilmID" value="#Film.FilmID#">
 </cfoutput>
</cfif>

<table align="center" bgcolor="orange">
 <tr>
  <th colspan="2">
   <cfoutput>
   <font size="+1">#FormTitle#</font>
```

Listing 14.17 (CONTINUED)

```
       </cfoutput>
     </th>
    </tr>
    <tr>
     <td>
      Movie:
     </td>
     <td>
      <cfinput type="Text"
               name="MovieTitle"
               value="#MovieTitle#"
               message="MOVIE TITLE is required!"
               required="Yes"
               validateAt="onSubmit,onServer"
               size="50"
               maxlength="100">
     </td>
    </tr>
    <tr>
     <td>
      Tag line:
     </td>
     <td>
      <cfinput type="Text"
               name="PitchText"
               value="#PitchText#"
               message="TAG LINE is required!"
               required="Yes"
               validateAt="onSubmit,onServer"
               size="50"
               maxlength="100">
     </td>
    </tr>
    <tr>
     <td>
      Rating:
     </td>
     <td>
      <!--- Ratings list --->
      <cfselect name="RatingID"
               query="ratings"
               value="RatingID"
               display="Rating"
               selected="#VARIABLES.RatingID#">
      </cfselect>
     </td>
    </tr>
    <tr>
     <td>
      Summary:
     </td>
     <td>
      <cfoutput>
      <textarea name="summary"
               cols="40"
```

Listing 14.17 (CONTINUED)

```
                        rows="5"
                        wrap="virtual">#Summary#</textarea>
         </cfoutput>
        </td>
      </tr>
      <tr>
       <td>
        Budget:
       </td>
       <td>
        <cfinput type="Text"
                 name="AmountBudgeted"
                 value="#AmountBudgeted#"
                 message="BUDGET must be a valid numeric amount!"
                 required="NO"
                 validate="integer"
                 validateAt="onSubmit,onServer"
                 size="10"
                 maxlength="10">
       </td>
      </tr>
      <tr>
       <td>
        Release Date:
       </td>
       <td>
        <cfinput type="Text"
                 name="DateInTheaters"
                 value="#DateInTheaters#"
                 message="RELEASE DATE must be a valid date!"
                 required="NO"
                 validate="date"
                 validateAt="onSubmit,onServer"
                 size="10"
                 maxlength="10">
       </td>
      </tr>
      <tr>
       <td>
        Image File:
       </td>
       <td>
        <cfinput type="Text"
                 name="ImageName"
                 value="#ImageName#"
                 required="NO"
                 size="20"
                 maxlength="50">
       </td>
      </tr>
      <tr>
       <td colspan="2" align="center">
        <cfoutput>
        <input type="submit" value="#ButtonText#">
        </cfoutput>
```

Listing 14.17 (CONTINUED)

```
    </td>
  </tr>
</table>

</cfform>

<!--- Page footer --->
<cfinclude template="footer.cfm">
```

There are only three changes in Listing 14.17. All `<cfquery>` tags have been removed and replaced by `<cfinvoke>` tags (obtaining the data from `movies.cfc`). The `action` has been changed to point to a new file—`movie_process.cfm`. In addition, look at the `RatingID` field. It uses a new tag named `<cfselect>`. This tag, which can be used only within `<cfform>` and `</cfform>` tags, simplifies the creation of dynamic data-driven `<select>` controls. The code

```
<cfselect name="RatingID"
          query="ratings"
          value="RatingID"
          display="Rating"
          selected="#VARIABLES.RatingID#">
</cfselect>
```

is functionally the same as

```
<select name="RatingID">
 <cfoutput query="ratings">
  <option value="#RatingID#"
   <cfif ratings.RatingID IS VARIABLES.RatingID>
    selected
   </cfif>>
   #Rating#</option>
 </cfoutput>
</select>
```

Obviously, using `<cfselect>` is much cleaner and simpler. It creates a `<select>` control named `RatingID` that is populated with the `ratings` query, using the `RatingID` column as the value and displaying the `Rating` column. Whatever value is in the variable `RatingID` will be used to pre-select the selected option in the control.

Listings 14.18 calls the appropriate `movies.cfc` methods to add or update movies.

Listing 14.18 `movie_process.cfm`—Movie Insert and Update

```
<!---
Name:        movie_process.cfm
Author:      Ben Forta (ben@forta.com)
Description: Process edit page
Created:     07/01/07
--->

<!--- Edit or update? --->
<cfif IsDefined("FORM.FilmID")>
 <cfset method="update">
<cfelse>
```

Listing 14.18 (CONTINUED)

```
  <cfset method="add">
</cfif>

<!--- Do it --->
<cfinvoke component="movies"
          method="#method#">
 <!--- FilmID only if update method --->
 <cfif IsDefined("FORM.FilmID")>
  <cfinvokeargument name="FilmID"
                    value="#FORM.FilmID#">
 </cfif>
 <cfinvokeargument name="MovieTitle"
                   value="#Trim(FORM.MovieTitle)#">
 <cfinvokeargument name="PitchText"
                   value="#Trim(FORM.PitchText)#">
 <cfinvokeargument name="AmountBudgeted"
                   value="#Int(FORM.AmountBudgeted)#">
 <cfinvokeargument name="RatingID"
                   value="#Int(FORM.RatingID)#">
 <cfinvokeargument name="Summary"
                   value="#Trim(FORM.Summary)#">
 <cfinvokeargument name="ImageName"
                   value="#Trim(FORM.ImageName)#">
 <cfinvokeargument name="DateInTheaters"
                   value="#DateFormat(FORM.DateInTheaters)#">
</cfinvoke>

<!--- When done go back to movie list --->
<cflocation url="movies.cfm">
```

Listing 14.18 uses a `<cfif>` statement to determine which method to invoke (`add` or `update`). It then uses a `<cfinvoke>` tag set containing a `<cfinvokeargument>` for each argument.

TIP

`<cfinvokeargument>` tags may be included conditionally, as is the case here for the `FilmID` argument. This is an advantage of `<cfinvokeargument>` syntax over `name=value` syntax.

Listing 14.19 simply invokes the CFC `delete` method to delete a movie. The code in Listings 14.18 and 14.19 provide no user feedback at all. Instead, they return to the administration screen using the `<cflocation>` tag as soon as they finish processing the database changes. `<cflocation>` is used to switch from the current template being processed to any other URL, including another ColdFusion template. The following sample code instructs ColdFusion to switch to the `movies.cfm` template:

```
<cflocation URL="movies.cfm">
```

This way, the updated movie list is displayed, ready for further processing, as soon as any change is completed.

TIP

This example could be further enhanced by not making the action page determine which CFC method to invoke. Instead, you could have a single update method that (based on passed arguments) creates or updates a row as needed. This approach would be preferable.

Listing 14.19 `movie_delete.cfm`—Movie Delete Processing

```
<!---
Name:        movie_delete.cfm
Author:      Ben Forta (ben@forta.com)
Description: Delete a movie
Created:     07/01/07
--->

<!--- Check that FilmID was provided --->
<cfif NOT IsDefined("FilmID")>
 <h1>You did not specify the FilmID</h1>
 <cfabort>
</cfif>

<!--- Delete a movie --->
<cfinvoke component="movies"
          method="delete"
          filmid="#URL.FilmID#">

<!--- When done go back to movie list --->
<cflocation url="movies.cfm">
```

And there you have it: a complete *n*-tier application featuring data display, edit and delete using data-drill down, and reusable data-driven add and edit forms—all in under 300 lines of code, including comments. Extremely powerful, and not complicated at all.

Beyond HTML Forms: ColdFusion-Powered Ajax

You've used HTML forms extensively in the past few chapters, and forms will undoubtedly play an important role in all of the applications you build. HTML forms are easy to create and work with, but they are also very limited and not overly capable.

For example, HTML form controls lack commonly needed controls such as date choosers and data grids. They lack any real form field validation, as discussed previously. They also are also essentially bound to the page request model of the Web: every change requires a roundtrip back to the server and a subsequent page refresh.

HTML forms leave much to be desired, and Web developers have acquired something of a love-hate relationship with forms, appreciating their simplicity but despising the lack of functionality that this simplicity causes.

To get around these problems and limitations, ColdFusion has constantly sought new and innovative technologies to include with the product for you to use. From Java applets to Adobe Flash controls to XForms abstractions, as new options become available, ColdFusion tries to take advantage of them.

ColdFusion 8 continues this pattern with powerful new HTML controls and with simplified Ajax support. This chapter explores these new options.

NOTE

Coverage of XForms and Adobe Flash forms are beyond the scope of this book and are thus not discussed in this chapter.

Using the Extended Controls

An example provides the best introduction to ColdFusion's extended form controls. In Chapter 14, "Using Forms to Add or Change Data," you created a series of forms to allow users to insert and update movie data in the Films table. One of those fields was a date field that required users to enter a valid movie release date.

Asking users to enter dates is always asking for trouble. Some users will enter digits for months and others will spell out or abbreviate months, some users will enter two-digit years and others will enter four-digit years, some users will enter hyphens as separators and others will use slashes—you get the idea. Rather than asking the user to enter a date manually, you really need a date control: a pop-up calendar that lets users browse months and click desired dates. But, as already noted, there is no date control in HTML forms.

Fortunately, there is one in `<cfform>`, and it does exactly what we want. To create a date field, all you need to do is use `<cfinput>` and change type to `type="datefield"`—it's that simple.

Listing 15.1 is an updated insert form (based on the one created in Chapter 14); Figure 15.1 shows the new form.

Listing 15.1 `insert1.cfm`—New Movie Form

```
<!---
Name:        insert1.cfm
Author:      Ben Forta (ben@forta.com)
Description: Advanced HTML controls
Created:     07/07/07
--->

<!--- Get ratings --->
<cfquery datasource="ows" name="ratings">
SELECT RatingID, Rating
FROM FilmsRatings
ORDER BY RatingID
</cfquery>

<!--- Page header --->
<cfinclude template="header.cfm">

<!--- New movie form --->
<cfform action="insert2.cfm">

<table align="center" bgcolor="orange">
 <tr>
  <th colspan="2">
   <font size="+1">Add a Movie</font>
  </th>
 </tr>
 <tr>
  <td>
   Movie:
  </td>
  <td>
   <cfinput type="Text"
            name="MovieTitle"
            message="MOVIE TITLE is required!"
            required="Yes"
            validateAt="onSubmit,onServer"
            size="50"
            maxlength="100">
  </td>
 </tr>
```

Listing 15.1 (CONTINUED)

```
<tr>
 <td>
  Tag line:
 </td>
 <td>
  <cfinput type="Text"
           name="PitchText"
           message="TAG LINE is required!"
           required="Yes"
           validateAt="onSubmit,onServer"
           size="50"
           maxlength="100">
 </td>
</tr>
<tr>
 <td>
  Rating:
 </td>
 <td>
  <!--- Ratings list --->
  <cfselect name="RatingID"
            query="ratings"
            display="Rating"
            value="RatingID" />
 </td>
</tr>
<tr>
 <td>
  Summary:
 </td>
 <td>
  <cftextarea name="summary"
              richtext="true"
              toolbar="Basic"
              height="150"
              wrap="virtual" />
 </td>
</tr>
<tr>
 <td>
  Budget:
 </td>
 <td>
  <cfinput type="Text"
           name="AmountBudgeted"
           message="BUDGET must be a valid numeric amount!"
           required="NO"
           validate="integer"
           validateAt="onSubmit,onServer"
           size="10"
           maxlength="10">
 </td>
</tr>
<tr>
 <td>
```

Listing 15.1 (CONTINUED)

```
    Release Date:
  </td>
  <td>
   <cfinput type="DateField"
            name="DateInTheaters"
            message="RELEASE DATE must be a valid date!"
            required="NO"
            validate="date"
            validateAt="onSubmit,onServer"
            size="10"
            maxlength="10">
  </td>
 </tr>
 <tr>
  <td>
   Image File:
  </td>
  <td>
   <cfinput type="Text"
            name="ImageName"
            required="NO"
            size="20"
            maxlength="50">
  </td>
 </tr>
 <tr>
  <td colspan="2" align="center">
   <input type="submit" value="Insert">
  </td>
   </tr>
</table>

</cfform>

<!--- Page footer --->
<cfinclude template="footer.cfm">
```

Most of Listing 15.1 should be self-explanatory by now. A <cfquery> is used to retrieve ratings to be used in a subsequent <cfselect> control, and <cfform> is used to create the actual form. The DateInTheaters field is now of type type="datefield", which creates the nice pop-up date field seen in Figure 15.1.

I also stuck another goodie in the code without telling you. The <cftextarea> box is no longer a simple text control; it is now an actual editor that lets you highlight text to make it bold, and so on. To use this feature, all you need to do is add richtext="true" to the <cftextarea> tag.

The real beauty of these controls is that they work as-is—no plug-ins are needed, and they have no special browser requirements. All current browsers on all major operating systems are supported.

NOTE

The rich text control is highly configurable, providing full control over the toolbars and buttons as well as the color schemes (via skins). In this example, the Basic toolbar was used. The other built-in toolbar is Default, and it contains several rows of buttons (far more than we need here). You can also create custom toolbars if necessary. Consult the ColdFusion documentation for information on creating and modifying toolbars.

Figure 15.1

ColdFusion offers enhanced form controls, including a rich text editor and a date field.

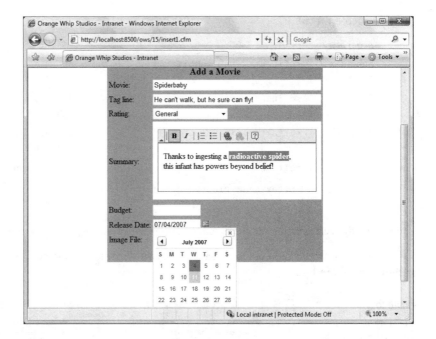

ColdFusion Extended Form Controls

You've seen examples of two of ColdFusion's extended form controls. But what other control types are supported? Table 15.1 lists the form controls along with their CFML syntax and usage notes (and notes those that support Ajax use, which will be described later in this chapter).

Table 15.1 Extended Forms Controls

CONTROL	SYNTAX	NOTES
Auto Suggest	`<cfinput type="text" autosuggest="">`	Supports simple and Ajax use.
Button	`<cfinput type="button">`	Functions just like HTML `<input type="button">`.
Check Box	`<cfinput type="checkbox">`	Functions just like HTML `<input type="checkbox">`.
Data Grid	`<cfgrid>`	Supports simple and Ajax use.
Date Field	`<cfinput type="datefield">`	Not supported in HTML.
Hidden	`<cfinput type="hidden">`	Functions just like HTML `<input type="hidden">`.
Password	`<cfinput type="password">`	Functions just like HTML `<input type="password">`.
Select	`<cfselect>`	Supports simple and Ajax use.

Table 15.1 (CONTINUED)

CONTROL	SYNTAX	NOTES
Submit	`<cfinput type="submit">`	Functions just like HTML `<input type="submit">`.
Text	`<cfinput type="text">`	Functions just like HTML `<input type="text">`.
Textarea	`<cftextarea>`	Functions just like HTML `<textarea>`.
Tree	`<cftree>`	Supports simple and Ajax use.
Rich Text	`<cftextarea richtext="true">`	

You've already seen examples of the date field and rich text editor; let's look at a few more controls.

The `<cfgrid>` control is used to create data grids: two-dimensional spreadsheet–type views of data as shown in Figure 15.2.

Figure 15.2

ColdFusion's data grid makes it easy to display multiple rows in a scrollable grid.

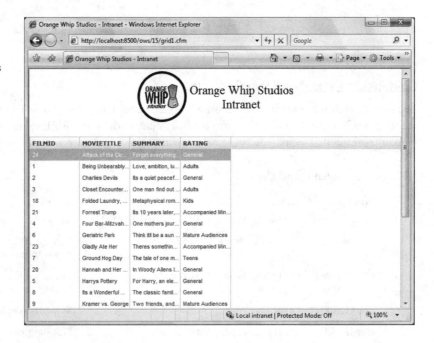

Listing 15.2 contains the code that created the grid shown in Figure 15.2.

Listing 15.2 grid1.cfm—Basic Data Grid

```
<!---
Name:         grid1.cfm
Author:       Ben Forta (ben@forta.com)
Description:  Basic data grid
```

Listing 15.2 (CONTINUED)

```
Created:     07/07/07
--->

<!--- Get movies --->
<cfinvoke component="movies"
          method="list"
          returnvariable="movies">

<!--- Page header --->
<cfinclude template="header.cfm">

<!--- Display grid --->
<cfform>
<cfgrid name="movieGrid"
        width="100%"
        format="html"
        query="movies" />
</cfform>

<!--- Page footer --->
<cfinclude template="footer.cfm">
```

Listing 15.2 invokes the list method in movies.cfc to obtain a list of movies. It then creates a data grid using <cfgrid>, passing the query to it.

Listing 15.3 is the list method used to populate the grid.

Listing 15.3 List Method

```
<!--- Get movie list --->
 <cffunction name="list"
             returntype="query"
             hint="List all movies">

   <!--- Create local variables --->
   <cfset var movies="">

   <cfquery datasource="#ds#"
            name="movies">
   SELECT FilmID, MovieTitle, Summary, Rating
   FROM Films, FilmsRatings
   WHERE Films.RatingID=FilmsRatings.RatingID
   ORDER BY MovieTitle
   </cfquery>
   <cfreturn movies>

 </cffunction>
```

This is all it takes to populate a data grid. Data in the grid can be sorted by clicking column headers (click once to sort in ascending order and click again to sort in descending order), and columns can be resized and moved as needed.

By default, `<cfgrid>` displays all of the columns in the passed query, using the column names as the grid headers. This behavior can be changed by using the `<cfgridcolumn>` tag, as seen in Listing 15.4, which creates an updated data grid.

Listing 15.4 `grid2.cfm`—Controlling the Data Grid Display

```
<!---
Name:        grid2.cfm
Author:      Ben Forta (ben@forta.com)
Description: Controlling data grid display
Created:     07/07/07
--->

<!--- Get movies --->
<cfinvoke component="movies"
          method="list"
          returnvariable="movies">

<!--- Page header --->
<cfinclude template="header.cfm">

<!--- Display grid --->
<cfform>
<cfgrid name="movieGrid"
        width="100%"
        format="html"
        query="movies">
   <cfgridcolumn name="FilmID"
                 display="no">
   <cfgridcolumn name="MovieTitle"
                 header="Title"
                 width="200">
   <cfgridcolumn name="Rating"
                 header="Rating"
                 width="100">
   <cfgridcolumn name="Summary"
                 header="Summary"
                 width="400">
</cfgrid>
</cfform>

<!--- Page footer --->
<cfinclude template="footer.cfm">
```

The updated listing explicitly prevents the FilmID column from being displayed and then provides alternate headers and widths for the other three columns.

TIP

The `<cfgridcolumn>` attribute also can be used to control the order in which grid columns appear.

NOTE

Additional `<cfgridcolumn>` attributes enable control of fonts, colors, and much more.

Another useful control, one that does not exist in HTML itself, is the auto-suggest control. This is actually less a control and more a change to the way that text input controls usually work.

Imagine that you have a form that prompts the user to enter an address. There are lots of possible options for the `City` field, but if you have lots of city names already stored in your database tables, you can assist the user by providing a drop-down list of suggestions (which the user can select or just ignore). This type of control is called an auto-suggest control, and it usually pops up only if the user pauses, giving you the opportunity to suggest text options.

There is no auto-suggest control in HTML. Creating an auto-suggest control requires writing some pretty sophisticated JavaScript—unless you are using ColdFusion that is, in which case you don't have to write any JavaScript at all.

To turn `<cfinput type="text">` into an auto-suggest control, all you need to do is provide the suggestions. For example, the following code creates an auto-suggest control:

```
<cfinput type="text"
         name="fruit"
         autosuggest="apple,banana,lemon,lime,mango,orange,pear">
```

If you were to save and run this code, you would see a regular text input control. But if you typed the letter *L* and paused, you'd see a pop-up box containing the two options that begin with the letter *L*.

Of course, the list need not be hard-coded. Listing 15.5 contains a complete auto-suggest example that creates the screen shown in Figure 15.3.

Listing 15.5 autosuggest1.cfm—Basic Auto-Suggest

```
<!---
Name:        autosuggest1.cfm
Author:      Ben Forta (ben@forta.com)
Description: Basic auto-suggest
Created:     07/07/07
--->

<!--- Get ratings --->
<cfquery datasource="ows" name="ratings">
SELECT Rating
FROM FilmsRatings
ORDER BY Rating
</cfquery>
<!--- Convert to list --->
<cfset list=ValueList(ratings.Rating)>

<!--- Page header --->
<cfinclude template="header.cfm">

<!--- Search form --->
<cfform>

<table align="center" bgcolor="orange">
 <tr>
  <th colspan="2">
```

Listing 15.5 (CONTINUED)

```
      <font size="+1">Find a Movie</font>
     </th>
    </tr>
    <tr>
     <td>
      Rating:
     </td>
     <td>
      <cfinput type="Text"
               name="Rating"
               autosuggest="#list#"
               size="50"
               maxlength="100">
     </td>
    </tr>
    <tr>
     <td colspan="2" align="center">
      <input type="submit" value="Search">
     </td>
     </tr>
  </table>

 </cfform>


 <!--- Page footer --->
 <cfinclude template="footer.cfm">
```

Figure 15.3

Auto-suggest lists can be hard-coded and populated programmatically.

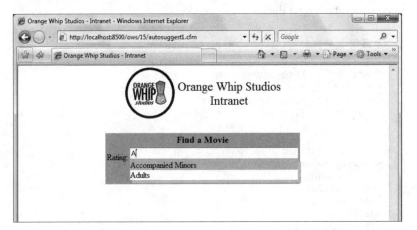

The code is Listing 15.5 gets a list of ratings using `<cfquery>`. Auto-suggest values need to be passed as a comma-delimited list, and so a list is constructed using the `ValueList()` function, which takes the name of a query column and returns a comma-delimited list of all of the values in that column. That list is then passed to `<cfinput>` as `autosuggest="#list#"`.

NOTE

All of the controls discussed here use JavaScript internally and require that JavaScript be enabled in the browser. If you view the source code on the generated page, you'll see the JavaScript that is included and generated.

Working with Ajax

All of the controls used thus far have embedded data (queries, lists, and so on) inside of the controls themselves. That works in many situations, but consider the following scenarios.

What if your auto-suggest values are being populated by a table that contains thousands of entries? You don't want to load all of these entries into a list in the control itself. For starters, that will increase the page size significantly and seriously affect performance, but also, you don't want to show your user that many options. What you really want is no data at all in the auto-suggest control; when the user types some text and pauses, you want your application to send that text to Cold-Fusion, which then returns the relevant auto-suggest entries. And of course, you want this process to work without refreshing the page.

Or suppose that the data grid we created previously displayed all of the movies at once. This is fine here, because our table contains only 23 movies. But what if the database table had hundreds or even thousands of entries? You wouldn't want them all displayed at once. Instead, you to show a page of data at a time, allowing users to scroll back and forth as needed. And of course, this process too would have to work without refreshing the page.

Is this doable?

The answer is yes, and this is where Ajax comes into play. Ajax (which stands for Asynchronous JavaScript and XML) is not a product or a technology. Actually, it's not any single thing you can point to. Rather, it is a technique that combines DHTML and JavaScript with the (until fairly recently unnoticed and unused) capability of Web browsers to make asynchronous HTTP calls.

If that sounds obscure, don't worry. What it simply means is that JavaScript (the scripting language supported by just about every Web browser) has the capability to issue Web page requests under programmatic control—requests that don't actually update or refresh the screen. By coupling that capability with some clever JavaScript and DHTML, you can make Web browsers do some very interesting things, including addressing the scenarios just mentioned.

➔ Ajax, and indeed ColdFusion's Ajax support, cannot be covered fully in one introductory chapter. In this chapter, you learn the basics; for more information, see Chapter 34, "Advanced ColdFusion-Powered Ajax," in *ColdFusion 8 Web Application Construction Kit, Volume 2: Application Development.*

Chapter 11, "The Basics of Structured Development," introduced ColdFusion Components (which we have been using ever since). Well, ColdFusion Components are the key to the way that Cold-Fusion's Ajax controls work. As just explained, Ajax controls make calls back to the server as needed, and in ColdFusion those calls are to CFCs.

Let's revisit the auto-suggest example, this time using an Ajax auto-suggest control. First we'll look at the CFC method needed to power the control. Listing 15.6 shows the code.

Listing 15.6   `lookupMovie` Method

```
<!--- Lookup used for auto suggest --->
 <cffunction name="lookupMovie"
             access="remote"
             returntype="string"
             hint="Lookup method for Ajax auto-suggest">
```

Listing 15.6 (CONTINUED)

```
        <cfargument name="search"
                    type="any"
                    required="false"
                    default="">

        <!--- Define variables --->
        <cfset var data="">

        <!--- Do search --->
        <cfquery datasource="#ds#" name="data">
        SELECT MovieTitle
        FROM Films
        WHERE UCase(MovieTitle) LIKE UCase('#ARGUMENTS.search#%')
        ORDER BY MovieTitle
        </cfquery>

        <!--- And return it --->
        <cfreturn ValueList(data.MovieTitle)>
    </cffunction>
```

Most of the code in Listing 15.6 is code you have seen before, but there are some very important points to note here. First, the method contains an attribute of access="remote". Usually, CFC methods can be invoked only by other ColdFusion code running on the same server, but a CFC method that needs to be invoked by a Web browser (as is the case with Ajax controls) needs to be explicitly granted that right, and that is what access="remote" does.

NOTE

Any CFC methods that include access="remote" can be invoked remotely, even by other users. Be very careful with the methods you expose, and pay attention to CFC security (discussed in Chapter 26, "Building Reusable Components," and 27, "Creating Advanced ColdFusion Components," both in Vol. 2, *Application Development*).

The lookupMovie method accepts an argument—the string the user has entered thus far—uses that text in <cfquery>, and then returns a comma-delimited list containing the matches (the format required by the auto-suggest control).

Now let's look at the client-side code that uses a <cfinput> control that uses the lookupMovie method. Listing 15.7 contains the code, and the result is shown in Figure 15.4.

Listing 15.7 autosuggest2.cfm—Ajax Auto-Suggest

```
<!---
Name:       autosuggest2.cfm
Author:     Ben Forta (ben@forta.com)
Description: Ajax auto-suggest
Created:    07/07/07
--->

<!--- Page header --->
<cfinclude template="header.cfm">

<!--- Search form --->
<cfform>
```

Listing 15.7 (CONTINUED)

```
<table align="center" bgcolor="orange">
 <tr>
  <th colspan="2">
   <font size="+1">Find a Movie</font>
  </th>
 </tr>
 <tr>
  <td>
   Movie:
  </td>
  <td>
   <cfinput type="Text"
            name="MovieTitle"
            autosuggest="cfc:movies.lookupMovie({cfautosuggestvalue})"
            size="50"
            maxlength="100">
  </td>
 </tr>
 <tr>
  <td colspan="2" align="center">
   <input type="submit" value="Search">
  </td>
  </tr>
</table>

</cfform>

<!--- Page footer --->
<cfinclude template="footer.cfm">
```

Figure 15.4

Ajax-powered
auto-suggest
controls retrieve
their suggestions
by making calls
back to ColdFusion.

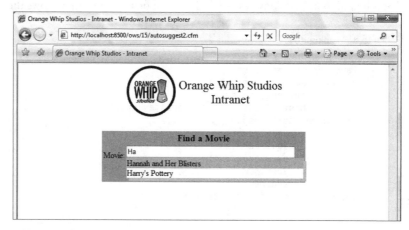

The first thing you'll notice about Listing 15.7 is that it contains no database query and no
<cfinvoke> to invoke a CFC method. Instead, we've added the following line to the <cfinput>
control:

```
autosuggest="cfc:movies.lookupMovie({cfautosuggestvalue})"
```

Unlike the example in Listing 15.5, autosuggest does not contain a list. Rather, it points to a CFC, in this case a CFC named movies (in the current folder), and a method named lookupMovie (the method in Listing 15.6). The lookupMovie method expects a string to be passed to it, the text that the user has typed thus far. Rather than requiring you to write JavaScript to extract that value, ColdFusion allows you to refer to a special client-side variable named cfautosuggestvalue, which will automatically be replaced by the actual value entered by the user when the CFC method is invoked. The cfautosuggestvalue variable is enclosed within curly braces ({ and }), which Cold-Fusion uses to delimit expressions within client-side code (in much the same way as server-side code uses # to delimit expressions).

NOTE

A full path is not needed when pointing to a CFC in the current folder. To point to a CFC in another folder, a fully qualified path is needed.

Save the code and give it a try. Each time you type text and pause, an asynchronous call is made to the CFC method, data is retrieved and returned, and suggestions are made.

You've now created an Ajax-powered control without having to worry about what Ajax actually is and without having to write a single line of JavaScript.

And that's why we love ColdFusion!

Let's look at another, more complex example: a data grid that must handle any amount of data, supporting paging as needed.

Again, the solution has two parts: the CFC that actually accesses the data, and the client-side code that is bound to it. Let's look at the CFC method first; Listing 15.8 shows the code.

Listing 15.8 lookupMovie Method

```
<!--- Browse movies --->
<cffunction name="browse"
            access="remote"
            returntype="struct"
            hint="Browse method for Ajax grid">
    <cfargument name="page"
                type="numeric"
                required="yes">
    <cfargument name="pageSize"
                type="numeric"
                required="yes">
    <cfargument name="gridsortcolumn"
                type="string"
                required="no"
                default="">
    <cfargument name="gridsortdir"
                type="string"
                required="no"
                default="">

    <!--- Local variables --->
    <cfset var movies="">
```

Listing 15.8 (CONTINUED)

```
            <cfquery datasource="#ds#"
                   name="movies">
            SELECT FilmID, MovieTitle, Summary, Rating
            FROM Films, FilmsRatings
            WHERE Films.RatingID=FilmsRatings.RatingID
             <cfif ARGUMENTS.gridsortcolumn NEQ ""
                   and ARGUMENTS.gridsortdir NEQ "">
               ORDER BY #ARGUMENTS.gridsortcolumn# #ARGUMENTS.gridsortdir#
             </cfif>
            </cfquery>

            <!--- And return it as a grid structure --->
            <cfreturn QueryConvertForGrid(movies,
                                          ARGUMENTS.page,
                                          ARGUMENTS.pageSize)>
       </cffunction>
```

Listing 15.8 contains a method named browse that is used to browse through rows in a table. The browse method returns data, one page at a time, and so it has to know the page that is requested as well as the number of rows per page. That way, if there are 10 rows per page and page 3 is requested, browse will know to return rows 21 to 30, and so on. These values must be passed by the client with each request, and indeed they are the first two arguments in this method. In addition, as mentioned previously, users can sort data grid contents by clicking column headers, and so the current sort column and direction are also passed by the client (if the user sorted data).

The method then uses <cfquery> to retrieve the data, optionally appending a SQL ORDER BY clause if the user sorted data.

Finally, the ColdFusion QueryConvertForGrid() function extracts the data for the desired page and formats it as needed by <cfgrid>, and the results are returned.

The client-side code creates the <cfgrid> control that uses the browse method. Listing 15.9 contains the code, and the result is shown in Figure 15.5.

Listing 15.9 grid3.cfm—Ajax Data Grid

```
   <!---
   Name:       grid3.cfm
   Author:     Ben Forta (ben@forta.com)
   Description: Ajax data grid
   Created:    07/07/07
   --->

   <!--- Page header --->
   <cfinclude template="header.cfm">

   <!--- Display grid --->
   <cfform>
   <cfgrid name="movieGrid"
           width="100%"
           format="html"
           pagesize="10"
           striperows="yes"
```

Listing 15.9 (CONTINUED)

```
            bind="cfc:movies.browse({cfgridpage},
                                    {cfgridpagesize},
                                    {cfgridsortcolumn},
                                    {cfgridsortdirection})">
    <cfgridcolumn name="FilmID"
                  display="no">
    <cfgridcolumn name="MovieTitle"
                  header="Title"
                  width="200">
    <cfgridcolumn name="Rating"
                  header="Rating"
                  width="100">
    <cfgridcolumn name="Summary"
                  header="Summary"
                  width="400">
    </cfgrid>
    </cfform>

    <!--- Page footer --->
    <cfinclude template="footer.cfm">
```

Figure 15.5

An Ajax-powered data grid supports record paging as well as on-demand sorting.

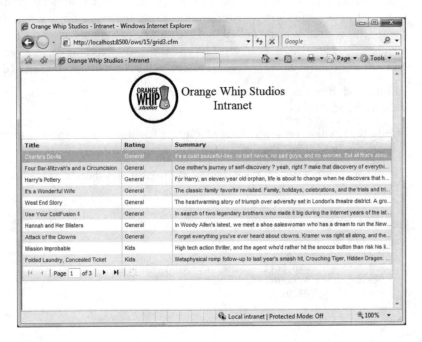

This `<cfgrid>` control is similar to the one in Listing 15.4. The big change is that the query attribute (which passes an actual query) has been replaced by a new bind attribute. The bind attribute points to a CFC method, using the same syntax as in the auto-suggest example previously. As already explained, the CFC method expects up to four arguments (the first two, current page and size, are required, and the last two, sort column and direction, are optional). Again, ColdFusion provides special variables that can be used in place of actual values: {cfgridpage} is replaced by the current page, {cfgridpagesize} is replaced by the value passed to the pagesize attribute, and so on.

All you need to do is save and run the code. To display the first page of data, JavaScript in the Web browser invokes the CFC method, obtaining the first set of rows. Then, as you browse from page to page or as you sort and resort data, that CFC method is called asynchronously, in the background, and the grid is updated.

NOTE

The <cfgrid> control supports data editing too, but that function is not covered in this chapter.

Using Bindings

You have already seen examples of bindings: The Ajax-powered auto-suggest control and data grids both used bindings to refer to ColdFusion Component methods on the server.

Bindings can also be used on the client side, allowing one control to refer to, and interact with, other controls. Let's look at some basic examples .

→ For full coverage of ColdFusion Ajax bindings, refer to Chapter 34.

We'll start with yet another data grid, but one with an interesting twist. As shown in Figure 15.6, this new data grid has a <textarea> box alongside it, so that when a movie is selected in the grid, the detailed summary is displayed in the box on the right. This type of user interface obviously requires interaction between controls, and thus it requires bindings.

Figure 15.6

Bindings allow controls to interact with other controls.

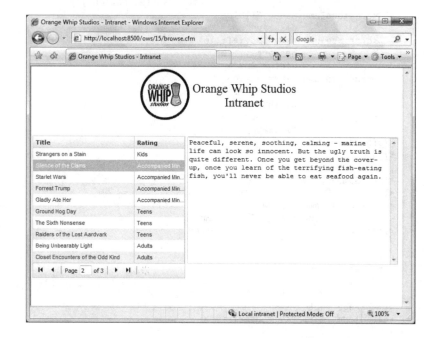

The CFC method that powers this new data grid is the same as the one used previously, so we won't revisit it here. But the client-side code, shown in Listing 15.10, warrants a closer look.

Listing 15.10 browse.cfm—Ajax Data Grid

```
<!---
Name:        browse.cfm
Author:      Ben Forta (ben@forta.com)
Description: Demonstrate using bindings
Created:     07/07/07
--->

<!--- Page header --->
<cfinclude template="header.cfm">

<!--- Display --->
<cfform>

<table>
<tr valign="top">

<!--- The grid --->
<td>
<cfgrid name="movieGrid"
        format="html"
        pagesize="10"
        striperows="yes"
        bind="cfc:movies.browse({cfgridpage},
                                {cfgridpagesize},
                                {cfgridsortcolumn},
                                {cfgridsortdirection})">
    <cfgridcolumn name="FilmID"
                  display="no">
    <cfgridcolumn name="MovieTitle"
                  header="Title"
                  width="200">
    <cfgridcolumn name="Rating"
                  header="Rating"
                  width="100">
    <cfgridcolumn name="Summary"
                  display="no">
</cfgrid>
</td>

<!--- Summary box --->
<td>
<cftextarea name="summary" rows="15"  cols="50"
            bind="{movieGrid.summary}" />
</td>

</tr>
</table>
</cfform>

<!--- Page footer --->
<cfinclude template="footer.cfm">
```

Aside from some table tags and control sizing, most of Listing 15.8 is used unchanged. The big change is the following code:

```
<cftextarea name="summary" rows="15"  cols="50"
            bind="{movieGrid.summary}" />
```

Here, a `<cftextarea>` area is created and named, and its size specified. Then `bind` is used to connect `<cftextarea>` to `movieGrid.summary` (the `summary` column in `movieGrid`, the data grid). This way, whenever the selection in the `movieGrid` data grid changes, the value in `<cftextarea>` is updated automatically.

Let's look at one final example: a more complex use of bindings. We've used `<select>` controls several times, and those controls have typically been populated with data retrieved from a database.

But what if you want multiple related `<select>` controls? What if you want a `<select>` control that lists all of the movie ratings and then another `<select>` control that lists the movies for whatever rating was selected in the first control? Obviously this scenario requires a way to make calls to ColdFusion to obtain the ratings initially and then a way to obtain a new list of movies whenever the rating changes. An example of the desired results is shown in Figure 15.7. How can we achieve these results?

Figure 15.7

Bindings can be used to trigger asynchronous calls to ColdFusion as needed.

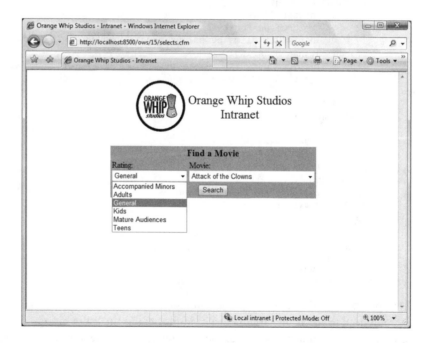

Well, if you have not figured it out yourself, the answer is to use bindings and Ajax-type asynchronous calls to ColdFusion Components.

We need two methods for this example: one to populate each of the `<select>` controls. Let's look at the CFC methods, shown in Listing 15.11, first.

Listing 15.11 getRatings and getFilms Methods

```
<!--- Get array of ratings types --->
<cffunction name="getRatings"
            access="remote"
            returnType="query"
            hint="Get ratings for Ajax SELECT">
  <!--- Define variables --->
  <cfset var data="">

  <!--- Get data --->
  <cfquery name="data" datasource="#ds#">
  SELECT RatingID, Rating
  FROM FilmsRatings
  ORDER BY Rating
  </cfquery>

  <!--- And return it --->
  <cfreturn data>
</cffunction>


<!--- Get films by rating --->
<cffunction name="getFilms"
            access="remote"
            returnType="query"
            hint="Get films by rating for Ajax SELECT">
  <cfargument name="RatingID"
              type="numeric"
              required="true">

  <!--- Define variables --->
  <cfset var data="">

  <!--- Get data --->
  <cfquery name="data" datasource="#ds#">
  SELECT FilmID, MovieTitle
  FROM Films
  WHERE RatingID = #ARGUMENTS.RatingID#
  ORDER BY MovieTitle
  </cfquery>


  <!--- And return it --->
  <cfreturn data>
</cffunction>
```

As before, both methods return queries, and both are access="remote". The getRatings method does not need to accept any arguments; it simply obtains the list of ratings. The getFilms method accepts a single argument, RatingID, and then retrieves just the movies that match that rating, which are then returned.

Simple enough. But what about the client side? The code is in Listing 15.12.

Listing 15.12 `selects.cfm`—Related SELECT Controls

```
<!---
Name:        selects.cfm
Author:      Ben Forta (ben@forta.com)
Description: Related SELECT controls
Created:     07/07/07
--->

<!--- Page header --->
<cfinclude template="header.cfm">

<!--- Search form --->
<cfform>

<table align="center" bgcolor="orange">
 <tr>
  <th colspan="2">
   <font size="+1">Find a Movie</font>
  </th>
 </tr>
 <tr>
  <td>
   Rating:<br>
   <cfselect name="RatingID"
             bind="cfc:movies.getRatings()"
             display="Rating"
             value="RatingID"
             bindonload="true" />
  </td>
  <td>
   Movie:<br>
   <cfselect name="FilmID"
             bind="cfc:movies.getFilms({RatingID})"
             display="MovieTitle"
             value="FilmID" />
  </td>
 </tr>
 <tr>
  <td colspan="2" align="center">
   <input type="submit" value="Search">
  </td>
  </tr>
</table>

</cfform>


<!--- Page footer --->
<cfinclude template="footer.cfm">
```

The code in Listing 15.12 contains two `<cfselect>` controls, both of which have a `bind` attribute connecting them to our two CFC methods. But there are two important differences between the controls.

The first <cfselect> control, RatingID, is simply bound to the getRatings method, and no arguments are passed (none are needed). However, getRatings would never be called because no event would force that call (unlike with the data grid used previously, which automatically requests the first page, <cfselect> bindings occur when something triggers them). This is why bindonload="true" is added; it tells the JavaScript code to trigger a server call as soon as the control is loaded, and that way the first <cfselect> control is automatically populated and ready for use. As the asynchronous server call returns a query, display and value are used to specify the columns to be used for the generated <option> tags.

The second <cfselect> control, FilmID, is bound to the getFilms method, which requires that a RatingID argument be passed to it. Thus, {RatingID} (the name of the first <cfselect> control) is passed as an argument to getFilms, and {RatingID} is replaced by the actual RatingID value when the call is made. This way, whenever the value in RatingID (the first <cfselect> control) changes, the binding on the second <cfselect> control is fired, and the list is updated—clean and simple.

And there you have it: extensions to HTML form controls that you can use as needed, and simple yet powerful Ajax functionality when that is called for.

CHAPTER 16

Graphing, Printing, and Reporting

Many ColdFusion applications involve some type of data reporting. If you're building an online store, for instance, you'll want to generate printable invoices or create a series of report-style pages that show the number of products sold per month. If you're building a community site, you might create a page that shows how many people log on during which parts of the day, or run a report of daily usage. Or, if you're building a Web site for a movie studio (ahem), you might create reports that show the expenses to date for each film, and which films are in danger of going over budget.

It'd be easy to imagine how each of these pages would turn out, if you could only use the skills you have already learned in this book. The pages would be easy to create with various uses of the <cfquery> and <cfoutput> tags, and they could be packed with useful information. You might even come up with some really attractive, creative uses of HTML tables to make the information easier to digest.

As the saying goes, a picture is often as good as a thousand words—or a thousand totals or subtotals. ColdFusion provides exciting and revolutionary features that let you dynamically create charts and graphs, printable documents, and complete reports that can be used to report on whatever data you want.

Generating Graphs

We'll start with an overview of the charting features included in ColdFusion. ColdFusion comes with a series of tags that will allow you to:

- Create many different types of graphs, including pie charts, bar graphs, line graphs, and scatter charts.

- Format your graphs options that control fonts, colors, labels, and more.

- Display the graphs on any ColdFusion page as JPEG images, PNG images, or interactive Flash charts.

- Allow users to drill down on data shown in your charts. For instance, you could have people click the wedges in a pie chart, revealing the data represented in that wedge.

- Combine several different charts, displaying them together on the page. For instance, you might create a scatter chart that shows individual purchases over time, and then add a line chart on top of it that shows users' average spending.

- Save the charts to the server's drive for later use.

Building Simple Charts

Now that you have an idea of what you can do with ColdFusion's charting features, let's get started with some basic examples. Most of the time, you will create charts with just two CFML tags, `<cfchart>` and `<cfchartseries>`.

Introducing `<cfchart>` and `<cfchartseries>`

To display a chart on a ColdFusion page, you use the `<cfchart>` tag. This tag controls the height, width, and formatting of your chart, but it doesn't display anything. Within the `<cfchart>` tag, you use the `<cfchartseries>` tag, which determines the type of chart (like bar or pie) and the actual data to show on the chart.

NOTE

Actually, you will occasionally want to place multiple `<cfchartseries>` tags within a `<cfchart>` tag. See the "Combining Multiple Chart Series" section, later in this chapter.

Table 16.1 shows the most important attributes for the `<cfchart>` tag, and Table 16.2 shows the most important attributes for `<cfchartseries>`.

Table 16.1 Basic `<cfchart>` Tag Syntax

ATTRIBUTE	DESCRIPTION
chartwidth	Optional. The width of the chart, in pixels. The default is `320`.
chartheight	Optional. The height of the chart, in pixels. The default is `240`.
xaxistitle	Optional. The text to display along the chart's x-axis.
yaxistitle	Optional. The text to display along the chart's y-axis.
url	Optional. The URL of a page to send the user to when various sections of the chart are clicked. You can pass variables in the URL so you know what part of the chart the user clicked. See "Drilling Down from Charts," later in this chapter.
format	Optional. The type of image format in which the chart should be created. The valid choices are `flash` (the default), `jpg`, and `png`.
seriesplacement	Optional. For charts that have more than one data series, you can use this attribute—`cluster`, `stacked`, `percent`, or `default`—to control how the series are combined visually. Use `cluster` if the data series represent related pieces of information that should be presented next to one another, rather than added together visually. Use `stacked` or `percent` if the data series represent values that should be added up to a single whole value for each item you're plotting. See "Combining Multiple Chart Series," later in this chapter.

NOTE

Because these tags have a large number of attributes (more than 40 in all), we are introducing only the most important attributes in these tables. Others are introduced later in this chapter.

Table 16.2   Basic `<cfchartseries>` Syntax

ATTRIBUTE	DESCRIPTION
type	Required. The type of chart to create. Usually, you will set this to either `bar`, `line`, `area`, or `pie`. Other chart types are `cone`, `curve`, `cylinder`, `scatter`, `step`, and `pyramid`. The ColdFusion documentation includes some nice pictures of these more unusual types of graphs.
query	Optional. The name of a query that contains data to chart. If you don't provide a `query` attribute, you will need to provide `<cfchartdata>` tags to tell ColdFusion the data to display in the chart.
valuecolumn	Required if a `query` is provided. The name of the column that contains the actual value (the number to represent graphically) for each data point on the chart.
itemcolumn	Required if a `query` is provided. The name of the column that contains labels for each data point on the chart.

NOTE

In this chapter, you will often see the term data point. Data points are the actual pieces of data that are displayed on a chart. If you're creating a pie chart, the data points are the slices of the pie. In a bar chart, the data points are the bars. In a line or scatter chart, the data points are the individual points that have been plotted on the graph.

NOTE

You don't have to have a query object to create a chart. You can also create data points manually using the `<cfchartdata>` tag. See "Plotting Individual Points with `<cfchartdata>`," near the end of this chapter.

Creating Your First Chart

Listing 16.1 shows how to use `<cfchart>` and `<cfchartseries>` to create a simple bar chart. The resulting chart is shown in Figure 16.1. As you can see, it doesn't take much code to produce a reasonably helpful bar chart. Anyone can glance at this chart and instantly understand which films cost more than the average, and by how much.

Listing 16.1   `Chart1.cfm`—Creating a Simple Bar Chart from Query Data

```
<!---
Name:        Chart1.cfm
Author:      Ben Forta
Description: Basic bar chart
Created:     07/10/2007
--->

<!--- Get information from the database --->
<cfinvoke component="ChartData"
```

Listing 16.1 (CONTINUED)

```
              method="GetBudgetData"
              returnvariable="ChartQuery"
              maxrows="10">

<html>
<head>
<title>Chart: Film Budgets</title>
</head>

<body>
<h2>Chart: Film Budgets</h2>

<!--- This defines the size and appearance of the chart --->
<cfchart chartwidth="750"
         chartheight="500"
         yaxistitle="Budget">

  <!--- within the chart --->
  <cfchartseries type="bar"
                 query="chartquery"
                 valuecolumn="amountbudgeted"
                 itemcolumn="movietitle">

</cfchart>

</body>
</html>
```

Figure 16.1

It's easy to create simple charts with <cfchart> and <cfchartdata>.

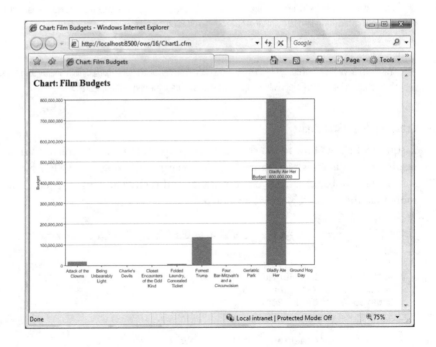

First, an ordinary <cfinvoke> tag is used to select invoke a CFC method that returns film and budget information from the database. Then a <cfchart> tag is used to establish the size of the chart, and to specify that the word Budget appear along the y-axis (that is, at the bottom of the chart). Finally, within the <cfchart> block, a <cfchartseries> tag is used to create a bar chart. ColdFusion is instructed to chart the information in the ChartQuery record set, plotting the data in the Amount-Budgeted column and using the MovieTitle column to provide a label for each piece of information.

NOTE

For this example and the next few listings, we are using maxrows="10" (passed to the <cfquery> tag) to limit the number of films displayed in the chart to ten. This keeps the pictures of the graphs simple while you're learning how to use the charting tags. Just eliminate the maxrows attribute to see all films displayed in the chart.

The charts created here are Adobe Flash charts, as that is the default chart format generated by ColdFusion. Charts may also be generated as static images (in JPG and PNG formats), although static charts aren't as functional or feature rich.

TIP

Data is presented in the chart in the order in which it's retrieved from the database. To change the order, just sort the query differently using the appropriate SQL ORDER BY clause.

Changing the Chart Type

The first chart we created was a bar chart. It's easy to change your code so that it displays a different kind of graph. Just change the type attribute of the <cfchartseries> tag. Figure 16.2 shows the pie chart created by the Chart2.cfm, the code for which is shown in Listing 16.2. The differences are that type="Pie" is used in the <cfchartseries> tag.

Figure 16.2

Changing the chart type is simply a matter of changing the type attribute.

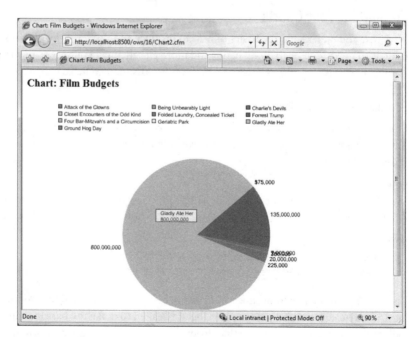

Listing 16.2 `Chart2.cfm`—Creating a Simple Pie Chart from Query Data

```
<!---
Name:        Chart2.cfm
Author:      Ben Forta
Description: Basic pie chart
Created:     07/10/2007
--->

<!--- Get information from the database --->
<cfinvoke component="ChartData"
          method="GetBudgetData"
          returnvariable="ChartQuery"
          maxrows="10">

<html>
<head>
<title>Chart: Film Budgets</title>
</head>

<body>
<h2>Chart: Film Budgets</h2>

<!--- This defines the size and appearance of the chart --->
<cfchart chartwidth="750"
         chartheight="500"
         yaxistitle="Budget">

<!--- within the chart --->
 <cfchartseries type="pie"
                query="chartquery"
                valuecolumn="amountbudgeted"
                itemcolumn="movietitle">

</cfchart>

</body>
</html>
```

Formatting Your Charts

Now that you understand the basics of how to produce simple charts, let's learn some formatting options to make your charts look better and more closely meet your users' needs. In general, your goal should be to make the charts as easy on the eyes as possible—it helps people concentrate on the data.

Adding Depth with 3D Charts

One of the easiest ways to make a basic chart look more sophisticated is to give it a 3D look. Table 16.3 shows the `<cfchart>` options available for adding a 3D effect to your charts. Get out the red-and-blue glasses!

NOTE

Whether the 3D effect makes a chart easier to read depends on the situation. It tends to look nice in simple creations, especially bar charts with relatively few data points. Once a chart displays many data points, the 3D effect becomes distracting.

NOTE

The `xoffset` and `yoffset` attributes have no discernible effect on pie charts. You can make a pie chart display with a 3D appearance using `show3d="Yes"`, but you can't control the offsets.

Listing 16.3 shows how to produce a 3D graph by adding these attributes to the code from Listing 16.1. The `xoffset` and `yoffset` have been tweaked to make the bars look like they are being looked at from the top a bit more than from the side. The results are shown in Figure 16.3.

Figure 16.3

Add 3D chart effects to better display chart details.

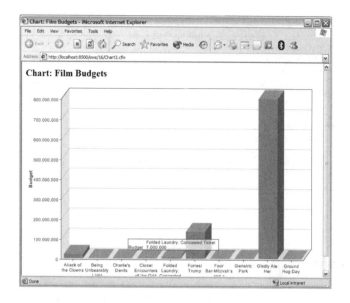

Table 16.3 `<cfchart>` Options for a 3D Effect

ATTRIBUTE	DESCRIPTION
show3d	Whether to show the chart with a 3D effect. The default is No.
xoffset	The amount that the chart should be rotated on the x-axis. In other words, this controls to what extent the chart appears to be viewed from the side. You can use a value anywhere from -1 to 1, but in general you will want to experiment with low, positive numbers (between .01 and .3) for best results. A value of 0 means no 3D effect horizontally. The default is .1.
yoffset	Similarly, the amount that the chart should be turned around its y-axis. This controls the extent the chart seems to be viewed from the top. Again, you will probably want to experiment with low, positive numbers (between .01 and .3) for best results. A value of 0 means no 3D effect vertically. The default is .1.

Listing 16.3 `Chart3.cfm`—Adding a 3D Appearance

```
<!---
Name:        Chart3.cfm
Author:      Ben Forta
Description: 3D bar chart
Created:     07/10/2007
--->

<!--- Get information from the database --->
<cfinvoke component="ChartData"
          method="GetBudgetData"
          returnvariable="ChartQuery"
          maxrows="10">

<html>
<head>
<title>Chart: Film Budgets</title>
</head>

<body>
<h2>Chart: Film Budgets</h2>
```

Listing 16.3 (CONTINUED)

```
<!--- This defines the size and appearance of the chart --->
<cfchart chartwidth="750"
         chartheight="500"
         yaxistitle="Budget"
         show3d="yes"
         xoffset=".03"
         yoffset=".06">

  <!--- within the chart --->
  <cfchartseries type="bar"
                 query="chartquery"
                 valuecolumn="amountbudgeted"
                 itemcolumn="movietitle">

</cfchart>

</body>
</html>
```

Controlling Fonts and Colors

ColdFusion provides a number of formatting attributes that you can use to control fonts, colors, and borders. Some of the attributes are applied at the <cfchart> level and others at the <cfchartseries> level, as listed in Table 16.4 and Table 16.5, respectively.

NOTE

All of the attributes that control color can accept Web-style hexadecimal color values, such as FFFFFF for white or 0000FF for blue. In addition, any of the following named colors can be used: Aqua, Black, Blue, Fuchsia, Gray, Green, Lime, Maroon, Navy, Olive, Purple, Red, Silver, Teal, White, and Yellow.

Table 16.4 <cfchart> Formatting Options

ATTRIBUTE	DESCRIPTION
showborder	Whether a border should be drawn around the entire chart. The default is No.
showlegend	Whether to display a legend that shows the meaning of each color used in the graph. This is applicable only to pie charts, or charts that use more than one <cfchartseries> tag. The default is Yes.
backgroundcolor	The background color of the portion of the chart that contains the actual graph (that is, excluding the space set aside for axis labels and legends).
databackgroundcolor	The background color of the space set aside for axis labels and legends (everywhere except the part where the actual graph is shown).
tipbgcolor	The background color for the pop-up tip window that appears when you hover the pointer over a data point.
foregroundcolor	The foreground color to use throughout the chart. This controls the color of all text in the chart, as well as the lines used to draw the x- and y-axes, the lines around each bar or pie slice, and so on.
font	The font to use for text in the chart, such as legends and axis labels. In ColdFusion, you can choose between Arial, Times, and Courier. In addition, you can choose arialunicodeMS, which you should use when using double-byte character sets. The default is Arial.

Table 16.4 (CONTINUED)

ATTRIBUTE	DESCRIPTION
fontsize	The size of the font, expressed as a number. The default is 11.
fontbold	Whether text is displayed in bold. The default is No.
fontitalic	Whether text is displayed in italics. The default is No.
tipstyle	Optional. Can be set to mouseOver (the default), mouseDown, or off. By default, a hint or tip message will display when users hovers their pointer over a data point in a graph (an example of this is shown in Figure 16.1). The tip message includes the label and value of the data point, as well as the series label, if given. If you want the tip to be shown only when the user clicks a data point, you can use tipstyle="mouseDown", but this works only if format="flash". If you don't want any tip to be shown at all, use tipstyle="off".
pieslicestyle	Relevant only for pie charts. If sliced (the default) is used, the pie is shown with its slices separated by white space (this effect is sometimes called exploded). If solid is used, the pie is shown with its slices together in a circle, the way you normally think of a pie chart. Unfortunately, there is no way to explode just one slice at a time, which is a common way to present pie charts. In general, you will probably want to use pieslicestyle="solid".

Table 16.5 <cfchartseries> Formatting Options

ATTRIBUTE	DESCRIPTION
seriescolor	A color to use for the main element of the data series.
serieslabel	A label or title for the data series.
paintstyle	A style to use when filling in solid areas on the chart for this series. The default is plain, which uses solid colors. You can also use raise, which gives each area a raised, button-like appearance; shade, which shades each area with a gradient fill; or light, which is a lighter version of shade.
colorlist	Relevant for pie charts only. A comma-separated list of colors to use for the slices of the pie. The first slice will have the first color in the list, the second slice will have the second color, and so on.
markerstyle	Relevant only for line, curve, and scatter charts. The look of the marker that appears at each data point. Can be set to rectangle (the default), triangle, diamond, circle, letter, mcross, snow, or rcross.

Listing 16.4 and Figure 16.4 show how some of these formatting attributes can be combined to improve the appearance of the bar charts you have seen so far.

Controlling Grid Lines and Axis Labels

One of the most important aspects of nearly any chart are the numbers and labels that surround the actual graphic on the x- and y-axes. The graphic itself is what lends the chart its ability to convey a message visually, but it's the numbers surrounding the graphic that give it a context. ColdFusion provides you with a number of options for controlling the *scale* of each axis (that is, the distance between the highest and lowest values that could be plotted on the chart), and for controlling how many different numbers are actually displayed along the axes.

Figure 16.4

The ColdFusion charting tags provide extensive control over chart formatting.

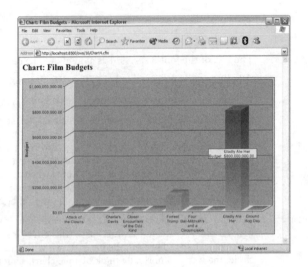

Table 16.6 shows the `<cfchart>` attributes related to grid lines and axis labels.

Table 16.6   `<cfchart>` Options for Grid Lines and Labels

ATTRIBUTE	DESCRIPTION
scalefrom	The lowest number to show on the y-axis. For instance, if you want one of the budget chart examples shown previously to start at $20,000 instead of $0, you can do so with `scalefrom="20000"`.
scaleto	The highest number to show on the y-axis. If the highest budget shown in the budget chart examples is $750,000, providing `scaleto="1000000"` will cause the scale to go all the way up to 1 million, even though there aren't any data points that go up that high. The result is extra "empty space" above the highest value, giving the viewer the sense that the values plotted in the chart could have been higher than they actually are.
gridlines	The number of grid lines to show for the data axis (generally the y-axis). This also affects the number of labeled tick marks along the axis. If you don't provide a value, ColdFusion attempts to use a sensible default value based on the size of the graph. For instance, in Figure 16.2 there are ten grid lines and tick marks (one for `0`, one for `83,300`, and so on), which seems about right.
showygridlines	Whether to display grid lines for the y-axis. On most charts, grid lines make it easier to grasp the value of each piece of data. These grid lines are shown in Figure 16.1 (the horizontal lines) and Figure 16.2 (the vertical lines). The default is `Yes`.
showxgridlines	Whether to display grid lines for the x-axis. The default is `No`.
sortxaxis	Sorts the data in the x-axis (that is, the labels) alphabetically. In general, I recommend that you use `order by` to reorder the records within a normal `<cfquery>` tag, before your code gets to the `<cfchart>` tag; that approach will be much more flexible.
labelformat	The format for the labels along the y-axis (in our examples so far, the labels that show the increasing amounts of money). You can set this to `number` (the default), `currency` (which on English-language systems adds a dollar sign [$]), `percent` (which multiplies by 100 and adds a percent sign [%]), or `date` (appropriate only if the data you're plotting are dates).

NOTE

You can't adjust the scale in such a way that it would obscure or chop off any of the actual data being shown in the chart. If your `scalefrom` value is higher than the lowest data point on the graph, ColdFusion will use the data point's value instead. For instance, if the lowest budget being plotted in one of the budget chart examples is $34,000 and you provide `scalefrom="50000"`, ColdFusion will start the scale at $34,000. The inverse is also true; if you provide a `scaleto` value that is lower than the highest data point, that point's value will be used instead.

Listing 16.4 shows how formatting, axis, and grid line options can be added to a chart to give it more appeal, and the axis labels have been formatted as currency (Figure 16.4). You can't see the colors in this book, but different shades of light blue have been used for the data background and the overall chart background. The text is in a dark navy type, and the bars of the chart themselves have a green gradient. Also note that the number of grid lines (that is, the number of numbered tick marks along the horizontal axis) has been set to 6 with the `gridlines` attribute. This means that there will be five tick marks (in addition to the first one), evenly distributed across the range.

Listing 16.4 `Chart4.cfm`—Add Formatting, Grid Line, and Axis Options

```
<!---
Name:        Chart4.cfm
Author:      Ben Forta
Description: Extensive chart formatting
Created:     07/10/2007
--->

<!--- Get information from the database --->
<cfinvoke component="ChartData"
          method="GetBudgetData"
          returnvariable="ChartQuery"
          maxrows="10">

<html>
<head>
<title>Chart: Film Budgets</title>
</head>

<body>
<h2>Chart: Film Budgets</h2>

<!--- This defines the size and appearance of the chart --->
<cfchart chartwidth="750"
         chartheight="450"
         yaxistitle="Budget"
         <!--- 3D appearance --->
         show3d="yes"
         xoffset=".04"
         yoffset=".04"
         <!--- Fonts and colors --->
         showborder="yes"
         foregroundcolor="003366"
         backgroundcolor="99dddd"
         databackgroundcolor="66bbbb"
         tipbgcolor="ffff99"
         fontsize="11"
```

Listing 16.4 (CONTINUED)

```
            fontbold="yes"
            fontitalic="yes"
            <!--- gridlines and axis labels --->
            scalefrom="0"
            scaleto="1500000"
            gridlines="6"
            showygridlines="yes"
            labelformat="currency">

  <!--- within the chart --->
  <cfchartseries type="bar"
                 seriescolor="green"
                 serieslabel="Budget Details:"
                 query="chartquery"
                 valuecolumn="amountbudgeted"
                 itemcolumn="movietitle"
                 paintstyle="light">
  </cfchart>

  </body>
  </html>
```

NOTE

When providing hexadecimal color values, the traditional number sign (#) is optional. If you provide it, though, you must escape the # by doubling it, so ColdFusion doesn't think you're trying to reference a variable. In other words, you could provide `backgroundcolor="99DDDD"` or `backgroundcolor="##99DDDD"` as you prefer, but not `backgroundcolor="#99DDDD"`.

Using Multiple Data Series

Now that you've been introduced to the basic principles involved in creating and formatting charts, we'd like to explain some of the more advanced aspects of ColdFusion charting support. In the next section, you will learn how to combine several chart types into a single graph. Then you will learn how to create charts that users can click, so they can drill down on information presented in the graph.

Combining Multiple Chart Series

So far, all the charts you've seen have contained only one `<cfchartseries>` tag. This makes sense, considering that the charts have presented only one set of information at a time. But it's also possible to create charts that represent more than one set of information, simply by adding additional `<cfchartseries>` tags within the `<cfchart>` block. The additional `<cfchartseries>` tags can each display different columns from the same query, or they can display information from different queries or data sources altogether.

The bar chart examples so far all show the budget for each film. It might be helpful to show not only the budget for each film but also the actual expenses to date, so that a glance at the chart will reveal which films are over budget and by how much.

Figure 16.5 shows just such a chart. There are now two bars for each film, clustered in pairs. One bar shows the budget for the film and the other shows the actual expenses for the film to date, as recorded in the Expenses table. Listing 16.5 shows the code used to produce this chart.

Figure 16.5

Multiple data series can be used in a single chart.

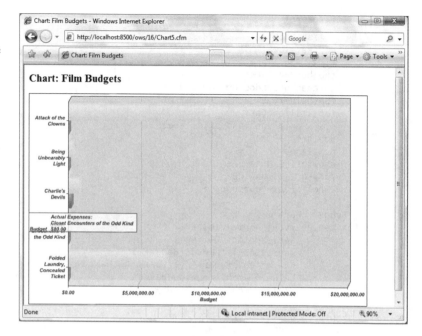

Listing 16.5 Chart5.cfm—Plotting Two Related Sets of Data

```
<!---
Name:        Chart5.cfm
Author:      Ben Forta
Description: Using multiple data series
Created:     07/10/2007
--->

<!--- Get information from the database --->
<cfinvoke component="ChartData"
          method="GetExpenses"
          returnvariable="ChartQuery"
          maxrows="5">

<html>
<head>
<title>Chart: Film Budgets</title>
</head>

<body>
<h2>Chart: Film Budgets</h2>

<!--- This defines the size and appearance of the chart --->
<cfchart chartwidth="750"
         chartheight="450"
         yaxistitle="Budget"
         seriesplacement="cluster"
           <!--- 3D appearance --->
         show3d="yes"
```

Listing 16.5 (CONTINUED)

```
                    xoffset=".01"
                    yoffset=".03"
                    <!--- Fonts and colors --->
                    showborder="yes"
                    databackgroundcolor="dddddd"
                    fontbold="yes"
                    fontitalic="yes"
                    <!--- gridlines and axis labels --->
                    scaleto="800000"
                    gridlines="5"
                    showxgridlines="yes"
                    showygridlines="no"
                    labelformat="currency">

    <!--- Budget chart --->
    <cfchartseries type="horizontalbar"
                    seriescolor="99ff99"
                    serieslabel="Amount Budgeted:"
                    query="chartquery"
                    valuecolumn="amountbudgeted"
                    itemcolumn="movietitle">

    <!--- Expenses chart --->
    <cfchartseries type="horizontalbar"
                    seriescolor="ff4444"
                    serieslabel="Actual Expenses:"
                    query="chartquery"
                    valuecolumn="expensetotal"
                    itemcolumn="movietitle"
                    paintstyle="light">

</cfchart>

</body>
</html>
```

Nearly any time you have multiple columns of information in the same query, you can display them using code similar to that used in this listing. The unspoken assumption is that the data in the first row of the AmountBudgeted and ExpenseTotal columns are related to the same real-world item. In this case, that real-world item is the first film.

Combining Series of Different Types

You're free to use different type values (line, bar, area, scatter, and so on) for each <cfchartseries> tag in the same chart. For instance, you might want to modify Listing 16.5 so that one series uses area and the other line. Line graphs are generally used to represent a single concept that changes over time, rather than blocks of individual data like film budgets, but in this particular case the result is rather effective. You're invited to experiment with different combinations of bar charts to see the various possibilities for yourself.

NOTE

You can't combine pie charts with other types of charts. Any <cfchartseries> tags that try to mix pie charts with other types will be ignored.

You can also experiment with the `seriesplacement` attribute to tell ColdFusion to change the way your chart series are combined. For instance, you can use `seriesplacement="stacked"` to have the bars shown stacked (as seen in Figure 16.6).

Figure 16.6

Multiple data series can be used in a single chart.

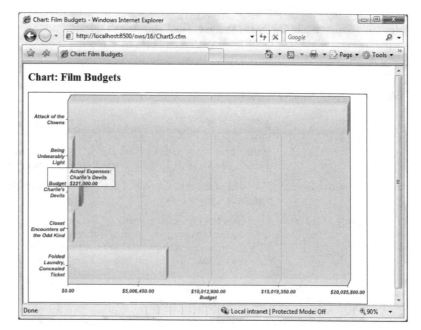

Drilling Down from Charts

The `<cfchart>` tag supports a URL attribute that you can use to create *clickable* charts, where the user can click the various data points in the chart to link to a different page. Of course, the page you bring users to when they click the chart is up to you. Generally, the idea is to allow users to zoom in or drill down on the data point they clicked.

For instance, if a chart displays information about film expenses, as in the examples above, then clicking one of the expense bars might display an HTML table that lists the actual expense records. Or it might bring up a second chart, this one a pie chart that shows the distribution of the individual expenses for that particular film. In either case, your clickable chart can be thought of as a navigation element, not unlike a toolbar or a set of HTML links. It's a way for users to explore your data visually.

Creating a Clickable Chart

To create a clickable chart, simply add a URL attribute to the `<cfchart>` tag. When the user clicks one of the data points in the chart (the slices of a pie chart, the bars in a bar chart, the points in a line graph, and so on), they will be sent to the URL you specify. So, if you want the browser to navigate to a ColdFusion page called `FilmExpenseDetail.cfm` when a chart is clicked, you would use url="FilmExpenseDetail.cfm". You can use any type of relative or absolute URL that is acceptable to use in a normal HTML link.

For the detail page to be dynamic, however, it will need to know which data point the user clicked. To make this possible, ColdFusion lets you pass the actual data that the user is clicking as URL variables. To do so, include any of the special values shown in Table 16.7 in the url attribute. Cold-Fusion will create a dynamic URL for each data point by replacing these special values with the actual data for that data point.

Table 16.7 Special Values for Passing in <cfchart> URLs

VARIABLE	DESCRIPTION
$value$	The value of the selected row (that is, the value in the valuecolumn attribute of the <cfchartseries> tag for the data point that was clicked). This is typically the value that you're most interested in passing in the URL.
$itemlabel$	The label of the selected row (that is, the value in the itemcolumn for the data point that was clicked).
$serieslabel$	The series label (that is, the value of the serieslabel attribute of the <cfchartseries> tag). It's usually only necessary to include this value in the URL if you have multiple <cfchartseries> tags in your chart; this value becomes the way that the target page knows which series the user clicked.

For instance, consider the following <cfchart> tag:

```
<cfchart url="FilmExpenseDetail.cfm?MovieTitle=$itemlabel$">
```

When the user clicks the slices in this pie chart, the title of the film they clicked on will be passed to the FilmExpenseDetail.cfm page as a URL parameter named MovieTitle. Within FilmExpenseDetail.cfm, the value will be available as URL.MovieTitle, which can be used just like any other variable in the URL scope.

Listing 16.6 shows how the URL attribute can be used to create a clickable chart. This listing creates a pie chart that breaks down the overall budget for Orange Whip Studios by film. When users click a slice of the pie, they are presented with the detail page shown in Figure 16.7. You'll see the code for the detail page in a moment.

Listing 16.6 Chart6.cfm—Creating Chart with Drill-Down Functionality

```
<!---
Name:        Chart6.cfm
Author:      Ben Forta
Description: Display a pie chart with drill-down support
Created:     07/10/2007
--->

<!--- Get information from the database --->
<cfinvoke component="ChartData"
          method="GetExpenses"
          returnvariable="ChartQuery"
          maxrows="10">
```

Listing 16.6 (CONTINUED)

```html
<html>
<head>
<title>Chart: Film Budgets</title>
</head>

<body>
<h2>Chart: Film Budgets</h2>

<!--- This defines the size and appearance of the chart --->
<cfchart chartwidth="550"
         chartheight="300"
         pieslicestyle="solid"
         show3d="yes"
         yoffset=".9"
         url="FilmExpenseDetail.cfm?MovieTitle=$ITEMLABEL$">

  <!--- Within the chart --->
  <cfchartseries type="pie"
                 query="chartquery"
                 valuecolumn="amountbudgeted"
                 itemcolumn="movietitle">

</cfchart>

</body>
</html>
```

Figure 16.7

Graph details can be displayed using chart drill-down functions.

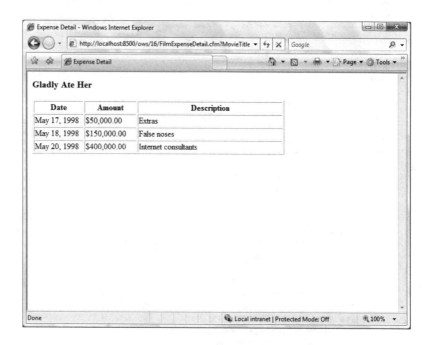

Date	Amount	Description
May 17, 1998	$50,000.00	Extras
May 18, 1998	$150,000.00	False noses
May 20, 1998	$400,000.00	Internet consultants

Creating the Detail Page

Creating the detail page shown in Figure 16.7 is relatively straightforward. Just use the URL para-meters passed by the URL attribute of the <cfchart> in Listing 16.6 to query the database for the appropriate Expense records. The records can then be displayed using normal <cfoutput> and HTML table tags.

There is one bit of unpleasantness to deal with, though. Unfortunately, <cfchart> doesn't provide a straightforward way to pass a unique identifier in URLs generated by <cfchart>. The only things you can pass are the actual label and value of the data point displayed on the graph (with the special $ITEMLABEL$ and $VALUE$ values, respectively).

So, for the example at hand (see Listing 16.7), the only pieces of information that can be passed to the FilmExpenseDetail.cfm page are the film's title and budget, since those are the only values that the chart is aware of. Ordinarily, it would be far preferable to pass the FilmID in the URL, thereby elimi-nating any problems that would come up if there were two films with the same title. Since this isn't currently possible in ColdFusion, the film will have to be identified by its title (and budget) alone.

NOTE

Keep this limitation in mind when creating drill-down applications with <cfchart>. If a data point can't be safely and uniquely iden-tified by the combination of the label and value displayed in the graph, you probably won't be able to implement drill-down.

Listing 16.7 FilmExpenseDetail.cfm—Detail Page Displayed on Drill-Down

```
<!---
Name:        FilmExpenseDetail.cfm
Author:      Ben Forta
Description: Movie drill-down
Created:     07/10/2007
--->

<!--- These URL parameters will be passed by the chart --->
<cfparam name="URL.MovieTitle" type="string">

<!--- Get information from the database --->
<cfinvoke component="ChartData"
          method="GetFilmID"
          returnvariable="FilmID"
          movietitle="#URL.MovieTitle#">

<!--- Show an error message if we could not determine the FilmID --->
<cfif FilmID IS -1>
  <cfthrow message="Could not retrieve film information."
           detail="Unknown movie title provided.">
</cfif>

<!--- Now that we know the FilmID, we can select the --->
<!--- corresponding expense records from the database --->
<cfinvoke component="ChartData"
          method="GetExpenseDetails"
          returnvariable="ExpenseQuery"
          filmid="#FilmID#">
```

Listing 16.7 (CONTINUED)

```
<html>
<head>
<title>Expense Detail</title>
</head>

<body>

<cfoutput>
 <!--- page heading --->
 <h3>#URL.MovieTitle#</h3>

 <!--- html table for expense display --->
 <table border="1" width="500">
  <tr>
   <th width="100">Date</th>
   <th width="100">Amount</th>
   <th width="300">Description</th>
  </tr>

  <!--- for each expense in the query... --->
  <cfloop query="expensequery">
   <tr>
    <td>#LSDateFormat(ExpenseDate)#</td>
    <td>#LSCurrencyFormat(ExpenseAmount)#</td>
    <td>#Description#</td>
   </tr>
  </cfloop>

 </table>
</cfoutput>

</body>
</html>
```

The purpose of the method invocation is to determine the FilmID that corresponds to the MovieTitle parameter passed to the page (from the chart in Listing 16.6). As a precautionary measure, the Budget parameter is also included in the query criteria. This means that if two films happen to have the same title, they can still be correctly identified as long as their budgets are different. For the rest of the page, FilmID holds the ID number for the film and can be used to retrieve any related information from the database.

NOTE

If no films are retrieved from the database (or if more than one is retrieved), an error message is displayed with the <cfthrow> tag.

Drilling Down to Another Chart

You may want to drill down to a different chart that shows a different view or subset of the data, rather just drilling down to a simple HTML page. The second chart page, in turn, could drill down to another page, and so on. You could use any of the drill-down techniques discussed in this section to put together such a multilayered data-navigation interface.

Additional Charting Topics

The remainder of this chapter introduces various topics related to ColdFusion charting features.

Plotting Individual Points with `<cfchartdata>`

The most common way to provide the actual data to a `<cfchartseries>` tag is to specify a QUERY attribute, then tell ColdFusion which columns of the query to look in by specifying `itemcolumn` and `valuecolumn` attributes. All of the examples you've seen so far in this chapter have supplied their data in this way.

It's also possible to omit the `query`, `itemcolumn`, and `valuecolumn` attributes and instead plot the data points individually using the `<cfchartdata>` tag, nested within your `<cfchartseries>`. The `<cfchartdata>` approach can come in handy if you want to permanently hard-code certain data points onto your charts, if you need to format your data in a special way, or if you come across a situation where you can't extract the desired data from a query in a completely straightforward manner.

Table 16.8 shows the syntax for the `<cfchartdata>` tag.

Table 16.8   `<cfchartdata>` Syntax

ATTRIBUTE	DESCRIPTION
item	The item associated with the data point you're plotting, such as a film title, a category of purchases, or a period of time—in other words, the information you would normally supply to the `itemcolumn` attribute of the `<cfchartseries>` tag.
value	The value of the data point (a number). This is what you would normally supply to the `valuecolumn` attribute of `<cfchartseries>`.

For instance, if you have a query called ChartQuery with two columns, ExpenseDate and ExpenseAmount, and you wanted to make sure the date was formatted to your liking when it was displayed on the chart, you could use:

```
<cfchartseries type="line">
 <cfloop query="ChartQuery">
  <cfchartdata item="#DateFormat(ExpenseDate, 'm/d/yy')#"
               value="#ExpenseAmount#">
 </cfloop>
</cfchartseries>
```

instead of:

```
<cfchartseries type="line"
               query="ChartQuery"
               valuecolumn="ExpenseAmount"
               itemcolumn="ExpenseDate">
```

This technique is also useful when creating charts based on data that are not query based. Using `<cfchartdata>` you can pass any data to a chart.

Using Charts with Flash Remoting

It's possible to use the name attribute to capture the binary content of a chart and then make it available to the Adobe Flash Player via Flash Remoting. This capability allows you to create a Flash movie that displays dynamically generated charts on the fly, perhaps as a part of a sophisticated data-entry or reporting interface, all without reloading the page to display an updated or changed chart. This topic is beyond the scope of this book.

Creating Printable Pages

It's long been a hassle to easily generate printable content from within Web pages, and this is a source of serious aggravation for Web application developers (all developers, not just ColdFusion developers). Considering that a very significant chunk of Web application development tends to be data reporting and presentation type applications, this is a big problem.

The truth is, Web browsers just don't print Web pages properly, so developers have had to resort to complex and painful work-arounds to put content in a printable format.

ColdFusion solves this problem simply with the <cfdocument> family of tags.

Using the <cfdocument> Tag

We'll start with a really simple example. Listing 16.8 contains simple text wrapped within a pair of <cfdocument> tags. The generated output is seen in Figure 16.8.

Figure 16.8

Adobe PDF format is the most commonly used printable document format on the Web.

Hello world!

Listing 16.8 `Print1.cfm`—Basic PDF Generation

```
<!---
Name:        Print1.cfm
Author:      Ben Forta
Description: Simple printable output
Created:     07/10/2007
--->

<cfdocument format="pdf">
Hello world!
</cfdocument>
```

The code in Listing 16.8 couldn't be simpler. By wrapping text in between <cfdocument> and </cfdocument> tags, content between those tags is converted into a PDF file on the fly, and embedded in the page.

Of course, you're not limited to static text; you can use dynamic CFML within the document content, too. Listing 16.9 uses a mixture of HTML, CFML, and dynamic data to create a printable report (seen in Figure 16.9).

Listing 16.9 `Print2.cfm`—Data-Driven Document Generation

```
<!---
Name:        Print2.cfm
Author:      Ben Forta
Description: Data driven printable output
Created:     07/10/2007
--->

<!--- Get budget data --->
<cfinvoke component="ChartData"
          method="GetBudgetData"
          returnvariable="BudgetData">

<!--- Generate document --->
<cfdocument format="pdf">

<!--- Header --->
<table align="center">
 <tr>
<td>
 <img src="../images/logo_c.gif"
      alt="Orange Whip Studios">
</td>
<td align="center">
<font size="+2">Orange Whip Studios<br>Movies</font>
</td>
 </tr>
</table>

<!--- Title --->
<div align="center">
<h2>Budget Data</h2>
</div>
```

Listing 16.9 (CONTINUED)

```
<!--- Details --->
<table>
 <tr>
  <th>Movie</th>
  <th>Budget</th>
 </tr>
 <cfoutput query="BudgetData">
  <tr>
   <td><strong>#MovieTitle#</strong></td>
   <td>#LSCurrencyFormat(AmountBudgeted)#</td>
  </tr>
 </cfoutput>
</table>

</cfdocument>
```

Figure 16.9

Printable output may contain HTML, CFML, and more.

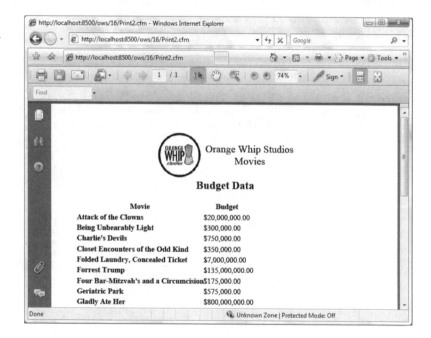

What Is Supported by `<cfdocument>`?

You'll notice that the code in Listing 16.9 uses a mixture of HTML (including tags like `<font>`, which generally should be avoided), an image, tables, CFML expressions, and more. The `<cfdocument>` tag supports all of the following:

- HTML 4
- XML 1

- DOM level 1 and 2

- CSS1 and CSS2

In other words, `<cfdocument>` should be more than able to convert all sorts of pages into printable PDF.

Creating Printable Versions of Pages

You will likely often need to create printable versions of existing pages. It would be tempting to try and simply conditionally include `<cfdocument>` tags in existing pages, but unfortunately that won't work: ColdFusion won't parse the page correctly because it thinks your tags aren't properly paired.

The solution to this problem is to create a wrapper page, one that defines the printable document and includes the original page. Listing 16.10 is a modified version of a page we created in Chapter 11, "The Basics of Structured Development"; it simply displays movie details. The modified page is seen in Figure 16.10.

Figure 16.10

It's often convenient to provide links to printable versions of pages.

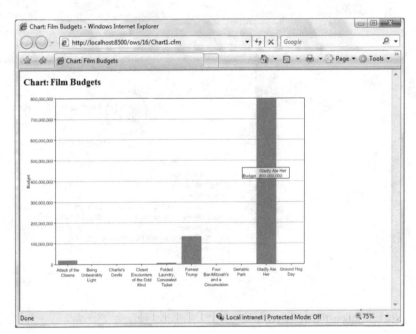

Listing 16.10 `details.cfm`—Movie Details Page

```
<!---
Name:        details.cfm
Author:      Ben Forta (ben@forta.com)
Description: CFC driven data drill-down details
             with complete validation
Created:     07/10/2007
```

Listing 16.10 (CONTINUED)

```
--->

<!--- Movie list page --->
<cfset list_page="movies.cfm">

<!--- Make sure FilmID was passed --->
<cfif not IsDefined("URL.filmid")>
 <!--- it wasn't, send to movie list --->
 <cflocation url="#list_page#">
</cfif>

<!--- Get movie details --->
<cfinvoke
 component="ows.11.movies"
 method="GetDetails"
 returnvariable="movie"
 FilmID="#URL.filmid#">

<!--- Make sure we have a movie --->
<cfif movie.RecordCount IS 0>
 <!--- It wasn't, send to movie list --->
 <cflocation url="#list_page#">
</cfif>

<!--- Build image paths --->
<cfset image_src="../images/f#movie.FilmID#.gif">
<cfset image_path=ExpandPath(image_src)>

<!--- Create HTML page --->
<html>
<head>
 <title>Orange Whip Studios - Movie Details</title>
</head>

<body>

<!--- Display movie details --->
<cfoutput query="movie">

<table>
 <tr>
  <td colspan="2">
   <!--- Check if image file exists --->
   <cfif FileExists(image_path)>
    <!--- If it does, display it --->
    <img src="../images/f#filmid#.gif"
       alt="#movietitle#"
       align="middle">
   </cfif>
   <b>#MovieTitle#</b>
  </td>
 </tr>
 <tr valign="top">
  <th align="right">Tag line:</th>
```

Listing 16.10 (CONTINUED)

```
   <td>#PitchText#</td>
  </tr>
  <tr valign="top">
   <th align="right">Summary:</th>
   <td>#Summary#</td>
  </tr>
  <tr valign="top">
   <th align="right">Released:</th>
   <td>#DateFormat(DateInTheaters)#</td>
  </tr>
  <tr valign="top">
   <th align="right">Budget:</th>
   <td>#DollarFormat(AmountBudgeted)#</td>
  </tr>
 </table>

 <p>

 <!--- Links --->
 [<a href="detailsprint.cfm?FilmID=#URL.FilmID#">Printable page</a>]
 [<a href="#list_page#">Movie list</a>]

 </cfoutput>

 </body>
 </html>
```

The big change to this page is a line added to the links section at the bottom. A new link to a Printable page has been created; when clicked, it opens detailsprint.cfm passing the FilmID to that page. The code for that page is remarkably simple, as seen in Listing 16.11.

Listing 16.11 detailsprint.cfm—Printable Movie Details Page

```
 <!---
 Name:        detailsprint.cfm
 Author:      Ben Forta (ben@forta.com)
 Description: Printable version of details page
 Created:     07/10/2007
 --->

 <cfdocument format="pdf">
 <cfinclude template="details.cfm">
 </cfdocument>
```

Listing 16.11 creates a document using <cfdocument> tags, and includes the existing details page to generate the printable output seen in Figure 16.11.

NOTE

The links in details.cfm work in the generated printable output.

Figure 16.11

Generated documents may contain page headers and footers.

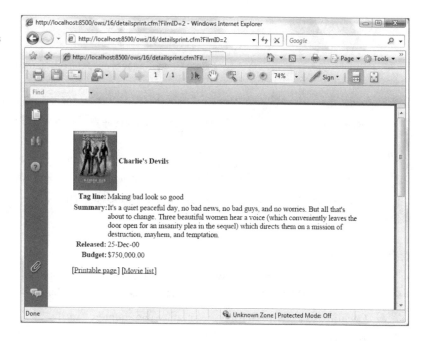

In addition to the format attribute used here, `<cfdocument>` supports a whole series of attributes to give you greater control over printed output. Table 16.9 lists the supported attributes.

Table 16.9 `<cfdocument>` Attributes

ATTRIBUTE	DESCRIPTION
`backgroundvisible`	Whether or not to display page background; default is `no`.
`encryption`	Optional encryption, `128-bit` or `40-bit` (used by PDF only).
`filename`	Optional file name, if specified document is saved to disk instead of being served in the browser.
`fontembed`	Whether or not to embed used fonts, `yes`, `no`, or `selective` (default).
`format`	`pdf` or `flashpaper`, this attribute is required.
`marginbottom`	Page bottom margin, use `unit` to specify unit of measure.
`marginleft`	Page left margin, use `unit` to specify unit of measure.
`marginright`	Page right margin, use `unit` to specify unit of measure.
`margintop`	Page top margin, use `unit` to specify unit of measure.
`name`	Optional variable name to contain generated output.
`orientation`	Page orientation, `portrait` (the default) or `landscape`.
`overwrite`	Whether or not to overwrite existing documents (if using `filename`).
`ownerpassword`	Optional owner password (used by PDF only).

Table 16.9 (CONTINUED)

ATTRIBUTE	DESCRIPTION
pageheight	Page height (used if pagetype="custom"), use unit to specify unit of measure.
pagetype	Page size, supports legal, letter, A4, A5, B5, and custom.
pagewidth	Page width (used if pagetype="custom"), use unit to specify unit of measure.
scale	Scaling factor, default is calculated by ColdFusion automatically.
unit	Unit of measure, in (inches) or cm (centimeters).
userpassword	Optional user password (used by PDF only).

Saving Generated Output

<cfdocument> embeds generated output in your Web page. You may opt to save the generated files to disk instead of serving them in real time. Reasons to do this include:

- Caching, so as to not have to regenerate pages unnecessarily

- Emailing generated content

- Generating pages that can be served statically

To save generated output, simply provide a file name in the filename attribute.

Controlling Output Using the <cfdocumentitem> Tag

<cfdocumentitem> is used within a <cfdocument> tag set to embed additional items. <cfdocumentitem> requires that a type be specified. Table 16.10 lists the supported types.

Table 16.10 <cfdocumentitem> Types

TYPE	DESCRIPTION
footer	Page footer.
header	Page header.
pagebreak	Embed a page break; this type takes no body.

NOTE

Page breaks are calculated automatically by ColdFusion. Use <cfdocumentitem type="pagebreak"> to embed manual breaks.

Listing 16.12 is a revised printable movie listing, with more options specified.

Listing 16.12 `Print3.cfm`—Printable Output with Additional Items

```
<!---
Name:       Print3.cfm
Author:     Ben Forta
Description: Printable output with additional options
Created:    07/10/2007
--->

<!--- Get budget data --->
<cfinvoke component="ChartData"
          method="GetBudgetData"
          returnvariable="BudgetData">

<!--- Generate document --->
<cfdocument format="pdf">

<!--- Header --->
<cfdocumentitem type="header">
OWS Budget Report
</cfdocumentitem>
<!--- Footer --->
<cfdocumentitem type="footer">
<p align="center">
<cfoutput>
#CFDOCUMENT.currentpagenumber# of #CFDOCUMENT.totalpagecount#
</cfoutput>
</p>
</cfdocumentitem>


<!--- Header --->
<table align="center">
 <tr>
  <td><img src="../images/logo_c.gif" alt="Orange Whip Studios"></td>
  <td align="center"><font size="+2">Orange Whip Studios<br>Movies</font></td>
 </tr>
</table>

<!--- Title --->
<div align="center">
<h2>Budget Data</h2>
</div>

<!--- Page break --->
<cfdocumentitem type="pagebreak" />

<!--- Details --->
<table>
 <tr>
  <th>Movie</th>
  <th>Budget</th>
 </tr>
 <cfoutput query="BudgetData">
  <tr>
   <td><strong>#MovieTitle#</strong></td>
   <td>#LSCurrencyFormat(AmountBudgeted)#</td>
```

Listing 16.12 (CONTINUED)

```
    </tr>
   </cfoutput>
  </table>

</cfdocument>
```

Listing 16.12 warrants some explanation. The `<cfdocument>` content now contains the following code:

```
<!--- Header --->
<cfdocumentitem type="header">
OWS Budget Report
</cfdocumentitem>
```

This code defines a page header, text that will be placed at the top of each page. A footer is also defined as follows:

```
<!--- Footer --->
<cfdocumentitem type="footer">
<p align="center">
<cfoutput>
#CFDOCUMENT.currentpagenumber# of #CFDOCUMENT.totalpagecount#
</cfoutput>
</p>
</cfdocumentitem>
```

This page footer contains two special variables. Within a `<cfdocument>` tag, a special scope exists named CFDOCUMENT. It contains two variables, as listed in Table 16.11. These variables may be used in headers and footers, as used in this example.

Table 16.11   CFDOCUMENT Scope Variables

TYPE	DESCRIPTION
currentpagenumber	Current page number.
totalpagecount	Total number of generated pages.

In addition, the code in Listing 16.12 embeds a manual page break using this code:

```
<!--- Page break --->
<cfdocumentitem type="pagebreak" />
```

`<cfdocumentitem>` must always have an end tag, even when no body is specified. The trailing / is a shortcut that you can use. In other words, the above tag is functionally identical to:

```
<!--- Page break --->
<cfdocumentitem type="pagebreak"></cfdocumentitem>
```

Defining Sections with `<cfdocumentsection>`

As you have seen, you have a lot of control over generated pages using the `<cfdocument>` and `<cfdocumentitem>` tags. But sometimes you may want different options in different parts of the same document. For example, you may want a title page to have different margins than other pages. Or you may want different headers and footers in different parts of the document.

To do this, you use <cfdocumentsection> tags. A <cfdocument> tag pair may contain one or more sections, each defined using <cfdocumentsection> tags. Within each section you can specify alternate margins, and can use <cfdocumentitem> tags to specify headers and footers for each section.

NOTE

> When using <cfdocumentsection>, all content must be in sections. ColdFusion ignores any content outside of sections.

Generating Reports

<cfdocument> is designed to create printable versions of Web pages. These Web pages may be reports (many will be), and may involve such features as:

- Banded reports

- Calculated totals and sums

- Repeating and nonrepeating regions

- Embedded charts

Understanding the ColdFusion Report Builder

While these reports can indeed be created manually, there is a better way, using the ColdFusion Report Builder. The ColdFusion Report Builder is a stand-alone program used to define Cold-Fusion Report templates. It can be run on its own, and also directly from within Dreamweaver by double-clicking on a report file.

NOTE

> At this time, the ColdFusion Report Builder is a Windows-only utility. But reports created using the Report Builder can be processed by ColdFusion on any platform, and reports can be viewed on any platform.

The ColdFusion Report Builder creates and edits a special ColdFusion file with a .cfr extension. Unlike .cfm and .cfc files, .cfr files can't be edited with a text editor; the ColdFusion Report Builder must be used. .cfr files are report templates that may be used as is, or invoked from CFML code as needed (as we'll explain below).

To launch the Report Builder select ColdFusion Report Builder from the Windows Adobe > ColdFusion 8 program group.

NOTE

> The ColdFusion Report Builder needs to be installed on a Windows machine. If you do not have it installed, you can download it from Adobe.com. There is a link to this download on the book Web page: http://forta.com/books/032151548X.

Using the Setup Wizard

The first time the ColdFusion Report Builder is run, a setup wizard will be launched (as seen in Figure 16.12). This wizard configures the Report Builder so it's ready for use.

Figure 16.12

The ColdFusion Report Builder setup wizard configures the Report Builder for use.

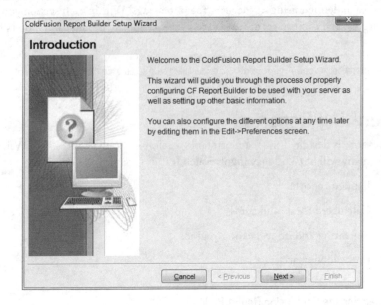

Click the Next button to provide basic information pertaining to measurement units. Once you have made your selections, click Next and you will be asked to specify how the Report Builder should connect to ColdFusion (as seen in Figure 16.13).

Figure 16.13

The Report Builder needs to know how to connect to ColdFusion.

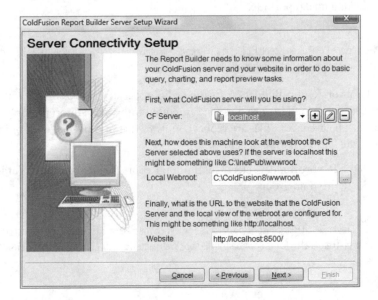

The ColdFusion Report Builder uses RDS to connect to ColdFusion, and you will be prompted for the server name and login information (as seen in Figure 16.14).

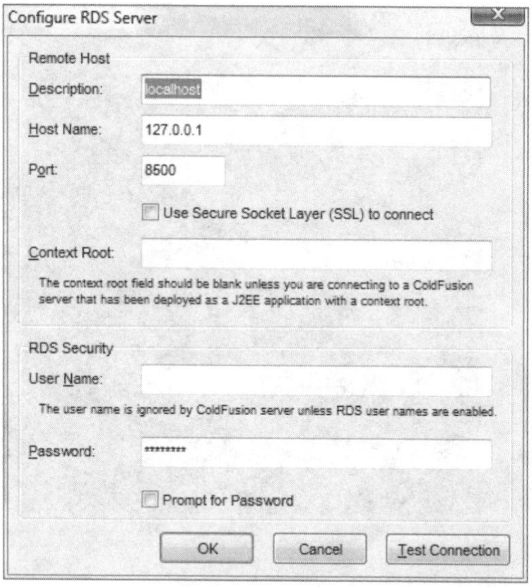

Figure 16.14

RDS login information must be provided to gain access to full Report Builder functionality.

NOTE

You can use the ColdFusion Report Builder without RDS, but you won't be able to use the Query Builder, Chart Wizard, and some other functionality.

Once you have completed the wizard, you'll be ready to start building reports.

NOTE

You can rerun the setup wizard at any time by selecting File > New in the Report Builder, and then selecting the Server Setup Wizard option.

Introducing the ColdFusion Report Builder

The ColdFusion Report Builder screen looks a lot like other report writing tools that you may have used. The screen, seen in Figure 16.15, contains several sections you should be aware of:

- The large open space in the middle of the Report Builder is where reports are defined and edited.

- The toolbox on the left contains buttons to insert images, fields, subreports, and more into reports, as well as buttons used to manage element alignment.

- On the top of the screen are toolbars for file opening, editing, fonts, etc.

- The Properties panel at the upper right displays the properties for any report item, and allows for quick property editing.

- The Fields and Parameters panel on the lower right is used to access query columns, calculated fields, and input parameters.

Figure 16.15

The Report Builder interface is used to define and edit ColdFusion reports.

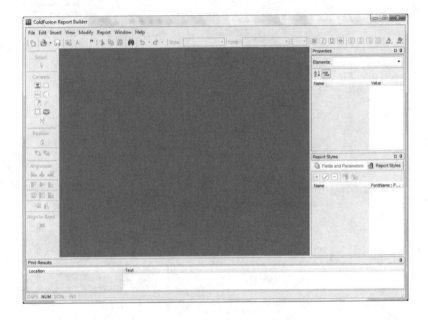

The ColdFusion Report Builder allows for multiple .cfr files to be open at once if needed.

Using the Report Wizard

The simplest way to create a report, and indeed the fastest way to learn the Report Builder, is to use the Report Creation Wizard. We'll start by creating a report of movie expenses. Here are the steps to follow:

1. Select File > New (or click the New button) to display the ColdFusion Report Builder Gallery dialog (seen in Figure 16.16).

Figure 16.16

The ColdFusion Report Builder Gallery is used to create new blank reports or to launch the report wizard.

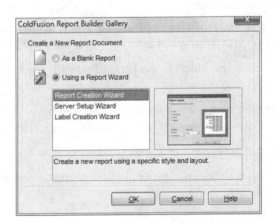

2. Select Report Creation Wizard, and click OK to launch the wizard. First we need the query columns to be used in the report. You may click Add to add the query columns manually, Import to import a query from an existing report, or Query Builder to launch the Query Builder (seen in Figure 16.17). We'll use the Query Builder, so click that button.

Figure 16.17

The SQL Query Builder simplifies the process of generating report SQL statements.

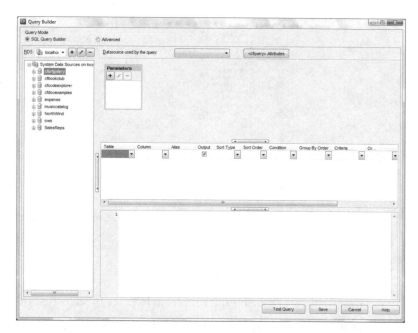

3. The SQL Query Builder has two modes, Figure 16.17 shows the SQL Query Builder interactive mode; you can also click the Advanced check box to enter the SQL manually. We'll use the SQL Query Builder mode. On the left you'll see a list of available data sources; expand the ows data source and then expand Tables to display the available tables.

NOTE

You won't see available data sources if RDS isn't used.

4. Drag the Films and Expenses tables into the SQL Query Builder (as seen in Figure 16.18). Notice how the SQL statement changes to reflect the table selections.

5. The Report Builder will attempt to figure out table relationships automatically, as it did here (seen in Figure 16.18). If necessary, you can also join tables manually. For example, to join the Films and Expenses tables, select the FilmID column in one of the tables and drag it to the FilmID column in there. A link will indicate that the tables are joined.

Figure 16.18

The SQL Query Builder shows SQL changes as selections are made.

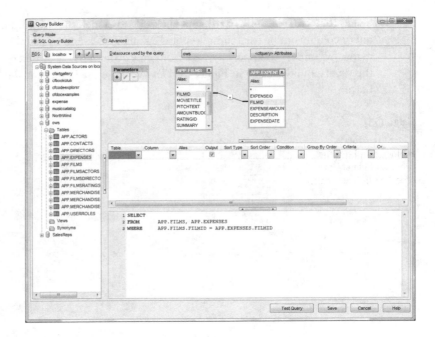

To change the join type, right-click on the box in the line that links the tables.

6. Double-click on the MovieTitle column in Films to select that column.

7. Double-click on the ExpenseDate, Description, and ExpenseAmount columns in Expenses (in that order) to select those three columns.

8. The report needs to be sorted by MovieTitle and then by ExpenseDate, so click on the Sort Type column for MovieTitle and select Ascending, then do the same for ExpenseDate (as seen in Figure 16.19).

9. Now that the SQL selection is complete, test it by clicking the Test Query button. The query results will be displayed in a pop-up window.

10. Close the query results window, and click Save to save the query (and columns) into the wizard (Figure 16.20).

11. Click Next, and the wizard will prompt you for any report grouping (used to create report bands). We want the report grouped by movie, so double-click MoveTitle to move it to the Group by Fields column. Then click Next.

Figure 16.19

SQL ORDER BY clauses can be created by selecting the desired sort type and sequence.

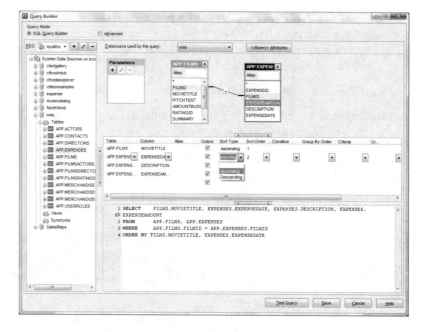

Figure 16.20

The SQL Query Builder inserts selected columns back into the wizard.

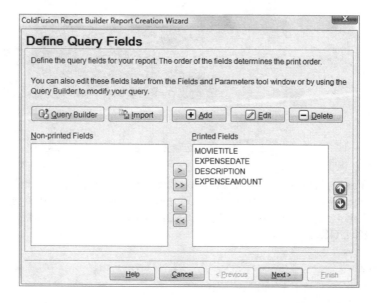

12. You will then be prompted for a report layout, page orientation, and paper size. Select Left Aligned, and then click Next.

TIP

As you click on any report layout, a sample preview shows you what it will look like.

13. You will then be prompted for the report style. Default should be used for all reports except subreports (reports embedded in other reports). You can also specify whether or not to generate totals for numeric fields, as well as the number of columns desired. Leave all the values as is, and click Next.

14. To select a color theme to use, pick one of the colors, then click Next.

15. The final wizard screen prompts for a title, headers, and footers. Enter Move Expenses as the title, and click Finish to generate your report.

16. When the wizard ends, your new report will be displayed in the Report Builder (as seen in Figure 16.21).

Figure 16.21

The wizard generates a complete report and displays it in the Report Builder.

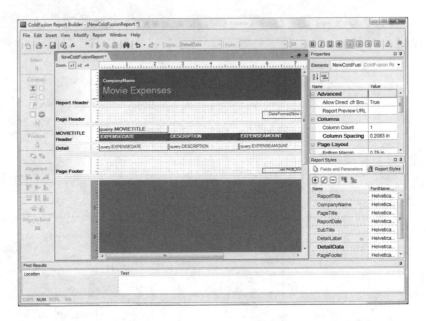

17. The report has a title already, but it has a generic CompanyName at the top. CompanyName is static text, and it can be edited by simply double-clicking on the text to display the Edit Label Text dialog box (see Figure 16.22). Change the text to Orange Whip Studios and click OK.

Figure 16.22

Static text can be edited by double-clicking on it.

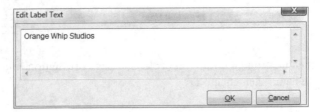

18. Save your new report (select File > Save, or click the Save button), name it `expenses.cfr`, and save it in the `/ows/16` folder.

19. The final step is to preview the report, to make sure that it's working as intended. Click the Preview button (the one with a globe with a lightning bolt through it), or press F12. A preview (in FlashPaper format, by default) will be displayed (as seen in Figure 16.23).

Figure 16.23

Preview your reports using the integrated preview feature.

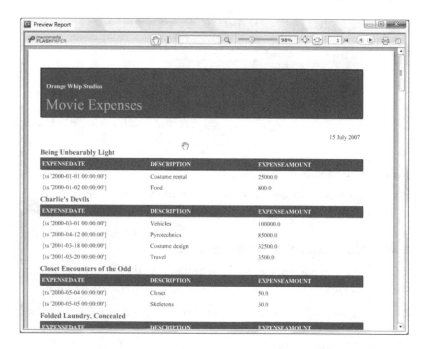

Notice that the query fields and calculated fields in the Fields and Parameters panel have been populated with the information provided to the wizard. You can edit these if needed.

Here is a very important item: The report displays expense dates, but these are not formatted properly. Double-click the `query.EXPENSEDATE` field and you'll see a screen like the one seen in Figure 16.24. This is the Expression Builder, and it can be used to embed any CFML expressions into your report. If you want to convert text to uppercase, access special variables, or perform any special processing, you can do so using CFML expressions. For now, change `query.EXPENSEDATE` so that it reads `DateFormat(query.EXPENSEDATE)`. Do the same for `query.EXPENSEAMOUNT`, changing it to `DollarFormat(query.EXPENSEAMOUNT)`, and then click OK. Now the date and amount will be formatted properly. This is one of ColdFusion Report Builder's most powerful features.

TIP

You can zoom in on the report you're working on by clicking the `x1`, `x2`, and `x4` buttons above each report.

Figure 16.24

Use Query Fields to edit database query fields, and Calculated Fields to define calculated fields for your report.

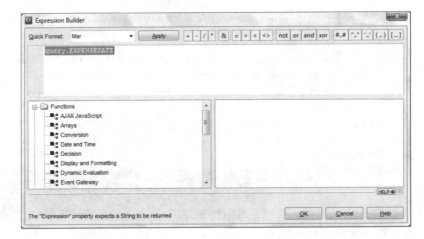

Running Your Reports

To run your report, invoke the full URL to it from within your browser. The report will be displayed, exactly as it was when previewed in the ColdFusion Report Builder.

Invoking Reports from Within ColdFusion Code

Being able to run reports in browsers is useful, but other reporting tools can do that, too. What makes ColdFusion reports unique is their ability to be altered at runtime.

Look at Listing 16.13. It uses a tag named <cfreport> to embed a report into a .cfm file.

Listing 16.13   Report1.cfm—Basic Report Invocation

```
<!---
Name:        Report1.cfm
Author:      Ben Forta
Description: Invoke a ColdFusion report
Created:     07/10/2007
--->

<cfreport template="Expenses.cfr"
          format="PDF" />
```

If you were to run this code, it would generate the same report as before, but now you're generating it in your own CFML instead of it's being generated automatically. Why is this of value? Look at Listing 16.14, a modified version of this code.

Listing 16.14   Report2.cfm—Passing a Query to a Report

```
<!---
Name:        Report2.cfm
Author:      Ben Forta
Description: Invoke a ColdFusion report
Created:     07/10/2007
--->
```

Listing 16.14 (CONTINUED)

```
<cfquery name="Expenses" datasource="ows">
SELECT    Films.MovieTitle, Expenses.ExpenseDate,
          Expenses.Description,
          Expenses.ExpenseAmount
FROM      Films, Expenses
WHERE     Expenses.FilmID = Films.FilmID
ORDER BY  Films.MovieTitle, expenses.expensedate
</cfquery>

<cfreport template="Expenses.cfr"
          query="Expenses"
          format="PDF" />
```

Listing 16.14 uses <cfquery> to create a database query, and then passes that query to the
<cfreport> tag overriding the query within the report. This query is exactly the same as the one
used within the report, but now that you can see how queries can be created and passed to reports,
you can start to see this feature's power. After all, you already know how to dynamically create
queries; using that knowledge, you can create a form that prompts for the information to be
included in the report, allowing you to create truly dynamic reports.

Let's look at an example. Listing 16.15 is a simple form; it allows for the selection of a movie or
specifying all movies.

Listing 16.15 ReportForm1.cfm—Report Front End

```
<!---
Name:        ReportForm1.cfm
Author:      Ben Forta
Description: Report form front end
Created:     07/10/2007
--->

<!--- Get movie list --->
<cfquery datasource="ows" name="movies">
SELECT FilmID, MovieTitle
FROM Films
ORDER BY MovieTitle
</cfquery>


<html>

<head>
<title>Orange Whip Studios Expenses Report</title>
</head>

<body>

<cfform action="Report3.cfm">
Select movie:
<cfselect name="FilmID"
          query="movies"
          display="MovieTitle"
          value="FilmID"
```

Listing 16.15 (CONTINUED)

```
                queryPosition="below">
  <option value="">--- ALL ---</option>
</cfselect>
<br>
<cfinput name="sbmt"
         type="submit"
         value="Report">
</cfform>

</body>

</html>
```

The form in Listing 16.15 prompts for a movie, and passes FilmID to Report3.cfm, shown in
Listing 16.16.

Listing 16.16 Report3.cfm—Dynamic Report

```
<!---
Name:        Report3.cfm
Author:      Ben Forta
Description: Invoke a ColdFusion report
Created:     07/10/2007
--->

<cfparam name="FilmID" default="">

<cfquery name="Expenses" datasource="ows">
SELECT    Films.MovieTitle, Expenses.ExpenseDate,
          Expenses.Description,
          Expenses.ExpenseAmount
FROM      Films, Expenses
WHERE     Expenses.FilmID = Films.FilmID
<cfif FilmID NEQ "">
 AND Films.FilmID = #FilmID#
</cfif>
ORDER BY  Films.MovieTitle, expenses.expensedate
</cfquery>

<cfreport template="Expenses.cfr"
          query="Expenses"
          format="PDF" />
```

Listing 16.16 is the same as Listing 16.14, but this time the <cfquery> is being created dynamically,
so the query can select either all expenses or just expenses for a specific movie. The same
<cfreport> tag is used, but now the report can display expenses for all movies, or just a single
movie.

This functionality is so important that the ColdFusion Report Builder can actually automatically
create calling CFML code for you. To try this, return to the ColdFusion Query Builder (with the
expenses.cfr report open), and click on the Code Snippet button (the one with tags on it). You will
see a screen that contains calling CFML code, either a single .cfm (Figure 16.25) or a .cfc and .cfm.

(Figure 16.26). You can select the code style using the radio buttons at the bottom of the page, and then click Save to save the generated ColdFusion code ready for you to use (and modify, if needed).

Figure 16.25

The Report Builder can generate calling CFML code.

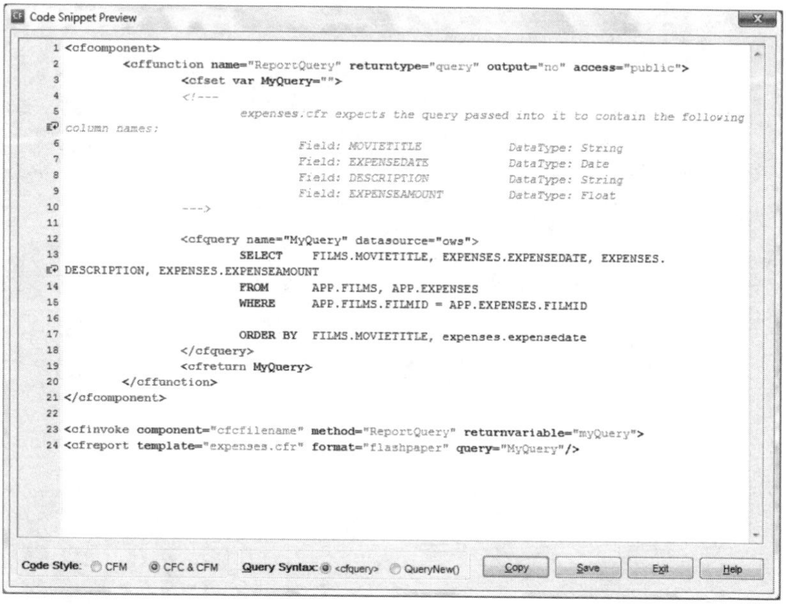

Figure 16.26

The Report Builder can also generate a .cfc containing the query, and a .cfm invoking that query and calling the report.

And a Whole Lot More, Too

We've only scratched the surface. The ColdFusion Report Builder is a powerful tool that in truth is deserving of far more space than can be devoted here. But it is also an easy-to-use tool, and one that you are encouraged to experiment with. Some features worth paying attention to are:

- The various properties available when clicking on different report sections and elements.

- The Chart button, which launches a Chart Wizard used to embed charts within reports (actually, the Wizard generates `<cfchart>` tags, the same tags used earlier in this chapter).

- The Subreport button, used to embed one report inside of another.

- The Print When property that can be used to conditionally include or exclude parts of reports.

- Input parameters, used to pass `name=value` pairs to reports at runtime.

- Text Styles, which allow styles to be used for formatting.

NOTE

Be sure to visit the book Web site at `http://www.forta.com/books/032151548X` for online lessons and tutorials on these features.

17

Debugging and Troubleshooting

Troubleshooting ColdFusion Applications

As with any development tool, sooner or later you're going to find yourself debugging or troubleshooting a ColdFusion problem. Many applications and interfaces have to work seamlessly for a ColdFusion application to function correctly. The key to quickly isolating and correcting problems is a thorough understanding of ColdFusion, data sources, SQL syntax, URL syntax, and your Web server—and more importantly, how they all work with each other.

If the prospect of debugging an application sounds daunting, don't panic. ColdFusion has powerful built-in debugging and error-reporting features. These capabilities, coupled with logical and systematic evaluation of trouble spots, will let you diagnose and correct all sorts of problems.

This chapter teaches you how to use the ColdFusion debugging tools and introduces techniques that will help you quickly locate the source of a problem. More importantly, because an ounce of prevention is worth a pound of cure, we introduce guidelines and techniques that help prevent common errors from occurring in the first place.

NOTE

This chapter does not discuss the new ColdFusion 8 interactive step debugger. See *ColdFusion 8 Web Application Construction Kit, Volume 3: Advanced Application Development* in this series for more information on this powerful new solution to aid in understanding and debugging ColdFusion applications.

Understanding What Can Go Wrong

As an application developer, sooner or later you are going to have to diagnose, or *debug*, a ColdFusion application problem. Because ColdFusion relies on so many other software components to work its magic, there are a lot of places where things can go wrong.

Since you're reading this chapter, the following assumptions are made:

- You are familiar with basic ColdFusion concepts.

- You understand how ColdFusion uses data sources for all database interaction.

- You are familiar with basic SQL syntax and use.

- You know how to use the ColdFusion Administrator.

- You are comfortable using Adobe Dreamweaver.

If you aren't familiar with any of these topics, I strongly recommend you read the chapters about them before proceeding.

→ See Chapter 1, "Introducing ColdFusion," for more information on how ColdFusion works and how all the pieces fit together to create a complete application.

→ See Chapter 3, "Accessing the ColdFusion Administrator," to learn how to enable debugging options using the ColdFusion Administrator.

→ See Chapter 5, "Building the Databases," for a detailed explanation of databases, tables, rows, columns, keys, and other database-related terms.

→ See Chapter 6, "Introducing SQL," for more information about data sources and how ColdFusion uses them for all database interaction.

Almost all ColdFusion problems fall into one of the following categories:

- Web server configuration problems

- Database driver errors

- SQL statement syntax or logic errors

- ColdFusion syntax errors

- URL and path problems

- Form problems

Let's look at each of these potential problem areas.

Debugging Web Server Configuration Problems

You should almost never encounter problems caused by Web server misconfiguration during routine, day-to-day operations. These types of problems almost always occur either during the initial ColdFusion setup or while testing ColdFusion for the first time. After ColdFusion is installed and configured correctly, it will stay that way.

The only exception to this is the possibility of you receiving an error telling you that ColdFusion isn't running. This error will only occur if you're using an external HTTP server (not ColdFusion's integrated web server), and will be generated when the Web server ColdFusion extensions can't communicate with the ColdFusion Application Server.

Obviously, the Application Server must be running for ColdFusion to process templates. Steps to verifying that the server is running, and starting it if it isn't, differ based on your operating system:

- If you're running ColdFusion on a Windows NT-based machine (including Windows 2000 and Windows XP), you should run the Services applet. It will show whether the service is running and will enable you to start it if it isn't.

- If you're running ColdFusion on Unix/Linux, use the `ps` command (or `ps -ef|grep cfusion`) to list running processes to see whether ColdFusion is running.

TIP

Windows services can be started automatically every time the system is restarted. The service Startup option must be set to Automatic for a service to start automatically. Windows 9x users can automatically start ColdFusion by ensuring that the ColdFusion Application Server is in the Programs, Startup group. This setting is turned on by the ColdFusion installation procedure and typically should be left on at all times. However, if the service doesn't automatically start, check these options.

TIP

If your operating system features a mechanism by which to automatically start services or daemons upon system restart, use it.

One other situation worth noting is when you are prompted to save a file every time you request a ColdFusion page. If this is the case, one of two things is happening:

- ColdFusion isn't installed on the server correctly (if not using the integrated HTTP server).

- You are accessing URLs locally (using the browser File > Open option) instead of via the Web server.

Debugging Database Driver Errors

ColdFusion relies on database drivers (JDBC or ODBC) for all its database interaction. You will receive database driver error messages when ColdFusion can't communicate with the appropriate driver or when the driver can't communicate with the database.

Database driver error messages are always generated by the driver, not by ColdFusion. ColdFusion merely displays whatever error message it has received from the database driver. Unfortunately these error messages are often cryptic or even misleading.

Database driver error messages always contain an error number, which in and of itself is pretty useless. A text message that describes the problem follows the error number, however. The text of these messages varies from driver to driver, so it would be pointless to list all the possible error messages here. Instead, the more common symptoms and how to fix the problems that cause them are listed.

TIP

You can use the ColdFusion Administrator to verify that a data source is correctly set up and attached to the appropriate data file.

Receiving the Error Message Data Source Not Found

ColdFusion communicates with databases via database drivers. These drivers access data sources—external data files. If the database driver reports that the data source could not be found, check the following:

- Make sure you have created the data source.

- Verify that the data source name is spelled correctly. Data source names are not case sensitive, so you don't have to worry about that.

- If you're using ODBC drivers, note that Windows ODBC data sources are *user login specific*. This means if you create a data source from within the ODBC Control Panel applet while logged in as a user without administrator privileges, only that user will have access to that ODBC data source.

Receiving the Error Message File Not Found

You might get the error message `File not found` when trying to use a data source you have created. This error message applies only to data sources that access data files directly (such as Microsoft Access, Microsoft Excel, and Borland dBASE), and not to client/server database systems (such as Microsoft SQL Server and Oracle).

`File not found` simply means that the database driver could not locate the data file in the location it was expecting to find it. To diagnose this problem, perform the following steps:

1. Data files must be created before data sources can use them. If you haven't yet created the data file, you must do so before proceeding.

2. Check the data source settings, verify that the file name is spelled correctly, and ensure that the file exists.

3. If you have moved the location of a data file, you must manually update any data sources that reference it.

Receiving Login or Permission Errors When Trying to Access a Data Source

Some database systems, such as Microsoft SQL Server, Sybase, and Oracle, require that you log on to a database before you can access it. When setting up a data source to this type of database, you must specify the login name and password the driver should use to gain access (whether you're working in the ColdFusion Administrator or using the `<cfquery>` tag's `UserName` and `Password` attributes).

The following steps will help you locate the source of this problem:

1. Verify that the login name and password are spelled correctly. (You won't be able to see the password—only asterisks are displayed in the password field.)

2. On some database systems, passwords are case sensitive. Be sure that you haven't left the Caps Lock key on by mistake.

3. Verify that the name and password you are using does indeed have access to the database to which you are trying to connect. You can do this using a client application that came with your database system.

4. Verify that the login being used actually has rights to the specific tables and views you are using and to the specific statements (SELECT, INSERT, and so on). Many better DBMSs enable administrators to grant or deny rights to specific objects and specific operations on specific objects.

TIP
When you're testing security- and rights-related problems, be sure you test using the same login and password as the ones used in the data source definition.

Receiving the Error Message Unknown Table

After verifying that the data source name and table names are correct, you might still get unknown table errors. A very common problem, especially with client/server databases such as Microsoft SQL Server, is forgetting to provide a fully qualified table name. You can do this in two ways:

- **Explicitly provide the fully qualified table name whenever it is passed to a SQL statement.** Fully qualified table names are usually made up of three parts, separated by periods. The first is the name of the database containing the table; the second is the owner name (usually specified as dbo); the third is the actual table name itself.

- **Some database drivers, such as the Microsoft SQL Server driver, let you specify a default database to be used if none is explicitly provided.** If this option is set, its value is used whenever a fully qualified name isn't provided.

TIP
If your database driver lets you specify a default database name, use that feature. You can then write fewer and simpler hard-coded SQL statements.

Debugging SQL Statement or Logic Errors

Debugging SQL statements is one of the two types of troubleshooting you'll spend most of your debugging time doing (the other is debugging ColdFusion syntax errors, which we'll get to next). You will find yourself debugging SQL statements if you run into either of these situations:

- ColdFusion reports SQL syntax errors. Figure 17.1, for example, is an error caused by misspelling a table name in a SQL statement. If you see only partial debug output, as shown in Figure 17.2, access the ColdFusion Administrator and turn on the Enable Robust Exception Information option in the Debugging Settings screen.

- No syntax errors are reported, but the specified SQL statement didn't achieve the expected results.

Figure 17.1

ColdFusion displays SQL error messages as reported by the database driver.

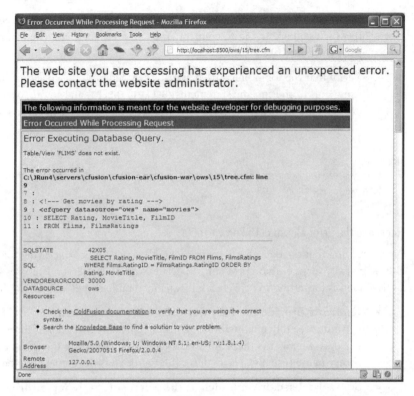

Figure 17.2

During development, be sure that Enable Robust Exception Information is turned on in the ColdFusion Administrator, or you won't see complete debug output.

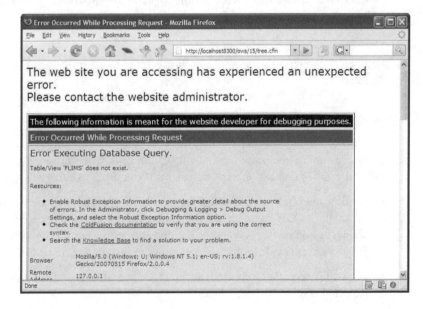

Obviously, a prerequisite to debugging SQL statements is a good working knowledge of the SQL language. I'm assuming you are already familiar with the basic SQL statements and are comfortable using them.

➔ See Chapter 7, "SQL Data Manipulation," for information about basic SQL statements and examples of their uses.

The keys to successfully debugging SQL statements are as follows:

- Isolate the problem. Debugging SQL statements inside ColdFusion templates can be tricky, especially when creating dynamic SQL statements. See the section "Viewing Dynamically Generated SQL" later in this chapter for help on viewing that SQL. Try executing the same statement from within another database client, replacing dynamic parameters with fixed values if appropriate.

- The big difference between ColdFusion SQL statements and statements entered into any other database client is the use of ColdFusion fields. If you are using ColdFusion fields within your statement, verify that you are enclosing them within quotation marks when necessary. If the value is a string, it must be enclosed in single quotation marks. If it's a number, it must *not* be enclosed in quotation marks. (And be sure double quotation marks are never used within SQL statements, because this will terminate the statement prematurely.)

- Look at the bigger picture. Dynamic SQL statements are one of ColdFusion's most powerful features, but this power comes at a price. When you create a dynamic SQL statement, you are effectively relinquishing direct control over the statement itself and are allowing it to be changed based on other conditions. This means that the code for a single ColdFusion query can be used to generate an infinite number of queries. Because some of these queries might work and others might not, debugging dynamic SQL requires that you be able to determine exactly what the dynamically created SQL statement looks like. Again, ColdFusion makes this an easy task, as you will see later in this chapter in the section "Viewing Dynamically Generated SQL."

- Break complex SQL statements into smaller, simpler statements. If you are debugging a query that contains subqueries, verify that the subqueries properly work independently of the outer query.

CAUTION

Be careful to not omit number signs (#) from around variable names in your SQL code. Consider the following SQL statement:

```
DELETE Actors
WHERE ActorID=ActorID
```

What the code is supposed to do is delete a specific actor, the one whose ID is specified in `ActorID`. But because the number signs were omitted, instead of passing the actor ID, the name of the actor ID column is passed. The result? Every row in the `Actors` table is deleted instead of just the one—all because of missing number signs. The correct statement should have looked like this:

```
DELETE Actors
WHERE ActorID=#ActorID#
```

Incidentally, this is why you should always test WHERE clauses in a SELECT before using them in a DELETE or UPDATE.

Whenever a SQL syntax error occurs, ColdFusion displays the SQL statement it submitted (if you selected Enable Robust Exception Information in the Administrator debug output settings). The fully constructed statement is displayed if your SQL statement was constructed dynamically. The field names are displayed as submitted if the error occurred during an INSERT or UPDATE operation, but the values are replaced with question marks (except for NULL values, which are displayed as NULL).

NOTE

If you ever encounter strange database driver error messages about mismatched data types or incorrect numbers of parameters, check to see if you have mistyped any table or column names and that you have single quotation marks where necessary. More often than not, that is what causes that error.

TIP

If you're using Dreamweaver, you can completely avoid typos in table and column names by using the database drag-and-drop support. To do this, open the Application panel and select the Database tab, select the desired data source, and expand the tables to find the table and column you need. You can then click the table or column name and just drag it to the editor window, where it will be inserted when you release the mouse key.

If you're using Eclipse instead and have installed the ColdFusion plug-ins for Eclipse, you can also find and drag and drop table and column names in the view ColdFusion RDS Dataview.

Viewing Dynamically Generated SQL

As discussed earlier in this chapter, a common challenge in debugging SQL problems in Cold-Fusion is identifying the SQL statement generated dynamically within a <cfquery> tag, because any valid CFML can be used to create any valid SQL. Fortunately, there are several solutions, some new in recent releases.

Perhaps the most traditional approach is to use the ColdFusion debugging information, which can be enabled in the ColdFusion Administrator. The Debug Output Settings page contains a check box labeled Database Activity, and during development, you can enable this option to display the full SQL statement and data source name (and with the Enable Robust Exception Information option, this information is displayed in any database-related error messages.) The debugging options are discussed further in the section "Using the ColdFusion Debugging Options" later in this chapter.

Newer options have become available since ColdFusion MX 7, and these can be of particular value when you cannot enable debugging. ColdFusion MX 7 added a new Result attribute for <cfquery> (and other tags), which enables you to name a variable whose value will be a structure containing metadata about the tag after its execution. In the case of a <cfquery> tag, one of the resulting keys is SQL, which holds the dynamically generated SQL.

Now ColdFusion 8, on a data source definition screen (under Advanced Settings), offers a Log Activity option, where you can name a log file to which ColdFusion will write the details of all database calls for that data source.

Debugging ColdFusion Syntax Errors

Debugging ColdFusion syntax errors is the other type of troubleshooting you'll find yourself doing. Thankfully, and largely as a result of the superb ColdFusion error-reporting and debugging capabilities, these are usually the easiest bugs to find.

ColdFusion syntax errors are usually one of the following:

- Mismatched number signs or quotation marks

- Mismatched begin and end tags; a `<cfif>` without a matching `</cfif>`, for example

- Incorrectly nested tags

- A tag with a missing or incorrectly spelled attribute

- Missing quotation marks around tag attributes

- Using double quotation marks instead of single to delimit strings when building SQL statements

- Illegal use of tags

If any of these errors occur, ColdFusion generates a descriptive error message, as shown in Figure 17.3. The error message lists the problematic code (and a few lines before and after it) and identifies exactly what the problem is.

Figure 17.3

ColdFusion generates descriptive error messages when syntax errors occur.

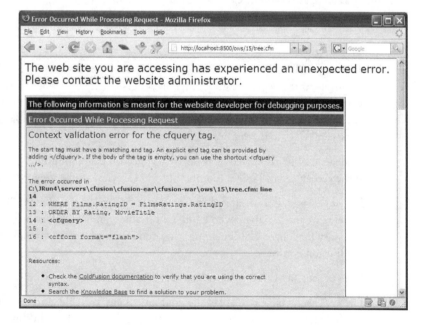

If your template contains HTML forms, frames, or tables, you might have trouble viewing generated error messages. If an error occurs in the middle of a table, for example, that table will never be terminated, and there's no way to know how the browser will attempt to render the partial table. If the table isn't rendered and displayed properly, you won't see the error message.

If you think an error has occurred but no error message is displayed, you can view the source in the browser. The generated source will contain any error messages that were included in the Web page but not displayed.

One of the most common ColdFusion errors is missing or mismatched tags. Indenting your code, as shown in the following, is a good way to ensure that all tags are correctly matched:

```
<cfif some condition here>
 <cfoutput>
  Output code here
  <cfif another condition>
   Some other output code here
  </cfif>
 </cfoutput>
<cfelse>
 Some action here
</cfif>
```

Dreamweaver users should take advantage of the available features designed to help avoid common mismatching problems. Color coding is one of these (if the code isn't colored correctly, you've done something wrong), as is right-click support for Tag Editors.

➔ See Chapter 2, "Choosing a Development Environment," for more information about Adobe Dreamweaver.

Inspecting Variable Contents

Sometimes problems throw no errors at all. This occurs when your code is syntactically valid but a logic problem exists somewhere. Aside from using the interactive debugger (which is discussed in Vol. 3 of this series), the primary way to locate this type of bug is to inspect variable contents during processing. Several ways to do this are available:

- Embed variable display code as necessary in your page, dumping the contents of variables to the screen (or to HTML comments you can view using View Source in your browser).

- The `<cfdump>` tag (introduced in Chapter 8, "The Basics of CFML") can display the contents of any variable, even complex variables, and can be used to aid debugging when necessary (and as of ColdFusion 8, this dump output can be directed to a log file or the ColdFusion console).

- The `<cflog>` tag can display the contents of any variable, writing its output to a log file.

- The `<cftrace>` tag can display the contents of any variable, and its operation can be enabled and disabled via the Administrator, as discussed later in this chapter, in the section "Using Tracing." By displaying variable contents, you usually can determine what various code blocks are doing at any given point during page processing.

You can use `<cfabort>` anywhere in the middle of your template to force ColdFusion to halt further processing. You can move the `<cfabort>` tag farther down the template as you verify that lines of code work.

During development, when you find yourself alternating between needing debugging information and not needing it, you can enclose debug code in `<cfif IsDebugMode()>` and `</cfif>`. This way, your debug output will be processed only if debugging is enabled.

Identifying HTML Syntax Errors

To help you catch syntax errors before your site goes live, Dreamweaver has an integrated validation engine. The validation engine can be used to check for mismatched tags, unknown variables, missing number signs, and other common errors—and not just CFML errors, either.

To use the validator, open the file to be checked in Dreamweaver and then open the Results panel and select the Validation tab. Click the Validate button (the green arrow at the top left of the panel) and select what it is you'd like to validate (the first option is the one you should use to validate the current document). Dreamweaver then validates your code and lists any errors in a results window at the bottom of the screen, as seen in Figure 17.4.

Figure 17.4

The Dreamweaver validation engine lists any errors in the Results panel.

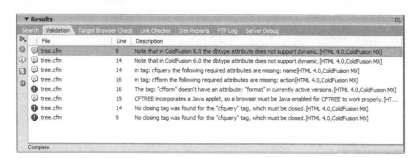

To quickly jump to the problematic code, click on any error message in the Results panel. As seen in Figure 17.5, Dreamweaver goes to the appropriate line of code and even highlights the trouble spot for you. This lets you fix errors before you roll out your application.

Figure 17.5

The Dreamweaver validation engine can flag problem code for you.

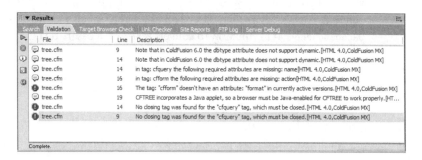

Ctrl-Shift-F7 is a Windows shortcut that takes you directly to the Validation tab.

You can customize the behavior of the validation engine, including specifying what gets validated and which tags to validate. To do this, open the Preferences screen, and then select the Validator tab.

Debugging URL and Path Problems

URL- and path-related problems are some of the easiest to diagnose and resolve because they tend to be binary in nature—they either work consistently or they fail consistently.

Images Are Not Displayed

If image files (and other files) aren't always displayed when you reference them from within ColdFusion, the problem might be path related. If you're using relative paths (and you generally should be), be sure that the path being sent to the browser is valid. Having too many or too few periods and slashes in the path is a common problem.

Most browsers let you check image paths (constructing full URLs from relative paths in your code) by right-clicking (Windows) or Control-clicking (Mac) the image and viewing the properties.

Passing Parameters That Aren't Processed

Parameters you pass to a URL may not be processed by ColdFusion, even though you see them present in the URL. URLs are finicky little beasts, and you have to abide by the following rules:

- URLs can have only one question mark character in them. The question mark separates the URL itself from the query string.

- Each parameter must be separated by an ampersand (&) to pass multiple parameters in the URL query string section.

- URLs must not have spaces or other special characters in them. If you are generating URLs dynamically based on table column data, be sure to trim any spaces from those values. If you must use spaces, replace them with plus signs. ColdFusion correctly converts the plus signs to spaces when used. You can also use the ColdFusion `URLEncodedFormat()` function to convert text to URL-safe text.

ColdFusion debug output, discussed in the following section, lists all passed URL parameters. This is an invaluable debugging tool.

Debugging Form Problems

If a form is submitted without data, it can cause an error. Web browsers submit data to Web servers in two ways. These ways are called GET and POST, and the submission method for use is specified in the `<form>` or `<cfform>` method attribute.

As a rule, forms being submitted to ColdFusion should always be submitted using the POST method. The default method for <form> is GET, so if you omit or misspell method="POST", ColdFusion may be incapable of processing your forms correctly.

You might occasionally get a variable is undefined error message when referring to form fields in the action template. Radio buttons, check boxes, and list boxes aren't submitted if no option was selected. It's important to remember this when referring to form fields in an action template. If you refer to a check box without first checking for its existence (and then selecting it), you'll generate an error message.

The solution is to always check for the existence of any fields or variables before using them using the isdefined function. Alternatively, you can use the <CFPARAM> tag to assign default values to fields, thereby ensuring that they always exist. (This discussion also applies to the detection and handling of undefined URL variables.)

➔ See Chapter 12, "ColdFusion Forms," for more information about working with form fields and working with specific form controls.

How can you check which form fields were actually submitted and what their values are? Enable ColdFusion debugging (as explained shortly) any time you submit a form. Its action page contains a debugging section that describes the submitted form. This is shown in Figure 17.6. A field named FORM.FIELDNAMES contains a comma-delimited list of all the submitted fields, as well as a list of the submitted fields and their values.

Figure 17.6

ColdFusion displays form-specific debugging information if debugging is enabled.

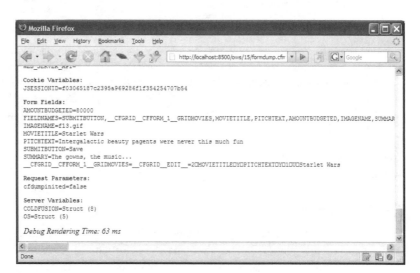

Here are some other things to look for in your form definition:

- Be sure all form fields have names.

- Be sure related check boxes or radio buttons have the same name (unless using Flash Forms, in which case check boxes must be uniquely named).

- Be sure form field names are specified within double quotation marks.

- Be sure form field names have no spaces or other special characters in them.

- Be sure that all quotation marks around attribute values match.

- When all else fails, dump the contents of the FORM scope with <cfdump var="#form#">.

All these are HTML related, not ColdFusion related. But every one of them can complicate working with forms, and HTML itself may not generate errors upon form display.

Using the ColdFusion Debugging Options

The ColdFusion debugging options are enabled or disabled via the ColdFusion Administrator, as explained in Chapter 3.

TIP

You can restrict the display of debugging information to specific IP addresses. If you enable debugging, you should use this feature to prevent debugging screens from being displayed to your site's visitors.

CAUTION

At a minimum, the local host IP address (127.0.0.1) should be specified. If no IP address is in the list, debugging information will be sent to anyone who browses any ColdFusion page.

TIP

A long-time problem for ColdFusion developers has been getting their administrators to let them access the Administrator so that they can change options such as those discussed in this section. In ColdFusion 8, an administrator can define username and password combinations to permit individuals to access the Administrator. Using this capability plus the Sandbox Security feature (in ColdFusion Enterprise), debugging can be restricted further, to one or more applications on a server. See Chapter 64, "Creating Server Sandboxes," in Vol. 3, *Advanced Application Development*, for more information on the new per-user admin configuration and Sandbox Security.

ColdFusion supports three different debugging modes. They all provide the same basic functionality, but with different interfaces.

Classic Debugging

The *classic* debugging interface appends debugging information to the end of any generated Web pages, as shown in Figure 17.7. The advantage of this format is that it doesn't use any complex client-side technology, so it's safer to use on a wide variety of browsers.

To select this option, select classic.cfm as the debug format in the ColdFusion Administrator.

NOTE

This is known as the classic format because it's the format supported in ColdFusion since the very first versions of the product.

Figure 17.7

ColdFusion can append debugging information to any generated Web page.

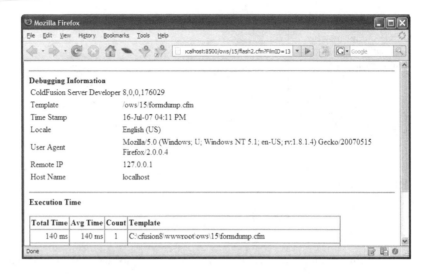

Dockable Debugging

ColdFusion also features a powerful DHTML-based debugging interface. As seen in Figure 17.8, debug information is displayed in a tree control in a separate pop-up window, or docked to the output itself, as seen in Figure 17.9. The advantage of this format (aside from a much cleaner and easier-to-use interface) is that the debug output doesn't interfere with the page itself.

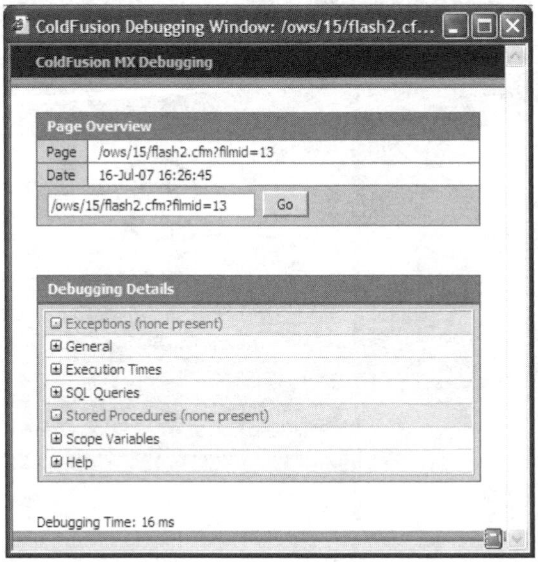

Figure 17.8

ColdFusion debug output can be displayed in a pop-up DHTML-based window.

Figure 17.9

Debug output may be "docked" to the page, if preferred.

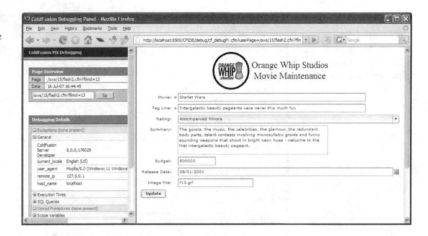

To select this option, select `dockable.cfm` as the debug format in the ColdFusion Administrator.

Dreamweaver Debugging

Debug output is also accessible from within Dreamweaver itself, as seen in Figure 17.10. Any Cold-Fusion page can be debugged from within Dreamweaver by clicking the Server Debug button on top of the Dreamweaver editor window, or selecting Server Debug from the View menu. Debug output is displayed in the Results panel below in a tree format.

Figure 17.10

Within Dreamweaver, ColdFusion debug output is displayed in the Results panel.

Using Debugging Options

Regardless of how the debugging information is accessed (through any of the options just listed) you'll have access to the same information:

- Execution time, so you can locate poorly performing code.

- Database activity, so you can determine exactly what was passed to the database drivers (post any dynamic processing) and what was returned.

- Tracing information (explained below).

- Variables and their values.

As you move from page to page within your application, the debug output will provide insight into what's actually going on within your code.

NOTE

The exact information displayed in debug output is managed by options in the ColdFusion Administrator.

Using Tracing

In addition to all the invaluable information provided by the debugger, you may on occasion want to generate your own debug output. For example, you may want to:

- Check the values of variables within a loop.

- Determine which code path or branch (perhaps in a series of `<cfif>` statements) is being followed.

- Inspect SESSION or other variables.

- Check for the presence of expected URL parameters or FORM fields.

- Display the number of rows retrieved by a query.

- Check the timing of a block of code.

This kind of information is useful in debugging logic problems—those annoying situations where code is valid syntactically, but some logic flaw (or unexpected situation) is preventing it from functioning as expected.

To insert your own information in debug output, use the `<cftrace>` tag, which embeds trace information. `<cftrace>` takes a series of attributes (all optional) that let you dump variable contents, display text (dynamic or static), abort processing, and more. As seen in Figure 17.11, the generated trace output is included with the standard debug output (if that option is enabled in the ColdFusion Administrator, see the Tracing Information option on the Debug Output Settings page).

Figure 17.11

Trace output (generated using `<CFTRACE>`) is included with debug output.

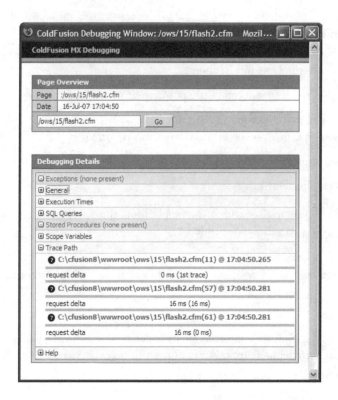

To use `<cftrace>`, simply embed `<cftrace>` tags at strategic locations in your code. For example, if you're trying to figure out why variables are being set to specific values, use `<cftrace>` statements at the top of the page, before and after any `<cfinclude>` statements and any other statements that could set variable values, and so on.

To output simple text use the following `<cftrace>` syntax:

```
<cftrace text="Just before the cfinclude">
```

To display variable values, you could do the following:

```
<cftrace text="firstname at top of page" var="firstname">
```

Note that the `<cftrace>` tag writes its output both to the debugging output and to a `cftrace.log` file (in the ColdFusion logs directory). You can also cause it to display its output at the point where the tag is executed, using the `Inline="yes"` attribute.

Also note that tracing can be enabled and disabled within the ColdFusion Administrator, so that you can leave the tags in your source code even in production. They will not generate any output or use any resources if the tracing information option in the Administrator is disabled.

Additional `<cftrace>` attributes allow for message categorization and prioritization, but the two examples here are usually all you need. By embedding `<cftrace>` blocks in your code you'll get a clear and systematic view into what happened, when, and why.

Code Timing

Another challenge in solving problems with ColdFusion code entails understanding how long some piece or section of code takes to execute. Fortunately, ColdFusion offers several tools to help identify code timing:

- `GetTickCount()`
- `<cftrace>`
- `<cftimer>`
- `cfquery.executiontime`
- `Result` attribute
- Server monitor profiling feature

One of the oldest ways to identify code timing is to use the `getTickcount()` function, which returns a number of milliseconds since a point in the past. This function can be used to compare the count of milliseconds at one point to the count at a later point.

However, it can be simpler to use a similar, built-in feature of the `<cftrace>` tag. When this tag executes, it displays the elapsed time since a previous `<cftrace>` tag was executed. You can surround a code block you want to time with `<cftrace>` tags.

ColdFusion also has added a tag that is devoted to this specific purpose: `<cftrace>`.

If you want to know how long a given `<cfquery>` tag took to execute, note that the available variable, `cfquery.executiontime`, holds the number of milliseconds. That shows the value for the last query executed, but as of ColdFusion 7, you can use the available `Result` attribute on any query, returning a structure that includes an `executiontime` value with the same timing information for that specific query (and disabling `cfquery.executiontime`).

Finally, the ColdFusion 8 server monitor includes new profiling functionality that can show the time taken to execute each tag in an application. The server monitor is discussed in Vol. 3, Chapter 56, "Monitoring System Performance," in Vol. 3, *Advanced Application Development*.

Using the ColdFusion Log Files

ColdFusion logs all warnings and errors to log files, which aids you and Adobe Technical Support in troubleshooting problems. ColdFusion log files are created when the ColdFusion service starts. You can delete these log files if they get too large, or move them to another directory for processing. If you do move or delete the log files, ColdFusion creates new ones automatically.

Most of the ColdFusion log files are plain-text, comma-delimited files. You can import these files into a database or spreadsheet application of your choice for analysis.

The ColdFusion Administrator lists all available log files (see Figure 17.12), and includes a sophisticated log file viewer that enables you to browse (see Figure 17.13), search, and analyze log file data as necessary.

Figure 17.12

The ColdFusion Administrator lists all available log files.

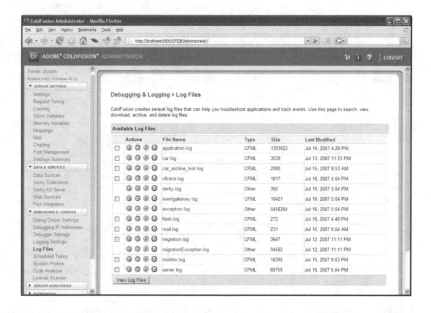

Figure 17.13

The Log Viewer supports browsing through log file entries.

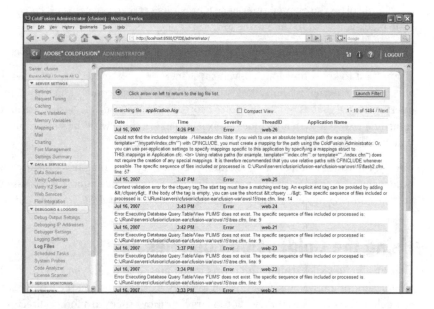

More sophisticated analysis filtering is supported (see Figure 17.14), allowing you to include or exclude filter conditions to locate exactly the logged messages you need. This is particularly useful on very busy systems, where multiple requests could be logging messages at the same time. Being able to filter by thread ID and time ranges helps find logging needles in the log file haystack.

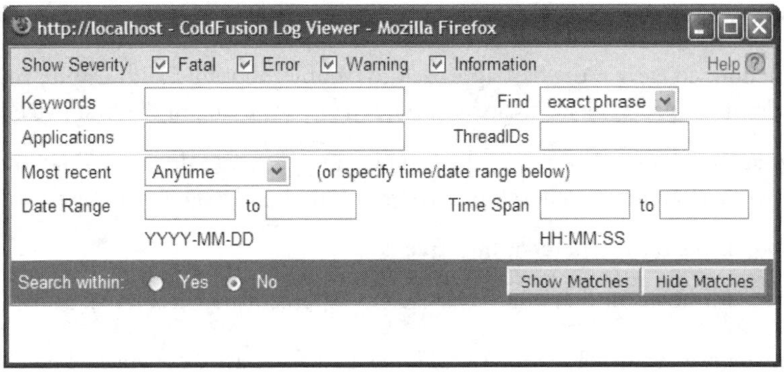

Figure 17.14

Use the Log Viewer
Filter window to
search for specific log
file entries.

Additionally, the ColdFusion 8 Eclipse plug-ins for ColdFusion add a new ColdFusion log viewer
that permits access to and display of the log files from within that editor. The plug-ins were introduced in Chapter 2.

ColdFusion creates several log files. Some of the important ones are:

- `application.log`—Contains generated CFML errors, syntax errors, and other runtime
  error conditions and messages.

- `cftrace.log`—Contains entries made using the `<cftrace>` tag.

- `eventgateway.log`—Contains errors and status messages related to the Event Gateway
  engine.

- `exception.log`—Contains Java exceptions thrown when errors occur.

- `flash.log`—Contains errors generated during Flash generation.

- `migration.log` and `migrationExceptoin.log`—Contains errors generated while migrating
  settings during ColdFusion reinstallations and upgrades.

- `server.log`—Contains information about the ColdFusion Application Server itself,
  including server stop and start times.

- `schedule.log`—Logs scheduled event execution.

In addition to the standard log files, specific operations (such as restoring an archive) can create
their own log files, too.

As a rule, you should monitor and browse log files regularly, as these often contain the first indica-
tion of problems occurring. For added convenience, the log file viewer in the ColdFusion Administrator allows filtering, sorting, downloading for further analysis and archiving.

TIP

Some errors are browser related. If you're having a hard time reproducing reported error messages, try to determine which version of
which browser the user was running and on which platform. You may have run into browser bugs (some versions of popular browsers
are very buggy). To help you find these problems, the log files list any identification information provided by a browser, along with the
error message.

Preventing Problems

As mentioned earlier, the best approach to troubleshooting ColdFusion problems (and indeed any development problems) is to prevent them from occurring in the first place.

Bugs are inevitable. As the size of an application grows, so does the likelihood of a bug being introduced. As an application developer, you need to have two goals in mind:

- Develop 100 percent bug-free code.

- In the event that your code isn't 100 percent bug-free, make sure it's easy to debug.

As an application developer myself, I know that these are lofty goals. The reality is that application development almost always takes longer than planned, and sacrifices have to be made if release dates are to be met. Code quality is usually the first thing that gets sacrificed.

Sooner or later these sacrifices will come back to haunt you. Then come the long debugging sessions, rapid code fixes, software upgrades, and possibly even data conversion. Then, because the rapidly patched code often introduces bugs of its own, the whole cycle starts again.

Although there is no surefire way of preventing all bugs, some guidelines and coding practices can both help prevent many of them and make finding them easier when they do occur. Here are my 10 Commandments of ColdFusion Development:

1. **Plan Before You Code.** We've all done it, and probably more than once. ColdFusion makes it so easy to start coding that you're often tempted to start projects by firing up an editor and creating CFM files. That's a bad thing indeed. Nothing is more harmful to your development efforts than failing to plan properly. You should be spending more time planning than coding—and I don't mean planning your IPO and subsequent retirement. Planning involves thinking through every aspect of your application, from database design to UI considerations, from resource management to schedules and deliverables, and from feature lists with implementation details to language and presentation. You'd never build a house without detailed blueprints (well, you might try, but you'd never get the necessary permits to start work), and building an application is no different. I'm constantly amazed by the number of applications I'm asked to look at that have no supporting documentation. And these aren't just from small development shops; I'm talking about some of the largest and most respected corporations. Scalability problems? I wouldn't doubt it. I'd actually be amazed if such an application ever did scale. You can't expect scalability from an application that grew in spite of its developers. Nor can you expect it to be bug free, manageable, or delivered on time. Yes, I know that detailed planning takes time, time none of us have. But in the long run you'll come out ahead.

2. **Organize Your Application.** An extension of planning your application is organizing it (along with any other applications). Applications are made up of lots of little bits and pieces, and keeping them organized is imperative. This includes directory structures and determining where common files should go, moving images to their own directory (or server), breaking long files into smaller, more manageable (and more reusable) ones (including CFCs), and even ensuring consistent organization among different

applications. Going back to the prior commandment, Plan Before You Code, all organization should be documented in detail as part of that plan. You should also consider using ColdFusion frameworks such as Fusebox, Model Glue, and Mach II to help you structure your applications, especially if you work in a large team or have multiple developers performing maintenance on a project over time.

3. **Set Coding Standards.** This is an interesting one, and one I get asked about often. Adobe hasn't published formal recommendations on coding standards, nor in my opinion should they. Adobe's job is to create killer tools and products for developers, and our job is to use them however works best for us. I don't believe that a single set of coding standards would work for all developers. At the same time, I don't believe any developer should be writing code that doesn't adhere to some standard—any standard. Coding standards include everything from file-naming and directory-naming conventions to variable-naming conventions, to code organization and ordering within your source, to error handling, to componentization, and much more. For example, if all variables that contain dates begin with `dt`, for example, then references to a variable named `dtOrderDate` become self-explanatory. The purpose of coding standards is to ensure some level of consistency in your code. Whether it's to allow other developers to understand and work with your code, or simply so that you'll know what the heck you did (and why) six months down the line, coding standards provide a mechanism to create code that describes and explains itself. There is no right or wrong coding standard, as long as one is used.

4. **Comment Your Code.** This is an obvious one, but apparently few of us have the time to pay attention to the obvious. So, I'll say it once again: All code must be commented. (For the record, I'd fire an employee on the spot for turning in code that wasn't commented; that's how serious an offense I believe this one to be.) Every source code file needs a descriptive header listing a description, the author information, the creation date, a chronological list of changes, any dependencies and assumptions, and any other relevant information. In addition, every conditional statement, every loop, every set of variable assignments, and every include or component reference must be commented with a simple statement explaining what is being done and why. It's a pain, I know. But the next time you (or anyone else) have to work with the code, you'll appreciate the effort immeasurably. And you might even be able to safely make code changes without breaking things in the process.

5. **Never Make Changes on a Live Server.** This is another obvious one, but one worth stating anyway. All development and testing should occur on servers established for just that purpose. Yes, this means you'll need additional hardware, but the cost of a new box is nothing compared to the cost of bringing down your application because that little change wasn't as little as you expected. Write your code, test it, debug it as necessary, deploy it to a testing server, test it some more, and test it some more, and then finally deploy it to your live production server. And don't repeat this process too often. Instead of uploading slightly changed versions of your application every day, collect the changes, test them some more, and deploy them monthly, or weekly, or whenever works best for

you. The key here is that your production server is sacred; don't touch it at all unless you have to—and the less frequently, the better. And never, ever, make changes on live servers, even minor ones. Nothing is ever as minor and as isolated as it seems, and there is no change worth crashing a server over.

6. **Functionality First, Then Features.** This is yet another obvious one, and a common beginner's mistake. Yes, writing fancy code or using DHTML menu-generation code (or Ajax or Flash Forms features) is far more fun that writing or using data-entry validation routines (especially server side), but validation routines are typically far more important to the success and reliability of your application. Concentrate on creating a complete working application; then pretty it up as necessary. Do so and increase the chance that you'll finish on schedule for a change. The final result might not be as cool as you'd like, but there is something to be said for an application that actually works, even an uncool one. Furthermore, (as explained in the next commandment) debugging logic problems is difficult when the code is cluttered with fancy formatting and features.

7. **Build and Test Incrementally.** Testing and debugging complete applications is difficult. The bigger an application is, the more components are used, and the more developers working on a project, the harder debugging and testing is. When you develop core components of your application, test them. Write little test routines, create stubs to return hard-coded values, or use smoke-and-mirrors as necessary, but however you do it, do it. Every component you write must have its own test utility. Feel free to use unit testing tools or solutions if they help, or create your own. Obviously, you'll have to test your complete application when you're finished and some problems won't come to light until then, but the more you can test code blocks in isolation, the better.

8. **Never Reinvent the Wheel, and Plan Not To.** This is one I have written about extensively. Write code with reuse in mind, and reuse code whenever possible. When designing your code, put in the extra time up front to ensure it isn't hard-coded or highly task specific unless it absolutely has to be. The benefits? Being able to reuse existing code shortens your development time. You stand a far greater chance of creating bug-free code when you use components that have already been used and tested. Plus, if you do make subsequent fixes and corrections, all code that uses the improved components benefit. This has a lot of benefits and no downside whatsoever.

9. **Use All the Tools at Your Disposal, Not Just ColdFusion.** ColdFusion applications usually aren't stand-alone entities. They rely on database servers, mail servers, etc. In addition, ColdFusion can leverage Web Services, Java, Flex, Ajax, Flash Remoting, LiveCycle Data Services, COM, CORBA, C/C++ code, and more. Use these tools, as many as necessary, and always try to select the best one for a specific job. The best ColdFusion applications aren't the ones written purely in ColdFusion; they are the ones that leverage the best technologies for the job, all held together by ColdFusion.

10. **Implement Version Control and Source Code Tracking.** Source code will change, and changes are dangerous. As your applications grow, so does the need for tracking changes and source code control. Select a version control package that works for you, and

use it. Key features to look for are the ability to lock files (so no one else edits a file while you edit it—if that does happen, someone's changes will be lost) or merge concurrent changes, the ability to view change history (what changed, by whom, and when), the ability to roll back complete applications (so that when the latest upgrade bombs you can easily roll back an entire application to a prior known state), the ability to create and check file dependencies (so you'll know what other code is affected by changes you make), and reporting. In addition, if you can integrate the product with Adobe Dreamweaver, that's even better. The bottom line: I don't care which product you use, just use one.

➔ Chapter 26, "Building Reusable Components," in *ColdFusion 8 Web Application Construction Kit, Volume 2: Application Development,* teaches the basics of code reuse and creating your own components.

➔ Chapter 54, "Development Methodologies, online, introduces several independent coding methodologies and standards, including the most popular one: Fusebox.

PART III

Building ColdFusion Applications

CHAPTER 18

Planning an Application

Getting Started on Your Application

When many developers get a new project to work on, their first instinct is usually to start coding right away. It's easy to understand why. Those first few hours or days of coding can be a lot of fun. The "inner geek" in each of us gets a special thrill from sinking our teeth into a new project, watching an application take shape, and carving something unique and useful out of thin air. Plus, there's often a deadline looming, so it seems best to start writing code as soon as humanly possible.

The problem is that even the simplest applications have a way of becoming much more complicated than they seemed at first. Nine times out of ten, if you take the time to plan your application and development process right from the start, you will do a better job in less time. Of course, people say that about almost everything in life. But in Web application development, it really is true.

Admit it! Your inner geek is already telling you to skip this chapter and get on with the coding. Resist the geek, if you can. The advice in this chapter will mean a bit more work for you up front. You might find that you even need to write a few documents. But you probably will end up doing more cool stuff and less tedious work if you know exactly where your application is headed at all times. Really. Seriously. Honest. Your inner geek might even buy you a drink when you're done.

Defining the Project

The first thing to do is to ensure that the project is as completely defined as possible. You need to know exactly what type of application to build, and that usually means doing some research and asking lots of questions.

In a perfect world, you would already have a written description of the application that defines its every aspect. You would know exactly what the expectations are for the project, and who will be testing it, using it, and benefiting from it. You would have complete understanding of every aspect of the project, from what technologies should be used to how the database should look.

In reality, you might have only a short description, such as, "We want to personalize our online store," or, "We need an accounting section in the company intranet." Sounds great, but you can't exactly start working yet.

The Importance of Being Inspired

If you can, try to have a vision about the project early on. Make it ambitious. Figure out how people are thinking about the project, and try to come up with some twist or feature that takes it to a whole new level—something an end user would be happy to see, and that you would be proud to implement. Why? Because it's important for you to be as interested in the project as you can be. If you're having fun during the development process, the application will turn out better. If at first the application sounds like something you've done or seen a million times before, try to think of something to add to make it unique. Even if the project already sounds difficult or daunting, think of some way to make it even more of a challenge.

Then, after you've gotten yourself excited about the project, try to get everyone else excited about it, too. Come up with a trademark-like name or code name for the project (perhaps from a favorite movie or a play on words based on the name of your competition). Talk about the project as if it were the cure for all diseases, as if it were going to save the world. Sell the thing. Even if it's filled with irony, your enthusiasm will bubble over onto the next desk or into the next room. At the very least, the project will be a little bit more fun. And how can that not be a good thing?

Understanding the Project

Now that you're enthused about the project, you need to get yourself educated as well. Before going further, be sure you know the answers to these questions:

- **Internet, intranet, or extranet?** Most projects will fall into one of these categories. Be sure you know which one yours falls into, and why. It is usually obvious that a project is an Internet project because it targets end users. Sometimes the difference between intranets and extranets can be more subtle, especially if the application is meant to be used by your company's business partners as well as in house. Even though it's just a word, be sure you and your client (or boss) agree on the word.

- **Totally new or "Version 2.0"?** You should know whether you are replacing an existing Web application. If so, why? What exactly is wrong with the current one? To what extent should you be using the existing application as a guide? Is the original just showing its age, or was it a total disaster from its very conception?

- **New process or existing process?** You should know whether your application is creating something totally new ("We have never had anything in place to do this"), or a modification of a current process ("We have always done this, but it was partly on paper and partly in a spreadsheet").

- **Integrating with existing site?** You should know whether your application is going to sit within the context of a larger Web site. If so, how will people get to your part of the site? How will they get back? Do you need to keep the navigation consistent?

- **Integrating with other systems?** Does any back-end or legacy integration need to be done? Perhaps your application needs to receive periodic updates from some type of batch process that occurs within the organization. If so, learn as much about the existing systems as you can. Also, find out if the project calls for the use of any Web Services that are currently available or are in the progress of being built. ColdFusion makes it easy to use ("consume") functionality provided by Web Services.

- **Existing database schemas?** Often, there is some type of existing database that at least part of your application will need to be aware of. Perhaps a table of customers and their IDs already exists somewhere in the organization. Find out whether your application can add tables and columns to this database or whether it should have its own database. Remember that ColdFusion generally has no problem dealing with information from multiple databases.

Conducting a Few Interviews

We recommend that you conduct a few informal interviews among the people who might actually be using your application when it's completed. Depending on the project, that might mean people within the company or potential end users on the street. Ask these people what they would like to see in the application. How could it be even more useful to them?

NOTE

A fun question to ask is, "If there were only a single button to click in this new application, what should it be?" At first, you might get sarcastic answers, such as, "It should find me a better husband," or "It should do my job for me," but you'll also get serious answers that can be quite telling.

These potential users will likely tell you more about how your application will actually be used than your normal contacts within the company can. They often are more likely to be able to describe what they need in ordinary terms. You might find that you think about the project differently after a couple of these short interviews, and you may end up reevaluating the importance of various features.

TIP

If your application is meant to replace or improve a process that these people perform manually or with an existing application, you might want to observe them doing their jobs for a short time. You might find that users spend most of their time doing task X, while you intended the application to assist primarily with task Y.

This interview process serves another, more subtle purpose as well. It associates a real person—a face, or several faces—with the project for you. When you reach a stumbling block later, or when you design a form, you can have these people in mind. Perhaps without totally realizing it, you will actually be creating the application *for* these people. When it's finished, you are likely to have improved their day-to-day work experiences or somehow made things more fun or easier for people using your application at home. You'll find it more rewarding, and your application will have much more perceived value.

Setting Expectations

This is perhaps the most important thing to nail down as early as possible. Even the savviest people have a way of expecting things from an application that they never told you about. Setting appropriate expectations is perhaps the most important thing to nail down as early as possible in the process.

Discussing the finer points of the project with your client can go a long way toward establishing reasonable expectations. Keep in mind that many of these items are matters of give and take. You might frame the discussion by clearly defining the choices: "The upside of doing this would be X, but the downside would be Y." Consider:

- **Screen resolution.** Most developers and graphic artists have great computer monitors that display lots of pixels at a time. But many people use monitors that have a lower screen resolution. If those people are important to you but the current design calls for a luxurious, cinematic layout that uses a lot of horizontal space, it's helpful to point out that some people are going to have to use the scroll bar at the bottom of the browser window to see all elements on the page.

- **The importance of security.** You should know to what extent your application needs to be secure. Many applications need some level of security (based on a password of some kind, as discussed in Chapter 23, "Securing Your Applications," online), but do they need more? Should the pages be further secured using HTTPS and SSL, or restricted according to IP address? Or should it be secured even further, using client certificates? Where will the application reside in relation to the company's firewall, assuming the company has one?

- **Concurrent Users.** If your client is thinking about the application getting a million hits per minute, but you have only an old computer to use to host the thing, that could be a problem. Of course, ColdFusion's multiple deployment options make it inherently scalable, and you could always use a cluster of better servers later, but it can't hurt to ensure that you and your client agree on load expectations.

- **Browser compatibility.** Does the application need to be capable of looking great with every browser ever made, from the first beta of Netscape Navigator to the latest service pack for Internet Explorer? Probably not. But you do need to determine exactly what the expectations are. Point out that if you are using client-side features, such as JavaScript or Dynamic HTML, the more browsers you need to support, and the more testing you might need to do. Note that using Adobe Flash in place of DHTML can go a long way toward avoiding browser compatibility issues.

- **Platform.** Unfortunately, today's Web browsers often display the same page differently on Macs and Windows machines. If you need to support only one platform (you're building an intranet for a strictly Linux shop, for example), your job might be a lot easier. Again, just be sure you and your client agree on what's expected.

Knowing the Players

Unless you are producing every aspect of the application on your own—including artwork, testing, and deployment—you need to know who is going to be working on the various aspects of the project. Depending on the circumstances, you might need to assemble a team on your own.

A team usually consists of the following basic positions. Even if one person performs more than one function, be sure you know who is who:

- **ColdFusion coders.** How many people will program the application? Just you, or a team of 20? Are the coders all under your control, or do they have their own chains of command or other responsibilities?

- **Graphic artists.** Who will provide graphics, banners, and buttons? Who will design the overall look and feel of the application? Who will design the site's navigation and structure?

- **Database people.** Who will determine the new database structure or make changes to any existing databases? Does that person see himself as a developer (designing tables for applications and so on), or more of a database administrator (tuning the database, adjusting indexes, scheduling maintenance, and the like)?

- **Project managers.** Who will ensure that the various elements of the project are completed on time and meeting all requirements? Who will keep an eye on everyone's schedules? Who will that person report to within the company? Who will report to that person within your team?

Fact Finding

Next, it's time to do a bit of research. This might sound like a lot of work, but the truth is you can often do the research suggested here in a couple of hours. It is almost always time well spent.

Looking at Similar Sites

Spend some time searching the Internet for sites that are similar to your project. Even if you can't find a Web site that does the exact same thing as the application you're building, at least try to find a few sites that are in the same conceptual space or that have pages that present the same type of information that your application will present.

For example, say one of your pages is going to be an "Advanced Search" page and another will present data in rows and columns. Find the best examples you can of such pages. What do you like about them? What don't you like? How does the use of color or spacing affect your opinion of the existing pages? When do the best sites use a button instead of a link, and why? When do graphics help, and when do they just get in the way?

Decide Which Technologies to Use

You also should research and decide which technologies you will use. Most likely, ColdFusion will give you most of the functionality you need, but you still need to answer a few questions:

- **What's the database?** Assuming your application requires a database of some kind, you need to decide which type of relational database management system (RDBMS) you will use. Many smaller Web applications are built using Access (.mdb) tables or delimited text files as their information stores, and there is nothing wrong with this for smaller applications. Most people will advise you to consider a server-based database product (such as Oracle, MySQL, or Microsoft's SQL Server) for larger-scale applications.

- **Any scripting or Ajax?** ColdFusion makes all its decisions on the server side, just before a page is delivered to the browser. Sometimes your application will benefit from some type of client-side scripting using JavaScript or perhaps Ajax. If so, decide where you will use scripting, and to what end.

- **Any Flash, video, or other multimedia?** Depending on the project, you might need to include dynamic, interactive content such as Adobe Flash movies, Shockwave presentations, or 3D worlds in your pages. These days, most computers are already equipped with the Flash player; with the Flash 8 player you can also deliver sound and video without an additional plug-in. Other types of multimedia content may require a plug-in installed on each user's browser. Such plug-ins generally can be installed automatically for Internet Explorer users (especially under Windows) but usually they must be downloaded and installed manually for other browsers and platforms. Keep these issues in mind as you discuss the project.

- **Any custom tags, user-defined functions (UDFs), or ColdFusion Components (CFCs)?** You should decide whether you will build reusable items while you construct your application. If you will, you might want to sketch out what each custom tag, UDF, or CFC will do and what each tag's attributes might be. (CFML custom tags and CFCs are discussed in Chapter 26, "Building Reusable Components," in *ColdFusion 8 Web Application Construction Kit, Volume 2: Application Development*. UDFs are discussed in Chapter 24, "Building User-Defined Functions," in Vol. 2, *Application Development*.)

- **Any custom-built extensions?** Depending on the situation, you might want (or need) to code certain parts of your application using a different programming language, such as C++, Java, or .NET. For example, you might compile a CFX tag to use within your ColdFusion templates. Or, you might create a COM object, servlet, or Java class, which you can also invoke within your ColdFusion template code. These subjects are not discussed in this book, but they are discussed in great detail in *ColdFusion 8 Web Application Construction Kit, Volume 3: Advanced Application Development*.

Investigating Existing Custom Tags, UDFs, and ColdFusion Components

The ColdFusion Developer's Exchange site is a great place to look for existing custom tags, UDFs, or ColdFusion Components that might help you build your application more quickly. Using these prebuilt extensions to ColdFusion often enables you to get your application finished more easily. Why reinvent the wheel if someone else has already done the work and is willing to share it with you for free (or for a nominal charge)?

The Developer's Exchange is located at `http://www.macromedia.com/cfusion/exchange/index.cfm`.

The Common Function Library Project (`http://www.cflib.org`) is an excellent resource for UDFs. CFCZone (`http://www.cfczone.org`) is a repository of ColdFusion Components.

Searching the ColdFusion Forums

Another good place to go during the planning phase is the Online Support Forums for ColdFusion, where users discuss problems and answer questions for each other. Support engineers from Adobe also participate in the forum discussions.

Try running searches for the type of application you are building or, for specific features you might not have fully formed in your mind yet. It's likely you'll find message threads that discuss various approaches of displaying the type of information you need to present, as well as any pitfalls or gotchas to keep in mind. You'll probably find code snippets and examples you can adapt as well.

The ColdFusion Support Forums are located at `http://www.adobe.com/cfusion/webforums/forum/index.cfm?forumid=1`.

Investigating Standard or Third-Party Extensions

As mentioned, ColdFusion can invoke and communicate with Java classes and .NET objects. ColdFusion can also invoke and communicate with Web Services. You don't have to write Java, C++, or .NET code to use these items; instead, you use them through CFML's `createObject()` function or through the `<cfobject>` tag. The basic idea is the same as when using custom tags: Why reinvent the wheel when someone has already done the work for you?

Therefore, it is worth a quick look on the Internet to see whether third-party Web Services, Java classes, or ActiveX controls are available to help with some part of the functionality your application is meant to provide:

- **Java classes.** It is also worth checking for Java classes that could provide specific chunks of functionality you need. For example, if you need a platform-agnostic way to deal with reading the public keys associated with a server's SSL certificate, you could take a look at the classes provided by the `java.security.cert` package in the standard Java Development Kit (JDK) from `http://www.javasoft.com`. Of course, you could look beyond the JDK as well; a great number of third-party products can be invoked through Java, which generally means you can invoke them via ColdFusion.

- **.NET classes.** ColdFusion 8 adds support for easily creating and working with .NET classes. You can use any .NET object as easily as you would a Java class.

- **Third-party Web Services.** As of this writing, Web Services are really coming into their own as another way of integrating other people's work into your own application. Instead of installing something on your ColdFusion server, you simply access the information exposed by the Web Service over the Internet. Nearly all Web Services can be used via a simple call to the `<cfinvoke>` tag or the `createObject()` function.

NOTE

A complete discussion of how to use these objects in your ColdFusion templates is beyond the scope of this book. See Vol. 3, *Advanced Application Development*, for complete explanations and examples.

Planning the Process

By now, you have probably met with your client a few times and have done your initial research. You have a pretty good idea about what your application is going to be about. You probably also are beginning to have a strong sense about how it will be laid out. In other words, you should be able to see the application in your mind. Time to get that down on paper. Then you can start doing the real work!

Design Documents

Even the most accomplished developers sometimes jump in without writing anything down on paper first. Those same developers will tell you that in most instances, working this way turns out to be a mistake. Sooner or later you realize you forgot some feature your client was expecting. Without documents, whether you really forgot the feature—or whether your client simply didn't mention it—can't be proven. In short, it simply can't hurt to put things down on paper.

Specification Document

At the very least, you should have some type of project specifications document that describes the application in plain English (or whatever) and lists all the critical elements or features. This document should also include approximations of how long you think each item will take to complete.

The document should have a big picture or executive summary portion that, if read by an outsider, will provide an explanation of the project. It should also have a detailed portion that is as specific as possible about individual features.

You also might want the document to prioritize the various elements or features; it could be that a shopping cart and an events calendar are both required elements, but that the events calendar is to be your primary focus. Most importantly, the specifications document should include the expectations that you have agreed upon for the project (see the section "Setting Expectations," earlier in this chapter).

Flowcharts and Storyboards

Depending on the project and your client, you might want to put together some visual aids, such as flowcharts or storyboards, that visually explain the various pages that will make up your application and what elements will be visible on each.

If you own a copy of the software product called Visio, you could use it to lay out flowcharts or storyboards. You could also use just about any other drawing program (such as PowerPoint) or just plain old paper or whiteboards. These flowcharts might be *logical* (mapping out the flow of decisions a template will make or the flow of choices your users might make) or *physical* (representing the pages in your application and the sequence or links from one to the other).

You might even end up with sketches of each page. In any case, be sure the important elements and features from your specification document are represented.

Milestones Document

Just as most therapists stress the importance of setting boundaries in your personal life, most developers recommend establishing *milestones* during the development of an application. Milestones are like checkpoints along the way to an application's completion. You might try to set five milestones, say, each representing approximately 20 percent of the application's features or pages. After each milestone, your client should take a look, give you preliminary feedback, and generally let you know that you are on the right track.

Milestones are good for everyone involved. Your client gets a positive feeling of progress whenever a milestone is reached. You also get a positive feeling of accomplishment, but more importantly, you are ensuring that your client is reasonably satisfied with the development at a number of junctures. This involvement also protects you—if your client has reviewed your progress as you reach these milestones, you know there's little chance of their disliking the whole project at the end because of some misunderstanding.

Planning the Testing Phase

You should now have a good roadmap for the development of your project, in the form of your specifications and milestones documents (see the previous section). Next, you should put together a similar type of roadmap for the testing phase. No matter how great a coder you are, your application is bound to have at least one bug the first time around. It's important that you and your client expect and leave time for some type of beta or testing phase.

Who Can Help with QA?

Somebody should be assigned the job of overseeing quality assurance (QA) for your application. In other words, someone should put the application through its paces to ensure that everything works as intended. Do all the links work? What if certain form fields are left out? What if a user submits a form more than once?

The QA folks also can be the ones ensuring that your application meets all the expectations agreed upon earlier (see the section "Setting Expectations," earlier in this chapter). If you agreed on a maximum download time for modem users, trying some of the pages using a modem can be part of the QA process. If you agreed on Internet Explorer and Netscape compatibility, someone should view the application using each relevant browser.

You also might want to make a list of all the items in your application that should be tested whenever you update the code. That way, your QA team (which might be just you) has a checklist of links, mouse clicks, and form submissions, for example, that must function properly before an iteration of the application can be said to be complete.

Beta Testing

In addition to internal QA work, it's often a good idea to have some kind of semi-public beta test in which real users get to put the application through its paces. Everyday users have a way of finding even the most obscure problems. Navigation elements that seem intuitive to you might be baffling to average folks. They might consistently overlook the most important button on the page, for instance.

Depending on the application, the appropriate beta testers can be select people within the company (perhaps the same folks you interviewed while you were defining the project, as discussed above), or a group of the company's customers. Or you might decide to open the beta site to the general public. There are also a variety of automated load-testing tools available that can test how your application will perform when used by many users at once.

Tracking Bug Reports

You might want to set up a way for people to report bugs in the application so that a list of unresolved issues will exist in a central place. Doing so will also keep your client off your back as you complete the project. Let's face it: People like to see progress. Anyone who can report bugs through some type of official channel—and see that the bug has been fixed a few days later—will be impressed with your professionalism.

You can approach bug tracking in many ways. Various commercial project-management applications include bug-tracking functionality. You can also find open source projects that provide bug tracking: for example, Lighthouse Pro (`http://lighthousepro.riaforge.org`).

➜ If you do create a Web-based bug tracker, you could include a link to it whenever a ColdFusion error message gets displayed for whatever reason. See "Customizing the Look of Error Messages" in Chapter 19, "Introducing the Web Application Framework," for details.

Separate Development Environment

Plan to have a separate development environment (server or set of servers) that will be used only by you and the rest of your development team, if there is one. While your QA people are checking out the application and finding bugs, you can be working on those bugs without worrying whether the QA people can still work while you're making changes. Many people achieve this by installing a private copy of the ColdFusion server and database server on their own workstations. Performance might not be optimal, but it is usually fine for development.

Staging/Production

Most developers recommend having separate staging and production environments. The *staging* environment is a server or set of servers your client visits to review your progress. It's also the server your QA or beta users visit. The *production* server is where the final code goes after everyone is satisfied with it, and it is the server your actual end users visit. Any updates to the code are made first to staging tested there, and then moved to production.

Ideally, the staging and production environments should be as identical as possible (same hardware, same software versions, and so on), so no surprise incompatibilities or other issues occur.

While You Are Working

The last thing to plan before you start coding is how you will continue to document the project as you go along. After all, if you've worked to create all those great flowcharts and other design documents, it would be silly to not keep them up to date while you work.

Charting Page Flow

One of the most valuable things to have at any time is an up-to-date list of important pages and the links between them. Dreamweaver CS3 can help you with this by letting you organize your application files maintaining links between all the templates in your project. But sometimes there's just no replacement for a proper paper document (perhaps a Visio drawing) that you can keep pegged to your wall for reference.

If you keep your page-flow document up to date throughout, you'll have that much more to refer to if you need to make adjustments to the application a year from now. And let's not forget that clients and bosses always like to see documents with recent dates on them, no matter what's actually in the documents.

Include Files and Custom Tags

Another handy document to keep current while you work is a list of include files and custom tags. You learned about include files in Chapter 9, "Programming with CFML," and you will learn about custom tags in Chapter 26. Although both types of files are handy because they enable you to isolate and reuse your code, it can be easy to forget which files rely on which other files. A simple spreadsheet or document that keeps track of these interdependencies can really help.

Commenting Style

Throughout this book, we encourage you to comment your code as much as possible. Any code, ColdFusion or otherwise, is a hundred times more valuable if it is thoroughly commented. And it becomes a *thousand* times more valuable if all the code for an application is commented in a consistent style.

You should decide ahead of time how you will comment your code, and stick to it while you work. For instance, you might make resolutions like these:

- Each .cfm file should have a header comment that lists the purpose of the file, when it was first written, and the original author's name.

- When anyone makes a significant change to the file, the header comment should be amended, explaining which portions were added or changed. Over time, you'll develop a detailed revision history for each file.

- The header comment should list the variables used within the template and what they are for. If the file is a custom tag, each attribute should be listed and explained.

- Each significant change or addition to a file should be noted in place with an explanation, date, and the developer's initials.

- There should be at least one line of comment before each CFML tag—perhaps a few exceptions can be made for self-explanatory tags such as <CFOUTPUT>, however.

Naming Conventions

Some developers are strict about naming conventions—for very good reason. We're not going to suggest any specific sets of naming conventions here because different people have different ideas about what makes sense. It's something you and your team should decide for yourselves.

That said, here are a few ideas:

- Because short variable names can result in cryptic-looking code, you might require that every variable name consist of at least two words, with the first letter of each word in uppercase. So instead of variable names such as tot and fn, you would have names such as CurrentTotal and FirstName.

- Many coders like to use the first letter of each variable's name to suggest the type of information the variable will hold. For example, you could use sFirstName and sShipAddress instead of FirstName and ShipAddress to instantly see that the actual values will be strings. Similarly, you might use dFirstVisit for dates and nCurrentPrice or iProductsOrdered for numbers. You also could use similar naming conventions for the columns in your database tables.

- Similarly, some people find that having the names of their database tables start with a t or tbl, such as tCustomers or tblCustomers, is useful. Sometimes people also choose to come up with a convention to indicate the relationship between related tables, such as calling a table tCustomers_Orders or rCustomers2Orders if the table relates rows from the tCustomers and tOrders tables.

- Some developers like to put all forms into a separate include file and start the file name with frm, as in frmNewUser.cfm or perhaps frm_NewUser.cfm. Other people do something similar with each <cfquery> tag, ending up with files with names such as qryGetDirectors and so on. See Chapter 54, "Development Methodologies," online, for more information.

Keeping the Directory Structure in Mind

There are no hard and fast rules about how to organize your ColdFusion templates and other files into folders, but you should put some real thought into it and come up with a scheme that makes sense to you.

Here are some things to keep in mind:

- Make every effort to keep the directory structure of your application as organized as possible. For instance, it often makes sense to have a folder that corresponds to each high-level section of the site (the sections that appear on your main navigation bar, or the sections accessible from the application's home page).

- Folders are like friends. Unless they are too full of themselves, the more you have, the better. It is almost always better to have lots of directories with relatively few files in them, rather than a few directories with hundreds of files in each.

- Decide where your images and other media files will be kept. For instance, this book calls for keeping them all in a single folder named images. You might decide to maintain a number of subfolders within images. Of course, you could also decide to use an entirely different strategy, perhaps keeping your image files in the same folders as the templates that use them. Just choose a method and stick with it.

- In general, it is most convenient to use long, descriptive file names. However, if you will be displaying a link to a particular template many, many times on a page (for each record in a database, say), a long file name might add to the size of the final HTML code your template generates. Try to use somewhat shorter file names for templates that will be linked to extremely often. The same goes for images that will be included in pages frequently.

TIP

The Yahoo! site is a good place to look for an example of a site that uses a very sensible, hierarchical URL structure, but where each portion of the URL is kept very short (often just a letter or two).

Moving Targets and Feature Creep

Unless you are particularly blessed by the gods of application development, you will deal with the twin evils of *Moving Targets* and *Feature Creep*. These scorned, ugly creatures are sometimes so filthy and wretched as to be barely distinguishable from one another. Moving Targets, of course, are those aspects of an application that your client keeps changing their mind about from one day to the next.

Feature Creep is what happens if little extra features keep getting piled onto the application while you work. Either one will keep you from getting your project done on time.

On the other hand, it's only natural that the best suggestions and most exciting "Eureka!" moments will come while the application is being built. Development is a creative process, and you or others might stumble upon a really brilliant idea that must be in there. Therefore, you should plan on making a few concessions or adjustments during the development process. Have some type of agreement in place about how to deal with incoming ideas.

CHAPTER 19

Introducing the Web Application Framework

ColdFusion provides a small but very important set of features for building sophisticated Web applications. The features have to do with making all your ColdFusion templates for a particular site or project behave as if they were related to one another—that is, to make them behave as a single application. These features are referred to collectively as the Web application framework.

The Web application framework is designed to help you with the following:

- **Consistent look and feel.** The application framework enables you to easily include a consistent header or footer at the top and bottom of every page in your application. It also lets you apply the same look and feel to user error messages. You can also use it to keep things like fonts and headings consistent from page to page.

- **Sharing variables between pages.** So far, the variables you have worked with in this book all "die" when each page request has been processed. The Web application framework gives you a variety of ways to maintain the values of variables between page requests. The variables can be maintained on a per-user, per-session, or application-wide basis.

- **Before and after processing.** The application framework gives you an easy way to execute custom code you want just *before* each page request. A common use for this capability is to provide password security for your application. You can also execute custom code just *after* the request. Along with executing code before and after a request, you can execute code when the application starts and when it expires. This lets you specify application-wide variables when it starts up, and doing cleanup once the application expires.

- **Handling errors.** In a perfect world, developers would never make mistakes, but for those of us who live in this world, mistakes happen. The application framework provides a simple way to handle errors. It also handles requests for missing ColdFusion templates.

Considered together, it's the Web application framework that really lets you present a Web experience to your users. Without these features, your individual templates would always stand on their own, acting as little mini-programs. The framework is the force that binds your templates together.

Using `Application.cfc`

To get started with the Web application framework, you first must create a special file called `Application.cfc`. In most respects, this file is just an ordinary ColdFusion component. (Components are discussed in depth in Chapter 26, "Building Reusable Components," in *ColdFusion 8 Web Application Construction Kit, Volume 2: Application Development*.) Only two things make `Application.cfc` special:

- The code in your `Application.cfc` file will be automatically executed just before any of your application pages.

- You can't visit an `Application.cfc` page directly. If you attempt to visit an `Application.cfc` page with a browser, you will receive an error message from ColdFusion.

The `Application.cfc` file is sometimes referred to as the application component. It might not sound all that special so far, but you will find that the two special properties actually go a long way toward making your applications more cohesive and easier to develop.

NOTE

On Unix/Linux systems, file names are case sensitive. The `Application.cfc` file must be spelled exactly as shown here, using a capital A. Even if you are doing your development with Windows systems in mind, pay attention to the case so ColdFusion will be capable of finding the file if you decide to move your application to a Linux or Unix server later.

NOTE

Previous versions of ColdFusion used another file, `Application.cfm`, to enable the application framework. This still works in the current version of ColdFusion. However, the use of `Application.cfc` is now recommended instead of `Application.cfm`.

Placement of `Application.cfc`

As we said, the code in your `Application.cfc` file is automatically executed just before each of the pages that make up your application. You might be wondering how exactly ColdFusion does this. How will it know which files make up your application and which ones don't?

The answer is quite simple: Whenever a user visits a `.cfm` page, ColdFusion looks to see whether a file named `Application.cfc` exists in the same directory as the requested page. If so, ColdFusion automatically executes it. Later on, you'll see exactly which methods of the CFC are executed.

If no `Application.cfc` exists in the same folder as the requested page, ColdFusion looks in that folder's parent folder. If no `Application.cfc` file exists there, it looks in *that* parent's folder, and so on, until there are no more parent folders to look in.

All this means is that you should do something you were probably already going to do anyway, namely, put all the ColdFusion templates for a particular application within a single folder, somewhere within your Web server's document root. Let's call that directory your application folder.

Within the application folder, you can organize your ColdFusion templates any way you choose, using any number of subfolders, sub-subfolders, and so on. If you put an Application.cfc file in the application folder, it will be executed when any the application's templates are run. It's that simple.

For instance, consider the fictional folder structure shown in Figure 19.1. Here, the application folder is the folder named MyApp, which is sitting within the Web server's document root. Some basic Web pages are located in there, such as the company's Home page (Index.cfm), a How To Contact Us page (ContactUs.cfm), and a Company Info page (CompanyInfo.cfm). There is also a SiteHeader.cfm template there, which we intend to include at the top of each page.

Because a file called Application.cfc also exists in this folder, it's automatically included every time a user visits Index.cfm or ContactUs.cfm. It's also included whenever a user visits any of the Cold-Fusion templates stored in the Intranet or Store folders, or any of the subfolders of the Intranet folder. No matter how deep the subfolder structure gets, the Application.cfc file in the MyApp folder will be automatically included.

NOTE

Don't worry about re-creating this folder structure yourself. None of the code examples for this chapter rely on it. We're just trying to clarify where your Application.cfc template might go in a real-world application.

Figure 19.1

The Application .cfc file gets included before any of your application's templates.

Application.cfc **Structure**

As you will learn in Chapter 26, "Building Reusable Components," a ColdFusion Component is a collection of methods and data. You can think of it as a package of information (the data) and things you can do with the information (the methods). The Application.cfc file lets you do just that—create both data and methods. However, some methods are special. For example, if you create a method called onRequestStart, the method will execute before each and every page request. Table 19.1 lists these methods and how they work. Later in the chapter we will demonstrate how these work.

Table 19.1 Application.cfc Methods

METHOD	PURPOSE
onApplicationStart	Run when the application begins. This will run the first time a user executes a page inside the application. This method can be used to initialize application variables.

Table 19.1 (CONTINUED)

onApplicationEnd	Executed when the application ends. All applications have a timeout, defined either by the application itself or the default application timeout value specified in the ColdFusion Administrator. An application times out when no one requests a file. You can use this method to record the status of application variables to a database, log to a file, or even send an email notifying you that the application has timed out.
onRequestStart	Executed before each page request. This could be used to specify Request scoped variables needed for pages in the application, check security credentials, or perform other checks that need to happen on every page request.
onRequestEnd	Executed before each page request. This could be used to specify Request scoped variables needed for pages in the application, check security credentials, or perform other checks that need to happen on every page request.
onRequest	Executed immediately after onRequestStart. Can be used to filter requests and modify the result.
onSessionStart	Executed when a user's session starts. Sessions are covered in Chapter 20, "Working with Sessions."
onSessionEnd	Executed when a user's session ends.
onError	Executed when an error occurs. This will be covered in greater depth later in the chapter.
onMissingTemplate	Executed when a request for a ColdFusion template is made and that template does not exist.

In our examples for this chapter, we will focus mainly on the onApplicationStart, onRequestStart, onError, and onMissingTemplate methods. Chapter 20 will cover onSessionStart and onSessionEnd.

A Basic Application.cfc Template

Take a look at Listing 19.1, a simple Application.cfc file. This example makes use of the onRequestStart method. Because the two <cfset> tags are executed before each page request, the dataSource and companyName variables can be referred to within any of the application's ColdFusion templates. For instance, the value of the dataSource variable will always be ows.

If you save this listing, be sure to save it as Application.cfc, not Application1.cfc.

Listing 19.1 Application1.cfc—A Simple Application Template

```
<!---
  Filename: Application.cfc (The "Application Component")
  Created by: Raymond Camden (ray@camdenfamily.com)
  Purpose: Sets "constant" variables and includes consistent header
--->

<cfcomponent output="false">
```

Listing 19.1 (CONTINUED)

```
    <cffunction name="onRequestStart" returnType="boolean" output="true">
        <!--- Any variables set here can be used by all our pages --->
        <cfset REQUEST.dataSource = "ows">
        <cfset REQUEST.companyName = "Orange Whip Studios">

        <!--- Display our Site Header at top of every page --->
        <cfinclude template="SiteHeader.cfm">

        <cfreturn true>
    </cffunction>

</cfcomponent>
```

As you will learn in Chapter 26, all components begin and end with the `<cfcomponent>` tag. This component only uses one method, `onRequestStart`. This method will execute before each request. The method begins by defining two REQUEST scope variables, `dataSource` and `companyName`.

In addition, the `<cfinclude>` tag in Listing 19.1 ensures that the company's standard page header will be shown at the top of each page. Listing 19.2 shows the `SiteHeader.cfm` template itself. Note that it can use the `CompanyName` variable that gets set by `Application.cfc`.

If this were your application, you would no longer have to put that `<cfinclude>` tag at the top of the `Index.cfm` or `CompanyInfo.cfm` pages (see Figure 19.1), and you wouldn't have to remember to include it in any new templates. ColdFusion would now be taking care of that for you.

Listing 19.2 `SiteHeader.cfm`—Simple Header Included on Each Page

```
<!---
 Filename: SiteHeader.cfm
 Created by: Nate Weiss (NMW)
 Please Note Included in every page by Application.cfc
--->

<html>
<head>
<title><cfoutput>#REQUEST.companyName#</cfoutput></title>
<style>
.header {
  font-size: 18px;
  font-family: sans-serif;
}
.footer {
  font-size: 10px;
  color: silver;
  font-family: sans-serif;
}
body {
  font-family: sans-serif;
}
.error {
  color: gray;
}
```

Listing 19.2 (CONTINUED)

```
    </style>
    </head>

    <body>

    <!--- Company Logo --->
    <img src="../images/logo_c.gif" width="101" height="101" alt=""
        align="absmiddle" border="0">
    <cfoutput><span class="header">#REQUEST.companyName#</span></cfoutput>
    <br clear="left">
```

Using onRequestEnd()

The Web application framework also reserves the special OnRequestEnd method, which is executed automatically at the end of every page request, rather than at the beginning. Listing 19.3 is a modification of Listing 19.1. This time our Application.cfc includes an onRequestEnd method. It has just one line of code, a simple <cfinclude> tag to include the SiteFooter.cfm template at the bottom of every page. Listing 19.4 shows the SiteFooter.cfm file itself, which displays a copyright notice. The net effect is that the copyright notice is displayed at the bottom of every page in the application, as shown in Figure 19.2.

Figure 19.2

The application framework makes it easy to keep things consistent throughout your site.

Of course, there are other ways to get this effect. You could forget about this OnRequestEnd() business and just put the <cfinclude> tag at the bottom of every page in your application. But that might be tedious, and you might occasionally forget to do it. Or, you could just put the copyright notice in the OnRequestEnd method and get rid of the SiteFooter.cfm file altogether. That would be fine, but leaving them in separate files keeps things more manageable if the footer becomes more complicated in the future.

If you save Listing 19.3, be sure to save it as Application.cfc, not Application2.cfc.

Listing 9.3 Application2.cfc—Including a Site Footer at the Bottom of Every Page

```
<!---
 Filename: Application.cfc (The "Application Component")
 Created by: Raymond Camden (ray@camdenfamily.com)
 Purpose: Sets "constant" variables and includes consistent header
--->

<cfcomponent output="false">

  <cffunction name="onRequestStart" returnType="boolean" output="true">
    <!--- Any variables set here can be used by all our pages --->
    <cfset REQUEST.dataSource = "ows">
    <cfset REQUEST.companyName = "Orange Whip Studios">

    <!--- Display our Site Header at top of every page --->
    <cfinclude template="SiteHeader.cfm">

    <cfreturn true>
  </cffunction>

  <cffunction name="onRequestEnd" returnType="void" output="true">

      <!--- Display our Site Footer at bottom of every page --->
      <cfinclude template="SiteFooter.cfm">

  </cffunction>

</cfcomponent>
```

Listing 19.4 SiteFooter.cfm—Simple Footer That Gets Included by OnRequestEnd()

```
<!---
 Filename: SiteFooter.cfm
 Created by: Nate Weiss (NMW)
 Please Note Included in every page by OnRequestEnd.cfm
--->

<!--- Display copyright notice at bottom of every page --->
<cfoutput>
  <p class="footer">
  (c) #year(now())# #REQUEST.companyName#. All rights reserved.
  </p></cfoutput>

</body>
</html>
```

NOTE

The expression #year(now())# is a simple way to display the current year. You also could use #dateFormat(now(),"yyyy")# to get the same effect.

Listing 19.5 provides preliminary code for Orange Whip Studio's home page. As you can see, it's just a simple message that welcomes the user to the site. Of course, in practice, this is where you would provide links to all the interesting parts of the application. The point of this template is to demonstrate that the site header and footer are now going to be automatically included at the top and bottom of all ordinary ColdFusion templates in this folder (or its subfolders), as shown in Figure 19.2. Note that this template is also able to use the REQUEST.companyName variable that was set in the Application.cfc file.

If you save this file, be sure to save it as index.cfm, not index1.cfm.

Listing 19.5 Index1.cfm—A Basic Home Page for Orange Whip Studios

```
<!---
 Filename: Index.cfm
 Created by: Nate Weiss (NMW)
 Please Note Header and Footer are automatically provided
--->

<cfoutput>
<blockquote>
<p>Hello, and welcome to the home of
#REQUEST.companyName# on the web! We certainly
hope you enjoy your visit. We take pride in
producing movies that are almost as good
as the ones they are copied from. We've
been doing it for years. On this site, you'll
be able to find out about all our classic films
from the golden age of Orange Whip Studios,
as well as our latest and greatest new releases.
Have fun!
</blockquote>
</cfoutput>
```

Using Application Variables

So far in this chapter, you have seen how ColdFusion's Web application framework features help you maintain a consistent look and feel throughout your application. You've also seen how easy it is to set up "before and after" processing with the special Application.cfc component and the onRequestStart and onRequestEnd methods. In other words, your pages are starting to look and behave cohesively.

Next, you will learn how your application's templates can start sharing variables between page requests. Basically, this is the part where your application gets a piece of the server's memory in which to store values. This is where it gets a brain.

What Are Application Variables?

Pretend it's Oscar season. Orange Whip Studios feels that all of its films are contenders. Tensions are high, and the president wants a new "Featured Movie" box on the studio's home page to help create more "buzz" than its bitter rival, Miramax. The featured movie should be different each time the home page is viewed, shamelessly rotating through all of the studio's movies. It's your job to get this project done, pronto.

Hmmm. You could retrieve all the movies from the database for each page request and somehow pick one at random, but that wouldn't guarantee that the same movie wouldn't get picked three or four times in a row. What you want is some way to remember your current spot in the list of movies, so they all get shown evenly, in order. You consider making a table to remember which movies have been shown and then deleting all rows from the table when it's time to rotate through them again, but that seems like overkill. You wish there was some kind of variable that would persist between page requests, instead of dying at the bottom of each page like the ColdFusion variables you're used to.

Well, that's exactly what application variables are for. Instead of setting a variable called `lastMovieID`, you could call it `APPLICATION.lastMovieID`. After you set this variable value to 5, say, it remains set at 5 until you change it again (or until the server is restarted). In essence, application variables let you set aside a little piece of ColdFusion's memory that your application can use for its own purposes.

When to Use Application Variables

Generally, you can use application variables whenever you need a variable to be shared among all pages and all visitors to your application. The variable is kept in ColdFusion's memory, and any page in your application can access or change its value. If some code on one of your pages changes the value of an application variable, the next hit to any of your application's pages will reflect the new value.

NOTE

This means you should not use application variables if you want a separate copy of the variable to exist for each visitor to your site. In other words, application variables shouldn't be used for anything personalized, because they don't distinguish between your site's visitors.

→ Chapter 20 explains how to create variables that are maintained separately for each visitor.

Consider application variables for:

- Rotating banner ads evenly, so that all ads get shown the same number of times

- Rotating other types of content, such as the featured movie problem mentioned previously, or products that might be on sale

- Keeping counters of various types of events, such as the number of people currently online or the number of hits since the server was started

- Maintaining some type of information that changes only occasionally or perhaps doesn't change at all, but can take time to compute or retrieve

Do *not* use application variables for per-user tasks, such as these:

- Maintaining a shopping cart

- Remembering a user's email address or username from visit to visit

- Keeping a history of the pages a user has visited while he has been on your site

Using the `Application.cfc` Component

We've already discussed the special purpose of the `Application.cfc` file. What we didn't mention was that by including an `Application.cfc` file, you automatically enable the use of Application variables. Application variables are one type of persistent variable; you will learn about two other types—client and session variables—in Chapter 20.

So far, the example `Application.cfc` files we have shown have only demonstrated methods. Components can also contain data. There are two main scopes in a component used to store data: `VARIABLES` and `THIS`. Earlier we mentioned that components can use any method names you want. But in the `Application.cfc` component, some method names were special. The same applies to the `THIS` scope. By setting particular values in the `THIS` scope you can control how the application behaves. For now we will focus on just two of those values, demonstrated in Table 19.2.

Table 19.2   `THIS` Scope Values Relevant to Application Variables

ATTRIBUTE	DESCRIPTION
name	A name for your application. The name can be anything you want, up to 64 characters long. ColdFusion uses this name internally to store and look up your application variables for you. It should be unique by server.
applicationTimeout	Optional. How long you want your application variables to live in the server's memory. If you don't provide this value, it defaults to whatever is set up in the Memory Variables page of the ColdFusion Administrator. See the section "Application Variable Timeouts," later in this chapter. The maximum value can't be higher than the maximum value specified in the Memory Variables page of the ColdFusion Administrator.

NOTE

ColdFusion maintains your application variables based on the `THIS scopes NAME` value. Therefore, it's important that no other applications on the same ColdFusion server use the same `NAME`. If they do, ColdFusion will consider them to be the same application and will share the variables among all the combined pages. Changing a variable in one also changes it in the other, and so on. It's conceivable to find yourself in a situation where this is actually what you want (if for some reason all the pages in your application simply can't be nested within a single folder); otherwise, make sure that each `Application.cfc`'s `THIS scope` gets its own `NAME`.

Using Application Variables

Now that application variables have been enabled, using them is quite simple. Basically, you create or set an application variable the same way you would set a normal variable, generally using the `<cfset>` tag. The only difference is the presence of the word `APPLICATION`, followed by a dot. For instance, the following line would set the `APPLICATION.ourHitCount` variable to `0`. The variable would then be available to all pages in the application and would hold the value of `0` until it was changed:

```
<cfset APPLICATION.ourHitCount = 0>
```

You can use application variables in any of the same places you would use ordinary ones. For instance, the following code adds one to an application variable and then outputs the new value, rounded to the nearest thousandth:

```
<cfset APPLICATION.ourHitCount = APPLICATION.ourHitCount + 1>
<cfoutput>#round(APPLICATION.ourHitCount / 1000)># thousand</cfoutput>
```

You also can use application variables with ColdFusion tags, such as <cfif>, <cfparam>, and <cfoutput>. See Chapter 8, "The Basics of ColdFusion," and Chapter 9, "Programming with CFML," if you want to review the use of variables in general.

Initializing Application Variables

Application variables are persistent. That simply means that once you create them, they stick around. Because of this, there is no reason to set them on every request. Once you create an Application variable, you don't need to create it. Once simple way to handle that would be with the isDefined() function.

```
<cfif not isDefined("APPLICATION.dsn")>
  <cfset APPLICATION.dsn = "ows">
</cfif>
```

This code will check to see if the variable, APPLICATION.dsn exists. If it doesn't, it will create it. However, the Application.cfc component provides an even easier way to do this. One of the special methods mention in Table 19.1 is the onApplicationStart() method. This method will execute only when the application starts. Conversely, there is also an onApplicationEnd() method. This could be used to do a variety of things. Listing 19.6 shows a newer version of the Application.cfc worked on earlier.

If you save this file, be sure to save it as Application.cfc, not Application3.cfc.

Listing 19.6 Application3.cfc—Using onApplicationStart and onApplicationEnd

```
<!---
  Filename: Application.cfc (The "Application Component")
  Created by: Raymond Camden (ray@camdenfamily.com)
  Purpose: Sets "constant" variables and includes consistent header
--->

<cfcomponent output="false">

  <cfset THIS.name = "ows19">

  <cffunction name="onApplicationStart" returnType="boolean" output="false">
    <!--- When did the application start? --->
    <cfset APPLICATION.appStarted = now()>

    <cfreturn true>
  </cffunction>

  <cffunction name="onApplicationEnd" returnType="void" output="false">
    <cfargument name="appScope" required="true">
```

Listing 19.6 (CONTINUED)

```
        <!--- Log how many minutes the application stayed alive --->
        <cflog file="#THIS.name#" text=
"App ended after #dateDiff('n',ARGUMENTS.appScope.appStarted,now())# minutes.">

    </cffunction>

    <cffunction name="onRequestStart" returnType="boolean" output="true">
        <!--- Any variables set here can be used by all our pages --->
        <cfset request.dataSource = "ows">
        <cfset request.companyName = "Orange Whip Studios">

        <!--- Display our Site Header at top of every page --->
        <cfinclude template="SiteHeader.cfm">

        <cfreturn true>
    </cffunction>

    <cffunction name="onRequestEnd" returnType="void" output="true">

    <!--- Display our Site Footer at bottom of every page --->
    <cfinclude template="SiteFooter.cfm">

    </cffunction>

</cfcomponent>
```

There's a lot of new code here, so let's tackle it bit by bit. The first new line is:

```
<cfset THIS.name = "ows19">
```

This line uses the THIS scope to name the application. Remember, every name for your application should be unique. If you use the same name for multiple Application.cfc files, they will essentially act as the same application. Notice that this line of code is outside any method. This line will be run when the Application.cfc file is loaded by ColdFusion.

The next set of new code is the onApplicationStart method. This method really does only one thing: it creates a variable called APPLICATION.appStarted initialized with the current time. The idea is to simply store the time the application started. ColdFusion automatically calls this method when the application is first started by a user. You don't have to do anything special to enable this function—ColdFusion handles it for you.

Next we have the onApplicationEnd method. This method will fire when the application ends. Normally the only way to execute ColdFusion code automatically is with the ColdFusion Scheduler. Outside of that, ColdFusion code only executes when someone requests a file. The onApplicationEnd method (as well as the onSessionEnd method) runs without anyone actually requesting a ColdFusion document.

That said, you can't output anything from this method. Even if you did, no one could see it! What you can do is clean up the application. This can include logging information to a database or file, firing off an email, or doing any number of things that would make sense when an application ends. Let's examine the method line by line. The first line is:

```
<cfargument name="appScope" required="true">
```

This simply defines an argument sent to the method. In our case, the ColdFusion server automatically sends a copy of the Application scope (all the data you stored in it) to the onApplicationEnd method. This is important. You can't access the APPLICATION scope they way you can normally. Instead, you have to use the copy passed in the method. The next line will show an example of this:

```
<cflog file="#THIS.name#" text=
"App ended after #dateDiff('n',ARGUMENTS.appScope.appStarted,now())# minutes.">
```

The <cflog> tag simply logs information to a file. We are only using two of the attributes in this line. The file attribute simply tells <cflog> what name to use for the file. When providing a file name, you don't add the ".log" to the name; <cflog> will do that for you. In our code, we use the value of the Application's name. Recall that we set the name using the THIS scope earlier in the component. The text attribute defines what is sent to the file. If you remember, we stored the time the application loaded in a variable called APPLICATION.appStarted. As we said above, we can't access the Application scope in the onApplicationEnd method. Instead, we have to use the copy passed in. We called this argument appScope, so we can access our original value as ARGUMENTS.appScope.appStarted. We use the dateDiff function to return the number of minutes between when the application started and the current time. This lets us log the total time the application was running before it timed out.

The rest of the file simply duplicates the onRequestStart and onRequestEnd methods we described earlier.

Putting Application Variables to Work

Application variables can make it relatively easy to get the little featured movie widget up and running. Again, the idea is for a callout-style box, which cycles through each of Orange Whip Studio's films, to display on the site's home page. The box should change each time the page is accessed, rotating evenly through all the movies.

Listing 19.7 shows one simple way to get this done, using application variables. Note that the template is broken into two separate parts. The first half is the interesting part, in which an application variable called MovieList is used to rotate the featured movie correctly. The second half simply outputs the name and description to the page.

Listing 19.7 FeaturedMovie.cfm—Using Application Variables to Track Content Rotation

```
<!---
 Filename: FeaturedMovie.cfm
 Created by: Nate Weiss (NMW)
 Purpose: Displays a single movie on the page, on a rotating basis
 Please Note Application variables must be enabled
--->

<!--- List of movies to show (list starts out empty) --->
<cfparam name="APPLICATION.movieList" type="string" default="">

<!--- If this is the first time we're running this, --->
<!--- Or we have run out of movies to rotate through --->
<cfif listLen(APPLICATION.movieList) eq 0>
```

Listing 19.7 (CONTINUED)

```
<!--- Get all current FilmIDs from the database --->
<cfquery name="getFilmIDs" datasource="#REQUEST.dataSource#">
SELECT FilmID FROM Films
ORDER BY MovieTitle
</cfquery>

<!--- Turn FilmIDs into a simple comma-separated list --->
<cfset APPLICATION.movieList = valueList(getFilmIDs.FilmID)>
</cfif>

<!--- Pick the first movie in the list to show right now --->
<cfset thisMovieID = listFirst(APPLICATION.MovieList)>
<!--- Re-save the list, as all movies *except* the first --->
<cfset APPLICATION.movieList = listRest(APPLICATION.movieList)>
<!--- Now that we have chosen the film to "Feature", --->
<!--- Get all important info about it from database. --->
<cfquery name="GetFilm" datasource="#REQUEST.dataSource#">
 SELECT
 MovieTitle, Summary, Rating,
 AmountBudgeted, DateInTheaters
 FROM Films f, FilmsRatings r
 WHERE FilmID = #thisMovieID#
 AND f.RatingID = r.RatingID
</cfquery>

<!--- Now Display Our Featured Movie --->
<cfoutput>
 <!--- Define formatting for our "feature" display --->
 <style type="text/css">
 TH.fm { background:RoyalBlue;color:white;text-align:left;
 font-family:sans-serif;font-size:10px}
 TD.fm { background:LightSteelBlue;
 font-family:sans-serif;font-size:12px}
 </style>

 <!--- Show info about featured movie in HTML Table --->
 <table width="150" align="right" border="0" cellspacing="0">
 <tr><th class="fm">
 Featured Film
 </th></tr>
 <!--- Movie Title, Summary, Rating --->
 <tr><td class="fm">
 <b>#getFilm.MovieTitle#</b><br>
 #getFilm.Summary#<br>
 <p align="right">Rated: #getFilm.Rating#</p>
 </td></tr>
 <!--- Cost (rounded to millions), release date --->
 <tr><th class="fm">
 Production Cost $#round(getFilm.AmountBudgeted / 1000000)# Million<br>
 In Theaters #dateFormat(getFilm.DateInTheaters, "mmmm d")#<br>
 </th></tr>
 </table>
 <br clear="all">
</cfoutput>
```

As you can see, the top half of the template is pretty simple. The idea is to use an application variable called `movieList` to hold a list of available movies. If 20 movies are in the database, the list holds 20 movie IDs at first. The first time the home page is visited, the first movie is featured and then removed from the list, leaving 19 movies in the list. The next time, the second movie is featured (leaving 18), and so on until all the movies have been featured. Then the process begins again.

Looking at the code line by line, you can see how this actually happens:

The `<cfparam>` tag is used to set the `APPLICATION.movieList` variable to an empty string if it doesn't exist already. Because the variable will essentially live forever once set, this line has an effect only the first time this template runs (until the server is restarted). This line could be moved to the `onApplicationStart` method of the `Application.cfc` file. We are keeping it here to make it a bit simpler to see what is going on with this template.

The `<cfif>` tag is used to test whether the `movieList` variable is currently empty. It is empty if this is the first time the template has run or if all the available movies have been featured in rotation already. If the list is empty, it is filled with the list of current movie IDs. Getting the current list is a simple two-step process of querying the database and then using the `valueList` function to create the list from the query results.

The `listFirst()` function is used to get the first movie's ID from the list. The value is placed in the `thisMovieID` variable. This is the movie to feature on the page.

Finally, the `listRest()` function is used to chop off the first movie ID from the `APPLICATION.movieList` variable. The variable now holds one fewer movie. Eventually, its length will dwindle to zero, in which case the `<cfif>` tag will again test whether the `movieList` variable is currently empty, repeating the cycle.

Now that the movie to be featured has been picked (its in the `thisMovieID` variable), actually displaying the movie's name and other information is straightforward. The `<cfquery>` in the second half of Listing 19.7 selects the necessary information from the database, and then a simple HTML table is used to display the movie in a nicely formatted box.

At this point, Listing 19.7 can be visited on its own, but it was really meant to show the featured movie on Orange Whip's home page. Simply include the template using the `<cfinclude>` tag, as shown in Listing 19.8.

Figure 19.3 shows the results.

Listing 19.8 `Index2.cfm`—Including the Featured Movie in the Company's Home Page

```
<!---
 Filename: Index.cfm
 Created by: Nate Weiss (NMW)
 Please Note Header and Footer are automatically provided
--->

<cfoutput>
 <p>Hello, and welcome to the home of
```

```
#REQUEST.companyName# on the web! We certainly
hope you enjoy your visit. We take pride in
producing movies that are almost as good
as the ones they are copied from. We've
been doing it for years. On this site, you'll
be able to find out about all our classic films
from the golden age of Orange Whip Studios,
as well as our latest and greatest new releases.
Have fun!<br>
</cfoutput>

<!--- Show a "Featured Movie" --->
<cfinclude template="FeaturedMovie.cfm">
```

Figure 19.3

Application variables enable the featured movie to be rotated evenly among all page requests.

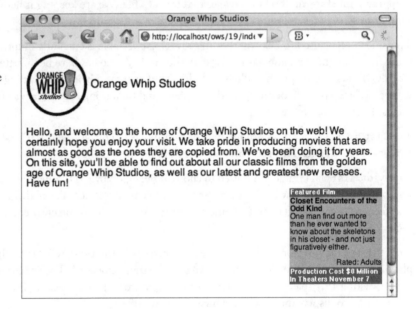

Customizing the Look of Error Messages

The Web application framework provides a simple way to customize the look of error messages that can occur while users are accessing your pages. As you know, error messages might appear because of syntax problems in your code, because of database connection problems, or just because users have left out one or more required fields while filling out a form.

The application framework lets you customize any of these error messages. You can even hide them from the user's view entirely if you want. This enables you to maintain a consistent look and feel throughout your application, even when those dreaded error messages occur. You even have multiple ways to handle exceptions. We will cover both, dealing with the simplest solution first.

Introducing the `<cferror>` Tag

You use the `<cferror>` tag to specify how error messages should be displayed. Customizing the error messages that appear throughout your application is generally a two-step process:

1. First, you create an *error display template*, which displays the error message along with whatever graphics or other formatting you consider appropriate.

2. Next, you include a `<cferror>` tag that tells ColdFusion to display errors using the error display template you just created. In general, you place the `<cferror>` tag in your `Application.cfc` file.

Table 19.3 shows the attributes supported by the `<cferror>` tag.

The next two sections discuss how to customize the error messages displayed for *exception errors* (syntax errors, database errors, and so on) and *validation errors* (when the user fails to fill out a form correctly).

Table 19.3   `<cferror>` Tag Attributes

ATTRIBUTE	DESCRIPTION
type	The type of error you want to catch and display using your customized error display template. The allowable values are `Request`, `Validation`, and `Exception`. The `Validation` type is no longer recommended for use and will not be covered. If you don't supply this attribute, it is assumed to be `Request`, but it's best to always supply it.
template	Required. The relative path and file name of your customized error display template. You specify the file name in the same way as you would specify an include file with the `<cfinclude>` tag.
mailto	Optional. An email address for a site administrator that the user could use to send some type of notification that the error occurred. The only purpose of this attribute is to pass an appropriate email address to your error display template. It doesn't actually send any email messages on its own.
exception	Optional. The specific exception that you want to catch and display using your customized error display template. The default value is `Any`, which is appropriate for most circumstances. See Chapter 51, "Error Handling," online, for a discussion of the other values you can supply here.

Request vs. Exception Error Templates

If you want to customize the way error messages are displayed, you first must create an error display template. This template is displayed to the user whenever a page request can't be completed because of some type of uncaught error condition.

ColdFusion actually allows you to create two types of error display templates:

- **Request error display templates.** The simplest way to show a customized error message. You can include whatever images or formatting you want so that the error matches your site's look and feel. However, CFML tags, such as `<cfoutput>`, `<cfset>`, or `<cfinclude>`, are not allowed. CFML functions and variables also are not allowed. Request error templates provide a last-resort way to handle errors. They normally are run after an exception error template fails.

- **Exception error display templates.** These are more flexible. You can use whatever CFML tags you want. For instance, you might want to have ColdFusion automatically send an email to the webmaster when certain types of errors occur. The main caveat is that ColdFusion can't display such a template for certain serious errors.

In general, the best practice is to create one template of each type. Then the exception template is displayed most often, unless the error is so serious that ColdFusion can't safely continue interpreting CFML tags, in which case the request template is displayed. The request template also kicks in if the exception template *itself* causes an error or can't be found.

NOTE

If you don't care about being able to use CFML tags in these error display templates, you can just create the request template and skip creating the exception one.

NOTE

For those history buffs out there, the request type of error display template is a holdover from earlier versions of ColdFusion. At one time, you could never respond intelligently to any type of error. Thankfully, those days are over.

Creating a Customized Request Error Page

To create the request display template, do the following:

1. Create a new ColdFusion template called `ErrorRequest.cfm`, located in the same directory as your `Application.cfc` file. Include whatever images or formatting you want, using whatever `<img>` or other tags you would normally. Remember to *not* put any CFML tags in this template.

2. Include the special `ERROR.diagnostics` variable wherever you want the actual error message to appear, if you want it to appear at all. Contrary to what you are used to, the variable should not be between `<cfoutput>` tags.

3. If you want, you can include the special `ERROR.mailTo` variable to display the email address of your site's webmaster or some other appropriate person. You also can use any of the other variables shown in Table 19.4.

4. Include a `<cferror>` tag in your `Application.cfc` file, with the `type` attribute set to `Request` and the `template` attribute set to `ErrorRequest.cfm`. This is what associates your error display template with your application.

Table 19.4   Special ERROR Variables Available in an Error Display Template

ATTRIBUTE	DESCRIPTION
ERROR.browser	The browser that was used when the error occurred as reported by the browser itself. This is the same value that is normally available to you as the #CGI.http_user_agent# variable, which generally includes the browser version number and operating system.
ERROR.dateTime	The date and time the error occurred, in the form MM/DD/YY HH:MM:SS. You can use the dateFormat() function to format the date differently in an exception template, but not in a request template.
ERROR.diagnostics	The actual error message. In general, this is the most important thing to include (or not to include) in an error display template. Please note that the exact text of this message can be affected by the settings currently enabled in the Debugging Settings page of the ColdFusion Administrator. See Chapter 17, "Debugging and Troubleshooting," for details.
ERROR.generatedContent	The actual HTML that had been generated by the requested ColdFusion template (and any included templates, and so on) up until the moment that the error occurred. You could use this to display the part of the page that had been successfully generated.
ERROR.HTTPReferer	The page the user was coming from when the error occurred, assuming that the user got to the problem page via a link or form submission. This value is reported by the browser and can sometimes be blank (especially if the user visited the page directly by typing its URL). Note the incorrect spelling of the word referrer.
ERROR.mailTo	An email address, presumably for a site administrator or webmaster, as provided to the <cferror> tag. See the following examples to see how this actually should be used.
ERROR.queryString	The query string provided to the template in which the error occurred. In other words, everything after the ? sign in the page's URL. This is the same value that is normally available to you as the #CGI.query_string# variable.
ERROR.remoteAddress	The IP address of the user's machine. This is the same value that is normally available to you as the #CGI.remote_addr# variable.
ERROR.template	File name of the ColdFusion template (.cfm file) in which the error occurred.

Listing 19.9 is a good example of a request error display template. Note that no <cfoutput> or other CFML tags are present. Also note that the only variables used are the special ERROR variables mentioned previously.

Listing 19.9 `ErrorRequest.cfm`—Customizing the Display of Error Messages

```
<!---
 Filename: ErrorRequest.cfm
 Created by: Nate Weiss (NMW)
 Please Note Included via <CFERROR> in Application.cfc
--->

<html>
<head><title>Error</title></head>
<body>

<!--- Display sarcastic message to poor user --->
<h2>Who Knew?</h2>
<p>We are very sorry, but a technical problem prevents us from
showing you what you are looking for. Unfortunately, these things
happen from time to time, even though we have only the most
top-notch people on our technical staff. Perhaps all of
our programmers need a raise, or more vacation time. As always,
there is also the very real possibility that SPACE ALIENS
(or our rivals at Miramax Studios) have sabotaged our website.
<p>That said, we will naturally try to correct this problem
as soon as we possibly can. Please try again shortly.

<!--- Provide "mailto" link so user can send email --->
<p>If you want, you can
<a href="mailto:#ERROR.mailTo#">send the webmaster an email</a>.
<p>Thank you.<br>

<!--- Maybe the company logo will make them feel better --->
<img src="../images/logo_b.gif" width="73" height="73" alt="" border="0">

<!--- Display the actual error message --->
<blockquote>
<hr><span class="error">#ERROR.diagnostics#</span></blockquote>

</body>
</html>
```

→ ColdFusion also provides the `<cftry>` and `<cfcatch>` tags, which enable you to trap specific errors and respond to or recover from them as appropriate. See Chapter 51 for details.

Listing 19.10 shows how to use the `<cferror>` tag in your `Application.cfc` file. Note that the email address webmaster@orangewhipstudios.com is being provided as the tag's `mailTo` attribute, which means that the webmaster's email address will be inserted in place of the `ERROR.mailTo` reference in Listing 19.9. Figure 19.4 shows how an error message would now be shown if you were to make a coding error in one of your templates.

To test this listing, save it as `Application.cfc`, not `Application4.cfm`.

Figure 19.4

Customized error pages help maintain your application's look and feel.

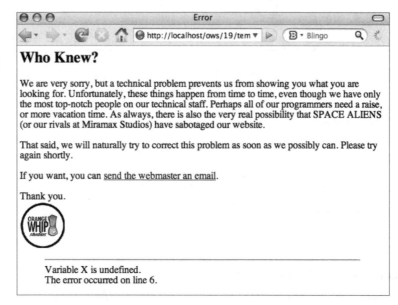

Listing 19.10 Application4.cfm—Use of the `<cferror>` Tag in `Application.cfc`

```
<!---
 Filename: Application.cfc (The "Application Component")
 Created by: Raymond Camden (ray@camdenfamily.com)
 Purpose: Sets "constant" variables and includes consistent header
--->

<cfcomponent output="false">

  <cfset THIS.name = "ows19">
  <cferror type="Request" template="ErrorRequest.cfm"
          mailto="webmaster@orangewhipstudios.com">

  <cffunction name="onApplicationStart" returnType="boolean" output="false">
    <!--- When did the application start? --->
    <cfset APPLICATION.appStarted = now()>

    <cfreturn true>
  </cffunction>

  <cffunction name="onApplicationEnd" returnType="void" output="false">
    <cfargument name="appScope" required="true">

    <!--- Log how many minutes the application stayed alive --->
    <cflog file="#THIS.name#" text=
"App ended after #dateDiff('n',ARGUMENTS.appScope.appStarted,now())# minutes.">

  </cffunction>

  <cffunction name="onRequestStart" returnType="boolean" output="true">
    <!--- Any variables set here can be used by all our pages --->
```

Listing 19.10 (CONTINUED)

```
        <cfset request.dataSource = "ows">
        <cfset request.companyName = "Orange Whip Studios">

        <!--- Display our Site Header at top of every page --->
        <cfinclude template="SiteHeader.cfm">

        <cfreturn true>
    </cffunction>

    <cffunction name="onRequestEnd" returnType="void" output="true">

        <!--- Display our Site Footer at bottom of every page --->
        <cfinclude template="SiteFooter.cfm">

    </cffunction>

</cfcomponent>
```

Additional ERROR Variables

In Listing 19.9, you saw how the ERROR.diagnostics variable can be used to show the user which specific error actually occurred. A number of additional variables can be used in the same way. You will see several of these used in Listing 19.11 in the next section.

NOTE

Note that the ERROR.generatedContent variable is not available in request error display templates.

TIP

These are the only variables you can use in request error display templates. You can use all types of ColdFusion variables in exception error display templates, discussed next.

Creating a Customized Exception Error Page

You have seen how to create a request error display template, in which you are prevented from using any CFML tags or functions. Now you can create an exception error template, in which you *can* use whatever CFML tags and functions you want.

For instance, Listing 19.11 is similar to Listing 19.10, but it doesn't display the ERROR.diagnostics message to the user. This means that the user won't know which type of error actually occurred. After all, your users might not care about the specifics, and you might not want them to see the actual error message in the first place. In addition, instead of allowing the user to send an email message to the webmaster, this template has ColdFusion send an email message to the webmaster automatically, via the <cfmail> tag.

Now all you have to do is add a second <cferror> tag to your Application.cfc file, this time specifying type="Exception" and template="ErrorException.cfm". You should put this <cferror> tag right after the first one, so the first one can execute if some problem occurs with your exception error display template. Since this modification is so simple, it won't be listed in the chapter. It is available at the book Web site with the name `Application5.cfc`.

Listing 19.11 `ErrorException.cfm`—Sending an Email When an Error Occurs

```
<!---
Filename: ErrorException.cfm
Created by: Nate Weiss (NMW)
Please Note Included via <CFERROR> in Application.cfc
--->

<html>
<head><title>Error</title></head>
<body>

<!--- Display sarcastic message to poor user --->
<h2>Who Knew?</h2>
<p>We are very sorry, but a technical problem prevents us from
showing you what you are looking for. Unfortunately, these things
happen from time to time, even though we have only the most
top-notch people on our technical staff. Perhaps all of
our programmers need a raise, or more vacation time. As always,
there is also the very real possibility that SPACE ALIENS
(or our rivals at Miramax Studios) have sabotaged our website.<br>
<p>That said, we will naturally try to correct this problem
as soon as we possibly can. Please try again shortly.
Thank you.<br>

<!--- Maybe the company logo will make them feel better --->
<img src="../images/logo_b.gif" width="73" height="73" alt="" border="0">

<!--- Send an email message to site administrator --->
<!--- (or whatever address provided to <cferror>) --->
<cfif ERROR.mailTo neq "">
 <cfmail to="#ERROR.mailTo#" from="errorsender@orangewhipstudios.com"
 subject="Error on Page #ERROR.Template#">
 Error Date/Time: #ERROR.dateTime#
 User's Browser: #ERROR.browser#
 URL Parameters: #ERROR.queryString#
 Previous Page: #ERROR.HTTPReferer#
 ----------------------------------
 #ERROR.diagnostics#
 </cfmail>
</cfif>
```

NOTE

Because sending automated error emails is a great way to show how exception templates can be used, the `<cfmail>` tag has been introduced a bit ahead of time here. Its use in Listing 19.11 should be self-explanatory: The ColdFusion server sends a simple email message to the webmaster. The email will contain the error message, date, browser version, and so on because of the **ERROR** variables referred to between the opening and closing `<cfmail>` tags.

➜ See Chapter 21, "Interacting with Email," online, for details.

➜ The webmaster could also look in ColdFusion's logs to see any errors that might be occurring throughout the application. See Chapter 17 for details.

Using the `OnError` Method

As we discussed earlier in the chapter, the `Application.cfc` contains a set of special methods that are executed depending on certain situations. We demonstrated how the `onApplicationStart` and `onApplicationEnd` methods are executed automatically based on the life of the ColdFusion application. One more special method is the `onError` method. As you can probably guess, this method is called whenever an exception occurs. Unlike the `<cferror>` tag, which is tied to a specific error type or exception, the `onError` method will fire on *any* error.

So how can you use this method? The method could do many of the things demonstrated in the listings we've already covered. You can mail the error to the administrator, or log the error to a file or database. You can even display a message to the user, but remember that the `onError` method will be run for any error. So for example, if your `onApplicationEnd` method throws an error, the `onError` method will run. The output won't be displayed, obviously, since no one is there to actually see it.

Another option to consider when using the `onError` method is to use it to handle the non-visual portions of the error (emailing the administrator, logging, etc.), and use the `<cfthrow>` tag to let your `<cferror>` tags take over. The `<cfthrow>` tag is discussed in Chapter 51. Think of the `onError` method as simply taking care of the error temporarily, and then passing it back to ColdFusion. If you have already created your request, exception, and validation templates, this approach lets you continue using those templates, while adding a bit of extra functionality to your application. Listing 19.12 demonstrates the latest version of our `Application.cfc` file, this time with an `onError` method. If you save this template, be sure to save it as `Application.cfc`, not `Application6.cfc`.

Listing 19.12 `Application6.cfc`—Working with `onError`

```
<!---
 Filename: Application.cfc (The "Application Component")
 Created by: Raymond Camden (ray@camdenfamily.com)
 Purpose: Sets "constant" variables and includes consistent header
--->

<cfcomponent output="false">

  <cfset THIS.name = "ows19">
  <cferror type="Request" template="ErrorRequest.cfm"
           mailto="webmaster@orangewhipstudios.com">
  <cferror type="Exception" template="ErrorException.cfm"
           mailto="webmaster@orangewhipstudios.com">

  <cffunction name="onApplicationStart" returnType="boolean" output="false">
    <!--- When did the application start? --->
    <cfset APPLICATION.appStarted = now()>

    <cfreturn true>
  </cffunction>

  <cffunction name="onApplicationEnd" returnType="void" output="false">
    <cfargument name="appScope" required="true">

    <!--- Log how many minutes the application stayed alive --->
    <cflog file="#THIS.name#" text=
```

Listing 19.12 (CONTINUED)

```
        "App ended after #dateDiff('n',ARGUMENTS.appScope.appStarted,now())# minutes.">

    </cffunction>

    <cffunction name="onRequestStart" returnType="boolean" output="true">
      <!--- Any variables set here can be used by all our pages --->
      <cfset request.dataSource = "ows">
      <cfset request.companyName = "Orange Whip Studios">

      <!--- Display our Site Header at top of every page --->
      <cfinclude template="SiteHeader.cfm">

      <cfreturn true>
    </cffunction>

    <cffunction name="onRequestEnd" returnType="void" output="true">

  <!--- Display our Site Footer at bottom of every page --->
  <cfinclude template="SiteFooter.cfm">

    </cffunction>

    <cffunction name="onError" returnType="void" output="false">
      <cfargument name="exception" required="true">
      <cfargument name="eventName" type="string" required="true">

      <!--- Use the cflog tag to record info on the error --->
      <cfif arguments.eventName is "">
        <cflog file="#THIS.name#" type="error"
               text="#arguments.exception.message#">
      <cfelse>
        <cflog file="#THIS.name#" type="error"
  text="Error in Method [#arguments.eventName#] #arguments.exception.message#">
      </cfif>

      <!--- Let the <cferror> tags do their job. --->
      <cfthrow object="#arguments.exception#">

    </cffunction>

  </cfcomponent>
```

The only thing new in this template is the onError method at the end, so we'll focus on that portion. The onError method is automatically passed two arguments. The first is the exception itself. This is just like the ERROR structure discussed earlier. It has the same values and we can use it to email, log to a file, or anything else. The second argument passed to the method is the name of the event that was running when the exception occurred. This argument will only have a value when the error occurs within the Application.cfc file itself. So for example, if the onApplicationStart method threw an error, that method name would be passed to the onError method. The onError method in Listing 19.12 checks to see if an eventName argument has a value. If it doesn't, it simply logs the error. Note that it uses the same file value as the onApplicationEnd's <cflog> tag. The value passed to the log is just the exception message. If the eventName argument wasn't blank, the text passed to the log is modified slightly to contain the event name as well. Lastly, we use the `<cfthrow>` tag to pass the error back out again from the `onError` method. Don't worry too much about this tag now; it's covered later in Chapter 51. Just consider the `onError` method here as being part of a "chain" of code blocks that will handle the error.

→ ColdFusion also provides the `<cftry>` and `<cfcatch>` tags, which allow you to trap specific errors and respond to or recover from them as appropriate. See Chapter 51 for details.

Handling Missing Templates

One of the new features of ColdFusion 8 is the ability to handle requests for ColdFusion files that do not exist. In the past, handling these requests was problematic and required updating of the Web server settings. Now you can simply add another method to your `Application.cfc` file to handle these missing templates.

Note though that this support for missing templates helps only with requests for missing ColdFusion files. If a user requests `dharma.html` (notice that the extension is `html`, not `cfm`), then ColdFusion can't help you.

Using onMissingTemplate

The new method that we'll be adding to our `Application.cfc` file is the `onMissingTemplate` function. This method is passed one argument: the name of the script that was requested. Listing 19.13 shows the latest version of the `Application.cfc` file. Be sure to save this file as `Application.cfc`, not `Application7.cfc`.

Listing 19.13 `Application7.cfc`—Working with onMissingTemplate

```
<!---
 Filename: Application.cfc (The "Application Component")
 Created by: Raymond Camden (ray@camdenfamily.com)
 Purpose: Sets "constant" variables and includes consistent header
--->

<cfcomponent output="false">

  <cfset THIS.name = "ows19">
  <cferror type="Request" template="ErrorRequest.cfm"
           mailto="webmaster@orangewhipstudios.com">
  <cferror type="Exception" template="ErrorException.cfm"
           mailto="webmaster@orangewhipstudios.com">

  <cffunction name="onApplicationStart" returnType="boolean" output="false">
    <!--- When did the application start? --->
    <cfset APPLICATION.appStarted = now()>

    <cfreturn true>
  </cffunction>

  <cffunction name="onApplicationEnd" returnType="void" output="false">
    <cfargument name="appScope" required="true">
```

Listing 19.13 (CONTINUED)

```
      <!--- Log how many minutes the application stayed alive --->
      <cflog file="#THIS.name#" text=
"App ended after #dateDiff('n',ARGUMENTS.appScope.appStarted,now())# minutes.">

  </cffunction>

  <cffunction name="onRequestStart" returnType="boolean" output="true">
    <!--- Any variables set here can be used by all our pages --->
    <cfset request.dataSource = "ows">
    <cfset request.companyName = "Orange Whip Studios">

    <!--- Display our Site Header at top of every page --->
    <cfinclude template="SiteHeader.cfm">

    <cfreturn true>
  </cffunction>

  <cffunction name="onRequestEnd" returnType="void" output="true">

    <!--- Display our Site Footer at bottom of every page --->
    <cfinclude template="SiteFooter.cfm">

  </cffunction>

  <cffunction name="onError" returnType="void" output="false">
    <cfargument name="exception" required="true">
    <cfargument name="eventName" type="string" required="true">

    <!--- Use the cflog tag to record info on the error --->
    <cfif arguments.eventName is "">
      <cflog file="#THIS.name#" type="error"
             text="#arguments.exception.message#">
    <cfelse>
      <cflog file="#THIS.name#" type="error"
 text="Error in Method [#arguments.eventName#] #arguments.exception.message#">
    </cfif>

    <!--- Let the <cferror> tags do their job. --->
    <cfthrow object="#arguments.exception#">

  </cffunction>


  <cffunction name="onMissingTemplate" returnType="boolean" output="false">
    <cfargument name="targetpage" type="string" required="true">

    <!--- log it --->
    <cflog file="#THIS.name#" text="Missing Template: #arguments.targetpage#">
    <cflocation
url="404.cfm?missingtemplate=#urlEncodedFormat(arguments.targetpage)#"
addToken="false">

  </cffunction>

</cfcomponent>
```

Let's focus on the new code in this document: the `onMissingTemplate` method. As stated earlier, this method takes one argument: the name of the template being requested. So if you requested `dharma.cfm` and that file did not exist, that is the value that would be passed to the function. The complete path is passed as well as the name, so you would really end up with something like this: `/ows/c19/dharma.cfm`. We do two things in the method. First we log the fact that a missing-template event occurred. This is important because if you commonly see people loading a file that does not exist, you may want to add the file anyway. Second, we send the user to a file named `404.cfm`. We pass the template as a URL variable. `404.cfm` will display a nice error message for the user. You can see this in Listing 19.14.

Listing 19.14 `404.cfm`—Handling Missing Templates

```
<!--- Filename: 404.cfm
  Created by: Raymond Camden (ray@camdenfamily.com)
  Purpose: Display an message about a missing file.
--->

<cfparam name="URL.missingtemplate" default="">

<cfoutput>
<p>
Sorry, we could not load #URL.missingtemplate#. Please try our <a
href="index.cfm">home page</a> instead.
</p>
</cfoutput>
```

This file doesn't do very much. It first ensures that the URL variable, `missingtemplate`, has a default value. It then tells the user that the requested file didn't exist and kindly provides a link back to the home page.

Special Considerations

In some circumstances, ColdFusion will notice if you request a subdirectory that does not contain an index page. An index page is any file that the Web server recognizes as a file to run in a folder if no particular file name is specified. If no such file exists, the Web server may respond with a list of files. Typically, though, this is not done because it presents a security risk. If you do want this behavior, then you need to specify a new `THIS` scope variable named `welcomeFileList`. This variable consists of a list of files that match the index files specified by your Web server. It tells ColdFusion when it should and should not run `onMissingTemplate` for a subdirectory. However, this scenario applies only to the embedded JRun Web server. It does not apply to common Web servers such as Apache or IIS.

Using Locks to Protect Against Race Conditions

ColdFusion is a *multithreaded* application, meaning that the server can process more than one page request at a time. Generally speaking, this is a wonderful feature. Because the server can in effect do more than one thing at a time, it can tend to two or three (or 50) simultaneous visitors to your application.

But as wonderful as multithreading is, it also means that you need to think carefully about situations where more than one person is accessing a particular page at the same time. Unless you take steps to prevent it, the two page requests can be reading or changing the same application variable at the very same moment. If you are using Application variables to track any type of data that changes over time, and the integrity of the data is critical to your application (such as any type of counter, total, or statistic), you must tell ColdFusion what to do when two page requests are trying to execute the same "shared data-changing" code at the same time.

NOTE

This isn't something that only ColdFusion programmers face. In one fashion or another, you'll run into these issues in any multi-threaded programming environment. ColdFusion just makes the issue really easy to deal with.

Of course, ColdFusion provides solutions to help you deal with concurrent page requests quite easily. Either of the following can be used to control what happens when several page requests are trying to read or change information in the application scope:

- You can use the `<cflock>` tag to mark the areas of your code that set, change, access, or display application variables. The `<cflock>` tag ensures that those potentially problematic parts of your code don't execute at the same time as other potentially problematic parts. As you will learn in this section, your locking instructions will cause one page to wait a moment while the other does its work, thus avoiding any potential problems. In other words, you keep your code thread-safe yourself.

- In the Server Settings page of the ColdFusion Administrator, you can set the Limit Simultaneous Requests To value to 1. Doing so guarantees that your whole application will be thread-safe because only one page request will be processed at once. Therefore, you can use application variables freely without having to worry about locking them. However, you probably don't want to do this unless your application is used only occasionally or by just a few users, because you will be giving up the benefits of multithreading. See Chapter 28, "ColdFusion Server Configuration," in Vol. 2, *Application Development*, for details.

NOTE

This discussion assumes that you are developing applications for ColdFusion MX or a more recent version. Previous versions of ColdFusion required you to use locks far more frequently, even when there wasn't a race condition issue at hand. Basically, you needed to lock every line of code that used application or session variables. This is no longer the case. Beginning in ColdFusion MX, you need only lock application or session variables if you are concerned about race condition issues, as explained in the next section.

NOTE

If you use the `onApplicationStart` method, you don't need to use any `<cflock>` tags. All application variables created there are entirely thread-safe. The same applies for `onSessionStart`.

What Is a Race Condition?

It's time to pause for just a moment of theory. You need to understand the concept of a race condition and how such conditions can occur in your ColdFusion applications. Simply put, a race condition is any situation where two different page requests can change the same information at the very same moment in time. In many situations, race conditions can lead to undesired results. In other situations, you may not care about them at all.

NOTE

We seriously recommend taking a few moments to really visualize and understand this stuff, especially if you are going to be using application variables to hold values that change over time (especially values that increment numerically as your application does its work).

Here's an example that should make this really easy to understand. Imagine an application variable called APPLICATION.HitCount. The purpose of this variable is to track the number of individual page views that an application has responded to since the ColdFusion server was started. Simple code like the following is used in the onRequestStart method to advance the counter by one every time a user visits a page:

```
<cfset APPLICATION.hitCount = APPLICATION.hitCount + 1>
```

So far, so good. The code seems to do what it's supposed to. Every time a page is viewed, the variable's value is increased by one. You can output it at any time to display the current number of hits. No problem.

But what happens if two people visit a page at the same time? We know that ColdFusion doesn't process the pages one after another; it processes them at the very same time. Keeping that in mind, consider what ColdFusion has to do to execute the <cfset> tag shown above. Three basic mini-steps are required to complete it:

1. ColdFusion gets the current value of APPLICATION.hitCount.

2. It adds one to the value.

3. Finally, it sets the APPLICATION.hitCount to the new, incremented value.

The big problem is that another page request may have changed the value of the variable between steps 1 and 2, or between steps 2 and 3. Just for fun, let's say the hit count variable is currently holding a value of 100. Now two users, Bob and Jane, both type in your application's URL at the same time. For whatever reason, Jane's request gets to the server a split moment after Bob's. Bob's request performs the first mini-step (getting the value of 100). Now, while Bob's request is performing the second mini-step (the addition), Jane's request is doing its first step: finding out what ColdFusion has for the current value of the application variable (uh-oh, still 100). While Bob's request performs the *third* mini-step (updating the counter to 101), Jane's request is still doing its *second* step (adding one to 100). Jane's request now finishes its third step, which sets the application variable to, you guessed it, 101. That is, when both requests are finished, the hit count has only increased by one, even though two requests have come through since hit number 100. A bit of information has been lost.

Granted, for a simple hit counter like this, a teensy bit of information loss probably isn't all that important. You may not care that the hit count is off by one or two every once in a while. But what if the application variable in question was something more like `APPLICATION.totalSalesToDate`? If a similar kind of "mistake" occurred in something like a sales total, you might have a real problem on your hands.

NOTE

Again, it is important to note that this isn't a problem specific to ColdFusion. It's a simple, logical problem that would present itself in almost any real-world situation where several different "people" (here, the people are Web users) are trying to look at or change the same information at the same time.

NOTE

By definition, the chances of a race condition problem actually occurring in an application will increase as the number of people using the application increases. That is, these kinds of problems tend to be "stealth" problems that are difficult to catch until an application is battle-tested.

The solution is to use `<cflock>` tags to make sure that two requests don't execute the `<cfset>` tag (or whatever problematic code) at the same exact moment. For example, `<cflock>` tags would cause Jane's request to wait for Bob's request to be finished with that `<cfset>` before it started working on the `<cfset>` itself.

NOTE

Does all this "two related things happening at the same moment in different parts of the world" stuff sound like something out of a Kieslowski film? Or remind you of bad song lyrics, perhaps something cut from The Police's "Synchronicity" album? Perhaps, but this kind of freak coincidence really can and will happen sooner or later. So, no, I can't promise that Irene Jacob, Julie Delpy, and Juliette Binoche will all happen to show up at your doorstep at the same time someday, any more than I can promise you tea in the Sahara. But I can assure you that some kind of unexpected results will occur someday if this kind of race condition is allowed to occur, unchecked, in your code. How's that for fatalism?

`<cflock>` **Tag Syntax**

Now that you know what race conditions are and how they can lead to unpredictable results, it's time to learn how to use locking to avoid them. We'll get into the nuances shortly, but the basic idea is to place opening and closing `<cflock>` tags around any part of your code that changes application variables (or session variables, which are discussed in the next chapter) or any other type of information that might be shared or changed by concurrent page requests. Table 19.5 takes a closer look at the tag's syntax.

Table 19.5 `<cflock>` Tag Syntax

ATTRIBUTE	DESCRIPTION
type	Optional. The type, or strength, of the lock. Allowable values are `Exclusive` and `ReadOnly`. You should use `Exclusive` to indicate blocks of code that change the values of shared variables. Use `ReadOnly` to indicate blocks of code that aren't going to be changing any shared values, but that always need to be reading or outputting the most recent version of the information. If you don't provide a `type`, the default of `Exclusive` is assumed.
scope	The type of persistent variables you are using between the `<cflock>` tags. Allowable values are `Application`, `Session`, `Request`, and `Server`. You would use a `<cflock>` with `scope="Application"` around any code that uses application variables. You would set this value to `Session` around code that uses session variables, which are discussed in the next chapter. If the code must be locked on a per-request basis, use the `Request` value. The use of server variables is not discussed in this book and is generally discouraged.
name	Optional. You can provide a `name` attribute instead of `scope` to get finer-grained control over your locks. This is discussed in the "Using Named Locks" section, later in this chapter. You must always provide a `name` or a `scope`, but you can't provide both.
timeout	Required. The length of time, in seconds, that ColdFusion will wait to obtain the lock. If another visitor's request has a similar `<cflock>` on it, ColdFusion will wait for this many seconds for the locked part of the other request to finish before proceeding. Generally, `10` is a sensible value to use here.
throwOnTimeout	Optional. The default is `Yes`, which means an error message will be displayed if ColdFusion can't obtain the lock within the `timeout` period you specified. (You can catch this error using `<cfcatch>` to deal with the situation differently. See Chapter 51 for details.)

Using `Exclusive` Locks

As Table 19.5 shows, there are two types of locks: `Exclusive` and `ReadOnly`. Let's start off simple, and talk about `<cflock>` tags of `type="Exclusive"`. If you want, you can solve your race condition problems using only `Exclusive` locks.

`Exclusive` locks work like this. When your template gets to an opening `<cflock>` tag in your code, it requests the corresponding lock from the server. There is only one available lock for each scope (`Application`, `Session`, `Request`, or `Server`), which is why it's called "exclusive." Once this `Exclusive` lock has been bestowed upon your template, it stays there until the closing `</cflock>` tag in your code, at which point the lock is released and returned to the server. While your template has the lock (that is, while the code between the `<cflock>` tags is running), all other templates that want an application-level lock must wait in line. ColdFusion pauses the other templates (right at their opening `<cflock>` tags) until your template releases the lock.

The code shown in Listing 19.15 shows how to place `Exclusive` locks in your code. This listing is similar to the previous version of the Featured Movie template (Listing 19.7). The only important difference is the pair of `<cflock>` tags at the top of the code. Note that the `<cflock>` tags surround the entire portion of the template that is capable of changing the current value of the `APPLICATION.movieList` variable.

Listing 19.15 `FeaturedMovie2.cfm`—Using Exclusive Locks to Safely Update Application Data

```
<!---
Filename: FeaturedMovie.cfm
Created by: Nate Weiss (NMW)
Purpose: Displays a single movie on the page, on a rotating basis
Please Note Application variables must be enabled
--->

<!--- Need to lock when accessing shared data --->
<cflock scope="APPLICATION" type="Exclusive" timeout="10">

  <!--- List of movies to show (list starts out empty) --->
  <cfparam name="APPLICATION.movieList" type="string" default="">

  <!--- If this is the first time we're running this, --->
  <!--- Or we have run out of movies to rotate through --->
  <cfif listLen(APPLICATION.movieList) eq 0>
    <!--- Get all current FilmIDs from the database --->
              <cfquery name="getFilmIDs" datasource="#REQUEST.dataSource#">
              SELECT FilmID FROM Films
              ORDER BY MovieTitle
              </cfquery>

              <!--- Turn FilmIDs into a simple comma-separated list --->
              <cfset APPLICATION.movieList = valueList(getFilmIDs.FilmID)>
  </cfif>

  <!--- Pick the first movie in the list to show right now --->
  <cfset thisMovieID = listFirst(APPLICATION.movieList, 1)>
  <!--- Re-save the list, as all movies *except* the first --->
  <cfset APPLICATION.movieList = listRest(APPLICATION.movieList, 1)>
</cflock>


<!--- Now that we have chosen the film to "Feature", --->
<!--- Get all important info about it from database. --->
<cfquery name="GetFilm" datasource="#REQUEST.dataSource#">
 SELECT
 MovieTitle, Summary, Rating,
 AmountBudgeted, DateInTheaters
 FROM Films f, FilmsRatings r
 WHERE FilmID = #thisMovieID#
 AND f.RatingID = r.RatingID
</cfquery>

<!--- Now Display Our Featured Movie --->
<cfoutput>
        <!--- Define formatting for our "feature" display --->
        <style type="text/css">
        TH.fm { background:RoyalBlue;color:white;text-align:left;
        font-family:sans-serif;font-size:10px}
        TD.fm { background:LightSteelBlue;
        font-family:sans-serif;font-size:12px}
        </style>

        <!--- Show info about featured movie in HTML Table --->
```

Listing 19.15 (CONTINUED)

```
        <table width="150" align="right" border="0" cellspacing="0">
        <tr><th class="fm">
        Featured Film
        </th></tr>
        <!--- Movie Title, Summary, Rating --->
        <tr><td class="fm">
        <b>#getFilm.MovieTitle#</b><br>
        #getFilm.Summary#<br>
        <p align="right">Rated: #getFilm.Rating#</p>
        </td></tr>
        <!--- Cost (rounded to millions), release date --->
        <tr><th class="fm">
        Production Cost $#round(getFilm.AmountBudgeted / 1000000)# Million<br>
        In Theaters #dateFormat(getFilm.DateInTheaters, "mmmm d")#<br>
        </th></tr>
        </table>
        <br clear="all">
    </cfoutput>
```

The purpose of the `<cflock>` tag in Listing 19.15 is to ensure that only one instance of the block is ever allowed to occur at the very same moment in time. For example, consider what happens if two different users request the page within a moment of each other. If by chance the second page request gets to the start of the block before the first one has exited it, the second request will be forced to wait until the first instance of the block has completed its work. This guarantees that funny race condition behavior doesn't take place (like one of the movies getting skipped or shown twice).

TIP

> If it helps, think of locks as being like hall passes back in grade school. If you wanted to go to the bathroom, you needed to get a pass from the teacher. Nobody else was allowed to go to the bathroom until you came back and returned the pass. This was to protect the students (and the bathroom) from becoming, um, corrupted, right?

Using `ReadOnly` Locks

Okay, you've seen how `Exclusive` locks work. They simply make sure that no two blocks of the same `scope` are allowed to execute at once. If two requests need the same lock at the same time, the first one blocks the second one. But in some situations this can be overkill, and lead to more waiting around than is really necessary.

ColdFusion also provides `ReadOnly` locks, which are less extreme. `ReadOnly` locks don't block each other. They only get blocked by `Exclusive` locks. In plain English, a `ReadOnly` lock means, "If the variables in this block are being changed somewhere else, wait until the changes are finished before running this block." Use a `ReadOnly` lock if you have some code that definitely needs to read the correct, current value of an application variable, but isn't going to change it at all. Then just double-check that all code that *does* change the variable is between `Exclusive` locks. This way, you are guaranteed to always be reading or displaying the correct, most current value of the variable, but without the unwanted side effect of forcing other page requests to wait in line.

Do this whenever you are going to be reading the value of a variable a lot, but changing its value only occasionally.

NOTE

> In other words, `ReadOnly` locks don't have any effect on their own. They only have an effect when some other page request has an `Exclusive` lock.

To demonstrate how much sense this all makes, let's adapt the featured movie example a bit. So far, the featured movie has rotated with every page request. What if you still wanted the movies to rotate evenly and in order, but instead of rotating with every page request, you want the movie to change once every five minutes (or ten minutes, or once an hour)?

Here is an adapted version of the featured movie template that gets this job done (see Listing 19.16). The code is a bit more complicated than the last version. For the moment, don't worry about the code itself. Just note that the portion of the code that makes changes in the APPLICATION scope is in an `Exclusive` lock. The portion of the code that grabs the current feature movie from the APPLICATION scope (which is also really short and quick) is inside a `ReadOnly` lock.

Listing 19.16 FeaturedMovie3.cfm—Using Exclusive and ReadOnly Locks

```
<!---
 Filename: FeaturedMovie.cfm
 Created by: Nate Weiss (NMW)
 Purpose: Displays a single movie on the page, on a rotating basis
 Please Note Application variables must be enabled
--->

<!--- We want to obtain an exclusive lock if this --->
<!--- is the first time this template has executed, --->
<!--- or the time for this featured movie has expired --->
<cfif (not isDefined("APPLICATION.movieRotation"))
 or (dateCompare(APPLICATION.movieRotation.currentUntil, now()) eq -1)>

  <!--- Make sure all requests wait for this block --->
  <!--- to finish before displaying the featured movie --->
  <cflock scope="APPLICATION" type="Exclusive" timeout="10">

      <!--- If this is the first time the template has executed... --->
      <cfif not isDefined("APPLICATION.movieRotation")>

          <!--- Get all current FilmIDs from the database --->
          <cfquery name="GetFilmIDs" datasource="#REQUEST.dataSource#">
          SELECT FilmID FROM Films
          ORDER BY MovieTitle
          </cfquery>

          <!--- Create structure for rotating featured movies --->
          <cfset st = structNew()>
          <cfset st.movieList = valueList(getFilmIDs.FilmID)>
          <cfset st.currentPos = 1>

          <!--- Place structure into APPLICATION scope --->
          <cfset APPLICATION.movieRotation = st>
```

Listing 19.16 (CONTINUED)

```
    <!--- ...otherwise, the time for the featured movie has expired --->
    <cfelse>
      <!--- Shorthand name for structure in application scope --->
      <cfset st = APPLICATION.movieRotation>

      <!--- If we haven't gotten to the last movie yet --->
      <cfif st.currentPos lt listLen(st.movieList)>
        <cfset st.currentPos = st.currentPos + 1>
      <!--- if already at last movie, start over at beginning --->
      <cfelse>
        <cfset st.currentPos = 1>
      </cfif>

    </cfif>

    <!--- In any case, choose the movie at the current position in list --->
    <cfset st.currentMovie = listGetAt(st.movieList, st.currentPos)>
    <!--- This featured movie should "expire" a short time from now --->
    <cfset st.currentUntil = dateAdd("s", 5, now())>
    </cflock>

  </cfif>

  <!--- Use a ReadOnly lock to grab current movie from application scope... --->
  <!--- If the exclusive block above is currently executing in another thread, --->
  <!--- then ColdFusion will 'wait' before executing the code in this block. --->
  <cflock scope="APPLICATION" type="ReadOnly" timeout="10">
    <cfset thisMovieID = APPLICATION.movieRotation.currentMovie>
  </cflock>


  <!--- Now that we have chosen the film to "Feature", --->
  <!--- Get all important info about it from database. --->
  <cfquery name="GetFilm" datasource="#REQUEST.dataSource#">
   SELECT
   MovieTitle, Summary, Rating,
   AmountBudgeted, DateInTheaters
   FROM Films f, FilmsRatings r
   WHERE FilmID = #thisMovieID#
   AND f.RatingID = r.RatingID
  </cfquery>

  <!--- Now Display Our Featured Movie --->
  <cfoutput>
   <!--- Define formatting for our "feature" display --->
   <style type="text/css">
   TH.fm { background:RoyalBlue;color:white;text-align:left;
   font-family:sans-serif;font-size:10px}
   TD.fm { background:LightSteelBlue;
   font-family:sans-serif;font-size:12px}
   </style>

   <!--- Show info about featured movie in HTML Table --->
   <table width="150" align="right" border="0" cellspacing="0">
   <tr><th class="fm">
```

Listing 19.16 (CONTINUED)

```
Featured Film
</th></tr>
<!--- Movie Title, Summary, Rating --->
<tr><td class="fm">
<b>#getFilm.MovieTitle#</b><br>
#getFilm.Summary#<br>
<p align="right">Rated: #getFilm.Rating#</p>
</td></tr>
<!--- Cost (rounded to millions), release date --->
<tr><th class="fm">
Production Cost $#round(val(getFilm.AmountBudgeted) / 1000000)# Million<br>
In Theaters #dateFormat(getFilm.DateInTheaters, "mmmm d")#<br>
</th></tr>
</table>
<br clear="all">
</cfoutput>
```

The first thing this template does is check whether changes need to be made in the APPLICATION scope. Changes will be made if the template hasn't been run before, or if it's time to rotate the featured movie. (Remember, the rotation is now based on time.) If changes are called for, an Exclusive lock is opened. Within the lock, if the template hasn't been run before, a list of movies is retrieved from the database and stored as a value called movieList, just as before. In addition, a value called currentPos is set to 1 (to indicate the first movie). This value will increase as the movies are cycled through. Execution then proceeds to the bottom of the <cflock> block, where the current movie id is plucked from the list, and a value called currentUntil is set to a moment in time a few seconds in the future.

On the other hand, if the lock was opened because the currentUntil value has passed (we're still inside the Exclusive lock block), then it's time to pick the next movie from the list. As long as the end of the list hasn't already been reached, the only thing required is to advance currentPos by one. If the last movie *has* already been reached, the currentPos is reset to the beginning of the list.

NOTE

At any rate, the entire Exclusive lock block at the top of the template executes only once in a while, when the movie needs to change. If you are rotating movies every 10 minutes and have a fair number of visitors, the lock is needed only in the vast minority of page requests.

Underneath, a second <cflock> block of type="ReadOnly" uses a <cfset> to read the current featured movie from the APPLICATION scope into a local variable. The ReadOnly lock ensures that if the featured movie is currently being changed in some other page request, the <cfset> will wait until the change is complete. Since the change occurs only once in a while, the page is usually able to execute without having to wait at all.

TIP

Think of ReadOnly locks as a way of optimizing the performance of code that needs some kind of locking to remain correct. For instance, this template could have been written using only Exclusive locks, and doing so would have made sure that the results were always correct (no race conditions). The introduction of the ReadOnly lock is a way of making sure that the locks have as little impact on performance as possible.

NOTE

You'll encounter the notion of explicitly locking potentially concurrent actions in database products as well. Conceptually, database products use the SQL keywords `BEGIN TRANSACTION` and `COMMIT TRANSACTION` in a way that's analogous to Cold-Fusion's interpretation of beginning and ending `<cflock>` tags.

→ See Chapter 41, "More About SQL and Queries," online, for details about database transactions.

Using Named Locks instead of SCOPE

You've seen why locks are sometimes needed to avoid race conditions. You've seen the simplest way to implement them—with `Exclusive` locks. You've seen how to avoid potential bottlenecks by using a mix of `Exclusive` and `ReadOnly` locks. Hopefully, you've noticed a pattern emerging: If you're worried about race conditions, your goal should be to protect your data with `<cflock>`, but to do so in the least obtrusive way possible. That is, you want your code to be "smart" about when page requests wait for each other.

So far, all of the `<cflock>` tags in this chapter have been *scoped locks*. Each has used a `scope="Application"` attribute to say, "This lock should block or be blocked by all other locks in the application." As you have seen, scoped locks are really simple to implement once you "get" the conceptual issue at hand. The problem with scoped locks is that they often end up locking too much.

There's no problem when you're using only application variables to represent a single concept. For instance, the various versions of the Featured Movie template track a few different variables, but they are all related to the same concept of a featured movie that rotates over time.

Consider what happens, though, if you need to add a rotating Featured Actor widget to your application. Such a widget would be similar to the featured movie but it would rotate at a different rate or according to some other logic. Just for the heck of it, pretend there's also a Featured Director widget, plus a couple of hit counters that also maintain data at the application level, and so on. Assume for the moment that these various widgets appear on different pages, rather than all on the same page.

Using the techniques you've learned so far, whenever one of these mini-applications needs to change the data it keeps in the APPLICATION scope, it will use a `<cflock>` with `scope="Application"` to protect itself against race conditions. The problem is that the `scope="Application"` lock is not only going to block or be blocked by instances of that same widget in other page requests. It's going to block or be blocked by all locks in the entire application. If all of your widgets are only touching their own application variables, this approach is overkill. If the Featured Actor widget doesn't touch the same variables that the featured movie widget uses, then there's no possibility of a race condition. Therefore, allowing reads and writes by the two widgets to block one another is a waste of time, but `scope="Application"` doesn't know that.

ColdFusion gives you further control over this kind of problem by supporting named locks. To add named locks to your code, you use a `name` attribute in your `<cflock>` tags, instead of a `scope` attribute. Named lock blocks will only block or wait for other lock blocks that have the same `name`.

For instance, instead of using a scoped lock, like this:

```
<cflock
  scope="Application"
  type="Exclusive"
  timeout="10">
```

you could use a named lock, like this:

```
<cflock
  name="OrangeWhipMovieRotation"
  type="Exclusive"
  timeout="10">
```

This way, you can feel comfortable manipulating the variables used by the featured movie widget, knowing that the `Exclusive` lock you've asked for will affect only those pieces of code that are also dealing with the same variables. Page requests that need to display the Featured Movie or Featured Director widget won't be blocked needlessly.

The name of the lock is considered globally for the entire server, not just for your application, so you need to make sure that the name of the lock isn't used in other applications. The easiest way to do this is to always incorporate the application's name (or something similar) as a part of the lock name. That's why the `<cflock>` tag shown above includes `OrangeWhip` at the start of the `name` attribute. Another way to get the same effect would be to use the automatic `APPLICATION.applicationName` variable as a part of the `name`, like so:

```
<cflock
  name="#APPLICATION.applicationName#MovieRotation"
  type="Exclusive"
  timeout="10">
```

The Web site for this book includes a `FeauturedMovie4.cfm` template, which is almost the same as `FeaturedMovie3.cfm`, shown in Listing 19.16. The only difference is that it uses `name=` `"OrangeWhipMovieRotation"` (as shown above) instead of `scope="Application"` in each of the `<cflock>` tags.

NOTE

So it turns out that the `scope="Application"` attribute is really just a shortcut. Its effect is equivalent to writing a named lock that uses the name of your application (or some other identifier that is unique to your application) as the `name`.

Nested Locks and Deadlocks

It's usually okay to nest named locks within one another, as long as the `name` for each lock block is different. However, if they aren't nested in the same order in all parts of your code, it's possible that your application will encounter deadlocks while it runs. Deadlocks are situations where it's impossible for two page requests to move forward because they are each requesting a lock that the other already has. Consider a template with an `Exclusive` lock named `LockA`, with another `<cflock>` named `LockB` nested within it. Now consider another template, which nests `LockA` within `LockB`. If both templates execute at the same time, the first page request might be granted an `Exclusive` lock for `LockA`, and the second could get an `Exclusive` lock for `LockB`. Now neither template can move forward. Both locks will time out and throw errors. This is deadlock.

Entire books have been written about various ways to solve this kind of puzzle; there's no way we can tell you how to handle every possible situation. Our advice is this: If you need to nest named locks, go ahead as long as they will be nested in the same combination and order in all of your templates. If the combination or order needs to be different in different places, use scoped locks instead. The overhead and aggravation you might encounter in trying to manage and debug potential deadlocks isn't worth the added cost introduced by the scope shorthand.

Don't confuse this discussion (nesting locks with different names) with nesting locks that have the same name or scope. In general, you should never nest <cflock> tags that have the same scope or name. A ReadOnly lock that is nested within an Exclusive lock with the same scope or name has no additional benefit (it's always safe to read if you already have an Exclusive lock). And if the Exclusive lock is nested within a ReadOnly lock, then the Exclusive lock can never be obtained (because it needs to wait for all ReadOnly locks to end first), and thus will always time out and throw an error.

Locking with ColdFusion 5 and Earlier

The advice about when and how to use locks given in this chapter applies only to ColdFusion MX and later. Previous versions of ColdFusion approached locking differently within the guts of the server. The result was that *every* read or write of any shared variable needed to be locked, regardless of whether there was a possibility of a logical race condition. Without the locks, ColdFusion's internal memory space would eventually become corrupted, and the server would crash or exhibit strange and unstable behavior. In other words, locks were needed not only to protect the logical integrity of shared data, but also to protect the ColdFusion server from itself. Thankfully, this shortcoming has gone away as of ColdFusion MX, because shared variables end up being synchronized internally by the new Java-based runtime engine.

This means that if you are writing an application that you want to be backward compatible with ColdFusion 5 and earlier, you must lock every single reference to any application, session, or server variable, even if you are just outputting its value. Even isDefined() tests and <cfparam> tags must be locked under ColdFusion 5 and earlier.

Application Variable Timeouts

By default, application variables are kept on the server almost indefinitely. They die only if two whole days pass without any visits to any of the application's pages. After two days of inactivity, ColdFusion considers the APPLICATION scope to have expired, and the onApplicationEnd method of the Application.cfc file is called, if it exists. Whether or not this method exists, all associated application variables are flushed from its memory.

If one of your applications uses a large number of application variables but is used very rarely, you could consider decreasing the amount of time that the APPLICATION scope takes to expire. Doing so would let ColdFusion reuse the memory taken up by the application variables. In practice, there might be few situations in which this flexibility is useful, but you should still know what your options are if you want to think about ways to tweak the way your applications behave.

Two ways are available to adjust the application timeout period from its two-day default value. You can use the ColdFusion Administrator or the `applicationTimeout` value of the `THIS` scope in the `Application.cfc` file.

Adjusting Timeouts Using `APPLICATIONTIMEOUT`

The `Application.CFC THIS` scope takes an optional `applicationTimeout` value. You can use this to explicitly specify how long an unused `APPLICATION` scope will remain in memory before it expires.

The `applicationTimeout` value expects a ColdFusion *time span* value, which is a special type of numeric information used to describe a period of time in terms of days, hours, minutes, and seconds. All this means is that you must specify the application timeout using the `createTimeSpan()` function, which takes four numeric arguments to represent the desired number of days, hours, minutes, and seconds, respectively.

For instance, to specify that an application should time out after two hours of inactivity, you would use code such as this:

```
<cfset THIS.applicationTimeout="#CreateTimeSpan(0,2,0,0)#">
```

NOTE

If you don't specify an `applicationTimeout` attribute, the Default Timeout value in the Variables page of the ColdFusion Administrator is used. See the next section, "Adjusting Timeouts Using the ColdFusion Administrator," for details.

NOTE

If you specify an `applicationTimeout` that exceeds the Maximum Timeout value in the Variables page of the ColdFusion Administrator, the Maximum Timeout in the Administrator is used instead. See the next section, "Adjusting Timeouts Using the Cold-Fusion Administrator," for details.

Don't forget that you can now execute code when the application times out. Listing 19.6 demonstrated a simple use of the `onApplicationEnd` method.

Adjusting Timeouts Using the ColdFusion Administrator

To adjust the amount of time that each application's `APPLICATION` scope should live before it expires, follow these steps:

1. Navigate to the Memory Variables page of the ColdFusion Administrator.

2. Under Default Timeout, fill in the days, hours, minutes, and seconds fields for application variables, as shown in Figure 19.5.

3. If you want, you also can adjust the Maximum Timeout for application variables here. If any developers attempt to use a longer timeout with the `applicationTimeout` value in the `Application.cfc THIS` scope, this value will be used instead (no error message is displayed).

4. Click Submit Changes.

Figure 19.5

You can adjust when an application expires using the Variables page of the ColdFusion Administrator.

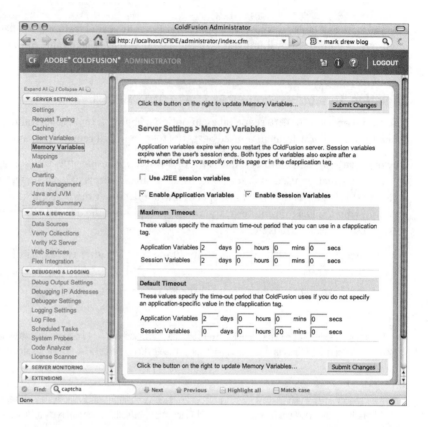

Using onRequest()

So far we have seen examples of how you can run code before and after a page request, as well as during the startup and end of the application. Another way to modify the behavior of your pages is with the onRequest method. This method is executed after the onRequestStart method, and before the onRequestEnd method. It takes one argument, the template currently being executed. If you don't actually include the template, using <cfinclude>, then your page won't show up.

Using this method has some serious drawbacks. The mere existence of this method won't allow any Flash Remoting or Web Services calls. The method also tends to "leak" variables into the template itself. If all of this sounds confusing, don't worry. Typically you won't need to use the onRequest method. If you simply want to wrap a page with a header and footer, for example, you can just use onRequestStart and onRequestEnd.

With that in mind, let's look at a simple example of where the onRequest method can be helpful. You may have seen some Web sites that have "Print" versions of their articles. These are versions of the article that normally have much reduced HTML. This is easy to build to do with advanced style sheets, or dynamically with ColdFusion, but what if you have old content, or pages, that weren't built to support a Print version? We can use the onRequest method to handle this situation. Listing 19.17 shows a modified version of our latest Application.cfc file. Since we are only modifying two methods and adding the onRequest method, we only list them below. The book Web site has the entire file.

Listing 19.17 `Application8.cfc`—Using onRequest

```coldfusion
<cffunction name="onRequestStart" returnType="boolean" output="true">
  <!--- Any variables set here can be used by all our pages --->
  <cfset request.dataSource = "ows">
  <cfset request.companyName = "Orange Whip Studios">

  <!--- Display our Site Header at top of every page --->
  <cfif not isDefined("URL.print")>
    <cfinclude template="SiteHeader.cfm">
  </cfif>

  <cfreturn true>
</cffunction>

<cffunction name="onRequestEnd" returnType="void" output="true">

  <!--- Display our Site Footer at bottom of every page --->
  <cfif not isDefined("URL.print")>
    <cfinclude template="SiteFooter.cfm">
  </cfif>

</cffunction>

<cffunction name="onRequest" returnType="void" outout="true">
  <cfargument name="targetPage" type="string" required="true">
  <cfset var content = "">

  <cfif not isDefined("URL.print")>
    <cfinclude template="#arguments.targetPage#">
  <cfelse>
    <!--- Show the Print version --->
    <!--- First we let the file run and save the result --->
    <cfsavecontent variable="content">
      <cfinclude template="#arguments.targetPage#">
    </cfsavecontent>

    <!--- Remove HTML --->
    <cfset content = reReplace(content,"<.*?>","","all")>
    <cfoutput><pre>#content#</pre></cfoutput>

  </cfif>
</cffunction>
```

Let's start with the onRequestStart and onRequestEnd methods. Both of these methods are the same as in the earlier version, except now they check for the existence of a URL variable print. If the variable exists, these methods don't include the header and footer. Now let's look at the onRequest method. This method takes one argument, the file name of the template being executed. You must include this template or it will never show up. Once again we check for the existence of the URL variable print. If it doesn't exist, we simply include the file.

The interesting part comes up when the variable *does* exist. First, we <cfinclude> the template, but wrap it with the <cfsavecontent> tag. This runs the template and saves all the content into a variable, in this case, content. Next, we use a regular expression (discussed in the *ColdFusion 8 Web Application Construction Kit, Volume 3: Advanced Application Development*) to remove the HTML.

Don't worry too much about this code—just know that it will remove all the HTML and leave the text behind. Lastly, we output the result wrapped in `<pre>` tags. The net result is that HTML that looks like so:

```
<h1>Welcome to our Site</h1>
Thanks for <b>visiting!</b>.
```

will be rendered like so:

```
Welcome to our Site
Thanks for visiting!
```

Now a Print version of your site can be generated by just adding a `print=1` to the current URL.

Working with Sessions

In Chapter 19, "Introducing the Web Application Framework," you learned about application variables, which live in your ColdFusion server's memory between page requests. You also learned that application variables are shared between all pages in your application. There are plenty of uses for application variables, but because they aren't maintained separately for each user, they don't go far in helping you create a personalized site experience.

This chapter continues the discussion of the Web application framework, focusing on the features that let you track variables on a per-user basis. This opens up all kinds of opportunities for keeping track of what each user needs, wants, has seen, or is interacting with. And in true ColdFusion style, it's all very easy to learn and use.

Addressing the Web's Statelessness

The basic building blocks of the Web—TCP/IP, HTTP, and HTML—don't directly address any notion of a "session" on the Web. Users don't log in to the Web, nor do they ever log out. So without some additional work, each page visit stands alone, in its own context. Content is requested by the browser, the server responds, and that's the end of it. No connection is maintained, and the server isn't notified when the user leaves the site altogether.

Out of the box, HTTP and HTML don't even provide a way to know who the users are or where they are. As a user moves from page to page in your site—perhaps interacting with things along the way—there's no way to track their progress or choices along the way. As far as each page request is concerned, there's only the current moment, with no future and no past. The Web is thus said to be "stateless" because it doesn't provide any built-in infrastructure to track the *state* (or status or condition) of what a user is doing.

What does the Web's statelessness mean to you as a Web developer? It means that without some type of server-side mechanism to simulate the notion of a session, you would have no way to remember that a user has put something into a shopping cart, say, or to remember the fact that the user has logged in to your site. The Web itself provides no short-term memory for remembering the contents of shopping carts and other types of choices users make during a visit. You need something to provide that short-term memory for you. That's exactly what you will learn about in this chapter.

The Problem of Maintaining State

The fact that HTTP and HTML are stateless is no accident. A main reason the Web is so wildly popular is the fact that it is so simple. It probably wouldn't have gotten so big so fast if a whole infrastructure needed to be in place for logging in and out of each Web server, or if it assumed that you needed to maintain a constant connection to a server to keep your current session open.

The simplicity of the sessionless approach also enables the tremendous scalability that benefits Web applications and the Web as a whole. It's what makes Web applications so thin and lightweight and what allows Web servers to serve so many people simultaneously. So the Web's statelessness is by design, and most people should be glad that it is.

Except for us Web developers. Our lives would probably be a lot easier if some kind of universal user ID existed, issued by, um, the United Nations or something. That couldn't be faked. And that could identify who the user was, no matter what computer they were sitting at. Until that happens, we need another way to track a user's movements as they move through our own little pieces of the Web.

Solutions Provided by ColdFusion

Expanding on the Web application framework—which already sets aside part of the server's brain to deal with each application—ColdFusion provides three types of variables that help you maintain the state of a user's visit from page to page and between visits.

Similar to application variables (which you learned about in the last chapter), all three of these are persistent variables because they stay alive between page requests. However, they are different from application variables because they are maintained separately for each browser that visits your site. It's almost as if ColdFusion had a tiny little part of its memory set aside for each visitor.

Cookies

Cookies are a simple mechanism for asking a browser to remember something, such as a user's favorite color or perhaps some type of ID number. The information is stored in the client machine's memory (or on one of its drives). You can store only a small amount of information using cookies, and users generally have a way to turn off cookies in their browsers' settings. Cookies have gotten a lot of bad press in the past few years, so many users turn them off at the browser level.

NOTE

Cookies aren't a ColdFusion feature per se, but a browser/Web server feature. ColdFusion just makes it easy to work with them.

Client Variables

Client variables are like cookies, except that the information is stored on the server, rather than on the client machine. The values are physically stored in the server's Windows Registry or in a database. Client variables are designed to hold semi-permanent data, such as preferences that should live for weeks or months between a user's visits.

Session Variables

Similar to client variables, *session variables* are stored on the server. However, instead of being stored physically, they are simply maintained in the server's RAM. Session variables are designed to hold temporary data, such as items in a shopping cart or steps in some type of wizard-style data-entry mechanism that takes the user several pages to complete.

Choosing Which Type of Variables to Use

With three types of per-visitor variables from which to choose, developers sometimes have a hard time figuring the best type to use for a particular task. We recommend that you look through this whole chapter before you start using any of them in your own application. However, in the future, you might want to refresh your memory about which type to use. Table 20.1 lists the major pros and cons of cookies, client variables, and session variables.

Table 20.1 Pros and Cons of Cookies, Client Variables, and Session Variables

VARIABLE TYPE	PROS	CONS
COOKIE	Not ColdFusion specific, so are familiar to most developers. Simple values only (no arrays, structures or queries).	Can persist for same visit only, or until a specific date/time. Limited storage capacity. User can turn them off. Have a bad reputation.
CLIENT	Much larger storage capacity. Values never leave the server. Persist between server restarts. Cookies not needed to retain values during single visit. Stored in server's registry or in any SQL database.	Can persist for months. Cookies required to remember values between visits. Simple values only (no arrays, structures, and so on), but see <CFWDDX> note in this chapter.
SESSION	High performance; stored in ColdFusion server's RAM only. Complex values allowed (arrays, structures, and so on). Can be used without cookies.	Values do not persist between server restarts.

Using Cookies to Remember Preferences

Cookies are simple variables that can be stored on a client machine. Basically, the server asks the browser to remember a variable with such-and-such a name and such-and-such a value. The browser returns the variable to the server as it requests successive pages from that same server. In other words, after the server sets the value on the browser, the browser continues to remind the server about it as the user moves from page to page. The net effect is that each site essentially has a small portion of the browser's memory in which to store little bits of information.

NOTE

Cookies first appeared in early versions of Netscape Navigator and have since been adopted by nearly all browser software. As of this writing, the original specification document for cookies is still available at `http://www.netscape.com/newsref/std/cookie_spec.html`. It is interesting to read, if only because it underscores how important Netscape's early innovations have become to today's Web. No substantive changes have been made to the cookies since.

Introducing the COOKIE Scope

Cookies aren't something specific to ColdFusion. Any server-side scripting programming environment can set them, and they can even be set by client-side languages such as JavaScript. Depending on the language, the actual code necessary to set or retrieve a cookie varies a bit, of course. The best implementations keep coders from having to understand the details of the actual communication between the browser and server. It's best if the coder can just concentrate on the task at hand.

In ColdFusion, the notion of cookies is exposed to you via the simple, elegant COOKIE scope. Similar to the APPLICATION scope you learned about in the previous chapter, the COOKIE scope is automatically maintained by ColdFusion. Setting a variable within the COOKIE scope instructs the browser to remember the cookie. Referring to a variable within the COOKIE scope returns the value of the cookie on the browser's machine.

For instance, the following line asks the user's browser to remember a cookie variable called MyMessage. The value of the cookie is "Hello, World!":

```
<cfset COOKIE.myMessage = "Hello, World!">
```

From that point on, you could output the value of #COOKIE.myMessage# in your CFML code, between <cfoutput> tags. The "Hello, World" message would be output in place of the variable.

A Simple Cookie Exercise

This simple exercise will illustrate what happens when you use cookies. First, temporarily change your browser's preferences so that you will receive notice whenever a cookie is being set.

To be notified when a cookie is set on your browser, follow these guidelines:

- If you are using Firefox, choose Tools and then Options. On the Privacy tab in the Cookie section, change Keep Until to Ask Me Every Time.

- If you are using Internet Explorer (version 5 or later), select Internet Options from the Tools menu, and then select the Security tab. Make sure the appropriate zone is selected;

then select Custom Level and check the Prompt options for both Allow Cookies That Are Stored on Your Computer and Allow Per-Session Cookies.

- If you are using some other browser or version, the steps you take might be slightly different, but you should have a way to turn on some type of notification when cookies are set.

Now use your browser to visit the CookieSet.cfm template shown in Listing 20.1. You should see a prompt similar to the one shown in Figure 20.1. The prompt might look different depending on browser and version, but it generally will show you the name and value of the cookie being set. (Note that you can even refuse to allow the cookie to be set.) Go ahead and let the browser store the cookie by clicking OK.

Figure 20.1

Click OK to let the browser store the cookie.

If you now visit the CookieShow.cfm template shown in Listing 20.2, you will see the message you started your visit at:, followed by the exact time you visited the code in Listing 20.1. Click your browser's Reload button a few times, so you can see that the value doesn't change. The value persists between page requests. If you go back to Listing 20.1, the cookie will be reset to a new value.

Close your browser, reopen it, and visit the CookieShow.cfm template again. You will see an error message from ColdFusion, telling you that the COOKIE.TimeVisitStart variable doesn't exist. By default, cookies expire when the browser is closed. Therefore, the variable is no longer passed to the server with each page request and is unknown to ColdFusion.

Listing 20.1 CookieSet.cfm—Setting a Cookie

```
<!---
 Filename: CookieSet.cfm
 Created by: Nate Weiss (NMW)
 Purpose: Sets a cookie to remember time of this page request
--->

<html>
<head><title>Cookie Demonstration</title></head>
<body>

<!--- Set a cookie to remember the time right now --->
<cfset COOKIE.TimeVisitStart = timeFormat(now(), "h:mm:ss tt")>

The cookie has been set.

</body>
</html>
```

Listing 20.2 `CookieShow.cfm`—Displaying a Cookie's Value

```
<!---
Filename: CookieShow.cfm
Created by: Nate Weiss (NMW)
Please Note Displays the value of the TimeVisitStart cookie,
which gets set by CookieSet.cfm
--->

<html>
<head><title>Cookie Demonstration</title></head>
<body>

<cfoutput>
 You started your visit at:
 #COOKIE.TimeVisitStart#<br>
</cfoutput>

</body>
</html>
```

Using Cookies

You can easily build on the last example to make it more useful in the real world. For instance, you wouldn't want the Time Started value to be reset every time the user visited the first page; you probably want the value to be recorded only the first time. So it would make sense to first test for the cookie's existence and only set the cookie if it doesn't already exist. It would also make sense to remember the full date/time value of the user's first visit, rather than just the time.

So, instead of

```
<cfset COOKIE.TimeVisitStart = timeFormat(now(), "h:mm:ss tt")>
```

you could use

```
<cfif not isDefined("COOKIE.VisitStart")>
 <cfset COOKIE.VisitStart = now()>
</cfif>
```

In fact, the `isDefined` test and the `<cfset>` tag can be replaced with a single `<cfparam>` tag:

```
<cfparam name="COOKIE.VisitStart" type="date" default="#now()#">
```

This `<cfparam>` tag can be placed in your `Application.cfc` file so it is encountered before each page request is processed. You can now be assured that ColdFusion will set the cookie the first time the user hits your application, no matter what page the user starts on, and that you will never get a `parameter doesn't exist` error message, because the cookie is guaranteed to always be defined. As discussed previously, the cookie will be reset if the user closes and reopens the browser.

→ If you need a quick reminder on the difference between `<cfset>` and `<cfparam>`, see Chapter 8, "he Basics of CFML," and Chapter 9, "Programming with CFML."

You could then output the time elapsed in your application by outputting the difference between the cookie's value and the current time. You could put this code wherever you wanted in your application, perhaps as part of some type of header or footer message. For instance, the following code would display the number of minutes that the user has been using the application:

```
<cfoutput>
 Minutes Elapsed: #dateDiff("n", COOKIE.VisitStart, now())#
</cfoutput>
```

The next two listings bring these lines together. Listing 20.3 is an `Application.cfc` file that includes the `<cfparam>` tag shown previously. Listing 20.4 is a file called `ShowTimeElapsed.cfm`, which can be used to display the elapsed time in any of the current application's pages by using `<cfinclude>`. You also can visit Listing 20.4 on its own—Figure 20.2 shows what the results would look like.

Figure 20.2

Cookies can be used to track users, preferences, or, in this case, elapsed times.

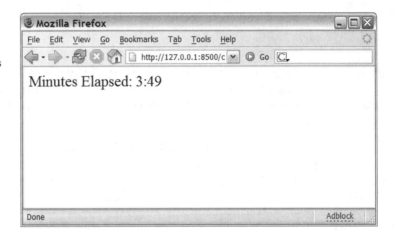

Be sure to save Listing 20.3 as `Application.cfc`, not `Application1.cfc`.

Listing 20.3 `Application1.cfc`—Defining a Cookie Variable in `Application.cfc`

```
<!---
 Filename: Application.cfc
 Created by: Raymond Camden (ray@camdenfamily.com)
 Handles application events.
--->

<cfcomponent output="false">

  <cffunction name="onRequestStart" output="false" returnType="boolean">
    <cfparam name="COOKIE.VisitStart" type="date" default="#now()#">
    <cfreturn true>
  </cffunction>

</cfcomponent>
```

Listing 20.4 `ShowTimeElapsed.cfm`—Performing Calculations Based on Cookies

```
<!---
 Filename: ShowTimeElapsed.cfm
 Created by: Nate Weiss (NMW)
 Please Note Can be <CFINCLUDED> in any page in your application
--->

<!--- Find number of seconds passed since visit started --->
<!--- (difference between cookie value and current time) --->
<cfset secsSinceStart = dateDiff("s", COOKIE.VisitStart, now())>
<!--- Break it down into numbers of minutes and seconds --->
<cfset minutesElapsed = int(secsSinceStart / 60)>
<cfset secondsElapsed = secsSinceStart MOD 60>

<!--- Display the minutes/seconds elapsed --->
<cfoutput>
 Minutes Elapsed:
 #minutesElapsed#:#numberFormat(secondsElapsed, "00")#
</cfoutput>
```

NOTE

What is the meaning of `output="false"` and `returnType="boolean"` in the methods in Listing 20.3? These are optional arguments that help define how CFC methods run. By using `output=false`, we limit the white space generated by the methods. Using `returnType=boolean` simply means that the method returns true or false. Again, these are optional attributes, but it's good practice to use them.

Because `COOKIE.VisitStart` is always a ColdFusion date/time value, getting the raw number of seconds since the visit started is easy—you use the `dateDiff` function. If the difference in seconds between the cookie value and the present moment (the value returned by the `now` function) is 206, you know that 206 seconds have passed since the cookie was set.

Because most people are more comfortable seeing time expressed in minutes and seconds, Listing 20.4 does some simple math on the raw number of seconds elapsed. First, it calculates the number of whole minutes that have elapsed, by dividing `SecsSinceStart` by 60 and rounding down to the nearest integer. Next, it calculates the number of seconds to display after the number of minutes by finding the modulus (which is the remainder left when `SecsSinceStart` is divided by 60).

Gaining More Control with `<cfcookie>`

You already have learned how to set cookies using the `<cfset>` tag and the special `COOKIE` scope (Listings 20.1 to 20.3). Using that technique, setting cookies is as simple as setting normal variables. However, sometimes you will want more control over how cookies get set.

Introducing the `<cfcookie>` Tag

To provide you with that additional control, ColdFusion provides the `<cfcookie>` tag, which is an alternative syntax for setting cookie variables. Once set, you can access or display the cookies as you have learned so far, by referring to them in the special `COOKIE` scope.

Table 20.2 introduces the attributes available when using `<cfcookie>`.

Table 20.2 `<cfcookie>` Tag Syntax

ATTRIBUTE	PURPOSE
NAME	Required. The name of the cookie variable. If you use NAME="VisitStart", the cookie will thereafter become known as COOKIE.VisitStart.
VALUE	Optional. The value of the cookie. To set the cookie's value to the current date and time, use VALUE="#Now()#".
EXPIRES	Optional. When the cookie should expire. You can provide any of the following:
	A specific expiration date (such as 3/18/2002) or a date/time value.
	The number of days you want the cookie to exist before expiring, such as 10 or 90.
	The word NEVER, which is a shortcut for setting the expiration date far into the future, so it effectively never expires.
	The word NOW, which is a shortcut for setting the expiration date in the recent past, so it is already considered expired. This is how you delete a cookie.
	If you don't specify an EXPIRES attribute, the cookie will do what it does normally, which is to expire when the user closes the browser. See "Controlling Cookie Expiration," later in this chapter.
DOMAIN	Optional. You can use this attribute to share the cookie with other servers within your own Internet domain. By default, the cookie is visible only to the server that set it. See "Controlling How Cookies Are Shared," later in this chapter.
PATH	Optional. You can use this attribute to specify which pages on your server should be able to use this cookie. By default, the cookie can be accessed by all pages on the server once set. See "Controlling How Cookies Are Shared," later in this chapter.
SECURE	Optional. You can use this attribute to specify whether the cookie should be sent back to the server if a secure connection is being used. The default is No. See "Controlling How Cookies Are Shared," later in this chapter.

Controlling Cookie Expiration

The most common reason for using `<cfcookie>` instead of a simple `<cfset>` is to control how long the cookie will exist before it expires. For instance, looking back at the Application.cfc file shown in Listing 20.3, what if you didn't want the Elapsed Time counter to start over each time the user closed the browser?

Say you wanted the elapsed time to keep counting for up to a week. You would replace the `<cfparam>` line in Listing 20.3 with the following:

```
<!--- If no "VisitStart" cookie exists, create it --->
<cfif not isDefined("COOKIE.VisitStart")>
 <cfcookie
 name="VisitStart"
 value="#now()#"
 expires="7">
</cfif>
```

Controlling How Cookies Are Shared

Netscape's original cookie specification defines three additional concepts that haven't been discussed yet. All three have to do with giving you more granular control over which pages your cookies are visible to:

- **A domain can be specified as each cookie is set.** The basic idea is that a cookie should always be visible only to the server that set the cookie originally. This is to protect users' privacy. However, if a company is running several Web servers, it is considered fair that a cookie set on one server be visible to the others. Specifying a domain for a cookie makes it visible to all servers within that domain. An example of this could be a server named `www.foo.com` that wants to share a cookie with the server `store.foo.com`, which is in the same domain.

- **A path can be specified as each cookie is set.** This enables you to control whether the cookie should be visible to the entire Web server (or Web servers), or just part. For instance, if a cookie will be used only by the pages within the `ows` folder in the Web server's root, it might make sense for the browser to not return the cookie to any other pages, even those on the same server. The path could be set to `/ows`, which would ensure that the cookie is visible only to the pages within the `ows` folder. This way, two applications on the same server can each set cookies with the same name without overwriting one another, as long as the applications use different paths when setting the cookies.

- **A cookie can be marked as secure.** This means that it should be returned to the server only when a secure connection is being used (that is, if the page's URL starts with `https://` instead of `http://`). If the browser is asked to visit an ordinary (nonsecure) page on the server, the cookie isn't sent and thus isn't visible to the server. This doesn't mean that the cookie will be stored on the user's computer in a more secure fashion; it just means that it won't be transmitted back to the server unless SSL encryption is being used.

As a ColdFusion developer, you have access to these three concepts by way of the `domain`, `path`, and `secure` attributes of the `<cfcookie>` tag. As Table 20.2 showed, all three attributes are optional.

Let's say you have three servers, named `one.orangewhip.com`, `two.orangewhip.com`, and `three.orangewhip.com`. To set a cookie that would be shared among the three servers, take the portion of the domain names they share, including the first dot. The following code would set a cookie visible to all three servers (and any other servers whose host names end in `.orangewhip.com`):

```
<!--- Share cookie over our whole domain --->
<cfcookie
name="VisitStart"
value="#now()#"
domain=".orangewhip.com">
```

The next example uses the `path` attribute to share the cookie among all pages that have a `/ows` at the beginning of the path portion of their URLs (the part after the host name). For instance, the following would set a cookie that would be visible to a page with a path of /ows/Home.cfm and /ows/store/checkout.cfm, but not /owintra/login.cfm:

```
<!--- Only share cookie within ows folder --->
<cfcookie
name="VisitStart"
value="#now()#"
path="/ows">
```

Finally, this last example uses the secure attribute to tell the browser to make the cookie visible only to pages that are at secure (https://) URLs. In addition, the cookie will expire in 30 days and will be shared among the servers in the orangewhip.com domain, but only within the /ows portion of each server:

```
<!--- This cookie is shared but confidential --->
<cfcookie
name="VisitStart"
value="#Now()#"
expires="30"
domain=".orangewhip.com"
path="/ows"
secure="Yes">
```

NOTE

You can specify that you want to share cookies only within a particular subdomain. For instance, domain=".intranet. orangewhip.com" shares the cookie within all servers that have .intranet.orangewhip.com at the end of their host names. However, there must always be a leading dot at the beginning of the domain attribute.

You can't share cookies based on IP addresses. To share cookies between servers, the servers must have Internet domain names.

The domain attribute is commonly misunderstood. Sometimes people assume that you can use it to specify other domains to share the cookies with. But domain can be used only to specify whether to share the cookies with other servers in the same domain.

Sharing Cookies with Other Applications

Because cookies aren't a ColdFusion-specific feature, cookies set with, say, Active Server Pages are visible in ColdFusion's COOKIE scope, and cookies set with <cfcookie> are visible to other applications, such as PHP, Perl, or JavaServer Pages. The browser doesn't know which language is powering which pages. All it cares about is whether the requirements for the domain, path, security, and expiration have been met. If so, it makes the cookie available to the server.

TIP

If you find that cookies set in another language aren't visible to ColdFusion, the problem might be the path part of the cookie. For instance, whereas ColdFusion sets the path to / by default so that the cookie is visible to all pages on the server, JavaScript sets the path to match that of the current page by default. Try setting the path part of the cookie to / so that it will behave more like one set with ColdFusion. The syntax to do this varies from language to language.

Cookie Limitations

There are some pretty serious restrictions on what you can store in cookies, mostly established by the original specification:

- **Only simple strings can be stored.** Because dates and numbers can be expressed as strings, you can store them as cookies. But no ColdFusion-specific data types, such as arrays and structures, can be specified as the value for a cookie.

- **A maximum of 20 cookies can be set within any one domain.** This prevents cookies from eventually taking up a lot of hard drive space. Browsers might or might not choose to enforce this limit.

- **A cookie can be only 4 KB long.** The name of the cookie is considered part of its length.

- **The browser isn't obligated to store more than 300 cookies.** (That is 300 total, counting all cookies set by all the world's servers.) The browser can delete the least recently used cookie when the 300-cookie limit has been reached. That said, many modern browsers choose not to enforce this limit.

Using Client Variables

Client variables are similar to cookies, except that they are stored on the server, rather than on the client (browser) machine. In many situations, you can use the two almost interchangeably. You're already familiar with cookies, so learning how to use client variables will be a snap. Instead of using the COOKIE prefix before a variable name, you simply use the CLIENT prefix.

Okay, there's a little bit more to it than that, but not much.

NOTE

Before you can use the CLIENT prefix, you must enable ColdFusion's Client Management feature. See the section "Enabling Client Variables," later in this chapter.

NOTE

It's worth noting that client variables can also be configured so that they are stored on the browser machine, if you take special steps in the ColdFusion Administrator. They then become essentially equivalent to cookies. See the section "Adjusting How Client Variables Are Stored," later in this chapter.

How Do Client Variables Work?

Client variables work like this:

1. The first time a particular user visits your site, ColdFusion generates a unique ID number to identify the user's browser.

2. ColdFusion sets this ID number as a cookie called CFID on the user's browser. From that point on, the browser identifies itself to ColdFusion by presenting this ID.

3. When you set a client variable in your code, ColdFusion stores the value for you on the server side, without sending anything to the browser machine. It stores the `CFID` number along with the variable, to keep them associated internally.

4. Later, when you access or output the variable, ColdFusion simply retrieves the value based on the variable name and the `CFID` number.

For the most part, this process is hidden to you as a developer. You simply use the `CLIENT` scope prefix in your code; ColdFusion takes care of the rest. Also note that a second cookie, `CFTOKEN`, is also sent by the server. This helps secure data because the browser must supply the correct token along with the ID value.

Enabling Client Variables

Before you can use client variables in your code, you must enable them using an `Application.cfc` file. In the last chapter, you learned how to use this file to enable application variables. You can modify the behavior of the application using `THIS`-scope variables. Table 20.3 lists values relevant to client variables.

Table 20.3   Additional `Application.cfc` `THIS`-Scope Values Relevant to Client Variables

ATTRIBUTE	DESCRIPTION
name	Optional. A name for your application. For more information about the `NAME` attribute, see the section "Using Application Variables" in Chapter 19."
clientManagement	Yes or No. Setting this value to Yes enables client variables for the application.
clientStorage	Optional. You can set this attribute to the word `Registry`, which means the actual client variables will be stored in the Registry (on Windows servers). You can also provide a data source name, which will cause the variables to be stored in a database. If you omit this attribute, it defaults to `Registry` unless you have changed the default in the ColdFusion Administrator. For details, see "Adjusting How Client Variables Are Stored," later. Another option is `Cookie`, which tells ColdFusion to store the client variables as cookies on the user's browser.
setClientCookies	Optional. The default is Yes, which allows ColdFusion to automatically set the `CFID` cookie on each browser, which it uses to track client variables properly for each browser. You can set this value to No if you don't want the cookies to be set. But if you do so, you will need to do a bit of extra work. For details, see "Adjusting How Client Variables Are Stored," later.
setDomainCookies	Optional. The default is No, which tells ColdFusion to set the `CFID` cookie so that it is visible only to the current server. If you have several ColdFusion servers operating in a cluster together, you can set this to Yes to share client variables between all your ColdFusion servers. For details, see "Adjusting How Client Variables Are Stored," later.

For now, just concentrate on the `clientManagement` attribute (the others are discussed later). Listing 20.5 shows how easy it is to enable client variables for your application. After you save this code in the `Application.cfc` file for your application, you can start using client variables. (Be sure to save Listing 20.5 as `Application.cfc`, not `Application2.cfc`.)

NOTE

If you attempt to use client variables without enabling them first, an error message will be displayed.

Listing 20.5 `Application2.cfc`—Enabling Client Variables in `Application.cfc`

```
<!---
 Filename: Application.cfc
 Created by: Raymond Camden (ray@camdenfamily.com)
 Handles application events.
--->

<cfcomponent output="false">

  <cfset this.name="OrangeWhipSite">
  <cfset this.clientManagement=true>

</cfcomponent>
```

Using Client Variables

Client variables are ideal for storing things like user preferences, recent form entries, and other types of values that you don't want to force your users to provide over and over again.

Remembering Values for Next Time

Consider a typical search form, in which the user types what they are looking for and then submits the form to see the search results. It might be nice if the form could remember what the user's last search was.

The code in Listing 20.6 lets it do just that. The basic idea is that the form's search criteria field will already be filled in, using the value of a variable called `SearchPreFill`. The value of this variable is set at the top of the page and will be set to the last search the user ran, if available. If no last search information exists (if this is the first time the user has used this page), it will be blank.

Listing 20.6 `SearchForm1.cfm`—Using Client Variables to Remember the User's Last Search

```
<!---
 Filename: SearchForm1.cfm
 Created by: Nate Weiss (NMW)
 Please Note Maintains "last" search via Client variables
--->

<!--- Determine value for "Search Prefill" feature --->
<!--- When user submits form, save search criteria in client variable --->
<cfif isDefined("FORM.searchCriteria")>
 <cfset CLIENT.lastSearch = FORM.searchCriteria>
 <cfset searchPreFill = FORM.searchCriteria>
```

Listing 20.6 (CONTINUED)

```
<!--- If not submitting yet, get prior search word (if possible) --->
<cfelseif isDefined("CLIENT.lastSearch")>
 <CFSET searchPreFill = CLIENT.lastSearch>

<!--- If no prior search criteria exist, just show empty string --->
<cfelse>
 <cfset searchPreFill = "">
</cfif>


<html>
<head><title>Search Orange Whip</title></head>
<body>
 <h2>Search Orange Whip</h2>

 <!--- Simple search form, which submits back to this page --->
 <cfform action="#cgi.script_name#" method="post">

 <!--- "Search Criteria" field --->
 Search For:
 <cfinput name="SearchCriteria" value="#searchPreFill#"
 required="Yes"
 message="You must type something to search for!">

 <!--- Submit button --->
 <input type="submit" value="Search"><br>

 </cfform>

</body>
</html>
```

The first part of this template (the <cfif> part) does most of the work because it's in charge of setting the searchPreFill variable that provides the "last search" memory for the user. There are three different conditions to deal with. If the user currently is submitting the form to run the search, their search criteria should be saved in a client variable called CLIENT.lastSearch. If the user isn't currently submitting the form but has run a search in the past, their last search criteria should be retrieved from the lastSearch client variable. If no last search is available, the isDefined("CLIENT.lastSearch") test will fail, and searchPreFill should just be set to an empty string.

The rest of the code is an ordinary form. Note, though, that the value of the searchPreFill variable is passed to the <cfinput> tag, which presents the user with the search field.

If you visit this page in your browser for the first time, the search field will be blank. To test the use of client variables, type a word or two to search for and submit the form. Of course, no actual search takes place because no database code yet exists in the example, but the form should correctly remember the search criteria you typed. You can close the browser and reopen it, and the value should still be there.

NOTE

Assuming that you haven't changed anything in the ColdFusion Administrator to the contrary, the value of CLIENT.LastSearch will continue to be remembered until the user is away from the site for 90 days.

Using Several Client Variables Together

No limit is set on the number of client variables you can use. Listing 20.7 builds on the search form from Listing 20.6, this time allowing the user to specify the number of records the search should return. A second client variable, called `lastMaxRows`, remembers the value, using the same simple `<cfif>` logic shown in the previous listing.

Listing 20.7 `SearchForm2.cfm`—Using Client Variables to Remember Search Preferences

```
<!---
 Filename: SearchForm2.cfm
 Created by: Nate Weiss (NMW)
 Please Note Maintains "last" search via Client variables
--->

<!---
  When user submits form, save search criteria in Client variable
--->
<cfif isDefined("FORM.searchCriteria")>
 <cfset CLIENT.lastSearch = FORM.searchCriteria>
 <cfset CLIENT.lastMaxRows = FORM.searchMaxRows>
<!--- if not submitting yet, get prior search word (if possible) --->
<cfelseif isDefined("CLIENT.lastSearch") and
          isDefined("CLIENT.lastMaxRows")>
 <cfset searchCriteria = CLIENT.lastSearch>
 <cfset searchMaxRows = CLIENT.lastMaxRows>
<!--- if no prior search criteria exist, just show empty string --->
<cfelse>
 <cfset searchCriteria = "">
 <cfset searchMaxRows = 10>
</cfif>

<html>
<head><title>Search Orange Whip</title></head>
<body>

<h2>Search Orange Whip</h2>

<!--- Simple search form, which submits back to this page --->
<cfform action="#cgi.script_name#" method="post">

<!--- "Search Criteria" field --->
Search For:
<cfinput name="SearchCriteria" value="#searchCriteria#"
required="Yes"
message="You must type something to search for!">

<!--- Submit button --->
<input type="Submit" value="Search"><br>

<!--- "Max Matches" field --->
<i>show up to
<cfinput name="SearchMaxRows" value="#searchMaxRows#" size="2"
required="Yes" validate="integer" range="1,500">
```

Listing 20.7 (CONTINUED)

```
message="Provide a number from 1-500 for search maximum.">
matches</i><br>
</cfform>
<!--- If we have something to search for, do it now --->
<cfif searchCriteria neq "">
  <!--- Get matching film entries from database --->
  <cfquery name="getMatches" datasource="ows">
  SELECT FilmID, MovieTitle, Summary
  FROM Films
  WHERE MovieTitle LIKE '%#SearchCriteria#%'
  OR Summary LIKE '%#SearchCriteria#%'
  ORDER BY MovieTitle
  </cfquery>

  <!--- Show number of matches --->
  <cfoutput>
  <hr><i>#getMatches.recordCount# records found for
  "#searchCriteria#"</i><br>
  </cfoutput>

  <!--- Show matches, up to maximum number of rows --->
  <cfoutput query="getMatches" maxrows="#searchMaxRows#">
  <p><b>#MovieTitle#</b><br>
  #Summary#<br>
  </cfoutput>
</cfif>

</body>
</html>
```

Next, the actual search is performed, using simple LIKE code in a <cfquery> tag. When the results are output, the user's maximum records preference is provided to the <cfoutput> tag's maxrows attribute. Any rows beyond the preferred maximum aren't shown. (If you want to brush up on the <cfquery> and <cfoutput> code used here, see Chapter 10, "Creating Data-Driven Pages.")

Not only does this version of the template remember the user's last search criteria, but it also actually reruns the user's last query before they even submit the form. This means the user's last search results will be redisplayed each time they visit the page, making the search results appear to be persistent. The results are shown in Figure 20.3.

You easily could change this behavior by changing the second <cfif> test to isDefined("FORM. SearchCriteria"). The last search would still appear prefilled in the search form, but the search itself wouldn't be rerun until the user clicked the Search button. Use client variables in whatever way makes sense for your application.

TIP

To improve performance, you could add a cachedwithin or cachedafter attribute to the <cfquery> tag, which enables ColdFusion to deliver any repeat searches directly from the server's RAM memory. For details, see Chapter 31, "Improving Performance," in *ColdFusion 8 Web Application Construction Kit, Volume 2: Application Development*..

Figure 20.3

Client variables make maintaining the state of a user's recent activity easy.

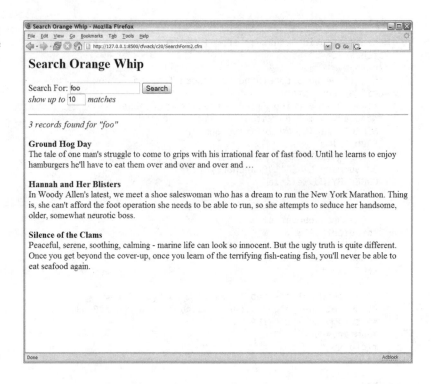

Deleting Client Variables

Once set, client variables are stored semi-permanently: they're deleted only if a user's browser doesn't return to your site for 90 days. In the next section, you learn how to adjust the number of days that the variables are kept, but sometimes you will need to delete a client variable programmatically.

NOTE

It's important to understand that a client doesn't have its own expiration date. Client variables don't expire individually; the whole client record is what expires. So, it's not that a client variable is deleted 90 days after it is set. Rather, the client variable (and all other client variables assigned to the user's machine) is deleted after the user lets 90 days pass before revisiting any pages in the application. For more information about tweaking the expiration system, see "Adjusting How Long Client Variables Are Kept," in the next section.

ColdFusion provides a `deleteClientVariable()` function, which enables you to delete individual client variables by name. The function takes one argument: the name of the client variable you want to delete (the name isn't case sensitive). Another handy housekeeping feature is the `getClientVariablesList()` function, which returns a comma-separated list of the client-variable names that have been set for the current browser.

Listing 20.8 shows how these two functions can be used together to delete all client variables that have been set for a user's browser. You could use code such as this on a start-over type of page, or if the user has chosen to log out of a special area.

Listing 20.8 `DeleteClientVars.cfm`— Deleting Client Variables Set for the Current Browser

```
<!---
 Filename: DeleteClientVars.cfm
 Created by: Nate Weiss (NMW)
 Purpose: Deletes all client variables associated with browser
--->

<html>
<head><title>Clearing Your Preferences</title></head>
<body>

<h2>Clearing Your Preferences</h2>

<!--- For each client-variable set for this browser... --->
<cfloop list="#getClientVariablesList()#" index="thisVarName">
 <!--- Go ahead and delete the client variable! --->
 <cfset deleteClientVariable(thisVarName)>

 <cfoutput>#thisVarName# deleted.<br></cfoutput>
</cfloop>

<p>Your preferences have been cleared.</p>

</body>
</html>
```

Along with `deleteClientVariable()`, you can also treat the `CLIENT` scope like a structure. So for example, you can remove the client variable name using `structDelete(CLIENT,"name")`.

Adjusting How Client Variables Are Stored

Out of the box, ColdFusion stores client variables in the server's Registry and will delete all client variables for any visitors who don't return to your site for 90 or more days. You can, of course, tweak these behaviors to suit your needs. This section discusses the client-variable storage options available.

Adjusting How Long Client Variables Are Kept

Normally, client variables are maintained on what amounts to a permanent basis for users who visit your site at least once every 90 days. If a user actually lets 90 days pass without visiting your site (for shame!), all of their client variables are purged by ColdFusion. This helps keep the client-variable store from becoming ridiculously large.

To adjust this value from the default of 90 days, do the following:

1. Open the ColdFusion Administrator.

2. Navigate to the Client Variables page.

3. Under Storage Name, click the Registry link.

4. Change the Purge Data for Clients That Remain Unvisited For value to the number of days you want; then click Submit Changes.

> **NOTE**
>
> Remember, there isn't a separate timeout for each client variable. The only time client variables are automatically purged is if the client browser hasn't visited the server at all for 90 days (or whatever the purge-data setting has been set to).

Storing Client Variables in a Database

ColdFusion can store your client variables in a database instead of in the Registry. This will appeal to people who don't like the idea of the Registry being used for storage, or who find that they must make the Registry very large to accommodate the number of client variables they need to maintain. The ability to store client variables in a SQL database is particularly important if you are running several servers in a cluster. You can have all the servers in the cluster keep your application's client variables in the same database, thereby giving you a way to keep variables persistent between pages without worrying about what will happen if the user ends up at a different server in the cluster on their next visit. See the section "Sharing Client Variables Between Servers," later.

> **NOTE**
>
> When using the term *Registry*, we are referring to the Windows Registry, assuming that ColdFusion Server is installed on a Windows machine. On other platforms, ColdFusion ships with a simple Registry replacement for storage of client variables. Linux and Unix users can still use the default client storage mechanism of the Registry. However, the Registry replacement isn't a high-performance beast, and isn't recommended for applications that get a lot of traffic.

> **NOTE**
>
> Although the Registry provides a quick and simple way to use client variables, using it is almost never recommended for a live Web site.

To store your client variables in a database, follow these steps:

1. Create a new database to hold the client variables. You don't need to create any tables in the database; ColdFusion will do that on its own. If you want, you can use an existing database, but we recommend that you use a fresh, dedicated database for storing client variables.

2. Use the ColdFusion Administrator to create a new data source for your new database. See Chapter 6, "Introducing SQL," for details.

3. Navigate to the Client Variables page of the ColdFusion Administrator.

4. Select your new data source from the drop-down list, then click the Add button. The page for adding to or editing the client store appears, as shown in Figure 20.4.

5. Adjust the Purge Data for Clients That Remain Unvisited For value as desired. This value was described in "Adjusting How Long Client Variables Are Kept," above. As the page in the Administrator notes, if you are using the client variable database in a cluster situation, this option should be enabled for only one server in the cluster. If you aren't using a cluster, you should keep this option enabled.

6. Check the Disable Global Client Variable Updates check box unless you are particularly interested in the accuracy of the `hitcount` and `lastvisit` properties. In general, we recommend that you check this option, because it can greatly lessen the strain on the

database. The only side effect is that client variables will be purged based on the last time a client variable was set or changed, rather than the last time the user visited your site.

Figure 20.4

You can have ColdFusion store your application's client variables in a database, rather than in the Registry.

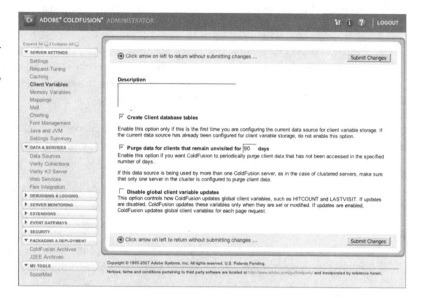

7. Leave the Create Client Database Tables option checked, unless you have already gone through that process for this database in the past.

8. Click the Submit Changes button.

You now can supply the new data source name to the `clientStorage` value in the `THIS` scope from the `Application.cfc` file (refer to Table 20.3). All of your application's client variables now will be stored in the database instead of in the Registry.

TIP

If you go back to the Client Variables page of the ColdFusion Administrator and change the Default Storage Mechanism for Client Sessions value to the data source you just created, it will be used for all applications that don't specify a `clientStorage` attribute (refer to Table 20.3).

Sharing Client Variables Between Servers

As explained at the beginning of this section, ColdFusion tracks each browser by setting its own client-tracking cookie called `CFID`. Normally, it sets this cookie so that it is sent back only to the server that set it. If you have three ColdFusion servers, each visitor will be given a different `CFID` number for each server, which in turn means that client variables will be maintained separately for each server.

In many situations, especially if you are operating several servers in a cluster, you will want client variables to be shared between the servers, so that a `CLIENT.lastSearch` variable set by one server will be visible to the others.

To share client variables between servers, do the following:

1. Have ColdFusion store your application's client variables in a database, rather than in the Registry. Be sure to do this on all servers in question. For instructions, see the section "Storing Client Variables in a Database," above.

2. Add a `setDomainCookies="Yes"` attribute to your application's `THIS` scope in the `Application.cfc` file. This causes ColdFusion to set the `CFID` cookie in such a way that it will be shared among all servers in the same Internet domain. This is the rough equivalent of using the `DOMAIN` attribute in a `<cfcookie>` tag.

Now you can use client variables in your code as you normally would. No matter which server a user visits, ColdFusion will store all client variables in the common database you set up.

NOTE

For cookies to be shared between servers, they all must be members of the same top-level Internet domain (for instance, `orangewhip.com`).

TIP

For more information about using client variables in a clustered environment, see Chapter 59, "Managing Session State in Clusters," in *ColdFusion 8 Web Application Construction Kit, Volume 3: Advanced Application Development.*

Backing Up Your Server's Client Variables

If you are keeping client variables in a database, you can back them all up by simply backing up the database itself. If it's an Access or some other file-based database, that entails making a backup copy of the database (`.mdb`) file itself. Otherwise, you must use whatever backup facility is provided with your database software.

If you are using a Windows server and are keeping client variables in the Registry, you can make a copy of the appropriate portion of the Registry. Just follow these steps:

1. Open the Registry Editor by selecting Run from the Windows Start menu and then typing `regedit` in the Run dialog box

2. Navigate to the following Registry branch (folder): `HKEY_LOCAL_MACHINE\SOFTWARE\Adobe\ColdFusion\CurrentVersion\Client`.

3. Select Export Registry File from the Registry menu, then save the file wherever you want. Be sure to leave the Selected Branch option enabled.

Storing Client Variables As a Cookie

Somewhat paradoxically, you can tell ColdFusion to store your application's client variables in cookies on the user's machine, rather than on the server side. You do this by setting the `clientStorage` value in the `THIS` scope from the `Application.cfc` file to `Cookie`. This basically lets you continue using the `CLIENT` prefix even if you want the variables to essentially be stored as cookies.

This might be useful, for instance, in situations where you are selling your code as a third-party application and want your licensees to have the option of using a server-side or client-side data store. Unfortunately, the size limitations for cookies will apply (see the section "Cookie Limitations," above). This is a somewhat esoteric subject, so it isn't discussed in full here. Please consult the ColdFusion documentation for more information about this feature.

NOTE

The cookie-storage mechanism for client variables can be useful in a clustered environment or a site that gets an extremely large number of discrete visitors.

NOTE

For more information about using client variables in a clustered environment, see Chapter 59.

Using Client Variables Without Requiring Cookies

Above, you learned that ColdFusion maintains the association between a browser and its client variables by storing a CFID cookie on the browser machine. That would seem to imply that client variables won't work if a browser doesn't support cookies or has had them disabled. Don't worry; all isn't completely lost.

Actually, ColdFusion normally sets two cookies with which to track client variables: the cfid value already mentioned and a randomly generated cftoken value. Think of cfid and cftoken as being similar to a username and password, respectively. Only if the cfid and cftoken are both valid will ColdFusion be capable of successfully looking up the appropriate client variables. If the browser doesn't provide the values, for whatever reason (perhaps because the user has configured the browser not to use cookies or because a firewall between the user and your server is stripping cookies out of each page request), ColdFusion won't be able to look up the browser's client variables. In fact, it will be forced to consider the browser to be a new, first-time visitor, and it will generate a new cfid and cftoken for the browser—which, of course, means that all client variables that might have been set during previous page visits will be lost.

You can still use client variables without requiring cookies, but it takes a bit more work. Basically, you need to make the cfid and cftoken available to ColdFusion yourself, by passing the values manually in the URL to every single page in your application.

So, if you want your client variables to work for browsers that don't (or won't) support cookies, you must include the cfid and cftoken as URL parameters. So, a link such as

```
<a href="MyPage.cfm">Click Here</a>
```

would be changed to the following, which would need to be placed between <cfoutput> tags:

```
<a href="MyPage.cfm?CFID=#CLIENT.cfid#&CFTOKEN=#CLIENT.cftoken#">Click Here</a>
```

ColdFusion provides a shortcut property you can use to make this task less tedious. Instead of providing the cfid and cftoken in the URL, you can just pass the special CLIENT.urlToken property, which always holds the current cfid and cftoken name/value pairs together in one string, including the & and = signs. This means the previous line of code can be shortened to the following, which would still need to be placed between <cfoutput> tags:

```
<a href="MyPage.cfm?#CLIENT.urlToken#">Click Here</a>
```

You must be sure to pass CLIENT.urlToken in every URL, not just in links. For instance, if you are using a <form> (or <cfform>) tag, you must pass the token value in the form's action, such as this:

```
<form action="MyPage.cfm?#CLIENT.urlToken#" method="Post">
```

If you are using frames, you must pass the token value in the src attribute, such as this:

```
<frame src="MyPage.cfm?#CLIENT.urlToken#">
```

And so on. Basically, you must look through your code and ensure that whenever you see one of your .cfm templates in a URL of any type, you correctly pass the token value.

ColdFusion provides yet another shortcut as well. The URLSessionFormat function will actually detect whether the current browser can accept cookies. You pass a URL, and ColdFusion will return either the URL as is (if the browser accepts cookies) or the URL with the token information. If you use this function, the form tag becomes:

```
<form action="#URLSessionFormat("MyPage.cfm")" method="Post">
```

NOTE

Remember that the URLSessionFormat value must always be placed between <cfoutput> tags, unless the URL is being passed as an attribute to a CFML tag (any tag that starts with CF, such as <cfform>).

TIP

If users bookmark one of your pages, the cfid and cftoken information should be part of the bookmarked URL, so that their client variables aren't lost even if their browsers don't support cookies. However, if they just type your site's URL into their browsers directly, it's unlikely that they will include the cfid and cftoken. ColdFusion will be forced to consider them as new visitors, which in turn means that the prior visit's client variables will be lost. ColdFusion will eventually purge the lost session (see the section "Adjusting How Long Client Variables Are Kept," earlier in this chapter).

NOTE

In addition to the cfid, cftoken, and urlToken properties mentioned here, several other automatically maintained properties of the CLIENT scope are available, including hitCout, lastVisit, and timeCreated.

Storing Complex Data Types in Client Variables

As mentioned earlier, you can store only simple values (strings, numbers, dates, and Boolean values) in the CLIENT scope. If you attempt to store one of ColdFusion's complex data types (structures, arrays, queries, and object references) as a client variable, you get an error message.

You can, however, use the <cfwddx> tag to transform a complex value into an XML-based string. In this serialized form, the value can be stored as a client variable. Later, when you want to use the variable, you can use <cfwddx> again to transform it from the string format back into its complex form.

There isn't space here to discuss the `<cfwddx>` tag fully, but the following code snippets will be enough to get you started. For more information about the Web Distributed Data Exchange (WDDX) technology in general and how it can be used to do much more than this, consult Vol. 3 in this series or visit http://www.openwddx.org.

Assuming, for instance, that myStruct is a structure, the following would store it in the CLIENT scope:

```
<cfwddx
 action="CFML2WDDX"
 input="#myStruct#"
 output="CLIENT.myStructAsWddx">
```

Later, to retrieve the value, you could use the following:

```
<cfwddx
 action="WDDX2CFML"
 input="#CLIENT.myStructAsWddx#"
 output="myStruct">
```

You then could refer to the values in myStruct normally in your code. If you made any changes to the structure, you would need to store it anew using the first snippet.

NOTE

You can use the `isSimpleValue()` function to test whether a value can be stored in the CLIENT scope without using this WDDX technique. You can use the `isWDDX()` function to test whether a client variable actually contains a valid WDDX value.

Using Session Variables

We have already has covered a lot of ground in this chapter. You have learned about cookies and client variables and how they can be used to make an application aware of its individual users and what they are doing. ColdFusion's Web application framework provides one more type of persistent variable to discuss: session variables.

What Are Session Variables?

Session variables are similar to client variables in that they are stored on the server rather than in the browser's memory. Unlike client variables, however, session variables persist only for a user's current session. Later you'll learn exactly how a session is defined, but for now, think of it as synonymous with a user's visit to your site. So session variables should be seen as per-visit variables, whereas client variables are per-user variables intended to persist between each user's visits.

Session variables aren't stored physically in a database or the server's Registry. Instead, they are stored in the server's RAM. This makes sense, considering that they are intended to persist for only a short time. Also, because ColdFusion doesn't need to physically store and retrieve the variables, you can expect session variables to work a bit more quickly than client variables.

Enabling Session Variables

As with client variables, you must enable session variables using an `Application.cfc` file before you can use them in your code. Table 20.4 lists the additional attributes relevant to session variables. In general, all you need to do is specify a `name` and then set `sessionManagement="Yes"`.

Table 20.4 `<CFAPPLICATION>` Attributes Relevant to Session Variables

ATTRIBUTE	PURPOSE
name	A name for your application.
sessionManagement	Yes or No. Set to Yes to enable the use of session variables. If you attempt to use session variables in your code without setting this attribute to Yes, an error message will be displayed when the code is executed.
sessionTimeout	Optional. How long you want your session variables to live in the server's memory. If you don't provide this value, it defaults to whatever is set up in the Variables page of the ColdFusion Administrator. See the section "When Does a Session End?" later. The ColdFusion Administrator specifies a maximum setting for session timeouts. If you specify a value higher than the maximum set in the Administrator, the value specified in the Administrator will be used instead.

For example, to enable session management, you might use something such as this in your `Application.cfc` file:

```
<!--- Name application and enable Session and Application variables --->
<cfset this.name="OrangeWhipSite">
<cfset this.sessionManagement="Yes">
```

NOTE

Session variables can be disabled globally (for the entire server) in the ColdFusion Administrator. If the Enable Session Variables option on the Memory Variables page of the Administrator has been unchecked, you will not be able to use session variables, regardless of what you set the `sessionManagement` attribute to.

The Web site for this book includes an `Application3.cfc` template, which enables session management. It is identical to the `Application2.cfc` template used earlier to enable client variables (Listing 20.5), except that `sessionManagement` is set to `Yes`, rather than to `clientManagement`.

Using Session Variables

After you have enabled session variables using `sessionMangement`, you can start using them in your code. ColdFusion provides a special `SESSION` variable scope, which works similarly to the `CLIENT` and `COOKIE` scopes you are already familiar with. You can set and use session variables simply by using the `SESSION` prefix in front of a variable's name.

For instance, instead of the `CLIENT.lastSearch` used in the `SearchForm.cfm` examples above, you could call the variable `SESSION.lastSearch`. The examples would still work in essentially the same way. The only difference in behavior would be that the memory interval of each user's last search would be short (until the end of the session), rather than long (90 days, by default).

For something such as search results, the shorter memory provided by using session variables might feel more intuitive for the user. That is, a user might expect the search page to remember their last search phrase during the same visit, but they might be surprised—or irritated—if it remembered search criteria from weeks or months in the past.

You will often find yourself using session and client variables together in the same application. Generally, things that should be remembered for only the current visit belong in session variables, whereas things that should be remembered between visits should be kept in client variables.

Using Session Variables for Multiple-Page Data Entry

Session variables can be especially handy for data-entry processes that require the user to fill out a number of pages. Let's say you have been asked to put together a data-entry interface for Orange Whip Studios' intranet. The idea is for your users to be able to add new film records to the studio's database. A number of pieces of information will need to be supplied by the user (title, director, actors, and so on).

The most obvious solution would be to just create one long, complex form. However, suppose further that you have been specifically asked not to do this because it might confuse the interns the company hires to do its data-entry tasks.

After carefully considering your options, you decide to present the data-entry screens in a familiar wizard format, with Next and Back buttons the users can use to navigate between steps. However, it's important that nothing actually be entered into the database until the user has finished all the steps. This means the wizard must remember everything the user has entered, even though they may be moving freely back and forth between steps.

Hmm. You could pass everything from step to step as hidden form fields, but that sounds like a lot of work, and it feels wrong to put the burden of remembering all that data on the client. You'd like to keep the information on the server side. You could create some type of temporary tables in your database, and keep updating the temporary values until the user is finished, but that also sounds like a lot of work. Plus, how would you keep the values separate for each user? And what if the user abandons the wizard partway through?

The answer, of course, is to use session variables, which are perfect for this type of situation. You only need to track the information for a short time, so session variables are appropriate. Also, session variables aren't kept permanently on the server, so you won't be storing any excess data if the user doesn't finish the wizard.

Maintaining Structures in the SESSION Scope

The following code snippet creates a new structure called SESSION.movWiz. It contains several pieces of information, most of which start out blank (set to an empty string). Because the variable is in the SESSION scope, a separate version of the structure is kept for each user, but only for the user's current visit. The stepNum value is in charge of tracking which step of the data-entry wizard each user is currently on:

```
<cfif not isDefined("SESSION.movWiz")>
  <!--- If structure is undefined, create/initialize it --->
  <cfset SESSION.movWiz = structNew()>
  <!--- Represents current wizard step; start at one --->
  < cfset SESSION.movWiz.stepNum = 1>
  <!--- We will collect these from user; start blank --->
  <cfset SESSION.movWiz.movieTitle = "">
  <cfset SESSION.movWiz.pitchText = "">
  <cfset SESSION.movWiz.directorID = "">
  <cfset SESSION.movWiz.ratingID = "">
  <cfset SESSION.movWiz.actorIDs = "">
  <cfset SESSION.novWiz.starActorID = "">
</cfif>
```

Updating the values in the SESSION.movWiz structure is simple enough. Assume for the moment that the wizard contains Back and Next buttons named goBack and goNext, respectively. The following snippet would increment the stepNum part of the structure by 1 when the user clicks the Next button, and decrement it by 1 if the user clicks Back:

```
<!--- If user clicked Back button, go back a step --->
<cfif isDefined("FORM.goBack")>
  <cfset SESSION.movWiz.stepNum = SESSION.movWiz.stepNum - 1>
<!--- If user clicked Next button, go forward one --->
<cfelseif isDefined("FORM.goNext")>
  <cfset SESSION.MovWiz.stepNum = SESSION.movWiz.stepNum + 1>
</cfif>
```

The other values in the movWiz structure can be accessed and updated in a similar way. For instance, to present the user with a text-entry field for the new movie's title, you could use something such as this:

```
<cfinput
name="MovieTitle"
value="#SESSION.movWiz.movieTitle#">
```

The input field will be prefilled with the current value of the movieTitle part of the movWiz structure. If the previous snippet was in a form and submitted to the server, the value the user typed could be saved back into the movWiz structure using the following line:

```
<cfset SESSION.movWiz.movieTitle = FORM.movieTitle>
```

Putting It All Together

The code in Listing 20.9 combines all the previous snippets into a simple, intuitive wizard interface that users will find familiar and easy to use. The listing is a bit longer than usual, but each part is easy to understand.

The idea here is to create a self-submitting form page that changes depending on which step of the wizard the user is on. The first time the user comes to the page, they see Step 1 of the wizard. They submit the form, which calls the template again, they see Step 2, and so on.

This data-entry wizard will collect information from the user in five steps, as follows:

1. The film's title, a one-line description, and the rating, which eventually will be placed in the `Films` table.

2. The film's director (the user can list only one), which is inserted in the `FilmsDirectors` table.

3. The actors in the movie (the user can list any number), which will be inserted in the `FilmsActors` table.

4. Which of the film's actors gets top billing, which sets the `IsStarringRole` column of the `FilmsActors` table to true.

5. A final confirmation screen, with a Finish button.

The following examples use variables in the `SESSION` scope without locking the accesses by way of the `<cflock>` tag. While extremely unlikely, it is theoretically possible that simultaneous visits to this template *from the same browser* could cause the wizard to collect information in an inconsistent manner. See the section "Locking Revisited," later in this chapter.

Listing 20.9 `NewMovieWizard.cfm`— Using Session Variables to Guide through a Multistep Process

```
<!---
 Filename: NewMovieWizard.cfm
 Created by: Nate Weiss (NMW)
 Please Note Session variables must be enabled
--->

<!--- Total Number of Steps in the Wizard --->
<cfset numberOfSteps = 5>

<!--- The SESSION.movWiz structure holds users' entries --->
<!--- as they move through wizard. Make sure it exists! --->
<cfif not isDefined("SESSION.movWiz")>
 <!--- If structure undefined, create/initialize it --->
 <cfset SESSION.movWiz = structNew()>
 <!--- Represents current wizard step; start at one --->
 <cfset SESSION.movWiz.stepNum = 1>
 <!--- We will collect these from user; start blank --->
 <cfset SESSION.movWiz.movieTitle = "">
 <cfset SESSION.movWiz.pitchText = "">
 <cfset SESSION.movWiz.directorID = "">
 <cfset SESSION.movWiz.ratingID = "">
 <cfset SESSION.movWiz.actorIDs = "">
 <cfset SESSION.movWiz.starActorID = "">
</cfif>


<!--- If user just submitted MovieTitle, remember it --->
<!--- Do same for the DirectorID, Actors, and so on. --->
<cfif isDefined("FORM.movieTitle")>
 <cfset SESSION.movWiz.movieTitle = FORM.movieTitle>
 <cfset SESSION.movWiz.pitchText = FORM.pitchText>
 <cfset SESSION.movWiz.ratingID = FORM.ratingID>
```

Listing 20.9 (CONTINUED)

```
<cfelseif isDefined("FORM.directorID")>
 <cfset SESSION.movWiz.directorID = FORM.directorID>
<cfelseif isDefined("FORM.actorID")>
 <cfset SESSION.movWiz.actorIDs = FORM.actorID>
<cfelseif isDefined("FORM.starActorID")>
 <cfset SESSION.movWiz.starActorID = FORM.starActorID>
</cfif>


<!--- If user clicked "Back" button, go back a step --->
<cfif isDefined("FORM.goBack")>
 <cfset SESSION.movWiz.stepNum = URL.stepNum - 1>
<!--- If user clicked "Next" button, go forward one --->
<cfelseif isDefined("FORM.goNext")>
 <cfset SESSION.movWiz.stepNum = URL.stepNum + 1>
<!--- If user clicked "Finished" button, we're done --->
<cfelseif isDefined("FORM.goDone")>
 <cflocation url="NewMovieCommit.cfm">
</cfif>


<html>
<head><title>New Movie Wizard</title></head>
<body>

<!--- Show title and current step --->
<cfoutput>
 <b>New Movie Wizard</b><br>
 Step #SESSION.movWiz.StepNum# of #NumberOfSteps#<br>
</cfoutput>


<!--- Data Entry Form, which submits back to itself --->
<cfform
 action="NewMovieWizard.cfm?StepNum=#SESSION.movWiz.stepNum#"
 method="POST">

 <!--- Display the appropriate wizard step --->
 <cfswitch expression="#SESSION.movWiz.stepNum#">
 <!--- Step One: Movie Title --->
 <cfcase value="1">
 <!--- Get potential film ratings from database --->
 <cfquery name="getRatings" datasource="ows">
 SELECT RatingID, Rating
 FROM FilmsRatings
 ORDER BY RatingID
 </cfquery>

 <!--- Show text entry field for title --->
 What is the title of the movie?<br>
 <cfinput
 name="MovieTitle"
 SIZE="50"
 VALUE="#SESSION.movWiz.MovieTitle#">
```

Listing 20.9 (CONTINUED)

```
<!--- Show text entry field for short description --->
<p>What is the "pitch" or "one-liner" for the movie?<br>
<cfinput
name="pitchText"
size="50"
value="#SESSION.movWiz.pitchText#">

<!--- Series of radio buttons for movie rating --->
<p>Please select the rating:<br>
<cfloop query="getRatings">
<!--- Re-select this rating if it was previously selected --->
<cfset isChecked = ratingID EQ SESSION.movWiz.ratingID>
<!--- Display radio button --->
<cfinput
type="radio"
name="ratingID"
checked="#isChecked#"
value="#ratingID#"><cfoutput>#rating#<br></cfoutput>
</cfloop>
</cfcase>

<!--- Step Two: Pick Director --->
<cfcase value="2">
<!--- Get list of directors from database --->
<cfquery name="getDirectors" datasource="ows">
SELECT DirectorID, FirstName || ' ' || LastName As FullName
FROM Directors
ORDER BY LastName
</cfquery>

<!--- Show all Directors in SELECT list --->
<!--- Pre-select if user has chosen one --->
Who will be directing the movie?<br>
<cfselect
size="#getDirectors.recordCount#"
query="getDirectors"
name="directorID"
display="fullName"
value="directorID"
selected="#SESSION.movWiz.directorID#"/>
</cfcase>

<!--- Step Three: Pick Actors --->
<cfcase value="3">
<!--- get list of actors from database --->
<cfquery name="getActors" datasource="ows">
SELECT * FROM Actors
ORDER BY NameLast
</cfquery>

What actors will be in the movie?<br>
<!--- For each actor, display checkbox --->
<cfloop query="GetActors">
<!--- Should checkbox be pre-checked? --->
<cfset isChecked = listFind(SESSION.movWiz.actorIDs, actorID)>
```

Listing 20.9 (CONTINUED)

```
<!--- Checkbox itself --->
<cfinput
type="checkbox"
name="actorID"
value="#actorID#"
checked="#isChecked#">
<!--- Actor name --->
<cfoutput>#nameFirst# #nameLast#</cfoutput><br>
</cfloop>
</cfcase>


<!--- Step Four: Who is the star? --->
<cfcase value="4">
<cfif SESSION.movWiz.actorIDs EQ "">
Please go back to the last step and choose at least one
actor or actress to be in the movie.
<cfelse>
<!--- Get actors who are in the film --->
<cfquery name="getActors" DATASOURCE="ows">
SELECT * FROM Actors
WHERE ActorID IN (#SESSION.movWiz.ActorIDs#)
ORDER BY NameLast
</cfquery>

Which one of the actors will get top billing?<br>
<!--- For each actor, display radio button --->
<cfloop query="getActors">
<!--- Should radio be pre-checked? --->
<cfset isChecked = SESSION.movWiz.starActorID EQ actorID>
<!--- Radio button itself --->
<cfinput
type="radio"
name="starActorID"
value="#actorID#"
checked="#isChecked#">
<!--- Actor name --->
<cfoutput>#nameFirst# #nameLast#</cfoutput><br>
</cfloop>
</cfif>
</cfcase>


<!--- Step Five: Final Confirmation --->
<cfcase value="5">
You have successfully finished the New Movie Wizard.<br>
Click the Finish button to add the movie to the database.<br>
Click Back if you need to change anything.<br>
</cfcase>
</cfswitch>


<p>
<!--- Show Back button, unless at first step --->
<cfif SESSION.movWiz.stepNum GT 1>
<input type="submit" name="goBack" value="&lt;&lt; Back">
</cfif>
```

Listing 20.9 (CONTINUED)

```
<!--- Show Next button, unless at last step --->
<!--- If at last step, show "Finish" button --->
<cfif SESSION.movWiz.stepNum lt numberOfSteps>
<input type="submit" name="goNext" value="Next &gt;&gt;">
<CFELSE>
<input type="submit" name="goDone" value="Finish">
</cfif>
</cfform>

</body>
</html>
```

NOTE

To help keep this code as clear as possible, Listing 20.9 doesn't prevent the user from leaving various form fields blank. See Listing 20.11 for a version that validates the user's entries, using the techniques introduced in Chapter 13, "Form Data Validation."

First, a variable called `numberOfSteps` is defined, set to 5. This keeps the 5 from needing to be hard-coded throughout the rest of the template. Next, the `SESSION.movWiz` structure is defined, using the syntax shown in the first code snippet that appeared before this listing. The structure contains a default value for each piece of information that will be collected from the user.

Next, a `<cfif>` / `<cfelseif>` block is used to determine whether the step the user just completed contains a form element named `movieTitle`. If so, the corresponding value in the `SESSION.movWiz` structure is updated with the form's value, thus remembering the user's entry for later. The other possible form fields are also tested for this block of code in the same manner.

Next, the code checks to see whether a form field named `goBack` was submitted. If so, it means the user clicked the Back button in the wizard interface (see Figure 20.5). Therefore, the `stepNum` value in the `movWiz` structure should be decremented by 1, effectively moving the user back a step. An equivalent test is performed for fields named `goNext` and `goFinish`. If the user clicks `goFinish`, they are redirected to another template called `NewMovieCommit.cfm`, which actually takes care of inserting the records in the database.

Figure 20.5

Session variables are perfect for creating wizard-style interfaces.

The rest of the code displays the correct form to the user, depending on which step they are on. If it's step 1, the first cfcase tag kicks in, displaying form fields for the movie's title and short description. Each of the form fields is prefilled with the current value of the corresponding value from SESSION.movWiz. That means the fields will be blank when the user begins, but if they later click the Back button to return to the first step, they will see the value that they previously entered. That is, a session variable is being used to maintain the state of the various steps of the wizard.

The other <cfcase> sections are similar to the first. Each presents form fields to the user (check boxes, radio buttons, and so on), always prefilled or preselected with the current values from SESSION.movWiz. As the user clicks Next or Back to submit the values for a particular step, their entries are stored in the SESSION.movWiz structure by the code near the top of the template.

The last bit of code simply decides whether to show Next, Back, and Finish buttons for each step of the wizard. As would be expected, the Finish button is shown only on the last step, the Next button for all steps except the last, and the Back button for all steps except the first.

Deleting Session Variables

Like the CLIENT scope, SESSION values are treated like a struct. This means the structDelete() function can be used to delete SESSION values.

For instance, to delete the SESSION.movWiz variable, you could use the following line:

```
<cfset structDelete(SESSION, "movWiz")>
```

TIP

Don't use the structClear() function on the SESSION scope itself, as in structClear(SESSION). This erases the session itself, rather than all session variables, which can lead to undesirable results.

TIP

If you need to delete all variables from the SESSION scope at once, see the section "Expiring a Session Programmatically," later in this chapter.

Listing 20.10 is the NewMovieCommit.cfm template, which is called when the user clicks the Finish button on the last step of the New Movie Wizard (refer to Listing 20.9). Most of this listing is made up of ordinary <cfquery> code, simply inserting the values from the SESSION.MovWiz structure into the correct tables in the database.

After all of the records are inserted, the movWiz variable is removed from the SESSION structure, using the syntax shown previously. At that point, the user can be directed back to the NewMovieWizard.cfm template, where they can enter information for another movie. The wizard code will see that the movWiz structure no longer exists for the user, and therefore will create a new structure, with blank initial values for the movie title and other information.

Listing 20.10 NewMovieCommit.cfm—Deleting Unnecessary Session Variables

```
<!---
   Filename: NewMovieCommit.cfm
   Created by: Nate Weiss (NMW)
```

Listing 20.10 (CONTINUED)

```
Purpose: Inserts new movie and associated records into
database. Gets called by NewMovieWizard.cfm
--->


<!--- Insert film record --->
<cftransaction>
  <cfquery datasource="ows">
   INSERT INTO Films(
   MovieTitle,
   PitchText,
   RatingID)
   VALUES (
   '#SESSION.MovWiz.MovieTitle#',
   '#SESSION.MovWiz.PitchText#',
   #SESSION.MovWiz.RatingID# )
  </cfquery>
  <!--- Get ID number of just-inserted film --->
  <cfquery datasource="ows" name="getNew">
   SELECT Max(FilmID) As NewID FROM Films
  </cfquery>
</cftransaction>

<!--- Insert director record --->
<cfquery datasource="ows">
 INSERT INTO FilmsDirectors(FilmID, DirectorID, Salary)
 VALUES (#getNew.NewID#, #SESSION.MovWiz.DirectorID#, 0)
</cfquery>
<!--- Insert actor records --->
<cfloop list="#SESSION.movWiz.actorIDs#" index="thisActor">
 <cfset isStar = iif(thisActor eq SESSION.movWiz.starActorID, 1, 0)>
 <cfquery datasource="ows">
 INSERT INTO FilmsActors(FilmID, ActorID, Salary, IsStarringRole)
 VALUES (#getNew.newID#, #thisActor#, 0, #isStar#)
 </cfquery>
</cfloop>


<!--- Remove MovWiz variable from SESSION structure --->
<!--- User will be started over on return to wizard --->
<cfset structDelete(SESSION, "movWiz")>


<!--- Display message to user --->
<html>
<head><title>Movie Added</title></head>
<body>
 <h2>Movie Added</h2>
 <p>The movie has been added to the database.</p>

 <!--- Link to go through the wizard again --->
 <p><a href="NewMovieWizard.cfm">Enter Another Movie</a></p>

</body>
</html>
```

NOTE

When we insert the movie into the database, we follow it up with a query to get the ID of the last inserted record. It is possible that multiple people could run this code at the same time. In order to prevent a situation where the ID returned is not the ID of the movie we just created, we use the `<cftransaction>` tag to "lock" our code.

→ You can read more about `<cftransaction>` in Chapter 41, "More About SQL and Queries," online.

One interesting thing about the wizard metaphor is that users expect wizards to adapt themselves based on the choices they make along the way. For instance, the last step of this wizard (in which the user indicates which of the movie's stars gets top billing) looks different depending on the previous step (in which the user lists any number of stars in the movie). You also could decide to skip certain steps based on the film's budget, add more steps if the director and actors have worked together before, and so on. This would be relatively hard to do if you were collecting all the information in one long form.

As you can see in Listing 20.10, this version of the wizard doesn't collect salary information to be inserted into the `FilmsActors` and `FilmsDirectors` tables. Nor does it perform any data validation. For instance, the user can leave the movie title field blank without getting an error message. If you want, take a look at the `NewMovieWizard2.cfm` and `NewMovieCommit2.cfm` templates (Listings 20.11 and 20.12). This slightly expanded version of the wizard adds some data validation for the form elements and adds another step in which the user enters financial information.

The following examples use variables in the `SESSION` scope without locking the accesses with the `<cflock>` tag. This is an acceptable practice here; however, in other situations it would be advisable to add locks to prevent undesired concurrent requests. See the section "Locking Revisited," later in this chapter.

Listing 20.11 `NewMovieWizard2.cfm`— Expanded Version of New Movie Wizard

```
<!---
 Filename: NewMovieWizard2.cfm
 Created by: Nate Weiss (NMW)
 Please Note Session variables must be enabled
--->

<!--- Total Number of Steps in the Wizard --->
<cfset NumberOfSteps = 6>

<!--- The SESSION.movWiz structure holds users' entries --->
<!--- as they move through wizard. Make sure it exists! --->
<cfif not isDefined("SESSION.movWiz")>
 <!--- If structure undefined, create/initialize it --->
 <cfset SESSION.movWiz = structNew()>
 <!--- Represents current wizard step; start at one --->
 <cfset SESSION.movWiz.stepNum = 1>
 <!--- We will collect these from user; start blank --->
 <cfset SESSION.movWiz.movieTitle = "">
 <cfset SESSION.movWiz.pitchText = "">
 <cfset SESSION.movWiz.directorID = "">
 <cfset SESSION.movWiz.directorSal = "">
 <cfset SESSION.movWiz.ratingID = "">
 <cfset SESSION.movWiz.actorIDs = "">
```

Listing 20.11 (CONTINUED)

```coldfusion
  <cfset SESSION.movWiz.staractorID = "">
  <cfset SESSION.movWiz.miscExpense = "">
  <cfset SESSION.movWiz.actorSals = structNew()>
</cfif>


<!--- If user just submitted movieTitle, remember it --->
<!--- Do same for the directorID, Actors, and so on. --->
<cfif isDefined("Form.movieTitle")>
 <cfset SESSION.movWiz.movieTitle = Form.movieTitle>
 <cfset SESSION.movWiz.pitchText = Form.pitchText>
 <cfset SESSION.movWiz.ratingID = FORM.ratingID>
<cfelseif isDefined("Form.directorID")>
 <cfset SESSION.movWiz.directorID = Form.directorID>
<cfelseif isDefined("Form.actorID")>
 <cfset SESSION.movWiz.actorIDs = Form.actorID>
<cfelseif isDefined("Form.starActorID")>
 <cfset SESSION.movWiz.starActorID = Form.starActorID>
<cfelseif isDefined("Form.directorSal")>
 <cfset SESSION.movWiz.directorSal = Form.directorSal>
 <cfset SESSION.movWiz.miscExpense = Form.miscExpense>
 <!--- For each actor now in the movie, save their salary --->
 <cfloop LIST="#SESSION.movWiz.actorIDs#" index="thisActor">
 <cfset SESSION.movWiz.actorSals[thisActor] = FORM["actorSal#thisActor#"]>
 </cfloop>
</cfif>


<!--- If user clicked "Back" button, go back a step --->
<cfif isDefined("FORM.goBack")>
 <cfset SESSION.movWiz.stepNum = URL.stepNum - 1>
<!--- If user clicked "Next" button, go forward one --->
<cfelseif isDefined("FORM.goNext")>
 <cfset SESSION.movWiz.stepNum = URL.stepNum + 1>
<!--- If user clicked "Finished" button, we're done --->
<cfelseif isDefined("FORM.goDone")>
 <cflocation url="NewMovieCommit2.cfm">
</cfif>


<html>
<head><title>New Movie Wizard</title></head>
<body>

<!--- Show title and current step --->
<cfoutput>
 <b>New Movie Wizard</b><br>
 Step #SESSION.movWiz.stepNum# of #numberOfSteps#<br>
</cfoutput>


<!--- Data Entry Form, which submits back to itself --->
<cfform
 action="NewMovieWizard2.cfm?StepNum=#SESSION.movWiz.StepNum#"
 method="POST">
```

Listing 20.11 (CONTINUED)

```
<!--- Display the appropriate wizard step --->
<cfswitch expression="#SESSION.movWiz.stepNum#">
<!--- Step One: Movie Title --->
<cfcase value="1">
<!--- Get potential film ratings from database --->
<cfquery name="getRatings" datasource="ows">
SELECT ratingID, Rating
FROM FilmsRatings
ORDER BY ratingID
</cfquery>

<!--- Show text entry field for title --->
What is the title of the movie?<br>
<cfinput
name="movieTitle"
size="50"
required="Yes"
message="Please don't leave the movie title blank."
value="#SESSION.movWiz.movieTitle#">

<!--- Show text entry field for title --->
<p>What is the "pitch" or "one-liner" for the movie?<br>
<cfinput
name="pitchText"
size="50"
required="Yes"
message="Please provide the pitch text first."
value="#SESSION.movWiz.pitchText#">

<!--- Series of radio buttons for movie rating --->
<p>Please select the rating:<br>
<cfloop query="getRatings">
<!--- Re-select this rating if it was previously selected --->
<cfset isChecked = ratingID EQ SESSION.movWiz.ratingID>
<!--- Display radio button --->
<cfinput
type="radio"
name="ratingID"
checked="#isChecked#"
value="#ratingID#"><cfoutput>#rating#<br></cfoutput>
</cfloop>
</cfcase>

<!--- Step Two: Pick Director --->
<cfcase value="2">
<!--- Get list of directors from database --->
<cfquery name="getDirectors" datasource="ows">
SELECT directorID, FirstName+' '+LastName As FullName
FROM Directors
ORDER BY LastName
</cfquery>
<!--- Show all Directors in SELECT list --->
<!--- Pre-select if user has chosen one --->
Who will be directing the movie?<br>
<cfselect
```

Listing 20.11 (CONTINUED)

```
size="#getDirectors.recordCount#"
query="getDirectors"
name="directorID"
display="fullName"
value="directorID"
required="Yes"
message="You must choose a director first."
selected="#SESSION.movWiz.directorID#"/>
</cfcase>

<!--- Step Three: Pick Actors --->
<cfcase value="3">
<!--- Get list of actors from database --->
<cfquery name="getActors" datasource="ows">
SELECT * FROM Actors
ORDER BY NameLast
</cfquery>

What actors will be in the movie?<br>
<!--- For each actor, display checkbox --->
<cfloop query="getActors">
<!--- Should checkbox be pre-checked? --->
<cfset isChecked = listFind(SESSION.movWiz.actorIDs, actorID)>
<!--- Checkbox itself --->
<cfinput
type="checkbox"
name="actorID"
value="#actorID#"
required="Yes"
message="You must choose at least one actor first."
checked="#isChecked#">
<!--- Actor name --->
<cfoutput>#nameFirst# #nameLast#</cfoutput><br>
</cfloop>
</cfcase>


<!--- Step Four: Who is the star? --->
<cfcase value="4">
<cfif SESSION.movWiz.actorIDs EQ "">
Please go back to the last step and choose at least one
actor or actress to be in the movie.
<cfelse>
<!--- Get actors who are in the film --->
<cfquery name="getActors" datasource="ows">
SELECT * FROM Actors
WHERE actorID IN (#SESSION.movWiz.actorIDs#)
ORDER BY NameLast
</cfquery>

Which one of the actors will get top billing?<br>
<!--- For each actor, display radio button --->
<cfloop query="getActors">
<!--- Should radio be pre-checked? --->
<cfset isChecked = SESSION.movWiz.StaractorID EQ actorID>
```

Listing 20.11 (CONTINUED)

```
<!--- Radio button itself --->
<cfinput
type="radio"
name="staractorID"
value="#actorID#"
required="Yes"
message="Please select the starring actor first."
checked="#isChecked#">
<!--- Actor name --->
<cfoutput>#NameFirst# #NameLast#</cfoutput><br>
</cfloop>
</cfif>
</cfcase>


<!--- Step Five: Expenses and Salaries --->
<cfcase value="5">
<!--- Get actors who are in the film --->
<cfquery name="getActors" datasource="ows">
SELECT * FROM Actors
WHERE actorID IN (#SESSION.movWiz.actorIDs#)
ORDER BY NameLast
</cfquery>

<!--- Director's Salary --->
<p>How much will we pay the Director?<br>
<cfinput
type="text"
size="10"
name="directorSal"
required="Yes"
validate="float"
message="Please provide a number for the director's salary."
value="#SESSION.movWiz.directorSal#">

<!--- Salary for each actor --->
<p>How much will we pay the Actors?<br>
<cfloop query="getActors">
<!--- Grab actor's salary from ActorSals structure --->
<!--- Initialize to "" if no salary for actor yet --->
<cfif not structKeyExists(SESSION.movWiz.actorSals, actorID)>
<cfset SESSION.movWiz.actorSals[actorID] = "">
</cfif>
<!--- Text field for actor's salary --->
<cfinput
type="text"
size="10"
name="actorSal#actorID#"
required="Yes"
validate="float"
message="Please provide a number for each actor's salary."
value="#SESSION.movWiz.actorSals[actorID]#">
<!--- Actor's name --->
<cfoutput>for #nameFirst# #nameLast#<br></cfoutput>
</cfloop>
```

Listing 20.11 (continued)

```
<!--- Additional Expenses --->
<p>How much other money will be needed for the budget?<br>
<cfinput
type="text"
name="miscExpense"
required="Yes"
validate="float"
message="Please provide a number for additional expenses."
size="10"
value="#SESSION.movWiz.miscExpense#">
</cfcase>


<!--- Step Six: Final Confirmation --->
<cfcase value="6">
You have successfully finished the New Movie Wizard.<br>
Click the Finish button to add the movie to the database.<br>
Click Back if you need to change anything.<br>
</cfcase>
</cfswitch>


<p>
<!--- Show Back button, unless at first step --->
<cfif SESSION.movWiz.stepNum gt 1>
<INPUT type="Submit" NAME="goBack" value="&lt;&lt; Back">
</cfif>
<!--- Show Next button, unless at last step --->
<!--- If at last step, show "Finish" button --->
<cfif SESSION.movWiz.stepNum lt numberOfSteps>
<INPUT type="Submit" NAME="goNext" value="Next &gt;&gt;">
<cfelse>
<INPUT type="Submit" NAME="goDone" value="Finish">
</cfif>
</cfform>

</body>
</html>
```

Listing 20.12 NewMovieCommit2.cfm—Expanded Version of Wizard Commit Code

```
<!---
Filename: NewMovieCommit2.cfm
Created by: Nate Weiss (NMW)
Date Created: 2/18/2001
--->

<!--- Compute Total Budget --->
<!--- First, add the director's salary and miscellaneous expenses --->
<cfset TotalBudget = SESSION.movWiz.miscExpense + SESSION.movWiz.directorSal>
<!--- Now add the salary for each actor in the movie --->
<cfloop list="#SESSION.movWiz.ActorIDs#" index="ThisActor">
 <cfset thisSal = SESSION.movWiz.ActorSals[thisActor]>
 <cfset totalBudget = totalBudget + thisSal>
</cfloop>
```

Listing 20.12 (CONTINUED)

```
<!--- Insert Film Record --->
<cftransaction>
  <cfquery datasource="ows">
   INSERT INTO Films(
   MovieTitle,
   PitchText,
   RatingID,
   AmountBudgeted)
   VALUES (
   '#SESSION.movWiz.movieTitle#',
   '#SESSION.movWiz.pitchText#',
   #SESSION.movWiz.ratingID#,
   #totalBudget#)
   </cfquery>

  <!--- Get ID number of just-inserted film --->
  <cfquery datasource="ows" name="getNew">
   SELECT Max(FilmID) As NewID FROM Films
   </cfquery>
</cftransaction>

<!--- Insert director record --->
<cfquery datasource="ows">
 INSERT INTO FilmsDirectors(FilmID, DirectorID, Salary)
 VALUES (#getNew.newID#, #SESSION.movWiz.directorID#, #SESSION.movWiz.directorSal#)
 </cfquery>

<!--- Insert actor records --->
<cfloop list="#SESSION.movWiz.actorIDs#" index="thisActor">
 <cfset isStar = iif(thisActor EQ SESSION.movWiz.starActorID, 1, 0)>
 <cfquery datasource="ows">
 INSERT INTO FilmsActors(FilmID, ActorID, Salary, IsStarringRole)
 VALUES (#getNew.newID#, #thisActor#, #SESSION.movWiz.actorSals[thisActor]#,
#isStar#)
 </cfquery>
</cfloop>

<!--- Remove movWiz variable from SESSION structure --->
<!--- User will be started over on return to wizard --->
<cfset structDelete(SESSION, "movWiz")>


<!--- Display message to user --->
<html>
<head><title>Movie Added</title></head>
<body>
 <h2>Movie Added</h2>
 <p>The movie has been added to the database.</p>

 <!--- Link to go through the wizard again --->
 <p><a href="NewMovieWizard2.cfm">Enter Another Movie</a></p>
</body>
</html>
```

One item of note in these slightly expanded versions is that the new `actorSals` part of the `SESSION.movWiz` structure is itself a structure. The fact that you can use complex datatypes such as structures and arrays is one important advantage that session variables have over client variables and cookies.

NOTE

See the "Other Examples of Session Variables" section at the end of this chapter for a list of other listings in this book that use session variables.

When Does a Session End?

Developers often wonder when exactly a session ends. The simple answer is that by default, Cold-Fusion's Session Management feature is based on time. A particular session is considered to be expired if more than 20 minutes pass without another request from the same client. At that point, the `SESSION` scope associated with that browser is freed from the server's memory.

That said, ColdFusion provides a few options that you can use to subtly change the definition of a session, and to control more precisely when a particular session ends.

J2EE Session Variables and ColdFusion

ColdFusion includes an option that allows you to use J2EE session variables. This new option is different from the "classic" ColdFusion implementation of session variables, which have been available in previous versions.

The traditional implementation uses ColdFusion-specific `cfid` and `cftoken` cookies to identify the client (that is, the browser). Whenever a client visits pages in your application within a certain period of time, those page requests are considered to be part of the same session. By default, this time period is 20 minutes. If more than 20 minutes pass without another page request from the client, the session "times out" and the session information is discarded from the server's memory. If the user closes the browser and then reopens it and visits your page again, the same session will still be in effect. That is, ColdFusion's classic strategy is to uniquely identify the machine, then define the concept of "session" solely in terms of time.

The J2EE session variables option causes ColdFusion to define a session somewhat differently. Instead of using `cfid` and `cftoken` cookies, which persist between sessions, to track the user's machine, it uses a different cookie, called `jSessionID`. This cookie isn't persistent, and thus expires when a user closes the browser. Therefore, if the user reopens their browser and visits your page again, it is an entirely new session.

To enable the J2EE session variables feature, select the Use J2EE Session Variables check box on the ColdFusion Administrator's Memory Variables page.

Once you enable this option, sessions will expire whenever the user closes their browser, or when the session timeout period elapses between requests (whichever comes first).

NOTE

The use of the jSessionID cookie is part of the Java J2EE specification. Using J2EE session variables makes it easy to share session variables with other J2EE code that may be working alongside your ColdFusion templates, such as Java Servlets, Enterprise Java-Beans, JSPs, and so on. In other words, telling ColdFusion to use J2EE session variables is a great way to integrate your ColdFusion code with other J2EE technologies so they can all behave as a single application. The assumption here is that the closing of a browser should be interpreted as a desire to end a session.

Default Behavior

Again, by default, a session doesn't automatically end when the user closes the browser. You can see this yourself by visiting one of the session examples discussed in this book, such as the New Movie Wizard (refer to Listing 20.9). Fill out the wizard partway, then close your browser. Now reopen it. Nothing has happened to your session's copy of the SESSION scope, so you still are on the same step of the wizard that you were before you closed your browser. As far as ColdFusion is concerned, you just reloaded the page.

Adjusting the Session Timeout Period

You can adjust the session timeout period for your session variables by following the same basic steps you take to adjust the timeout period for application variables. That is, you can adjust the default timeout of 20 minutes using the ColdFusion Administrator, or you can use the session-Timeout attribute in the THIS scope defined in your Application.cfc file to set a specific session timeout for your application.

→ For specific instructions, see the section "Application Variable Timeouts" in Chapter 19.

Expiring a Session Programmatically

If you want a session in your code to expire, there are a few ways to handle it. In the past, you could use the <cfapplication> tag with a sessionTimeout value of 0 seconds. A more appropriate way, however, would be to simply remove the session values by hand using the structDelete() function. For instance, if you wanted to give your users some type of log-out link, you could use structDelete() to remove the session variables you set to mark a user as being logged on.

Ending the Session when the Browser Closes

The simplest way to make session variables expire when the user closes their browser is by telling ColdFusion to use J2EE session variables, as explained earlier in the "J2EE Session Variables and ColdFusion" section. When in this mode, the ColdFusion server sets a nonpersistent cookie to track the session (as opposed to the traditional session-variable mode, in which persistent cookies are set). Thus, when the browser is closed, the session-tracking cookie is lost, which means that a new session will be created if the user reopens their browser and comes back to your application.

Assuming that you aren't using J2EE session variables, one option is to set the setClientCookies attribute in the THIS scope in your Application.cfc file to No, which means that the cfid and cftoken cookies ColdFusion normally uses to track each browser's session (and client) variables will not be maintained as persistent cookies on each client machine. If you aren't using client variables, or don't need your client variables to persist after the user closes their browser, this can be a viable option.

If you do decide to set setClientCookie="No", you must manually pass the cfid and cftoken in the URL for every page request, as if the user's browser did not support cookies at all. See the section "Using Client Variables Without Requiring Cookies," earlier in this chapter, for specific instructions.

If you want to use setClientCookie="No" but don't want to pass the cfid and cftoken in every URL, you could set the cfid and cftoken on your own, as nonpersistent cookies. This means the values would be stored as cookies on the user's browser, but the cookies would expire when the user closes their browser. The most straightforward way to get this effect is to use two <cfset> tags in your Application.cfc's onSessionStart method, as follows:

```
<!--- Preserve Session/Client variables only until browser closes --->
<cfset Cookie.cfid = SESSION.cfid>
<cfset Cookie.cftoken = SESSION.cftoken>
```

This technique essentially causes ColdFusion to lose all memory of the client machine when the user closes their browser. When the user returns next time, no cfid will be presented to the server, and ColdFusion will be forced to issue a new cfid value, effectively abandoning any session and client variables that were associated with the browser in the past. The expiration behavior will be very similar to that of J2EE session variables.

NOTE

Please note that by setting the cfid and cftoken cookies yourself in this way, you will lose all session and client variables for your application when the user closes their browser. If you are using both client and session variables, and want the client variables to persist between sessions but the session variables to expire when the user closes their browser, then you should use either the technique shown next or J2EE session variables as discussed earlier.

A completely different technique is to set your own nonpersistent cookie, perhaps called COOKIE.browserOpen. If a user closes the browser, the cookie no longer exists. Therefore, you can use the cookie's nonexistence as a cue for the session to expire programmatically, as discussed in the previous section.

Unfortunately, there is a downside to this technique. If the browser doesn't support cookies or has had them disabled, the session will expire with every page request. However, as long as you know that cookies will be supported (for instance, in an intranet application), it will serve you well.

Using Session Variables Without Requiring Cookies

Unless you take special steps, the browser must accept a cookie or two in order for session variables to work correctly in ColdFusion. If your application needs to work even with browsers that don't (or won't) accept cookies, you need to pass the value of the special SESSION.URLToken variable in each URL, just as you need to pass CLIENT.urlToken to allow client variables to work without using cookies. This will ensure that the appropriate cfid, cftoken, or jSessionID values are available for each page request, even if the browser can't provide the value as a cookie. See "Using Client Variables Without Requiring Cookies," earlier in this chapter, for specific instructions. As before, you can use the URLSessionFormat to put the URLToken value in the URL for you.

Other Examples of Session Variables

A number of our other examples use session variables. You might want to skim through the code listings outlined here to see some other uses for session variables:

- In Chapter 23, "Securing Your Applications," online, session variables are used to track the logged-in status of users.

- In Chapter 21, "Interacting with Email," online, session variables are used to help users check their email messages from a ColdFusion template.

- The Ad Server examples in Chapter 38, "Generating Non-HTML Content," in Vol. 2, *Application Development*, use session variables to track which ads have been shown on which pages on a per-visit basis.

Working with `onSessionStart` and `onSessionEnd`

Earlier in the chapter, we talked about how session variables can be enabled in the `Application.cfc` file and how handy they are for tracking information about your users. Another feature you may find handy is the ability to run code at both the beginning and end of a session. There are many ways this can be useful. Let's say that you want to note when a user first enters your system. You can do this easily with this code:

```
<cfset SESSION.entered = now()>
```

This line of code is simple enough. However, you want to run it only once. You could use the `isDefined` function to check whether the variable exists, but an even easier approach is to use the `onSessionStart` method of the `Application.cfc` file. This is a special method run only at the beginning of a user's session. Conversely, it may be handy to notice when a user's session ends. In the past, doing this was (mostly) impossible in ColdFusion. But now that we have the powerful features provided by the `Application.cfc` file, we can handle scenarios like this. The `onSessionEnd` method is fired whenever a user's session times out. One simple use of this feature is to log to a text file. Because we are noting when a user first enters the system, we can log the total time the user is on the system. Listing 20.13 presents an example of this. Be sure to save the file as `Application.cfc`.

Listing 20.13 `Application4.cfc`—Supporting Session Events

```
<!---
 Filename: Application.cfc
 Created by: Raymond Camden (ray@camdenfamily.com)
 Handles application events.
--->

<cfcomponent output="false">
```

Listing 20.13 (CONTINUED)

```
<cfset THIS.name="OrangeWhipSite_c20">
<cfset THIS.sessionManagement=true>
<cfset this.sessiontimeout = createtimespan(0,0,0,10)>

<cffunction name="onSessionStart" returnType="void">
  <cfset SESSION.created = now()>
</cffunction>

<cffunction name="onSessionEnd" returnType="void">
  <cfargument name="theSession" type="struct" required="true">
  <cfset var duration = dateDiff("s",arguments.theSession.created,now())>
  <cflog file="#THIS.name#" text="Session lasted for #duration# seconds.">
</cffunction>

</cfcomponent>
```

Let's take a look at the two methods in this component. The onSessionStart method simply sets the created variable to the current time. The onSessionEnd method is going to use this variable. First note that inside the onSessionEnd method, you can't access the SESSION scope directly. Instead, the SESSION scope is passed as an argument to the method. We create a variable to store the number of seconds that the session was alive and then log this information to a text file. You may have noticed the dramatically short sessiontimeout value. This value was shortened so that this scenario would be easier to test. You don't have to log only to a file. You can also store the results in a database. This log would provide a handy way to see how long users stick around on your Web site.

Locking Revisited

Like application variables, session variables are kept in the server's RAM. This means that the same types of race condition problems can occur if session variables are being read and accessed by two different page requests at the same time. (See the section "Using Locks to Protect Against Race Conditions" in Chapter 19.)

➜ If you haven't yet read "Using Locks to Protect Against Race Conditions" in Chapter 19, please take a look at that section before you continue.

Sessions and the `<cflock>` Tag

Just as it's possible to run into race conditions with application variables, it's also possible for race conditions to crop up when using session variables. In general, it's much less likely that race conditions will occur at the session level than at the application level, as there is usually only one page request coming from each session at any given time. Even though it's unlikely in the grand scheme of things, it still is quite possible that more than one request could be processed from a session at the same time. Here are some examples:

- Pages that use frames can allow a browser to make more than one page request at the same time. If, say, a frameset contains three individual frame pages, most browsers will issue all three follow-up requests at once.

- If for whatever reason (perhaps network congestion or a heavy load on your ColdFusion server) a particular page is taking a long time to come up, many users tend to click their browser's Reload or Refresh button a few times. Or they might submit a form multiple times. In either case, it's quite possible that a second or third request might get to the server before the first request does.

- If you are using `<cfcontent>` to serve up images, as in the Ad Server examples in Chapter 38, and there are three or four such images on a page, most browsers will make the requests for the images concurrently.

In other words, although race conditions are probably less likely to occur with session variables than they are with application variables, it is still possible to encounter them. Therefore, if the nature of your session variables is such that concurrent access would be a bad thing, you need to use the `<cflock>` tag. In general, you will use `<cflock>` just as it was shown in Chapter 19, except you use `scope="Session"` instead of `scope="Application"`.

Remember, though, that in *most* cases you don't need to care about locking. For example, most session variables are set once (when you log in, for example) and read many times. There is no need to lock these session variables, even if your site uses frames or cfcontent.

NOTE

Locks of `SCOPE="Session"` will affect only those locks that have been issued to the same session, which is of course what you want. In plain English, a `<cflock>` with `scope="Session"` means "don't let other page requests from this session interfere with the code in this block."

PART IV

Appendixes

Installing ColdFusion and Development Environments

This appendix is divided into three parts: the ColdFusion installation process, the IDE installation processes, and instructions on how to install the sample files used in the lessons in this book.

ColdFusion 8

ColdFusion 8 is supported on Windows, Mac OS X, Linux, and Unix systems. All of these platforms are supported by the exact same ColdFusion; all that differs is the installer. Thus, although the exact installation steps vary based on the platform, once ColdFusion is installed everything about it is consistent regardless of the platform used.

NOTE

Links to download ColdFusion and other files mentioned in this appendix can be found at the book Web page: http://www.forta.com/books/032151548X.

The Different Flavors of ColdFusion 8

ColdFusion 8 comes in three editions:

- ColdFusion Developer Edition
- ColdFusion Standard
- ColdFusion Enterprise

As already explained, there is a single ColdFusion installation program, and a single ColdFusion application. The different editions are activated based on the serial number specified.

NOTE

ColdFusion Developer Edition is functionally equivalent to ColdFusion Enterprise, but has IP address restrictions.

Preinstallation Checklist

To be sure ColdFusion will work at peak performance on your hardware platform, make sure you follow the steps listed here:

- Check the system requirements in the installation documentation.

- Check your hardware's specs. If your RAM or disk space is inadequate, or your processor can't handle the load, an upgrade will be necessary.

The complete list of supported platforms and the system requirements for each can be found at http://www.adobe.com/products/coldfusion/productinfo/systemreqs/.

Choosing Your Hardware

You probably already know which hardware platform you will use for ColdFusion: the hardware you already own. But if you're still deciding, keep the following points in mind:

- Virtually all ColdFusion code will execute perfectly across all supported platforms. So if you jump ship to another platform during or after development, your applications will require little, if any, porting.

- From a ColdFusion perspective, there is no real difference between hardware platforms. The decision as to which platform to use should be driven by cost, experience, support, and other factors.

Checking Your Web Server

As explained in Chapter 1, "Introducing ColdFusion," Web servers are separate software programs that enable two-way communication between your system and other Web servers. A great number of Web servers are available for a great number of operating systems. You must choose the Web server that is compatible with your operating system and ColdFusion.

ColdFusion is primarily used with Microsoft IIS (Internet Information Server) and Apache. In addition, an embedded Web server is also available, allowing you to do development without needing to install and configure a Web server.

- Microsoft's Internet Information Server (IIS) is free and comes bundled with Windows. One of IIS's principal advantages is its capability to use Windows' user lists and security options. This eliminates the complexity of maintaining multiple lists of passwords and security privileges.

- Apache is one of the oldest and still the most popular Web server on the Net. The Apache Web server is a free, open source software project available for most operating systems, including Windows, Linux, and Solaris. Despite its popularity, Apache is harder to install and manage than IIS.

Because the applications you develop with ColdFusion are portable among all supported Web servers, your production Web server can differ from the Web server used for development with minimal changes in your ColdFusion code.

After you have installed a Web server, you must verify that it is working properly. To do this, start a Web browser and go to the URL http://localhost/. If everything is working, your Web server's default home page should appear.

If the home page doesn't display, you must do a little troubleshooting. First, type ping 127.0.0.1 at a command prompt. If the ping is successful, TCP/IP is working. More than likely, the problem lies with the Web server. For more information, consult the Web server's documentation.

Installing ColdFusion on Windows and MAC OS X

You install ColdFusion on Windows and Mac OS X systems using an interactive installation program. You must have administrative privileges to be able to install ColdFusion.

During the installation you will be prompted for information:

- Product serial number (which will activate ColdFusion as either ColdFusion Standard or ColdFusion Enterprise). You can omit the serial number if installing ColdFusion as a Developer Edition or installing the 30-day free trial. (The trial edition will revert to a Developer Edition after 30 days unless a serial number is provided.)

- If installing ColdFusion Enterprise or ColdFusion Developer Edition, you will be prompted for the installation type. You may install a stand-alone installation (integrated J2EE server, single instance only), JRun+ColdFusion, or additional instances of top of an existing J2EE server. ColdFusion Standard edition always installs using the stand-alone configuration.

- The Web server to be used. ColdFusion will display a list of detected Web servers, as well as offering you the option of using the internal HTTP server (to be used on development systems only).

- Passwords to be used to secure the ColdFusion Administrator and RDS access (used by the Report Builder, Dreamweaver, and Eclipse to provide access to databases and more).

TIP

Stand-alone mode is the simplest to use for development, as no Web server is needed. Most of the examples in this book assume that stand-alone mode is being used.

With this information complete and verified, the installer will install and configure ColdFusion, and will create Start menu icons to access ColdFusion documentation and the ColdFusion Administrator.

Installing ColdFusion on Linux and Unix

To install ColdFusion on Linux and Unix machines, make sure that the appropriate attributes have been assigned to the install file. The install file must be made executable using the chmod command as follows:

```
chmod 755 filename
```

You must be logged on as an administrator to install ColdFusion.

During the installation you will be prompted for information:

- Product serial number (which will activate ColdFusion as either ColdFusion Standard or ColdFusion Enterprise). You may omit the serial number if installing ColdFusion as a Developer Edition or installing the 30-day free trial. (The trial edition will revert to a Developer Edition after 30 days unless a serial number is provided.)

- If installing ColdFusion Enterprise or ColdFusion Developer Edition, you will be prompted for the installation type. You may install a stand-alone installation (integrated J2EE server, single instance only), JRun+ColdFusion, or additional instances of top of an existing J2EE server. ColdFusion Standard edition always installs using the stand-alone configuration.

- The location and account information for Apache (if not using the integrated HTTP server).

- Passwords to be used to secure the ColdFusion Administrator and RDS access (used by Dreamweaver to provide access to databases and more).

TIP

Stand-alone mode is the simplest to use for development, as no Web server is needed. Most of the examples in this book assume that stand-alone mode is being used.

Installing the ColdFusion Report Builder

The ColdFusion Report Builder is a Windows application (although reports created with it can be processed by all editions of ColdFusion on all platforms).

The ColdFusion Report Builder installer can be downloaded from Adobe. You can run this installer to manually install the Report Builder on development machines.

NOTE

Links to download the ColdFusion Report Builder and other files mentioned in this appendix can be found at the book Web page: http://www.forta.com/books/032151548X.

Dreamweaver CS3

The Dreamweaver CS3 installation is straightforward. Dreamweaver support Windows and Mac and uses standard installers on each platform.

During the installation process, you will be prompted for information:

- Installation location.

- Files to associate Dreamweaver with. For ColdFusion development, make sure that `.cfm` and `.cfc` are selected.

- Activation serial number. Activation requires that you be connected to the Internet. Without activation, Dreamweaver will run as a trial edition.

Although Dreamweaver ships with built-in ColdFusion support, updated support for ColdFusion 8 is available for download as a Dreamweaver extension. To install the extension, download it, and then simply run the MXP file on each machine with Dreamweaver installed.

NOTE

Links to download the Dreamweaver extension and other files mentioned in this appendix can be found at the book Web page: `http://www.forta.com/books/032151548X`.

Eclipse

ColdFusion 8 comes with Eclipse plug-in extensions. Obviously, to use these, Eclipse must be installed.

- If you already have Eclipse 3.1 or later installed (perhaps because you are using Adobe Flex Builder), then you can install the ColdFusion extensions in that same Eclipse installation.

- If you do not have Eclipse installed, then you will need to download a copy from `http://www.eclipse.org/` (or any of the many other distribution locations).

You will likely also want to install the community-created CFEclipse plug-in, which can be found at `http://www.cfeclipse.org/`.

And finally, you will want to install the ColdFusion Eclipse extensions, which can be downloaded from Adobe. These are distributed as an Eclipse archive (a special ZIP file).

NOTE

Links to all of the downloads mentioned here, as well as to other files mentioned in this appendix, can be found at the book Web page: `http://www.forta.com/books/032151548X`.

Samples and Data Files

The best way to learn a product is by using it, and in this book you learn ColdFusion by building applications, some really simple and some quite sophisticated. The applications you'll create are for a fictitious company named *Orange Whip Studios*, or *OWS* for short.

Building the applications involves writing code, using databases, and accessing images and other files. You don't need to create all of these manually—they're available for download from the book Web page. You can install all of these files or just the ones you need; the choice is yours.

NOTE

The OWS data files and links to other files mentioned in this appendix can be found at the book Web page: http://www.forta.com/books/032151548X.

What to Install

The OWS files are distributed in two downloadable ZIP files.

The owsdata.zip file contains a folder named ows containing the Apache Derby database used by the lessons and examples in this book.

The ows.zip file contains subdirectories that each contain the files that make up the applications. Note the following subdirectories:

- The images directory contains GIF and JPEG images used in many of the applications.

- The sql directory contains a SQL query utility used in Chapters 6, "Introducing SQL," and 7, "SQL Data Manipulation."

- The numbered directories contain files created in specific chapters in this book with the directory number corresponding to the chapter number. For example, directory 8 contains the files created in Chapter 8, "The Basics of CFML."

All readers should install the database and images directories. This book walks you through the processes for creating the tables and designing the images. Without the databases most of the examples won't work, and without the images your screens won't look like the screen shots in the book.

The sql directory is optional and should only be installed if you have no other tool or utility with which to learn SQL.

CAUTION

To ensure database and server security, don't install the files in the sql directory on production servers.

The numbered directories should *not* be installed unless you plan to not try the examples yourself (which would be a pity). These files are provided so you can refer to them as needed, or even copy specific files to save time. To really learn ColdFusion you'll want to perform every lesson in the book and create the files yourself.

Installing the OWS Files

The default location for ColdFusion databases is the ColdFusion database folder (the `db` folder under the ColdFusion root; on Windows machines, this will usually be `C:\coldfusion8\db`). The `owsdata.zip` file contains a folder named `ows`, which you should save in the database folder.

Install the `ows.zip` contents under the Web server root. If you are using ColdFusion in stand-alone mode (on Windows) using installation defaults, then the Web root will be:

```
c:\coldfusion8\wwwroot
```

If you are using Microsoft IIS, the Web root will likely be:

```
c:\inetpub\wwwroot
```

To install the OWS files, do the following:

1. Create a directory named `ows` beneath the Web server root.

2. Copy the `images` directory into the just-created `ows` directory. You can copy the entire directory; you don't need to copy the files individually.

3. Copy the `sql` directory, if needed.

4. Copy the chapter directories, if needed. If you plan to create the files yourself—which we recommend—you'll be creating your own files in the ows directory as you work through the book. As such, you may want to copy these files into another location (not the newly created ows directory) so they will be readily available for browsing if needed, but not in the way of your own development.

And with that, you're ready to start learning ColdFusion.

Sample Application Data Files

Sample Application Data Files

"Orange Whip Studios" is a fictitious company used in the examples throughout this book. The various examples and applications use a total of 12 database tables, as described in the following sections.

NOTE

The sample applications use Apache Derby as a database (this database engine is included with ColdFusion). Because of limitations in the datatypes supported by Apache Derby, all money or currency fields are represented as real types, and all bit fields are represented by single character types.

The Actors Table

The Actors table contains a list of all the actors along with name, address, and other personal information. Actors contains the columns listed in Table B.1.

Table B.1   The Actors Table

COLUMN	DATATYPE	DESCRIPTION
ActorID	Numeric (Identity)	Unique actor ID
NameFirst	Text (50 chars)	Actor's (stage) first name
NameLast	Text (50 chars)	Actor's (stage) last name
Age	Numeric	Actor's (stage) age
NameFirstReal	Text (50 chars)	Actor's real first name
NameLastReal	Text (50 chars)	Actor's real last name
AgeReal	Numeric	Actor's real age
IsEgomaniac	Small Integer	Egomaniac flag
IsTotalBabe	Small Integer	Total babe flag
Gender	Text (1 char)	Gender (M or F)

Primary Key

- `ActorID`

Foreign Keys

- None

The `Contacts` Table

The `Contacts` table stores all contacts, including mailing list members and online store customers. `Contacts` contains the columns listed in Table B.2.

Table B.2   The `Contacts` Table

COLUMN	DATATYPE	DESCRIPTION
ContactID	Numeric (Identity)	Unique contact ID
FirstName	Text (50 chars)	Contact first name
LastName	Text (50 chars)	Contact last name
Address	Text (100 chars)	Contact address
City	Text (50 chars)	Contact city
State	Text (5 chars)	Contact state
Zip	Text (10 chars)	Contact ZIP
Country	Text (50 chars)	Contact country
Email	Text (100 chars)	Contact email address
Phone	Text (50 chars)	Contact phone number
UserLogin	Text (50 chars)	Contact user login
UserPassword	Text (50 chars)	Contact login password
MailingList	Small Integer	Mailing list flag
UserRoleID	Numeric	ID of the associated role

Primary Key

- `ContactID`

Foreign Keys

- The `UserRoleID` column is related to the primary key of the `UserRoles` table.

The Directors Table

The Directors table stores all movie directors. Directors contains the columns listed in Table B.3.

Table B.3 The Directors Table

COLUMN	DATATYPE	DESCRIPTION
DirectorID	Numeric (Identity)	Unique director ID
FirstName	Text (50 chars)	Director first name
LastName	Text (50 chars)	Director last name

Primary Key

- DirectorID

Foreign Keys

- None

The Expenses Table

The Expenses table lists the expenses associated with listed movies. Expenses contains the columns in Table B.4.

Table B.4 The Expenses Table

COLUMN	DATATYPE	DESCRIPTION
ExpenseID	Numeric (Identity)	Unique expense ID
FilmID	Numeric	Movie ID
ExpenseAmount	Real	Expense amount
Description	Text (100 chars)	Expense description
Expense Date	Date Time	Expense date

Primary Key

- ExpenseID

Foreign Keys

- FilmID related to primary key in Films table

The `Films` Table

The `Films` table lists all movies and related information. `Films` contains the columns in Table B.5.

Table B.5 The `Films` Table

COLUMN	DATATYPE	DESCRIPTION
FilmID	Numeric (Identity)	Unique movie ID
MovieTitle	Text (255 chars)	Movie title
PitchText	Text (100 chars)	Movie one-liner
AmountBudgeted	Currency (or numeric)	Movie budget (planned)
RatingID	Numeric	Movie rating ID
Summary	Memo (or text)	Movie plot summary
ImageName	Text (50 chars)	Movie poster image file name
DateInTheaters	Date Time	Date movie is in theaters

Primary Key

- `FilmID`

Foreign Keys

- `RatingID` related to primary key in `FilmsRatings` table

The `FilmsActors` Table

The `FilmsActors` table associates actors with the movies they are in. `FilmsActors` contains the columns in Table B.6. Retrieving actors with their movies requires a three-way join (`Films`, `Actors`, and `FilmsActors`).

Table B.6 The `FilmsActors` Table

COLUMN	DATATYPE	DESCRIPTION
FARecID	Numeric (Identity)	Unique film actor ID
FilmID	Numeric	Movie ID
ActorID	Numeric	Actor ID
IsStarringRole	Small Integer	Is star flag
Salary	Real	Actor salary

Primary Key

- `FARecID`

Foreign Keys

- `FilmID` related to primary key in `Films` table
- `ActorID` related to primary key in `Actors` table

The `FilmsDirectors` Table

The `FilmsDirectors` table associates directors with their movies. `FilmsDirectors` contains the columns in Table B.7. Retrieving actors with their movies requires a three-way join (`Films`, `Directors`, and `FilmsDirectors`).

Table B.7   The `FilmsDirectors` Table

COLUMN	DATATYPE	DESCRIPTION
`FDRecID`	Numeric (Identity)	Unique films director ID
`FilmID`	Numeric	Movie ID
`DirectorID`	Numeric	Director ID
`Salary`	Real	Director salary

Primary Key

- `FDRecID`

Foreign Keys

- `FilmsID` related to primary key in `Films` table
- `DirectorID` related to primary key in `Directors` table

The `FilmsRatings` Table

The `FilmsRatings` table lists all movie ratings. `FilmsRatings` contains the columns in Table B.8.

Table B.8   The `FilmsRatings` Table

COLUMN	DATATYPE	DESCRIPTION
`RatingID`	Numeric (Identity)	Unique rating ID
`Rating`	Text (50 chars)	Rating description

Primary Key

- RatingID

Foreign Keys

- None

The Merchandise Table

The Merchandise table lists the movie-related merchandise for sale in the online store. Merchandise contains the columns in Table B.9.

Table B.9 The Merchandise Table

COLUMN	DATATYPE	DESCRIPTION
MerchID	Numeric (Identity)	Unique merchandise ID
FilmID	Numeric	Movie ID
MerchName	Text (50 chars)	Merchandise name
MerchDescription	Text (100 chars)	Merchandise description
MerchPrice	Real	Merchandise price
ImageNameSmall	Text (50 chars)	Item's small image file name
ImageNameLarge	Text (50 chars)	Item's large image file name

Primary Key

- MerchID

Foreign Keys

- FilmID related to primary key in Films table

The MerchandiseOrders Table

The MerchandiseOrders table stores online merchandise order information. MerchandiseOrders contains the columns in Table B.10.

Table B.10 The MerchandiseOrders Table

COLUMN	DATATYPE	DESCRIPTION
OrderID	Numeric (Identity)	Unique order ID
ContactID	Numeric	Buyer contact ID
OrderDate	Date Time	Order date

Table B.10 (CONTINUED)

COLUMN	DATATYPE	DESCRIPTION
ShipAddress	Text (100 chars)	Ship to address
ShipCity	Text (50 chars)	Ship to city
ShipState	Text (5 chars)	Ship to state
ShipZip	Text (10 chars)	Ship to ZIP
ShipCountry	Text (50 chars)	Ship to country
ShipDate	Date Time	Ship date

Primary Key

- OrderID

Foreign Keys

- ContactID related to primary key in Contacts table

The MerchandiseOrdersItems Table

The MerchandiseOrdersItems table contains the items in each order. MerchandiseOrdersItems contains the columns in Table B.11.

Table B.11 The MerchandiseOrdersItems Table

COLUMN	DATATYPE	DESCRIPTION
OrderItemID	Numeric (Identity)	Unique order item ID
OrderID	Numeric	Order ID
ItemID	Numeric	Ordered item ID
OrderQty	Numeric	Number of items ordered
ItemPrice	Real	Item sale price

Primary Key

- OrderItemID

Foreign Keys

- OrderID related to primary key in MerchandiseOrders table
- ItemID related to primary key in Merchandise table

The UserRoles Table

The UserRoles table defines user security roles used by secured applications. UserRoles contains the columns in Table B.12.

Table B.12 The UserRoles Table

COLUMN	DATATYPE	DESCRIPTION
UserRoleID	Numeric (Identity)	Unique user role ID
UserRoleName	Text (20 chars)	Role name
UserRoleFunction	Text (75 chars)	Role purpose

Primary Key

- UserRoleID

Foreign Keys

- None

Online Content

Additional material for this volume is available online at http://www.forta.com/books/032151548X. These chapters are published in printable PDF format and include supporting downloadable code listings.

- Chapter 21, "Interacting with Email," introduces ColdFusion's email capabilities. ColdFusion enables you to create SMTP-based email messages using its <cfmail> tag. You learn how to send email messages containing user-submitted form fields, how to email the results of a database query, and how to do mass mailings to addresses derived from database tables. Additionally, you learn how to retrieve mail from POP mailboxes using the <CFPOP> tag.

- Chapter 22, "Online Commerce," teaches you how to conduct real-time e-commerce, including credit card authorization. You build an entire working shopping cart application—one you can use as a stepping stone when writing your own shopping applications.

- Chapter 23, "Securing Your Applications," introduces important security concepts and explains which you should worry about and why. You learn how to create login screens, access control, and more.

INDEX